The Complete Semi-Slav

Peter Wells

An Owl Book
Henry Holt and Company
New York

Henry Holt and Company, Inc.
Publishers since 1866
115 West 18th Street
New York, New York 10011

Henry Holt® is a registered
trademark of Henry Holt and Company, Inc.

Copyright © 1994 by Peter Wells
All rights reserved.
First published in the United States in 1994 by
Henry Holt and Company, Inc.
Published in Great Britain in 1994 by B. T. Batsford Ltd.

Library of Congress Catalog Card Number: 94—77218

ISBN 0-8050-3288-6 (An Owl Book: pbk.)

First American Edition—1994

Printed in the United Kingdom
All first editions are printed on acid-free paper. ∞

10 9 8 7 6 5 4 3 2 1

Adviser: R. D. Keene, GM, OBE
Technical Editor: Graham Burgess

Contents

Bibliography

Periodicals (the numbers indicate the most recent issue which could be consulted)
Informator (58)
New in Chess Magazine (1993/8)
New in Chess Yearbook (30)
FIDE Chess
ChessBase Magazine (37)
British Chess Magazine
Chess Monthly

Books
Donaldson & Silman, *Semi-Slav: Non-Meran Variations,* Summit Press.
Donaldson, *Meran Defense*, Chess Enterprises. Coraopolis 1987.
Encyclopaedia of Chess Openings, vol. D, 2nd edition, Šahovski Informator. Belgrade 1987.
Polugaevsky, *Slawisch*, Sportverlag Berlin. 1988.
Kondratiev, *Slavyanskaya Zashchita*, Fizkultura i Sport. Moscow 1985.
Harding & Whiteley, *Queen's Gambit Declined: Semi-Slav*, Batsford. London 1981.
Richmond, *Anti-Meran Gambit*, The Chess Player. Nottingham 1988.
Varnusz, *Semi-Slawisch*, Schachverlag Reinhold Dreier.
Beliavsky & Mikhalchishin, *D44*, Šahovski Informator. Cyprus 1993.

Introduction

The basic position of the Semi-Slav, to which almost the entire book is devoted, is shown in the first diagram. I shall discuss the variety of move orders by which it is reached later in the introduction. For the moment 1 d4 d5 2 c4 c6 3 ♘f3 ♘f6 4 ♘c3 e6 *(1)* will serve as an example.

1
W

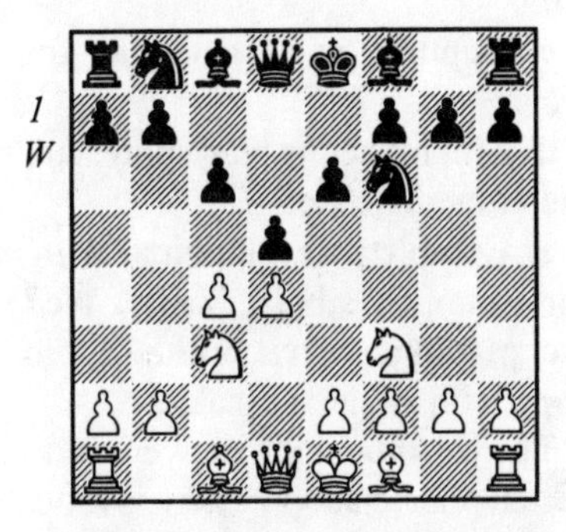

The opening is old and has a great pedigree. The Meran Variation (see Section 2) took on a recognizable form as long ago as the 1920s. An important part of the theory of Section 1, covering the uncompromising 5 ♗g5 was worked out by Botvinnik. What is remarkable is that in the last couple of years an opening which has always enjoyed a steady following has suddenly shot to unprecedented popularity.

Garry Kasparov gives it the occasional outing, but in the repertoires of a large proportion of the young players in the world's elite -- Kramnik, Anand, Shirov, Chernin, Illescas to name but a few – it plays a key role. One Grandmaster, upon hearing that I was working on this book, said to me recently 'In Biel it was getting ridiculous. Every other game was a Semi-Slav. The opening can't be that good!'

So why this truly extraordinary boom? I believe it is because the opening combines the solidity of many of the other 1 d4 d5 openings with great opportunities to complicate and play for the full point. It is consequently compatible with a wide range of styles. Moreover, whilst as in all openings a really determined bore with the white pieces can usually contrive to use the first move to deaden the game to a degree, there are few if any chances to do that and aspire after a plus.

The Basic Idea of the Semi-Slav

Why ...e6 and ...c6? To those unfamiliar with the opening it may seem a strange combination, since at the risk of over-generalizing a little, in most variations of the Queen's Gambit Declined (QGD)

Black plays for the break ...c5. I think the 'point' of the Semi-Slav can be understood in two stages:

1) Very important is that in comparison with the pure QGD White has to think twice about playing 5 ♗g5, since Black has a choice of methods to extract a cost from White for this extravagance. He can either capture on c4 (the complicated but fascinating material of the first seven chapters of the book) a pawn which White cannot recover without heading for a position of great structural imbalance; or he can play 5...h6, (Chapter 8) when White must relinquish the bishop pair or offer a probably rather dubious pawn sacrifice. So, one point of ...c6 is that it threatens to grab a pawn and rather crudely keep hold of it with ...b5.

2) The upshot of this is that many players of the white pieces opt to defend c4 immediately with 5 e3, already a slight concession compared with the QGD. This position leads us to the second stage of the explanation of Black's set-up, namely its FLEXIBILITY. This is best illustrated by the material in Section 3, where after 5 e3 ♘bd7, White avoids the tempo loss implicit in the Meran variation (6 ♗d3 dxc4) and opts for the popular 6 ♕c2 ♗d6 7 ♗e2 *(2)*. Here Black still has no less than five conceptually distinct approaches available:

2
B

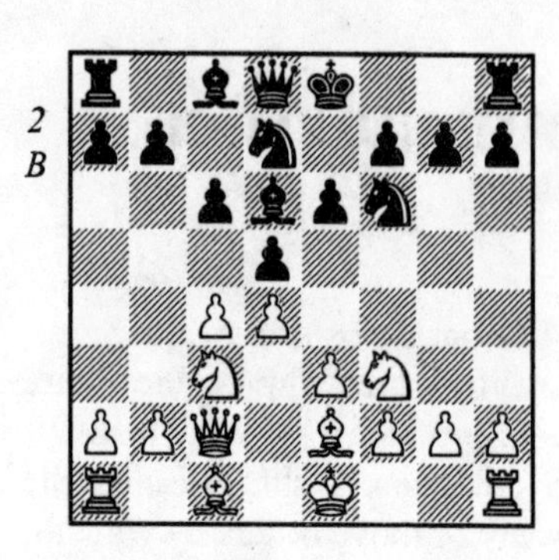

a) Capture on c4 and play for ...b5 and an eventual ...c5.

b) Capture on c4 and play for ...e5.

c) Capture on c4 and play for ...c5.

d) Aim for active piece play with the immediate ...e5.

e) Complete development with, for example, ...b6, ...♖e8, ...♕e7 etc placing pieces optimally to cope with White's break.

There is no 'right answer' as to which plan to adopt. There is room for personal taste, style, a richness of strategy which is hard to match.

Reaching Diagram 1

As I mentioned earlier, there are many routes to the basic position, and here I will hope to outline the advantages and disadvantages of each of the main options:

a) The Slav move order 1 d4 d5 2 c4 c6 3 ♘f3 ♘f6 4 ♘c3 e6 is one of the most common. For me it has one overwhelming drawback, namely that White may avoid the

Semi-Slav with the far from entertaining 3 cxd5 - the Exchange Variation. This is notoriously lifeless and also not entirely innocuous. In addition, there is a slight complication in that White may play 4 e3, not a very ferocious move in itself, but it does enable White to answer 4...e6 with 5 ♗d3 or 5 ♘bd2. On the other hand, since the Slav proper is also having quite a purple patch in world chess at the moment, many players are opting for 3 ♘c3 ♘f6 4 e3 with White after which 4...e6 guarantees reaching the Semi-Slav while even circumventing the complex ♗g5 variations. This would be a useful tip for players keen to play the theory in this book with the white pieces.

b) The 1...♘f6, 2...e6 move order. This is only appropriate as part of a wider repertoire, but since the principal requirement is the sound and popular Nimzo-Indian Defence, this may appeal to many readers. The idea is to play the Nimzo against 3 ♘c3, but to meet 3 ♘f3 with 3...d5 when in a majority of cases White replies 4 ♘c3 and then 4...c6 leads to diagram 1. I have often used this move order, with the sharp Vienna Variation for use against 4 ♗g5.

c) Perhaps the most highly recommended move order for maximizing the number of Semi-Slavs is 1 d4 d5 2 c4 e6 3 ♘c3 c6. This has the advantage that 4 cxd5 can be met by 4...exd5 with a favourable version of the Queen's Gambit Exchange Variation for Black since the knight is not yet committed to f6. For players more comfortable in the Meran and other non-♗g5 sections it also may help that many players will shy away from 4 ♘f3 since in addition to the material here, Black can try the very sharp 4...dxc4. White will often choose 4 e3 ♘f6 5 ♘f3, leading to Sections 2 and 3. The only drawback, if drawback it be, is that White can try 4 e4, the Marshall Gambit, the subject of the penultimate chapter of the book. However, if Black studies this thoroughly it should not be a cause for any concern. I personally enjoy playing both sides of this fascinating gambit.

To conclude, there are many routes to the basic position of the Semi-Slav and those seeking to play the opening with Black will find that it arises in a majority of their 1 d4 games. It is worth considering a little which route offers alternatives with which you will be most at home.

About the Book

The explosion of interest in the Semi-Slav in recent years has led to a deluge of material. This has forced an element of concentration on the sharpest, most topical lines where a knowledge of the moves as well as just understanding is essential. Hence, there is a heavy concentration on 5 ♗g5, the Meran, 6 ♕c2 and the Marshall Gambit. Sometimes the theory is inevitably complicated, but I have tried to maximize explanatory comment and have placed the opening in the context of complete games to make the theory accessible to the widest possible audience. I hope that some contribution will here be made to the process of popularizing this fascinating opening at all levels.

Finally I would like to thank all those who helped with materials, including Richard Britton, Malcolm Pein, Jonathan Wilson, Glenn Flear (who opened up his library to me for a few days) and Rajko Vujatovic who generously made some original analysis available for my use.

Graham Burgess deserves credit for great dedication – always with patience and good humour – that this ever-expanding book was eventually produced.

On a more personal note, a big thank you to my parents who have given unwavering support to my chess career through thick and thin and to whom I dedicate this book. Last, but by no means least, to Noemi who has shown great patience and offered loyal support through a long series of missed deadlines.

Peter Wells
March 1994

Section 1 5 ♗g5 Introduction

The assessment of 5...dxc4 is fundamental to the appeal of the Semi-Slav for aggressive counter-attacking players; White has no escape from complications. So, a word on how the main lines come about:

After 5...dxc4 White usually continues 6 e4 (all early alternatives are examined in Chapter 7).

Black must defend c4, or else his relinquishing of the centre has no justification, so 6...b5 *(3)*.

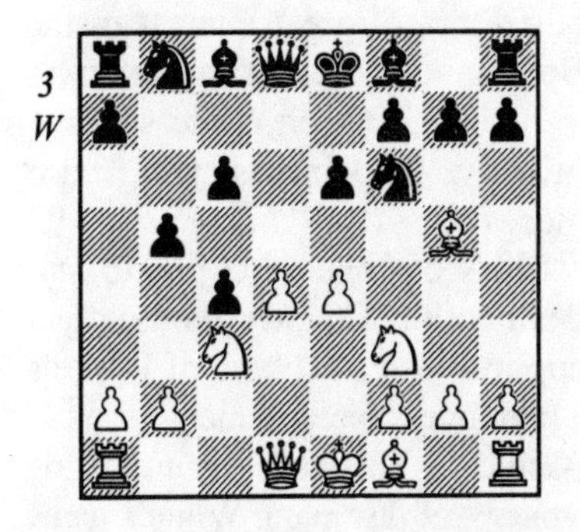

Now there are a range of possibilities – sometimes White sacrifices one or two pawns, sometimes Black, but there are very few variations of equal material! For the sake of simplicity, I will here divide the material into four parts (of which the fourth is by far the most important).

1) 7 a4 (see chapter 7) is an attempt to undermine Black's queenside expansion: It does not seem too troublesome, although Black should be well prepared before heading for the lines where he keeps the gambit pawn with 7...♕b6!?.

7 e5 is clearly the critical test of Black's play. Black is forced to save his piece with the sequence 7...h6 8 ♗h4 g5. Here White is faced with the fundamental decision whether to win back his material with interest, or to sacrifice a second pawn.

2) 9 exf6 (Chapter 6) is the second option. After 9...gxh4 10 ♘e5! White launches a very sharp and rapid assault on Black's weak points, most vividly f7, and in conjunction with the modern treatment 11 a4 he tries too to undermine the queenside phalanx. This has lost some popularity (it is two pawns), but is in my view still fertile research ground.

3) The main line runs 9 ♘xg5 when Black has the very interesting but probably not quite correct deviation 9...♘d5 (Chapter 5).

4) Black answers 9...hxg5 10 ♗xg5 ♘bd7 *(4)* (Chapters 1-4).

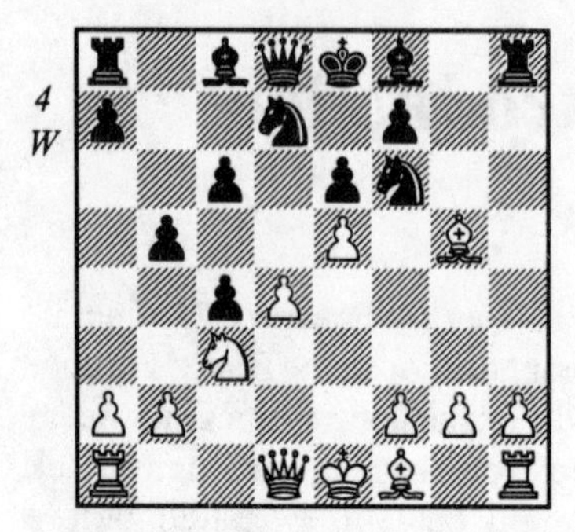

The key basic position of the Botvinnik. White will normally recapture on f6 and, since Black should not self-pin by ...♘xf6 without clear reason, White will be at least temporarily a pawn up. In addition, White has a passed h-pawn, and if he elects to fianchetto his king's bishop (undoubtedly best!) his king has good cover from Black's half-open files too. Black's position has plus points too, however. His phalanx of queenside pawns can be very strong in an ending, and he is well placed to launch an assault on White's vulnerable d-pawn. The battle of these relative advantages is well illustrated in the old main line (Chapters 1 and 2). Note that the 17 a3 of Chapter 1 is typical of the process of attacking Black's pawn phalanx to chip away at the shield it provides Black's king from the white rooks.

More topical are Black's attempts to avoid these main lines. One plus of Black's position is that whichever 11th move White chooses (11 exf6 or 11 g3) he can interrupt the smooth flow of White's game. Chapter 3 examines 11 exf6. The problem here for White is that after 11...♗b7 12 g3 Black has a split-second opportunity to force the d-pawn forward with 12...c5!. After 13 d5 this pawn can be further attacked. In current fashion, 13...♗h6!? (Game 4) to exchange off the bishop on g5, weakening f6 and by implication d5 too, is taking over from the also complex 13...♘xf6 (Game 3) as the hottest topic of debate.

This is an argument for 11 g3, but then Black can prevent White's planned exf6 by putting the question to White's bishop with 11...♖g8!? (Game 6). This is the other area of great interest in the Botvinnik at present in particular the debate between White's rook + initiative *vs* Black's two minor pieces after 12 h4!? ♖xg5.

Black has one other possibility, dealt with in Chapter 4, but in fact applicable against both of White's 11th move choices, namely 11...♕a5 (Game 5). This hails the interesting strategy of disrupting White's game on the a6-f1 diagonal and it is sufficient to discourage the fianchetto. Here the queenside pawn phalanx is used as a weapon early in the game. Success or failure will depend on whether its advance strengthens or weakens it. Here the verdict of fashion is not so kind, but in general the Botvinnik is looking as full of possibilities for Black as ever.

1 Botvinnik System: Main Line 17 a3

Game 1
Yusupov-Tukmakov
Leningrad 1987

1 d4	**♘f6**
2 c4	**e6**
3 ♘f3	**d5**
4 ♘c3	**c6**
5 ♗g5	**dxc4**
6 e4	**b5**
7 e5	**h6**
8 ♗h4	**g5**
9 ♘xg5	**hxg5**
10 ♗xg5	**♘bd7**
11 exf6	**♗b7**
12 g3	**c5**
13 d5	**♕b6**
14 ♗g2	**0-0-0**

The move order here is of considerable significance. Alternatives for both sides in ...♕b6 positions are dealt with in Game 6 note 'e' to Black's 11th.

15 0-0	**b4**
16 ♘a4	**♕b5**
17 a3 *(5)*	

5
B

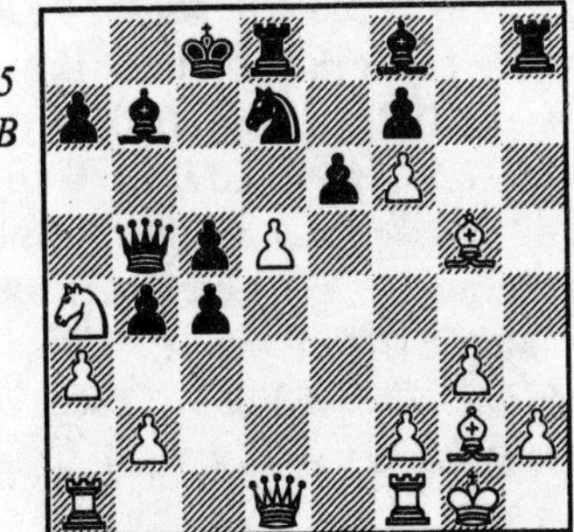

Without a doubt still the main line, 17 a3 has been analysed in extraordinary detail. White aims to break up Black's queenside pawns, and launch an attack on Black's king by opening the a-file, hence targeting the a7 pawn. Sometimes, as Kasparov showed in his fantastic career with the line, White will not shirk sacrificial means to blast open the c-file too.

17 ...	**♘b8**

In a sense the most ambitious move. Black seeks to capture the d5 pawn without further compromising his own structure or opening the e-file. In addition, once the d5 pawn's fate has been clarified, the knight is often headed for c6 to bolster the a7 weakness. Black has tried two other moves. The first is interesting since the 'approved refutation' gives Black the chance to transpose to the very topical note 'b' to White's 19th below. White has other plausible moves, but there is at the very least scope for fresh research for Black here. The second, once the main line, is still the source of fascinating new ideas for both sides, but is not currently fashionable, it must be said on balance, with good reason:

a) **17...♘e5!?** met with swift retribution, viz. **18 axb4** cxb4 19 ♕d4

(19 ♕e2? ♖xd5!) 19...♖xd5? 20 ♕xa7 ♘c6 21 ♘b6+ ♔c7 22 ♘xd5+ exd5 23 ♗f4+ etc. in Malishauskas-Cichocki, Miedzybrodzie 1991. This was in line with the received wisdom, but not the end of the story since with 19...♘c6! we reach the controversial queen sacrifice mentioned above. This may not be everyone's cup of tea so it is worth considering how White can profitably deviate. Attention has focused on **18 ♕e2** ♘d3 (18...♗d6 19 f4 ♘d3 20 dxe6 ♗xg2 21 ♕xg2 fxe6 22 axb4 cxb4 23 ♕a8+ ♗b8 24 b3! ♕d5 25 ♕xd5 exd5 26 ♖ad1+- Mikhalchishin, although 26...a5!? Δ27 bxc4?! ♗a7+ does not look too bad) 19 axb4 (Also possible is 19 dxe6 ♗xg2 20 ♔xg2 ♕c6+ 21 f3 fxe6∞. Black has as many weaknesses as White has passed pawns, but there is definite counterplay based on ...♖d5-e5/h5, and the beast on d3) 19...cxb4 20 b3! exd5! (20...c3? 21 ♖fd1! ♖xd5 22 ♗xd5 ♕xd5 23 f3 ♗a6? 24 ♘b6+ ±) 21 ♕g4+ ♔b8 Maximenko-Scherbakov, Berlin 1993 and now 22 ♕d4! ♗c5 23 ♘xc5 ♕xc5 24 ♗e3! ♕xd4 25 ♗xd4 a6 26 ♖fb1 Δ♗f1 gives White a clear positional plus – Mikhalchishin.

b) **17...exd5 18 axb4 cxb4** *(6)* and White has a wide choice of largely promising lines. A summary:

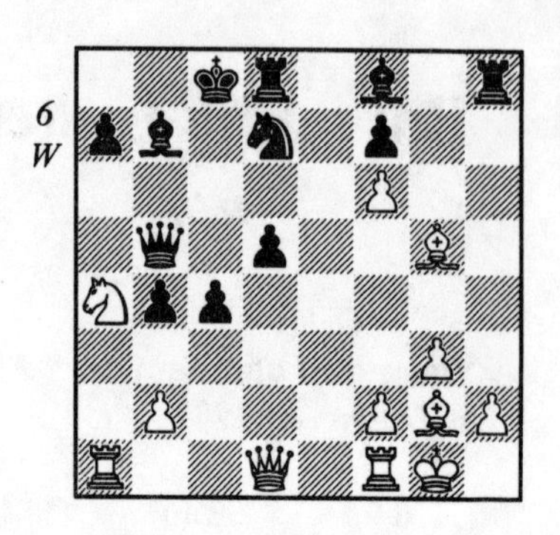

6
W

b1) **19 ♖e1** and now:

b11) **19...♗h6** 20 ♗xh6 ♖xh6 21 ♕d4 ♖xf6 22 ♗h3 ♖d6 23 ♘c5 ♕b6 24 ♖ed1 ♔c7 25 ♗xd7 ♖8xd7 26 ♘xd7 ♕xd4 27 ♖xd4 ♔d7± Stean-Rivas, Marbella Z 1982. Black has some compensation for the exchange, but it is uncertain whether enough.

b12) **19...d4!?** is a further try. 20 ♕xd4 ♗xg2 21 ♔xg2 ♕xg5 22 ♕xc4+ ♔b8 23 ♖ad1 ♕a5 24 ♖d5 ♕c7! 25 ♕d3 ♕c6! (25...♗h6? enabled White to gain very strong pressure in spite of the queen exchange after 26 ♖e7 ♕c6 29 ♕b5+ ± in Dolmatov-Rivas, Minsk 1982) and Black still has chances to defend (Polugaevsky).

b13) **19...♘c5** 20 ♕g4+!? (20 ♖e7!? {Smejkal-Sveshnikov, Sarajevo 1983} 20...♘e6! 21 ♖xf7 ♘xg5 22 ♕g4+ ♖d7 23 ♖xd7 ♕xd7 24 ♕xg5 ♗c6 gives counterchances – Sveshnikov) 20...♕d7 21 ♕d4! ♘xa4 22 ♕xa7 ♗c5 (22...♘c5 23 ♖e7! ♕c6 24 ♗f4+-) 23 ♕xa4 ♕xa4 24 ♖xa4

♖he8 25 ♖e7!± Riskin-Andrianov, Minsk 1982.

b2) **19 ♕g4** d4 (the loose bishop on g5 plays an important role in Black's defence, but 19...♗d6 may be OK too) 20 ♗xb7+ ♔xb7 21 ♕e4+! ♕c6 22 ♕xd4 ♗d6 23 ♖fe1 ♖de8! (still playing for ...♘e5) 24 ♖xe8 ♖xe8 25 ♗e3 ♗b8 26 ♕xd7+ ♕xd7 27 ♘c5+ ♔c8 28 ♘xd7 ♔xd7 29 ♖a4! a5! 30 ♖xa5 ♗e5! with counterplay in an ending typical of the Botvinnik; Zarabin-Andrianov, USSR 1982.

b3) **19 ♗e3!? ♘c5** and White can choose between:

b31) **20 ♕g4+** and now not **20...♔b8?** 21 ♕d4! ♘xa4 22 ♕xa7+ ♔c7 23 ♖xa4! ♖a8 24 ♕xa8 ♗xa8 25 ♖xa8 c3 (Black's kingside pieces are hopelessly tied up. The text is the only, forlorn, hope of counterplay) 26 bxc3 bxc3 27 ♗f4+ with a winning attack in Agzamov-Chandler, Belgrade 1982, but **20...♖d7!** 21 ♘xc5 ♗xc5 22 ♖fe1 ♔c7!∞ (Nikolić).

b32) **20 ♘xc5** ♗xc5 21 ♕g4+ ♔b8 22 ♕f4+ ♔a8 23 ♕c7 (Black was threatening ...d4) 23...♖c8 24 ♕xf7 ♖hf8 25 ♕g7 ♖g8 and drawn, since White was reluctant to leave the seventh rank and permit ...d4, in Kharitonov-Dorfman, Volgodonsk 1981.

b4) **19 ♕d4!?** is an interesting recent addition to White's armoury. **19...♘c5 20 b3!** *(7)*.

7
B

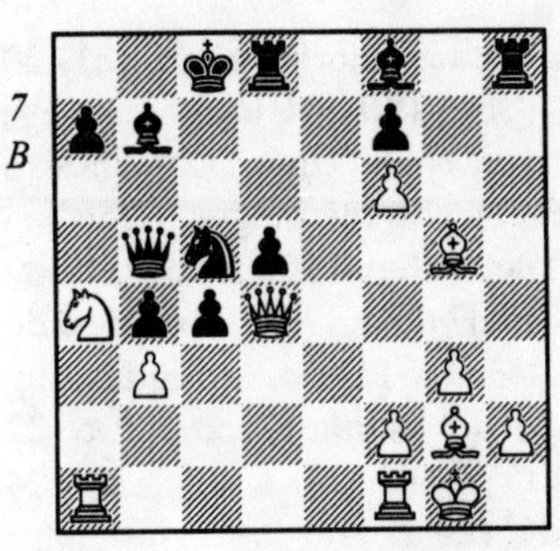

A recognized strategy to open lines by attacking Black's queenside pawn phalanx whilst at the same time defending a4, but here deserving special credit since it is based on a fine tactical sequence. 20...♘xb3 21 ♕xa7 ♘xa1 22 ♗f4! ♔d7 (If 22...♗d6 23 ♘b6+ ♕xb6 24 ♕xb6 ♗xf4 25 ♖xa1 ♗d6, which would be thus far quite acceptable to Black on material grounds alone, White breaks through with 26 ♖a7 ♖d7 27 ♖xb7!±) 23 ♗xd5! (an important improvement on Nikolac-Kishnev, Munich 1992/3 which favoured Black after 23 ♘b6+?! ♔c6 24 ♘xd5 ♖xd5 25 ♖d1 ♖hh5! and now White should have tried 26 g4) 23...♕xd5! 24 ♘b6+ ♔c6 25 ♘xd5 ♖xd5 26 ♖xa1 ♗h6! 27 ♕e3 (27 ♖a6+ ♗xa6 28 ♕xa6+ ♔c5 29 ♗b6!?) 27...♗xf4 28 ♕xf4± Dokhoian.

b5) **19 h4!?** is another new idea. White gains the new possibility ♗h3+, but it is hard to believe it is the most critical. 19...♘e5 (Dokhoian gives 20 ♖e1 as a reply to 19...♘c5, but is this more dangerous timing than in 'a' above?) 20 ♖e1 ♗d6 (20...d4 looks very aggressive, but White has tactics to prevent a long diagonal mishap and net material after 21 ♗h3! ♖d7 22 ♗xd7+ ♔xd7 23 ♕xd4+ ♗d6 24 ♖e3 ♕c6 25 ♘c5+ ± liquidating in the nick of time) 21 ♕d4 ♘c6 22 ♕xd5 ♕xd5 23 ♗xd5 ♘d4 24 ♖ad1! (24 ♗xb7+ ♔xb7 just helps Black's king to come to the aid of his queenside pawns) was played in Yusupov-Dokhoian, Bundesliga 1992, and now with 24...♘f3+! 25 ♗xf3 ♗xf3 26 ♖d4 c3! 27 bxc3 b3! 28 ♖b1 ♖he8! Black's domination of the key light squares around the white king would give enough compensation for the pawns.

18 axb4 cxb4 *(8)*

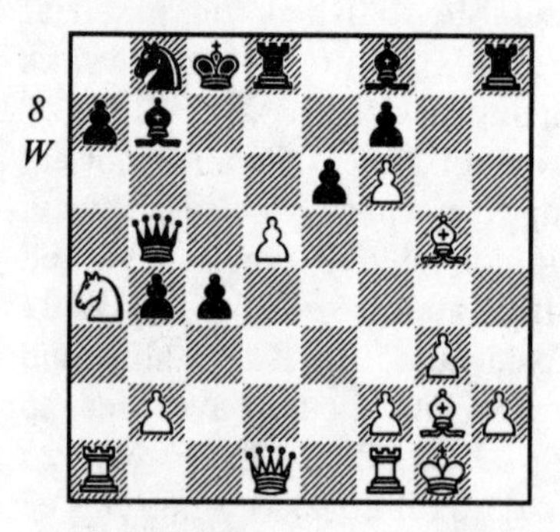

8
W

19 ♕g4

A very major parting of the ways. For a long time the choice here was between the text and 19 ♗e3. Three games with, and superb analysis of the latter by the World Champion predictably focused great attention on it, but it now seems that with correct play Black is OK. Since 1990 the amazing correspondence game Krausser-Gunther has given White a fascinating alternative: 19 ♕d4!? and the ensuing queen sacrifice considered below. It may yet be premature to attempt a definitive assessment of this intriguing possibility. Black's defences have certainly been strengthened since the first successful outing, but no clear refutation of this dangerous idea has yet been found. Still, I decided to focus the main game on 19 ♕g4 which still poses problems for Black and is perhaps most guaranteed to prove to be of durable worth. The (major) alternatives in turn:

a) **19 ♗e3** is directed against Black's weak spot on a7, and leads to a plethora of attacking possibilities, and White sacrifices on c3 to open the c-file as well as the a-file almost routinely. **19...♗xd5 20 ♗xd5 ♖xd5 21 ♕e2 ♘c6 22 ♖fc1** *(9)*.

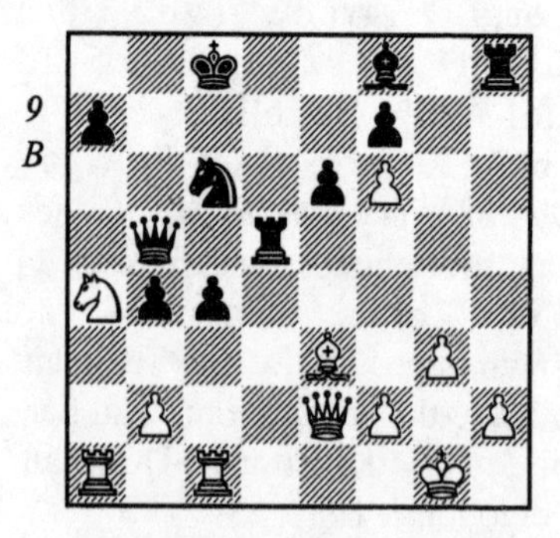

9
B

Now Black has a number of moves. The first two are clearly inadequate, so Black's choice essentially comes down to which square his knight should occupy. Interestingly, the extra possibilities for the knight which come from controlling d3, f3, and g4 count for more than blocking the a-file. Thus:

a1) **22...♔b7** 23 ♖xc4 ♘a5 24 b3! ♗d6 25 ♕a2± Anikaev-Sveshnikov, Volgodonsk 1981.

a2) **22...c3** (with hindsight, it seems illogical for Black to play this voluntarily) 23 ♕xb5 ♖xb5 24 ♘xc3! bxc3 25 ♖xc3 ♔d7 26 ♖a6 ♘e5! 27 ♖xa7+ ♔d6 28 ♗f4 ♔d5 29 ♗xe5 ♔xe5 30 ♖xf7 and the pawns outweigh the extra piece; Novikov-Ivanchuk, USSR 1983.

a3) In early games Black tried **22...♘a5?! 23 b3! c3 24 ♘xc3!** (The fundamental motif of the variation. White generates a ferocious attack down the two files, which in many cases persists even after the exchange of queens) **24...bxc3 25 ♖xc3+ ♔d7** (25...♔b7 26 ♕c2 ♗d6 27 b4! reveals a further drawback of the knight's placement) **26 ♕c2 ♗d6 27 ♖c1 ♕b7 28 b4! ♕xb4** (28...♖xh2 29 ♕a4+ ♕b5 30 ♕xb5+ ♖xb5 31 ♔xh2 ♖xb4 32 ♗xa7± was no improvement either in Cvitan-Marjanović, Yugoslav Ch 1982) **29 ♖b1 ♕g4 30 ♗xa7!**. Note the catastrophic situation of the black knight on a5, and that the black queen is tied to defending a4. Kasparov demonstrated the strength of White's position twice(!) at the 1981 USSR Championship in Frunze:

a31) Kasparov-Timoshchenko continued **30...e5** 31 ♕a2 (immediately exploiting the loosening of the rook on d5) 31...♖d1+ (31...♕f5 32 ♖b7+! ♘xb7 33 ♕xd5±) 32 ♖xd1 ♕xd1+ 33 ♔g2 ♕h5 34 ♕a4+ ♔e6 35 h4 and the black knight was lost.

a32) Little better for Black was **30...♗e5** 31 ♖c5! ♖xc5 32 ♗xc5 ♘c6 33 ♕d3+ ♔c8 34 ♖d1! ♘b8 35 ♖c1 ♕a4 36 ♗d6+ +- with which Dorfman was duly dispatched.

a4) **22...♘e5!** (Tal's move) 23 b3 (Kasparov's original notes indicated that if 23 ♗xa7?! ♔b7! 24 ♗e3 ♖d3! Black obtains some counterplay. Goldenberg-Meleghegyi, corr. 1986 confirmed this after 25 ♖f1 ♗d6 26 f4 ♘g4 27 ♕xg4 ♖xe3-+, and 25 ♘b6 ♖xe3! 26 ♕xe3 ♗c5 27 ♕e4+ ♔xb6 is no better) 23...c3 24 ♘xc3 bxc3 25 ♖xc3+ ♔b8! 26 ♕c2 (26 ♗xa7+ ♔b7 27 ♕e4 ♕b4!∓ Kasparov) ♗d6 27 ♗xa7+ ♔b7 28 b4 (Kasparov-Tal, Moscow 1983) and now 28...♖d3! would be the cleanest equalizer.

b) **19 ♕d4!?** introduces the aforementioned queen sacrifice. Acceptance now must be critical; without entering into the main fray Black does not generate enough play to compensate for the loss of the key a7-pawn:

b1) Two games with **19...♖xd5?!** confirm this: 20 ♕xa7! ♘c6 21 ♘b6+ ♔c7 (21...♕xb6!? 22 ♕xb6 ♗c5 23

♖a8+? {23 ♕xb7+!?; 23 ♕xc6+ ±} 23...♗xa8 24 ♕a6+ ♗b7 25 ♕a4 ♘d4∞) 22 ♗f4+ ♗d6 23 ♘xd5+ exd5 24 ♗xd6+ ♔xd6 25 ♕e3 ♔c7 (25...d4 26 ♖fd1 ♔c7 27 ♕f4+ ♔b6 28 ♖xd4 ♘xd4 29 ♕xd4+ **1-0** Malishauskas-Cichocki, Beskidy 1991) 26 ♖fe1 ♖d8 27 b3 d4 28 ♕f4+ ♔b6 29 ♖e7! 1-0 Shirov-Oll, Tilburg 30 min 1992.

b2) **19...♘c6 20 dxc6!** – the point. Without this intriguing queen sacrifice, for which White gains two pieces, a passed pawn on the seventh rank and a host of tricks, 19 ♕d4 would be absurd. As it is, a really convincing antidote has yet to be found. **20...♖xd4 21 cxb7+** *(10)*.

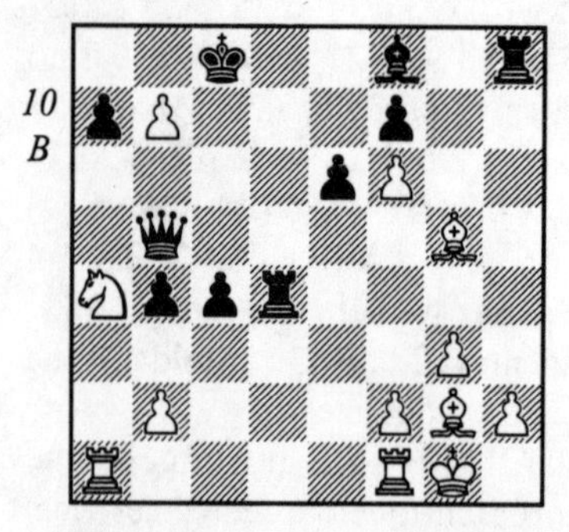

10
B

b21) The stem game, Krausser-Gunther, corr. 1990, went **21...♔b8** 22 ♗e3 e5 (Drazić analysed 22...♗c5?! 23 ♘xc5 ♕xc5 24 ♖a6 ♖hd8 25 h4!±) 23 b3! (Black obtains a passed pawn, but more importantly the knight on a4 becomes well supported) 23...c3 (23...cxb3?! 24 ♖fc1 ♗d6 25 ♗xd4 exd4 26 ♖c6 ♗c7 27 ♘c5 b2 28 ♖b1 ♖d8 29 ♖xb2 d3 30 ♖xb4+- Vujatović) **24 ♖ad1 ♗h6** (24...♖xd1 25 ♖xd1 ♗h6 26 ♗c5 a5 27 ♗d6+ ♔a7 28 b8♕+ ♖xb8 29 ♗c5+! ♕xc5 30 ♖d7+ **1-0** was Rantanen-Kokkila, corr. 1991) 25 ♗xd4 exd4 26 ♖xd4 c2?! 27 ♖c4 c1♕ 28 ♖fxc1 ♗xc1 29 ♖xc1 and Black was helpless. However, Vujatović claims that 24 ♖ad1 was inaccurate on account of **24...♖d6!** when after 25 ♖xd6 ♗xd6 26 ♖a1! ♕e2 27 ♗xa7+ ♔c7 28 ♗b6+ ♔d7 29 ♗e3 White has only a slight edge. Instead he prefers **24 ♖fd1!** when **24...♖d6??** fails of course to 25 ♗xa7+, and Krausser's **24...♗h6** 25 ♗xd4 exd4 26 ♖xd4 c2 27 ♖c4 ♕e5 '∞' seems to fail to 28 ♖f1 c1♕ 29 ♖fxc1 ♗xc1 30 ♖xc1 ♕xf6 and just the quiet 31 h3 preparing ♖c6 and ♘c5 is strong.

b22) **21...♔c7!?** 22 ♗e3 **e5?!** 23 ♘c3!! (looks more convincing than 23 b3 which has however also been the subject of some interesting analysis, viz. 23...c3 24 ♖ad1?! ♖xd1 25 ♖xd1 ♗h6! 26 ♗c5 c2 27 ♗d6+ ♔d7 28 ♗h3+ ♔e8 29 ♖e1 ♕xb7 favoured Black in Maiwald-Shabalov, Neu Isenberg 1992. However, again Vujatović's creative analysis seems to strengthen White's play with 24 ♖fc1! and there is no clear defence to the threat of ♘xc3) 23...bxc3 24 bxc3 ♖d6 (Salov's 24...♗c5 25 ♖fb1 ♖d1+ 26 ♖xd1 ♗xe3 27 fxe3± keeps Black on the board, but is also clearly unsatisfactory) 25 ♖ab1 a6 26 ♖xb5 axb5 27 ♖a1 ♖d8 28 ♗e4 ♗h6 29 ♗c5 ♗f8 30 ♗a7+- Salov-Illescas, Madrid 1993. In view of this, Black may have to reconcile himself to Krausser's original suggestion **22...♖xd5** 23 ♗xa7 ♗d6 24 ♘b6 ♗c5! 25 ♘xd5+ exd5 26 b8+ ♖xb8 27 ♗xb8+ ♔xb8 28 ♗xd5± but clearly Black needs better to make the line attractive again.

The inescapable conclusion is that at present the onus is still on Black after 19 ♕d4.

19 ... ♗xd5

19...♖xd5 20 ♖fc1! c3 (20...♖xg5 fails simply to 21 ♕xc4+) 21 bxc3 ♖xg5 22 cxb4+ ♔d8 23 ♕d4+ ♖d5 24 ♕xa7 ♘c6 25 ♕b6+ ♕xb6 26 ♘xb6 ♖hh5 27 ♗xd5 ♖xd5 28 ♘xd5 exd5 29 b5 gave White a clear plus in Dvoirys-Sveshnikov, Sochi 1983.

20 ♖fc1 ♘c6

a) Considerable attention has also been devoted to **20...♘d7**, by which Black hopes to be able to recapture on d5 with a pawn, and hence provide much needed back-up to his c4 weakness. However, this currently looks no improvement due to 21 ♕f4! (Simplest; White logically wants to concentrate on the weakness of c4, and prepares to answer 21...♕c6 with 22 ♖xc4! ♕xc4 23 ♖c1 ♕xc1 24 ♕xc1+ ♔b7 25 ♗f4±; and 21...♗xg2 with 22 ♕xc4+ ±. To prepare ♗f1, ...♘e5 must also be cut out) 21...♘c5 22 ♘xc5 ♗xc5 (22...♕xc5 23 ♕g4 ♖d7 24 ♗e3±) 23 ♗f1 ♔b7 24 ♗xc4 ♗xc4 25 ♖xc4!± Magerramov-Savchenko, St. Petersburg 1992.

b) In addition, the refutation of the strange-looking **20...♕d7?** *(11)* is worth knowing, even if only for aesthetic reasons.

11
W

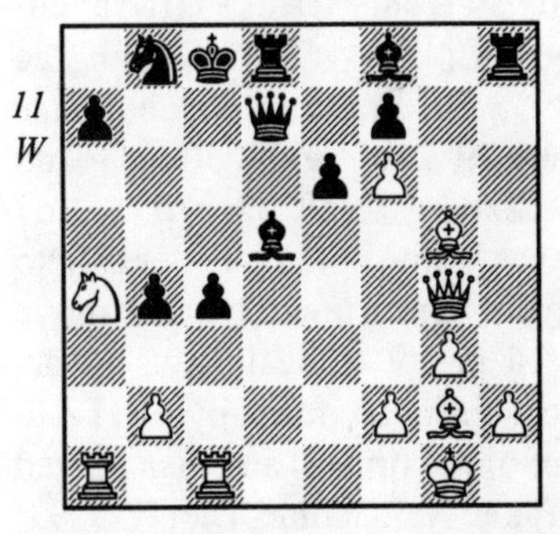

Tolstikh-Kozlov, USSR 1988 concluded 21 ♖xc4+! ♗xc4 22 ♕xc4 ♕c7 23 ♘b6+! axb6 24 ♗b7+! ♔xb7 (24...♔d7 25 ♕b5+ decides) 25 ♖a7+ ♔xa7 28 ♕xc7+ 1-0.

21 ♗xd5 ♖xd5

22 ♖xc4

Not 22 ♕xc4?? ♖d1+ winning heavy material; Van Wely(!)-Shabalov, New York Open 1993. An astonishing blunder from a young player who can boast many fine successes on the White side of the Botvinnik variation.

22 ... ♖xg5

22...♔d7? looked like an interesting attempt by Lembit Oll to avoid the far from straightforward defensive task which Black must undertake in the main line. Ivan

Sokolov, who incidentally awarded the ending from Yusupov-Tukmakov a '±' was duly impressed after **23 ♖ac1** ♖xg5 24 ♕e4 ♘d8! (24...♖d5 25 ♖xc6 ♕xc6 26 ♖xc6 ♔xc6 27 b3±) 25 ♕d4+ ♔e8 26 ♕xa7 ♕a5 27 ♕b8 ♕a4 28 ♖d4 that now instead of the disastrous **28...♖d5??** 29 ♖xd5 exd5 30 ♕c8!+- (♖e1+ is the intention) I.Sokolov-Oll, Wijk aan Zee 1993, **28...♕a5!** would equalize since 29 ♖xd8 ♕xd8 30 ♖c8 ♖d5 31 ♖xd8+ ♖xd8 32 ♕b5+ ♖d7 leaves White nothing better than to repeat. Unfortunately, the move has a pretty tactical flaw, apparently discovered first by FRITZ (a sign of the times!) and then played in Piket-Nalbandian, Biel IZ 1993: **23 ♖d1!** ♘e5 24 ♖c5!!± *(12)*.

12
B

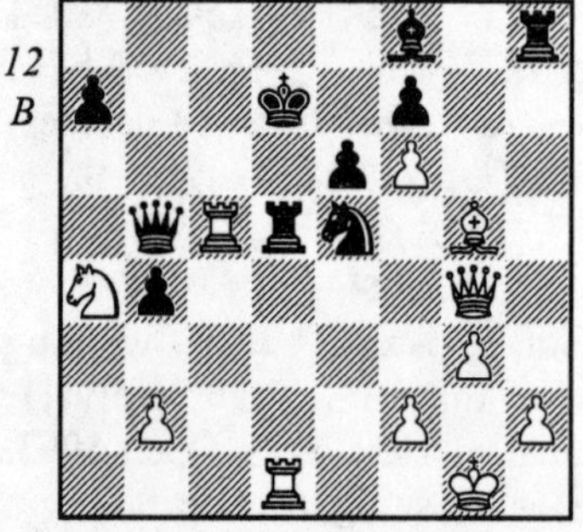

White won without difficulty after 24...♘xg4 25 ♖1xd5+ exd5 26 ♖xb5 ♘xh2 27 ♔g2 ♘g4 28 ♖xd5+ ♔e6 29 ♖d8 ♖h2+ 30 ♔f3 ♔f5 31 ♗e3 ♗h6 32 ♗xa7+-.

23 ♕d4!

Not **23 ♖xc6?** on account of 23...♔b7!∓. Now too Black's next is forced since if 23...♖d5 White has 24 ♕xa7 ♔d8 25 ♕xf7 ♕xc4 26 ♘b6+-.

23 ... ♔b8
24 ♖xc6! ♖xg3+!
25 fxg3 ♕xc6
26 ♖d1!

White both prevents ...♗d6, and prepares to answer 26...♖h5 with 27 ♕d8+ ♕c8 28 ♖d7! (Tukmakov).

26 ... ♗h6 *(13)*

13
W

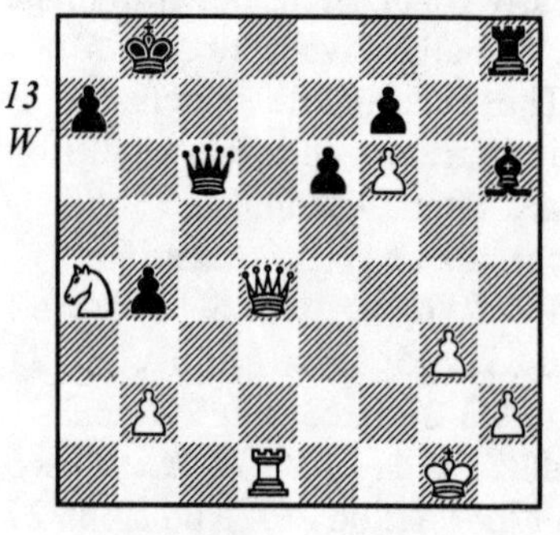

27 ♘c5

A key moment. White's plan of exchanging queens is logical since he can target the f7 pawn, the weakest on the board, while without the c-pawn Black's counterplay is weaker than in most Botvinnik Variation endgames. Moreover, with the bishop on h6 and the half-open h-file Black has some chances to attack the white king. However, Tukmakov mentions **27 ♕xb4+!?** ♔a8 28 ♕d4 in his notes, and there is a question mark over why in particular Shabalov in the later game refrained from this. Since **28...♕f3** 29 ♖d3 leads nowhere, and **28...e5** 29 ♕d5 is a bad ending, Black should perhaps investigate **28...♕c2!?**, threatening 29...♗e3+. Then if **29 ♘c3** simply 29...♕xb2 30 ♕e4+ ♕b7 is fine; or **29 ♖e1** ♗g5!? Δ 30 h4 ♗xh4. Interesting is **29 ♘b6+!?** axb6 (29...♔b7 30 ♘c4!±) 30 ♖a1+ ♔b7 31 ♕d7+ ♔b8 and now in view of the threat of mate from Black, White should give perpetual since if 32 ♕a7+? ♔c8 33 ♕a8+ ♔c7! 34 ♖a7+ ♔d6 White remarkably runs out of checks.

27 ... ♔a8
28 ♕e4! ♕xe4
29 ♘xe4 a5

Only now did Black deviate in Shabalov-Svensson, Gausdal 1991, with **29...♗e3+** 30 ♔g2 a5 31 h4!? ♔b8 32 b3 ♔c7 33 ♔f3 ♗b6 34 ♔e2 ♔c6 35 ♖d6+ ♔c7 36 ♖d3 ♔c6 37 ♘d6!? ♗c7 38 ♘xf7 ♖f8 39 g4!? (39 ♘g5 ♖xf6=/±) 39...♖xf7 40 g5 ♗f4 41 ♔f3 ♗e5 42 ♔e4 ♗xf6! 43 ♖f3 ♗xg5 44 ♖xf7 ♗xh4 and White could make Black suffer a little, but should have no realistic chances to win.

30 ♖a1

As Tukmakov points out, **30 ♖d7?** is a blunder in view of 30...a4 31 ♖xf7?! a3 32 bxa3 bxa3 33 ♖d7 a2 34 ♖d1 ♖b8 35 f7 ♗g7∓/-+. However, **30 ♔g2** Δ♔f3 may be more flexible than the text. In general, if White is careful this ending should be a little in his favour, but the bishop is strong with play on both sides, and it seems very hard to win.

30 ... ♗e3+
31 ♔g2 ♖h5
32 g4 ♖d5
33 b3 ♔b7
34 h4 ♔b6
35 ♖e1!

Not 35 ♔f3? ♖d3! 36 ♔e2 ♖xb3 37 ♘d6 ♗d4! and suddenly Black has the upper hand.

35 ... ♗f4?

A very serious error, which Black was lucky to get away with. Placing his bishop on the file of White's potential passed pawn enables White to put his rook behind it with gain of tempo. Better was **35...♗d4!** 36 g5 a4 37 bxa4 b3 **38 g6** fxg6 39 f7 ♖f5!; or **38 h5** b2 39 h6 ♖d8 holding the balance.

36 ♔f3?

Returning the compliment. **36 ♖f1** ♗e5 37 g5 a4 38 bxa4 b3 39 g6 fxg6 40 f7 was not so difficult, and after giving up the bishop Black should lose.

36 ... ♗e5
37 g5 a4
38 bxa4 b3
39 g6 fxg6
40 ♖b1

If 40 f7 ♗g7 41 ♘g5 ♖f5+ 42 ♔g4 ♔a5 43 ♘e6 ♗h6 – Tukmakov.

40 ... b2
41 f7

½-½

The two kings will arrive on the scene together: 41...♖d8 42 ♘g5 ♖f8 43 ♔g4 ♔a5 44 h5 gxh5 45 ♔xh5 ♔xa4 46 ♔g6 ♔b3.

2 Main Line – Uhlmann's 16 ♖b1 and 17 dxe6!? and other White alternatives

In this chapter, we examine the play when Black is ready to enter the theoretical minefield of 17 a3, but White thinks better of it.

The first of the two important lines is 16 ♖b1, which Uhlmann has practised with his characteristic loyalty across four decades but which now is perhaps regarded as less dangerous for Black than previously.

The other key option for White is 17 dxe6, featured here in our main game. For some time this looked like a move which should make Black think twice before heading for these main lines. Its combination of definite sting with considerable solidity has made it a favourite of such practical Grandmasters as Predrag Nikolić and Alexander Beliavsky. However, since Savchenko's truly excellent novelty 21...♖d4!! Black's kingside counterplay in the main lines suddenly looks a lot more dangerous, and whatever the theoretical assessment turns out to be, the line has lost a little of its appeal as a 'safe option'.

Game 2
Beliavsky-Piket
Amsterdam 1989

1 d4 ♘f6 2 c4 c6 3 ♘c3 d5 4 ♘f3 e6 5 ♗g5 dxc4 6 e4 b5 7 e5 h6 8 ♗h4 g5 9 ♘xg5 hxg5 10 ♗xg5 ♘bd7 11 g3 ♗b7 12 ♗g2 ♕b6 13 exf6 0-0-0 14 0-0 c5 15 d5 b4

16 ♘a4

White has two alternatives here, the latter of particular theoretical importance.

a) **16 dxe6?! ♗xg2 17 e7 ♗xf1** (17...♗xe7 18 fxe7 ♖dg8 has been proposed by Baturinsky and Polugaevsky; however, White could try 19 ♘d5!? ♕c6 {19...♕e6 20 ♘f4!} 20 e8♕+! ♖xe8 21 ♔xg2 ♘b6 {or 21...♖e5 22 ♕f3 ♖xd5 23 ♖ad1 ♘b6 24 h4±, although not 24 ♖xd5 ♘xd5 25 ♖d1?? ♘f4+ ∓} 22 ♕f3 ♘xd5 23 h4!±) **18 ♘d5 ♕e6** (Probably better than 18...♕b7 19 exd8♕+ ♔xd8 20 ♔xf1 ♖xh2 21 ♔g1 ♖h8 22 ♕f3 ♗d6 23 ♖d1 {23 ♕e4!?} 23...♗e5 24 ♕e2? {again 24 ♕e4 was more to the point} 24...c3! 25 bxc3 bxc3 26 ♕e4 c2! 27 ♕xc2 ♗d4 28 ♕e4 ♖e8 29 ♕h1

½-½ Suba-Tatai, Dortmund 1981) **19 exd8♕+ ♔xd8 20 ♔xf1** and Black has two viable choices:

a1) **20...♖xh2** 21 ♔g1 ♕h3! 22 ♕f3 ♘e5 23 ♕e4 ♕h5 (Δ...♘f3+) 24 ♕xe5 ♖h1+ 25 ♔g2 ♖h2+ etc. ½-½ in Kuschenko-Rapaport, corr. 1979.

a2) **20...♕h3+!?** (more ambitious) 21 ♔e1 ♕xh2 with counterplay eg. 22 ♘e3 ♗h6! 23 ♕d5! ♕g1+ 24 ♔e2 ♕xa1 25 ♕a8+ ♔c7 26 ♕xa7+ and White must give perpetual (Euwe).

b) **16 ♖b1!?** *(14)*.

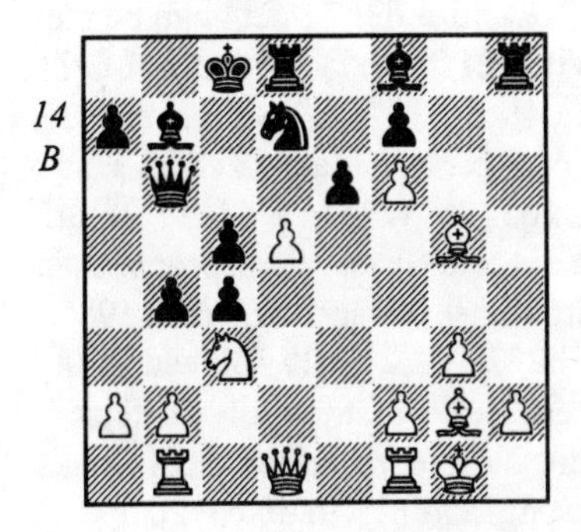

Uhlmann's patent, the immediate tactical justification of which is seen after **Δ16...bxc3?** 17 bxc3 ♕a6 18 ♖xb7! 19 dxe6 with a fearsome attack for White. More reasonable choices for Black are:

b1) **16...♗h6!?** 17 ♕c1 (17 f4?! ♕a6! 18 ♗xh6?! {perhaps 18 dxe6, although 18...♗xg2 19 ♔xg2 ♕xe6 looks fine for Black, e.g. 20 ♕d5? bxc3 21 ♕a8+ ♘b8 22 bxc3 ♕d5+} 18...♖xh6 19 ♘e4 ♘xf6 20 ♘xf6 ♖xf6 21 ♕g4 Yusupov-Sveshnikov, USSR Ch 1981, when 21...♖g6! would have at least equalized) 17...♗xg5 18 ♕xg5 and now 18...♖dg8! is Polugaevsky's recommendation. **19 ♕e3** ♘xf6 (∓ Polugaevsky) 20 ♘a4 ♕c7 21 ♘xc5 (21 dxe6 ♗xg2 22 ♔xg2 ♖xh2+) 21...♗xd5 looks fine for Black. However White should perhaps investigate **19 ♕f4!?** since Black's 18th does relax the pressure on d5 somewhat.

b2) **16...♕a6** (? – Polugaevsky) is not so clear. **17 dxe6** (17 b3?! {Δ17...bxc3 18 bxc4±} 17...♘b6! 18 bxc4 ♕xc4∓ Shabalov) **17...♗xg2 18 e7** and now:

b21) **18...♗a8** (18...bxc3 loses to 19 bxc3 Δ♖b8+; 18...♕c6 19 ♘b5! is also clearly inadequate). Now White has two choices, the selection between which seems to rest basically upon the validity of L.Santos' assessment in *Informator 46* of the very sharp position which arises after **19 ♘d5!? ♕b7** (the availability of this square for the queen is the justification of the 'full' bishop retreat) 20 exf8♕ ♖hxf8 21 ♘e7+ ♔c7 22 ♗f4+ ♘e5! 23 ♗xe5+ ♔b6. All this was published in *Informator 41* by Shabalov with the judgement ∓, which at first sight looks highly likely. Santos' contribution was the further 24 f3 ♖xd1 25 ♖bxd1 (15), reaching the diagram below with the implication of ample compensation.

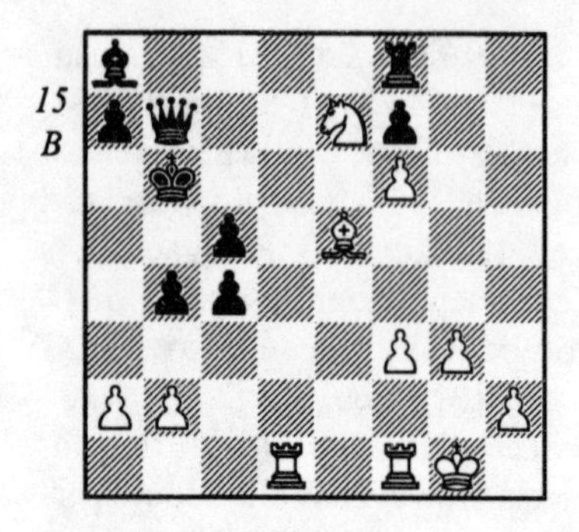

15
B

On reflection I am inclined to Santos' view. So is Uhlmann whose endorsement should count for something in this variation; at least that is the implication behind the opening in Uhlmann-Schön, Porz 1990. This game again highlighted the critical significance of the diagram position since Schön's attempt to improve after 19 ♘d5 with **19...♕e6(?)** 20 exf8♕ ♖dxf8 21 ♘e7+ ♔d8 22 f3 ♖h5 23 ♕d2 ♖fh8 24 h4 ♕e5 25 ♔g2 led to a clear plus for White.

Further relevance for all this is Black's success in holding his position together at present against White's other choice. Following **19 exd8♕+** ♔xd8 20 ♘e2 ♔c8 21 ♕c2 ♕e6 22 f3!? (after 22 ♘f4 ♕g4 23 ♖fe1 ♗h6! 24 ♗xh6 ♕f3 25 ♔f1 ♕h1 White would have been wise to reconcile himself to sharing the point in Ermolinsky-Shabalov, USSR 1986) 22...♗d6 23 ♖bd1 ♗c6! (directed against ♕a4. White's weakened kingside certainly gives Black some play for the exchange. Whether it is enough is a moot point, but Black seemed to have chances in the only practical test to date) 24 ♘f4 (24 ♗f4 ♗e5!) 24...♕e3+ 25 ♕f2 ♕xf2+ 26 ♖xf2 ♗e5 27 ♘d5 (27 ♔g2!?; but Black still has compensation) and now 27...♗xd5! 28 ♖xd5 ♗d4 would have maintained the balance in Ermolinsky-Makarov, USSR 1986.

b22) **18...♗xf1?!** and now:

b221) **19 ♕d5** seems to allow Black to equalize with precise play: 19...♗h6! (19...♗d3 20 ♗f4! is too dangerous) 20 exd8♕+ (now that Black's rooks are connected, 20 ♗xh6 ♗d3! 21 ♗f4 can be met with 21...♕b7) 20...♔xd8! 21 ♘e4! ♗h3! 22 ♘xc5 ♗e6! 23 ♘xe6 fxe6 24 ♕a8+ ♕c8 25 ♕xa7 ♗xg5 26 ♕a5+ ♕c7 27 ♕xg5 ♕e5+ and Black had no problems in Ermolinsky-Ivanchuk, Pinsk 1986.

b222) **19 ♔xf1!?** (played in the stem game, and initially criticized, this simple recapture now looks strong again) 19...bxc3 20 bxc3! (the real improvement on 20 ♕d5? ♗xe7 21 fxe7 c2!∓ Uhlmann-Alexandria, Halle 1981) 20...♗h6 21 ♗xh6! ♘xf6 (21...♖xh6 22 ♖b8+ ±) 22 exd8♕+ ♖xd8 23 ♖b8+ ♔xb8 24 ♕xd8+ ± Uhlmann. It seems that here the tempo spent on 16 ♖b1 is most self-evidently justified and hence Black should avoid 18...♗xf1.

16 ... ♕b5

Clearly the best. **16...♕a6** invites 17 a3, when 17...♕b5 is still best, and the tempo can be profitably used by 18 h4!? or 18 Re1!?.

17 dxe6 *(16)*

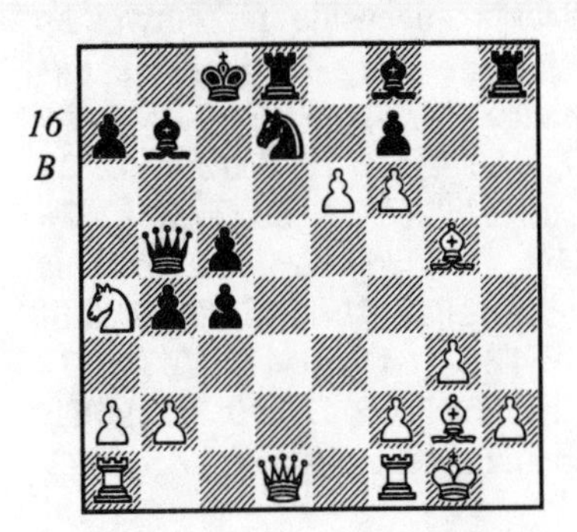

17 ... Bxg2
18 Kxg2

18 e7? is definitely not recommended here. Black had excellent play after 18...Bxf1 19 exd8Q+ Kxd8 20 Kxf1 Qc6! (the key diagonal. Not 20...Rxh2? 21 Kg1 Rh8 22 Qd5! when White seizes it advantageously) 21 Kg1 Bd6 (Δ...Ne5) 22 f4 Re8 23 Kf2 Kc7 in Ubilava-Timoshchenko, USSR Ch (First League) 1981.

18 ... Qc6+

18...Ne5!? has been a fairly popular alternative for Black here, but it seems to me to be based on a misapprehension. The idea is to force White's queen to e2 rather than c2 since, as we shall see, 19 Qc2 allows Black a fierce attack beginning with 19...Rxh2+!. So far so good, since the attack seems to be at least worth a draw. Less convincing is the claim that White's queen stands worse on e2. Praxis has seen:

a) **19 Qc2?!** Rxh2+! 20 Kxh2 Nf3+ 21 Kh3! (21 Kg2?? Qc6 or 21 Kh1?? Qc6 22 e7 Bxe7 23 fxe7 Rh8+ 24 Bh4 Nxh4+ both lose immediately) 21...Nxg5+ 22 Kg2 Qc6+ 23 f3 Qxe6 24 g4 Rd3 25 Rad1 (otherwise ...Qd5 is too strong) 25...Qd5 26 Rxd3 cxd3 27 Qd2 Bd6 (Black's kingside counterplay has shifted focus to the f4 weakness which White was obliged to create, and seems wholly adequate for the draw. Activating the a4 knight is an enduring problem for White) 28 Qe3 Ne6 29 Rd1 Kc7 30 b3 Nf4+ 31 Kf1 Qg5 32 Rxd3 Qh4 33 Rxd6 Qh1+ 34 Kf2 ½-½ since White cannot avoid perpetual check; Pal.Petran-Jo.Horvath, Siofok 1990, and(!) Wl.Schmidt-Cichocki, Polish Ch (Warsaw) 1990.

b) **19 Qe2! Qc6+ 20 f3 Qxe6 21 h4** and now:

b1) **21...Nd3?** 22 Qxe6+ fxe6 23 Rac1!! *(17)*.

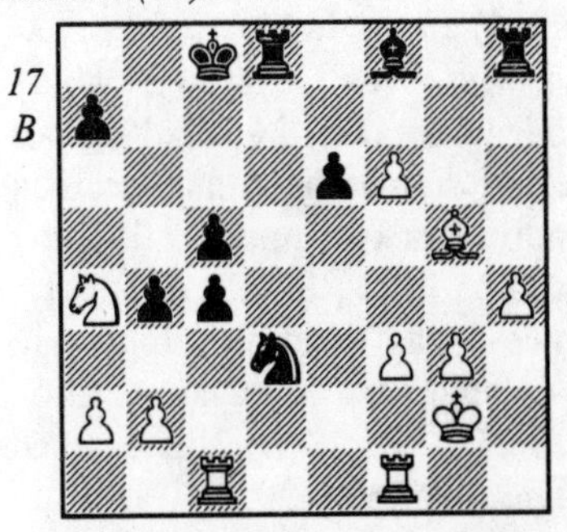

A very instructive moment. White has several trump cards: an extra pawn, the passed h-pawn, the potential weakness of Black's queenside pawns. Black's only real plus is the knight on d3, which in turn offers these queenside pawns some offensive prospects. Sacrificing the exchange to remove this knight card robs Black's position of all dynamic possibilities. 23...♘xd3 24 ♖xc1 ♔c7 (also hopeless was 24...♖d4 25 ♗e3 ♖d3 26 ♗xc5 ♗xc5 27 ♖xc4±) 25 ♖xc4 ♔c6 26 b3 ♖d4 27 ♖c2 ♖h7 28 g4 1-0 Kibalichenko-Khudoroshkov, corr. 1990-91.

b2) **21...♕d5!** is much more challenging. 22 a3 ♘d3 (22...♗h6?! 23 ♕e3 ♗xg5 24 ♕xg5 ♕d2+ 25 ♖f2 ♕xg5 26 hxg5 ♘d3 27 ♖c2 ♖de8 28 axb4 ♘e1+ 29 ♖xe1 ♖xe1 30 f4± {Nikolić} looks convincing) 23 ♕e3!? (Nikolić's 'improvement' on the 23 axb4 axb4 24 ♕e3 ♕d4 25 ♕xd4 ♖xd4 of Jasnikowski-Cichocki, Polish Ch {Warsaw} 1990 when Black's queenside phalanx offers some counterplay, although I still think ±) 23...♗d6 (queried by Nikolić, who gives 23...♕d4 24 ♕xd4 cxd4 {also after 24...♖xd4, does the omission of the exchange on b4 benefit Black so much?} 25 axb4 ♗xb4 26 ♖fd1 ♖he8 27 ♔f1 Δb3±. However, as Vujatović points out, Black can here force a repetition with 27...♘e5 28 ♔g2 ♘e5 when White must play 29 ♔f1 again to prevent invasion on e2. It is for this reason that I am not so convinced that 23 ♕e3!? is so significant) 24 axb4 ♖he8 25 ♘c3!. Thus White solves simply the problem of the a4 knight, usually his greatest bane in this variation. The destruction of Black's queenside far outweighs the impending loss of the exchange. 25...♖xe3 26 ♘xd5 ♖e2+ 27 ♔h3 ♘f2+ 28 ♖xf2 ♖xf2 29 ♖xa7 ♔b8 (if 29...♖xf3, 30 ♘e7+ ♔b8 31 ♘c6+ ♔c8 32 bxc5 is crushing) 30 ♖xf7 ♖xf3 31 ♗f4 ♗xf4 32 ♘xf4 cxb4 33 ♖e7 c3 34 bxc3 ♖xc3 35 f7 1-0 P.Nikolić-Brenninkmeijer, Wijk aan Zee 1992.

19 f3

19 ♕f3?? ♖xh2+ does not seem, as opening traps go, too well disguised but it can boast a fairly illustrious victim after Aseev-Bagirov, Helsinki 1992.

19 ...	**♕xe6**
20 ♕c2	**♘e5**
21 ♖ae1	**♕h3+?!**

Probably better than **21...♖d3?!** when White gained a significant plus with 22 h4 ♗d6 23 b3!? (introducing the possibility of ♘b2 at a moment when 23...c3? fails to 24 ♕xd3 ♘xd3 25 ♖xe6 fxe6 26 ♖d1) 23...♕d5 24 bxc4 ♘xc4 25 ♖d1! ♘e5 26 ♖xd3 (simpler than 26 ♘b2 ♖xd1) 26...♕xd3 27 ♕xd3 ♘xd3 28 ♖d1 c4 29 ♘b2 ♘xb2 30 ♖xd6. The ending is very favourable for White although Black has still a little counterplay which in P.Nikolić-Tal, Nikšić 1983 was combined with great genius to hold a draw.

However, for the time being at least, all attention in this variation is focused on **21...♖d4!** *(18)*.

18
W

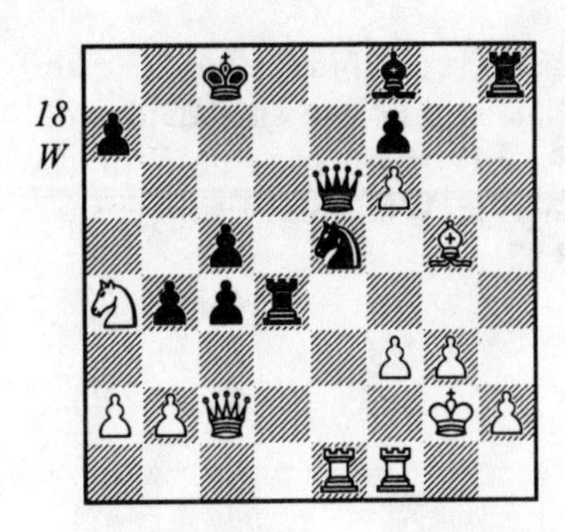

After **22 h4 ♗d6**, various moves have been tried:

a) **23 ♗e3?!** allows the point behind Black's aggressive set-up to be brutally revealed: 23...♖dxh4!! 24 gxh4 (24 ♖h1 ♖h2+!∓/-+) 24...♖xh4 25 ♔g1 (25 ♖h1 ♘xf3! 26 ♔xf3 ♕g4+ 27 ♔f2 ♗g3+ 28 ♔g1 ♗f4+! 29 ♔f2 {29 ♕g2 ♖xh1+ 30 ♔xh1 ♕h4+ 31 ♔g1 ♕xe1+ -+} 29...♕g3+ 30 ♔e2 ♕xe3+ 31 ♔d1 ♖xh1 32 ♖xh1 ♕f3+ ∓/-+) 25...♘d3! 26 ♕g2 (otherwise ...♕h3 is killing) 26...♗h2+ 27 ♕xh2 ♖xh2 28 ♔xh2 ♘xe1 29 ♖xe1 ♕xf6 and in view of the exposed white king and the fact that the knight on a4 cannot enter the game without jettisoning the b-pawn, Black's queen clearly outweighs the white pieces; Rublevsky-Savchenko, Helsinki 1992.

b) No more amenable was White's abrupt experience in Bareev-Oll, Moscow 30 min 1992, which continued **23 ♖e4?** ♕d5 24 ♗e3 (this move is still not safe!) 24...♘xf3! with a winning position.

c) White subsequently improved, but also failed to find anything especially convincing in P.Nikolić-Shirov, Wijk aan Zee 1993: **23 a3** ♕d5 24 ♕f5+ ♔c7 25 ♖e2 (25 ♗f4?! ♖xd4! looks like a strong exchange sacrifice, revealing another point of the versatile 21...♖d4!) **25...♔c6!!** *(19)*.

19
W

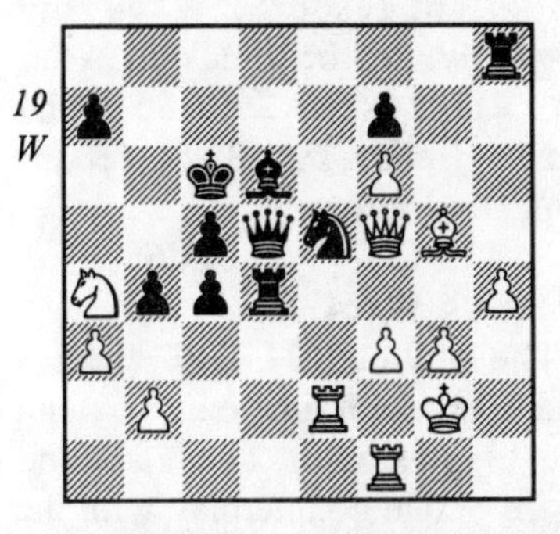

A very fine idea. Black plans to play ...♘d3, but must first give support to the c4 pawn (as we have seen so often the weak link in Black's game in this line) since the immediate **25...♘d3?** fails to 26 ♕xd5 ♖xd5 27 axb4 cxb4 28 ♖e4!. In fact from the diagram White also found an excellent active defence, and after 26 b3! c3! 27 axb4 cxb4 28 ♖a1 ♘d3 29 ♕xd5+ ♖xd5 30 ♖e4 ♔b5 31 ♖c4 ♖e8! 32 ♖a2! Black was only fractionally better.

d) **23 ♖e2!?** ♕d5 24 ♕f5+ ♔c7 25 ♖fe1 ♘d3 26 ♕xd5 ♖xd5 27 ♖e7+!? ♗xe7 28 ♖xe7+ ♔c6 29 ♖xf7 should be investigated since White gets interesting compensation for the exchange, with his fierce f-pawn.

22 ♔g1 ♘d3

Necessary to disrupt the coordination of White's defence. If **22...♗d6** for example, then simply 23 ♕g2 ♕h5 24 f4 and Black is confronted by more than a successful defence.

23 ♖e2

23 ♖e4 is weaker because the important resource ♕xc4 and ♕g4+ would be blocked. After 23...♗d6 24 ♖h4 ♖xh4 25 ♗xh4 ♗e5! (Beliavsky) Black retains dangerous threats.

23 ... ♗d6
24 ♕xc4

The obvious **24 ♖g2** enables Black to take a time out to defend the c-pawn with 24...♕e6! and again obtain counterplay with the ...♗d6-e5-d4 manoeuvre.

24 ... ♗xg3
25 ♕g4+!

By **25 ♕a6+** and 26 ♕b5+ White can give perpetual. The text rightly aims for more.

25 ... ♕xg4
26 fxg4 ♗c7

Weaker is **26...♗h4?** 27 ♖f5! ♖dg8 28 ♘xc5!±. After the move played, Black retains compensation in the form of pressure against White's g- and h-pawns, and the relative strengths of the two knights. It may be sufficient to retain the balance.

27 ♖f3

27 h4?! is rather looser and Black can exploit this by 27...♗g3! 28 h5 ♖d4. If **27 b3**, Beliavsky mentions an interesting idea of 27...♖h3 with the similar idea of 28...♖d4 again hassling White's kingside. White's choice prepares 28 h3.

27 ... ♘e5
28 ♖f5 ♖d1+
29 ♔g2 ♘d3? *(20)*

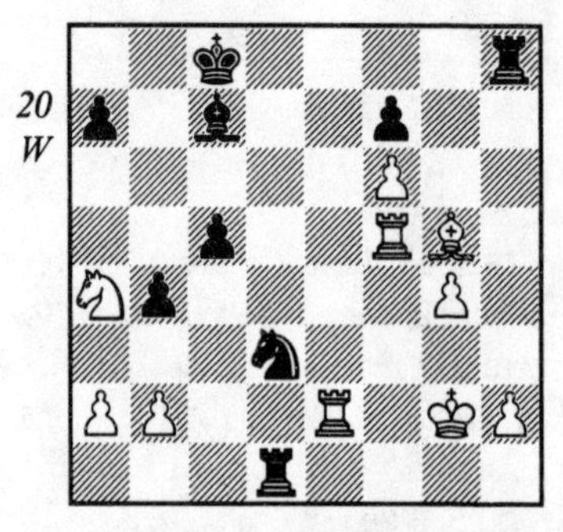

According to Beliavsky, the decisive mistake. Whilst **29...♘xg4** 30 h4± is even worse, **29...♘c6!** threatening both h2 and the fork on d4 would have sufficed to hold the balance after 30 ♗f4 ♘d4 31 ♖e7 (31 ♖xc5!?) 31...♗xf4 32 ♖xf4 ♖d2+ 33 ♖f2 ♖h2+ 34 ♔xh2 ♖xf2+ 35 ♔g3 ♖xf6 and Black is quite safe.

30 h4±

The game now concluded: **30...♘e1+ 31 ♔h3 ♘c2 32 ♖e7! ♗d6 33 ♘xc5! ♘d4** (33...♗xe7 34 fxe7 ♖e8 35 ♖xf7 is also crushing. Once White's king escapes from the checks, his pieces dominate the board and further resistance is futile) **34 ♖d5 ♖h1+ 35 ♔g2 ♖h2+ 36 ♔f1 ♖h1+ 37 ♔f2 ♖h2+ 38 ♔e3 ♗xe7 39 fxe7 ♘c6 40 ♘e4 ♖h3+ 41 ♔f4 1-0**.

3 Deviations from the Main Line after 11 exf6

The section introduction discussed at some length the relative merits of 11 exf6 and 11 g3. As mentioned, 11 exf6 offers more chances for Black to avoid the main lines of Chapters 1 and 2, but more need not necessarily be merrier. In addition, White need not automatically continue 12 g3 after the customary 11...♗b7. The king's fianchetto has been rightly hailed as in principle the correct handling of the variation, superseding the dubious 12 ♗e2 against which Botvinnik won justly famous masterpieces. However, White has recently explored the alternatives 12 h4!? and even more radically 12 ♕c2 13 0-0-0.

Our first game here will principally examine the logical attempts by Black to exploit White's temporary absence from the long diagonal after 11 exf6 ♗b7 12 g3 c5 13 d5, namely by 13...♘b6 and the new addition to the Black arsenal, 13...♘xf6. I believe the former to be virtually refuted, but the latter offers a lot of scope for new ideas and has recently been adopted at the highest level (albeit with mixed fortunes). The second game looks at the interesting 13...♗h6 which has a similar aim of deflecting White's bishop from g5, prior to capturing the f6 pawn and hence again pressuring White's centre. Peter Richmond in his very comprehensive but already somewhat dated (1988) book on the Anti-Meran strongly advocates the move and recently Shirov added his weight to its exponents, with a variation hitherto condemned by the theoreticians which has in recent months become high fashion.

Game 3
Vladimirov-Dzhandzhgava
Pavlodar 1987

1 d4 d5 2 c4 c6 3 ♘f3 ♘f6 4 ♘c3 e6 5 ♗g5 dxc4 6 e4 b5 7 e5 h6 8 ♗h4 g5 9 ♘xg5 hxg5 10 ♗xg5 ♘bd7

11 exf6 ♗b7

Devotees of the ...♕a5 and ...♗a6 lines discussed in Chapter 4 can consider **11...♕a5** with confidence here. White should almost certainly transpose with **12 g3**. The attempt to exploit Black's move order with **12 ♗e2** looks logical enough, but in fact seems to be weak: 12...♗b7 13 0-0 0-0-0 14 ♕c2 (14 ♕c1 c5! 15 dxc5 ♗xc5 16

♕f4 ♘e5!∓ Karolyi-Kaidanov, Budapest 1989 is no better either) 14...c5! 15 dxc5 ♗xc5 16 h4 ♖dg8! 17 ♘e4 ♕c7 18 ♖fd1 (now 18 g3 cannot be played because of 18...♗xe4 and ...♕xg3+) 18...♗xe4 19 ♕xe4 ♖xg5 20 ♖xd7 ♔xd7 21 ♖d1+ ♖d5 22 ♖xd5+ exd5 23 ♕xd5+ ♗d6 and Black is winning; Levitt-Kaidanov, Hastings Challengers 1990. I remember the *post-mortem* where a slightly shell-shocked Jon Levitt tried to work out where he had gone wrong, and his opponent, a leading 'Semi-Slavist' believing that avoiding 12 g3 was (of course!) a recipe for difficulties.

12 g3

The main line and probably the most reliable. 12 ♗e2 is now regarded as clearly inferior. Peter Richmond neatly summarized the advantages of 12 g3 thus: 'The h-pawn is covered down the diagonal, the f4 square is guarded, the bishop (on g2 as opposed to f3) is not vulnerable to ♘e5 at any stage, the g-file is neutralized and the queen has access to h5'. Once it became clear that 12 g3 works tactically (see note to 13...♘b6 below) 12 ♗e2 had little to offer. Still, the strengths of Black's position were revealed in some instructive and historically important Botvinnik games and a flavour of this should be given here: **12 ♗e2** ♕b6 (of course 12...♕a5 is also good – see Levitt-Kaidanov above) 13 0-0 0-0-0 14 a4 b4 15 ♘e4 c5 16 ♕b1 (16 ♘xc5?? ♘xc5 17 dxc5 ♕c7!∓/-+) 16...♕c7 17 ♘g3 cxd4 18 ♗xc4 ♕c6 19 f3 d3! 20 ♕c1 ♗c5+ 21 ♔h1 ♕d6! 22 ♕f4 ♖xh2+ 23 ♔xh2 ♖h8+ 24 ♕h4 ♖xh4+ 25 ♗xh4 ♕f4 0-1 Denker-Botvinnik, USA-USSR 1945.

However, White can consider two other ideas, both of which have had an encouraging recent outing. The line discussed here under 'b' is especially original:

a) **12 h4!?**. This was very successful in P.Nikolić-Blauert, Lugano 1989, which continued **12...♕b6?!** 13 a4!? ♗b4 (interestingly 13...b4 14 a5! ♕a6 15 b3!± was played in Korchnoi-NN, simul 1975; however, perhaps 13...**0-0-0** is playable) 14 ♕g4 **0-0-0** 15 ♗e2 c5 16 a5 ♗xa5 17 dxc5 ♘xc5 18 0-0 ♘b3 19 ♘xb5 ♕xb5 20 ♗xc4 ♕c6 21 ♗xb3 ♖d4 22 ♕h3 ♗c7 23 ♖ac1 ♕d6 24 ♖fd1 ♔b8 25 ♖xd4 ♕xd4 26 ♕e3 ♕g4 27 f3 ♕b4 28 ♕c3 ♕d6 29 f4 ♗b6+ 30 ♔h2 ♖c8 31 ♕e5! with a comfortably winning ending. Perhaps Black should avoid the a4-a5 idea with **12...♕a5!?** Δ...0-0-0 and sometimes ...b4 and ...c3.

b) **12 ♕c2!?** is quite different from White's other approaches since he intends to castle long. In Kanikevich-West, Sydney 1991 Black failed to adapt, and after **12...♕b6** 13 0-0-0 0-0-0 14 ♗e2 ♗h6 15 f4 Black had at best nothing much to show for the pawn minus. One idea to consider might be simply **12...♘xf6** now that White has lost the option of reinforcing the pin with ♕f3.

12 ... c5

As discussed, the text is the best route not only to the material considered here, but to the main line too. If Black plays first **12...♕b6** (see Game 6) he may have to reckon with a later ...c5 being met with dxc5. 12...♕b6 is interesting though, if Black eschews ...c5 altogether. One other line is exclusive to this move order but its neglect seems soundly based: **12...b4?!** 13 ♘e4 c5 14 ♗g2 (also good is 14 ♕g4 cxd4 15 ♗xc4 ♕b6 16 ♕e2) 14...cxd4 (14...♕b6 {Richmond} 15 ♖c1! {Vujatović} 15...cxd4 16 ♖xc4±) 15 ♕xd4±.

13 d5 ♘xf6!? *(21)*

21
W

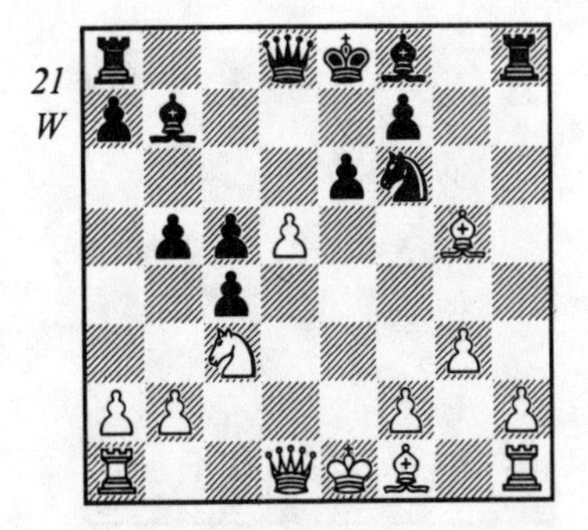

Attributed to the Georgian Master Bokuchava, the text has looked like a viable weapon in its albeit short career. Compared with 13...♘b6 the move has the obvious advantage of re-establishing material parity. On the minus side the pressure against d5 is clearly rendered less urgent since Black's knight is pinned. It is worth mentioning that the 'tactical justification' of White's play is seen after **13...b4?** 14 ♗xc4! when 14...bxc3 15 dxe6 is crushing. The viable alternatives **13...♗h6** and **13...♘e5!?** will be considered in Game 4.

The other choice, **13...♘b6**, was long under a cloud then somewhat rehabilitated again, but in my opinion the more cynical view better reflects its merits: **14 dxe6! ♗xh1** (14...♕xd1+!? 15 ♖xd1 fxe6 16 ♖g1 a6 is mentioned by Harding and Whiteley; I prefer White but it is no catastrophe) **15 e7** and now:

a) **15...♕xd1+ 16 ♖xd1 a6** (16...♗c6 17 ♗g2! Δ♘xb5±) **17 h4!!** *(22)*.

22
B

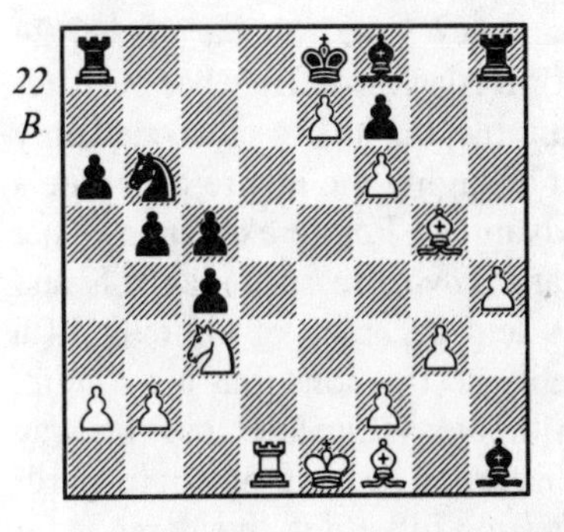

Polugaevsky's brilliant conception, for some time seen as an outright refutation. Much less convincing was **17 exf8♕+** ♔xf8! 18 ♖d6 ♖b8 19 ♗e3 ♖h5 20 ♗e2

♖e5 21 ♘d1 (21 ♗f4 ♖e8 22 ♗e3 ♖e5 should draw) 21...♔g8 22 ♗f4 ♖ee8 23 ♘e3 ♗e4! (otherwise f3 would be strong) 24 f3 ♗g6 and Black was somewhat better in Beliavsky-Bagirov, USSR 1981. White has a pawn and some play for the exchange, but Black's queenside pawn phalanx in conjunction with ideas such as ...♘a4 and ...♗b1 yields excellent counterplay.

Returning to the diagram position: 17...♗h6 18 f4!. A fantastic position - White has sacrificed a whole rook, but his kingside pawn chain exercises a decisive grip over Black's position. Moreover the extra rook is on h8, whence it hardly even has a good view. 18...b4 19 ♖d6! ♖b8! (19...bxc3 20 ♖xb6 cxb2 21 ♖xb2 leaves Black short of any potential freeing mechanism) 20 ♘d1 ♗xg5 21 fxg5 ♘d5! 22 ♗xc4 ♘xe7 23 fxe7 ♔xe7 24 ♖f6!. Black's defence has been admirable, but he has succeeded only in changing the nature of White's advantage. For the exchange White has a pawn, pressure against f7 and a6 and a choice of enticing fifth rank destinations for his knight. Although White later loses his way a little and in one moment jeopardizes the full point, this game is for me a modern Botvinnik Variation classic and well merits full coverage. 24...♖hf8 25 ♘e3 ♗e4 26 ♖xa6 ♖bd8 27 ♖f6 ♖d6 28 ♖f4 ♖d4 29 h5 ♗d3! 30 ♘d5+ ♔d6 31 ♖xd4 cxd4 32 ♗b3? (Rather sad, since 32 ♗xd3! ♔xd5 33 h6 ♖g8 34 h7 ♖h8 35 ♔d2 ♔d6 36 ♔c2 ♔e7 37 ♔b3 ♔f8 38 ♔b4 ♔g7 39 ♔c4 would not only have won much more cleanly, it also emphasize in a new context the helplessness of Black's king's rook) 32...♗c2! 33 ♗xc2 ♔xd5 34 ♗b3+? (34 h6 still wins comfortably) 34...♔e5 35 g4 ♔f4? (returning the favour; 35...d3 36 ♔d2 ♔d4 would have posed a more testing question) 36 g6! (back on track since 36...fxg6 37 hxg6 ♖e8+ 38 ♔d2 ♖e7 39 ♗f7! is decisive) 36...♔e3 37 g7 ♖c8 38 ♔f1 d3 39 ♔g2 ♔f4 40 h6 1-0 Polugaevsky-Torre, Moscow 1981.

b) **15...♕d7!?** *(23)* was Lukacs' celebrated improvement which in my view does not substantially revive Black's case.

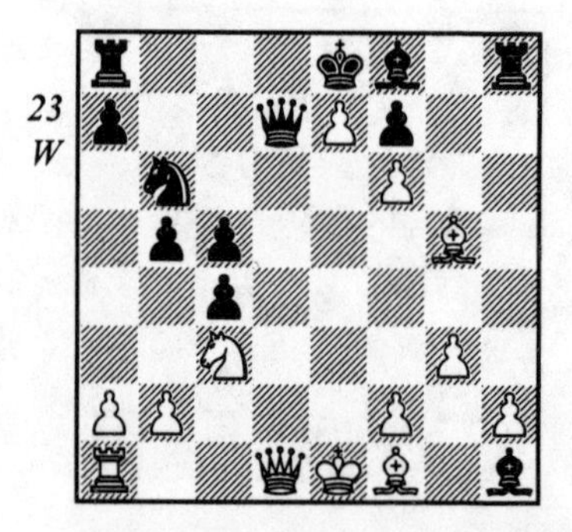

b1) Its first outing was a striking success after **16 f3?!** ♗xe7?! (better would have been 16...♖xh2! 17 ♕xd7+ {17 ♘e4 ♕xd1+! 18 ♖xd1 ♗xf3∓ since after 18 ♘d6+ ♔d7 White has no square for the rook and no lethal discovered check} 17...♘xd7! intending to meet 18 ♘b5 with 18...♘xf6! 19 ♗xf6 (19 exf8♕+ ♔xf8 20 ♗xf6 ♖e8+ ∓) 19...♗xe7 20 ♘c7+ ♔d7∓; or 18 ♘e4 with 18...♗xe7! 19 fxe7 f6!; or 18 ♘d5 with 18...♖c8 19 exf8+ ♘xf8 20 ♗e2 ♘e6. In all cases Black has a large advantage) 17 fxe7 f6 18 ♗xf6 ♖xh2 19 ♘e4? (19 ♕xd7+!) 19...♘d5 20 a4? (20 ♗h4∓) 20...♕e6 21 ♗h4 ♘xe7 22 ♗e2 ♖d8 23 ♕c1 ♖d3! 24 ♕g5 ♗xf3! 25 ♗xf3 ♖xf3 26 ♕h5+ ♖f7 27 ♕h8+ ♖f8 28 ♕h5+ ♕g6 29 ♕e5 ♖xe4 0-1 Bareev-Lukacs, Vrnjacka Banja 1987. However, White has interesting alternatives, and in my opinion 'b3' and 'b4' are both promising:

b2) **16 ♕e2?!** would be strong if Black becomes materialistic with **16...♗h6?** 17 ♖d1 ♕c6 **18 ♕d2!** – Vujatović. Dzhandzhgava and Bokuchava give only **18 ♗h3**, but the text appears to win on the spot in view of the threat of ♕d8+. Better, therefore is either **16...b4!?** or the solid **16...a6**, for example 17 ♖d1 ♕c6 18 ♕d2 ♗xe7 19 fxe7 f6 20 ♕d8+ ♔f7∓.

b3) **16 ♕xd7+!** ♔xd7 (16...♘xd7 can transpose to 'b4', which is good for White, but an additional attractive alternative is 17 ♘xb5 ♗xe7 18 fxe7 f6 19 ♗e3! ♔xe7 20 h4 ♗f3 21 ♗xc4 ♖hc8 22 ♖c1 ♘e5 Ionov-Scherbakov, Rostov-on-Don 1993, when White's pawns give excellent value for the exchange, and according to Ionov 23 b3 Δ♗f1 would have clarified this plus) 17 ♖d1+! (17 h4 ♔c6 18 0-0-0 ♗h6 19 f4 b4∞ Lukacs) 17...♔c6 18 ♖d8±.

b4) **16 exf8♕+!** ♔xf8 17 ♕xd7 ♘xd7 18 0-0-0 ♗c6 19 h4 ♘e5 *(24)* is given as ∞ by Lukacs.

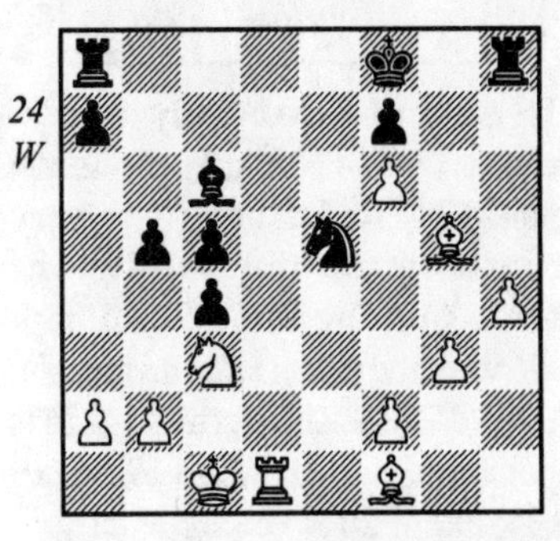

24
W

However, since White has a pawn for the exchange, Black's queenside pawns can become quite weak (20 ♗e3 might be enough to prove that 19...♘e5 was not very appropriate) and Black will have trouble mobilizing his rook on h8, White's chances seem significantly better.

14 ♗g2

This move was praised from the early days of this system, and while two alternatives merit attention, it is once again looking like the most testing choice.

a) **14 ♗xc4!?** *(25)* can be played either as a sacrifice or as a route to a queenless middlegame. The former is more threatening, although Black seems to have enough resources.

25
B

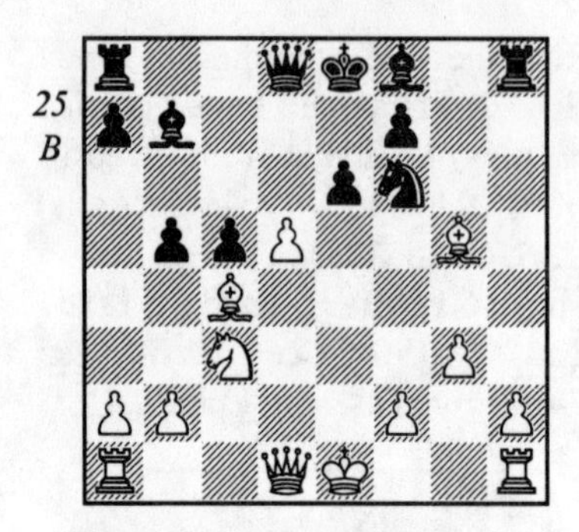

Thus after **14...bxc4** play divides:

a1) **15 ♕a4+** ♕d7 16 ♗xf6 ♕xa4 17 ♘xa4 ♖h6! (it is very important for the solidity of Black's structure that he take back on d5 with the pawn – for this reason 17...♗xd5 18 ♗xh8 ♗xh1 19 ♗f6 is unpalatable) 18 ♗g5 ♖g6 19 h4 (19 ♗e3?! exd5! 20 ♗xc5 ♖e6+ 21 ♔f1 d4! with strong counterplay) 19...exd5 20 0-0-0 ♖e6 and whilst the passed h-pawn gives White a clear plan, the two bishops and mobile passed d-pawn should enable Black to find at least enough play.

a2) **15 ♗xf6(!)** ♕xf6 16 ♕a4+ ♔d8 (16...♔e7? 17 d6+) 17 0-0-0 e5 18 f4 (an understandable urge to reopen the centre, but maybe a little premature. Shabalov considers also 18 ♕xc4 after which 18...♕g6!? could be examined, and 18 ♖he1) 18...exf4 19 d6 ♗xh1! 20 ♕a5+ ♔d7 21 ♕c7+ ♔e6 22 d7!? Shabalov-Ka.Müller, Pula 1989, and now Black could have consolidated with only slight inconvenience by 22...♕e5! 23 d8♕ ♖xd8 24 ♕xd8 ♗f3 25 ♖d7 ♔f5! 26 ♖xf7+ ♔g6 27 ♖xf8 ♕e1+ ∓/-+.

b) **14 dxe6!?** was for a long time universally dismissed with the comment '14...♗e7! 15 exf7+ ♔xf7∓', all the commentators presumably taking each other on trust. I am indebted here to Rajko Vujatović who some time ago suggested to me that the above assessment only clearly holds up in the event of 16 ♕xd8+?. If White plays the sensible 16 ♖g1 Black's compensation still has to be demonstrated.Analysiswas notconclusive,butcannowbesupplemented by a couple of ideas from praxis.

b1) **14...♗g7!?** 15 ♖g1 (Lobron preferred 15 ♕xd8+ ♖xd8 16 ♖g1) 15...♕b6 16 ♕e2 (16 exf7+ ♔xf7 17 ♗g2 ♖xh2 18 ♗xb7 ♕xb7 gives Black a clear plus according to Kramnik) 16...♕xe6 17 ♘xb5 ♕xe2+ 18 ♗xe2 ♘e4! 19 0-0-0 (simply retreating the bishop looks more logical; Kramnik gives 19 ♗f4∞) 19...♘xg5 20 ♘d6+ ♔f8 21 ♘xb7 ♖xh2 22 ♖gf1 ♗d4 and Black was exerting some pressure in Lobron-Kramnik, Dortmund 1993.

b2) **14...♗e7 15 exf7+ ♔xf7 16 ♖g1** *(26)*.

26
B

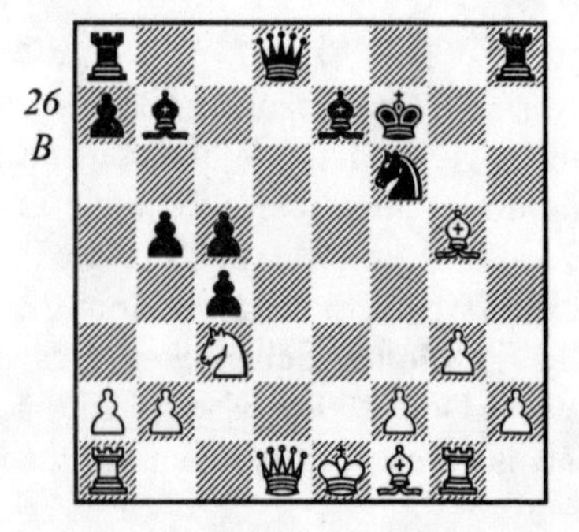

First a few thoughts on the position. Black is a pawn down, and indeed his whole kingside has disappeared. Whilst his king's situation is not immediately problematic, the total lack of potential pawn cover renders this a factor in some lines. Moreover, here and now the b5 pawn requires defence. On the plus side, White too has problems with his king, he will have to give a tempo with h4 to neutralize the h-file, and completing his development will not be a trivial exercise. Some concrete lines:

b21) **16...♕e8?!** is tricky, but 17 ♕c2! (Vujatović) is not easy to refute. White threatens 18 ♘xb5 and ♗xc4+ which prevents 17...♖xh2. Black's best may be 17...♘e4 18 ♗e3!± (better than 18 ♗xe7 ♕xe7 19 0-0-0 ♖xh2∞).

b22) **16...♕b6** 17 h4 (17 ♕c2!? might again merit consideration) 17...♖ad8 18 ♕c2 ♕e6+ 19 ♕e2 ♘e4 20 ♗xe7 ♕xe7 21 ♗g2 (21 ♘xe4 ♗xe4 22 ♗g2 ♖he8∓) 21...♖d2 22 ♕e3 ♖d3 23 ♕f4+ ♘f6+ 24 ♔f1 ♖e8 25 g4 (Ftaćnik condemns this, suggesting 25 ♗xb7 ♕xb7 26 a4!?) 25...♖d4 26 ♕f5 ♗c8 27 ♕c2 ♗xg4∓ 28 ♗f3 ♗h3+ 29 ♗g2 ♗g4 30 ♗f3 ♗h3+ 31 ♗g2 ♕d7 32 ♖h1 ♗xg2+ 33 ♔xg2 ♖g8+ 34 ♔f1 ♕g4 0-1 Kir.Georgiev-Dreev, Biel IZ 1993. A fine attacking display by Dreev.

Both practical tests leave the onus on White to show that 14 dxe6 is a serious try.

14 ... ♗e7

14...♗h6 was tried in Kasparov-Ivanchuk, Linares 1994: 15 ♗xf6 ♕xf6 16 0-0 0-0-0 17 ♘xb5 exd5 18 ♘xa7+ ♔b8 19 ♘b5 ♗g7 20 a4 ♕h6 21 h4 ♗f6 22 ♕e1! ♗xh4 23 ♕a5 ♗e7 24 ♕c7+ ♔a8 25 ♕a5+ ♔b8 26 ♕c7+ ♔a8 27 ♖fe1 ♗d6 28 ♕b6 ♗b8 29 a5 ♖d7 30 ♖e8!+-

15 0-0 ♘xd5
16 ♗xe7 ♔xe7
17 ♘xb5 ♕b6
18 ♘a3 *(27)*

In Quist-Karoly, Dieren 1988, White sought to improve by **18 ♘c3**, preferring to force the exchange of Black's strong knight on d5 while blockading, rather than targeting Black's c-pawns. However, Black retained sufficient play based on his control of the d-file to hold the balance comfortably after 18...♘xc3 19 bxc3 ♗xg2 20 ♔xg2 ♕c6+ 21 f3 (21...♖xh2(+) is the devastating reply to 21 ♔g1?? or 21 ♕f3??) 21...♖ad8 22 ♕e1 (22 ♕c1!? is also possible) 22...♖d3 23 ♖f2 ♕d5 24 ♖b1 ♖h5! 25 ♕e4 (otherwise 25...♖e5 will force White into passivity) 25...♖f5 26 ♖b7+ ♔f8 27 ♖b8+ ♔g7! 28 ♕g4+ ♖g5 29 ♕h4 ♖h5 30 ♕g4+ ♖g5 ½-½.

27
B

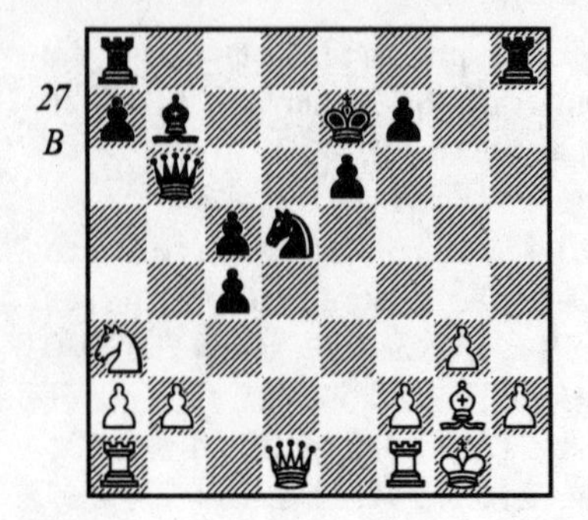

18 ... c3

It is not yet clear whether dissatisfaction with the text, or merely the belief that he had found something still better moved Kramnik to introduce the spectacular **18...♖h4!?** in the game Van Wely-Kramnik, Biel IZ 1993. The move has some nice points: if **19 gxh4?** then **19...♘f4?** seems to fail to 20 ♗xb7 ♕xb7 21 f3 ♖g8+ 22 ♔h1 ♕xb2 23 ♕d6+!!, but simply **19...♖g8!** leaves White facing too many threats, while **19 ♕c1** *is* met by 19...♘f4!.

However, in the game, White quickly attained the upper hand with **19 ♕d2(!) ♖d4?** 20 ♕g5+ ♘f6 21 ♗xb7 ♖g8 22 ♕e5 ♘d7 23 ♕e2 ♕xb7 24 ♘xc4 ♖h4 (the standard trick 24...♖xc4 and ...♘e5 fails since the c-pawn is loose with check, and so Black appears devoid of substantial compensation for the pawn) 25 f3 ♕c7 26 ♘e3 ♔f8 27 ♘g4 ♖h5 28 ♖ad1 ♖d5 29 ♕e4 ♕d6 30 ♘e3 with an indisputable plus. It is yet to be clearly established that the more plausible **19...♖g8!?** improves matters substantially: 20 f4! (Black threatens ...♘f4, and 20 f3 ♖d4 does not look dangerous) when it is difficult to defend c4 without becoming passive, and if **20...c3** 21 bxc3 c4+ 22 ♕d4! (22 ♕f2?! ♖xf4 23 ♕xb6 ♖xf1+∞; 22 ♖f2? ♖xf4∓; 22 ♔h1? ♘e3∓) 22...♕b2 23 ♖ab1 ♕xg2+ 24 ♔xg2 ♘xf4+ 25 ♔f2 ♖xh2+ (25...♘h3+ 26 ♔e3 gives nothing much for the exchange) 26 ♔e1 ♘g2+ 27 ♔d1 ♖d8 28 ♖xf7+! puts a firm stop to Black's little games, but Van Wely mentions the line **20...♘xf4!** 21 ♖xf4 (not 21 ♘xc4 ♕c7! – Oll) 21...♖xf4 22 ♕xf4 ♕xb2 but now Dautov gives 23 ♕d6+!! ♔f6 24 ♖f1+ winning.

Strangely, the young Bulgarian talent Veselin Topalov felt moved not to give up the ghost so easily and tried after 18...♖h4 19 ♕d2! to stop f4 by the most direct means possible, namely **19...♘f4!?** *(28)*, a very visual but not necessarily very convincing self-fork.

28
W

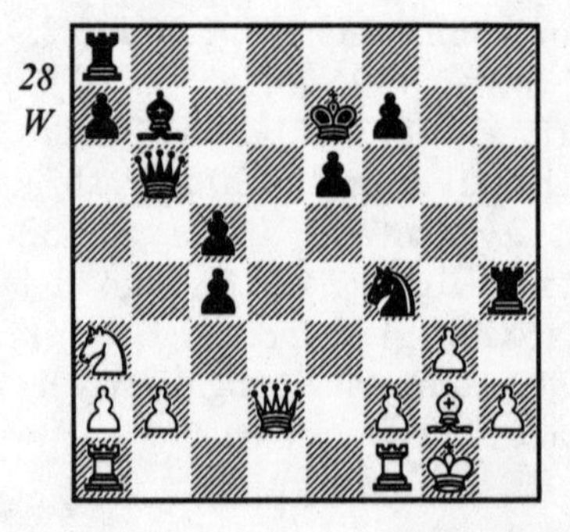

Sadly for this most creative idea, White was able to consolidate quickly with 20 Nxc4 Qc7? (20...Bxg2? 21 Nxb6 Bf3 22 Qxf4 Rxf4 23 Nxa8+-; 20...Qa6 21 Ne3± Oll) 21 f3 Nxg2 22 Qg5+ Kf8 23 gxh4 Nf4 24 Kh1 Rd8 25 Ne5 Rd5 26 Rae1 Nd3 27 Qh6+ 1-0 Oll-Topalov, Biel IZ 1993.

19 Nc4 **Qc7**
20 Qc1?!

Several sources have questioned this, some recommending **20 b3** instead. Perhaps more to the point is **20 bxc3!?** intending **20...Rag8** 21 Rb1!? or **20...Nxc3** 21 Qd2 Bxg2 22 Kxg2 (22 Qg5+ first also looks interesting) 22...Ne4 23 Qe3 Nf6 24 Qf3 Rab8 25 Rab1 Nd7 26 h4! Rb4 27 Rfc1 Rhb8 28 Rb3! Rxb3 (28...a5!?±) 29 axb3 Qb7 30 Qxb7 Rxb7 31 Ra1 with fair chances of converting to the full point; Van Wely-Dreev, Bern 1993. This could well be the line to which exponents of 13...Nf6 should devote most attention.

20 ... **Rag8**
21 f4 **cxb2?!**

Better, as Dzhandzhgava and Bokuchava indicate, was the simple plan of doubling on the h-file with **21...Rh7∓**. The text activates White's queen.

22 Qxb2 **Ba8**
23 Rac1

23 Qe5!± was more to the point, since Black's attacking prospects would be severely blunted by the exchange of queens. After Black's excellent reply White does not get another chance.

23 ... **Rh5!**
24 Rf2 **Rf5**
25 Ne5 **f6**
26 Nd3 **c4!**
27 Qd4 **Nb6** *(29)*

29
W

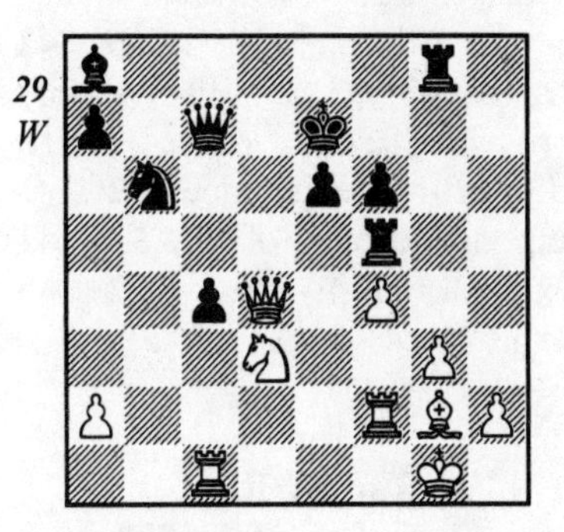

The pattern of the play has switched. White has successfully covered the immediate danger to his kingside, but Black still stands well since his passed c-pawn is now a major player, pushing back the white pieces.

The game now continued: **28 Bxa8 Rxa8 29 Qe4 Qd6! 30 Nb2 Qd5 31 Qe3 Qc5 32 Qc3?** (By now White should have accepted the exchange of queens, although after 32 Qxc5 Rxc5 33 Rfc2 Rac8 Black has a clear initiative since his c-pawn dictates the play) **32...Rd5 33 Qc2 f5 34 Qc3 Rd4!** (Preparing ...Nd5. The white pieces are curiously helpless against Black's patient encroachment. Not now 35 Nd3? Rxd3! 36 Qxd3 Qxf2+ +-) **35 Nd1 Nd5 36 Qb2 Rd8 37 Nc3**

♘e3 38 h3 (Forced in view of the threat of ...♘g4, but here the consequent weakness of the g- and h-pawns is easily demonstrated) **38...♖d3 39 ♔h2 ♕c6! 40 ♕b4+ ♔f7 41 ♔g1 ♘g4! 0-1**.

An attractive finish, the more so in that 41 ♔g1 was directed against the threat of ...♘g4!. If now **42 hxg4** ♖xg3+ 43 ♔f1 Black simply wins the rook on c1 with 43...♕h1+. Neither does **42 ♖g2** help on account of 42...♖d2 43 ♖xd2 ♖xd2 44 ♘e4 ♖g2+ 45 ♔xg2 ♕xe4+ 46 ♔f1 ♕f3+.

Game 4
Karpov-Ribli
Thessaloniki OL 1988

1 d4 d5 2 c4 c6 3 ♘f3 ♘f6 4 ♘c3 e6 5 ♗g5 dxc4 6 e4 b5 7 e5 h6 8 ♗h4 g5 9 ♘xg5 hxg5 10 ♗xg5 ♘bd7 11 exf6 ♗b7 12 g3 c5 13 d5

13 ... ♗h6!? *(30)*

30
W

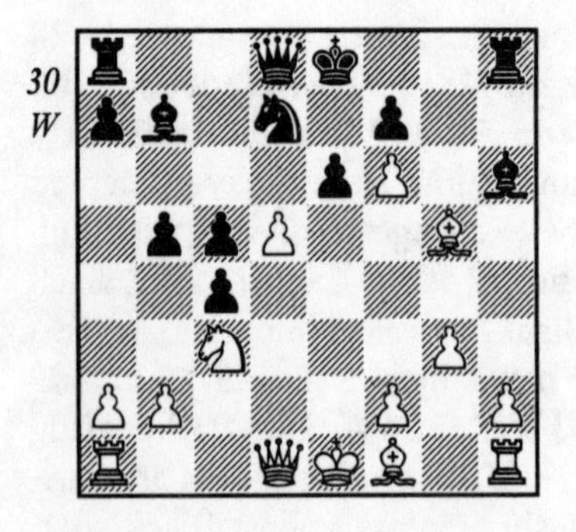

Since 13...♘b6 currently looks rather suspect, and 13...♘xf6 has yet to establish itself fully, the text may be Black's most respectable attempt to exploit 11 exf6. The idea is simple and logical – Black wants to capture on f6, further pressurizing d5 without permitting the unpleasant pin on the h4-d8 diagonal. The possible drawbacks may be that Black's rooks could be exposed on h6, and that Black's d6-square and c5-pawn are weakened by the exchange.

One other option merits attention here: **13...♘e5** *(31)*.

31
W

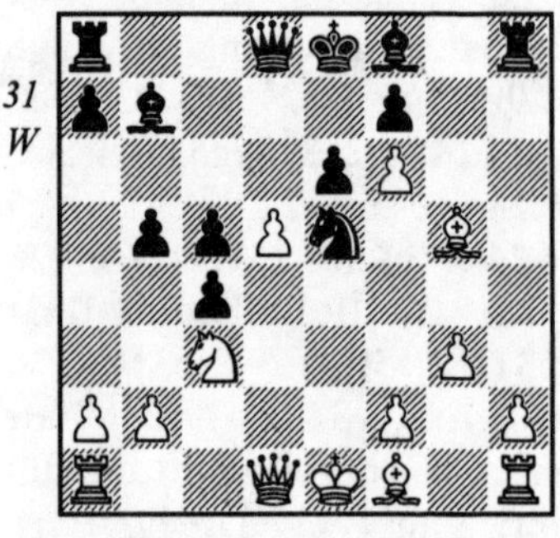

Here an entirely different consequence of White's move order is under the microscope – his delay in playing ♗g2 but his need to do so to protect d5 – affording the possibility of a disruptive check on d3. However, Black eschews attempts to regain material parity, and although there is no consistent condemnation in the theoretical verdicts, there is scepticism and a suspicion that Black's position is rather loose. The move, though older than its rivals, has never attracted a following. After **14 ♗g2** there is:

a) **14...b4** 15 Qa4+ Qd7 16 Qxd7+ Nxd7 17 Nb5 0-0-0 18 0-0-0 a6 19 Na7+ Kc7 20 dxe6 Bxg2 21 Bf4+ Kb7 22 e7! Bh6 23 exd8Q Rxd8 24 Bxh6 Bxh1 25 Rxh1 Ne5 (Brkljaca-Karaklajić, Bela Crkva 1984) when by 26 Be3! Nd3+ 27 Kc2 Kxa7 28 b3 White undermines the d3 knight in familiar fashion and clarifies his endgame advantage.

b) Also unpalatable for Black is **14...Bh6** 15 Qh5! (15 Bxh6 Nd3+ 16 Kf1 Rxh6 gives good chances of creating counterplay on the f-file) 15...b4 16 0-0! bxc3 17 Rae1! Qd6 18 Bxh6 cxb2 (18...0-0-0 19 bxc3!) 19 dxe6! Bxg2 20 Rxe5 0-0-0 21 Kxg2 Rxh6 22 Rxc5+ Kb8 23 Rb5+ Kc7 24 Qxf7+ 1-0 Ermolinsky-Yuneev, USSR 1984.

c) **14...Nd3+ 15 Kf1 Qd7** (15...exd5?? 16 Qe2+ wins; 15...Qb6 16 b3!? {16 dxe6 is good too} 16...0-0-0?! 17 bxc4 bxc4 18 Rb1 Qa5 19 Rxb7! gave White a very strong attack in Wells-Richmond, British Ch {Southport} 1983) and now:

c1) Black often has a surprising degree of counterplay in endgames where his queenside pawn mass is supported by the beast on d3: **16 Qe2 0-0-0** 17 dxe6 fxe6 18 Bxb7+ Kxb7 19 Qe4+ (19 b3!?) 19...Qc6 20 h4 Bd6 21 f4 b4 22 Qxc6+ Kxc6 23 Ne4 Kd5! and the situation was still not clear in J.Hansen-Bagirov, Moscow 1975.

c2) In view of the previous line, Polugaevsky's **16 dxe6**± needs some explaining since after 16...fxe6 it is not clear how White improves on 17 Qe2. 17 b3 Beliavsky-Illescas, Linares 1994.

c3) **16 Qf3!** is Vujatović's very interesting idea, simply threatening 17 dxe6, which 16...**0-0-0**? does nothing to combat. Black has problems, since the natural 16...exd5 runs into 17 h4! keeping Black's king in the centre, when White's initiative is very dangerous. Following the Beliavsky-Illescas encounter, Daily Telegraph correspondent Malcolm Pein faxed this idea to Kasparov, who agreed it was strong.

14 Bxh6 Rxh6

15 Qd2(!)

The text has become the standard try since Black's resources after the natural **15 Bg2** seem fully adequate. **15...b4 16 Ne4 Nxf6** *(32)* and now:

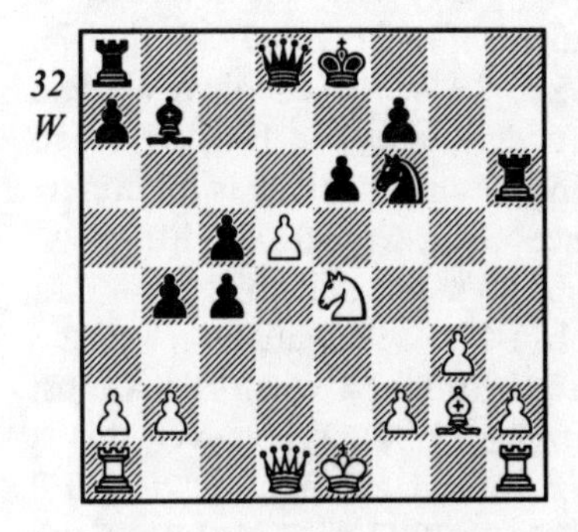

32
W

a) **17 Nxc5?! Bxd5 18 0-0** (18 Bxd5 Qxd5 19 Qxd5 Nxd5 20 Rc1 Rc8 21 Rxc4 Nb6 22 Rc1

♘a4 23 ♘d3 ♖xc1+ 24 ♘xc1 ♘xb2 ½-½ Azmaiparashvili-Dolmatov, USSR Ch 1986; 18 ♕a4+ transposes to 'b') **18...♗xg2 19 ♔xg2** and now two ways of exchanging queens seem fine, while Black may be more ambitious:

a1) **19...♕xd1** 19...♕xd1 20 ♖axd1 ♖c8 21 ♘a6 ♘d5 22 ♖fe1 ♖h5 23 g4 ♖g5 24 ♔g3∞ Bagirov.

a2) **19...♕d5+** 20 ♕xd5 exd5 21 ♖fe1+ ♔d8 22 ♘a6 ♔d7 23 ♖ad1 also with unclear play.

a3) **19...♕b6!?** (this is more ambitious) 20 ♕f3 (20 ♕a4+? ♔e7 21 ♘a6 ♘d5! gave Black very fierce counterplay with ...♖ah8 in Schneider-Dvoretsky, Frunze 1983) 20...0-0-0!? (again Black has legitimate alternatives in the safe 20...♖c8 21 ♘e4 ♘xe4 22 ♕xe4 ♕c6= {Dvoretsky}, or 20...♖d8 21 ♘e4 ♔e7!?, but the text is more active) 21 ♘a4 (21 ♖fd1? ♖xd1+ 22 ♖xd1 ♕xc5 23 ♕a8+ ♔c7 and Black's king is quite safe) 21...♕b7 22 ♕xb7+ ♔xb7 23 ♖ac1 ♖c8 when White's offside knight and Black's active king mean that Black is for preference; Suba-Crouch, Cardiff 1984.

b) **17 ♕a4+** and now:

b1) **17...♔f8!?** allows 18 ♘xc5 ♗xd5 19 ♕xb4 when Black must answer 19...♔g7; however, this is not so bad either after **20 0-0-0** ♕b6! or **20 f3** ♕c7 21 0-0-0 ♖ah8 22 ♘e4 ♗xe4 23 fxe4 ♘g4 with counterplay in Vladimirov-Bykhovsky, Irkutsk 1983.

b2) **17...♔e7** 18 ♘xc5 (both 18 d6+ ♔f8 19 ♘xf6 ♗xg2 20 ♘d7+ ♔g7 21 ♖g1 ♗f3 and 18 ♘xf6?! ♖xf6 19 d6+ ♕xd6 20 ♗xb7 ♕e5+ are good for Black according to Kuuksmaa) 18...♗xd5 19 0-0-0 (19 ♕xb4 ♕b6! - the point behind 17...♔e7 – 20 ♕a3 ♗xg2 21 ♘e4+ ♔e8 22 ♘d6+ ♔d7 23 ♘xc4 ♕c7 24 0-0-0+ ♘d5∓) 19...a5 20 ♖he1 ♔f8 21 ♗xd5 exd5 22 ♕c6 ♖c8 23 ♖xd5 ♖xc6 24 ♖xd8+ ♔g7 25 ♘b7 (Nesis-Kuuksmaa, corr. 1984) 25...♖xh2=.

c) **17 ♕c1?!** ♖h5! (Richmond) 18 ♕xc4 ♘xe4 19 ♗xe4 ♗xd5 with somewhat more than equality.

d) **17 ♕e2!?** (looks relatively the most promising) 17...♗xd5 18 ♖d1 (not 18 ♘xf6+ ♖xf6 19 ♖d1?? ♗xg2!) 18...♔f8 19 0-0 ♘xe4 20 ♗xe4 ♕g5 21 f4 ♕h5 22 ♗f3 ♗xf3 23 ♖xf3 c3! 24 bxc3 bxc3 **25 ♖e3?** ♖b8∓ was Razuvaev-Yusupov, USSR Ch 1983, but **25 ♖f2** would have given equal chances according to Yusupov.

15 ... ♖xf6

Black's best here is also a matter for debate. Three other moves have been seen in practice, and in addition, Richmond strongly advocates 15...♖h8!?. We shall consider:

a) **15...♖h5?** 16 ♗e2 ♗xd5 (16...♖h7 17 0-0-0 ♘xf6 18 ♘xb5 ♗xd5 19 ♕f4± Kasparov-Younglove, London satellite simul 1984) 17 0-0! leaves Black terribly loose.

b) **15...♖g6** 16 0-0-0 ♘xf6 17 ♕e3 ♕b6 18 ♗g2 ♔f8 (18...0-0-0? 19 dxe6! ♗xg2 20 ♖xd8+ ♕xd8 21 exf7 leaves the rook on g6 almost uniquely badly placed to meet the threat of ♕xc5+) 19 h4! (19 ♖he1 ♔g8? 20 dxe6 ♗xg2 21 exf7+ ♔xf7 22 ♘e2!! Δ♘f4 was the elegant continuation of Beliavsky-Pinter, Budapest 1984, but in view of the improvement 19...♔g7! when the most promising is probably 20 h4, the text is more flexible, since the rook is clearly well placed for this plan) 19...♖e8 20 h5 exd5 21 ♕d2 and White was better in Dolmatov-Steflisch, Sofia 1985.

c) **15...♖h8!?** is still generally ignored, but putting the rook out of harm's way has its virtues, e.g. 16 0-0-0! (16 ♗g2 ♘e5!? 17 0-0 b4 18 ♘e4 ♗xd5 19 ♘xc5 {19 ♖fe1!?} 19...♗xg2 20 ♕xd8+ ♖xd8= {Richmond}, but not 16 dxe6 ♘e5 17 ♕xd8+ ♖xd8 18 f3 ♘xf3+ 19 ♔f2 ♘xh2∓) 16...♘xf6 17 ♕e3 ♕b6 18 ♕e5!? (18 ♗g2?! 0-0-0! compare 'b') 18...♖h6 19 ♗g2± (at least).

d) **15...♕xf6** had been written off as inferior, but has gained credence from a recent outing by Alexei Shirov, and Yusupov's suggested improvement for Black. A number of recent games constitute a fully-fledged rehabilitation of the line, but as yet there has emerged no consensus as to White's best response.

d1) **16 ♗g2** ♘e5 17 0-0 0-0-0 and now not **18 ♕e3??** ♖xh2! 19 ♖fe1 ♖xg2+ 20 ♔xg2 ♘d3-+ Uhlmann-Enders, E.Germany 1985, but **18 ♖fe1** Δ♕e3 which Enders rates as ±.

d2) **16 0-0-0** has been the most common move:

d21) **16...♗xd5!?** 17 ♘xd5 exd5 18 ♗g2 (18 ♕xd5 ♘b6!? 19 ♖e1+ {19 ♕xc5 ♕xb2+!} 19...♔f8 20 ♕xc5+ ♔g8! Δ21 ♕e3 c3!∞ or 21 ♕e5 ♕xf2) 18...♘b6 19 ♕e3+ (the mistake according to Yusupov; he gives 19 ♗xd5 0-0-0 20 ♗b7+ ♔c7 21 ♕xd8+ ♕xd8 22 ♖xd8 ♔xd8 23 ♗a6±) 19...♔f8 20 ♕xc5+ ♔g8 21 ♕d4 ♖e8! 22 ♗xd5 ♕xd4 23 ♖xd4 ♖e2 24 ♗e4 c3!? (24...♖xf2 25 ♖d2=) 25 bxc3 ♘a4 26 ♗c2 ♘xc3 27 ♖d2 ♘xa2+ 28 ♔d1 ♘c3+ 29 ♔c1 ♖he6∓ (although later drawn) Yusupov-Shirov, Linares 1993.

d22) The 'latest word' here is **16...♔f8**, the point being to meet 17 ♗g2 (or 17 dxe6) with 17...♘e5. So far the practical results have been outstanding. After **17 f4** (17 g4 ♖g6! 18 h3 b4 19 ♘e4 c3! 20 bxc3 ♕f3 21 dxe6 ♗xe4 22 exd7 bxc3 23 d8♕+ ♔g7!! ∓Shirov) **17...♘b6**:

d221) **18 g4!?** deserves attention.

d222) **18 ♘xb5** exd5∓ Shirov.

d223) **18 ♘e4** ♕g7 (18...♕f5∓ Shirov) 19 ♗g2 ♗xd5 20 ♘c3 b4 21 ♘xd5 exd5 22 ♕f2 ♖c8 23 ♗xd5 c3 24 b3 c4 25 ♗xc4 ♘xc4

26 bxc4 b3 25 ♗xc4 ♘xc4 26 bxc4 b3 27 ♕d4 ♕xd4 28 ♖xd4 ♖a6 0-1 Vladimirov-Bareev, Tilburg 1993.

d224) **18 ♗g2 exd5** and now:

d2241) **19 ♘xd5** ♗xd5 20 ♗xd5 ♖d8 21 ♕g2 c3 Züger.

d2242) **19 ♘xb5** ♗c6 20 ♘c7 ♖d8∓ Alterman-Kamsky, Tilburg 1993.

d2243) **19 ♕f2** ♖c8! 20 ♘xb5 (20 g4 ♖g6) 20...♘a4! 21 ♕c2 ♕a6 22 ♘a3 (22 ♘c3 is met by 22...♘xc3 23 ♕xc3 ♕xa2 24 ♖xd5 ♗xd5 25 ♗xd5 ♖b8) 22...c3!! 23 ♗xd5 (23 bxc3 ♕a5 24 ♘b1 ♖b8!? Shirov) 23...♘xb2 24 ♕f5 (24 ♗xb7 ♕xa3 25 ♗xc8 ♘c4+ 26 ♔b1 ♖b6+ 27 ♔a1 ♕b2+ 28 ♕xb2 cxb2+ 29 ♔b1 ♘a3 mate) 24...♖f6! 25 ♕h7 (25 ♗xb7 fails to 25...♘d3+!) 25...♕xa3 26 ♕h8+ ♔e7 27 ♖he1+ ♔d7 28 ♕h3+ ♔d6! 29 ♗xb7+ ♘xd1+! 30 ♔xd1 ♕xa2 31 ♕g2 ♕b1+ 0-1 Kamsky-Shirov, Lucerne Wch teams 1993.

d3) The question, therefore, is why not **16 ♘e4** when theory gives 16...♕f3 (16...♕e5! 17 ♗g2 exd5 18 ♕xh6 exd4 19 0-0-0∞ Korchnoi) 17 ♘d6+ ♔e7 **18 ♘xb7 ♕xh1(?)** 19 d6+! ♔e8 20 ♕xh6 ♕xb7 (Shirov-Kamsky, Kapsukas 1987) 21 ♕h4!+-. Again Yusupov sheds some light on this, although much further analysis would be recommended. He gives instead **18...♖h5!**∞. Is this really so good? What if 19 ♖g1 Δ19...♖xd5 20 ♗e2!?, or 19...♖e5+ 20 ♗e2 exd5 21 ♔f1!? or 19...c3 20 bxc3 ♖e5+ 21 ♗e2 ♖xe2+ 22 ♕xe2 ♕xc3+ 23 ♔f1 ♕xa1+ 24 ♔g2 ♕d4 25 ♖d1 (Fritz2)? Black should have something concrete to venture down this path in future. Not in much doubt is that Yusupov's alternative for White in the above line, **18 ♖g1**, is not dangerous after either **18...♗xd5** or **18...♕xd5!?** 19 ♕xh6 ♕xd6, with compensation.

16 ♗g2

Karpov solidly defends his d5 pawn and prepares short castling. However, it is not completely clear that White cannot more ambitiously seek to refute Black's play. The tempting **16 ♘e4**, which Richmond regards as promising, does not seem to be the way to do it, since after 16...♗xd5! 17 ♘xf6+ Black should play 17...♘xf6! when if 18 ♖g1 Black has the embarrassing 18...♘e4 with a strong attack.

However **16 0-0-0** is interesting. Langeweg-Cuijpers, Dutch Ch 1984 continued 16...b4 17 ♘e4 exd5 (17...♗xd5 18 ♘xf6+ ♘xf6 meets with the nice refutation 19 ♕h6! and Black's compensation is patently inadequate) 18 ♘xf6+ ♕xf6 19 ♗xc4! ♘b6 20 ♖he1+ ♔f8 21 ♗f1 when Black has compensation, but I find it hard to believe it is enough. It is intriguing to speculate on what deterred Karpov from 16 0-0-0.

16 ... ♘e5

16...♘b6 intensifying the pressure on d5 would also bear examination.

17 0-0 **♘f3+**
18 ♗xf3 **♖xf3**
19 ♕e2

This has been questioned, since Black's resource on move 20 neutralizes all of the pressure. Ribli suggests the more aggressive **19 ♕h6!?** ♗xd5 20 ♖ad1 ♕f6 (20...♖d3 anyway?) 21 ♕xf6 ♖xf6 22 ♘xd5 exd5 23 ♖xd5 ♖c8 with a small endgame plus for White.

19 ... **♗xd5**
20 ♖fd1

Less accurate is **20 ♖ad1?!** since after 20...♖d3! 21 ♖xd3 cxd3 22 ♕xd3 ♗c4! 23 ♕xd8+ ♖xd8 the d-file (and bishop *vs* knight) gives Black the better prospects.

20 ... **♖d3!** *(33)*

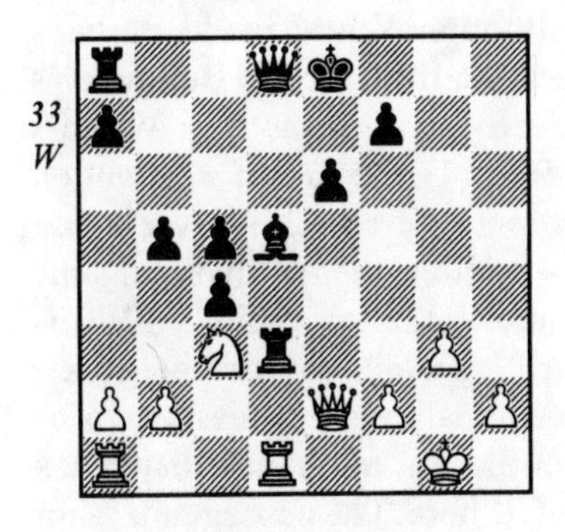

33
W

21 ♖xd3 **cxd3**
22 ♕xd3 **♗c6**
23 ♕e2

Ribli mentions also **23 ♕e3** ♕d4= as an alternative. However **23 ♕h7** would be false aggression, since simply 23...♕f6 would cover all danger and leave Black better centralized, with an immediate threat of ...♕f3.

23 ... **b4**
24 ♖d1 **♕e7**
25 ♘e4 **♖d8**
26 ♖c1!

Whilst in many positions queen and knight operate better than queen and bishop in the absence of other pieces, here the exchange of rooks **26 ♖xd8+ ♕**xd8 would favour Black. The white king is weak on the long diagonal, and the black queen can come to d4 to support the advance of the queenside. The text forces Black to relinquish the 'minor exchange' after which in the pure major piece ending Black's queenside majority proves just as mobile as White's h-pawn.

Play proceeded as follows: **26...♗xe4 27 ♕xe4 ♖d5! 28 h4 ♕d6 29 ♔g2 ♔f8 30 ♕e3 a5 31 b3 ♖e5 32 ♕f3 ♖f5 33 ♕e2** (33 ♕a8+?! ♔g7 34 ♕xa5 ♖xf2+! leaves White's king exposed) **33...♖e5 34 ♕c4 a4! 35 bxa4 ♕c6+ 36 ♔h3** (To effect the forced liquidation upon which White now embarks, his king must not be on the back rank since after 36 ♔g1 ♕xa4 37 ♕f4 ♖d5, 38 ♖xc5?? ♕d1+ enables the rook to be captured with impunity) **36...♕xa4 37 ♕f4 ♖d5 38 ♖xc5 ♖xc5 39 ♕d6+** ½-½.

After 39...♔g7 40 ♕xc5 ♕xa2 41 ♕xb4 ♕xf2 there is nothing left to play for.

4 Deviations from the Main Line after 11 g3

As was mentioned in the section introduction, this is arguably the most accurate move order for the player with White seeking to reach the main line since it affords Black the fewest possibilities to deviate. Game 5 examines the most popular of all Black's alternatives in Chapter 4, 11...♕a5. In fact this option is probably available against 11 exf6 too since after 11...♕a5, alternatives to 12 g3 do not look too promising (see Levitt-Kaidanov in the note to 11...♗b7 in Game 3). Our main game features the relatively new idea of delaying ...b4 in favour of the immediate ...♗a6, previously thought to be inferior but recently revived by Novikov and Kaidanov. The more common 12...b4 is also extensively covered. Neither move has in fact scored particularly impressively lately, but Black's position does offer a lot of scope for counterplay and their popularity is at least in part understandable.

Game 6 examines both Black's other options which are in fact genuinely exclusive to 11 g3, and some minor but interesting approaches which are equally valid against either 11th move.

The most important is 11...♖g8 (now clearly reckoned to be more accurate than after the insertion of 11...♗b7 12 ♗g2). This forces White either to relinquish the bishop pair with ♗xf6 or to play h4 which leads to complex rook *vs* two minor piece positions. This has recently been tested extensively at the highest level and is at the time of writing 11...♖g8 is the 'Main line' of 11 g3. The current theoretical wisdom is that 12 ♗xf6 is not enough for a plus (although White could perhaps invest a little time in Beliavsky's piece sacrifice (note to White's 15th in Game 6) and so attention is focussed on 12 h4. According to 'written theory' the endgame (note 'b222' to White's 12th) is still crucial, but recent praxis seems, albeit by omission, to be confirming my hunch that Black is OK here. The new agenda is for White to seek chances in the middlegame, and Black should be well prepared for this.

Of the other Black alternatives, 11...b4, which heralds a well-analysed queen sacrifice, looks sadly inadequate, but 11...♗b7 12 ♗g2 ♕c7!? might merit some study.

Also considered in the notes to Game 6 are two possibilities which did not fit in easily elsewhere!

1) The first is White's efforts to exploit the fact that if Black seeks to reach the main line against g3 he must play ...♕b6 before ...c5. This can give White the chance to avoid the advance d5 and all the complexity *that* introduces.

2) The second is an idea for Black: playing ...♕b6 without ...c5 usually in conjunction with ...♘e5 or ...♗h6, keeping the white pawn on d4 as a target.

Game 5
Komljenović-Kaidanov
Andorra 1991

1 d4 d5 2 c4 e6 3 ♘c3 c6 4 ♘f3 ♘f6 5 ♗g5 dxc4 6 e4 b5 7 e5 h6 8 ♗h4 g5 9 ♘xg5 hxg5 10 ♗xg5 ♘bd7

11 g3 ♕a5 *(34)*

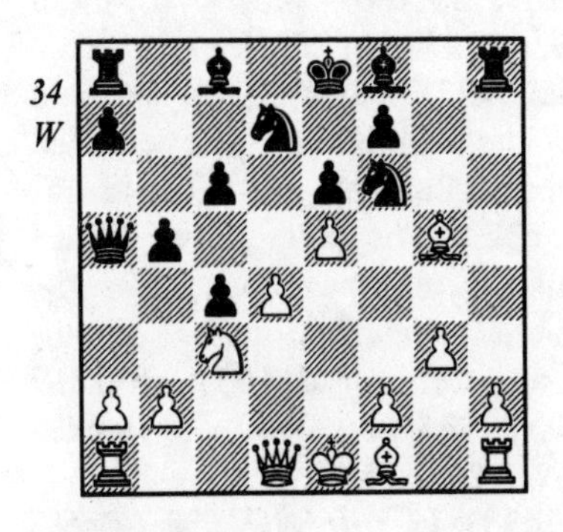

Black's other options are considered in Game 6.

12 exf6 ♗a6!?

The placing of the bishop on the f1-a6 diagonal, at once anticipating and discouraging White's intended fianchetto, is the main idea of the ...♕a5 lines. The text move was long thought to be inferior to the more popular 12...b4 (considered at length in note 'c' below) and is indeed still controversial since by 13 a3 White can hold up Black's queenside pawns and seek to render the a6 bishop irrelevant. Black's move claims in the first place that the threat of ...b4 is stronger than its execution and that 13 a3 weakens b3 and the loss of time can be exploited tactically. The importance of the issue of how to handle Black's queenside pawns (i.e. whether to advance them to make counterplay at the risk of loosening c4 or to keep them solid) has been alluded to before. Here is the debate in its starkest form. It is worth mentioning that whilst the case for ...b4 as part of Black's plan is strong, the apparently thematic follow-up ...c3 is usually only justified by a premature ♗g2 (see Timman-Pinter under 'c41'). If White has not fianchettoed, the weakening of Black's c-pawns is usually the most significant outcome. There are numerous instructive warning examples of Black rushing this advance – see Knaak-Zso.Polgar (line 'c6'). Before examining 12...b4 two other moves can be briefly considered:

a) **12...♗b7** transposes to line 'c' in the note to 11...♖g8 in Game 6.

b) **12...♗b4?!** 13 ♕f3 ♘b6!? (Δ14 ♕xf6+ ♗d7 15 ♕f3 ♖c8!? Kishnev) 14 ♗g2 ♗b7 15 0-0 **0-0-0?!** 16 ♘e2! ♖d7 17 ♕e3 ♘d5 18 ♕c1 (Δa4) 18...c3 19 a3 cxb2 20 ♕xb2 ♗f8?! (20...♗c3±) 21 ♖fc1 ♔b8 22 ♘f4 ♘b6 23 ♘d3!+- (Δ23...♘c4 24 ♖xc4 bxc4 25 ♘e5 ♖c7 26 ♘xc6) Kishnev-Maximenko, Lvov 1990 was clearly unsatisfactory for Black, although by **15...♗xc3** 16 bxc3 0-0-0⩲ Black could have retained some counterplay with ...♘a4.

c) **12...b4 13 ♘e4 ♗a6** *(35)*

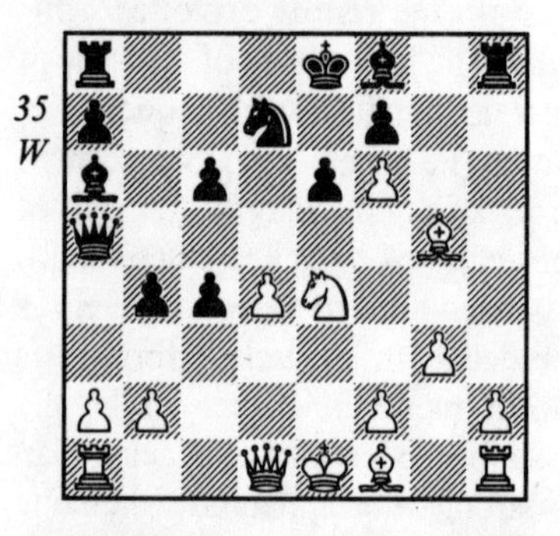

Offers White no less than four reasonable tries. First though, one mistake and one dubious idea:

c1) **14 ♗g2?** c3∓ since White's king is severely embarrassed. Not only the king suffered this fate in Kramer-Berliner, Washington 1948 after 15 bxc3? bxc3 16 ♕c2 ♖b8 17 a3 ♖b2 18 ♕xc3 ♗b4-+.

c2) **14 a3** looks so stupid that being better than it looks is scant consolation! 14...bxa3+ 15 ♗d2 ♕d5 16 ♗g2 axb2! (Δ17 ♖xa6 ♕b5) 17 ♖a5 ♗b5 (∓ Korchnoi) 18 0-0 (∞ Harding) gives White some but not sufficient compensation.

c3) **14 ♗e2** is solid enough, but does not really address effectively the question of where to put the white queen. After **14...0-0-0**:

c31) **15 h4?** is all wrong. Black gained an extra pawn and a strong attack by 15...♘c5! 16 ♘xc5 ♗xc5 17 0-0 ♗xd4 18 ♕c2 ♕d5 19 ♖ac1 ♖dg8 20 ♖fd1 ♖xg5 21 ♖xd4 ♕xd4 22 hxg5 ♕d5 23 f3 ♕xg5 in Fedorowicz-Novikov, New York Open 1991.

c32) **15 ♕c1 ♘b6 16 ♗e3** and now:

c321) **16...e5!?** was played in Brinck-Claussen – Lukacs, Espoo 1987:

c3211) **17 ♗g4+** ♔b7 18 ♘c5+ ♗xc5 19 dxc5 ♘a4! 20 0-0 ♘xc5 21 ♕c2 ♘d3 22 ♗f3 e4! 23 ♗xe4 ♕e5 24 ♗xd3 ♖xd3 25 ♖fd1 ♖hd8 26 ♖xd3 cxd3∓ Lukacs.

c3212) **17 dxe5!** ♕xe5 18 ♘g5 ♕xf6 19 0-0 ♘d5! 20 ♘e4 (20 ♗xa7 ♗h6!∞) 20...♕e6 21 ♗xc4 ♗xc4 22 ♕xc4 ♕h3 23 ♕xc6+ and White is obliged to give perpetual check (Lukacs).

c322) The older move **16...c3** also seems fine. Black had sufficient compensation in Furman-Zak, Leningrad 1951 after 17 ♗xa6+ ♕xa6 18 ♕c2 e5!? 19 bxc3 bxc3 20 dxe5 ♕c4.

c33) **15 0-0 ♕f5** (15...♘c5!? may be stronger. After 16 ♕c2 ♘xe4 17 ♕xe4 ♕d5! 18 ♗f3 ♕xe4 19 ♗xe4 ♖xd4 20 ♗xc6

Bh6! Black stood well in Schroer-Mercuri, USA 1986) **16 Qc2** (± Harding) **16...Nb6** (16...Qh3 17 Bh4±) **17 Rad1** and Black has two interesting possibilities:

c331) **17...Bb7** 18 g4!? Qh7 19 Bf4 (Polugaevsky mentions only 19 h4 Bh6!) 19...c5 20 dxc5! gave White a promising attack in Istvan-Nemeth, corr. 1982.

c332) **17...Qh3!?** 18 Bh4 Rxh4!? 19 gxh4 Bh6!? (19...Qxh4) 20 h5 c5! 21 d5 exd5 22 Ng3 Bg5 23 Qf5+ Qxf5 24 Nxf5 Bxf6 25 b3 Kc7 with a sharp ending in which Black has definite counterplay – Polugaevsky.

c4) **14 Qf3** has great theoretical significance not least because the positions discussed here may be reached after 12...Ba6!? 13 Qf3!? b4 14 Ne4 etc. Long castling, though not compulsory, seems the most flexible, and certainly the most frequent choice for Black, after which we reach another major crossroads after **14...0-0-0** *(36)* (14...Qd5!?) and now:

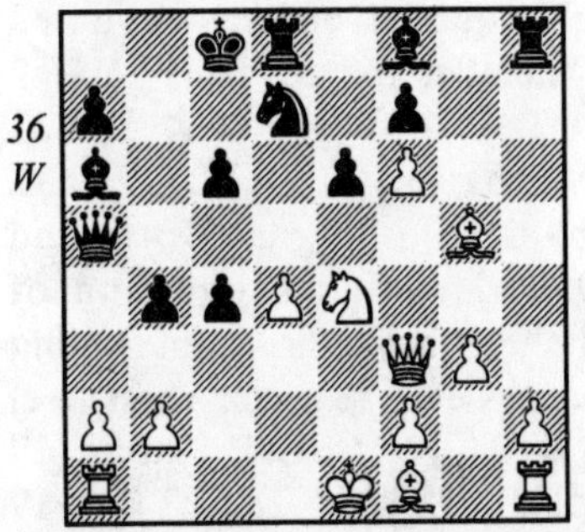
36
W

c41) **15 Bg2?** c3! 16 Nxc3 (16 bxc3?! bxc3 17 Nxc3 Nb8 18 Bd2 Rxd4 19 Rb1 Bb4 20 a3 Qxa3 21 Ne4 Rxe4+! 22 Qxe4 Bxd2+ 0-1 Bonin-Weldon, New York Open 1987 is clearly still worse for White. Perhaps 16 b3 ΔBf1 is safest, but hardly begins to justify White's 15th) 16...Nb8! 17 Ne4 Rxd4 18 Be3 b3+ (Pinter suggests plausibly that 18...Rd7 is also good) 19 Nc3 Ba3! 20 Bxd4 (20 axb3 Bxb2) 20...Bxb2 21 Bf1 Bb7 22 Bg2 Ba6 23 Bf1 Bxa1 24 Bxa6+ Qxa6 25 axb3 (25 Qe2 bxa2) 25...Rd8 26 Qe3 Timman-Pinter, Taxco IZ 1985, and now by the simple 26...Qa5 27 0-0 Rxd4 28 Qxd4 Bxc3 Black would have retained his large plus.

c42) **15 Be2!?** has scored quite well, but, whilst it is one of White's better options, the logical plan for Black of switching back to play on the a8-h1 diagonal should secure reasonable play. 15...Bb7! (15...Nb6?! has had rather a rough time of it: 16 Nc5! {16 Be3 Bb7 17 0-0 c5 18 dxc5 Na4? 19 Bxc4 Nxb2 20 c6! Bxc6 21 Rac1 Kb7 22 Bxe6!! fxe6 23 Rxc6 Kxc6 24 Rc1+ Kd7 25 f7 with a decisive attack; Magerramov-Oll, Klaipeda 1988} 16...Bb5 17 0-0 Rxd4 18 Nb3!± Kishnev-Thesing, Bad Wörishofen 1990) 16 0-0 Qd5 17 Be3 17...Rg8! 18 Rfc1 c5 19 Nd2 cxd4 20 Qxd5 exd5= Flohr.

c43) **15 Nc5!?** Nxc5!? (15...Ne5 16 dxe5 Bxc5 17 Be2! b3+ 18 Kf1 Rd5 19 Kg2 bxa2 20 Rhc1 Bd4 21 Rxc4! Δ21...Bxc4

22 ♗xc4 ♖c5 23 ♖xa2 was better for White in Garcia Gonzalez-Braga, Cuba 1984. One can sympathize with Black. 15 ♘c5 must have been hard to meet over the board, and indeed Vladimirov's logical recipe eluded annotators too for some time) 16 ♕xc6+ ♕c7 17 ♕xc7+ ♔xc7 18 dxc5 ♗b7! (the key point, since 18...♗xc5 19 ♖c1 is quite unsatisfactory) 19 ♖g1 ♖xh2 is unclear according to Vladimirov.

c44) **15 b3** may have been shorn of much of its terror in view of line 'c443' below:

c441) **15...cxb3?!** is weak: 16 ♗xa6+ ♕xa6 17 ♕xb3 ♕b5 18 ♖c1! (much more to the point than the previously known 18 **0-0-0** since Black's c-file problems more than outweigh the temporary restriction of the white king to the centre) 18...♘b6 19 ♗e3 a5?! (A bad plan, but even the better 19...♖d5 20 ♕c2 looks ±) 20 ♕c2 (20 ♘g5! was even stronger) 20...♔b7 21 ♕e2 ♕d5 22 f3 ♘d7 23 0-0 ♗h6 24 ♖f2! with great advantage for White in Kasparov-Miles, Basle (5) 1986.

c442) Possible too is **15...♕d5** 16 ♖d1 (16 ♗e3 ♘b6 {16...e5!?} 17 ♖c1 ♗b5 18 bxc4 ♘xc4 19 ♘d2!? ♘xd2 20 ♕xd5 ♖xd5 21 ♗xb5 ♖xb5 22 ♔xd2± ♔b7 23 g4?! {23 h4!±} 23...♖h3! 24 g5 ♗d6 25 ♖cg1? ♖a5!∓ Dinstuhl-Wells, Hastings Challengers 1992/3) 16...♘b6 17 bxc4! ♗xc4 (17...♘xc4!?) 18 ♗xc4 ♕xc4 19 ♖c1 ♕b5 20 ♕e2 and White was somewhat better in the ensuing endgame in Vladimirov-Neverov, USSR 1985.

c443) **15...♘b6!** *(37)*

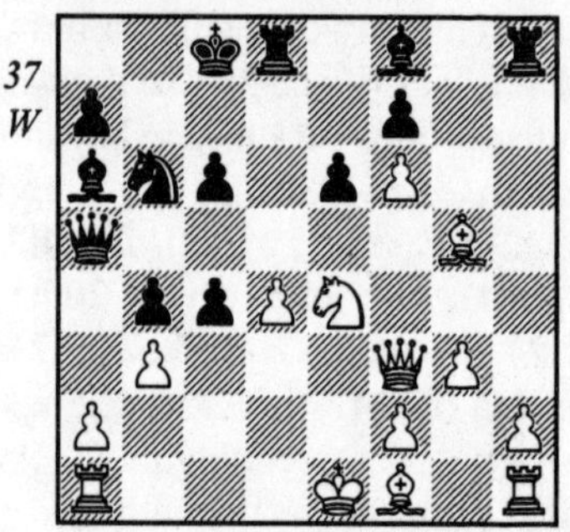
37
W

16 ♘c5 ♗b5 17 ♗e3 (17 bxc4 fails to 17...♗xc5 18 cxb5 b3+ 19 ♗d2 ♗b4 20 ♕xc6+ ♔b8∓/-+) 17...♖d5! 18 a4 bxa3+!! 19 ♗d2 ♕xd2+ 20 ♔xd2 ♗xc5 21 bxc4 ♖xd4+ 22 ♔c3 ♘xc4 with a crushing attack for Black in Oll-Kaidanov, Kuibyshev 1986.

c5) **14 ♗e3 0-0-0** (14...c3?! was an instructive positional error from Zsofia Polgar. Black's pawn on c3 was a liability, and the exchange of light-squared bishops favoured White after 15 bxc3 bxc3 16 ♕c2 ♗xf1 17 ♔xf1 ♕f5 18 ♔e2! ♗a3 19 ♖ab1 0-0 20 g4 ♕g6 21 f3± Knaak-Zso.Polgar, Dortmund 1990. Knaak's suggestion of 14...♕f5 however is interesting and may even be Black's best here) 15 ♕c2 ♘b6 16 b3 e5! 17 dxe5 (17 ♖d1!?) 17...♕xe5 18 ♖c1 ♖e8 19 f3 ♘d5 20 ♗d2 Khenkin-Feher, Cappelle la Grande 1992 and now

20...♕xf6! 21 ♗e2! ♕d4 22 ♗xc4 ♗xc4 23 ♕xc4 ♕xc4 24 bxc4 ♘f6 is about equal – Khenkin.

c6) **14 b3!?** *(38)*

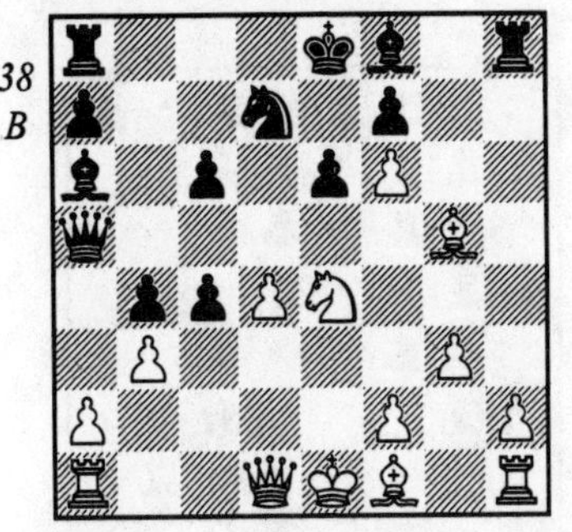

Described by Polugaevsky as the most principled continuation, White blocks out all tricks based on the a5-e1 diagonal, and seeks to clarify the queenside structure by attacking the loose black c-pawn. Now the alternatives to castling queenside read as a list of instructive mistakes!:

c61) **14...♘b6** 15 bxc4! ♘xc4 16 ♕b3 ♕f5!? 17 f3 ♘a5 18 ♕e3 ♗xf1 19 ♔xf1 **0-0-0** 20 ♖c1 ♕d5 21 ♕e2± Ruban-Bryson, Hastings Challengers 1992.

c62) **14...♕f5?** 15 f3 **0-0-0** 16 ♗xc4! ♗xc4 17 bxc4 ♘c5 18 g4! ♕g6 19 dxc5!! ♖xd1+ 20 ♖xd1 ♗h6 21 ♗xh6 ♕xh6 22 ♔e2 ♕h3 23 ♖dg1! and Black can do nothing constructive at all.

c63) **14...♕d5** 15 ♕c2 (it is the queen's position here that gives 14 b3 a special flavour) 15...♘b6 16 ♖c1! and the speed of White's ganging up on c4 gives Black no time to re-group.

c64) **14...0-0-0** 15 ♕c2 ♘b6 16 ♗e3 and now instead of **16...♔b7** 17 ♖c1 ♔a8 (as usual 17...c3?! 18 ♗xa6+ ♕xa6 19 ♕e2! is merely weakening) 18 ♗e2 ♗b7 19 0-0 ♕f5 20 h4± Komarov-Kamsky, USSR Ch 1987, Black should try **16...e5!** which transposes to 'c5' above and gives enough play.

13 a3 *(39)*

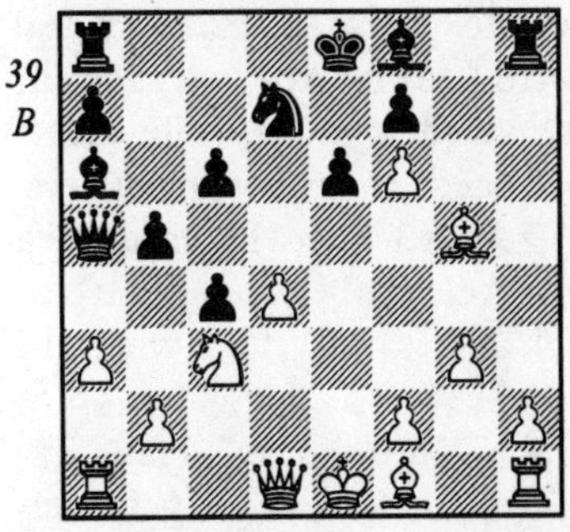

As discussed above, this is the critical test of Black's controversial 12th move. Other moves give Black the option of transposing back to the lines discussed above in the extensive notes to 12...b4, whilst having avoided the dangerous-looking 14 b3. However, White has tried to manufacture these transpositions and here we should assess the viability of Black's efforts to explore an independent path:

a) **13 ♕f3** is important since it seeks to reach one of White's better lines after 13...b4. Superficially interesting was I.Sokolov-Kamsky, Belgrade 1991 where Black tried **13...♖c8**, virtually the only independent try. However the main significance of the novelty was the decision to leave Black's king in the centre since after 14 ♗e2 Black continued 14...b4 anyway. After 15 ♘e4 c5 **16 dxc5** ♘xc5 17 ♘xc5 ♗xc5 18 0-0 ♗d4 19 ♕f4 ♕xe5 20 ♕xe5 ♗xe5 Black had good counterplay. However as Ivan Sokolov points out, by **16 d5!** he could have broken open lines against Black's king. He gives 16...exd5 17 0-0 ♗b7 18 ♖fe1 Δ♗xc4 'with attack', and indeed it looks quite nasty. Black needs an improvement here.

b) **13 ♗e3** gives Black quite a pleasant choice between 13...b4 (as ever) and 13...♘xf6!? when 14 ♕f3 ♘d5 15 ♗g2 b4 (Not 15...♗b7 16 0-0 ♘xc3 17 ♗d2±) 16 ♘xd5 (16 ♘e4 c3 generates serious counterplay) 16...cxd5 is unclear according to Kaidanov, but if anything I prefer Black.

c) **13 ♗e2** b4 14 ♘e4 transposes to 'c3' in the note to Black's 12th, which holds no terrors for Black.

13 ... 0-0-0
14 ♗e3

White wants to bolster the d4 pawn which as we shall see is a major target for Black's counterplay in this line, and at the same time retain options on the placement of his king's bishop. However, since 13 a3 has nullified the threat of ...b4, the natural **14 ♗g2** is an important move too. White has scored well with it in practice, but the theoretical position is far from clear: **14...♘c5 15 0-0 ♘b3 16 ♕f3 ♗b7** (if 16...♘xd4 17 ♕e4 ♗b7 18 ♖ad1 ♕b6 19 ♗e3 ♗c5 20 ♕e5 and Black's knight will be undermined, and his position with it) **17 ♖ad1** *(40)*:

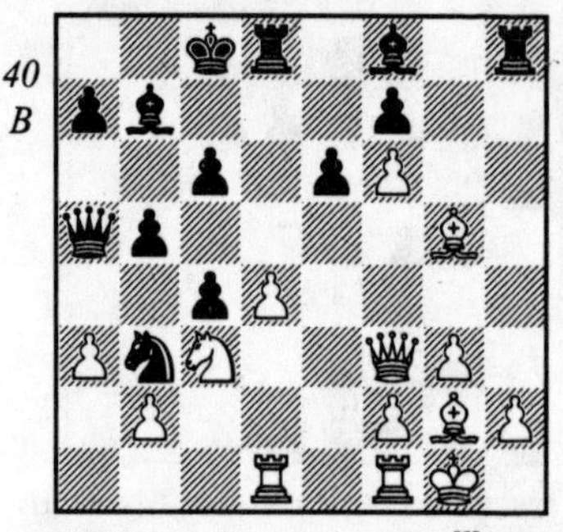

a) Beliavsky gave **17...♖d7!?** – to support the bishop on b7 preparing ...c5 – 18 ♕e3 ♕b6 19 ♘e2 c5 20 dxc5 ♗xc5 with good counterplay. 19 a4!? looks more fun, Δ19...b4?! 20 ♘e4! and the possibility of a5 immunises the d-pawn.

b) **17...b4!?** 18 ♘e4 bxa3 19 bxa3 ♗xa3 20 ♗e3! (20 h4?! ♗b4 21 ♗e3 ♕b5 22 ♘c5 a5 23 ♘xb7 ♔xb7 24 ♕e2 was Beliavsky-Novikov, USSR Ch 1990 and now 24...♖d5 with the simple idea of marching the a-pawn was strong according to Beliavsky) 20...♗b4? (it was important to try to exchange queens with 20...♕h5! again with the a-pawn as the main trump. In this case Black would not stand worse) 21 ♘c5! ♗xc5 22 dxc5 ♕b5 23 ♖xd8+ ♖xd8 24 ♕h5± c3 25 ♕xf7 ♘xc5 26 ♕e7 ♘d3 27 ♗h6! 1-0 Gomez-Novikov, Pamplona 1990/1.

14 ... ♘e5!?

Currently looks the best. It is very important that Black generates very rapid counterplay against White's d-pawn, since if White consolidates, Black will be weak on the h1-a8 diagonal and without ...b4 will be deprived of counterplay. White was better after **14...c5** (14...♘xf6!? Savchenko)15 ♗g2 cxd4 (15...♘e5 16 0-0 cxd4 17 ♗xd4 ♗c5 is the note to 17...♘e5 below) 16 ♗xd4 ♗c5 (not 16...♘c5 17 0-0 ♘b3 18 ♕f3 with a winning attack) 17 0-0! (17 ♕f3 ♗xd4 leads to no more than a perpetual) 17...♘xf6 (17...♘e5 18 ♗xe5 or 18 ♘d5!? are promising, but 17...♕b6!? merited attention, although still ±) 18 ♗xc5! ♖xd1 19 ♖axd1 with excellent play for the slight material deficit, the more so in that Black cannot try to redeploy his off-side bishop in view of 19...♗b7? 20 ♗b4! ♕b6 21 ♖d6!± in Savchenko-Novikov, Šibenik 1989.

15 f4 **c5!**

Black has no choice.

16 fxe5 **cxd4**
17 ♗xd4 **♗b7**
18 ♖g1 **♖xh2**
19 ♗e2 **♕c7!**
20 ♖c1 *(41)*

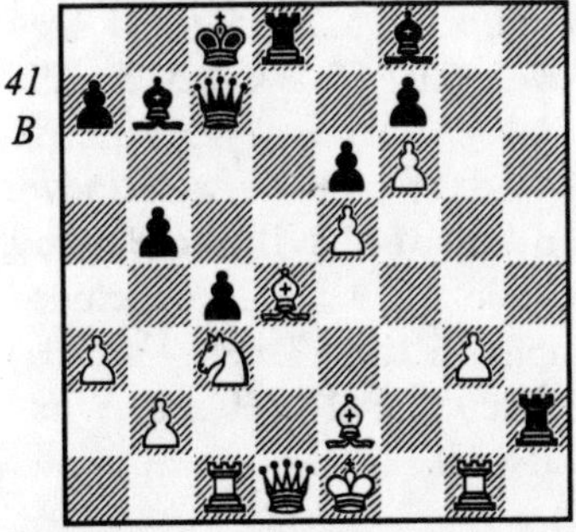

The previous moves, in spite of the highly unbalanced nature of the position, do not need much comment since they were fairly forcing. Black looks to have good play for the piece. White has no safe home for his king, and no simple way to break the pin on the d-file. 19...♕c7 threatened ...♗c5 (which would of course have previously been a blunder in view of ♗xc5) and 20 ♘xb5? would not have helped in view of 20...♕a5+ 21 ♘c3 ♗c5∓. However, there was a case for **20 b4!?** instead of the text, when, according to Kaidanov, Black's bishop should enter the fray from the other side after the precautionary 20...a6! Δ...♗h6-e3. My feeling is that this should give at least enough.

20 ... **♖xd4?**

Needlessly rushing things, always a temptation after the sacrifice of material. Solid, and retaining all threats was again **20...a6!**.

21 ♕xd4 **♗c5**
22 ♘xb5!

22 ♕g4 ♗xg1 23 ♘b5 ♕d8! 24 ♘d6+ ♔b8 25 ♖xc4 a5! (to stop 26 ♖b4) would be unclear, since the knight on d6 is 'pinned' to the possibility of ...♗f2+ and ...♕d2.

After the text Black should be struggling. Play continued: **22...♗xd4 23 ♘xc7 ♗xg1 24 ♖xc4 ♗f2+ 25 ♔d2?** (A self-pin which costs victory. After the simple 25 ♔d1!, 25...♗xg3 can be answered decisively by 26 ♘xe6+

♔b8 27 ♖g4 ♗xe5 28 ♖g8+ ♗c8 29 ♗a6+-. Now that White has to waste a tempo and a pawn unpinning, the game liquidates into an ending which is trivially drawn) **25...♗xg3 26 ♘xe6+ ♔b8 27 ♖g4 ♗xe5 28 ♖g8+ ♗c8 29 ♔e3 ♗xf6 30 ♗a6 ♖h8 31 ♖xh8 ♗xh8 32 ♗xc8 ♔xc8 33 ♘g5 ♗xb2 34 ♘xf7 ♔d7 35 ♔d3** (Kaidanov mentions one final trap: 35 a4?? ♔e7∓/-+) **35...♗xa3 ½-½.**

Game 6
I.Rogers-Kuijf
Wijk aan Zee 1987

1 d4 d5 2 c4 c6 3 ♘f3 ♘f6 4 ♘c3 e6 5 ♗g5 dxc4 6 e4 b5 7 e5 h6 8 ♗h4 g5 9 ♘xg5 hxg5 10 ♗xg5 ♘bd7 11 g3

11 ... ♖g8 *(42)*

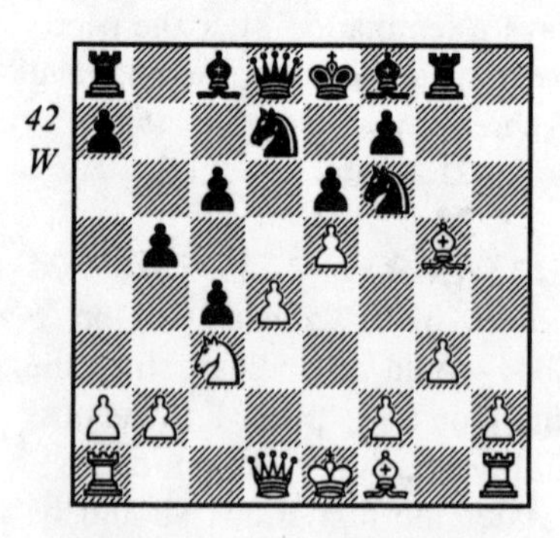

It is logical that when White has deferred recapturing the knight on f6, putting the question to the bishop on g5 should be an important option for Black. Here we shall consider Black's alternative ideas. One of these, the closely related 11...♗b7 12 ♗g2 ♖g8 seems in the key line with h4 to be inferior, but this will be pointed out in the text (see note 'b2224' to 12 ♗xf6).

a) **11...♘xe5?** is simply weak. Euwe's analysis 12 dxe5 ♕xd1+ 13 ♖xd1 ♘d5 14 ♘e4 ♗b4+ 15 ♔e2± makes a convincing impression.

b) **11...b4?!** and the queen sacrifice associated with it must also, sadly after so much labour of love and commitment devoted to trying to prove its correctness, be confined to the scrap-heap too. After 12 ♘e4 ♘xe4 13 ♗xd8 ♔xd8 Black has three pieces for the queen and pawn, but White is still active, the black pawns, notably c4, are weakened and his king is not so comfortable in the centre. 14 ♗g2 (Seems the simplest. Korchnoi suggests 14 ♕c2 f5 15 ♗xc4 but 15...♘b6 Δ...♗b7 and ...♘d5 gives some play. The text opens the position, and the evidence is that this benefits the queen more than the black pieces) 14...f5 15 exf6 (Also 15 f3!? is to be considered, e.g. 15...♘g5 16 f4 ♘e4 17 ♕c2 ♗b7 18 ♕xc4 Δ18...♖h6 19 g4 – Varnusz) 15...♘exf6 (15...♘dxf6 was the well-known blunder of P.Nikolić-Bagirov, Sarajevo 1980 which concluded abruptly 16 ♗xe4 ♘xe4 17 ♕f3!+-) 16 ♗xc6 ♖b8 17 0-0 and White standswell.

c) **11...♗b7 12 ♗g2 ♕a5!? 13 exf6** *(43)* and now:

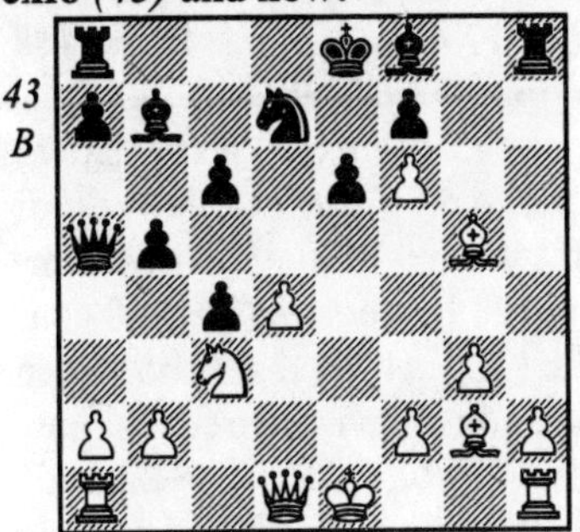

43
B

c1) **13...0-0-0**:

c11) **14 ♕f3!?** was played in Lilienthal-Botvinnik, USSR Ch 1944, a game which Black won, but the opening is universally given as clearly better for White after 14...♘b6 15 0-0!? ♖xd4 16 ♖fd1 ♖xd1+ 17 ♕xd1 ♘d5 18 ♘e4 b4 19 a3 bxa3 20 ♗d2 ♕b6 21 bxa3. The interesting question is why White has not repeated it. Despite Black's strong knight on d5, he has problems with both bishops, and the c4 pawn looks more a liability than an asset.

c12) **14 0-0** ♘e5!? 15 ♕e2 (15 dxe5?! is better for Black than the analogous and well known sacrifice with the black queen on b6 {see 'e'}: 15...♖xd1 16 ♖axd1 b4 17 ♘e4 ♕xe5 18 ♖fe1 ♕xb2 19 ♖d2 ♕e5 was Gaprindashvili-Pudkova, USSR 1985 when Black has counterplay. If Black feels this is worth avoiding, however, he may try 14...♘c5!?) 15...♘d3 16 ♘e4!? ♖xd4 17 ♗e3 ♖d7 18 b3 ♗a3 19 bxc4 bxc4 20 ♕c2 ♗a6 21 ♗d2 ♗b4 22 ♖ab1 ♗xd2 23 ♘xd2 ♕c5 24 ♘e4 ♕a3 25 ♘d2 ♕c5 ½-½ Piket-Pinter, Thessaloniki OL 1988.

c13) The other possibility, **14 ♕e2?!** is probably weak, since as L.Santos points out, it rather invites the idea of ...b4 and ...c3 Δ...♗a6.

c2) **13...b4?!** is an imaginative possibility, switching to play similar to Game 5, except with White's bishop already committed to g2. However the tempo which needs to be expended to redeploy Black's bishop to the a6-f1 diagonal seems to be more significant. Korchnoi's assessment of 14 ♘e4 c3 15 bxc3 ♗a6 16 ♗d2! as ± is if anything a bit modest. I can find nothing for Black here, and no one has felt moved to test the idea in practice.

d) **11...♗b7 12 ♗g2 ♕c7 13 exf6 c5** *(44)* and now White has two ways of obtaining the advantage:

44
W

d1) **14 0-0** ♗xg2 (14...b4? 15 ♗f4! (now that 15...♕b6 is answerable with 16 ♘a4) 15...e5 16

♘d5 ♗xd5 17 ♗xd5 0-0-0 18 dxe5 ♘xe5 19 ♗xe5 ♕xe5 20 ♕g4+ ±) 15 ♔xg2 ♕b7+ 16 f3 0-0-0 17 dxc5 ♘xc5 18 ♕e2 ♘d3 19 ♘e4 and Black was short on compensation in Ruban-Savchenko, Tbilisi 1989.

d2) **14 d5** ♕e5+ 15 ♕e2 0-0-0 (15...♕xg5? 16 dxe6 ♗xg2 17 exd7+ ♔xd7 18 f4!± Vera) 16 dxe6 (16 ♕xe5!? ♘xe5 17 ♘xb5 – Vujatović, looks rather materialistic but is not so easy to refute) 16...♕xe2+ 17 ♔xe2 ♗xg2 and now not **18 exd7+** ♖xd7 19 ♖hd1 b4 20 ♖xd7 ♔xd7 21 ♘d1 ♗e4! when Black's c4-pawn is far more significant than White's h-pawn (Legky-Savchenko, USSR 1987), but 18 e7! ♗xe7 19 fxe7 ♖dg8 20 ♗f4! ♖e8 (20...♗xh1 21 ♘xb5!) 21 ♘xb5 ♖xe7+ 22 ♔d2 ♗xh1 23 ♘d6+ ♔d8 24 ♖xh1± Knaak.

e) **11...♗b7 12 ♗g2 ♕b6 13 exf6 0-0-0** (13...c5?! 14 dxc5! really looks promising, as Black cannot follow up ...♘xc5 with ...0-0-0 for legal reasons) **14 0-0** and now:

e1) **14...c5** (This is Black's attempt to reach the main line examined in Chapters 1 and 2. The question here is whether White's deviations represent a problem. It is important to remember that the material here can arise after 11 exf6 too, at Black's behest) 15 dxc5!? ♘xc5 (Black has not fared well with 15...♗xc5: 16 ♕e2 ♖dg8 17 ♗xb7+ ♕xb7 18 ♘e4 ♕d5?! 19 ♖fd1 ♗d4 20 ♖xd4! ♕xd4 21 ♖d1 ♕e5 22 ♕f3!± Yuferov-Timoshchenko, USSR 1981) 16 ♕e2 ♗xg2 17 ♔xg2 ♗h6! 18 h4 (18 ♗xh6 ♖xh6 19 ♕f3!? Tal) 18...♗xg5 19 hxg5 ♕c6+ 20 f3 ♖h5!. An important move for Black's counterplay. Now Timman-Tal, Hilversum (2) 1988 continued 21 a4 b4 22 ♘b5 when Black could have secured his share of the play with 22...♕d5 23 ♖fd1 ♘d3 24 ♕e3 ♕g5 25 ♕e4 ♕d5 26 ♖xd3 cxd3∞ (Tal).

e2) **14...♘e5** 15 dxe5 ♖xd1 16 ♖fxd1 b4 (16...♗c5 17 ♘e4 ♗d4 18 ♘d6+ ♔c7 19 ♘xf7 ♖f8 20 ♘d6 ♗xe5 21 ♗e3 ♕a6 22 ♘e4 ♗c8 23 ♗c5 ♖xf6 24 ♘xf6 ♗xf6∞ Vilela-Frey, Havana 1985) 17 ♘e4 c5 18 a3! ♗d5 19 axb4 ♕b7 (de la Villa gives instead 19...cxb4 20 ♗e3 ♕c7 {20...♕c6 21 ♘g5! ♗xg2 22 ♘xf7 ♗c5 23 ♗xc5 ♗h1 24 ♘d6+ with favourable complications for White} 21 ♘d6+ ♗xd6 22 ♖xa7 ♕xa7 23 ♗xa7 ♗xe5 24 ♗xd5 exd5 25 ♖xd5 ♗xb2 26 ♖b5 ♗xf6 {26...♗c3 27 ♖b8+} 27 ♖xb4 with the better ending for White) 20 ♖xd5! exd5 21 ♘c3 cxb4?! (21...♕b4 22 ♘xd5 ♕xb2 is more critical) 22 ♘xd5 ♕d7 23 ♗e3 ♔b8 24 ♗f4 gave White too much play against the black king in Illescas-Morović, Spanish team Ch 1993.

12 ♗xf6

White has two alternatives of which 'b' is particularly important:

a) **12 ♗h4?!**:

a1) **12...♕b6?!** 13 exf6 e5!? 14 ♕e2! b4 15 ♘e4 ♗a6 16 0-0-0 0-0-0 17 d5 ♕a5 18 dxc6 ♕xa2 19 ♗h3 ♗h6+ 20 f4 exf4 21 cxd7+ ♔b8 22 ♕h5! ♖g5!! (against the possibility of ♕e5+) 23 ♗xg5 c3 24 ♘xc3! bxc3 25 bxc3 ♗xg5 ½-½ since if 26 ♕xg5 Black gives perpetual on a1 and a2; Vilela-Chekhov, Halle 1981. Great entertainment, but I suspect that Black can still better take advantage of the bishop's inability to return to e3.

a2) In this regard Magerramov-Savchenko, Helsinki 1992 looked tempting, reverting to play analogous to Game 5 with **12...♕a5** 13 exf6 ♗a6!? (13...b4) **14 a3** 0-0-0 15 ♗g2 ♘c5 16 0-0 ♘d3!? (16...♘b3!? looks as if it could improve on the Novikov games) 17 ♕f3 ♗b7 18 b4 ♕c7∞. However, simply **14 ♗g2!** b4 15 ♘e2 looks much better.

a3) Hence Savchenko's more recent try **12...♗b7**, which, remarkably, seems to be a novelty, looks best. Magerramov-Savchenko, Rostov-on-Don 1993 looked promising for Black after 13 ♗g2 ♕c7 14 exf6 0-0-0 15 ♕f3 (15 0-0 ♘e5! takes classic advantage of the bishop's new home on h4. 15 ♕h5!?∞ should be White's focus of research) 15...b4! 16 ♘e2 (16 ♘a4 c5! 17 ♕xb7+ ♕xb7 18 ♗xb7+ ♔xb7 19 0-0-0 ♔c6! gives Black good play too) 16...♘b6! 17 0-0 (if 17 0-0-0 simply ...♘d5 preparing ...c5 is strong, claims Savchenko plausibly) 17...c5 18 ♕xb7+ ♕xb7 19 ♗xb7+ ♔xb7 20 ♖fd1 and now instead of 20...♘a4!?, simply 20...♔c6! Δ...a5 appears to give Black an uncomplicated plus.

b) **12 h4!?** *(45)*

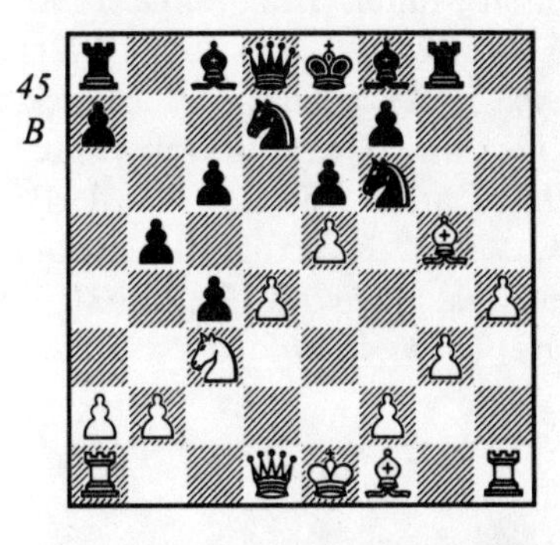

Probably the critical continuation, where White sacrifices two pieces for a rook and a middlegame attack or an endgame initiative, depending on how Black responds. Both are based on the open h-file and the disruptive qualities of the key move g6. The theoretical verdict has been generally in White's favour, but the recent upsurge of interest in 11...♖g8 may be a sign that things are not so clear. 11...♗b7 12 ♗g2 ♖g8 13 h4 will be considered too where it has independent value. Play continues **12...♖xg5** (12...b4? 13 ♘e4 ♖xg5 14 ♘xg5 ♘d5 15 ♘xe6! fxe6 16 ♕h5+ ♔e7 17 ♗e2! with a winning attack) **13 hxg5 ♘d5 14 g6! fxg6** and now:

b1) **15 ♖h7?!** (Kramnik also mentions 15 ♖h8!?) 15...♕a5 (15...♗e7 16 ♗h3(?!) ♘f8 looks rather passive, but Black quickly seized the upper hand after 17 ♖g7 ♘xc3! 18 bxc3 ♕d5 19 ♕g4 ♕h1+ 20 ♗f1 ♕h6 21 ♕f3 ♕xg7 22 ♕xc6+ ♔d8 23 ♕xa8 ♗a3∓ in Schön-Müller, Bundesliga 1990) 16 ♕f3 ♔d8 17 ♗h3 ♗b4 18 ♔f1 ♗xc3 19 ♗xe6 Knaak-Tischbierek, E.German Ch (Furstenwalde) 1981 and now instead of **19...♗xd4?** 20 ♗xd5, Black could get equal play with **19...♗xb2!**.

b2) **15 ♕g4(!)** *(46)*

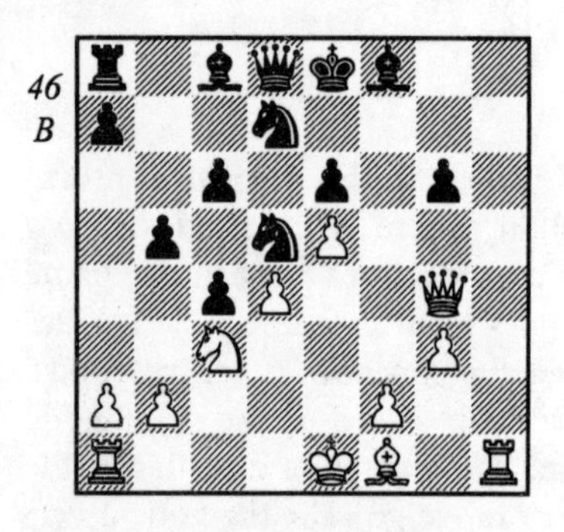

This looks more dangerous since Black must allow an ending where in practice the rook looks to have had an edge over the two pieces:

b21) The counterattacking **15...♕a5?** has been known to be bad since White's superb attacking display in the now famous Knaak-Van der Wiel, Lugano 1989: 16 ♕xe6+ ♔d8 17 ♗g2!!. Very cool! 17...♘xc3 18 ♔f1! ♘d5 19 ♕xc6 ♘5b6 20 ♖h8 ♕b4 21 e6! ♖b8 22 exd7 ♘xd7 23 a3 ♕e7 24 ♕xg6 ♕b6 25 ♕h5 ♖f6 26 ♖e1±.

b22) **15...♕e7** with the following possibilities:

b221) **16 ♗g2!?** was White's choice in Beliavsky-Kramnik, Linares 1993 which continued 16...♕f7 (awarded a (!) by Kramnik; 16...♗a6?! 17 ♕xg6+ ♕f7 18 ♗e4 ♗b4 19 ♖h7 ♕xg6+ 20 ♗xg6+ ♔d8 21 a3± Tolonen-Harding, corr. 1991; 16...♗b7 transposes to 11...♗b7 12 ♗g2 ♖g8) 17 ♗e4 ♘e7 18 **0-0-0** (When I first saw this game I could not understand why not 18 ♘xb5. According to Kramnik 18...cxb5 19 ♗xa8 ♘b6 20 ♗e4 ♘bd5 is ∓, and the more I look at it the more I agree Black's minor pieces are excellent. Instead Beliavsky gives 18 ♖h8!? ♕g7 19 ♕h3! followed by ♗c2 and ♘e4 keeping White's initiative) 18...♗a6 19 ♘e2 ♗g7 20 ♘f4 ♘f8 21 ♘h3 **0-0-0** (21...c3!? Δ22 bxc3 ♘d5 gave interesting play too) 22 ♘g5 ♕e8! 23 ♕f3 (23 ♘xe6? ♕d7∓/-+) 23...♘f5 24 ♕a3 ♗b7 25 ♕xa7 ♕e7 26 ♘f3 c5! with excellent play for Black.

b222) **16 ♕xg6+ ♕f7 17 ♕xf7+ ♔xf7 18 ♗g2** (18 0-0-0 ♘xc3! 19 bxc3 ♗a3+ 20 ♔c2 ♘f8 21 ♗g2?! {21 f4!?} 21...♗d7 22 f4 ♖b8 and Black had enough play on the queenside in Arbakov-Savchenko, USSR 1989; 18 ♘e4 ♗b4+ 19 ♔e2 c3! 20 bxc3 ♘xc3 21 ♘xc3 ♗xc3 22 ♖d1 b4! 23 ♗g2 ♗a6 24 ♔e3 ♖g8! 25 ♗xc6 ♘b6 gave Black sufficient play in Lobron-Shirov, Bundesliga 1993/4) and now:

b2221) **18...♘7b6** 19 ♘e4! ♗d7 20 ♔e2 ♗g7 21 ♘d6+ ♔g8 22 ♖h5! ♘a4 23 ♖g5 ♘xb2 24 ♗xd5! with the simple and effective plan of ♖h1-h4-g4± in the stem game Yusupov-Chekhov, USSR Ch (Vilnius) 1980.

b2222) **18...♗b4** 19 0-0-0 ♗xc3?! (Black can also play similarly to Arbakov-Savchenko above with 19...♘xc3, but the tempo lost will of course make his task more difficult) 20 bxc3 ♘f8 21 ♗xd5!± A frequently justified exchange in this variation which here presages the transfer of the rook to f6 with great force; Knaak-Kallai, Calimanesti 1984.

b2223) **18...♘xc3!? 19 bxc3 ♖b8!? 20 ♗xc6** (can this be wrong?) **20...♗b7 21 ♖h7+** (21 ♗xb7) **21...♔g6 22 ♖xd7 ♗xc6 23 ♖xa7** *(47)*

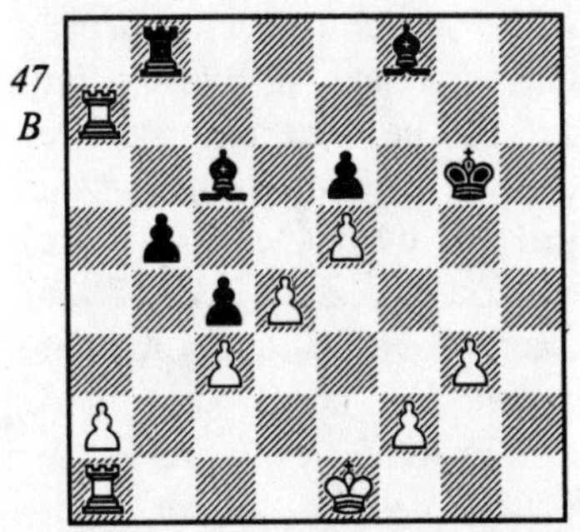

47
B

A very interesting position. At the expense of two pawns, Black has succeeded in activating his two bishops. In particular he has an excellent bind on the light squares.

b22231) In the game Shirov-Stisis, London Lloyds Bank 1990, Black played **23...♗f3** and after 24 ♔d2 ♗h6+ 25 ♔c2 ♖f8 26 ♔b2 Shirov found a safe place for his king on the queenside and eventually won by returning a rook for one of Black's bishops.

b22232) What of **23...b4!** however? In conjunction with a passed c-pawn Black's bishop pair can be really dangerous. This whole idea of Stisis' looks like Black's best bet against 12 h4.

b2224) **18...♗b7** is important since it can arise from the 11...♗b7 move order. Logically, and on the evidence here it looks as if this may be inaccurate. 19 ♘e4 ♗e7 20 ♘d6+! ♗xd6 21 ♖h7+ ♔g8 22 ♖xd7 ♗b4+ 23 ♔e2 ♗c8 24 ♖d8+ ♗f8 25 ♗xd5! (as above, a further generic argument for ...♘xc3!) 25...cxd5 26 ♖h1 and Black can do little but wait for White to organize a timely f5; Vladimirov-Conquest, Alma-Ata 1989.

b223) The latest wrinkle is **16 ♖h8!?** which led to very sharp play in Kamsky-Serper, Groningen PCA qualifier 1993: 16...♘xc3 17 bxc3 ♕f7 18 ♗g2 ♗b7 19 ♗e4 0-0-0 20 ♗xg6 ♕e7 21 a4 a6 22 ♖h7 ♗g7 23 ♗e4 ♖g8 24 ♕f3 ♔c7 25 axb5 axb5 26 ♖h4 ♖f8 27 ♖f4 ♗h6 28 ♖xf8 ♗xf8 29 ♔e2 ♗h6 30 ♖h1 ♕a3 31 ♖xh6 ♕b2+ 32 ♔d1 ♕a1+ 33 ♔d2 ♕b2+ 34 ♗c2 c5 35 d5 ♗xd5 36 ♕e3 b4 37 cxb4 cxb4 38

♕a7+ ♔c6 39 ♕a4+ ♔b6 40 ♕xd7 ♕c3+ 41 ♔c1 ♕e1+ 42 ♗d1 ♕c3+ 43 ♗c2 ♕a1+ 44 ♔d2 ♕c3+ 45 ♔d1 ½-½. Knife-edge stuff; those wishing to refute the line with 11...♖g8 will doubtless scour this game in search of improvements in the near future.

12 ... ♘xf6
13 exf6 ♕xf6

Black has also tried other queen moves, albeit generally prefaced with 11...♗b7 12 ♗g2 as discussed, but they cannot be regarded as improvements. So here **13...♗b7** 14 ♗g2 and now 14...♕b6 (14...♕c7 can be answered by either 15 a4 {± Sveshnikov} or 15 0-0 0-0-0 16 ♕c2 ♖xd4 17 a4 ♗c5 18 axb5 ♖d3 19 b6 ♗xb6 20 ♘e4 ♕e5 21 ♕xc4 with great advantage in Novikov-Thesing, Berlin 1991) 15 0-0 0-0-0 16 ♕h5! (another weak point in the ...♖g8 lines) 16...♖g6 17 a4! b4 18 a5 ♕xd4 19 a6 ♗a8 20 ♖ad1 ♕xf6 21 ♘e4 ♕xb2 22 ♖xd8+ ♔xd8 23 ♖d1+ ♔e8 24 ♕a5± P.Nikolić-Petursson, Skien 1979.

14 ♗g2 ♗b7 *(48)*

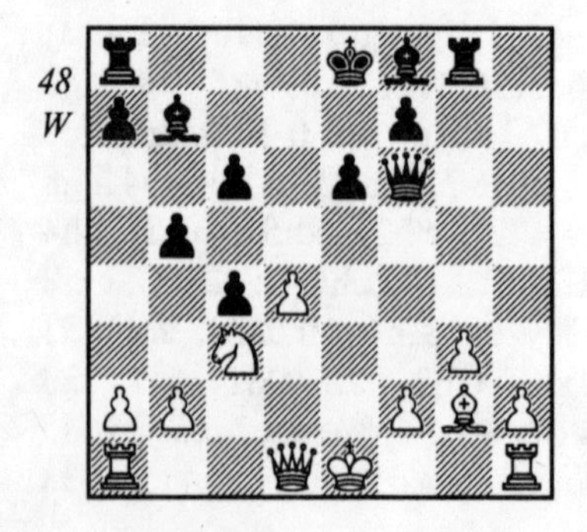

48
W

15 a4

Not **15 0-0** 0-0-0 when White's d-pawn is very weak.

However, **15 ♘xb5** is a legitimate alternative, strengthened by Beliavsky's piece sacrifice after 15...0-0-0 16 ♘xa7+ (16 ♘c3 e5! passes the initiative firmly to Black) 16...♔c7 17 0-0! ♖a8! 18 ♘xc6 ♗xc6 19 ♗xc6 ♔xc6 20 ♕e2 ♔d7 21 ♕xc4 ♖a5!. An interesting position. White has four pawns for the piece, but the weakness of d4 and of the squares around the white king can become important factors if Black consolidates his own king's position. Therefore Beliavsky chose to invest further with 22 d5!? ♖xd5 23 ♕a4+ ♔e7 24 ♖ac1 ♕f5! ½-½. Now that the king can escape to f6 the chances are still finely balanced; Beliavsky-Piket, Thessaloniki OL 1988.

15 ... 0-0-0!

White seems to reach at least a slight advantage if Black acquiesces in the weakening of his queenside without winning d4 in return: **15...b4** 16 ♘e4 ♕f5 17 ♖c1 c5 18 ♘d6+ ♗xd6 19 ♗xb7 ♖b8 20 ♗c6+ ♔e7 21 ♖xc4± Liberzon-Lombard, Biel IZ 1976.

16 axb5 cxb5
17 ♗xb7+ ♔xb7
18 ♘xb5 ♗b4+
19 ♘c3!

19 ♔f1?! is much weaker and Black soon built up a very powerful position in Novikov-Dreev,

Bern 1993: 19...a5 20 ♔g2 ♖g5! 21 ♕a4 e5! 22 ♘a3 e4! 23 ♖hf1 ♕f3+ 24 ♔g1 e3 25 ♘c2 e2 26 ♖fc1 ♖f5∓ (at least).

19 ... ♖xd4 *(49)*

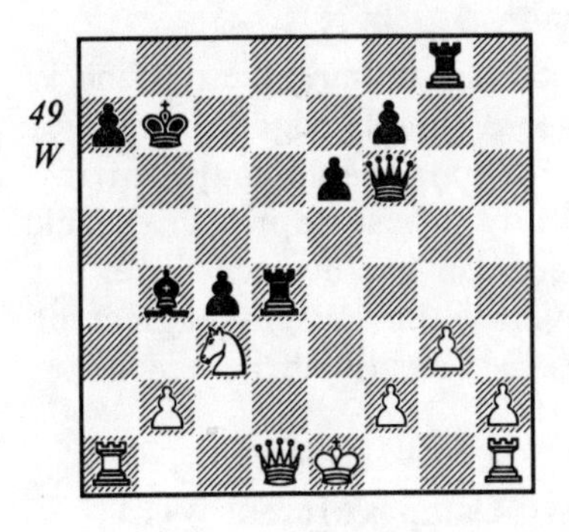

49
W

Here the endgame after **19...♕xd4?** 20 ♕xd4 ♖xd4 21 h4 is not a pleasant option.

However, Black may have a safer route to a satisfactory game with **19...a5!?** 20 0-0 ♖xd4 21 ♕e2 (21 ♕a4 ♕f5!∞) 21...♕f5 22 ♘d1 ♕d3 23 ♕h5 ♕f5= (Mikhalchishin).

20 ♕e2

20 ♖xa7+!? is worth consideration too since if **20...♔xa7?**, 21 ♕a4+ followed by ♕b4+ and 0-0 gives White a very strong attack for very little sacrifice. Also weak is **20...♔b6** 21 ♕a1±. Best seems to be **20...♔b8** 21 ♕a4 ♗xc3+ 22 bxc3 ♕e5+ 23 ♔f1 ♕d5! 24 ♖a8+ ♕xa8 25 ♕xa8+ ♔xa8 26 cxd4 ♔b7 when in view of the passed c-pawn and weak d4 pawn the ending looks tenable for Black.

20 ...	**♕f5**
21 0-0	**♖gd8**
22 ♘d1!	**♗d2**
23 ♘e3	**♕e4**
24 ♕h5	

White's knight manoeuvre was interesting, to target the c4 pawn and Black's king's position still gives cause for concern. Black had an alternative to 24...f5 in **24...a6** since if 25 ♕xf7+, then 25...♖8d7 followed by 26...♗xe3 is quite adequate. However, both here and in the game the patient **25 ♘d1!** would preserve a small plus.

Instead there followed: **24...f5 25 ♘xc4 ♖xc4 26 ♕f7+ ♔b8 27 ♕xa7+ ♔c8 28 ♖fd1 ♖dd4?** (Not yet a decisive mistake but Black makes his defensive task more difficult, and his intention to run with the king to the kingside is misguided. Better was 28...♖c2 when White can choose after 29 ♕a6+ ♔b8 between perpetual with 30 ♕a7+ or unclear complications with 30 b4) **29 ♕a6+ ♔d7 30 ♕b5+ ♔e7?** (This time the error is terminal. Black had to try 30...♕c6 31 ♖a7 ♔c8 and there is no clear win) **31 ♖a7+ ♔f6 32 ♕e8± ♗h6 33 ♖f1! ♕g4 34 ♖f7+ ♔e5 35 ♖e1+ ♖e4 36 ♕b8+ ♔d5 37 ♖d7+ ♔c5 38 ♕d6+ ♔b5 1-0**.

Since White mates in three beginning 39 ♖b7+.

5 9...♘d5!? – The Alatortsev Variation and 10...♗e7?!

I have the feeling that moves like 9...♘d5 often present some challenge to the objectivity of an author. Here at a really crucial early point *en route* to the main lines of the Botvinnik System is a daring, romantic, sacrificial option which sharpens still further the play and invites a tidal wave of tactical complexity. It is currently little played, but were it proved to be a sound option for Black, its impact on the theory of 5 ♗g5 would be enormous. So, the reality? My impression is that if White accepts the implicit challenge and the exchange with 10 ♘xf7, Black's resources are really generally quite impressive, with the single exception that 14 ♘g6 seen below under 'a21' looks problematic. It is also uncertain whether Black can reach fully satisfactory play against the quieter 10 ♘f3, but again I believe that theory is unnecessarily pessimistic. The simple strategy of piling up maximum pressure on the pinned white knight on c3, as for example in Bukic-P.Nikolić (see note to Black's 13th), leaves Black's kingside too vulnerable, as White impressively showed. Black should rather strike in the centre with ...c5, but his kingside weaknesses are such that opening the position is also a double-edged procedure. The main game may portray White's best approach. Black needs an improvement here, but overall the current neglect of 9...♘d5 seems rather overdone.

Game 7
Campos Moreno-Vera
Hospitalet 1988

1 d4 d5 2 c4 e6 3 ♘c3 c6 4 ♘f3 ♘f6 5 ♗g5 dxc4 6 e4 b5 7 e5 h6 8 ♗h4 g5 9 ♘xg5

9 ... ♘d5

One other alternative by which Black can avoid the theory of the preceding chapters is after **9...hxg5 10 ♗xg5** to break the pin with **10...♗e7**. This naturally obliges immediate clarification with **11 exf6 ♗xf6** *(50)*.

50
W

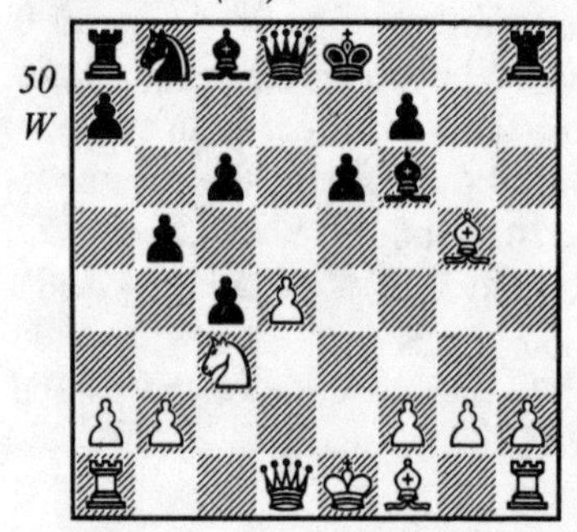

Once dismissed as too weakening of Black's dark squares, its reputation was vastly enhanced when Smyslov used it to secure a draw with Kasparov in their 1984 Candidates match. This and other games brought to light the possibilities for rapid counterplay against d4 and for a while the move even became quite fashionable. Now it seems again to be in trouble, ironically in particular in the variation where White eschews the exchange on f6. Consequently the coverage will be lighter than in preceding chapters. From the diagram White has:

a) **12 ♗xf6 ♕xf6** and now:

a1) **13 ♕d2?!** ♘a6 14 a4 ♖h4 15 axb5 ♖xd4 16 ♕e3 ♘b4∓ Wells-Flear, British Ch (Edinburgh) 1985.

a2) **13 g3** ♗b7 14 ♗g2 ♘a6!. The point; Black develops so as to facilitate pressure on d4. 15 ♘e4 (15 ♘xb5 0-0-0 16 ♘a3 {16 ♕a4 cxb5 17 ♗xb7+ leads to just a perpetual as in Jirovsky-Somlai, Mitropa Cup 1991} 16...♖xd4 17 ♕e2 ♘b4 18 0-0 ♗a6 19 ♕f3 ♕xf3 20 ♗xf3 ♖d2!= Uhlmann-Gauglitz, Dresden 1985) 15...♕e7 16 0-0 0-0-0 (16...f5!?) 17 a4 f5 (17...♔b8 18 ♕d2 b4 {18...♘b4 19 ♖fd1! e5 20 ♘c5 ♘d3 21 axb5± Paunović-Flear, Geneva 1986} 19 ♖ac1 f5 20 ♘g5 e5 21 ♖xc4 c5 22 ♗xb7 with advantage in Kasparov-Smyslov, Vilnius Ct 1984, although as mentioned above, White failed to convert) 18 ♘c3 e5!? 19 axb5 cxb5 20 ♘xb5 ♗xg2 21 ♖xa6! ♗b7 22 ♕a4! with a strong attack in Vidoniak-Nedobora, Lvov 1992.

a3) **13 a4!?** ♖h4 14 axb5 (14 g4?! ♕g7! {or 14...♕f4 ½-½ Krizsany-Belikov, Györ jr 1991} 15 h3 e5! 16 ♗g2 exd4 17 ♘xb5 cxb5 18 ♗xa8 b4 with excellent compensation in Dzhandzhgava-Ivanchuk, Lvov 1987) 14...♖xd4 15 ♕f3 ♕xf3 16 gxf3 ♗b7 17 ♖g1! ♘d7 (*editor's note:* 17...♔f8!? 18 ♖g4 c5 19 ♘e4 a6 20 b6 ♗xe4 21 fxe4 ♘d7 looked good for Black in Yuferov-Kula, Katowice 1992) 18 ♖g8+ ♘f8 19 bxc6 ♗xc6 20 ♖g4± Magerramov-Ivanov, USSR 1988.

b) **12 ♗e3!?** *(51)*

51
B

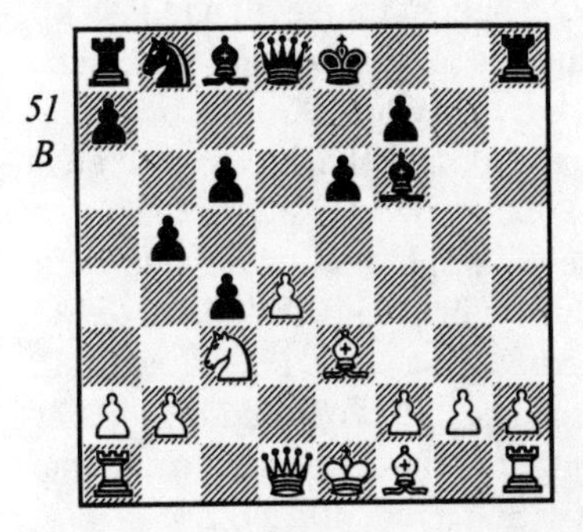

12...♗b7 (12...♘a6 13 a4 ♘c7 14 ♕f3! ♗d7 15 axb5 cxb5 16 ♗f4! seems to cause Black serious problems too. 16...♖c8 17 ♘e4 ♘d5 18 ♘d6+ ♔e7 19 ♘xc8+ ♕xc8 20 ♗e2±) 13 ♕f3! (Much stronger than 13 ♘e4? ♘a6 14 ♘xf6+ ♕xf6 15 ♕d2 0-0-0! 16 ♗g5 ♕f5 17 ♗xd8 ♖xd8 18 ♕c3 c5 19 dxc5 ♘xc5 with fantastic compensation in Vyzhmanavin-Ivanchuk, Irkutsk 1986. Also promising for White, however is 13 a4 b4 14 ♘e4 c5 15 ♘xc5 ♗d5 16 ♖c1 Nogueiras-Rogers, Dubai OL 1986) 13...♗xd4 (13...a6 14 ♘e4 and ♘c5 is strong) 14 **0-0-0** ♗xe3+ 15 fxe3 ♕e7 16 ♘e4 ♔f8 17 ♘c5! (threatening 18 ♖d8+) 17...♕xc5 (17...♗c8 is excruciatingly passive and White can build an attack on the f-file at leisure) 18 ♖d8+ ♔e7 19 ♖xh8 ♘d7 20 ♖xa8 ♗xa8 21 ♗e2 (Demirel-Fridman, Sas van Gent 1992) 21...c3 22 ♕f4 and Black has no compensation.

10 ♘f3

Naturally the alternative **10 ♘xf7** is also a critical test. White wins the exchange and a pawn, and Black's kingside is decimated. On the other hand the white knight on h8 is stranded, and Black can generate a lot of play by intensifying the pin on the c3 knight and undermining the centre with ...c5. After **10...♕xh4 11 ♘xh8 ♗b4** *(52)* (11...♘xc3? 12 bxc3 ♗g7 13 ♕c2! ♗xh8 14 ♕h7± Junge) White has two major alternatives and a rare offshoot:

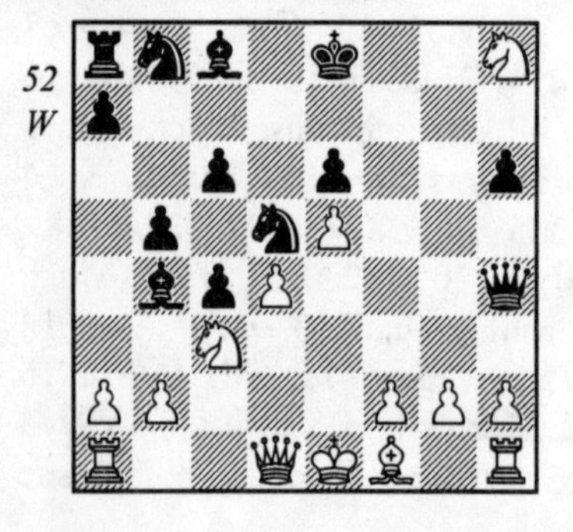

52
W

a) **12 ♕d2 c5** (12...♘d7 13 0-0-0 ♗b7 14 g3 ♗xc3! 15 gxh4! ♗xd2+ 16 ♖xd2 c5 17 ♖g1! is mentioned by Harding, but Black's compensation must be inadequate) and there is a further important parting of the ways:

a1) **13 dxc5 ♘d7** and now:

a11) **14 0-0-0** ♘xe5 transposes to 'a22' and may be the best.

a12) Also possible is **14 ♗e2** ♘xe5 15 0-0-0 (15 0-0 ♗b7 16 a3 ♗xc3 17 bxc3 ♘f4! is dangerous for White) 15...♗b7 16 g3 ♕f6 17 f4 (or 17 ♗h5+ ♔f8 18 ♘g6+ ♘xg6 19 ♕xh6+ ♕g7 20 ♕xg6 ♗xc3 21 bxc3 ♕xc3 with perpetual – Belavenets) 17...♘xc3!? (after 17...♕xh8 18 ♗h5+! ♘f7 19 ♕e2! ♔f8! 20 ♕xe6 ♕f6 21 ♗xf7! ♕xe6 22 ♗xe6 ♘xc3 23 bxc3 ♗a3+ Yudovich gives ∞ but whilst Black has good drawing chances only White can be better with 24 ♔d2) 18 ♗h5+! ♔f8 19 fxe5 ♘xa2+ 20 ♔b1 ♕f5+ 21 ♔xa2 ♗xd2 22 ♖hf1 (∞ Botterill). The position is finely balanced. Black's two bishops would be fearsome if he could consolidate, but White's forces are well placed to cause substantial short-term disruption.

a13) **14 g3?!** ♕h5 15 ♗g2 ♗b7 16 0-0 0-0-0! 17 ♕e2! (17 ♕d1 ♕xd1 18 ♖axd1 ♗xc3 19 ♘f7! ♗xb2∓) 17...♕xe2 18 ♘xe2 ♖xh8 19 ♘d4 ♘xe5 20 ♘xe6? (20 ♘xb5! ♗xc5 21 ♖ae1 a6 22 ♖xe5 axb5 23 ♖xe6= was already the best course for White) 20...♘d3!

and Black stood well in Timman-Henley, Indonesia 1983.

a2) **13 0-0-0(!) ♘c6** (13...cxd4 14 ♕xd4 ♕g5+ 15 f4! favours White after 15...♘xf4 16 ♘e4! ♘e2+ 17 ♔b1 ♘xd4 18 ♘xg5±) when White may try:

a21) **14 ♘g6!?** (seems a greater threat to Black than 'a22'):

a211) **14...♘xc3** 15 ♘xh4 ♘xa2+ 16 ♔b1 ♗xd2 17 ♖xd2 ♘ab4 18 ♘f3 Polugaevsky.

a212) **14...♗xc3** 15 bxc3 ♕g5 16 ♕xg5 hxg5 17 h4 ♔f7 18 h5 ♘xc3 19 ♖d2 cxd4 (19...♘xd4? 20 h6±) 20 g4! ♗b7 21 ♗g2 d3 22 f4 ♘e2+ 23 ♖xe2 dxe2 24 f5± Korchnoi. Black needs to find something here. This looks like the greatest problem in the entire 10 ♘xf7 complex.

a22) **14 dxc5** is considered the main line, but it appears to me that Black's resources are pretty fair: **14...♘xe5 15 f4!** (15 ♕e1 ♕g5+ 16 ♔b1 was once thought to be good too, but it now looks as if 16...♗xc3! 17 bxc3 ♗b7!? – Tatai, gives enough play) **15...♕xf4** (15...♗xc3 is also possible first, e.g. 16 bxc3 ♕xf4 17 ♕xf4 ♘xf4 18 g3 {18 c6!? Δ18...♘xc6 19 g3± looks still better since White's pieces coordinate OK without having to return material} 18...♘fd3+ 19 ♗xd3 ♘xd3+ 20 ♖xd3 cxd3 21 ♖e1±. Ironically the knight will finally emerge from h8 to be the better minor piece. Brinck-Claussen - Mikhalchishin, Copenhagen 1979) **16 ♕xf4 ♘xf4** and now:

a221) Polugaevsky's preference is **17 g3** ♘fd3+ 18 ♗xd3 ♘xd3+ (Razuvaev-Inkiov, Moscow 1986) and now 19 ♖xd3!? cxd3 20 ♘xb5 (20 ♘e4?! e5 21 g4 ♗xg4 22 ♘f6+ ♔e7 23 ♘xg4 ♖xh8 24 ♘xe5 ♖c8∞) 20...♖b8 21 ♘d6+ ♔f8 22 ♘g6+. However, I do not see what is the big problem here, since Black's two bishops still seem to give him fair counterchances.

a222) **17 ♘xb5** ♔e7! (clearly bad, and it would seem, maybe unfairly dealing a hefty blow to the reputation of the whole line, was 17...♖b8 which failed straightforwardly to 18 ♘d6+ ♔e7 19 ♘xc4± in Ribli-Nogueiras, Montpellier Ct 1985) 18 c6. Now Ribli gave only **18...♘fd3+** 19 ♗xd3 ♘xd3+ 20 ♔c2 ♘f2 21 ♖hf1 ♘xd1 22 ♘g6+ ♔d8 23 ♖xd1 when there is indeed no questioning White's advantage. After Polugaevsky's **18...♖b8!?** things are not so clear since if 19 ♘xa7 ♗a6 and the knight will suffer, and if it retreats then ...♘fd3+ gains considerably in force.

b) **12 ♖c1** and now:

b1) **12...♕e4+** is the only move discussed in most sources but seems to give White a choice of routes to advantage. **13 ♗e2 ♘f4** and now:

b11) **14 ♕d2!** ♘d3+ (14...♘xg2+ 15 ♔d1 ♘e3+ 16 ♕xe3 ♕xh1+ 17 ♔c2 ♕xh2 18 ♕f3 ♕h4 19 ♘xb5 cxb5 20 ♕xa8

♕xd4 21 ♗h5+ wins for White - Smyslov) 15 ♔f1 ♘xc1 16 ♕xc1! ♕xd4 17 ♕xh6 ♗xc3 18 bxc3 ♕xc3 19 g3! is assessed a bit modestly by Nemet as ± since White's attack is crushing, e.g. 19...♘d7 20 ♕g5! ♘xe5 21 ♗h5+ ♔d7 22 ♕g7+ ♔d6 23 ♘f7+ ♔d5 24 ♗f3+! and wins.

b12) **14 a3!?** ♘xg2+ 15 ♔f1 ♘e3+ 16 fxe3 ♕xh1+ 17 ♔f2 ♕xh2+ 18 ♔e1 ♗e7 (18...♗xc3+ 19 ♖xc3 a5 Δ...♖a7 may restrict White's plus, but it still doesn't seem in doubt) 19 ♔d2! c5? (Richmond gives 19...♗g5 20 ♕g1 ♕h4∞ but 20 ♘e4! looks strong. Overall White's position looks excellent value for a pawn. Still, the text hastens the end) 20 ♘xb5 cxd4 21 ♖xc4 ♘a6 22 ♖xd4 and White won quickly in Timman-Ljubojević, Buenos Aires 1980.

b2) **12...c5!** 13 dxc5 *(53)*

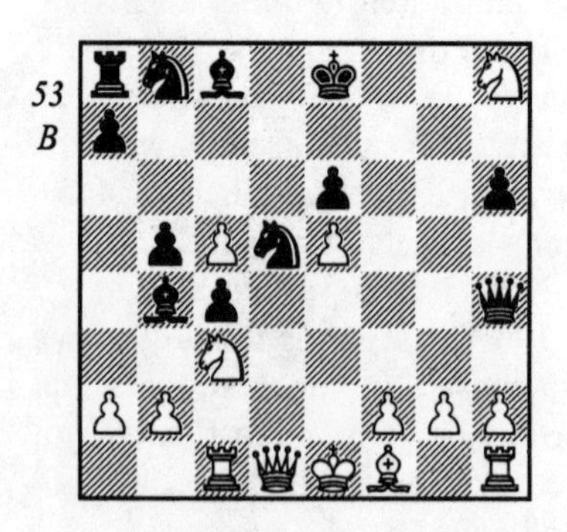

13...♕g5! (Weaker, and responsible for the neglect of this line was 13...♘d7 14 ♗e2 ♘xe5 15 0-0 ♗xc3 16 ♖xc3!! ♘xc3 17 ♗h5+ ♔f8 18 ♕d6+ ♔g8 19 ♕xe5 ♘d5 20 ♗f7+ ± Nemet-Karaklajić, Yugoslav Ch 1979) 14 ♗e2 ♗b7 15 ♗h5+! (The endgame was exceptionally interesting and probably slightly in Black's favour after 15 0-0 ♘xc3 16 ♗h5+ ♔f8 17 ♕d6+ ♔g8 18 ♕xe6+ ♔xh8 19 ♕e8+ ♕g8 20 ♕xg8 ♔xg8 21 bxc3 ♗xc5 in Timoshchenko-Kozlov, Tashkent 1982. Although materially White can be quite content, Black's bishop on c5 is a truly excellent piece, especially for blockading the white pawns) 15...♔f8 16 ♕f3+ ♔g7 17 0-0 ♔xh8 18 ♕f8+ ♕g8! (18...♔h7 19 ♗f3±) 19 ♕xh6+ 'and White has at least perpetual check' – Polugaevsky, after an analysis by Lanka. My impression however is that to attempt to play for more would be fraught with danger for White.

c) *editor's note:* **12 a3** ♘xc3 13 ♕f3 was a startling success in Stefansson-Inkiov, Gausdal 1990: 13...♕xd4 14 ♕h5+ ♔d8 15 axb4 ♕e4+ 16 ♗e2 ♘xe2 17 ♕xe2 ♕h7 18 ♕d2+ ♔c7 19 ♕d6+ ♔b7 20 ♖d1 ♕xh8 21 ♕e7+ ♗d7 22 f4 ♕e8 23 ♕g7 ♔c7 24 0-0 a5 25 f5 axb4 26 fxe6 ♕xe6 27 ♖d6 ♕e8 28 ♖xh6 c3 29 bxc3 b3 30 e6 b2 31 c4 ♖a2 32 cxb5 cxb5 33 ♕e5+ 1-0.

10 ... ♕a5
11 ♕d2

Possibly more accurate is **11 ♖c1** ♗b4 12 ♕d2. With the move order of the game, Black could consider also **11...b4!?**.

11 ... ♗b4
12 ♖c1 ♘d7
13 ♗e2 ♗b7

13...♘7b6?! is the classic example of the 'greedy' approach against which I warned in the discussion above. In this way Black neglected the kingside and was duly punished there after 14 0-0 (14 ♗f6 ♘xf6 15 exf6± is a common idea when the black knight runs to the queenside and here it is good too; Uhlmann-Tischbierek, E.Germany 1979) 14...♗xc3 (14...♘a4 15 ♗f6! ♖g8 16 ♕xh6 ♗xc3 17 ♕h7!± was Szilagyi-Perecz, Hungary 1992) 15 bxc3 ♘a4 16 ♗f6 (familiar?) 16...♖g8 17 ♕xh6 ♘axc3 18 ♖c2 ♗b7 19 ♘g5! with a strong attack in Bukić-Nikolić, Banja Luka 1981.

14 0-0 c5 *(54)*

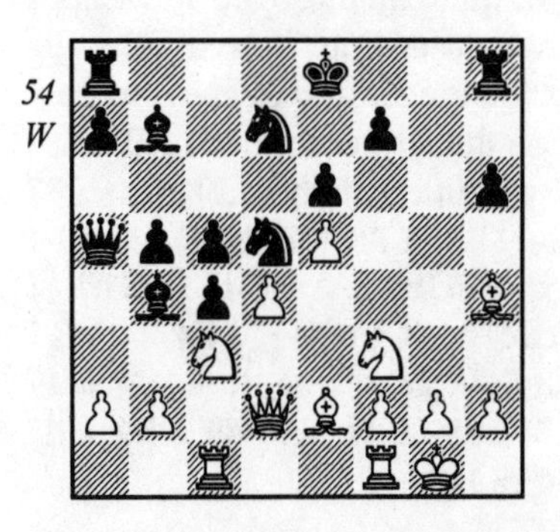

The text is without a doubt the right idea, and it seems the right moment too. Noteworthy, but not correct was Black's **14...♘f8?!** 15 ♗f6 (so not only when the knight goes to the queenside!) 15...♘xf6 16 exf6 ♕d8 17 ♘e5 ♕xf6 18 ♗f3 ♕c8 19 ♕e2 with good compensation for the pawn in Van der Heijden-Halldorsson, Corr. 1985.

15 a3!?

Again, possibly the most testing. By forcing the issue with regard to his pinned knight, White must sacrifice a pawn, but he obtains excellent play on the dark squares, a good square for the knight on d4, and the possibility of both bishops bearing down on Black's king. Black seems to have no trouble finding play against quieter tries:

a) **15 dxc5** ♘xc5 16 ♕d4 ♗xc3 17 bxc3 ♘a4 18 ♘d2?! (18 ♗f6!?) 18...♘axc3 19 ♗f3 ♕b6 20 ♕g4 ♔d7 21 ♕h5!? (21 ♕g7 is weaker, since 21...♖af8 22 a4 ♕d4∓ parried all threats in Kir.Georgiev-Nogueiras, Varna 1982) 21...♖af8 22 ♗xd5 ♘xd5 23 ♘e4∞ Uhlmann-Inkiov, Plovdiv 1986.

b) **15 ♖fd1** ♖c8 16 ♔f1 (16 ♕c2 ♗xc3 17 bxc3 ♘f4! 18 ♕d2 ♘xe2 19 ♕xe2 ♗d5! with a very comfortable position for Black in Nogueiras-Huerta, Santa Clara 1984) 16...♗xc3 17 bxc3 b4! 18 dxc5 bxc3 19 ♕d4 ♕xc5 20 ♕g4 ♕f8!? 21 ♕d4 ½-½ Gavrikov-Nogueiras, Tbilisi 1983.

15 ... ♗xc3
16 bxc3 ♕xa3
17 dxc5 ♕xc5

Perhaps **17...♘xc5** was a better try although White's attack after 18 ♘d4! ♘e4 19 ♕e1 ♘exc3 20 ♗h5 also looks well worth the material.

If 20...0-0 then 21 f4, with ideas of ♖f3, or ♗f6 etc.

18 ♘d4! ♘xe5
19 ♗h5 ♖g8!

Black guards against the threat of 20 ♘xe6 by utilizing his only asset on the kingside, the open g-file. It would now be answered with 20...♖xg2+ 21 ♔xg2 ♘f4+ 22 ♔g3 ♘xh5+ and wins. However, White's cool response also combines attack and defence.

20 ♖fe1 ♘e7
21 ♗g3 ♕d5
22 f3 ♖g5? *(55)*

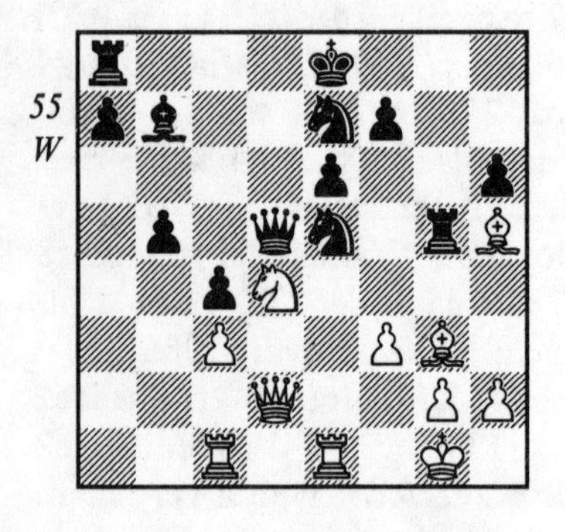

55
W

Up until here, Black has defended well, driving the bishop from h4, and forcing f3. The text is a blunder which allows White a very attractive liquidation. **22...♘5g6** closing the h5-e8 diagonal had to be tried, when White has no clear breakthrough.

23 ♕xg5!!

White now won convincingly: **23...hxg5 24 ♖xe5 ♕d7 25 ♘xe6 ♗d5 26 ♘xg5 ♔f8** (Since 26...0-0-0 fails immediately to 27 ♘xf7 ♗xf7 28 ♗g4+-) **27 ♗h4! ♘c6 28 ♘h7+ ♔g7 29 ♘f6 ♘xe5 30 ♘xd7 ♘xd7 31 ♖d1 ♗e6 32 ♗f2 ♘f6?** (Now the dust has cleared it is evident that while White's fine play netted him no material gain, the two bishops constitute a major asset in the 'race' of the three *vs* one pawn majorities. Still, the text, walking into an unpleasant pin, was a bad blunder. The natural 32...a5 would have offered much stiffer resistance) **33 ♗d4 ♔h6 34 ♗xf7 ♗xf7 35 ♗xf6 ♔g6 36 ♗d4** (The win is now quite simple, opposite bishops notwithstanding. Indeed, after the exchange of rooks they merely ease the task of rendering Black's pawns utterly impotent) **36...a5 37 ♖a1! ♗d5 38 ♔f2 b4?! 39 cxb4 axb4 40 ♖xa8 ♗xa8 41 ♗c5 b3 42 ♗d4 ♔h5 43 g4+ ♔h4 44 ♔g2 ♔g5 45 ♔g3 ♔h6 46 h4 ♗c6 47 h5 ♗d5 48 f4 ♗c6 49 ♔h4 ♗d7 50 f5 1-0.**

6 Botvinnik Anti-Meran 9 exf6!?

Instead of winning a pawn as in the main line with 9 ♘xg5, White sacrifices two, banking on his lead in development, knight outpost on e5 and the weakness of Black's f7 point to build a strong initiative. The line has been quite fashionable in the 1980s, receiving a lot of attention in particular in the former Soviet Union. The play is in general complicated. It is ironic that it is losing out in the popularity stakes to 9 ♘xg5 just at the moment when it seems its theoretical status has never been better!

Game 8
Tukmakov-M.Kuijf
Wijk aan Zee 1991

1 d4 d5 2 c4 c6 3 ♘f3 ♘f6 4 ♘c3 e6 5 ♗g5 dxc4 6 e4 b5 7 e5 h6 8 ♗h4 g5

9 exf6 gxh4
10 ♘e5 ♕xf6
11 a4 *(56)*

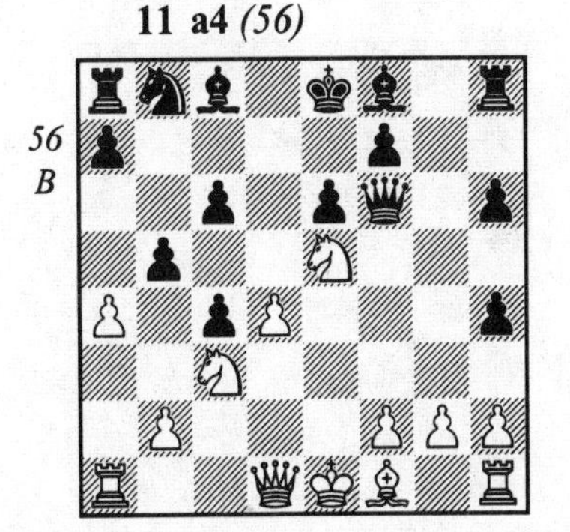

This is the move that revived 9 exf6. Early deviations will be dealt with in the next game.

11 ... ♗b7

Possibly Black's most natural reply once it is established that **12 axb5** is not a real threat in view of 12...c5!, e.g. 13 b6 cxd4 14 ♕a4+ ♔d8 15 ♕a5 ♗d6! 16 bxa7+ ♔e7±. In many positions, axb5 becomes a factor later on, but in the first instance 11 a4 should be understood in the context of White's first priority – maintaining his outpost on e5 by discouraging ...♘d7. Of Black's alternatives, 11...c5 will be the subject of Game 9.

The rest, in something like ascending order of significance:

a) **11...b4?** is simply the product of a misunderstanding of the position. Normally it is the threat of ...♗b4+ that holds back the otherwise powerful ♘e4. 12 ♘e4 ♕f4 13 ♕e2 c3 14 bxc3 bxc3 15 g3 ♕f5 16 ♕e3! Δg4±.

b) **11...♗d6** has been tried a few times lately. Play was complicated but not clearly bad for Black after 12 ♗e2!? (12 ♘e4? ♗b4+; to be considered however is 12 ♕e2 Δg3; 12 ♘g4 ♕e7 13 ♗e2 ♗b7 14 axb5 cxb5 15 ♗f3 ♘c6 16 0-0 {16 ♘xb5!? Knaak} 16...h5 17 ♘e3 a6

18 Nf5 Qc7 19 d5 exf5 20 dxc6 Bxc6 21 Re1+ Kf8 22 Qd4 Rg8 looked dangerous initially, but Black was at least holding on in Pal.Petran-Feher, Hungarian Ch 1989) 12...Bxe5 13 dxe5 Qxe5 14 axb4 (otherwise ...b4) 14...Bb7 15 0-0 Ke7! (15...cxb5 16 Bf3 Nc6 17 Re1 looks nasty) 16 Bf3 a6 17 Re1 Qd6 18 Qc2 Nd7 (It is still dangerous to clarify the queenside: 18...axb5 19 Rad1 Qc7 20 Ne4 Nd7 21 Qc3! with a fierce attack) 19 Rad1 (19 Ne4!? can make trouble too) 19...Qc7 20 Qe4 (The wrong coloured square. I would prefer the knight on e4 and the queen on the dark squares, when White's attack still looks dangerous) 20...axb5 21 Qxh4+ Kf8 22 Qd4 Ke7 and Black should be surviving; Moskalenko-Lugo, Holguin 1989. So, no clear refutation, but clearly a risky line for Black.

c) **11...Bb4?!** was for a long time the main line, but it now seems that White can avoid the worst of the complications and emerge with a clear plus: 12 Be2 c5 13 0-0! (13 Bf3 is a bit greedy – Black seems to enjoy sufficient compensation if White plays to win the exchange. I received recently a valuable reminder that it is not enough to know that a line is regarded as suspect, sometimes it is necessary also to prove it. Having forgotten 13 0-0, Wells-Lukacs, Budapest First Saturday 1993 went 13 Bf3 cxd4 14 Qxd4 Nd7 15 Bc6!? {15 Bxa8 Bc5! gives excellent compensation} 15...0-0 16 Bxd7 Bxd7 17 0-0!? {Theory gives 17 Qg4+ Kh8 18 Nxd7 Bxc3+ 19 Ke2 Qd8∞, but it looks very ropey to me. The text too is no threat to Black} 17...Rfd8 18 Qe4 Bxc3 19 Nxd7! Qd4 20 bxc3 Qxd7 21 Qh4 Kh7 22 axb5 Qxb5 23 Rxa7 Rxa7 ½-½) 13...cxd4 (also inadequate for equality was 13...Bxc3 14 bxc3 Bb7 15 Qb1! b4 16 Nxc4 Qf4 17 dxc5 Rg8 18 f3 h3 19 Rf2 in Pein-Icklicki, Brussels 1987) 14 Qxd4 Nd7 15 Qe4! (it transpires that again White will win material, this time with his king much more secure) 15...Qxe5 (15...Rb8? 16 Nxd7 Bxd7 17 Nd5! 1-0 was Novikov-Feher, Budapest 1989 and 16...Kxd7 is also hopeless after 17 Rfd1+ Kc7 18 Nxb5+ Kb6 19 Qe3+ Bc5 20 Rd6+!) 16 Qxa8 Bd6 17 f4 and Black's compensation is inadequate.

d) **11...h3!?** *(57)*

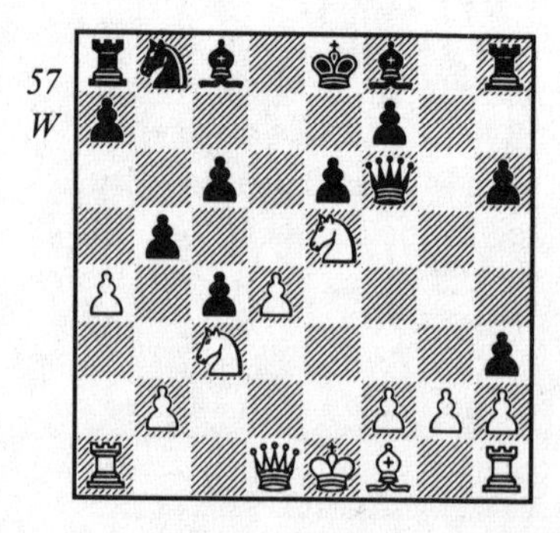

57
W

The latest try, presumably prompted by the discovery of 11...♗b7 12 ♗e2 h3 13 ♗h5! (see note below to Black's 12th). Its debut (see line 'd3') was spectacular. After **12 g3** (12 gxh3!? Khenkin) **12...c5!**:

d1) Khenkin gives **13 ♘xb5** cxd4 14 ♘c7+ ♔d8 15 ♕xd4+ ♘d7! (it may seem too banal to point out, but the possibility of ...♘d7 with the bishop still on c8 is part of the theoretical case for the approach here or in Game 9 rather than 11...♗b7) **16 ♘xa8?** ♗b4!∓. This is unsurprising, since it is analogous with 11...c5 12 ♘xb5 discussed in Game 9. Interesting is that in the event of **16 0-0-0!?** ♔xc7 17 ♕xc4+ ♘c5 18 ♕b5! compared with Ligterink-M.Kuijf, note 'b' to 12 ♘g4 in Game 9, White is deprived of ♗g2 but Black lacks the resource ...♕f4+xa4. The upshot is that after 18...♕xe5, White seems to have a draw with 19 ♕a5+ ♔b8 20 ♕b5+ ♔c7 (but not 20...♗b7 21 ♖d8+ ♔c7 22 ♕a5+ ♔c6 23 ♗b5#).

d2) On the other hand the insertion of ...h3 and g3 means that **13 ♘g4?!** can be answered by 13...♕xd4 14 ♘xb5 ♕e4+ when 15 ♘e3 is unclear.

d3) **13 ♗xh3** cxd4 14 ♘g4! ♕g7 15 ♕f3 dxc3 16 ♕xa8 (16 0-0 cxb2 17 ♖ad1 f5! 18 ♕xa8 ♕b7!∓ Khenkin) 16...cxb2 17 ♖d1 ♗b4+ 18 ♔e2 c3! 19 ♕xb8 **0-0** *(58)*

58
W

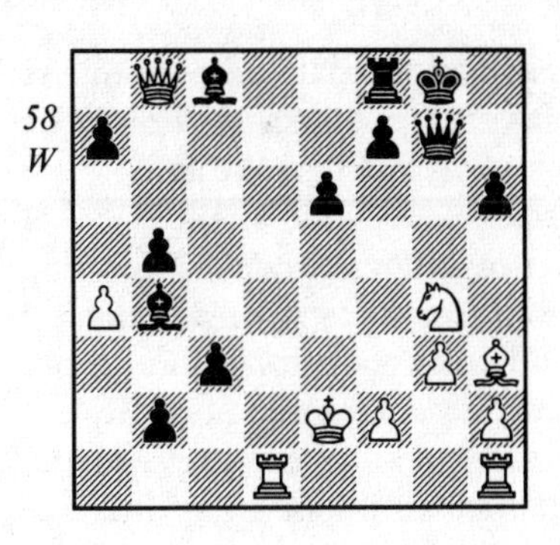

To an extent the dust has cleared, and Black's strong pawns combined with the exposed white king easily outweigh the rook deficit. 20 ♕xb5 (20 ♕c7 bxa4 and White has a new problem with which to contend!) 20...c2! 21 ♕xb4 ♗a6+ 22 ♔e3 ♖c8! 23 ♖c1! h5! (Black's lack of urgency about recouping his material is a pleasing feature of the attack) 24 ♔d2 ♕g5+ 25 ♘e3 ♕d8+ 0-1 Tukmakov-Khenkin, Iraklion 1992. Wonderful stuff – show this to anyone who thinks the Semi-Slav is dull.

Naturally though, some unanswered questions remain. Perhaps the most promising place to scrutinize is straight away, since 12 gxh3!? has the virtue of preventing 12...c5 as the g2 square is free.

12 ♗e2 c5

Initially the regular choice here, the text was for a while superseded by **12...h3** seeking to disrupt White's kingside in preparation for ...c5. When the play is so sharp it would be tempting fate to make categorical assessments, but at the time of writing Ikonnikov's 13 ♗h5 on 12...h3 looks very hard to meet. I studied in vain for a line to put 12...h3 back on the map. Still, it is safer to allow for a revival and attempt a full survey of the previously popular alternative.

a) Weak is **13 g3** ♗g7 14 0-0 0-0 15 ♗f3 b4 16 ♘e4 ♕e7 17 ♕e2 c5! (a disguised version of Black's classic break) 18 ♘xc5 ♗xf3 19 ♕xf3 ♗xe5∓ Glek-Shabalov, Philadelphia 1990 although after White's best 20 dxe5 ♕xc5 21 ♕g4+ ♔h8 22 ♕f4 playing for the win with 22...♕e7 (22...♔g7 repeats) involves a degree of risk.

b) **13 ♗f3** hxg2 14 ♖g1 (logically, mobilization should be a priority over the immediate recapture. However taking on g2 with the rook involves loss of a tempo, which respite Black uses to organize his defence. Therefore maybe 14 ♗xg2 is better. After 14...b4! 15 ♘e4 ♕f4 Shabalov suggests that either 16 ♕c1!? or simply 16 ♘xc4 give play) 14...b4 15 ♘e4 ♕f4 16 ♖xg2 ♘d7! 17 ♖g4 (17 ♘xd7 and 18 ♖c1 merited attention, but not 17 ♕c1 ♘xe5!) 17...♕xh2 18 ♖g2 ♕f4 and now repeating moves would have been wiser than 19 ♘xc4 in Moskalenko-Shabalov, Podolsk 1990.

c) **13 ♗h5(!)** *(59)*

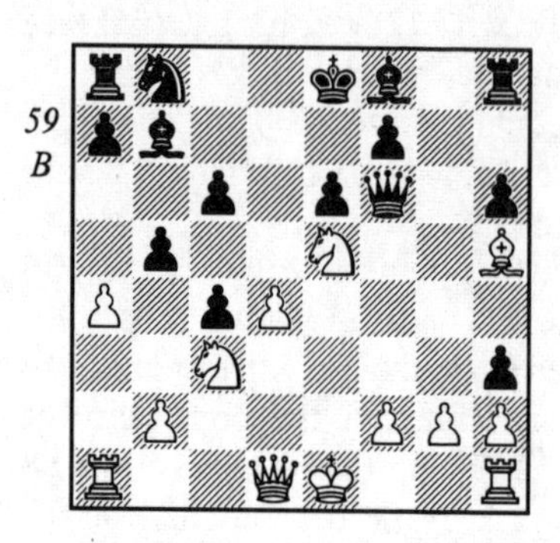
59
B

13...hxg2 14 ♖g1 ♖h7 (this looks passive, but 14...♗g7 looks far less plausible than in the similar position in the main game, because, for all its intended disruptive qualities 12...h3 simply does not threaten to undermine White in the centre in the way that 12...c5 does. After 15 ♗xf7+ ♔e7 White has time for 16 ♗h5, e.g. 16...♖d8 17 ♘e4! ♕f5 18 ♘g6+ with an awful position for Black) 15 ♗f3 a6? (but already depressing) 16 axb5 axb5 17 ♖xa8 ♗xa8 18 ♕a1± ♗b7 19 ♕a7 ♘d7 20 ♘xd7 ♕xf3 21 ♘e5 1-0 Ikonnikov-Godena, Vienna 1991.

13 ♗h5

A major alternative here is **13 ♘xb5**, when Black has a choice between preventing ♘c7+, or seeking counterplay in the centre and braving White's assault:

a) **13...cxd4** 14 ♘c7+ ♔d8 15 ♕xd4+ ♔xc7 16 ♕xc4+ ♘c6 17

♘xc6 ♗xc6 18 ♖c1 e5 19 b4! ♕g6 (neither is the 19...a5 20 b5 ♗b4+ 21 ♔f1 ♖ac8 of Piket-Van der Wiel, Leiden 1986 to be recommended since 22 ♕e4 ♔b8 23 bxc6 favours White) 20 b5 ♕xg2 21 ♕xc6+ ♕xc6 22 ♖xc6+ ♔d8 23 0-0± Lukacs. This seems most unsatisfactory for Black. He has retained his extra pawn, but it is useless, while he has difficulties persisting with both his development and even his king safety.

b) **13...♘a6** and now:

b1) **14 ♗h5?!** is no longer so appropriate. After 14...cxd4! 15 ♗xf7+ (of course not 15 ♘xf7 ♗b4+ Δ16...0-0) 15...♔e7 16 ♕xd4 Black was able to obtain counterplay by activating his rook by 16...♖d8! 17 ♕e3 ♖d5 18 f4 ♔d8! Van Gaalen-Okkes, Eindhoven 1986.

b2) The immediate **14 ♗f3** is possible too though, e.g. 14...♗xf3 15 ♕xf3 ♕xf3 when according to Meulders the simple 16 ♘xf3 is a slight advantage.

b3) **14 0-0** ♖g8 15 ♗f3 (White has secured the misplacement of the knight on a6, doubly significant since the security of the e5 knight is a linchpin of his game. He now neutralizes the pressure on the long light-square diagonal, and Black's position begins to look loose for no obvious compensation) 15...♗xf3 16 ♘xf3 (60).

60
B

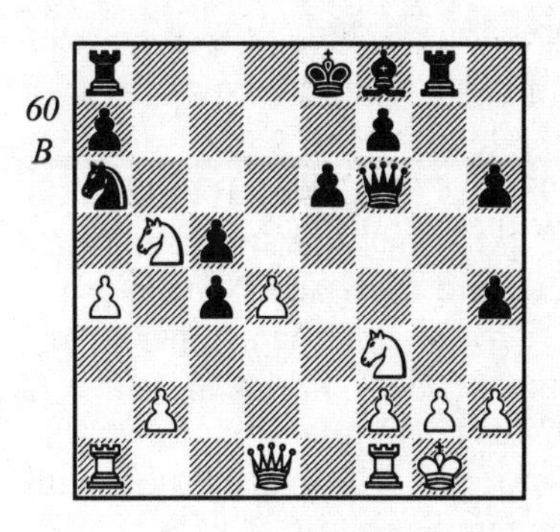

16...cxd4?! (One of the most difficult and challenging aspects of the 9 exf6 variation is the way in which a position can quickly be transformed from tactical *mêlée* into one where positional imperatives predominate. Here, as mentioned in the note above, this transformation basically favours White who has a safe haven for his king and better mobilization to bother Black's pawns. Hence Black should be trying still to create or perhaps maintain mess, and to this end Pinter's suggestion 16...h3 17 g3 ♖d8 looks more to the point, although I think it is still ±) 17 ♖c1! ♖c8 18 ♘fxd4 ♖c5 19 f4 ♘b4 20 f5 e5 21 ♕f3! ♗e7 22 ♘b3 ♖c8 23 ♘d2±. White will meet ...a6 with ♘c3, and has an excellent hold on the central light squares.

13 ... ♗g7

The alternative **13...♖h7** is passive, and White's advantage looks relatively uncomplicated after 14 axb5! (14 ♘xb5 leads to the standard 'messy' positions which is here quite unnecessary) 14...♕f4 (14...h3 15 ♗f3 ♗xf3 16 gxf3 ♕d8 17 dxc5± Piskov-S.Ivanov, USSR 1986) 15 ♘e2! ♕g5 16 ♗f3 ♗xf3 17 gxf3 (the same structure again; it is hard for Black to make counterplay, and meanwhile her development lags) 17...cxd4 (since if 17...♕f5, White can utilize the weakened Black queenside with the familiar motif 18 b6!) 18 ♕c2 and now the speculative **18...cxd4** 19 ♕xh7 ♕xe5+ 20 ♔f1 was insufficient for Black in Gaprindashvili-Arakhamia, Tskhaltubo Ct 1988, but **18...♕f5** is also ±.

14 ♗xf7+ ♔e7 *(61)*

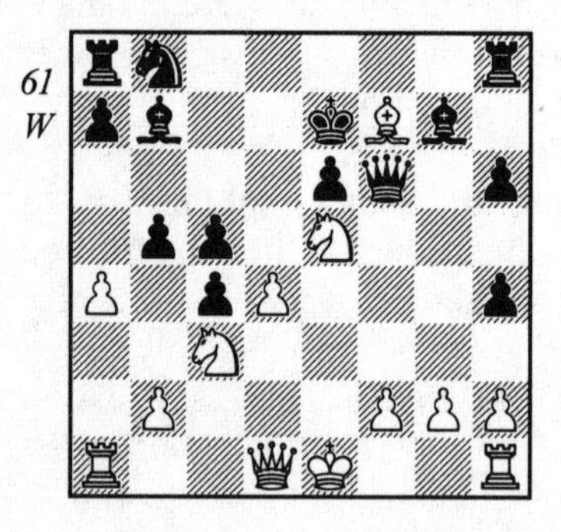

15 f4!?

Also possible is **15 ♗h5**, but the priority which the text puts upon maintaining the e5 outpost feels right in principle.

15 ... ♘c6

Tukmakov criticized the text, preferring either 15...♖d8, or the disruptive 15...♗xg2!?. The latter has the virtue of preventing 0-0, which would for example be the reply even to **15...h3?!**, and consequently gets my vote.

After **15...♗xg2!?** 16 ♖g1 h3 the threat of ...♕h4+ is also useful, and if **17 ♕g4** or **17 ♕h5** cxd4! I can find nothing concrete for White. Black's urge to get developed is laudable also, and despite the opening of the f-file, the possibility of exchanging queens ameliorates the worst effects of White's initiative.

15...♖d8 by contrast looks worse after 16 0-0 ♖xd4 17 ♕g4 with strong pressure.

16 0-0	**♘xe5**
17 fxe5	**♕g5**
18 d5!	**♕xe5**
19 ♗xe6	**♖hf8**
20 ♖e1	**♕d4+**
21 ♔h1	**♕xd1**
22 ♖axd1	**♗xc3!**

The last of a set of exchanges which were clearly mandatory for Black's defence, since not **22...b4** 23 ♗c8+ ♔d8 24 ♗xb7 ♖b8 25 ♘e4±. After the text, White can re-establish material parity, but although the black pawns paint a less aesthetic picture, he is attacking White's pawns which in turn curtails the activity of Tukmakov's pieces.

23 bxc3	**♔d6**
24 axb5	**♖ae8**
25 ♔g1	**h3!**

Thus a weak pawn is liquidated, since 26 g3?! or 26 gxh3?! allow the black rook to become active via f3.

At this point we could draw a veil, with the conclusion that Black has succeeded in fully justifying his opening play. Play continued: **26 ♗xh3 ♖xe1+ 27 ♖xe1 ♗xd5 28 ♖a1 ♖b8 29 ♖a5 ♖b7** (Black could also consider the immediate 29...♔e5 since 29 ♖a5 was a recognition that White {rightly} does not intend to exchange b-pawn for a-pawn) **30 ♔f2 h5 31 ♔e3 ♔e5 32 ♔d2 ♖g7 33 g3 ♖f7 34 ♔e2 ♗f3+ 35 ♔e3 ♗e4 36 ♖a3 ♗d5 37 ♔e2 ♗f3+ 38 ♔e1 ♗d5?!** (An inaccuracy which prolongs the struggle. White has been manoeuvring for 39 ♗f1 which both ties Black down to d5 and can prepare ♗e2 to hit h5. 38...♖b7 again was more watertight. After Black's premature 39...h4?! White gets a fleeting opportunity, but later there is little left to squeeze, and it is far from our focus of interest) **39 ♗f1! h4?! 40 gxh4 ♖h7 41 h3 ♗e6 42 ♖a6?!** (This was the key moment, and a rather curious mutual oversight. Simply 42 h5 threatens ♗e2, and after 42...♖xh5 43 ♖xa7 ♗xh3 44 ♗xc4 White has good winning chances. The rest is for the record only) **42...♖xh4 43 ♖xa7 ♗xh3 44 ♗e2 ♗g2 45 ♖g7 ♗d5 46 ♔d2 ♖h8 47 b6 ♖b8 48 ♖g5+ ♔d6 49 ♖g6+ ♔e5 50 ♗g4 ♗e4 51 ♖e6+ ♔f4 52 ♗e2 ♗d5 53 ♖h6 ♔e5 54 ♗g4 ♖g8 55 ♗h3 ♖f8 56 ♔e2 ♖g8 57 ♖h7 ♖b8 58 ♖h5+ ♔d6 59 ♖h6+ ♔e5 60 ♔e3 ♖f8 61 ♗g4 ♖f1 62 ♖h5+ ♔d6 63 ♖h6+ ♔e5 64 b7 ♖b1 ½-½.**

Game 9
Moskalenko-Kaidanov
Lvov 1988

1 d4 d5 2 c4 e6 3 ♘c3 c6 4 ♘f3 ♘f6 5 ♗g5 dxc4 6 e4 b5 7 e5 h6 8 ♗h4 g5 9 exf6 gxh4 10 ♘e5

10 ... ♕xf6

This obvious capture is invariably played, and Black's choice of alternatives is limited by the need to cover the threat of ♘xf7!. **10...c5?** for example left Black with no real compensation after 11 ♘xf7 ♕xf6 12 ♘xh8 cxd4 13 ♕h5+ ♔d7 14 0-0-0 in Ikonnikov-Alekseev, Vienna 1991.

However, **10...♖g8!?** needs to be considered.

a) The game Ikonnikov-Stojanovski, Plovdiv 1990 raised some interesting questions after **11 ♗e2(?!)** ♘d7! 12 ♗f3 (12 ♘xc6 ♕b6 13 ♗f3 ♗b7 14 d5 ♗xc6 15 dxc6 ♘xf6 {∞ Ikonnikov} 16 a4!?) 12...♗b7 (12...♘xe5 is probably a safer try provided that Black follows 13 dxe5 by attacking e5 with 13...♕c7! rather than 13...♕xd1 when 14 ♖xd1 ♗b7 15 ♘xb5 is ±) 13 ♗xc6 ♗xc6 14 ♘xc6 ♕c7 15 d5 ♘c5! with counterplay.

b) **11 g3(!)** is suggested by Rini Kuijf and it seems very logical. The only disadvantage over ♗e2 and ♗f3 is that the bishop will be momentarily undefended on g2. The advantages of g-file security in a host of variations must outweigh this. Also the line 11...♘d7 12 ♗g2 ♘xe5 13 dxe5 ♕c7 14 ♕e2 seems much more attractive than its counterpart with the bishop on f3.

11 a4!?

Again in modern practice the text is by far the most popular. However, older moves put in an occasional appearance:

a) **11 ♗e2** was the precursor to new main line. The lack of pressure on b5 means that Black should use the moment to challenge e5 with 11...♘d7! 12 ♘xc6 (12 0-0 ♘xe5 13 dxe5 ♕xe5! is not a very dangerous pawn sacrifice since 14 ♗f3 ♗b7 15 ♖e1 ♕d6 16 ♘xb5 ♕xd1 17 ♖exd1 cxb5! 18 ♗xb7 ♖b8 is ∓; Ree-Hamann, Netanya 1968) 12...♗b7 13 ♗f3 a6 14 0-0 ♗g7 (In view of the threat of 15 ♘d5, Black's choices are rather limited here. 14...♖c8!? 15 ♘d5 ♕g5 also gave White nothing immediate however in Ortega-Lugo, Santiago 1986) 15 a4! (15 d5 ♗xc6 16 dxc6 ♘e5 17 ♗e4 0-0 is good for Black who can slowly round up c6. White must play to weaken Black's queenside – the whole thinking behind the modern 11 a4 system!) 15...b4 16 ♘e4 ♕f4 17 ♕c1 ♕c7! 18 ♕xc4 ♗xc6 19 ♖ac1 0-0 20 ♕xc6 ♕xc6 21 ♖xc6 ♖a7! with equality; Barlov-Karaklajić, Yugoslavia 1987.

b) **11 g3** was the old main line, to which Jeroen Piket briefly turned the late-1980s spotlight by essaying it against Murshed and obtaining a plus. On closer examination it seems that its main interest will remain historical. **11...♘d7** and now:

b1) **12 f4** supporting e5 with the f-pawn, with a view to opening the f-file has now gone completely from fashion. F.Portisch-Ribli, Warsaw Z 1979 showed the way for Black: 12...♗b7 (12...hxg3 13 ♕f3!) 13 ♗g2 ♘xe5 14 fxe5 ♕e7 15 0-0 0-0-0 16 ♕h5 ♖xd4! 17 ♖xf7 ♕g5 18 ♕xg5 hxg5 19 ♘e4 h3! 20 ♗h1 ♖d5 21 ♖af1 ♗b4 22 a3 ♗a5 (an excellent manoeuvre to cover d6 from a safe square. If 23 ♘d6+ ♖xd6 24 exd6 ♗b6+ ∓) 23 ♗f3 ♗c7∓ since e5 is so weak.

b2) **12 ♕e2** with a further division:

b21) **12...c5(?!)**. So played Murshed, and theory does not condemn the move. White has a number of tries:

b211) **13 ♘xb5(?!)** ♗b7 (13...cxd4 14 ♘c6!±) 14 ♘xd7 ♔xd7 15 0-0-0 ♗xh1 16 dxc5+ ♗d5 and now both **17 ♘c3** and **17 ♗g2** merit consideration according to Piket, but the whole idea is a bit speculative.

b212) What however, of **13 ♘c6(!)** ? This is mentioned by Piket but without analysis, and earlier Whiteley/Harding gave 13 ♘c6! '±', but others have ignored it. I can find no refutation, and the threat of ♘d5 is not easy to meet. **13...♘b6** is legal, but 14 dxc5 Δ14...♗xc5 15 ♘e4 looks promising. Perhaps **13...♗b7!?** 14 ♘d5 ♗xc6 15 ♘xf6+ ♘xf6 16 ♖g1 cxd4 is worth investigating, but I would be surprised if the play quite merited the investment.

b213) **13 ♕e4** was hailed as an important discovery after Piket-Murshed, Palma GMA 1989, but as we have seen, White has other moves of interest here. 13...♖b8 14 ♘c6 ♗b7?! (best is 14...♖b7, when White can try 15 0-0-0 b4 16 ♘d5 ♕g6 17 ♕xg6 fxg6 18 ♗h3! with initiative, since if 18...exd5 then 19 ♖he1+ ♔f7 20 ♘d8+ ±) 15 ♘d5! ♕d8 16 ♘xd8 ♗xd5 17 ♕f4 ♖xd8 18 ♖g1 and White should be somewhat better.

b22) **12...♗b7** 13 ♗g2 ♘xe5! saves all this trouble. 14 dxe5 ♕e7 15 0-0-0 ♗g7 16 f4 0-0 17 ♖d6 (17 ♘e4 allows 17...h3 18 ♗xh3 c5∓ Martin-G.Flear, Hastings 1985/6) 17...♖ad8 18 ♖hd1 (overall here White clearly has a bind but at best it is just enough to compensate for the two pawn deficit) 18...♖xd6 19 exd6 ♕d8 20 ♘e4 ♕a5 21 ♔b1 h3! 22 ♗xh3 c5 23 ♘xc5 ♗d5 with a tremendously powerful bishop pair – Botvinnik.

11 ... c5!? *(62)*

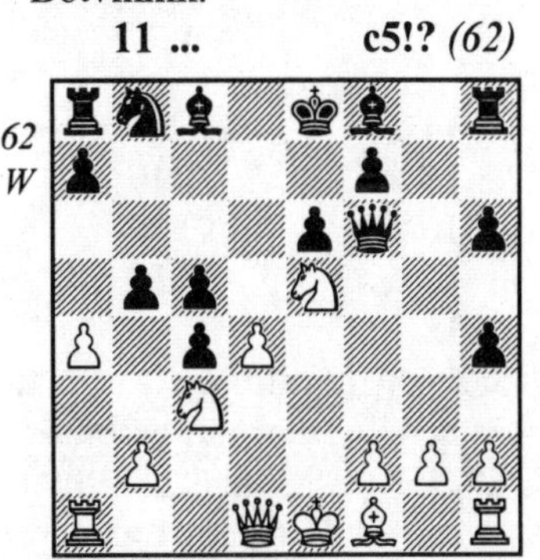

This fascinating move, answering the attempt to undermine Black's queenside pawns by seeking to counter-undermine White's centre is one of Black's most critical tries. In comparison with 11...♗b7 12 ♗e2 c5, all ideas with ♗h5 are cut out, and in the event of 12 ♘xb5 Black has the benefit of the bishop on c8 defending the knight on d7 (see also the discussion of 11...h3!?). Currently White's best seems to be the game continuation, and the note to Black's 13th is very significant for the entire 9 exf6 theory.

12 ♘g4!

Black's play is holding up well after other moves:

a) **12 ♗e2** cxd4! (12...♗b7 transposes to Game 8) 13 ♕xd4 ♘d7 14 ♕e4 ♖b8 15 ♘c6 ♘c5 16 ♘d5 (enterprising play by White, but unfortunately Black's only move is very strong) 16...♕xf2+! 17 ♔xf2 ♘xe4+ 18 ♔f1 exd5 19 ♘xb8 b4! 20 ♘c6 ♗c5 21 ♖d1 ♗d7! with terrific play for the exchange in Conquest-Novikov, Tbilisi 1988.

b) **12 ♘xb5** cxd4 13 ♘c7+ (13 ♕xd4 ♘d7! 14 0-0-0?! ♕xe5 15 ♕xe5 ♘xe5 16 ♘c7+ ♔e7 17 ♘xa8 ♗b7 18 ♘c7 h3! with excellent play for the exchange) 13...♔d8 14 ♕xd4+ ♘d7 15 0-0-0 ♔xc7 16 ♕xc4+ ♘c5 17 ♕b5!? (17 ♘d3? ♗a6!∓) 17...♕f4+! 18 ♖d2 ♕xa4 19 ♕xa4 ♘xa4 20 ♖c2+ ♘c5! 21 b4 ♖g8 22 bxc5 ♖g5∓ Ligterink-Kuijf, Dutch Ch 1988. Black has an extra pawn, but more importantly here, two bishops on an open board. Compare with the discussion of 11...h3 in Game 8.

12 ... ♕e7

Not **12...♕xd4** 13 ♘xb5 ♕xd1+ 14 ♖xd1 and Black's pawns will drop for no recompense.

13 dxc5

13 ♗e2 ♗g7 14 dxc5 (14 ♗f3 cxd4! 15 ♘b5! a6! 16 ♗xa8 (16 ♘xd4 ♖a7 Δ...♖d7∓) 16...axb5 17 f4! (Black threatens ...h5, and White's knight is needed to return to e5 to threaten the d- and c-pawns) 17...b4!∞ Dzhandzhgava/Bokuchava, but also 17...♕b4+!? looks interesting since 18 ♕d2 c3∓, or 18 ♔f1 **0-0** and White will have trouble untangling his kingside) 14...b4 15 ♘b5 0-0 16 0-0 (16 ♗f3!?) Epishin-Dzhandzhgava, Vilnius 1988, and now 16...a6 17 ♘d6 ♘d7∓ since the bishop on g7 is still the best minor piece.

13 ... ♗g7?!

Generally criticized, but the only move to have been tested in practice. The alternative, which may be critical, is **13...♗b7** when Kaidanov gives 14 ♕d4 e5 15 ♕xe5 ♕xe5 16 ♘xe5 ♗xc5∞ *(63)*.

63
W

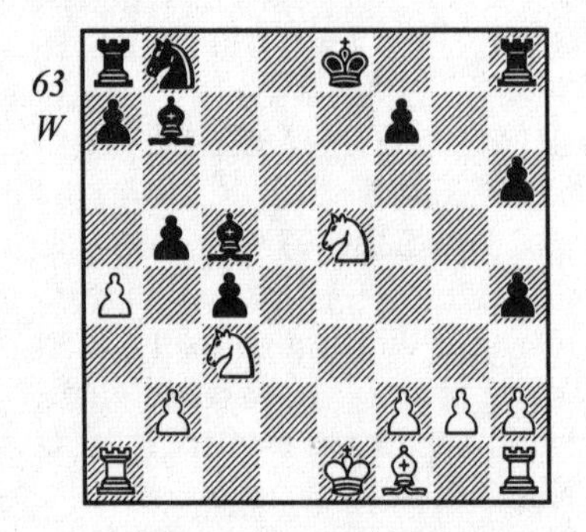

For example: 17 ♘xb5 (17 axb5!?) 17...♗b4+ 18 ♘c3 (18 ♔d1 ♘a6 19 ♗xc4 **0-0-0**+ is risky) 18...♘c6!? (18...**0-0** 19 ♗xc4±) **19 ♘xc6!?** ♗xc6 20 **0-0-0** ♗xc3 (20...h3?! 21 ♘d5!) 21 bxc3 h3 (21...♗xa4?! 22 ♖d4±) 22 ♖g1 ♗xa4 23 ♖d4 with approximate equality. The alternative **19 ♘xc4** by contrast could be asking for trouble since 19...**0-0-0** Δ...♘d4 gives Black a dangerous initiative.

14 axb5

Kaidanov suggested **14 ♕d6±** in his notes, but in his later encounter compatriot Moskalenko stayed loyal to his earlier choice, deviating as late as move 18. His scepticism towards the view that 14 ♕d6 leads to an uncomplicated plus seems justified. 14...♕xd6 15 cxd6 b4 16 ♘b5 ♗xb2 seems to give Black fair counterplay since 17 ♖b1 or 17 ♖d1 c3 affords him the tempo he needs to deal with the threat of ♘c7+.

14 ...	**♘d7**
15 ♕f3	**♖b8**
16 c6	**♘b6**
17 ♗e2	**♘d5!?**
18 0-0	

Kaidanov questioned the text, recommending the more ambitious **18 ♗xc4!?**. In Moskalenko-Summerscale, Andorra 1991 this received a test, and the initial evidence is promising, viz. 18...♘xc3 19 bxc3 **h5** *(64)*

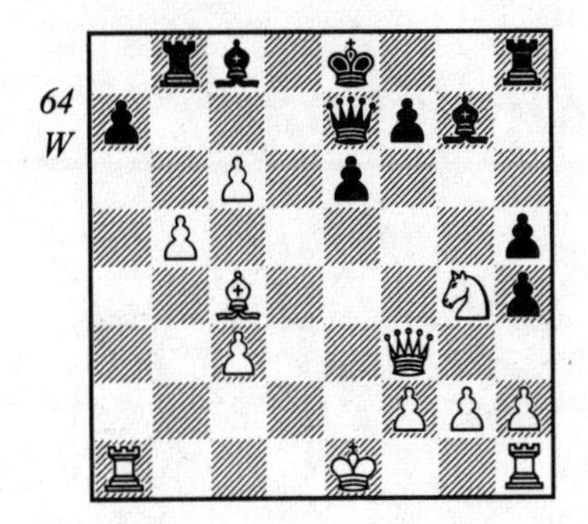

64
W

20 ♘e3 ♗xc3+ 21 ♔e2 ♗xa1 22 ♖xa1 ♕c5 23 ♕f6 0-0 24 f4 (White can try 24 g3!? with the point that 24...h3 is met by 25 g4! h4! and now not 26 g5? ♖xb5! 27 g6 ♕g5, but 26 ♖b1!? Δg5) 24...♖xb5 25 ♗xb5 ♕xb5+ 26 ♔f2 ♗a6 27 ♖a2 and White's chances on the kingside are quite serious. Interesting too is Kaidanov's original idea **19...f5** 20 ♕e3 (after 20 ♘e3 ♗xc3+ 21 ♔e2 ♗xa1 22 ♕h5+ ♔f8 23 ♖xa1 ♖h7 Black has reasonable defensive chances along the second rank) 20...fxg4 21 ♖xa7 ♕f6 22 0-0 and the combination of kingside threats and strong queenside pawns gives White quite good chances.

18 ...	**♘xc3**
19 bxc3	**♖xb5**
20 ♗xc4	**♖c5**
21 ♗a6	**0-0**

Also **21...♖xc3** 22 ♕e2 0-0 23 ♖ac1 is just equal.

22 ♗b7	**f5**
23 ♘e3	**f4**
24 ♘c2	**♖xc3**
25 ♕e4	**f3!?**
26 gxf3??	

A truly horrible way to go down. White could at just this moment secure the draw with a few tactics of his own, **26 ♗xc8** ♖xc8 27 ♖xa7! ♕g5 28 ♕xe6+ ♔h7 29 ♖xg7+! ♔xg7 30 ♕d7+ and Black must permit a perpetual.

26 ...	**♖xc2!**
27 ♕xc2	**♗xa1**

0-1

Since 28 ♖xa1 ♕g7+ decides.

7 7 a4 and Early Deviations

Game 10
Van Wely-Kramnik
Manila OL 1992

1 d4	**d5**
2 ♘f3	**c6**
3 c4	**♘f6**
4 ♘c3	**e6**
5 ♗g5	**dxc4**
6 e4	

The immediate **6 a4**, a strategy of preventing rather than attacking b5, is also playable, though not regarded as especially dangerous: **6...♗b4! 7 e4** (7 a5!? is an outrageous idea of Gutman's to take the a5 square from White's queen. He was successful in Gutman-Barbero, Frankfurt 1990, but it is very hard to believe: 7...♗xa5 8 e4 h6 {8...b5!? 9 e5 h6} 9 ♗xf6 gxf6 10 ♗xc4 b5 11 ♗b3 ♗b7 12 0-0 ♘d7 13 ♘h4 with fair play for a pawn) and now **7...b5** is note 'c' to 7...♗b7 below, while Black has a couple of alternatives:

a) **7...♗xc3+ 8 bxc3 ♕a5 9 e5 ♘e4** and now:

a1) **10 ♖c1** ♕d5 11 ♗e3 c5 12 ♗e2 ♘c6 13 0-0 0-0 14 ♕c2 cxd4 15 cxd4 c3 16 ♗d3 ♘b4 17 ♗xe4 ♘xc2 18 ♗xd5 ♘xe3 19 fxe3 exd5 20 ♖c7 ♗xa4 21 ♖xb7 with at best an edge for White in the endgame in Petursson-Kuijf, Wijk aan Zee 1990 but Black held.

a2) Perhaps more interesting is **10 ♗d2!?** ♕d5 (10...♘xd2 11 ♕xd2 b5 12 ♘g5!?; after 10...c5 11 ♗xc4 cxd4 12 cxd4 ♘xd2 13 ♘xd2 ♘c6 14 ♗b5 0-0 15 ♗xc6 bxc6 16 0-0 ♕d5 17 ♕c2 ♗a6 18 ♖fd1, as played in Lputian-Kaidanov, Lucerne Wch teams 1993, John Donaldson suggests 18...♕xd4=) 11 a5! (The text, threatening 12 ♕a4+ as an answer to ...c5, superseded 11 ♗e2?! c5 12 0-0 ♘c6 13 a5 0-0 14 ♖a4 cxd4 15 ♗xc4 ♕d7! 16 ♗b5 dxc3 17 ♖xe4 cxd2 18 ♕b1?! ♕e7 19 a6 h6 20 ♘xd2 ♖d8 21 ♕b2 ♘b8!! and Black will develop, simultaneously killing off White's initiative; Cebalo-Pinter, Yugoslavia 1987) 11...♘d7 12 ♗e2 b5 13 axb6 ♘xb6 14 0-0 h6 15 ♕c2 ♗b7 (15...♘xd2!?) 16 ♗e3 0-0 (Kiselev-Yakovich, USSR 1991) and now 17 ♖fd1 would have given White a significant pull.

b) **7...c5!?**:

b1) **8 e5?!** cxd4 9 exf6 gxf6 10 ♗h4 ♘c6 11 ♘xd4 ♘xd4 12 ♗xc4 ♔e7 13 ♕d2! was just about tenable for White in Lin Weiguo-Kaidanov, Lucerne Wch teams 1993.

b2) **8 ♗xc4** cxd4 9 ♘xd4 h6 10 ♗b5+ (10 ♗e3!? has historical interest since it was played in the last game of the Bronstein-Botvinnik match of 1951 for the World Championship. White needed to win, and came up with this remarkable offer. After 10...♘xe4 11 0-0 ♘f6?!, 12 ♘db5 would have given White dangerous play. Better is 11...♗xc3 12 bxc3 0-0 13 ♕c2 with some compensation for the pawn; Zaid-Ivanchuk, USSR 1985) 10...♘bd7! 11 ♗xf6 ♕xf6 12 ♘e2 a6 (Black is very comfortable) 13 ♗xd7 ♗xd7 14 0-0 ♗c6 15 ♕b3 ♗d6 16 ♖ad1 ♖d8 17 ♔h1 (17 ♘d4 ♗xh2+ ∓) 17...0-0 18 f4 ♗c5 19 ♕c4 ♕e7 20 h3 ♖c8 and the two bishops gave Black the advantage in Kiselev-Dreev, Helsinki 1992.

Perhaps a little under-rated and certainly not yet too theoretical is **6 e3** b5 7 a4 ♗b4 (7...a6!? 8 axb5 cxb5 9 ♘xb5 axb5 10 ♖xd8 ♗b4+ 11 ♘d2 ♗b7 is probably sufficient compensation for the exchange, e.g. 12 ♗xf6! gxf6 13 ♖a1 e5! 14 ♕h5 ♘c6 15 ♖d1 Koerholz-Karsa, Luxembourg 1986, and now 15...exd4! 16 ♕xb5 dxe3 17 fxe3 ♕e7∞ Karsa) 8 ♘d2! ♗b7!? (Taimanov's suggestion, hardly discussed in the literature, looks sensible) 9 ♕f3 (or 9 axb5 ♗xc3 10 bxc3 cxb5 11 ♕b1 ♕b6 12 ♗xf6 gxf6 13 ♘e4 ♘d7 and White has adequate compensation but no more; Blees-Lukacs, Budapest 1990) 9...h6!?∞.

6 ...	**b5**
7 a4	**♗b7**

The text move is the safest choice, but Black has three alternatives, the latter two of which are frequently seen in practice, and have the advantage of obliging White to play sharply. Line 'c' will receive relatively light coverage since it is in my opinion dubious against best play, and because it arises relatively rarely from the Semi-Slav move order:

a) **7...b4?!** 8 ♘b1 and now: **8...♗a6** 9 ♕c1 c3!? (otherwise White has a large positional plus after ♗xc4) 10 bxc3 ♗xf1 11 ♔xf1 h6 12 ♗xf6 ♕xf6 13 ♘bd2 bxc3 14 ♕xc3 with some advantage, although after 14...a5! Black was at least able to put his bishop on a good square on b4, so ±; Lerner-Chernin, USSR Ch 1984.

b) **7...♕b6!?** *(65)*.

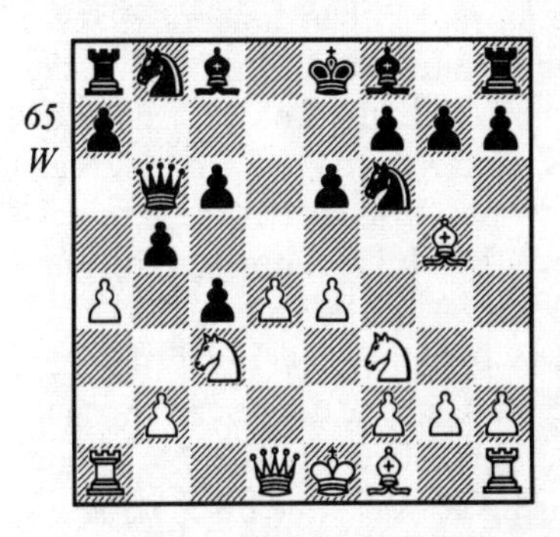
65
W

This move makes a real gambit of White's opening. White's only justification is to capture on f6, creating weaknesses and then to seek to open the position in the centre with d5, and to further pressure the queenside phalanx with b3. The order in which this can be done, however is quite subtle, and the assessment is not yet so clear. **8 ♗xf6 gxf6 9 ♗e2 a6** (it may be possible for Black to develop more naturally too, omitting ...a6. Eingorn-Dolmatov, USSR 1985 continued 9...♗b7 10 0-0 ♘d7 11 d5?! cxd5 12 exd5 b4 13 a5 ♕a6 14 dxe6 fxe6 15 ♘a4 ♖g8 16 ♕c2 0-0-0! with active play for Black. Dolmatov suggests rather 11 axb5 cxb5 12 b3! which seems the most logical attempt to exploit the omission of ...a6) **10 0-0** and now:

b1) **10...♗b7** performs OK against the immediate attempt to open the centre with **11 d5**, for example 11...♗c5!? 12 dxe6 fxe6 13 ♘h4 (13 e5 ♘d7 14 exf6 0-0-0∞ Lputian-Ribli, Sarajevo 1985) 13...♘d7 14 ♗g4 (14 ♗h5+ ♔e7 helps rather than hinders Black's mobilization) 14...♘d7 15 ♗xe6 ♔b8! 16 ♗xd7 ♗c8 17 ♘d5 exd5 18 ♗xc8 dxe4∞ Farago-Flear, Hastings 1984/5, but the immediate **11 b3!** seems stronger: 11...cxb3 12 ♕xb3 ♘d7 13 d5 cxd5 14 exd5 bxa4! (as if 14...♘c5 15 ♕b4 and the queen can swing to the kingside while Black's knight has no constructive discovered attack; Lerner-Kaidanov, Moscow 1985) 15 ♕xa4 ♕b4 16 ♖fb1 and White's pressure will persist after the exchange of queens.

b2) **10...♖a7** 11 b3! b4 12 a5 ♕d8 13 ♘a4 c3 14 ♘b6 ♘d7 15 ♘xc8 (although White's knight has toured in order only to exchange itself, the loss of the light-squared bishop is problematic for the defence) 15...♕xc8 16 d5± Lukacs-Hölzl, Budapest 1987.

c) **7...♗b4 8 e5 h6 9 exf6!** (9 ♗h4 g5 10 exf6 gxh4 11 ♘e5 c5! Ubilava-Shirov, Daugavpils 1989, gives Black much more scope for counterplay) **9...hxg5 10 fxg7 ♖g8 11 h4!** (11 g4!?; 11 g3 g4! 12 ♘h4 ♗b7 13 ♗g2 ♖xg7 is interesting, but I feel the strength of the text should render it academic):

c1) **11...♘d7** 12 hxg5 ♗b7 13 ♖h8 ♔e7 14 ♖xg8 ♕xg8 15 ♕d2± Moskalenko-Moroz, USSR 1986.

c2) **11...gxh4** 12 ♖xh4 ♘d7 13 ♖h8 ♔e7 14 ♕d2 ♖xh8 15 gxh8♕ ♕xh8 16 axb5 cxb5 17 ♘d5+ exd5 18 ♕xb4+ ± Ehlvest-Andrianov, Tallinn 1981. In both these cases, the opening of the h-file has a seriously disrupting effect on Black's game.

c3) **11...g4** 12 ♘e5 ♖xg7 13 h5! (13 ♗e2 ♗b7?! {13...f5 14 h5} 14 ♗xg4 ♘d7 15 ♗f3 ♘xe5 16 dxe5 ♕c7 17 ♔f1 ♗xc3 18 bxc3 a6 19 ♕d4± Bang-Jacobsen, Lyngby 1989) 13...f5 14 ♗e2 and now Oll & Yudasin give 14...♕g5! 15 ♕d2 with advantage to White.

8 e5?!

The marking may seem a little harsh, but the evidence is rather inescapable. This attempt to reach the main line from Game 8, namely the position after 9 exf6 gxh4 10 ♘e5 ♕xf6 11 a4 ♗b7, cutting out for example 11...c5 and 11...h3, is understandable, but allows Black a far more important possibility than those it avoids. Deviations for White along the way may be playable, but no more. The better move, and the only way to test 7...♗b7, is with 8 axb5!. White has the advantage that, although objectively equal, this quiet position may not appeal to Black players of the Botvinnik. After **8 axb5 cxb5 9 ♘xb5** (9 e5 h6 10 ♗d2?! ♘e4 11 ♘xb5 ♘xd2 12 ♕xd2 ♗xf3 13 gxf3 ♘c6 14 ♖d1 ♕b6 15 ♗xc4 ♗b4 16 ♘c3 0-0-0∓ was Scherbakov-Novikov, Blagoveshensk 1988) **9...♗xe4 10 ♗xc4** (10 ♗xf6 gxf6 11 ♗xc4 is worth consideration) practice has seen:

a) **10...♗e7** 11 ♘c3 ♗b7 12 ♗b5+ ♘fd7 13 ♗e3 0-0 14 0-0 a6 15 ♗e2 ♘c6 16 d5 exd5 17 ♘xd5 ♗c5 18 ♗g5 ♘e7 19 ♗c4 ♘b6 20 ♘xb6 ♕xb6 21 ♘e5 ♘g6 22 ♘xg6 hxg6= Gostiša-Vera, Portorož 1987.

b) **10...♗b4+** 11 ♘c3 ♘bd7 12 0-0 ♗xc3 13 bxc3 0-0 14 ♗d3 ♕c7 15 c4 ♖fe8 16 ♗xf6 ♘xf6 17 ♗xe4 ♘xe4 18 ♕d3 ♘f6 19 ♖a4 ♖ed8± (at the very most) Ribli-Inkiov, Dubai OL 1986.

8 ...	**h6**
9 ♗h4	

9 ♗xf6 should not be dangerous since the structural disruption is mild, and Black's pieces, especially the two bishops, are very active: 9...gxf6 10 axb5 cxb5 11 ♘xb5 ♕b6 12 ♕a4 (12 ♗xc4 a6 13 ♘c3 ♕xb2 14 ♖c1 ♗xf3! 15 gxf3 ♗b4 16 ♕d2 ♕xd2+ 17 ♔xd2 ♘c6∓ Lukacs, is if anything a rather modest assessment) 12...♘c6! 13 ♗xc4 (13 ♕xc4 ♗b4+ 14 ♘c3 0-0-0 looks better, with balanced chances) 13...a6 14 ♘a3 ♖g8! 15 0-0 0-0-0 with excellent counterplay for Black in D.Ilić-Lukacs, Vrnjacka Banja 1987.

9 ...	**g5**
10 exf6	**gxh4**
11 ♘e5	

Perhaps White's best option after 8 e5 is here the seemingly modest but in fact quite complex **11 ♗e2!?**. Matters were quite unclear in Dokhoian-Kuijf, Wijk aan Zee 1989, with 11...c5!? 12 dxc5 (12 axb5 ♘d7∞) 12...♘d7 13 c6! ♗xc6 14 ♘d4 ♗xg2 15 ♖g1 (15 ♘xe6 ♕b6 – Dokhoian) and now instead of **15...♗h3**, which defends e6 but leaves the bishop looking rather off-side, Dokhoian suggests **15...h3!?** 16 ♘xe6 ♕xf6!? (16...♕b6 17 ♘g7+ is also very unclear) 17 ♘c7+ ♔d8 with wild chances for both sides.

Also possible again here is **11 axb5**, but after 11...cxb5 12 ♘xb5 ♗b4+ 13 ♘c3 and now instead of **13...♕xf6+?!** after which 14 ♕a4+! causes a certain interruption in the flow of Black's game (Kir. Georgiev-Nogueiras, Sarajevo 1985), Black should play **13...0-0** since ...♕xf6 cannot be stopped, and Black's pieces, notably the bishop on b7, are more promisingly placed.

11 ...	**♘d7!** *(66)*

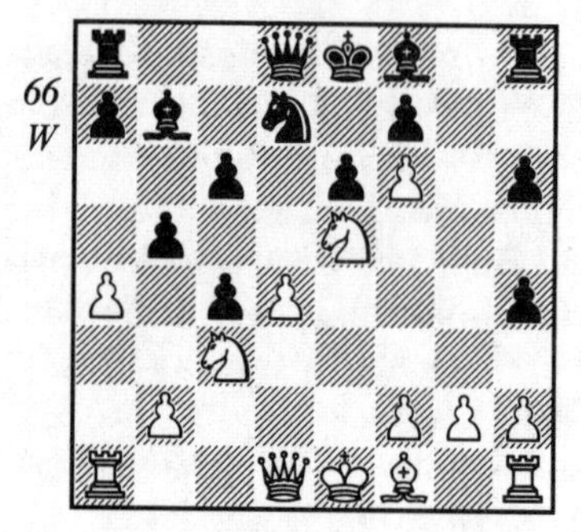

The point! With the move ...♗b7 already played, the black queen is defended from a8, and so the text cannot be answered with 12 ♘xf7? ♔xf7 13 ♕h5+ since simply 13...♔xf6 wins.

12 ♕h5

Van Wely's novelty, which, however is unlikely to attract a following. In reply to the immediate challenge to the e5 'strongpoint' White also has:

a) **12 ♗e2** ♘xe5 13 dxe5 ♕c7 14 ♕d4 h3 (this looks at least adequate, but Kramnik gives 14...b4!? 15 ♘e4 c5 16 ♕xc4 0-0-0 as even stronger) 15 0-0-0 hxg2 16 ♖hg1 bxa4 17 ♗xc4?! (17 ♘xa4 was better) 17...a3! and White's queenside will be similarly undermined; Kohlweyer-Ribli, Dortmund 1986.

b) **12 f4!?** ♘xf6 13 f5 ♗b4 (13...c5!? is also logical since White's very aggressive idea would backfire if queens were exchanged. However 14 fxe6 fxe6 15 ♕c2 ♖g8 is unclear and interesting, although I basically believe Black's position) 14 fxe6 fxe6 15 ♗e2 (15 ♕f3!? was more dangerous and Black should probably acquiesce in 15...♕xd4 16 ♕xf6 ♗xc3+ 17 bxc3 ♕e3+! 18 ♔d1 ♖d8+ 19 ♗d3 ♖xd3 20 ♘xd3 ♕xd3+ 21 ♔c1 ♕e3+ 22 ♔b2 ♕d2+ 23 ♔a3 ♕d6+ with perpetual) 15...0-0 16 0-0 c5! (Szilagyi-Somlai, Hungarian League 1990), when 17 ♘a2 would have kept the game complex with chances for both sides.

c) **12 axb5!?** is suggested by both Kramnik and Van der Sterren, the former giving 12...cxb5 13 ♘xb5 ♗b4+ 14 ♘c3 ♘xe5 15 dxe5 ♕b6∞ which looks to me quite encouraging for Black.

12 ... ♕xf6
13 ♘xd7 ♔xd7
14 axb5 cxb5

Black can also consider **14...♖g8** or **14...h3** (the latter presumably to free the black queen from f7 guard duty) according to Kramnik.

15 ♕xb5+ ♗c6
16 ♕xc4 ♗d6 *(67)*

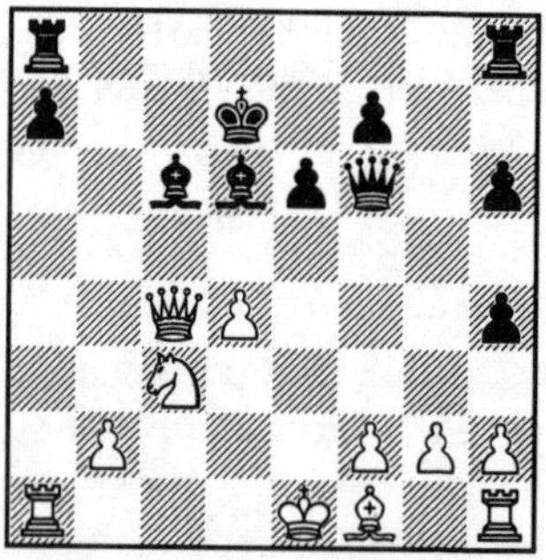

After a series of exchanges the position clarifies somewhat. Material balance has been restored and Black still has the tattered h-pawns characteristic of all the exf6 lines.

However, the position clearly favours Black. His king on d7 will not even feel serious discomfort in view of his excellent lead in development and raking bishops which are ideal for both attack and defence. The possibility of ...h3 (as so often with this structure) should also be taken very seriously. Kramnik's ∓ is for me an understatement. Clearly White's priority must be to remove part of Black's bishop pair. According to Kramnik the best way was **17 ♘b5!** ♕f4 18 ♘xd6 ♕xd6. It is not clear whether Van Wely's choice was the product of aggression or panic, but Black was unimpressed with the investment of material, and with precise counterattacking defence secures a large plus.

17 ♖a6?! ♖hc8
18 ♖xc6 ♖xc6
19 ♕a4 ♕g5
20 ♗b5 ♕xg2

Impressively cool. If **20...♕c1+** 21 ♘d1, White can subsequently castle and restrict Black's advantage.

21 d5

The only hope. If **21 ♖f1** simply 21...a6 22 d5 axb5 23 ♕xa8 exd5, and Black's king is quite safe.

21 ... ♕xh1+
22 ♔e2 ♔d8!

Much better than **22...♔e7** when White finally gets a realistic crack at the black king with 23 ♕xh4+ f6 24 ♕g4! ♔f8 25 ♕g6!∞.

23 ♗xc6 ♖b8
24 ♘b5

A defensive as well as offensive move, since the threat of ...♖xb2+ has to be met.

24 ... exd5!

The threat to exchange queens with ...♕e4+ always gives Black an extra defensive resource. Clearly too, the bishop on d6 is immune due to the drastic consequences of ...♖b2+.

25 ♕a5+ ♔e7
26 ♕xa7+ ♔f8
27 ♕e3 ♔g8!

Such an important part of great technique is recognizing when apparently strong continuations will still throw up problems. A good case in point is **27...♕e4?!** 28 ♕xe4 dxe4 29 ♘xd6 ♖xb2+ 30 ♔e3 ♖b6 31 ♘xf7 ♖xc6 32 ♘e5 and the win is not trivial (Kramnik).

In the game Black is able to exchange queens under more leisurely circumstances and there are few further problems, even with some time-trouble playing a role: **28 h3 ♗f8 29 ♕f4 ♕e4+ 30 ♕xe4 dxe4 31 ♔e3 ♖b6 32 ♗d7 ♖f6 33 b3 ♗c5+ 34 ♔xe4 ♖xf2 35 ♔d5 ♗b4 36 ♘d4 ♔g7 37 ♔c4 ♖f4!** (The opposite-coloured bishops enable White to delay matters, but once the black king is freed, the days of the light square blockade are numbered. It is no problem that this costs a pawn) **38 ♔d5 ♔f6 39 ♗c8 ♖f1 40 ♗g4 ♗c3 41 ♘f3 ♔g6! 42 ♘xh4+ ♔g5 43 ♘f3+ ♔f4 44 ♘h4 ♖f2!** (A nice finish. The knight is helpless) **45 ♗c8 ♔g5 0-1**.

8 5 ♗g5 h6 – Moscow Variation

Not everyone plays the Semi-Slav for a bloodbath. After 5 ♗g5 Black is by no means obliged to permit the tremendous complications examined in the previous chapters. For example Black can with 5...♘bd7 steer the game towards the Queen's Gambit Declined (QGD) in either its Orthodox or Cambridge Springs incarnations. However, these fall outside our ambit here. In addition though Black has one quiet option which keeps the Semi-Slav character, namely 5...h6. The move is compatible with the principle enunciated in the introduction, namely that White cannot play 5 ♗g5 without being forced into some concession, in this case either relinquishing the two bishops (6 ♗xf6 – the main line) or sacrificing a pawn (moreover after 6 ♗h4 dxc4 in a form generally regarded as an improvement for Black over the Botvinnik). Having declared that 5...h6 retains the 'Semi-Slav character' of the game I would like to add a qualification. In general the quieter and more positional the play, the more it bears comparison with other openings, and at times in the forthcoming chapter I have discussed comparisons with the QGD and even the Grünfeld to name but two.

The material is organized into two games; the first deals with the comparatively rare 6 ♗h4 and with all alternatives to 7 e3 after 6 ♗xf6 ♕xf6. The second deals exclusively with 7 e3(!), an emphasis which reflects a firm belief that this course for White offers both solidity and good prospects of a small plus. Overall, Black has to tolerate a fair degree of passivity in return for acquiring the bishop pair, and this is clearly not to everybody's taste. Nonetheless, the resulting positions are sound and solid for Black, and 5...h6 is a move which has attracted a devoted following of specialists, especially in the former Soviet Union.

There is one other option worth a mention, partly for a bit of light relief since the story of the move is quite amusing, partly because the willingness of Black players to 'experiment' with it seems to have mysteriously postdated the wide publication of its outright refutation. The move is 5...♕b6?! and the first culprit may well be Borges-Gomez, Cuba 1989 which continued 6 ♗xf6?! ♕xb2 7 ♕c1 ♕xc1 8 ♖xc1 gxf6 9 cxd5

♗b4 10 dxc6 ♘xc6 and Black certainly had no problems. All this caught the attention of Rainer Knaak who mentioned it as an interesting oddity in his *Trends* pamphlet. The big moment for 5...♕b6 came in P.Cramling-G.Flear in a key round of the Bern open 1992. Pia played the very logical 6 ♕c2! and Glenn followed with the consistent 6...♘e4? in accordance with his preparation. The game duly wound its way onwards with 7 cxd5 ♘xg5 8 ♘xg5 etc. It was later that Colin Crouch pointed out that 7 ♘xe4 dxe4 8 c5! wins at least a pawn, a rather simple idea missed not only by both players but by Glenn's far from weak team of analysts that morning, and by Ftaćnik annotating subsequently for *ChessBase Magazine*. Andrew Muir was the lucky beneficiary, and in the Manila Olympiad against local man Atotubo after 8...♕b5 9 a4 ♕a6 10 ♕xe4 b6 11 b4 ♕c4 12 ♗d2 a5? 13 ♕b1! Δe4 he was well on the way to the full point. Evidence of more recent outings is a bit anecdotal, but White should be prepared and keep hoping!

Game 11
Stohl-Kuczynski
Budapest Z 1993

1 d4 **d5**
2 c4 **c6**
3 ♘c3 **♘f6**
4 ♘f3 **e6**
5 ♗g5 **h6**
6 ♗xf6

This is the regular choice. In contrast with the Botvinnik Variation, after **6 ♗h4 dxc4** White is committed to offering a real gambit. Thought to be a bit speculative, it still has its adherents and since Garry Kasparov has essayed it on one occasion it should be examined with respect. After **7 e4 g5** (as a simpler method, 7...♗e7 8 e5 ♘d5 9 ♗xe7 ♕xe7 10 ♗xc4 ♕b4 11 ♗xd5 exd5 12 0-0 ♗g4 13 ♕d3 ♗xf3 14 gxf3 0-0 ½-½ Urban-Kuczynski, Polish Ch {Czestochowa} 1992 may have a future) **8 ♗g3** *(68)*:

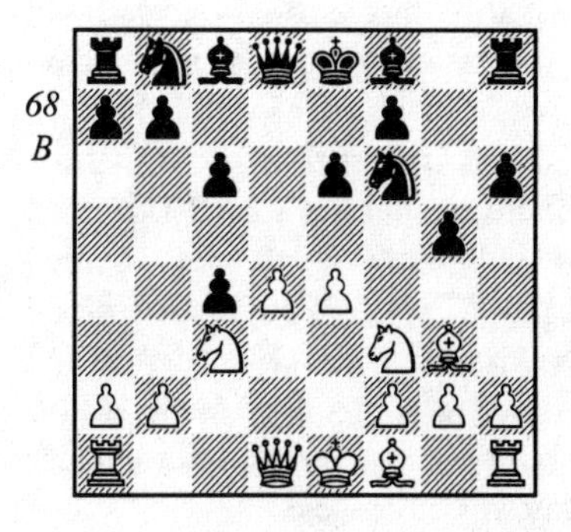

a) **8...♗b4** 9 ♗xc4 (9 ♕c2 is best met by 9...b5 10 e5 ♘d5 according to Yuneev and Yudasin, since the greedy 9...g4?! 10 ♘d2 ♕xd4? 11 0-0-0 is really asking for it; 9 ♗e5 ♘bd7 10 ♗xc4 ♘xe5 11 ♘xe5 ♘xe4 12 ♕f3 ♘d6 {Pytel-Minev,

Albena 1973} 13 **0-0** ♗xc3 14 bxc3 gives White compensation - Minev) 9...♘xe4 10 **0-0** ♘xg3 11 fxg3! ♘d7 and now instead of **12 ♕b3** ♗e7 13 ♖ae1 ♘b6 14 ♗d3 **0-0** 15 ♔h1?! (15 ♗b1) 15...c5! with no problems for Black (Lputian-Sveshnikov, USSR Ch (Lvov) 1985), **12 a3** (Lputian) or **12 ♕e2** Δ♖d1 and ♘e5 (Kondratiev) should be considered.

b) **8...b5** with two possibilities:

b1) **9 e5** gives rise to positions which can be reached via the Botvinnik move-order (5...dxc4 6 e4 b5 7 e5 h6 8 ♗h4 g5 9 ♗g3).

b11) **9...♘h5** is liable to transpose to Piket-Dreev below after 10 ♗e2 ♗b7.

b12) **9...♘d5** 10 h4!? leads to messy positions in which White probably has enough activity to compensate for the pawn, but no more, e.g. 10...♕a5 11 ♖c1 g4 12 ♘d2 ♗b4 and now Mikhalchishin's analysis runs **13 ♕c2** c5 14 dxc5 ♘d7 15 c6 ♘c5 16 ♗e2 ♗xc3 17 bxc3 ♕b6 18 **0-0** ♕xc6 19 ♗xg4 ♗b7 or **13 ♘de4** ♕xa2 14 ♖c2 ♕a5 15 ♗e2 ♘d7 16 0-0 ♗b7 17 ♗xg4 0-0-0, with unclear play in both cases.

b2) **9 ♗e2** is best met by the sensible **9...♗b7**, when White may try:

b21) **10 0-0** a6 (10...♗g7? 11 e5 Δ♘e4; 10...b4 11 ♘a4 ♘xe4 12 ♗xc4; 10...♗e7 11 ♘e5 ♘bd7 12 f4 ♘xe5 13 fxe5 ♘h7 14 ♗h5 0-0 15 ♕f3 {Kupreichik-Sveshnikov, USSR Ch 1985} 15...♕xd4+ 16 ♔h1 ♕d7!? Ftacnik) 11 ♘e5 ♗g7 12 f4 **0-0** 13 fxg5 hxg5 14 ♗h5 ♘xh5 15 ♕xh5 f6! 16 ♘g4 ♘d7 17 e5 ♕e8 18 ♘h6+ ♔h7 19 ♘f7+ ♔g8 20 ♘h6+ ♔h7 and now in Lputian-Sveshnikov, European Club Cup 1991, White should have settled for a draw.

b22) **10 e5** ♘d5 (10...♘h5 11 **0-0** ♘d7 12 a4 a6 13 ♔h1 ♘g7 14 ♘e4 ♘f5 {14...c5 15 ♘d6+} 15 ♘fd2 ♕b6 {15...♘xd4 16 ♘xc4} 16 ♗h5 ♕xd4 17 ♕g4 ♘c5 18 ♖ae1 ♘d3 19 ♖e2 ♗e7 20 f4 gave White a very dangerous attack in Piket-Dreev, Groningen 1991, but Dreev gives instead 17...c5! 18 ♖ae1 ♖h7 19 f4 0-0-0∓) 11 h4 ♕a5 12 ♖c1 g4 13 ♘d2 ♘xc3 (13...c5?! 14 ♘ce4 cxd4 15 **0-0** is good for White after either 15...♘c6 16 a4 a6 17 ♖a1! ♕d8 18 axb5 axb5 19 ♖xa8 ♕xa8 20 ♗xg4 or 15...h5 16 a4! a6 {Kasparov-Tal, Moscow IZ 1982} 17 ♗xc4 bxc4 18 ♘xc4 ♕b4 19 f3! ♘c6 20 ♗e1 ♕e7 21 ♘cd6+ ♔d8 22 ♖xc6! ♗xc6 23 ♗a5+ ♘c7 24 ♕xd4+-, as analysed by Kasparov) 14 bxc3 h5 and now White can choose between **15 ♘e4** ♘d7 16 **0-0** (better than 16 f3?! c5 17 ♘d6+ ♗xd6∓ Kishnev-Av.Bykhovsky, Moscow 1982) and **15 f3!?** ♘d7 16 fxg4 hxg4 17 0-0 ♗e7 18 ♗xg4 c5 19 ♗h5 with sharp play; Burlov-Volodin, Moscow 1985.

6 ... ♕xf6 *(69)*

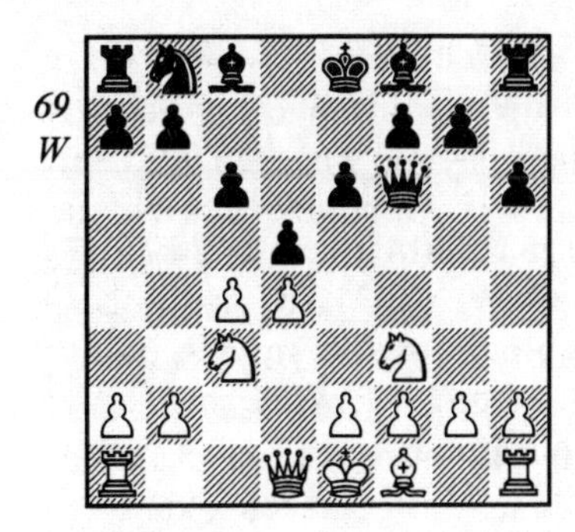

69
W

7 ♕b3

Of the alternatives to 7 e3, the text is the most popular. White is still usually aspiring to play e4 in one go by preventing ...♗b4+, while at the same time the move can prepare 0-0-0, or ♖d1. By defending c4, the move is also consistent with approaches where White would like to fianchetto his king's bishop without having to play in gambit style. Other moves:

a) **7 e4** is the most direct, but the current wisdom is that the displacement of the white king is irritating enough for Black to equalize, e.g. **7...dxe4 8 ♘xe4 ♗b4+ 9 ♔e2** and now:

a1) **9...♕d8** 10 g3 (10 c5 doesn't have the desired tempo-winning effect as Black can react energetically with 10...0-0 11 g3 b6! 12 a3 f5 13 ♘d6 ♗a6+ 14 ♔e3 f4+ 15 gxf4 bxc5 16 axb4 ♕xd6∓ Mageramov-Sveshnikov, USSR 1981) 10...0-0 11 ♕b3 ♗e7 (11...♗a5 or even 11...♕e7 merit attention too) 12 ♗g2 ♘d7 13 ♖hd1 ♕a5 (Black's correct strategy is to emphasize his dark-square chances by playing ...e5) 14 ♕c3 ♗b4 15 ♕c2 f5∞ Cebalo-Sveshnikov, Belgrade 1984.

a2) **9...♕f4!?** 10 ♕c2 (10 ♕d3 ♘d7 11 g3 ♕c7 12 ♗g2 {12 c5?! b6 13 ♘ed2 e5! is a classic undermining of White's centre} 12...♗e7 13 ♖he1 ♘d7 14 ♕c3 f5 {14...b6 looks adequate too} 15 ♘ed2 ♗f6∞) 10...f5 (also 10...0-0 11 ♘e5 ♘d7 12 g3 ♕f5 13 ♘xd7 ♗xd7 may equalize) 11 ♘c3 e5 12 g3 ♕g4 13 h3 ♕h5 14 dxe5 ♘d7 15 ♗g2 ♘xe5 16 ♔f1 ♘xe5 17 ♕e2+!= Uhlmann-Bagirov, Berlin 1989.

b) **7 a3**. No prizes for guessing White's intention here. White is looking for e4 without committing any of his pieces first. Still, the move is a little slow, and capturing on c4 leads to an interesting struggle, but one which holds few terrors for Black. After 7...dxc4 8 ♘e5 (8 e3 is illogical since at some stage after 8...b5 White will need the lever a4) 8...c5!? (8...b5 9 g3 gives fair compensation, but 8...♘d7 9 ♘xc4 ♘b6 10 e3 ♕d8 11 b4 ♗e7 12 ♕b3 0-0 was safe enough if a little unambitious in Staniszewski-Kuczynski, Polish Ch 1986) 9 ♘xc4 (9 ♕a4+ is interesting: 9...♘c6 10 ♘xc6 ♗d7 11 d5 exd5 12 ♘xd5 ♕d6 13 0-0-0 ♗xc6 14 ♕xc4 leaves White with some initiative; perhaps 9...♗d7 10 ♘b5 ♕d8 11 ♘xd7 ♘xd7 12 ♕xc4 a6= is safer) 9...cxd4 10 ♘b5

♕d8 11 ♕xd4 ♕xd4 12 ♘xd4 White's lead in development compensates for the bishop pair but not more. Kasparov-Sveshnikov, USSR Ch (Frunze) 1981 continued 12...♗d7 13 g3 ♗c5 14 ♘b3 ♗e7 15 ♘ca5 ♗c6 16 ♘xc6 ♘xc6 17 ♗g2 ♖c8 with no problems for Black.

c) **7 ♕c2** again prepares e4, this time with the intention of recapturing on e4 with the queen. Developing normally and permitting this plan is possible, but it is probably simpler for Black to capture on c4 and entice White into sharpening the play to win back his material. We shall consider:

c1) **7...♘d7** 8 e4 dxe4 (8...♗b4 9 e5!?⩲) 9 ♕xe4 ♗d6 (9...g6 10 ♗d3 ♗g7 11 **0-0 0-0** 12 ♕e3 b6 13 ♖fe1 ♗b7 14 ♘e4 ♕e7 15 c5± Khuzman-Timoshchenko, USSR 1982 illustrates a familiar theme that Black should beware of whenever he tries ...b6 in these positions) 10 ♗d3 c5 (10...g6!? should be considered, as in the main line White enjoys a comfortable initiative) 11 d5 ♘e5 12 ♘xe5 ♗xe5 (12...♕xe5!?) 13 **0-0** ♕f4 14 ♕xf4 ♗xf4 15 ♖ad1 **0-0** 16 ♖fe1 ♖d8 17 ♗e4 ♖b8 18 ♗f3 b6 19 h4± Agzamov-Gorelov, USSR 1982.

c2) **7...dxc4** 8 e3 (playing in true gambit spirit with 8 e4!? is interesting; Black should play 8...b5 9 ♗e2 ♗b7 and certainly ...♗b4 in reply to a4, but if White reserves a4 until after castling he obtains reasonable compensation. The optimal Black set-up is not so clear here. A strange hybrid was tried in Khalifman-Kir. Georgiev, Las Palmas 1993 with 8 g3!?. Black's response 8...♕f5!? was equally creative, and after 9 ♕xf5 exf5 10 ♘e5 ♗e6 11 e3 ♘d7 12 ♘xc4 ♗e7 13 ♗e2 **0-0-0** 14 **0-0** ♘f6 15 a3 g5 16 ♘e5 ♗d6 17 ♘c4 ♗c7 18 ♘d2 f4 he had good counterplay) 8...b5! 9 a4 (Maybe for a plus White has to go all-in with 9 ♘xb5 cxb5 10 ♕e4 ♗b4+ 11 ♔d1 **0-0** 12 ♕xa8 ♗d7! but Black has a lot of activity and White's king position will be a headache for a long time) 9...♗b7! 10 axb5 cxb5 11 ♘xb5 ♗b4+ 12 ♘c3 (12 ♘d2?! **0-0** 13 ♘c7 ♘d7 14 ♘xa8 ♖xa8 gives Black similar compensation to that found in the 5...dxc4 6 e3 line from Chapter 7, note to White's 6th. Black will follow up with ...e5, and if 15 ♗xc4 ♖c8!? 16 ♖xa7 ♗xg2 17 ♖g1 ♘b6! looks very good value for the material) 12...**0-0** 13 ♗e2 ♘d7 14 **0-0** ♖fd8 15 ♘d2 e5 16 ♗f3! ♗xf3 17 ♘xf3 ♕e6 Stohl-Sveshnikov, Leningrad 1984, and now 18 ♖fd1⩲.

d) **7 g3!?** has been quite a popular alternative to the main lines, quite logically since the exchange of White's dark-squared bishop on f6 makes a regular appearance in the related Catalan Opening. Black has tried three basic set-ups:

1) Keeping the queen on f6 and developing his king's bishop to b4

or d6 (not e7 which leaves the queen embarrassed);

2) Retreating the queen to d8 in preparation for ...♗e7;

3) Capturing on c4. Thus:

d1) **7...♘d7** 8 ♗g2 ♗b4 (8...♗d6 9 0-0 ♕e7 10 e4 dxc4 11 ♘d2 ♘b6 12 e5!? ♗c7 13 ♕e2 0-0 Bagirov-Fernandez, Cascais 1986, and now 14 ♖fd1 as preparation for ♘xc4 leaves White with some spacial plus) 9 ♕b3 (9 0-0 0-0 10 e4 dxc4 11 e5 ♕d8 12 a3 ♗e7 13 a4 ♖b8 14 ♘d2 b5 15 ♗xc6 b4 16 ♘e2 ♗a6 17 ♗b5⩲ Lputian-Conquest, Hastings 1986) 9...♕e7 10 0-0 0-0 11 a3 (11 e4!?) 11...♗a5 12 ♘d2 ♘f6 (12...e5 13 e3!⩲) 13 e4 dxe4 14 ♘dxe4 ♖d8 15 ♖ad1 ♘xe4 16 ♘xe4 e5 17 d5 cxd5! (Not 17...♗g4 18 d6! ♗xd1 19 ♖xd1 when White's enormous d-pawn gave a decisive advantage in Tukmakov-Sveshnikov, Moscow 1985) 18 ♖xd5 ♖xd5 19 cxd5 ♗b6! with reasonable counterplay; Kaidanov-Sveshnikov, Kuibyshev 1986.

d2) **7...♕d8** 8 ♗g2 ♘d7 (8...b5?! was revealed to be a premature attempt to generate activity in Kozlov-Sveshnikov, USSR 1986 after 9 cxb5 cxb5 10 ♘xb5 ♕b6 11 ♘c3 ♕xb2 12 0-0! ♗a3 13 ♕d3 ♗a6 14 ♕e3 ♗e7 15 ♘e5± since Black's development is dangerously retarded; neither is 8...♗e7 viable except for transposition: 9 0-0 0-0 10 e4 dxc4 11 ♕e2 b5 12 ♖fd1 b4 13 ♘b2 ♗a6 14 ♕c2 ♘d7 15 ♘d2 ♘b6 16 ♗f1 gave White a positional plus in Knaak-Kuczynski, Camaguey 1987) 9 0-0 ♗e7 10 e4!? (The sharpest. Arguably 10 ♕d3 is less testing: 10...0-0 11 e4 dxc4 12 ♕xc4 ♘b6 13 ♕e2 c5 14 ♖fd1 ♗d7 15 dxc5 {15 a4 may keep the pressure on Black a little better} 15...♗xc5 16 ♘e5 ♕e7 17 ♘xd7 ♘xd7 18 e5 ♖ab8 19 ♘e4 ♖fd8 20 ♖ac1 ♗b6 with only a nominal spacial edge for White in Oll-Sveshnikov, Minsk 1986) 10...dxe4 11 ♘xe4 0-0 12 c5! (An excellent move which may send Black back to the drawing board in this line. Black was able to match White in the fascinating complications which arose from the previous try 12 ♖c1 b6 13 d5!? in Agdestein-Speelman, Hastings 1991/2 by 13...cxd5 14 cxd5 exd5 15 ♕xd5 ♗a6 16 ♖fd1 ♘c5 17 ♕f5 ♘d3! 18 ♖c6 ♖c8 19 ♘e5 ♘xe5! 20 ♖xd8 ♖cxd8 21 ♖c1 ♘c6! 22 ♘c3 ♘d4 23 ♕e4 ♗g5 24 f4 ♖fe8 and Black's initiative was excellent value for the small material investment) 12...b6 13 ♕c2 ♕c7 14 ♖ac1 ♗b7 15 ♖fe1 ♖ad8 16 b4⩲ (at least) since Black has no assets to set against his lack of space; Komarov-Kramnik, USSR 1991.

d3) **7...♘d7 8 ♗g2 dxc4 9 0-0 ♗e7** *(70)* (9...♗d6 10 ♘e4 {10 e4? e5∓} 10...♕e7 11 ♘fd2 b5 12 a4⩲; apparently risky, the immediate 9...e5 was tried in Tukmakov-Illescas, Wijk aan Zee 1993. After 10 d5 ♘b6 11 ♘d2 {11 dxc6!?} 11...cxd5 12 ♘xd5 ♘xd5 13 ♗xd5 ♗e7 14 ♘xc4 0-0 15 ♕b3 ♗h3 16 ♖fd1 ♗c5 17 ♕f3 ♖ab8 White had at the most a slight edge) and now:

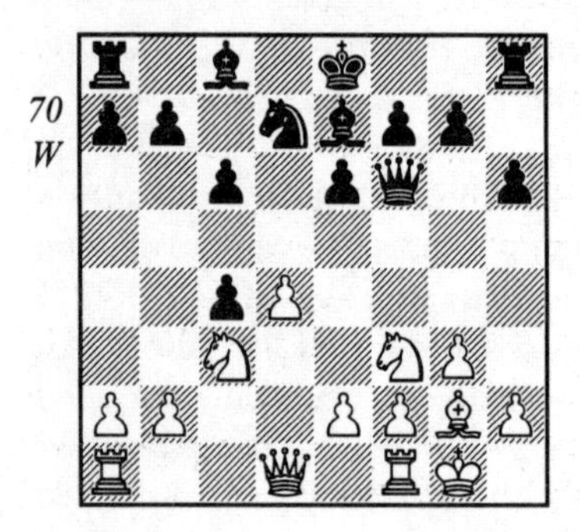
70
W

d31) **10 ♘e4** earned Tukmakov a nasty reversal in his long-running debate with Sveshnikov in this line (Sochi 1987) after 10...♕f5! **11 ♘fd2** ♘b6 12 a4 ♕a5 13 ♕c2 0-0 14 ♖fd1 ♖d8 15 e3?! e5! 16 dxe5 ♗g4 17 f3 ♗e6 18 f4 ♖d3 19 ♗f1? (19 ♔f2!∓) 19...♖xe3 20 ♗xc4 ♖xe4! 21 ♗xe6 ♖e2 22 ♗g4 ♕d5! 23 ♗xe2 ♗c5+ with decisive advantage for Black. **11 ♘ed2!?** may be a better try: 11...b5 12 a4 0-0 13 axb5 ♕xb5 14 ♕c2 ♗b7 15 ♘c4 c5 was Christiansen-M.Gurevich, Antwerp 1993 when Gurevich suggests 16 ♘a5!? ♗xf3 17 ♗xf3 ♖ac8 18 d5! exd5 19 ♗xd5±.

d32) **10 a4!?** is interesting. Loginov-Ivanov, Budapest 1990 continued 10...0-0 11 e3 e5 12 d5 ♘c5 13 ♘d2 ♖d8 14 ♕e2 ♘b3 15 ♖ad1±.

d33) **10 e3 0-0** 11 ♘d2! (11 ♕e2 e5 12 ♕xc4 exd4 13 ♘xd4 ♘e5 14 ♕b3 ♖d8 15 f4 ♘g4 16 ♘e4 ♕g6 17 f5 ♕h7 18 h3 ♘f6 19 g4 ♘xe4 20 ♗xe4 h5! and the black queen found a role from its unorthodox new home in Tukmakov-Sveshnikov, USSR 1986) 11...e5 (11...♘b6 12 a4 a5 13 ♘ce4 ♕f5 14 f4! ♗b4 15 ♖c1 ♗xd2 16 ♘xd2± Jovčić) 12 ♘xc4! (White overstretched with 12 d5?! ♘b6 13 ♘e4 ♕g6 14 d6 ♗d8 15 ♗f3 ♘d7 16 ♗h5 ♕e6 17 ♘c4 b6 18 ♗e2 f5 19 b3 ♗a6! and was driven back leaving his d-pawn looking very lonely in Kuijf-Spasov, Munich 1992) 12...exd4 13 exd4 ♘b6 14 ♘e3!? ♖d8 (14...♗b4!?) 15 d5 ♗e6 16 ♕b3 cxd5 17 ♘cxd5 ♘xd5 18 ♘xd5 ♗xd5 19 ♗xd5± with only a depressing defence in store for Black in Speelman-Sveshnikov, Biel IZ 1993.

7 ... a5!?

There are two main ideas attached to this interesting pawn push. The first is to advance ...a4, based on the tactic that if ♘xa4, Black can often capture on c4 and then fork with ...b5. If possible, Black may even seek to cause maximum disruption by pushing again to a3, emphasizing Black's superiority on the dark squares. The subsidiary point, which actually comes to the fore in our main game is once again to enable check on b4 in the event of an immediate e4. Other moves are:

a) **7...dxc4** (committal?) 8 ♕xc4 ♘d7 9 ♖d1 (9 0-0-0!?; 9 e4?! e5 10 d5 ♘b6 11 ♕b3 ♗c5 12 ♗e2 ♗g4 13 **0-0** ♗xf3 with definite counterplay on the dark squares in Kishnev-Lukacs, Budapest 1991) 9...♕e7!? 10 ♕b3 g6 11 e4 (11 g3!?) 11...♗g7 12 e5?! 0-0 13 ♘e4 c5 14 dxc5 ♘xc5 15 ♕a3 b6 16 ♘xc5 ♕xc5 17 ♕xc5 bxc5 18 ♗c4 ♗b7 19 ♔e2 ♗xf3+ 20 ♔xf3 ♗xe5 Brenninkmeijer-Novikov, New York 1993, and clearly only Black can realistically have eyes for the full point.

b) **7...♘d7** (Out of favour at present, but not necessarily deservedly so) 8 e4 (8 g3 ♕e7!? 9 cxd5?! exd5 10 ♗g2 ♘f6 11 0-0 ♗e6 12 ♘a4 ♕c7= Winants-Korchnoi, Brussels 1988) 8...dxe4 (8...dxc4 9 ♗xc4 b5 10 ♗d3 e5 is an interesting alternative. Perhaps White should consider 10 ♗e2!? – Veličković) 9 ♘xe4 ♕f4 10 ♗d3 e5! 11 **0-0** f5 12 ♘g3 e4 13 ♖fe1 ♔d8 14 ♗xe4 fxe4 15 ♖xe4 ♕f7 16 ♕c2 ♗d6 17 ♖ae1 ♘f6 18 ♘e5 ♗xe5 19 ♖xe5∞ Kishnev.

8 e4

Generally White has taken up the challenge in this way in recent practice. This is unsurprising, since none of the alternatives seem particularly threatening:

a) **8 ♖c1?** is worth mentioning because it allows the execution of Black's plan in all its glory: 8...a4! 9 ♘xa4 dxc4 10 ♕c2 ♗b4+ 11 ♔d1 b5∓ Suba-Sveshnikov, Sochi 1983 since 12 ♘b6 fails to 12...♖xa2!.

b) **8 cxd5** is possible, but ...a5 fits in to the QGD Exchange structures every bit as well as ♕b3. 8...exd5 9 e3 ♘a6!? 10 ♖c1 ♕d8 11 ♗d3 ♗d6 12 0-0 0-0 13 ♗b1 ♖e8 14 ♖fe1 ♗g4 15 ♘d2 ♕h4 was Tatai-Pomar, Las Palmas 1972, when Black's kingside play was as far advanced as anything White had to offer.

c) **8 a3** a4 9 ♕a2 (9 ♘xa4 dxc4 10 ♕c2 b5! 11 ♘b6 {11 ♘c3 b4!? 12 ♘e4 ♕f5 13 ♘e5 b3 with counterplay – Kondratiev} 11...♗b4+ 12 ♔d1 ♖a6 13 ♘xc8 ♕d8!∓ {not 13...0-0? 14 ♖c1}; also 9 ♕c2 dxc4 10 ♘e4 ♕d8 11 ♕xc4 ♕a5+ 12 ♘c3 ♘d7 etc is harmless) 9...♘d7 10 e4 dxe4 11 ♘xe4 ♕f4 12 ♗d3 e5 13 **0-0** exd4 14 ♘xd4 ♗e7 15 ♘f5! ♘e5! 16 ♘fd6+ ♗xd6 17 ♘xd6+ ♔e7 18 ♘xc8+ ♖fxc8 19 ♖ae1 ♔f8 and even when minor pieces are reduced to white bishop *vs* black knight, Black still enjoys some supremacy on the dark squares; Gomez-Tal, Seville 1992.

d) **8 g3** ♕d8 9 ♗g2 ♗e7 10 0-0 0-0 11 ♖fd1 ♘d7 12 e4 dxe4 13 ♘xe4 a4 14 ♕c2 ♕c7 15 ♘c3 a3 16 b3 ♖fd8 17 ♖ac1 ♘f6 18 ♘e5 ♗d7 19 c5 ♗e8 20 ♘c4 ♘d7 21 ♘a4 ♗f6 ½-½ Topalov-Kuczynski, Budapest Z 1993.

e) **8 e3** ♘d7 (8...a4!? looks interesting too, although Black has generally avoided it in practice. 9 ♘xa4 {9 ♕c2 a3!?∓} 9...dxc4 10

♕c2 b5 11 ♘b6 ♗b4+ 12 ♘d2 ♖a6 13 ♘xc8 ♕d8 looks quite healthy for Black) 9 ♗e2 ♕d8 10 0-0 ♗e7 11 e4 dxe4 12 ♘xe4 0-0 13 c5 e5 14 ♖ad1 exd4 15 ♖xd4 ♕c7 16 ♕c2 ♘e5 17 ♘d6 ♘xf3+ 18 ♗xf3 ♗e6 19 b3 ♖ad8= Gavrikov-Godena, Reggio Emilia 1992.

8 ... dxe4

Very interesting here is **8...a4!?** *(71)*:

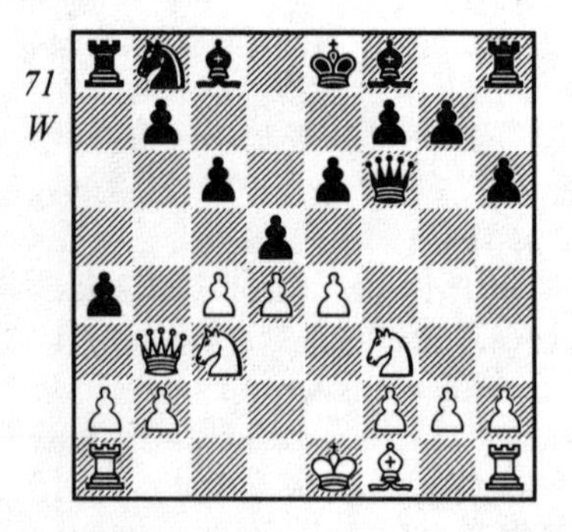

a) **9 ♕c2!?** dxe4 (9...a3!? is good if White can really do no better than 10 e5 axb2 11 ♕xb2 ♕d8 12 c5 ♘d7 13 ♖b1 ♕a5 14 ♗d3 b6, given by Varnusz as =, but I would prefer Black. However, why not 10 cxd5 axb2 11 ♕xb2 exd5 {11...♗a3 12 ♕c2 exd5 13 ♘xd5±} 12 exd5 ♗a3 13 ♕e2+ ♔d8 14 ♕c2±/∞) 10 ♘xe4 (10 ♕xe4 a3! 11 b3 ♗b4 12 ♖c1 c5 13 ♗e2 ♘c6 14 0-0 ♗xc3 15 ♖xc3 cxd4 16 ♖d3 e5 17 ♘xd4= Uhlmann) 10...♗b4+ 11 ♔d1 ♕d8 12 c5 0-0 13 a3 ♗a5 14 ♕xa4! b5 15 cxb6! (seems to lead to a slight but uncomplicated plus, which is not true of 15 ♕c2 e5 16 ♘d6 Uhlmann-Kuczynski, Dresden 1988, when with 16...♗g4! 17 ♗e2 exd4 18 ♕e4 ♗xf3 19 ♗xf3 ♘d7! Black could have kept matters very complex) 15...♗b7 16 ♘c5 ♗xb6 17 ♘xb7! ♖xa4 18 ♘xd8 ♖xd8 19 ♔c2 ♗xd4 20 ♔b3 ♖a7 21 ♘xd4 ♖xd4 22 ♔c3 ♖f4 23 ♖d1 ♘d7 24 ♖d2± Ivanchuk-Ribli, Reggio Emilia 1988/9?

b) **9 ♘xa4(?!)** dxe4 10 ♘b6?! (10 ♘e5 looks safer) 10...♖a5?! (It is surprising that Speelman did not elect to give 10...exf3! a try since 11 ♘xa8 ♕xd4 with compensation {Miles} looks very promising to me, and also typical of his style) 11 ♘e5 ♕d8 12 0-0-0 ♗d6 13 ♔b1 ♗c7 14 c5 ♗xb6 15 cxb6 0-0 16 ♗c4 ♘d7 17 ♘xd7 ♗xd7 18 ♖he1 and Black was very cramped, although he later won after a topsy-turvy tussle; Miles-Speelman, Dublin Z 1993

9 ♘xe4 ♗b4+
10 ♔d1

Various assessments have been offered of the ending arising after **10 ♕xb4** axb4 11 ♘xf6+ gxf6 12 c5 but I agree with Stohl that Black can obtain counterplay with ...♘d7 and ...b6.

10 ... ♕f4
11 ♗d3

The ending arising from **11 ♕e3?!** ♕xe3 12 fxe3 is in no way dangerous for Black, so long as he remembers to tuck his bishop the right side of the impending c5 with

12...♗e7 13 c5 ♘d7 as usual preparing ...b6 as the break to open the play for his pair of bishops.

11 ... **♗e7**

A major option here is **11...f5**, Dreev's move, by which Black tries to recapture a little space. Initially hailed as the end of the variation for White, and still given as the only move by Timman in *Informator 56*, it now seems that White has two ways to test it severely. After **12 ♘g3 c5** praxis has seen:

a) **13 d5?!** a4 14 ♕c2 0-0? (Black has to take advantage of White's 13th move omission to play 14...a3! himself and create a little disruption. After the text White can build his position at relative leisure) 15 a3 ♗a5 16 ♕e2! exd5 17 cxd5 ♗d7 18 ♕e5 ♗c7 19 ♕xf4 ♗xf4 Timman-Kuczynski, Tilburg 1992, and now the simple 20 ♖fe1 followed by ♘e5 would have been very unpleasant for Black.

b) **13 a3** a4 14 ♕c2 ♗a5 15 ♘e2! (The key moment. In the stem game Novikov-Dreev, Lvov Z 1990 White paid dearly for the natural pawn snatch on a4: 15 ♕xa4+? ♗d7 16 ♕c2 cxd4 17 ♘e2 ♕g4 18 ♘exd4 ♘c6 19 ♘b5 ♕xg2 20 ♔e2 ♕g4! 21 ♖g1 ♕h5 22 ♖g3 ♘e5 23 ♘bd5 ♘xf3 24 ♘xf3 ♗c6 25 b4 {a last-ditch attempt for counterplay which backfires completely after Black's elegant 27th} 25...♗xb4 26 axb4 ♖xa1 27 ♕b2 ♖g1!! 28 ♕e5 ♖xg3 29 ♕xe6+ ♔d8 30 ♕xd6+ ♔c8 0-1) 15...♕g4 16 ♘e5! ♕xg2 17 ♖g1 ♕xf2 18 ♕xa4+ ♘d7 19 b4! cxd4 20 ♖xg7 ♕f1+ 21 ♔c2 ♕xa1 22 ♘xd7 b5 23 ♕xb5 1-0 Novikov-Strokov, Alicante 1992.

12 ♘e5 **h5!**

It is already essential to give the queen some space. If **12...0-0?** 13 g3 ♕f5 14 ♘d6 ♕xf2 15 ♘xc8 ♖xc8 16 ♕xb7 is crushing.

13 g3 **♕h6** *(72)*

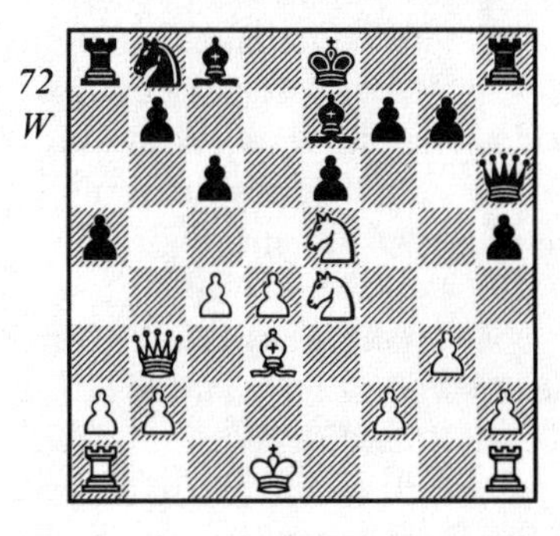

The position is exceptionally interesting. The usual features of this variation are present: White's space advantage and lead in development against Black's two bishops. Additionally though, Black's queen stands badly and ...a5 has created a few extra weak squares. Still, there is potential counterplay against d4, and White's king on the end of the d-file. In a sense the course of the game from here is thus quite logical. Black sacrifices pawns to emphasize the strong points of his game. I am not wholly convinced that Black always had enough, but Stohl's comments betray a man who was not wholly comfortable as White here.

14 ♕b6!

In this extremely sharp position White essays his novelty. **14 c5 0-0** 15 ♔e2 ♖d8 16 ♕c3 ♘d7 17 ♘xd7 ♗xd7 18 h4 ♗e8 19 ♖ad1 ♖d7 20 ♗c2 b5 21 cxb6?! (21 ♘d2=) 21...♖b7 22 ♘c5 ♖b6 23 b3 ♕f6 24 ♕d3 g6 25 ♘e4 ♕g7∓ was the much quieter course of Knaak-Sveshnikov, Novi Sad 1979. In this case the disadvantages of both sides' positions lose something of their acuteness. Here, White tries much more directly to impede Black's development.

14 ... f6!?

Looks strange, but **14...0-0** fails after 15 ♕c7! ♖e8, not to the brutal **16 ♘xf7?!** ♔xf7 17 ♘d6+ ♔f8 18 ♘xe8 ♘a6!, but rather to **16 c5!** (prophylaxis against ...♘a6). Stohl then mentions the interesting 16...♘d7 17 ♘xd7 ♗d8 18 ♕d6 ♗e7 19 ♘b6! ♗xd6 20 ♘xd6 ♗d7 21 ♘xd7 ♖ed8 22 ♘b6 with three very good pieces for the queen (±).

15 ♘g6! ♘d7
16 ♕b3

In this sharp position accuracy is required from both sides. A neat trap is **16 ♕c7??** ♕xg6! 17 ♘d6+ ♗xd6 18 ♗xg6+ ♔e7!-+.

16 ... a4
17 ♕c3

Of course not **17 ♕c2??** f5 18 ♘xe7 fxe4 19 ♘xc8 exd3-+.

17 ... f5
18 ♘xe7 fxe4
19 ♘xc8 ♖xc8
20 ♗xe4 ♘f6
21 ♗f3?

An error since the possibility of f4 is removed, which enhances Black's chances of play on the f-file. Instead. Stohl suggests **21 ♗g2!** 0-0 22 ♔e2. Black can no longer throw in the immediate **22...e5?** in view of simply 23 dxe5 ♘g4 24 f4±. 23 f4 also looks like a good reply to **22...h4!?**. Black could examine the ultra-sharp 23...g5, but this is looking a bit like an indication of desperation. I do not share Stohl's view that in the absence of radical action by Black the assessment is only ± or thereabouts.

21 ... 0-0
22 ♔e2 e5!?

White's inaccuracy has given Black a choice of ways to make play. If White's intention with 21 ♗f3 was to deny Black access to the g4 square, then it was misguided since even the immediate **22...♘g4!?** was interesting: 23 h3 (23 ♗xg4 hxg4 gives Black a lot of play on the light squares – notably e4, f3 and h3 – around the white king) 23...♖xf3! 24 ♕xf3 (24 ♔xf3 ♕f6+ 25 ♔e2 ♕f2+ 26 ♔d1 ♘e3+ 27 ♔d1 ♖d8! is risky for White) 24...♖f8 25 hxg4 ♖xf3 26 ♔xf3 hxg4+ 27 ♔g2 ♕g6= Stohl.

23 dxe5 ♘g4
24 ♗xg4 hxg4
25 ♖ad1 ♖ce8

26 ♖d3	**♖f5**
27 ♖e3	**♖ef8**
28 ♖f1	

Most of the preceding moves required little comment – Black was making direct threats, and White responding accordingly. **28 ♕e1?** ♕e6! was worse than the text, so Black wins back one pawn with White still rather tied up.

28 ...	**♕xh2**
29 ♕e1	**♕h6?!**

Commencing a period of inaccuracy! Better was **29...♕g2** when White has little alternative to creating a diversion with his e-pawn. Best play seems to lead to just equality after 30 e6 ♖f3! 31 e7 ♖xe3+ 32 ♔xe3 ♖e8 33 ♔d2 ♖xe7 34 ♕xe7 ♕xf1=.

30 ♔d1	**♖f3**
31 ♖xf3	**gxf3?!**

Perhaps a little over-concerned about the e-pawn, but the f-file was more important. **31...♖xf3!** 32 e6 ♕g6! 33 ♔c1 ♖f6! 34 e7 ♖e6 35 ♕b4 ♕g5± was better.

32 ♕e3?

Gives Black an unnecessary chance, just as White was on the point of consolidating since **32...♕xe3!** 33 fxe3 g5! 34 g4 ♖f7 35 ♖f2 ♔f8 36 ♔d2 ♔e7 37 ♔d3 ♔e6 38 ♔e4 c5! 39 ♖xf3 ♖xf3 40 ♔xf3 ♔xe5 leads surprisingly to a pawn ending where White can make no progress. This possibility could have been easily circumvented with **32 ♕d2!** ♕e6 33 ♕d4 with play similar to the game.

32 ...	**♕e6?**
33 ♕e4	**b5**
34 ♔c2!	**bxc4**
35 ♖d1	**♖e8**

35...♖f5 would require a certain accuracy from White, but he can win with 36 ♖d8+! ♔f7 37 ♖d6 ♕xe5 38 ♕xc6! ♕c5 (White's attack is too strong with queens on. 38...♕e2+ is just one check) 39 ♖d7+ ♔g8 40 ♖d8+ ♔h7 41 ♕xc5 ♖xc5 42 ♖f8±.

36 ♕xf3!	**♕xe5**
37 ♕xc6	**♕f5+**
38 ♔c1	**♕g5+?!**
39 f4	**♕e7**
40 ♕xc4+	**♔f8**
41 ♖h1	**♕e3+**
42 ♔b1	**1-0**

A very difficult game to play which, at least in the notes, illustrates Black's possibilities for counterplay. The theoretical assessment at this stage has to be that Black has some problems after Stohl's 14 ♕b6! and that maybe Black should examine 8...a4 more carefully.

Game 12
Yusupov-Dreev
Tilburg 1992

1 d4 d5 2 c4 c6 3 ♘f3 ♘f6 4 ♘c3 e6 5 ♗g5 h6 6 ♗xf6 ♕xf6

7 e3(!)

7 e3 might look more modest than the lines where White seeks to execute the e4 advance in one go, but I believe that it is White's most

effective choice. White is by no means eschewing e4. Whilst it might be thought that e4 is not entirely logical since the side with the two knights is seeking to open the play, opening the position is also the prerogative of the player with a spatial plus and this factor here generally weighs more heavily. However, whilst e4 remains a common idea, White's slower approach has the virtue of flexibility. A few thoughts to consider:

1) White first develops, usually reserving judgement on the best square for his queen (not true of 7 ♕b3 or 7 ♕c2 for example) and avoiding the inconvenience of king displacement not true of, for instance, 7 e4.

2) White can consider c5. If Black does not relish this prospect he may capture on c4 early. In this context however, it is likely that the e4 break is no longer appropriate – if e4 is answerable by ...e5 then White may begin to feel the absence of his dark-squared bishop. In our main game White prefers 11 ♘e4 in this context and builds uncomfortable pressure.

3) After the fairly fashionable deployment of the bishop to g7 for example, there is a stronger case for cxd5, again switching from the e4 plan to a closed centre with the bishop 'biting on granite' and White turning to the minority attack for his play.

In comparison with the sharp tactical emphasis of the early chapters, the slower, more strategic nature of the play here bears more generalities, and I hope these thoughts may act as a useful guide as we move on to consider some concrete variations.

7 ... **♘d7** *(73)*

By far the most frequent choice, the text must be the most flexible. The main alternative has been **7...♗d6**, but after 8 ♗d3 (8 a3 is also interesting) 8...♕e7 9 0-0 ♘d7 we reach a position considered in the note to Black's 8th.

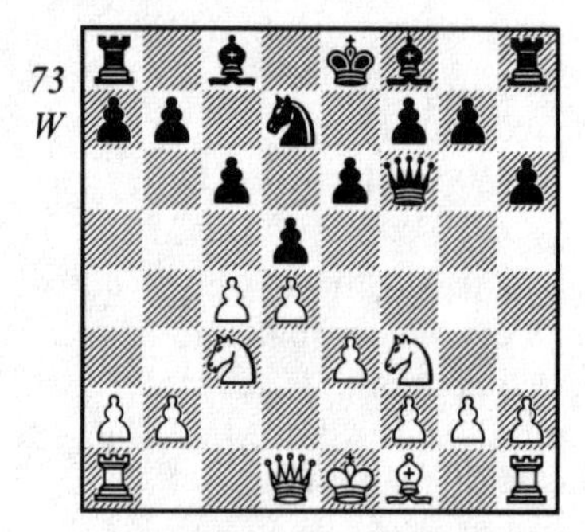

73
W

8 ♗d3

In my view, the natural text move is the most promising. Other moves are seen from time to time, and there is a major option in 8 a3. This changes the pecking order of the various Black set-ups, but seems sufficiently committal that Black can find enough play:

a) **8 cxd5** is not especially threatening here. 8...exd5 9 ♗d3 ♗d6 10 0-0 0-0 11 ♖e1 ♕d8 12 ♖b1 ♘f6

13 ♕c2 ♖e8 14 ♘d2 was Lputian-Sveshnikov, Sarajevo 1983, when 14...a5! would have given Black an easy game. In the Queen's Gambit Exchange Variation, with a similar structure, White usually only exchanges voluntarily on f6 if this assists immediately effecting the move b4.

b) **8 ♗e2** is motivated by the desire to avoid lines where White's break e4 is answered in the familiar Semi-Slav fashion with ...dxc4 and ...e5. Still, the bishop is too passive to cause Black problems: 8...♕d8 9 0-0 ♗e7 10 e4 dxe4 11 ♘xe4 0-0 12 ♕c2 ♕c7 13 ♖ad1 ♘f6 14 c5 b6 15 b4 a5 16 a3 axb4 17 axb4 ♗a6= Peev-Velikov, Plovdiv 1984.

c) **8 ♕c2** is maybe the most interesting of these minor alternatives if White continues with 0-0-0. Black's choice of ways to develop is similar to that after 8 ♗d3 to be discussed in detail in a later note. In brief: **8...g6** 9 0-0-0!? ♗g7 10 e4 ♕f4+ (10...dxc4 looks a bit risky here) 11 ♔b1 dxe4 12 ♘xe4 0-0 13 ♗e2 with an edge; L.B.Hansen-Mednis, Amsterdam 1989; or **8...a6!?** 9 0-0-0 (maybe White could look at 9 ♗d3 or 9 ♖d1 since short castling might better exploit the weaknesses created by a forthcoming ...b5) 9...♗b4 10 ♔b1 0-0 11 ♗d3 b5 with counterplay in Ree-Kuijf, Dutch Ch 1986.

A related idea, perhaps best treated here, was seen in the game Lobron-M.Gurevich, Munich 1993. White played 8 ♗d3 as in the main lines but after 8...♕d8 tried **9 ♕c2**. My suspicion is that White would do better to reserve judgement on the placing of the f1 bishop in conjunction with this whole **0-0-0** idea. Still, sharp play ensued after 9...♗e7 10 cxd5 exd5 11 0-0-0 ♘f6 (11...0-0?! 12 g4!) 12 h3 ♗d6 13 ♘e5 ♕e7 14 f4 ♗e6!? (short castling still involves considerable risk after 15 g4!) 15 ♔b1 0-0-0 16 ♖c1 (Gurevich gives 16 ♘b5 ♔b8 17 ♘xd6 ♖xd6 Δ...♖c8, ...♘e8, and ...f6 evicting the white knight from e5 with enough counterplay) 16...♔b8 17 g4 ♖c8 18 ♘a4 ♖c7 19 ♖h2 ♖hc8 20 ♕d1 and finally after much organization 20...c5! with chances for both sides.

d) **8 a3** *(74)* and now:

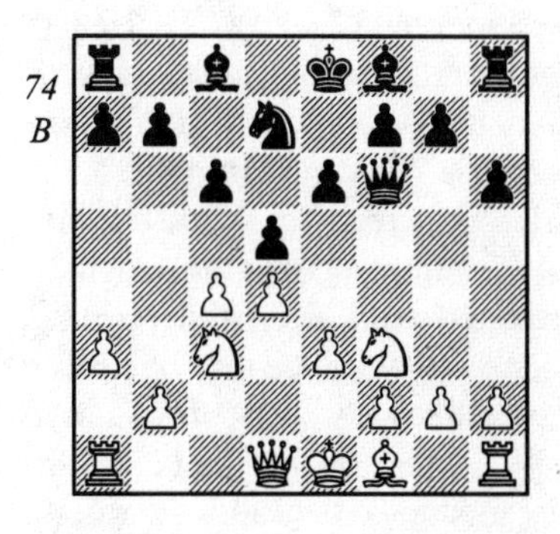

d1) **8...♗d6?!** is a little cooperative, justifying White's 8th after 9 e4! dxe4 10 ♘xe4 ♕e7 11 ♘xd6+ ♕xd6 12 c5 ♕c7 13 ♗c4 0-0 14 0-0 b6 15 b4 e5 16 ♖e1 exd4 17

♕xd4 with the more pleasant game for White in Browne-Bisguier, USA 1980.

d2) **8...g6!?**. As ever, against ...g6 White has a choice of exchanging on d5 leading to a structure with similarities to the Grunfeld (see note to 8 ♗d3 g6!? below) or playing for e4 and showing that extra space counts for more than the slight dark-square looseness. In I.Sokolov-Lautier, Corrèze (6) 1992, White opted for the former approach but my hunch is that a3 adds not too much to White's cause here. **9 ♗d3** (9 ♗e2!?) 9...♗g7 10 0-0 0-0 11 cxd5 exd5 12 b4 ♕d6 13 ♕b3 ♘b6 (½-½ Cs.Horvath-Todorčević, Nikšić 1991) 14 a4 ♗g4 (14...♗e6 is more normal since it by no means clear that the knight is worse on d2) 15 ♘d2 ♗e6 16 ♖fc1 ♘d7 17 ♘e2 (the immediate 17 b5 is well met by 17...c5!) 17...♖fe8 18 ♖ab1 and the minority attack is no more dangerous than Black's prospects on the centre and the kingside. More recently White tried the other approach, but although he emerged well from the opening, Black's play can be improved after **9 e4!?** dxe4 10 ♘xe4 ♕f4 11 ♗d3 ♗g7 12 0-0 0-0 **13 ♖e1** e5? (the key moment. Black should investigate either 13...♕c7 or 13...c5!? both of which look quite promising. The text leaves Black's queen rather embarrassed) 14 g3 ♕g4 15 ♘d6! exd4 16 ♖e4 ♕h3 17 ♗f1 ♕h5 18 b4! g5 (unfortunate necessity in view of the threat of g4) 19 ♘xd4! with a strong initiative which persists into the ensuing ending; Tukmakov-M.Gurevich, Wijk aan Zee 1993. In view of Black's clear improvement at move 13, White tried to preempt the loosening of his dark squares with **13 c5!?** in Neverov-Guliev, Nikolaev Z 1993. Now that Black has lost his ...c5 break on the one hand, and does not have to contend with the white rook motoring to e4 on the other, 13...e5 seems correct. This led to very sharp, and it seems to me well balanced play after 14 g3 ♕g4 15 ♖e1 exd4 16 ♗c4 b6 17 b4 bxc5 18 bxc5 ♕h5 19 ♖c1 ♘e5 20 ♘f6+ ♗xf6 21 ♘xe5 ♔g7 22 ♕xh5 gxh5 23 ♘xc6 ♗g4 and although the white c-pawn holds some dangers for Black, the two bishops are, as so often in the ...g6 lines, an important trump (*editor's note:* Chekhov gives 24 ♗a6 as '!±').

d3) **8...dxc4** 9 ♗xc4 ♗d6 also looks illogical, since White has gained a3 free of charge. Still, in Yusupov-M.Gurevich, Belgrade 1991 White was unable to exploit this especially after **10 ♘e4 ♕e7 11 ♘xd6** ♕xd6 12 0-0 ♕e7! (12...0-0 13 e4! Δe5 is quite serious) 13 ♕c2 (13 e4 e5 14 d5 ♘b6 Δ...♗g4 in traditional manner is fine for Black) 13...0-0 14 ♗a2 ♖d8 15 ♖ad1 a5!? 16 ♗b1 ♘f8 and Black is at worst somewhat cramped. However, I don't think the idea will catch on. Apart from anything else simply **10 0-0** or **11 0-0** will reach a position analogous to the main game when it is hard to believe that the extra a3 damages White's cause.

d4) **8...♕d8** has been the main line, but is not necessarily best. A few examples:

d41) **9 e4?!** is not best here since Black has an elegant freeing tactic: 9...dxe4 10 ♘xe4 ♗e7 11 g3 (11 ♗d3 e5! 12 dxe5 {12 d5?! is still worse positionally} 12...♘xe5 13 ♘xe5 ♕a5+ 14 ♕d2 ♕xe5 15 f4 ♕c7 16 0-0 ♗f5∓ Rashkovsky-Sveshnikov, USSR 1981 gave Black the two bishops and the d4 square at which to aim) 11...0-0 12 ♗g2 e5! with at least equal play in Korchnoi-Dreev, Manila IZ 1990.

d42) **9 ♕c2** led to a fascinating tussle between two of the world's finest young talents in Ivanchuk-Anand, Linares 1992: 9...♗e7 10 ♗d3 0-0 11 0-0 a6 12 ♘e2 (12 ♖ac1 ♖b8!? 13 ♖fd1 b5 14 cxd5 exd5 15 e4 dxe4 16 ♗xe4 ♗d6!= was Tukmakov-Illescas, Wijk aan Zee 1993) 12...♗d6 13 c5 ♗b8 14 e4 e5?! (too ambitious; 14...dxe4 15 ♗xe4 e5 16 ♖fd1 exd4 17 ♘exd4 ♕f6 would have adequately contended the central dark squares) 15 ♖ad1 f5!? 16 exd5 e4 17 d6 exf3 18 ♘f4 ♘f6 19 ♖fe1 ♗xd6 (otherwise White's bind is too strong) 20 cxd6 ♕xd6 21 g3 with a clear positional plus.

d43) After **9 ♗d3**, **9...g6** seems less appropriate here than on the previous move. Lerner-Dreev, USSR Ch 1989 favoured White after 10 e4 dxe4 (10...dxc4!?) 11 ♘xe4 ♘f6 12 c5 ♘xe4 13 ♗xe4 ♗g7 14 ♘e5 ♕g5 15 ♕d2! ♗xe5 16 ♕xg5 hxg5 17 dxe5 g4 18 f4! with an ending in which the relative worth of the respective bishops determines White's plus. Hence Black should play **9...♗e7** transposing to 8 ♗d3 ♕d8 note 'b4' below.

8 ... dxc4

The analysis of 8 a3 gave some preview of the range of possible piece configurations between which Black may choose here. This however is a good moment to describe these more systematically, and to attempt to shed a little light on their relative merits. Basically Black has tried four important independent ideas here (others are usually inferior or merely transpositional). In addition to the text:

1) The rationale for 7 e3 discussed above touched on the various possibilities arising from the main line where Black plays ...♗d6 and ...♕e7. The ideal case arises where Black delays capturing on c4, and White plays a premature e4 allowing the ...dxc4 and ...e5 break under the ideal circumstances of Black's bishop pair and control of the light squares. However, White can better try 10 c5! examined below, which gives

Black a rather passive and negative defensive task. The text move above is an attempt to pre-empt this, but again, so long as White avoids e4, he gains a position similar to many encountered in the QGD where Black's problems developing the c8 bishop satisfactorily provides ample compensation for the fact that it is part of a pair. I have to confess to finding the apparent enduring appeal of ...♗d6 lines rather masochistic.

2) 8...♕d8 and ...♗e7 was for a long time the main alternative mode of deployment. Black has lost time with his queen and again Black's game seems rather passive. White's best is to simply build quietly when Black usually feels obliged to stop e4 once and for all with ...f5, leading to a kind of Dutch Stonewall when the loss of knight for White's dark-squared bishop has some plus and minus points. It seems they do not cancel out to an equal game.

3) 8...g6!?, the modern idea, has again, as after 8 a3, caught my affections here. Interestingly When White plays for the minority attack with 9 cxd5 and a later b4, the play almost exactly transposes to the now quite unfashionable line of the Grünfeld which commences 1 d4 ♘f6 2 c4 g6 3 ♘c3 d5 4 ♘f3 ♗g7 5 ♗g5 ♘e4 6 cxd5 ♘xg5 7 ♘xg5 e6 8 ♘f3 exd5 9 e3 0-0 10 b4 etc. Whilst it is not exclusively at White's behest that this line is no longer in favour, and there are some differences of nuance from the Semi-Slav approach, it does seem to offer good equalizing prospects. If White eschews e5 then Black seems to obtain good play on the dark squares. If does he plays it, then this centre looks as if it should be vulnerable to nibbling commencing ...c5.

a) **8...♗d6 9 0-0** (9 e4!? dxe4 {9...dxc4 10 e5!±} 10 ♘xe4 ♗b4+ 11 ♔f1 ♕d8 12 c5 0-0 13 ♕e2!? ♗a5 14 ♖d1 ♗c7 15 h4 e5 16 ♗c2 exd4?! {16...♕e7! looks better although White's position is nevertheless not without attacking prospects} 17 ♖xd4 ♕e7 18 ♕d3!± and the black king is much the more inconvenienced; Stempin-Bany, Polish Ch 1987) **9...♕e7** *(75)* and now:

75
W

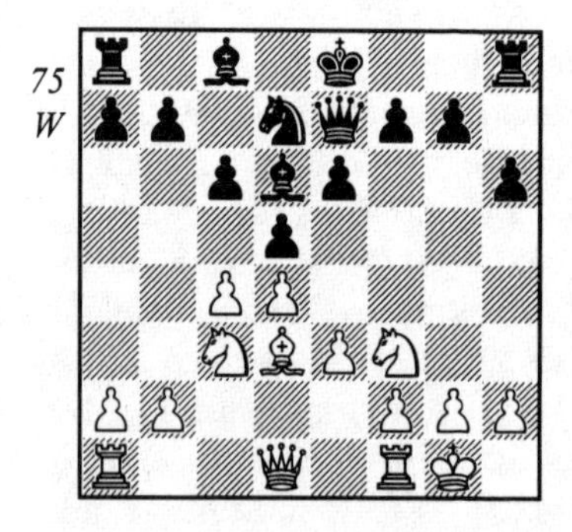

a1) **10 c5!** is the main drawback to this method for Black. The second player rarely activates his pieces sufficiently that the hole at d5 becomes a factor. **10...♗c7 11 e4 dxe4** (Black got into big trouble trying for too long to avoid ...dxe4 in Van der Sterren-Thesing, Nettetal 1992 after 11...0-0 12 ♖e1 ♕d8 13 b4 b6 14 ♕c2 ♗b7 15 ♖ab1 ♕c8 16 h3 a5 17 exd5! exd5 18 ♗f5 axb4 19 cxb6 bxc3 20 bxc7 ♕xc7 21 ♖e7 ♖ad8 22 ♘e5 ♗c8 and 1-0) **12 ♘xe4** (12 ♗xe4 is also promising) **12...0-0** and now:

a11) **13 ♕e2** ♖fd8 (This variation does not reward impatience, 13...e5? 14 ♘d6 ♗xd6 15 exd6 ♕xd6 16 dxe5 ♕e7 17 ♕e4 g6 18 e6± Danielian-Zoler, Duisburg 1992 being one warning example) 14 ♖fd1 (14 ♖ad1 ♘f8 15 a3 ♗d7 16 ♖fe1 f6!? 17 ♗c4 ♔h8 18 ♘g3 ♕f7 19 b4 ♖e8 20 ♕c2 ♘g6 21 ♕f5 ♖e7 22 ♕e4 ♖d8 23 ♗d3 ½-½ Sturua-Lputian, Protvino Z 1993 was typical of the outcome when Black successfully stabilizes his kingside) 14...♘f8 (the c8 bishop is often headed for e8 to bolster Black's kingside, giving the g6 square in particular much needed support) 15 ♘g3 ♘d7 16 ♘e4 ♘f8 17 ♘c3 (17 a3 ♗d7 18 b4 ♗e8 19 g3 ♘d7 20 ♗f1 ♘f8 21 ♕b2 f6 22 ♖e3 ♗f7 23 ♘ed2 ♕d7 24 ♖ae1 ♖ab8 25 ♕c3 ♖e8 26 a4 ♖bd8 27 b5 ♖e7 28 ♕b4 g5 29 ♘e4 ♘h7 30 b6 was an excellent controlled execution of White's plan in Ruban-Sveshnikov, Anapa 1991, and after 30...♗b8 31 bxa7 ♗xa7 32 ♘d6 ♗b8 33 ♘f5 ♖ee8 34 ♘xh6 White was reaping huge rewards) 17...♘d7 (without the above jockeying for position Komarov-Sveshnikov, USSR 1987 went here instead 15...♗d7 16 b4 ♗e8 17 ♗c2 b6 18 ♖ab1±. White can still threaten to take action on either side of the board, but as usual here, although Black is cramped no automatic plan is available) 18 ♗c2 ♘f6 19 ♘e5 ♗d7 20 ♘e4 ♘d5 21 ♘c3 ♗e8? (Impatience. After 21...♘f6 the onus would be on White to show that he can improve the position) 22 ♘xd5 cxd5 23 ♕d3 with advantage; C.Hansen-Sveshnikov, Palma de Mallorca 1989.

a12) **13 ♖e1** ♖d8 (After 13...♘f6 14 ♘xf6+ ♕xf6 15 ♕e2 ♖d8 16 b4 ♗d7 17 a4 ♗e8 18 ♖ab1 White also enjoyed a persistent initiative in Lautier-Bisguier, New York 1991. However, 13...b6!? 14 b4 a5 15 a3 ♗a6 16 ♗xa6 ♖xa6 17 ♕d3 ♖aa8 Sturua-Dolmatov, USSR 1978 is a defensive method worth consideration) 14 ♕c2 (14 ♖c1 ♘f8 15 b4 ♗d7 16 a4 ♗e8 17 ♕b3 ♖ab8 18 ♕c3 b6!? 19 cxb6 ♗xb6 20 ♘c5 ♗xc5 21 dxc5 ♕b7 22 ♖b1 ♘d7 23 ♗c2 ♘f6 24 ♘e5± Beliavsky-Anand, SWIFT Rapid 1992) 14...♘f8 15 ♘c3 ♗d7 16 ♖ad1 ♗e8 17 b4± Epishin-Sorokin, Norilsk 1987. White has the customary spatial plus.

a2) Also worth a mention was the course of Kiselev-Guliev, Azov teams 1991. Here White delayed c5, and a later ...a6 by Black seemed to enable it under still better circumstances, viz: **10 ♕c2!?**

0-0 11 ♖ac1 a6 12 c5(!) ♗c7 13 e4 dxe4 14 ♘xe4 e5 15 ♖fe1! exd4 16 ♘eg5 ♕xc5 17 ♕b3! ♕d5 18 ♕xd5 cxd5 19 ♘h7! ♗b6 20 ♘xf8 and although Black has two pawns for the exchange, his position is undeveloped and White can soon clarify his material and positional pluses.

b) **8...♕d8 9 0-0 ♗e7** (9...♗d6?! does not fit in well here, since after 10 e4 dxc4 11 ♗xc4 e5 12 dxe5 ♗xe5 {12...♘xe5 sadly loses a pawn here} 13 ♘xe5 ♘xe5 14 ♕xd8+ ♔xd8 15 ♗b3 ♔e7 16 f4 ♘d3 17 ♖ad1 ♘c5 18 f5! the ending clearly favours White; Karpman-Stripunsky, Ukrainian Ch 1990) and now White has a large choice although the fundamental choice is whether or not to go for an early e4. We shall consider:

b1) **10 ♕e2?!** strangely does not seem to fit in well either with e4, or with the 'Stonewall' structures arising from an early ...f5: 10...0-0 11 e4?! (11 ♖ac1 a6! 12 ♖fd1 f5 13 ♕c2 ♗d6 14 ♕b1?! {14 ♘e2=} 14...♕e7 15 cxd5 cxd5 16 ♗f1 g5!∓ Cvitan-Nikolić, Yugoslav Ch 1982) 11...dxc4 12 ♗xc4 b5 13 ♗d3 b4 14 ♘a4 ♕a5! 15 b3 ♗b7 16 ♖ac1 ♖fd8 17 ♘d2 c5 18 ♘c4 ♕c7∓ Ree-Sveshnikov, Wijk aan Zee 1981.

b2) **10 cxd5** exd5 11 a3 a5 12 ♕e2 0-0 13 ♖ab1 (White can also play in the centre. Bönsch-Sveshnikov, Sochi 1984 saw 13 ♖ad1 ♗d6 14 e4 dxe4 15 ♘xe4 ♘f6 16 ♘e5 ♗e6 17 ♖fe1∞) 13...♘f6 14 b4 ♗d6!? (14...axb4) 15 b5!? ♗xa3 16 bxc6 bxc6 17 ♘a4 ♕d6 18 ♘e5± Kunstowicz-Westerinen, Bochum 1981.

b3) **10 e4** dxc4 11 ♗xc4 b5 (Black was very restrained in Schmidt-Keitlinghaus, Prague 1990, playing 11...0-0 12 ♕e2 b6 13 ♖fd1 ♗b7 14 ♖ac1 ♖e8 15 a3 a6 16 ♗a2 ♕b8 17 ♗b1 ♕a7 18 ♕c2 ♖ad8 19 d5 ♘f8 20 dxe6 fxe6 ½-½. However, this would not have universal appeal!) 12 ♗d3! ♗b7 13 ♖c1 0-0 14 e5!? ♕b6 15 ♗e4 ♖fd8 16 ♕e2± Rastensis-Chernin, USSR 1985.

b4) **10 a3 0-0** and now:

b41) **11 ♕c2** (immediate breaks do not look very effective here: 11 e4 dxc4 12 ♗xc4 c5!? Sveshnikov; or 11 b4 ♕c7 12 ♕b3 dxc4 13 ♕xc4 e5 14 ♗c2 exd4 15 exd4 ♘f6 16 ♖fe1 a5= which was a previous Lerner-Sveshnikov tussle, USSR Ch 1979) 11...a6 12 ♖ac1 (12 e4 dxc4 13 ♗xc4 b5 14 ♗a2 c5 15 ♖ad1 cxd4 16 ♖xd4 ♕e7 was comfortable for Black in Gavrikov-Sveshnikov, USSR Ch 1981. 12 b4 is of course also possible here. Black should probably play again for a quick ...e5 with 12...dxc4 13 ♗xc4 ♗f6 etc. In the game Kramnik-M.Gurevich, Alcobendas (4) 1993 Black preferred the Dutch structure, but the circumstances were favourable for White after 12...f5?! 13 c5! ♗f6 14 a4 g5 15 b5 a5?! 16 ♘e2 ♗g7 17 ♖ab1 ♕e7 18 ♘d2±) 12...f5 (Black showed another approach which seems valid in Tukmakov-M.Gurevich, Wijk aan Zee 1993 with 12...♖b8 13 ♖fd1 b5 14 cxd5 cxd5 15 e4 dxe4 16 ♗xe4 ♗d6 17 g3 ♕b6 18 ♕e2 ♘f6=) 13 cxd5 cxd5 14 ♘a4 ♗d6 15 b4 ♖f7 16 ♕b2 ♖e7. Black has satisfactorily covered his weak points, and if White does nothing he can even look to the kingside. In Lerner-Sveshnikov, USSR Ch 1985, White played 17 ♘e5 ♘xe5 18 dxe5, but following 18...♗c7 intending the solid ...♗d7 and ...♖b8 it is not clear how White creates further threats. Note that ...a6 was an important preparation for ...f5 to prevent cxd5 and ♘b5 in reply.

b42) **11 ♖c1** a6 12 e4 dxc4 13 ♗xc4 b5 14 ♗a2 c5?! (14...♗b7 seems safer. The text allows White a very strong breakthrough in the centre) 15 d5! c4 16 e5! exd5 17 ♕xd5 ♖b8 18 e6 fxe6 19 ♕xe6+ ♔h8 20 ♖cd1 with tremendous pressure on the d- and e-files, and the constant motif of threats on the b1-h7 diagonal, hence ± Kramnik-M.Gurevich, Alcobendas (2) 1993.

c) **8...g6!? 9 0-0** (The recent addition of 9 h4 to White's armoury should be taken seriously. White's idea is as much to weaken Black on the light squares – f5 in particular – as to attack crudely on the kingside. P.Nikolić-Novikov, Bosna-Garant Donbass 1993 continued 9...♗g7 10 cxd5 {10 ♕c2!? ♕e7 11 0-0-0 ♘f6∞} 10...exd5 11 h5 g5 12 ♕c2 ♕e7 {12...♘b6!? 13 0-0-0 ♗g4 14 ♖dg1 0-0-0 15 ♘e5 ♗e6= Novikov is perhaps simpler} 13 0-0-0 ♘f6 14 ♔b1 ♗e6 15 ♘e5 ♘g4 16 ♘xg4 ♗xg4 17 ♖c1 0-0 18 ♘e2 ♗xe2 19 ♕xe2 ♖ad8 20 g4 ♖d6 21 ♗c2 ♖b8 22 ♕d3 b6=) **9...♗g7** *(76)* (for the popular alternative 9...dxc4 see 8...dxc4 9 ♗xc4 g6!? below) and now:

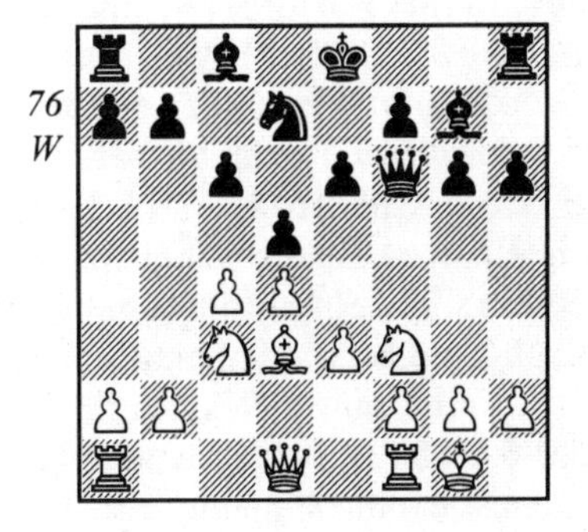

c1) **10 cxd5** exd5 11 b4 ♕d6! (probably the most accurate, intending to answer the immediate 12 b5 with ...c5!; 11...0-0 12 b5! ♕d6 13 bxc6 bxc6 14 ♖c1 c5 15 dxc5 ♘xc5 16 ♗c4! ♗e6 17 ♗xd5 ♖ad8 18 ♗xe6 ♕xe6 19 ♘d4 favoured White in Ruban-Lazić, Yugoslavia 1993) 12 ♕b3 ♘b6 13 a4 ♗e6 14 ♘d2 0-0 15 ♖fc1 ♘d7 16 ♖ab1 (16 ♘e2!) and now Black should have played the immediate 16...a5 since 17 b5 c5 is good, or 17 bxa5 ♖xa5 18 ♕c2 b6∞ (Serper).

c2) **10 e4** dxc4 (10...dxe4 11 ♘xe4 ♕e7 12 ♖e1±) 11 e5! (11 ♗xc4 e5! 12 d5 ♘b6 13 ♗e2 0-0 14 ♕b3 15 exd5 ♗f5∓ Finegold-Kuczynski, Groningen 1992) 11...♕e7 12 ♗xc4 0-0 (Partos suggests 12...c5 as a possible improvement, pointing out the line 13 d5 ♘xe5 14 ♗b5+ ♔f8 15 d6 ♘xf3 16 gxf3 ♕g5+ 17 ♔h1 ♗e5, and therefore preferring 13 ♘e4 0-0) 13 ♕c2 b6 (Fauland suggests 13...a6, e.g. 14 ♗d3 b5 15 ♗e4 ♗b7 16 ♖ac1 ♖fd8) 14 ♖fe1 a6 (14...♗b7 is best met by 15 ♖ad1, according to Fauland, to meet 15...c5 with 16 d5, and the passive 15...♖ad8 with 16 ♗a6) 15 ♗d3 ♗b7 16 ♗e4 ♖a7 17 ♖ac1 b5 18 ♕e3! b5 19 d5! led to trouble for Black in Kamsky-Kramnik, Lucerne Wch teams 1993.

d) **8...♗b4** is worth mentioning among the 'others' mainly because White's excellent early play in the game P.Nikolić-Korchnoi, Skellefteå 1989 was instructive for how to exploit a space advantage. The game went 9 0-0 0-0 (9...♕e7 10 a3 ♗xc3 Δ...dxc4 and ...e5 is a better attempt to free Black's game) 10 e4! dxe4 11 e5! ♕d8 12 ♗xc4 b6 13 ♘e4 ♗b7 14 ♕e2 ♖e8 15 ♖fd1 ♘f8 16 a3 ♗e7 17 h4! and White began the transition to a direct attack.

9 ♗xc4 ♗d6

In the analogous position covered earlier with 8 a3 added, Gurevich suggested 9...♗e7 intending to meet ♘e4 with ...♕f5. It remains untested, and I am a bit sceptical. However, the recent trend towards treating these positions with the kingside fianchetto has an important variant here, and **9...g6** has in the last couple of years become a major alternative to the text. A few examples after **10 0-0 ♗g7** *(77)*:

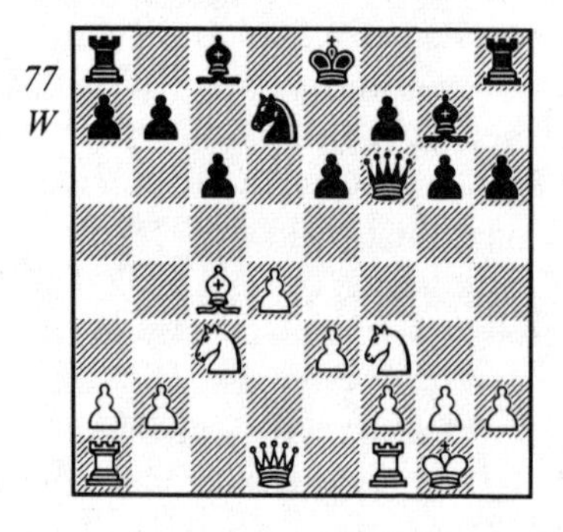
77
W

a) **11 ♖c1** 0-0 12 e4 (12 ♗b3 ♕e7 13 ♖e1 ♖d8 14 ♘e4 e5 15 ♕c2 ♘f8 16 ♘xe5 ♗xe5 17 dxe5 ♕xe5 18 f4 ♕f5 19 ♕b1 ♗e6= Rogozenko-Novikov, Debrecen 1992) 12...e5 13 d5 ♘b6 14 dxc6 bxc6 15 ♗e2 ♖d8 16 ♕c2 ♗g4 17 ♘b1 ♗xf3 18 ♗xf3 ♖d6 19 ♘d2 h5 20 ♘b3 a5 21 ♖fd1 ♖xd1+ 22 ♖xd1 ♕e6 23 a3 ♕c4 24 ♖c1 ♕xc2 25 ♖xc2 ♘a4 26 ♘c1 ♖b8 27 b3 ♗h6 28 ♗d1 ♘b2 29 ♖xb2 ♗xc1 30 ♖a2 ♖d8 31 ♗e2 ♖d2 32 ♖xd2 ♗xd2 33 ♗c4 ½-½ Van der Sterren-Kamsky, Wijk aan Zee Ct (7) 1994.

b) **11 ♘e4** ♕e7 12 ♖c1 0-0 13 ♗b3 b6!? 14 ♗a4 c5 15 ♗c6 ♖b8 16 ♕a4 ♗b7 17 ♗xb7 ♖xb7 18 dxc5 bxc5 with virtual equality in Lutz-Knaak, Baden-Baden 1992.

c) **11 ♕c2!? 0-0** 12 ♗b3 ♕e7 13 ♖ad1 b6 14 e4! ♗b7 15 ♖fe1 ♖fd8 16 e5 ♘f8 17 ♕e2 c5 18 d5 exd5 19 ♘xd5 ♗xd5 20 ♗xd5 ♖ac8 21 ♕c4 ♖e8 22 h4 with a slight pull for White, but later drawn in Chernin-Kuczynski, Debrecen 1992.

d) **11 b4!? 0-0** 12 ♖c1 ♕e7 (the immediate 12...e5 may be possible here, and it certainly fared better than the version one move later: 13 ♗b3 exd4 14 ♘xd4 ♖e8 15 ♕c2 ♕d6 16 b5 c5 17 ♘f3± at best in Aseev-Zviagintsev, Rostov 1993) 13 ♕b3 a5 (Here 13...e5 was beautifully punished by 14 b5! exd4?! 15 exd4 ♘b6 16 ♖fe1 ♕d6 17 bxc6 bxc6 18 ♗xf7+! ♖xf7 19 ♖e8+ ♗f8 20 ♘e5 ♕f6 21 ♘e4 ♕f4 22 ♖xc6 ♔g7 23 g3 ♕f5 24 g4 ♕f4 25 ♖xg6+ ♔h7 26 ♘f6+ 1-0 in Lutz-Kuczynski, Bundesliga 1993) 14 b5 ♕b4!? with fair play in Razuvaev-Zviagintsev, Moscow Tal mem 1992.

10 0-0

The possibility of check on b4 means that while **10 ♘e4** is playable it does not create special problems for Black. In Ribli-Dreev, Calcutta 1992 the players concluded a rapid peace treaty after 10...♗b4+ 11 ♔e2 ♕d8 12 ♕c2 0-0 13 ♖hd1 ♕c7 14 a3 ♗e7 15 ♖ac1 ♖d8 16 h3 b6 17 ♔f1 ½-½.

10 ... ♕e7

11 ♘e4

It seems that if White avoids the text, Black can effect a fairly problem-free ...e5 break: **11 ♕c2 0-0** 12 a3 (12 ♖ac1 e5 13 ♘e4 exd4 14 ♘xd6 ♕xd6 15 ♖fd1 ♘b6 16 ♖xd4 ♕e7 17 ♗b3 ♗e6= Stone-L.B.Hansen, Groningen 1992) 12...e5 13 ♗a2 ♘f6 14 dxe5 ♗xe5 15 ♘xe5 ♕xe5 16 ♖ae1 ♗e6 17 ♗b1 ♖ad8 18 f4 ♕d6 19 e4 ♕d4+ 20 ♕f2 ♗c4 21 ♕xd4 ♖xd4 22 ♖f3 ♖d2 23 b4 ♖fd8 24 e5 ♘e8 25 f5 ♘c7 26 ♖g3 ♔f8= I.Sokolov-Dreev, Biel IZ 1993.

11 ... ♗c7

An important position, the hallmark of which is slow manoeuvring with White trying to make something of his considerable spacial plus, often by playing on both sides, and in the centre (e4-e5). Black's role seems to be mostly one of prophylaxis – for example the key manoeuvre ...♘f8, ...♗d7-e8 followed by ...f6 and the use of the bishop on f7 and g6 covering direct threats. Black's main hope of the full point seems to lie in White overstretching, but this has happened often enough that GM Robert Kuczynski has virtually made a living from this position, while Mikhail Gurevich, Anand and in particular Dreev have shown a willingness to defend it. Black's position is indeed hard to break down, but I cannot escape the feeling that the task of the defence is none too enjoyable.

12 ♖c1 0-0

13 ♕c2

Since Black rarely plays for an early break ideas are more important than move order. Still **13 ♗b3** has appeared often: 13...♖d8 14 ♕e2 a5 (14...♘f8 15 ♘e5 ♖b8 16 f4 f6 17 ♘d3 ♔h8 18 ♘dc5 a5 19 a3 ♖a8 20 ♕c2 b6 21. ♘d3 ♗d7 22 ♕c4 ♖ac8 23 ♗a2 ♗e8 24 b4 ♗g6 25 ♘ef2± and White made further progress with a due e4-e5 in Cebalo-Kuczynski, Polanica Zdroj 1992) 15 a3 ♘f6(?!) – oddly this exchange of pieces seems in no way to benefit the defence – 16 ♘xf6+ ♕xf6 17 ♖fd1 ♗d7 18 ♖c5 ♗e8 19 ♕c2 ♕e7 20. ♗a2 ♗d6 21 ♖c3 ♖ac8 (21...e5!?) 22 h4! g6 23 e4± Bareev-Anand, Linares 1992.

13 ... ♖d8

Black tried an interesting idea to enable ...e5 by **13...♔h8!?** 14 a3 e5 15 ♘g3 ♘b6 16 ♗a2 exd4 17 ♘xd4 ♗d7 18 ♘df5 ♕f6 19 f4 g6 with reasonable success in P.Cramling-Knaak, Hamburg 1991.

14 ♖fd1

14 a3 a5 15 ♗a2 ♖b8 16 ♗b1 ♘f8 17 ♖fd1 ♗d7 18 ♘e5 ♗e8 19 f4 f6 20 ♘c4(?!) ♗g6 21 ♕c3 ♗h5 22 ♖e1 ♖a8 23 ♘c5 ♖a7 24 ♖f1 ♗f7 25 ♖f2 b6 26 ♘e4 ♖aa8 27 ♘cd2 ♖ec8 28 b4? ♗d6!∓ Savchenko-Kuczynski, Groningen 1992, is an instructive example of Black patiently defending, covering all weak spots until White mistimes his break.

14 ... a5

Dreev has often preferred **14...♘f8** first, although it is often transpositional. One independent example: 15 ♘c5!? ♗d6 16 ♘d3 ♗d7 17 e4 ♗e8± Chernin-Dreev, Moscow 1989, with typical play.

15 ♗b3	**♘f8**
16 a3	**♗d7**
17 ♘c5	**♖a7**

This looks like the most logical defence of b7 since the rook on the a-file is well placed if White plays for b4, and can help to defend a6 in the event that Black wants to evict White's intruding knight with ...b6. The alternative **17...♖b8** was tried, however, in Yusupov-M.Gurevich, Munich 1993 which went 18 e4! ♗c8 (18...♗e8 19 e5 ♗b6 20 ♘e4± Yusupov) 19 ♘d3 ♘g6 20 e5 ♘h4?! 21 ♘de1! ♘xf3+ (21...♘g6!?±) 22 ♘xf3 ♗d7 23 ♕e4 c5!? (I must admit, when I first saw this my reaction was that if Black wanted to play so actively he should have chosen a different variation! Still, whilst the counterplay is insufficient, he already had severe problems and it may be the best chance) 24 ♖xc5 ♗c6 25 ♕f4 ♗xf3!? 26 gxf3! b5 27 ♔h1± but with serious technical problems still to come.

18 e4	**♗e8**
19 e5	**♗b6** *(78)*

The same position only with the white bishop on a2 not b3 arose in Sakaev-Dreev, Brno 1992. There Black chose **19...b6** but the conclusion 20 ♘a4 ♖aa8 ½-½ suggests the players had other priorities than enlightening the public. 20 ♘e4 looks more to the point.

78
W

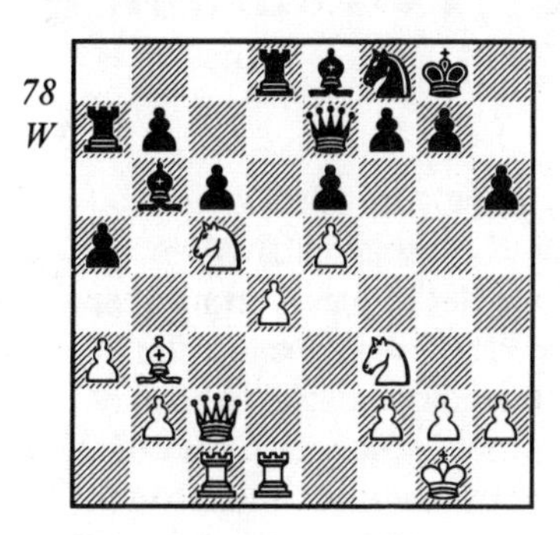

20 ♘e4	**♖aa8**
21 ♗a2	**♖d7**
22 ♕b3	**♗a7**

Necessary to cover c5. **22...♕d8** 23 ♘c5! is unpleasant.

23 ♘d6	**♕d8**

Black's plan of doubling rooks on the d-file has been forestalled since **23...♖ad8** would be met with 24 ♕c3 and defence of a5 is suddenly a problem. After the text, White should continue to build with **24 ♗b1**. Instead he impatiently grabs a pawn, and enables Black to sacrifice the exchange to secure dangerous counterchances.

24 ♘xb7?	**♖xb7!**
25 ♕xb7	**♗b6!**
26 d5!	

Seems to be the only way out for the white queen against Black's threat of ...♖a7. There is no good way to accumulate material for her majesty since **26 ♖xc6?** ♖b8 27 ♖xb6 ♖xb7 28 ♖xb7 ♗c6 embarrasses the rook in turn (29 ♖b3 ♗d5∓).

26 ...	**cxd5!**

But not **26...exd5?** 27 ♖xc6! ♖b8 28 ♖xb6 ♖xb7 29 ♖xb7 ♗c6 30 ♗xd5! ♗xd5 31 ♖b5±.

27 ♘d4	**♘g6**
28 ♘c6	**♗xc6**
29 ♕xc6	**♘xe5**
30 ♕c2	**♘g4**
31 ♖f1	**♖b8**
32 ♗b1	**g6**
33 h3	**♘f6**

The position has settled down and White's earlier indiscretion has cost him quite dear. Black has only one pawn for the exchange, but White's centre has collapsed, his two vs one on the queenside is immobile and it is clearly Black who derives attacking chances from the presence of the opposite-coloured bishops.

Still in the harsh real world, time-trouble rears its ugly head even in promising positions, and Dreev allows White to gain control of first the c-file and then, critically, the 8th rank to decisive effect: **34 ♕d2 ♔g7 35 ♖c6 ♕d7?!** (Better was 35...♗c7) **36 ♖fc1 ♕a7 37 ♕f4 ♖b7?! 38 ♖c8 ♘d7 39 ♕d6! ♗d4 40 ♔h1 ♗e5 41 ♕e7 1-0**.

White threatens 42 ♕d8 to which there is no satisfactory defence, e.g. 41...♕xf2 42 ♕d8 f5 43 ♕e7# or 41...h5 42 ♕e8 f5 43 ♕xe6 ♖b6 44 ♖g8+ ♔h7 45 ♕e7+ ♔h6 46 ♖cc8 ♗6 47 ♖h8+ ♔g5 48 ♕e3+ f4 49 h4+ Yusupov.

Section 2: 5 e3 ♘bd7 6 ♗d3 dxc4
The Meran Defence – Introduction

This section covers the historic Meran Defence which arises when White eschews the complications of 5 ♗g5, and adopts what may be viewed as his most natural mode of development. White does not fear losing a tempo playing first ♗d3 and then ♗xc4 since Black will have to play ...c6-c5 to attack White's centre, thus returning the compliment (White can of course avoid this tempo loss with 6 ♕c2 which is the main subject of Section 3).

The position after 6...dxc4 7 ♗xc4 bears some structural comparison to the Queen's Gambit Accepted. Here however White has already played ♘c3, which takes the sting out of approaches where White avoids e4 and plays an early a4 to attack Black's queenside pawns – see note on 9 0-0 to Game 20 (simply because if Black replies ...b4, the knight is better placed at home on b1, *en route* for c4 via d2). However, the fact that Black has not yet played ...c5, and that it takes a little preparation, gives White the possibility of a very quick e4 which takes us well away from analogies with the QGA.

As with the introduction to Section 1, I shall attempt to give a guide to the forthcoming chapters and break down a mass of material into a comprehensible form. After the basic sequence 6 ♗d3 dxc4 7 ♗xc4 b5, we can identify no less than six strategically independent possibilities:

a) 8 ♗b3 usually presages a quick advance of e4-e5 with a massive piece attack on e6, with sacrifices in the air. The drawback is that the bishop is (sorry about the cliché) biting on granite if this direct attack fails. It is hence out of favour – see Game 27.

b) 8 ♗e2 is discussed in detail in the introduction to Chapter 18 since it best discussed comparatively with 8 ♗d3. The tactical justification is the possibility of a quick e4 and answering ...b4 with e5 when the exchange of knights favours White in many cases.

c) 8 ♗d3 ♗b7 9 e4 is the subject of Chapters 9-11, and since after the further moves 9...b4 10 ♘a4 c5 White is virtually obliged to answer with 11 e5, a very distinctive structure arises. Black has certain clear strategic pluses (strong knight on d5; good diagonal for the bishop on b7; sometimes too, White's off-side knight on a4). Still, White has a spatial plus and a choice between emphasizing his lead in development with 12 0-0 (Chapters 9 and 10) or seeking to embarrass the black king with 12 dxc5 (Chapter 11).

d) 8 ♗d3 ♗b7 9 0-0 b4 (see Chapter 14). Again Black's strategy foresees the exchange of his c-pawn for White's d-pawn. However, in this case White's e-pawn is still on e3. This gives Black a little more space, but the absence of the strong points discussed under 'c' reduces his chances for counterplay. On the whole theory smiles more kindly on White here.

e) 8 ♗d3 a6 9 e4 c5 10 d5. Known after the English player Reynolds, this is discussed in two parts, according to whether Black plays an early ...♗b7 (Chapter 13 and 14 with ...♗b7, Chapter 15 without). In general, Black tries to compensate for a weak centre pawn by proving that his queenside majority is an asset. Play is very complex, and the use of the phalanx requires mature judgement, since if advanced too extravagantly it can be revealed as weak. On the whole though, Black is fine in the theoretical battle here. In addition the very distinctive consequences of 10...cxd3 11 dxe6 cxd3!? where Black seeks to compensate for his loose d3 pawn with his bishop pair and hold on the light squares (Chapter 16) is very interesting too.

f) 8 ♗d3 a6 9 e4 c5 10 e5 is described here as the 'Old Main Line' (Chapter 17). Recently less popular than 8...♗b7, I predict that this may change in the near future. Curiously, given the early expansion of the two sides, the battle is often between Black with a strong central pawn mass, against White, strong on the flanks. In any case, all the main lines are characterized by a dominating structural asymmetry. In all three of the main games here, Black can find interesting lines worth practical trial.

9 Wade Variation – The Modern Pawn Sacrifice 13 ♘xd4

Much of the recent revival of interest in the Semi-Slav in the former Soviet Union has centred around 8...♗b7 in the Meran. The move rightly bears the name of International Master Bob Wade, who fashioned it into a respected system in the 1950s. Larsen's regular adoption of the variation in the 1970s helped to produce a first peak of popularity, but in the early 1980s it went briefly out of favour. Recently it has almost totally superseded the 'old main line' 8...a6. The new, mainly young, generation of practitioners – Kaidanov, Dreev, Shirov, Chernin, to name but a few, have enjoyed tremendous success with the Wade Variation. This is no doubt due in part to the rather good positional foundations on which it is built. Initially however, the stubbornness with which White players have tried to blow it away with the pawn sacrifice to be examined here, in the face of increasingly discouraging results, helped to produce a score for Black which perhaps flattered just a little. At the time of writing White is investigating less frantic methods, of which perhaps the older 12 dxc5, and the early deviation 9 0-0 are the most promising. However, for all that the brief but intense experience with 13 ♘xd4 has been encouraging for Wade devotees, it would be foolish to rule out the possibility of improvements for White, and in any case, the extremely sharp nature of the play makes a detailed knowledge of this chapter especially essential for Black.

Game 13
I.Sokolov-Shirov
Stockholm 1990

1 d4	**d5**
2 c4	**c6**
3 ♘c3	**♘f6**
4 e3	**e6**
5 ♘f3	**♘bd7**
6 ♗d3	**dxc4**
7 ♗xc4	**b5**
8 ♗d3	**♗b7**
9 e4	**b4**
10 ♘a4	**c5**
11 e5	**♘d5**
12 0-0	**cxd4**
13 ♘xd4 *(79)*	

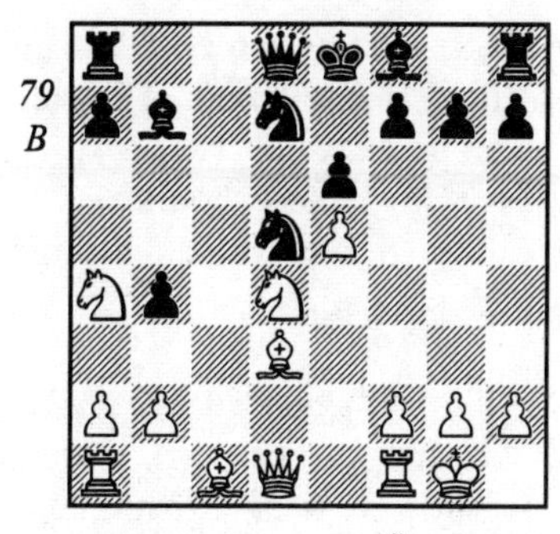

79
B

13 ... ♘xe5!

Acceptance of White's offer is clearly best. The alternatives in brief:

a) **13...♗e7** enables White to play 14 ♖e1, transposing to line 'b' in the note to Black's 13th in Game 14 in which White obtains an attack currently thought to be very dangerous.

b) **13...a6?** is even worse, as it fails to address White's major threat. It is hence surprising to see such an eminent theoretician falling victim to 14 ♘xe6! fxe6 15 ♕h5+ ♔e7 16 ♗g5+ ♘5f6 17 exf6+ gxf6 18 ♗h4 with an obvious advantage; Smagin-Sveshnikov, Sochi 1987.

c) **13...♘c7** prepares to meet **14 ♖e1?** with ...♘xe5, and bolsters the vulnerable e6 point, but the move is fundamentally too passive to equalize. In Chernin-Kaidanov, Lvov 1987 White stood better after **14 ♕e2** ♗e7 15 ♖d1 **0-0** 16 ♗f4 ♘d5 17 ♗g3 ♘7b6 18 ♘xb6 ♕xb6 19 ♘b5 ♗a6 20 ♕e4! g6 21 ♘d6.

d) **13...g6** is also thought to be inadequate. **14 ♕g4! ♗g7 15 ♗g5!** and now:

d1) **15...♕a5!?** 16 ♗b5!?.

d2) **15...♘xe5** 16 ♘xe6! ♘xg4 was Razuvaev-Bagirov, Jurmala 1987; now 17 ♗b5+ ♕d7 18 ♘xg7+ ♔f8 19 ♗xd7 ♘gf6 20 ♘xe6+ fxe6 21 ♗xe6 was the most crushing – Mikhalchishin.

d3) **15...♘e7** 16 ♗b5! ♖c8 17 ♖ac1 h6 18 ♖xc8 ♕xc8 19 ♖c1 ♕a8 20 ♘xe6 fxe6 21 ♗xd7+ ♔xd7 22 ♘c5+ ♔e8 23 ♗xe7 1-0 Van der Sterren-Mednis, Amsterdam 1989.

14 ♗b5+ ♘d7
15 ♖e1

The extraordinary idea **15 ♘c6?! ♕c7 16 ♕xd5** is rather trickier than might appear at first sight. However, I don't believe that it really merits any more than the two top level outings that it has enjoyed:

a) **16...exd5** 17 ♖e1+ ♗e7 18 ♘xe7 ♔d8(!) 19 ♗d2 (19 ♗g5 f6) 19...♕a5 20 ♗c6 ♖e8! 21 ♗xb7 ♖xe7 22 ♖xe7 ♔xe7 23 ♗xa8 (23 ♖e1+ ♔f6! 24 ♘c3!? ♘b6! 25 a3 bxc3! 26 ♗xc3 ♕xc3 27 bxc3 ♖d8 gives Black a better ending) 23...♕xa4 24 ♗d5 and with accurate play White could have held the ending in Piket-M.Gurevich, Ostend 1991.

b) However, satisfactory though this is for Black, it may be the simple plus which Bareev attained by declining the queen offer which finally halts interest in the line. He played **16...♗d6!?** 17 ♖e1 **0-0** (or 17...♔f8!? 18 ♕d4 a6 19 ♘xb4 axb5 20 ♘c3 ♗xh2+ 21 ♔h1 ♕d6 {Bareev} although White may consider 19 ♖d1!? Δ19...axb5 20 ♕xd6+ ♕xd6 21 ♖xd6 ♗xc6 22 ♖xc6 axb4 23 ♗d2!∞) 18 ♕c4! ♖fc8 and now instead of **19 ♗g5?!** ♗xc6 20 ♖ac1 ♘b8! 21 ♕g4 a6 22 ♗f6 ♗f8 23 ♗d3 ♘d7 24 ♗d4 ♕d6! 25 ♘c5 ♘xc5 26 ♖xc5 when 26...g6 should have rendered White's attack illusory in Christiansen-Bareev, Biel 1991, White should have bailed out into a slightly inferior ending with **19 ♘e7+** ♗xe7 20 ♕xc7 ♖xc7 21 ♗f4 e5 22 ♗xe5 ♘xe5, etc.

15 ... ♖c8

It is difficult to generalize about White's compensation for the pawn in this line. Most of the long-term positional trumps are held by Black.

He has the best minor piece – the knight on d5 – and White's knight on a4 is, as so often in the Wade variation, a serious liability. This, along with Black's solid pawn structure often enables Black to return some material to simplify to a superior ending. In short, White's sole strategy in this line is a quick knockout punch using his superior development and the often not so temporary insecurity of Black's king. Practice has shown that Black's resources are sufficient here.

The text is virtually forced:

a) **15...a6??** loses to either 16 ♘c6 or 16 ♗c6 ♕c7 17 ♘xe6! fxe6 18 ♕xd5.

b) **15...♗e7** is also terribly risky and while Mikhalchishin's **16 ♖xe6!?** may not be water-tight after 16...fxe6 17 ♘xe6 ♕a5!? (Van der Vliet), **16 ♘c6(!)** ♕c7 17 ♘xe7 ♔xe7 (17...♘xe7? 18 ♗f4) 18 ♗g5+ ♘7f6 19 ♖c1 should be sufficient to frighten off all but the most masochistic.

16 ♕h5

Speelman suggested **16 ♕e2!?** since in several lines ...g6 merely helps Black. **16 ♕g4** ♘f6 has been shown to be less dangerous: 17 ♕h3 a6 18 ♗xd7+ ♕xd7 19 ♘xe6 fxe6 20 ♘b6 ♕f7 21 ♖xe6+ ♗e7 22 ♖xf6?? ♖d8! **0-1** Ermolinsky-Dreev, Simferopol 1988.

16 ... g6

Still no such luxury as alternatives for the defender. **16...♘f6??** 17 ♘xe6 ♘xh5 18 ♘xg7 mate is one route to an early exit.

17 ♕e2

A major crossroads. In addition to the text, White can try:

a) **17 ♕h3** after which sacrifices on e6 are more than ever the major theme:

a1) **17...♗e7** 18 ♗h6 a6 19 ♗xd7+ ♕xd7 20 ♗g7 ♖g8 21 ♕xh7 ♖xg7 22 ♕xg7 (Buchman-Smagin, Šibenik 1988) 22...♗f6! 23 ♘xe6 ♗xg7 24 ♘ec5+ ♔d8 25 ♘xd7 ♔xd7∓.

a2) **17...a6** is also quite sound, but White seems to have the possibility of a draw with 18 ♗g5! (18 ♘xe6 is not sound in view of 18...fxe6 19 ♕xe6+ ♗e7 20 ♗xa6 ♗xa6 21 ♕xa6 ♘b8! 22 ♕e6 ♕d7 23 ♕e5 **0-0** 24 ♗h6 ♗f6∓/-+ Van der Vliet) 18...♗e7 19 ♗xe7

♕xe7! 20 ♘xe6 fxe6 21 ♖xe6 axb5 (one of many positions in the ♕h3 line where Black can profitably give up his queen) 22 ♖xe7+! (22 ♖ae1? ♕xe6+ ± Oll-Novikov, Tallinn 30 min 1988) 22...♔xe7 23 ♖e1+ ♔d8 24 ♕h4+ ♔c7 25 ♕g3+ ♔d8 26 ♕h4+ ½-½ C.Hansen-Rasmussen, Esbjerg 1988.

b) **17 ♕e5 ♕f6** *(80)* and now:

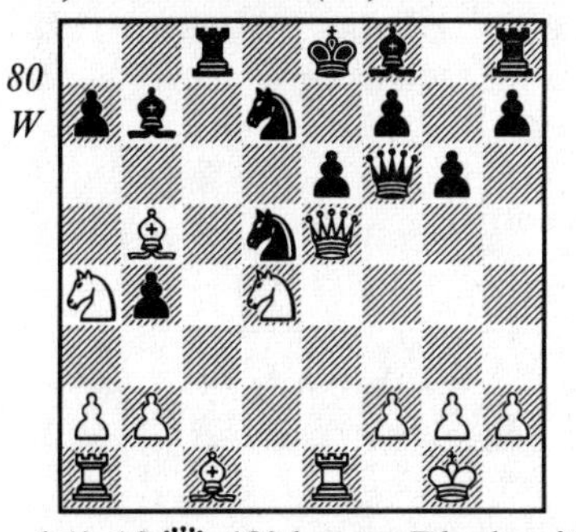

b1) **18 ♕e4?!** leaves Black with only one move, 18...♖c7!, but a good one (instead 18...♗g7? 19 ♘xe6! fxe6 20 ♗g5! is an attacking theme well worth remembering, from Mikhalchishin-Lanc, Trnava 1988). 19 ♕g4 ♗e7 20 ♗h6 a6! 21 ♗xd7+ ♔xd7! (Black's king runs comfortably to the queenside) 22 ♖ad1 ♔c8∓ Wells-Kaidanov, Dublin 1991.

b2) **18 ♕xf6** ♘xf6 19 ♗g5 ♗g7 20 ♗xf6 ♗xf6 was Ftačnik-Tukmakov, Biel 1988 when White could secure a draw but no more with 21 ♘xe6 fxe6 22 ♖xe6+ ♔f7 23 ♗xd7 ♖c7 24 ♖d6 ♔e7 25 ♖e6+!=.

b3) **18 ♘f3(!)** and now:

b31) **18...♗g7** seems quite satisfactory for Black:

b311) **19 ♕g3** ♕d8 20 ♘e5 ♗xe5 21 ♕xe5 0-0 and it is hard for White to exploit the dark squares around the black king; Aseev-Dreev, Lvov Z 1990. In the game White strayed further with 22 ♕d4 ♕f6 23 ♕xa7 ♖c7! and was already in trouble.

b312) **19 ♗xd7+** ♔xd7 20 ♕e2 ♕e7 21 ♕b5+ ♔c7 22 a3 (to open files against the king's new home) 22...♔b8 23 axb4 a6 24 ♕a5 ♕xb4 25 ♕xb4 ♘xb4 26 ♗f4+ ♔a7 27 ♗e3+ ♔b8! 28 ♗f4+ ½-½ Akopian-Dokhoian, USSR Ch 1991.

b32) **18...h6!?** 19 ♗f4?! (19 ♗e3 looks better, although Black must be OK) 19...♔d8! – a novel way of forcing off the queens! – 20 ♕xf6 ♘7xf6 21 ♗e5 ♗g7 22 ♖ac1 ♖xc1 23 ♖xc1 ♔e7 with clear advantage for Black – Obukhov.

17 ... ♕e7

In *NIC Yearbook 15*, Dreev gave this as the only move. It remains his choice, but in the meantime **17...a6!** has been rehabilitated and currently looks perfectly viable too. After **18 ♗xa6** (18 ♗g5? is unsound here in view of 18...♕xg5 19 ♘xe6 ♕xg2+ {the only move here, just as in our main game} 20 ♔xg2 ♘f4++ 21 ♔f1 ♘xe2 22 ♗xd7+ ♔xd7 23 ♘xf8+ ♖cxf8! and White has nothing for the pawn, or 22 ♖xe2 axb5 23 ♘c5+ ♔d8! 24 ♘xb7+ ♔c7 and wins) **18...♗xa6 19 ♕xa6** Black has tried three moves:

a) **19...♖a8?!** was found wanting in the highly instructive game Timman-Nogueiras, Rotterdam 1989, which damaged the reputation of 17...a6 for some time. The game continued 20 ♕c4 ♖xa4 21 ♕xd5 ♗e7 22 ♘xe6! fxe6 23 ♕xe6 ♖a5 (after 23...♖f8 24 ♗g5 ♖f7 25 ♖ad1 threatening ♗xe7 and ♕g8+ there is no defence) 24 ♗h6! ♖f8 25 ♗xf8 ♘xf8 26 ♕c4 ♕d6 27 ♖ad1 ♖e5 28 g3 ♕e6?! (the superiority of the rook and pawns over the minor pieces is more graphic in the endgame although White's superiority should in any case be decisive) 29 ♕xe6 ♖xe6 30 ♖xe6 ♘xe6 31 ♔f1 ♔f7 32 ♖d7 ♘c5 33 ♖a7 ♔e6 34 ♔e2 ♔d6 35 ♔e3 h5 36 ♔d4 ♗f6+ 37 ♔c4 ♗xb2 38 ♔xb4 ♘d3+ 39 ♔b5 ♘xf2 40 ♖a6+ ♔e5 41 ♖xg6 ♔f5 42 ♖c6 ♘g4 43 a4 ♘e5 44 ♖c7 ♗d4 45 a5 ♗g1 46 a6 ♘f3 47 ♖c5+ 1-0. An excellent technical display.

b) Most important for the rehabilitation of 17...a6 though was the discovery that the natural **19...♗g7!** is playable in view of the resource **20 ♗g5** (20 ♘xe6 fxe6 21 ♗g5 ♘c7! 22 ♖xe6+ ♔f7∓) **20...♘c7!**. White has been able to prove absolutely nothing here; on the contrary he has even struggled in the resulting ending.

b1) **21 ♕a5** ♖a8 22 ♗xd8 ♖xa5 23 ♗xc7 ♖xa4 24 ♖ed1 ♘f6 25 ♗e5! (since both the black minor pieces are superior, White ensures the exchange of one pair. The resulting ending is hard to win, since Black has only one queenside pawn, but there is no doubt that it is White on the defensive) 25...0-0 26 a3! ♘d5 27 ♗xg7 ♔xg7∓ I.Sokolov-Chernin, Wijk aan Zee 1991.

b2) **21 ♕b7** ♖b8 22 ♗xd8 ♖xb7 23 ♗xc7 ♖xc7 24 ♘b5 ♖c2 25 ♖ac1 ♖xc1 26 ♖xc1 **0-0!**∓ Vyzhmanavin-Novikov, Moscow 1990.

18 ♗g5

18 ♕g4 ♘f6 19 ♕h3 ♗d5 Vyzhmanavin-Dreev, Moscow 1989 was not too troublesome either for Black.

18 ...	**♕xg5**
19 ♘xe6	**♕xg2+!** *(81)*

81
W

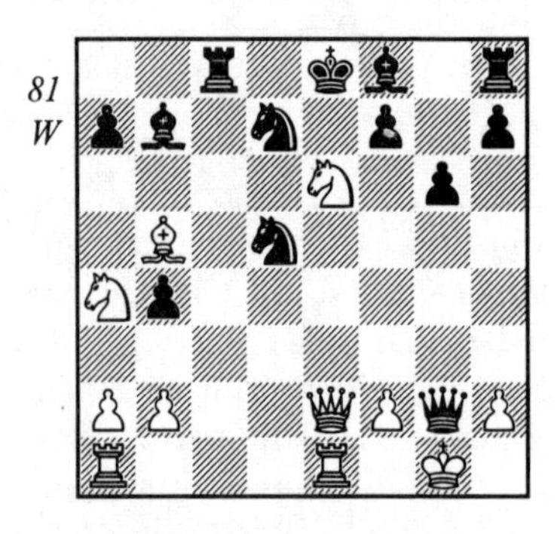

The point of Dreev's idea. After the following forced sequence, an endgame is reached where Black's compensation for the exchange is quite adequate. The position moreover is unbalanced, and Black is quite able to play for a win too.

20 ♔xg2	**♘f4+**
21 ♔f1	**♘xe2**
22 ♖ad1!	**fxe6!**
23 ♗xd7+	**♔f7**
24 ♗xc8	**♗xc8**
25 ♔xe2	**♗a6+** *(82)*

82
W

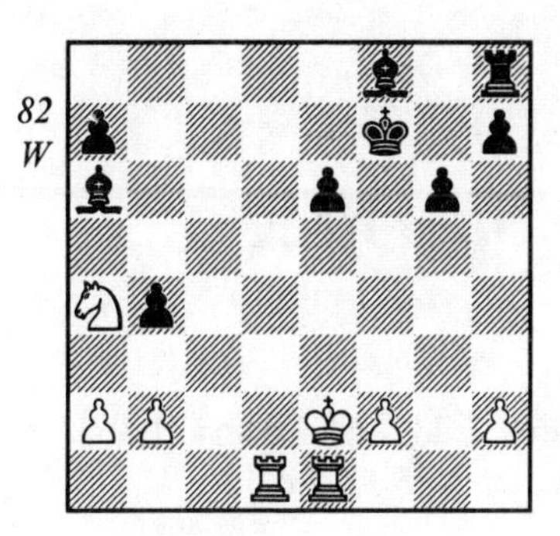

26 ♔e3!

White's attempt to improve with **26 ♔f3?!** in Nadera-Dreev, Manila OL 1992 backfired badly after 26...♗b7+ 27 ♔g3 ♗d5 28 b3 ♗d6+ 29 ♔h3 ♖f8 30 ♘b2 ♔g7 when White's king was up against some quite nasty threats. After he therefore returned the exchange 31 ♖xd5 exd5 32 ♔g2 ♔f6 Black was faced with (albeit not trivial) technical problems only.

26 ... ♗b5

Important to prevent White's rook invading on d7.

27 b3 ♗h6+
28 ♔f3 ♖c8

It was perhaps more solid to prevent the entry of the white rook by **28...♗c6+** 29 ♔g3 ♗d5 30 ♘c5 ♖c8. Still, since in addition to the strengths of his position – the two bishops, the poor position of the knight on a4 and the potential vulnerability of the white king - Black does have some genuine weaknesses – on e6 and a7 for example, it was not possible to have everything. Black preferred to keep the white knight badly placed, even at the expense of further material sacrifice – an interesting choice, typical of Shirov's aggressive style.

29 ♖d6 ♗c6+
30 ♔g3 ♗d5
31 ♖d7+ ♔f6
32 ♖xa7

If **32 ♖xh7** ♗g7! Shirov, and the rook will have a difficult time reentering the fray.

32 ... e5!
33 ♖a5 ♗f4+
34 ♔h3 ♗f3
35 ♘b6

Undoubtedly the main benefit for White in grabbing the a-pawn was the liberation of his knight. Now he had the luxury of two possible routes. Hence **35 ♘c5** ♖d8 36 ♘e4+ also came into consideration, although both 36...♔g7 and 36...♔f5 37 ♘g3+ ♔f6 were possible according to Shirov. After the text, Black's forces become very active, and directly threatening to White's king. White's decision to bail out with a perpetual seems correct.

35 ... ♖d8!
36 ♘c4 e4
37 ♘e3 ♖d2
38 ♘d5+ ♔e5
39 ♘e3+

Shirov suggests that **39 ♘xf4+** ♔xf4 40 ♖a7 ♖xf2 41 ♖f7+ ♔e5 42 ♖xh7 ♖xa2 would be too risky in view of the weakness of b3, and the persistent problem of the white king. Therefore...

39 ... ♔f6
40 ♘d5+ ♔e5
41 ♘e3+ ½-½

10 Wade Variation 12 0-0 – Avoiding the Pawn Sacrifice

After the modern 12 0-0, both sides have alternatives to the wild pawn sac lines considered in the preceding chapter. The main bulk of this chapter will be devoted to White's solid alternative 13 ♖e1. By defending the e-pawn first White hopes to bring his knight to the more active d4 square free of charge. Also keeping the knight on f3 supports a possible ♗g5 which is useful in several lines. Black also has a viable alternative: to avoid 12...cxd4, seeking to retain the tension in the centre and offering White a second chance to enter territory similar to that examined in the next chapter. The best such move is undoubtedly 12...h6 since it is useful in almost all lines where White captures on c5. After a brief spell where White tended to shy away from 9 e4, the material in this chapter is once again highly topical, and finely balanced.

Game 14
Stohl-Sakaev
Dortmund 1992

1 d4 d5 2 ♘f3 ♘f6 3 c4 c6 4 ♘c3 e6 5 e3 ♘bd7 6 ♗d3 dxc4 7 ♗xc4 b5 8 ♗d3 ♗b7 9 e4 b4 10 ♘a4 c5 11 e5 ♘d5 12 0-0

12 ... cxd4

Black has tried other moves. In ascending order of importance:

a) **12...♗e7?!** 13 ♖e1 ♖c8 14 ♘xc5 ♘xc5 15 dxc5 ♗xc5 16 ♘g5!? left Black a tempo down on normal ♘xc5 lines; Darga-Zaitsev, Graz 1979.

b) **12...♖c8** gives White the necessary time to make 13 ♘g5! really threatening. 13...♗e7 (13...cxd4 14 ♘xe6 is strong with White already castled. Compare 12 ♘g5!? discussed in the note to 12 dxc5 in the next chapter) 14 ♕h5 g6 15 ♕h6 ♗f8 16 ♘xe6 ♗xh6 17 ♘xd8 ♔xd8 18 ♗xh6 cxd4 19 ♗e4!± was Razuvaev-Dorfman, USSR 1973.

c) **12...h6!?** *(83)* has been extremely popular of late.

83
W

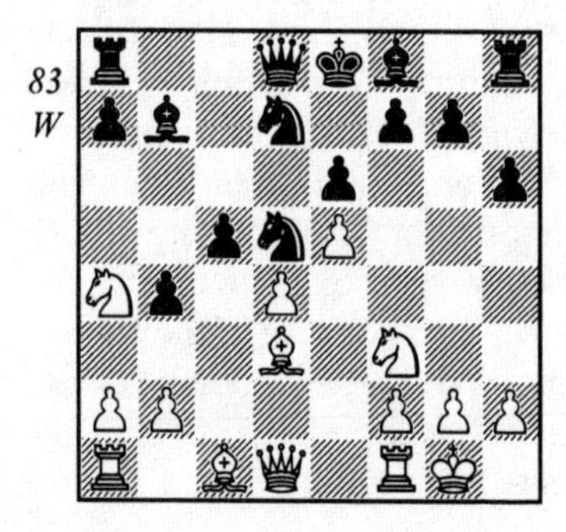

Black tries to show that White has no advantageous waiting moves and will at some stage have to capture on c5. This has both possible psychological (White has rejected these lines initially) and theoretical value. ...h6 is almost always a good move, cutting out ♗g5(+) and sometimes ♘g5. Of course **0-0** is useful for White too, but in some cases may not be critical.

c1) In particular, it is arguable that **13 dxc5 ♗xc5** 14 ♘xc5 ♘xc5 15 ♗b5+ ♔f8 (15...♔e7!?) transposes to a line in which White's **0-0** is not the most testing. Worth a mention is the possibly rather too ambitious **13...a6** 14 ♖e1 ♘xc5 15 ♘xc5 ♗xc5 16 ♘d2(!) ♕b6 17 ♘e4 ♗e7 18 ♕g4 g5 19 a3 ♖d8 20 ♕e2 ♕d4 21 ♗xa6 ♗xa6 22 ♕xa6 ♕xe5 23 ♕a4+ ♔f8 24 ♗d2 ♕xb2 25 axb4 with White somewhat for preference; San Segundo-Illescas, Madrid 1993. White has tried independently:

c2) **13 ♕e2** ♗c6!? 14 ♘xc5 ♘xc5 15 dxc5 ♗xc5 16 ♗d2 ♕b6 17 ♖ac1 ♖c8 18 ♗c4!? 0-0! 19 ♘e1 ♗d4 20 ♘d3 a5 21 ♕g4 ♔h7 22 ♕e4+ ♔g8 23 ♕g4 ♔h7= L.B.Hansen-Rasmussen, Danish Ch 1993.

c3) **13 ♖e1** ♖c8 14 dxc5 ♘xc5 15 ♗b5+ ♗c6 16 ♗xc6= Mikhalchishin-Reefschläger, Balatonbereny 1988.

c4) **13 ♗d2** ♖c8 14 ♕e2 ♗c6!? 15 b3!? ♗xa4 16 bxa4 cxd4 17 ♘xd4 ♗c5 18 ♘b3 ♗e7 19 ♗c4 0-0 20 ♗xd5 exd5 and Black looks fine; Olafsson-Dorfman, France v Iceland 1993.

c5) **13 a3** is in keeping with a tendency for White to try to make play on the queenside in these lines, but Black's resources look fine: 13...a6!? (13...♖c8 also turned out well for Black after 14 dxc5 ♘xc5 15 ♗b5+ ♘d7! 16 axb4 ♗xb4 17 ♘c3 ♗xc3 18 bxc3 ♘xc3 19 ♕xd7+ ♕xd7 20 ♗xd7+ ♔xd7 21 ♖xa7 ♖c7= Anitoaei-Breahna, Romanian Ch 1989) 14 ♖e1 (Perhaps 14 ♕e2 is critical. After 14...♗c6 {14...♗e7!?} 15 ♘xc5 ♗xc5 16 dxc5 ♘xc5 17 ♗c4 0-0 18 axb4 ♘xb4 19 ♖a3 ♗d5!= Black was OK in Psakhis-Gelfand, Tallinn 1989, but 18 b3!± was more promising, claims Psakhis) 14...♖c8!? (14...♕c7? 15 ♗d2 g5 16 dxc5! bxa3, Razuvaev-Shabalov, Jurmala 1987 should have favoured White, had he found 17 bxa3 ♗c6 18 ♖c1 ♗g7 19 ♘b6! ♘7xb6 20 ♗a5±. However, Shabalov's idea to play the immediate 14...g5!? looks a better try) 15 axb4 (15 dxc5 ♗xc5 16 ♘xc5 ♘xc5 17 ♗c2 bxa3 18 ♖xa3 ♘b4 is easy equality for Black, but still safer for White than the text) 15...c4! 16 ♗e4 ♗xb4 17 ♗d2 a5 18 ♘c3 ♘7b6 19 ♗c2 (19 ♕b1!?∓) 19...0-0 20 ♕e2 ♘e7! 21 ♖ad1 ♘g6 22 ♘e4 ♘d5 23 ♘d6 ♗xd6 24 exd6?! (24 ♗xg6!∓) 24...♘df4 25 ♗xf4 ♘xf4 26 ♕e5

♗xf3! 27 gxf3 ♕g5+ 28 ♕xg5 hxg5 *(84)* with a fantastic endgame for Black in Piket-Oll, Manila OL 1992. His domination of all the key squares is very visual.

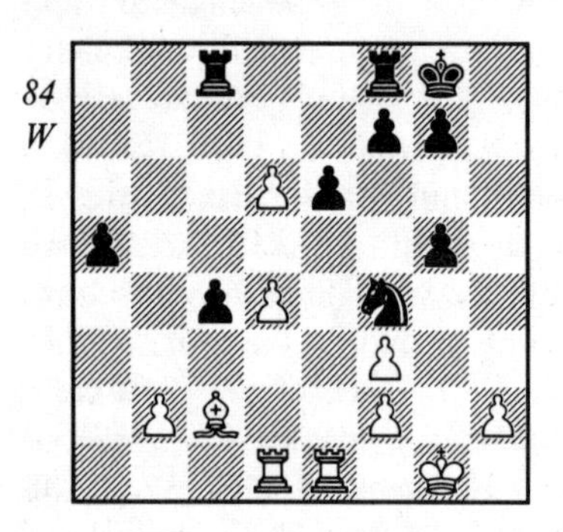

To sum up, 12...h6 is looking quite adequate for Black, but although White's switch to more positional ideas against 12...cxd4 is putting the squeeze on Black a little, 12...h6 is still a move trying to replace a good main line!

13 ♖e1 g6

It is logical to fianchetto here since White's advanced e-pawn can be targeted, and if the bishop develops along the a3-f8 diagonal Black's kingside lacks cover. We shall consider three other choices:

a) **13...♕a5?!** 14 ♘xd4 **0-0-0** was Ogaard-Barczay, Lublin 1975, an example of the least usual destination for Black's king in these lines. As Korchnoi points out in *ECO*, 15 ♗g5! ♗e7 16 ♗xe7 ♘xe7 17 ♘b5 would have left Black suffering on the dark squares.

b) **13...♗e7?!** allows White to fulfil his plan unhindered and he develops a very strong attack after **14 ♘xd4**:

b1) **14...♕a5** and here:

b11) **15 ♗b5!** (Liebert) looks unpleasant for Black after **15...♖d8** 16 ♕g4 g6 17 ♗h6!, **15...0-0-0** 16 ♗d2 or **15...a6!?** 16 ♗c6 ♕c7 17 ♗xb7 ♕xb7 18 ♕g4 g6 19 ♗h6. Thus it is not yet clear to me why Shabalov should be willing to defend this.

b12) Still, Kaidanov-Shabalov, New York 1993 went down an alternative route with **15 ♗d2** ♖d8 16 a3 ♘5b6 17 ♗b5 ♘xa4 18 ♗xb4! ♗xb4 19 axb4 ♕b6 20 ♗xd7+ ♖xd7 21 ♕a4 when Black was also struggling.

b2) **14...0-0** is best met by **15 ♕h5! g6 16 ♕h6!**. Various solutions have been posited for Black here, but none seem to ward off the attack satisfactorily:

b21) **16...♖e8?!** 17 ♗xg6! hxg6 18 ♘xe6 fxe6 (18...♗f8 19 ♘xd8 leaves White a good pawn ahead) 19 ♕xg6+ ♔h8 20 ♕h6+ ♔g8 21 ♖e4 ♘xe5 22 ♖xe5 ♗f6 23 ♕g6+ ♗g7 24 ♗h6 ♖e7 25 ♘c5! gives White a crushing attack (Boleslavsky's analysis)

b22) **16...♘c5** 17 ♘xc5 ♗xc5 18 ♘f3 (Larsen).

b23) **16...♘xe5!?** attempts to break the bind by radical means but 17 ♖xe5 ♘f6 18 ♕f4 ♗d6 19 ♕g3! (Taimanov) looks hard to refute.

b24) **16...♘c7** and **16...♕e8** are both untried and somewhat passive suggestions of Larsen.

c) **13...a6!?** *(85)*.

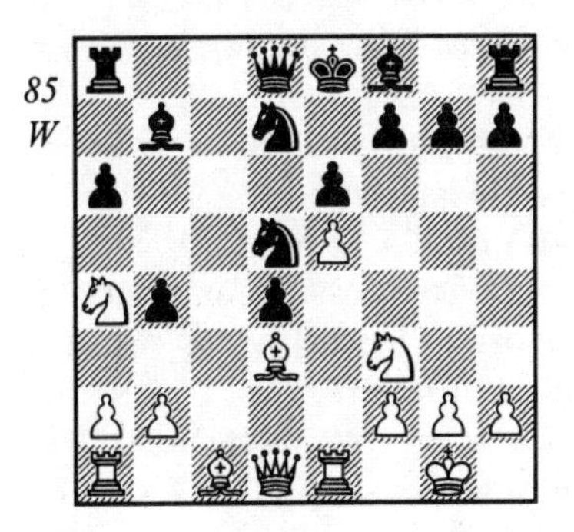

85
W

An interesting move, preventing ♗b5 which occurs in many 13...g6 lines, and leaving the option of where to place the dark-squared bishop. For example if White plays 14 ♘xd4 Black intends to reply 14...g6 since White has lost the ♗g5 option. So far so good, but precisely this line has had a bad press until now in view of 15 ♕g4. The details:

c1) **14 ♘xd4**:

c11) **14...g6 15 ♕g4**:

c111) Balashov-Garcia Martinez, Cienfuegos 1975 concluded **15...♗g7?!** 16 ♗g5 ♘e7 17 ♗c4! h6? 18 ♘xe6 fxe6 19 ♕xe6 ♖f8 20 ♗d3 1-0 which did little for the reputation of the line.

c112) In the earlier game Poch-Panno, Buenos Aires 1971 Black had run into problems as well with **15...♕a5** 16 b3 ♘c5 17 ♗c4!? ♘xa4 18 bxa4 ♕xa4 (18...b3!?) 19 ♗g5 h6 20 ♗f6 ♖g8 21 ♖ad1 with good attacking chances.

c113) However, the latter game seems to leave some unanswered questions, and the recent adoption of 13...a6 by both Kaidanov and Lautier suggests that all is not clear-cut. Though neither opponent has tested 15 ♕g4, Lautier's notes claim that Black is even slightly better after **15...♕a5** 16 b3 ♗g7. Positionally true, but I would closely scrutinize the thematic sacrifice 17 ♘xe6! fxe6 18 ♕xe6+ ♘e7 19 ♗g5 before venturing the line for Black. Not **19...♕d8?** 20 ♗c4 Δ♖ad1, but **19...♗f8** prepares to answer 20 ♗c4 with ...♗d5 giving chances to defend. Scope for much further enquiry!

c12) Another possibility for Black may be **14...♕b8**. This was hardly tested by **15 ♕e2** g6 16 ♗g5 ½-½ Scherbakov-Filipenko, Sochi 1989. The possibility of this square for the queen seems to be another attraction of preventing ♗b5, but M.Gurevich-Kramnik, Bundesliga 1993 removed any illusions that this was just a nice safe option for Black. In fact Kramnik managed to prove enough for the exchange to defend against White's critical try **15 ♕h5** g6 16 ♕h3 ♘xe5 17 ♗e4 (the immediate 17 ♘xe6 is tempting, but not so clear cut against 17...♗c8 18 ♗xg6 fxg6 19 f4 ♕a7+ 20 ♔h1 ♕f2∞ – Gurevich) 17...♕d6 18 a3!? ♗g7 19 axb4 ♕xb4 20 ♘c2 ♕e7 21 b3

0-0 22 ♗a3 ♕c7 23 ♗xf8 ♖xf8. Black has a bishop controlling a lot of dark squares, and a pawn for the rook and should not be worse. Much scope for further research.

c2) For the record Kožul-Lautier, Biel 1991 saw White go astray with **14 ♖e4?** g6 15 ♗g5 ♕a5 16 ♘d2 (16 ♘xd4 ♗g7 17 ♘f3 0-0 is nice for Black. If White is unable to remain active his structural weaknesses will leave him struggling) 16...♗c6! (contrast with 15 ♘d2 ♗c6? in the note to 14 ♗g5 below. The position of the rook on e4 gives Black extra tactical possibilities) 17 ♘c4 ♕xa4 18 b3 ♘c3! 19 ♕e1 ♕b5 20 ♘d6 ♗d6 21 ♗xb5 axb5 and Black has amassed ample for the queen.

c3) **14 ♗g5** is best met by **14...♕b8!?** rather than **14...♗e7** 15 ♗xe7 ♕xe7 16 ♘xd4 according to Lautier.

c4) In the spirit of the main game, White tried **14 ♗d2!?** in Razuvaev-Sorokin, Moscow 1992. That this is dealt with below, is indicative of Black's failure to find anything more distinctive than 14...g6.

14 ♗d2!?

A speciality of Boris Alterman's, this deceptively innocuous development has been scoring heavily and clearly deserves consideration, not least because Black is doing fine in the main line 14 ♗g5. We shall discuss this and also 14 ♗b5 which remains a respectable but almost untouched option. First one less testing move:

a) **14 ♘xd4?!** ♗g7 15 ♗b5 0-0 16 ♗xd7 ♕xd7 17 ♘c5 ♕e7 18 ♘xb7 ♕xb7 was at least equal in Dorfman-Doroshkevich, USSR 1975.

b) **14 ♗g5** gives Black two reasonable choices:

b1) **14...♗e7**:

b11) One possible drawback is that with **15 ♗h6** White virtually obliges **15...♗f8** when **16 ♗g5** repeats. Interesting after 15...♗f8 is **16 ♕d2** ♗c6(!) (16...♗xh6 17 ♕xh6 ♕a5 18 b3 ♘c3 19 ♘g5! ♖f8 20 ♘xh7 ♖g8 21 ♘xc3 bxc3 22 b4! {Tukmakov-Sveshnikov, USSR 1977} 22...♕b6! 23 ♕h4 g5!? 24 ♘xg5 0-0-0 25 ♗e4± according to Polugaevsky) 17 ♗xf8 ♔xf8 18 ♗e4 ♕a5 (18...♔g7!? Polugaevsky) 19 b3 ♗xa4 20 ♕h6+ ♔g8 21 bxa4 ♖c8 22 ♘xd4 ♘c3 23 ♗c2 Tukmakov-Polugaevsky, USSR Ch 1977. A difficult position to assess. As so often in this variation Black holds long-term positional trumps, while White must exploit Black's awkward development. In the game Black managed to free himself with ...♕c5-f8.

b12) **15 ♗xe7 ♕xe7 16 ♗b5 0-0 17 ♗xd7 ♕xd7 18 ♘c5** and now:

b121) **18...♕b5** 19 ♕xd4 ♘e7 (19...♖ad8 20 ♕h4) 20 ♘xb7 ♕xb7 21 ♖ad1 ♔g7 22 ♘g5 h6 23 ♘e4 ♘f5 24 ♕d2 ♖fd8 25

♘d6 ♘xd6 26 exd6± Gligorić-Ribli, Nikšić 1978.

b122) **18...♕e7!?** 19 ♕xd4 ♖ad8 20 ♖ac1 (20 ♘e4 ♗a8 21 ♘df6; or 20 ♘xb7 ♕xb7 21 ♘g5 ♔g7 22 ♘e4 ♕b6! with counterplay in both cases) 20...♘b6! 21 ♕xb4 ♗xf3 22 gxf3 ♖d5 with sufficient play for the pawn; Kožul-Tukmakov, Toronto 1990

b2) **14...♕a5** with two main alternatives:

b21) **15 ♘d2** was formerly the main line but 15...♗a6! (not 15...♗c6? 16 ♘c4! when Black must bail out with 16...♗xa4 but is clearly worse) 16 ♘c4 ♗xc4 17 ♗xc4 ♗g7 and now the piece sacrifice 18 ♕d4 is virtually forced but in view of the recent game L.B.Hansen-Ribli, Polanica Zdroj 1993 it may be worth reinvestigating. After 18...♕xa4 19 ♗xd5 exd5 20 ♕xd5 ♘b6 21 ♕d6! (21 ♕c5? ♗f8 22 ♕e3 ♕d7!∓) 21...♕d7 22 ♕xb4 and now 22...♗f8 23 ♕c3 ♕c8 24 ♕f3 Polugaevsky gives **24...♕e6!?** but Hansen thinks that White has chances after 25 ♗f6 ♖g8 26 ♖ad1. Ribli preferred **24...♗g7** and was OK after 25 e6!? 0-0! 26 ♗e7 fxe6! 27 ♗xf8 ♕xf8 28 ♕b3 ♕f7 29 ♖xe6 ♗xb2! 30 ♖d1 ♖b8= but it is clear that Black needs to take great care and be well prepared here.

b22) **15 ♘xd4** has been the recent preference. If now 15...♗g7?, then 16 ♗b5 gives White a clear plus, so best is **15...a6!** *(86)*. Jeroen Piket in particular has been amassing a lot of experience on the White side of this relatively solid and sober try. White has:

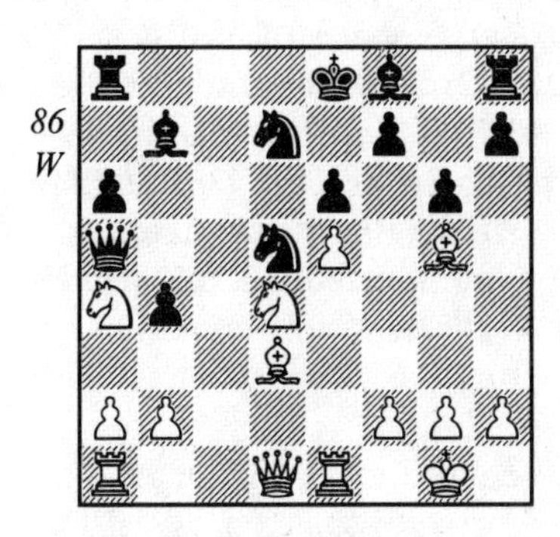

86
W

b221) **16 a3!?**, trying to prove that the black queen is embarrassed, seems fairly risk-free, but Black should not lose after 16...bxa3! (16...♗g7 17 axb4 is problematic, since both 17...♕xb4 18 ♖e4!±, and 17...♘xb4 18 ♗c4! favour White according to Lukacs) 17 bxa3 ♗g7 18 ♗d2 ♕d8 19 ♖b1 ♖b8 20 ♖xb7! (This forcing combination is the point of White's play. Although it nets a pawn, Black's position remains resilient since normal pluses such as the d5 square and pressure against e5 are retained) 20...♖xb7 21 ♗xa6 ♕a8 22 ♗xb7 ♕xb7 23 ♗b4!? (this interesting attempt to wrest back the initiative by returning the material gained, looks the most testing) 23...♘xb4 24 axb4 ♕xb4 25 ♘c6 ♕b7 26 ♕d6 ♗f8 27 ♘c5 ♗xd6 28 ♘xb7 ♗c7 29 ♘d6+ (Pinter-

Kaidanov, Budapest 1989) and now 29...♔f8 should lead towards a draw. This was confirmed at the highest level in Illescas-Kramnik, Madrid 1993 which wound up with 30 ♖a1 ♘xe5 31 ♖a8+ ♔g7 32 ♖xh8 ♘xc6 33 ♖c8 ♗xd6 34 ♖xc6 ♗f4 35 g4 f5 with a clear draw.

b222) **16 ♖c1** has been the focus of Piket's efforts. **16...♗g7 17 ♘c6 ♗xc6 18 ♖xc6 0-0 19 ♗c4!** *(87)*.

87
B

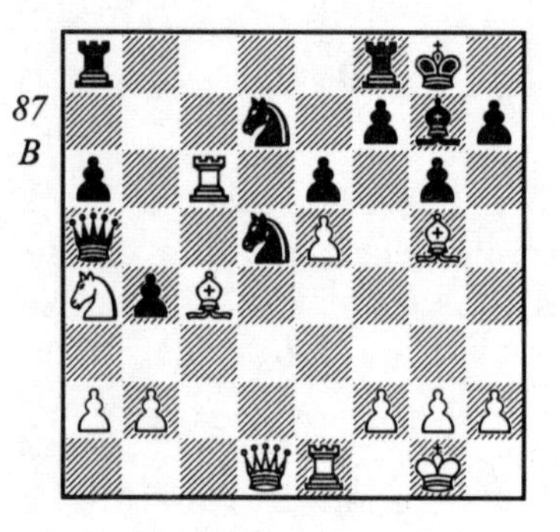

This novelty revived White's case here. 19 ♖e4?! h6 20 ♗h4 g5 21 ♗g3 ♖fc8 22 ♕c2 ♘e7!∓ was Kakageldiev-Beliavsky, USSR 1978. From the diagram:

b2221) **19...♗xe5** 20 ♘c5! (20 ♖xe5? ♘xe5 21 ♖c5 ♘xc4 gives too much for the queen) 20...♘xc5 21 ♖xe5 ♘d7 22 ♖e1 ♖fc8 (22...♘5b6!? Piket) 23 ♗xd5 ♕xd5 24 ♕xd5 exd5 25 ♖d6 ♘c5 26 ♖xd5 ♘e6 27 ♗f6 gave White a small but enduring initiative into the endgame in Piket-M.Gurevich, Belgium 1993.

b2222) Also possible is **19...♘5b6** 20 ♘xb6 ♘xb6 21 ♗b3 ♖fc8 22 ♖xc8 ♖xc8 (Piket-Anand, Dortmund 1992) and now Piket's suggestion 23 h4 Δ23...♗xe5 24 ♗d8 may keep some pressure.

b2223) **19...h6!?** is possibly the simplest in view of Kramnik's fine discovery three moves later. 20 ♗xd5 ♕xd5 21 ♕xd5 exd5 22 ♗f6 ♘xe5!! (Black will win back the piece, and the superiority of the g7 bishop in the endgame enables Black to jettison a pawn and still retain the balance. Supreme judgement from Kramnik) 23 ♗xe5 (the interesting calculation is the refutation of 23 ♖xe5? with 23...♖ac8! 24 ♗xg7 ♖xc6 25 ♗xh6 g5! 26 ♗xg5 f6 27 ♖xd5 fxg5 28 ♖xg5+ ♔h7 29 f3 ♖d8 when the pawns do not suffice for the exchange since the knight at a4 remains White's Achilles' Heel) 23...♖ae8 24 f4 f6 25 ♘b6 fxe5 26 ♘xd5 exf4 27 ♖xe8 ♖xe8 28 ♖xg6 ♔h7 29 ♖xa6 ♖e2 30 ♔f1 ♖xb2 31 ♘f4 ½-½ Piket-Kramnik, Amsterdam 1993.

c) **14 ♗b5** also merits consideration.

c1) If **14...♗g7?** 15 ♗g5 is strong, and 14...♖c8?! 15 ♕xd4 a6 16 ♗g5 ♗e7 17 ♗xe7 ♕xe7 18 ♗xd7+ ♕xd7 19 ♘c5 ♕e7 20 ♘e4! **0-0** 21 ♘d6 left White clearly better in Hort-G.Flear, Metz 1984.

c2) Best is **14...a6** when:

c21) White should avoid **15 ♗g5?** which would be good if met by **15...♛c8** 16 ♗f1! Δ17 ♖c1± but allows Black to get three pieces for the queen and the advantage with **15...axb5!** 16 ♗xd8 ♖xd8 17 ♘xd4 bxa4 18 ♛xa4 ♗g7! (A refinement over Dieren's original 18...♗c5 which is also not bad) 19 a3 0-0 20 ♛b5 ♗a8 21 ♘f3 ♘f4! 22 axb4 bxf3 23 gxf3 (Mirallès-G.Flear, Valras 1990) when 23...♘d5 would have set White very serious problems.

c22) The somewhat neglected **15 ♗c4** is much more promising. Hort-Rasmussen, Berlin 1984 looked very encouraging for White, who after 15...♗g7 16 ♛xd4 ♛a5 17 ♗b3 0-0 18 ♗d2 ♛b5 19 ♛h4 ♖fe8 20 ♖ad1 ♖ac8 21 ♗h6 ♗h8 22 ♘d4 ♛a5 23 f4 had consolidated his centre and could look forward to good kingside attacking prospects.

14 ... ♗g7

Since 14 ♗d2 has only recently received much attention, it is not at all clear what constitutes Black's best approach. We shall consider three other possibilities:

a) **14...♖c8** was Black's reply in the game Vasiukov-Votruba, Leningrad 1974, the only early example of the ♗d2 idea. In fact the move order was 14 ♗g5 ♗e7 15 ♗h6 ♗f8 16 ♗d2, which may account for why Black's apparently very reasonable move seems to have been overlooked by recent commentators. After 16...♖c8 17 ♘xd4 ♗g7 18 ♘f3 0-0 19 a3 a5 20 ♗b5 ♗c6 it is not clear that White has anything.

b) **14...a6** 15 ♗e4 is a little better for White according to Alterman, which looks plausible since being denied ...♗g7 is, to say the least, inconvenient. This passed a test in Razuvaev-Sorokin, Moscow 1992: 15...♛b8 16 a3 a5 17 axb4 axb4 18 ♗d3!? ♗g7 19 ♗b5 ♗c8 20 ♗c6 ♖a5 21 ♘d4 ♘e7 22 f4 0-0 23 ♗e4 ♖d8 24 ♘b3 ♖a6, and now 25 ♛e2!±.

c) **14...♗e7** 15 ♗h6 ♗f8 16 ♗d2 ♗e7 17 ♘xd4 0-0 18 ♗h6 ♖e8 19 ♛g4 ♗f8 (White threatened 20 ♘xe6!, and 19...♘7b6 20 ♗b5! is awkward) 20 ♗xf8 ♖xf8 21 h4 with some attack in Alterman-L.Spassov, Munich 1992. The combination of ...g6 and ...♗f8 constitutes something of a concession and is unlikely to equalize.

15 ♗b5 a6

In Alterman-Pinter, Beersheva 1991 Black played instead **15...♖c8** and White's notes for *Informator 53* share the implicit assumption that White's intended ♘c5 should be avoided. However White obtains good chances with 16 ♗g5 ♛a5 17 ♘xd4 ♖**c7** and now Alterman's suggestion 18 a3 0-0 19 ♗d2!. Stohl gives instead **17...a6** 18 ♗xd7+ ♔xd7 19 ♘b3 ♛b5 as only equal.

16 ♘c5 axb5

Ernst gives the surprising **16...♗c8!?** 17 ♗c6 ♖b8 18

♘xd7 ♗xd7 19 ♗xd5 exd5 20 ♗g5 ♕b6=, but whilst I cannot fault the analysis, I still slightly prefer White at the end after 21 ♘xd4.

17 ♘xb7 ♕b6
18 ♘d6+ ♔e7
19 ♘g5

Clearly the Russians had come to the conclusion that this was the way to combat 14 ♗d2. Igor Stohl, interestingly, seems to agree and is pessimistic about White's chances in the early phase of this game. After White's success in Alterman-Dreev, Manila OL 1992 however, attention may switch to the alternative **19 ♗g5+!?** ♔f8 20 ♖c1(!) (Stohl considered only 20 ♘xd4?!). This makes Black's task of freeing himself much more complex, and prepares to meet **20...♘xe5** with 21 ♘xe5 **♗xe5** 22 ♖xe5 ♕xd6 23 ♕xd4±, although **21...♕xd6!?** 22 ♖c6 ♕xe5 23 ♖xe5 ♗xe5 is worth considering for Black. The game continued **20...h6** 21 ♗h4 ♔g8 22 ♗g3 ♔h7 23 ♘xf7 ♖hf8 24 ♘d6 ♘f4 25 ♕d2 ♘h5 26 ♘xd4 ♘xg3 27 hxg3 ♗xe5 28 ♘xe6! ♗xd6 29 ♘xf8+ ♖xf8 30 ♖e6 and Black's minor pieces lined up on the d-file ran into some trouble.

19 ... ♖hf8

19...♘xe5 20 ♘dxf7 ♘xf7 21 ♖xe6+ ♕xe6 22 ♘xe6 ♔xe6 23 ♕b3! is dangerous (Stohl).

20 ♘xh7 *(88)*

88
B

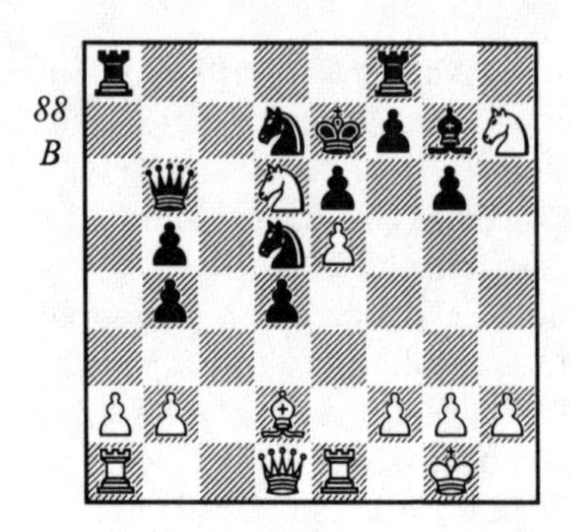

20 ... ♗xe5?

The crucial error according to Stohl. He believes Black was better after the alternative **20...♘xe5!** (not 20...♖h8 21 ♗g5+). He gives some interesting lines after 21 ♘e4! f5 (21...♖h8 22 ♗g5+ f6 23 ♘exf6! ♘xf6 24 ♘xf6 ♗xf6 25 ♖xe5 with a strong attack) but 22 ♘eg5 may be dangerous, since his intended 22...♖fd8 23 f4 ♘e3 seems to lose immediately to 24 ♗xb4+.

21 ♘xf8 ♔xf8
22 ♘e4 ♗g7
23 ♕b3 ♖a4

Black is tied down to defending b4 and with White seizing total control of the c-file, Black's compensation is clearly inadequate. The game concluded: **24 ♖ac1 ♕b8 25 ♘c5! ♘xc5 26 ♖xc5 ♗e5 27 ♖ec1 ♗xh2+ 28 ♔h1 ♕e5 29 ♕h3! ♗f4 30 ♖xd5! exd5** (A nice finish, White returns the exchange to open lines and commence a mating attack) **31 ♗xf4 ♕xf4 32 ♕h8+ ♔e7 33 ♖e1+ ♔d7 34 ♕e8+ ♔c7 35 ♖e7+ 1-0.**

11 Wade Variation 9 e4 – White Captures on c5

The early moves of the Wade variation are fairly forcing, but on move 12 White does have two significant alternatives to 12 ♖e1 (examined in the previous chapters), namely to capture on c5: either 12 dxc5 or 12 ♘xc5. Both have enjoyed a steady popularity ever since the Wade Variation first came to prominence. As mentioned in the previous chapter, these lines can also arise after 12 0-0 h6!? and since White's independent choices at this juncture are not notably promising, the material in this chapter may be of interest even to those who wish to make 12 0-0 their principal weapon.

Game 15
Pinter-Chernin
Hungary 1992

1 d4 d5 2 c4 c6 3 ♘c3 ♘f6 4 e3 e6 5 ♘f3 ♘bd7 6 ♗d3 dxc4 7 ♗xc4 b5 8 ♗d3 ♗b7 9 e4 b4 10 ♘a4 c5 11 e5

11 ... ♘d5 *(89)*

12 dxc5

The majority of this chapter will be devoted to White's two captures on c5, but first Chernin's fascinating analysis of **12 ♘g5!?** in *Informator 56* is worth a mention.

89
W

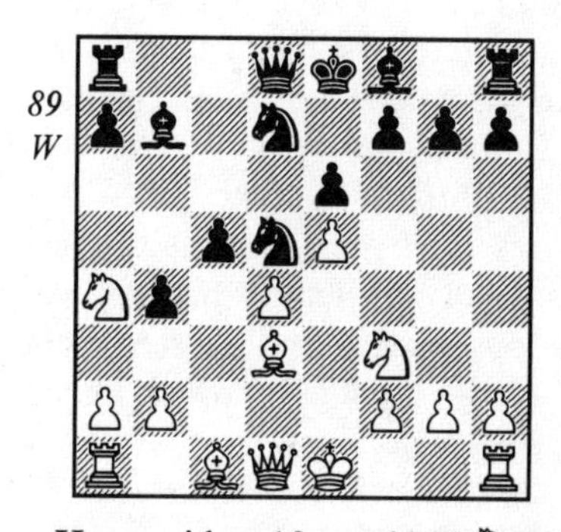

He considers 12...cxd4 13 ♘xe6! ♕e7 (13...fxe6 14 ♕h5+ and 15 ♗g5+ is too risky) 14 ♘xf8 ♕xe5+ 15 ♗e2 ♔xf8! 16 0-0 ♖e8 17 ♗c4! (Seems to be the best square for the bishop. 17 ♗f3? fails to 17...♗a6 and 17 ♗b5 ♘5f6! 18 ♗xd7 ♘xd7 19 ♗d2 ♕d6 20 a3 bxa3 21 ♖xa3 f6! Δ...♕d5 and ♔f7 seems OK. The loss of the two bishops blunts White's initiative) After 17 ♗c4 Chernin gives **17...♘5b6** 18 ♘xb6 ♘xb6 19 ♗d2 as ±. I agree. Black should seek counterplay more directly while White cannot challenge the e-file. To this end I like the suggestion **17...g5** Δ...♘f4 and if ♗xf4, then ...gxf4!. In any case, a lot of food for thought and scope for original ideas.

The currently popular 12 ♘xc5, shares strategic themes with the previous chapter. White exchanges off his bad knight on a4. Also, in some variations, White can displace the black king with ♗b5+. Indeed, 12 ♘xc5 and 12 dxc5 often transpose. The main differences rest with what one or the other avoids:

1) 12 dxc5 avoids the lines where Black keeps the two bishops without at the same time being committed to ...♕a5.

2) 12 ♘xc5 has the virtue that Black is obliged to recapture immediately. Whether this has any serious bearing on the assessment is a moot point upon which I hope to shed some light.

On to concrete analysis after **12 ♘xc5**:

a) **12...♗xc5 13 dxc5** and now:

a1) **13...♘xc5 14 ♗b5+** *(90)* with the further important divergence:

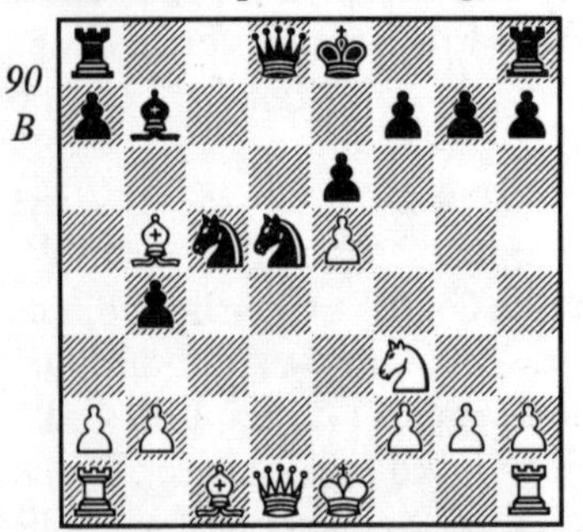

90
B

a11) **14...♔f8** 15 0-0 (15 ♕d4 is possible here too) 15...h6 16 a3!? (16 ♕d4 ♖c8 17 ♕g4 g6 18 h4 h5 19 ♕d4 ♕b6 20 ♗e2 ♘d7 21 ♕d1 ♗a6 22 ♗g5 ♔g7 23 ♗xa6 ♕xa6 24 a3 ♕b7 with chances for both sides in Dautov-Oll, Tbilisi 1989) 16...bxa3 17 ♖xa3 a6 18 ♗e2 g6 19 ♘d2 ♘f4 20 ♗f3 ♗xf3 21 ♖xf3 ♘d5 22 ♘c4± Tukmakov-Shabalov, Riga 1988.

a12) **14...♔e7** 15 ♕d4 (15 ♗g5+!?; 15 0-0 enables 15...♕b6 16 ♗c4 ♖hc8! which makes Black's position more comfortable) 15...♕b6 (15...♖c8 16 0-0 ♕b6 17 ♗c4 ♘d7 18 ♕h4+ f6 – the price of the h8 rook staying put – 19 ♗d2 a5 20 ♖e1± Peshina-Kaidanov, USSR 1987) 16 ♗c4 (16 ♕h4+!? looks a good alternative. After 16...♔f8 17 ♗c4 ♘e7 18 ♕f4 ♘g6 19 ♕e3 ♘d7 20 ♗e2 ♕xe3 21 ♗xe3 h6 22 0-0 ♔e7 23 a3! perhaps even 14...♔e7 begins to seem a bit doubtful) 16...♘d7 (16...h6!?) 17 ♕g4 (17 ♕h4+!?) 17...h6! (17...♖ag8? 18 0-0 h5 19 ♕h4+ f6 20 ♖d1 ♖d8 21 ♗d2 ♔f7 22 a3 b3 23 ♖ac1 left Black rather loose in Grünberg-Kaidanov, Moscow 1989) 18 0-0 a5 19 ♗d2 ♖hc8 20 ♖fc1 ♔f8 with only a tiny plus for White in Polugaevsky-Panno, Palma de Mallorca 1972.

I have to confess that in spite of the long pedigree of 13...♘xc5, I am suspicious of the full soundness of Black's position.

a2) **13...♕a5!?** 14 ♕e2 (the main move here 14 0-0! is a direct transposition into Pinter-Chernin) 14...♘c7! (The safest. Another game in the great Uhlmann-Larsen tussle from the 1971 Candidates suggested that 14...♘xc5 15 ♗b5+ ♔f8 16 0-0 h6 17 ♗e3! strongly favours White. Larsen later gave 15...♔e7 as favouring Black, offering the variation 16 ♗g5+ f6 17 exf6 gxf6 18 ♗d2 ♘b3. However, the whole idea looks risky. Even with the moves 0-0 and ...h6 inserted, Bagaturov-Nalbandian, Protvino Z 1993 found Black rapidly in difficulties with 17 ♘d4 ♕c7 18 ♗e3 a6 19 ♖ac1 ♘xe3 20 ♕xe3 axb5 21 ♖xc5!±) 15 **0-0** ♘xc5 16 ♗c4 ♘d7! 17 ♖e1 0-0 18 ♗d3 ♖fd8 19 ♗f4 ♘f8 20 a3! bxa3 21 bxa3 ♗a6 22 ♗xa6 ♘xa6 23 a4 ♘c5 24 ♗d2 ♕a6 25 ♕xa6 ♘xa6= Bareev-Smagin, Sochi 1988.

b) **12...♘xc5 13 dxc5 ♗xc5**. Now castling is clearly White's best option:

b1) **14 ♗b5+** is here merely a loss of time, since with the two bishops in his possession, the apparent vulnerability of the black king in the centre is a mere illusion. This was demonstrated in one of the classic expositions of Black's strategy in the Wade variation, Uhlmann-Larsen, Las Palmas Ct (6) 1971 which continued 14...♔e7 15 0-0 ♕b6 16 ♗d3 h6 17 ♕e2 ♖hd8 18 ♗d2 ♔f8 19 ♖ac1 *(91)*

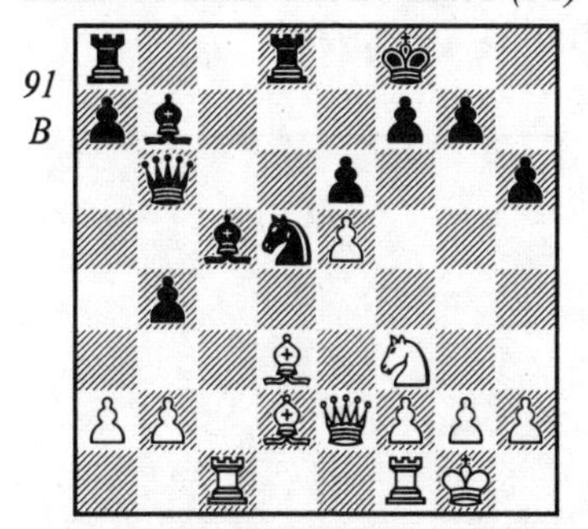

(Larsen's 19 a3!? was better since if White leaves the Black queenside unmolested he has no compensation for Black's superb knight on d5 and Black's excellent control of the a8-h1 and a7-g1 diagonals) 19...♖ac8 (19...a5 Δ20 ♖c2 ♘e7 may have been more precise) 20 ♖c2 a5 21 ♖fc1 ♔g8 22 h3 ♘e7 23 ♘e1?! (Black's king is perfectly safe, and White is short of an effective plan) 23...♗d4! 24 ♖xc8 ♖xc8 25 ♖xc8 ♘xc8 26 b3?! ♘e7 27 ♘f3 ♗c5 28 ♗e1 ♘f5 29 ♔f1 ♕c6 30 ♗b5 ♕c7 31 ♗d3 ♘d4 32 ♘xd4 ♗xd4 33 f4? ♕c1 34 ♕d2 ♕a1 35 ♕c2 ♗c3 36 ♕b1 ♗a6! 0-1.

b2) Also dubious for White is **14 ♘g5?! ♕c7!** 15 0-0 ♕xe5 16 ♕a4+ ♔e7 17 ♘xf7 ♔xf7! 18 ♕d7+ ♗e7 19 ♕xb7 ♖hb8 20 ♕a6 ♔g8∓ Liebert.

b3) **14 0-0!** *(92)*

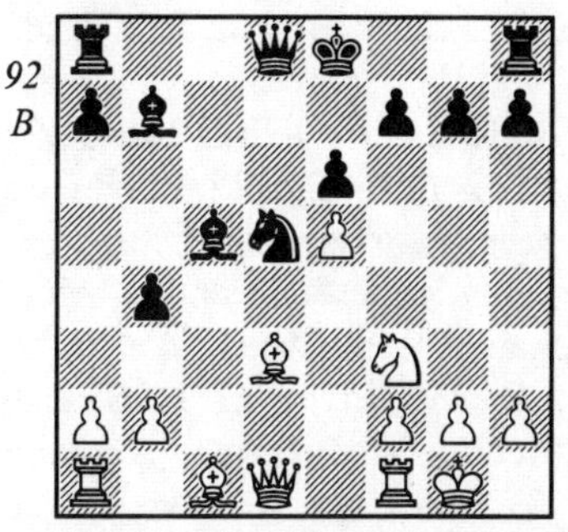

14...h6 (Necessary, since the refutation of 14...0-0? is as crushing as it is elegant: 15 ♗xh7+! ♔xh7 16 ♘g5+ ♔g6 17 ♕c2+ f5 18 exf6+ ♔xf6 19 ♕xc5 ♖c8 20 ♕xf8+!+- Kholmov) and now White can choose between:

b31) **15 ♕e2** again discourages castling since 16 ♕e4 would be strong, but does not seem dangerous after 15...♕b6 (15...g5!? Bangiev) 16 ♗d2 ♔f8 (16...♔e7 is quite valid too, eg. 17 h4?! ♖hd8 18 h5 ♔f8 19 ♖ac1 a5 20 ♖c2 ♘e7!∓ Lev-Pinter, Beersheba 1988; 17 ♖ac1 ♖hc8 18 ♕e4 ♔e8 19 ♕g4 ♔f8 might constitute something like 'correct play') 17 ♖ac1 ♖d8 18 ♖c2 g6 19 ♖fc1 ♗e7 20 ♗c4 ♖c8= Karpov-Polugaevsky, USSR 1975.

b32) **15 ♘d2(!)** and now:

b321) **15...0-0!?** is worth a look, if only because it calmly ignores what is supposed to be White's strong positional threat of ♘e4-d6. In Tukmakov-Dreev, Odessa 1989 Black levelled comfortably after 16 ♘e4 ♗d4 17 ♘d6 ♗c6 (not 17...♗xe5? 18 ♘xb7 ♕b6 19 ♕h5 ♗f4 20 ♘c5 ♕xc5 21 ♗xf4 ♕d4 22 ♗d6 ♕xd3 23 ♗xf8± Bareev-Shirov, Linares 1994) **18 ♗xh7+** ♔xh7 19 ♕xd4 f6! 20 ♗d2 fxe5. Black's play feels loose in the 'main' line below, and this may be a sound option. More dangerous seems to be **18 ♕e2**. After 18...f5 19 ♖d1 ♕e7?! 20 ♗a6 (Korchnoi-M.Gurevich, Antwerp 1993) Black should have played 20...♗b6 21 ♗d2 ♖ad8 22 ♖ac1 ♗a8 – M.Gurevich, but he still prefers White a little.

b322) **15...♘c3** 16 ♕c2 ♕d5 17 ♘f3 ♖d8 18 ♘e1 ♗d4 19 ♗d2! ♘b5 (not 19...♘e4 20 ♗xb4 ♗xe5 21 ♖d1± Dautov-Dreev, Tbilisi 1989) 20 ♗xb4 ♗xe5! 21 ♗c4 (21 ♖d1!?) 21...♕c6 22 ♕e2 ♘d4 23 ♕xe5 ♕xc4 24 ♕xg7 ♕xb4 25 ♕xh8+ ♔e7 26 ♕xh6 ♗a6 and Black's task is still not easy – Bagirov.

12 ... ♕a5

Black has a wider choice against 12 dxc5, but this does not necessarily imply a superior one!:

a) **12...♘xc5?!** is clearly inferior here in view of 13 ♗b5+ ♘d7 14 ♗g5 ♕a5 (14...♗e7 15 ♘c5! ♗xg5 16 ♗xd7+ ♔f8 17 ♗xe6!+-) 15 ♗xd7+ ♔xd7 16 0-0 ♗c6 17 b3± Balashov-Mariotti, Leningrad 1977.

b) **12...♗xc5** 13 dxc5 ♘xc5 14 ♗b5+ was covered in note 'a1' of the 12 ♘xc5 analysis above.

c) **12...♖c8!?** has been played with encouraging results to date by Kaidanov. If there is an argument against the 12 dxc5 move-order it is probably this. After **13 0-0** when Black has a choice:

c1) **13...♘xc5** is also possible now that c5 is covered, since 14 ♗b5+ ♘d7 15 ♗g5 ♗e7! (contrast note 'a') 16 ♗xe7 ♕xe7 17 ♕d4 0-0! 18 ♕xa7 ♗c6 19 ♗xc6 ♖xc6 20 ♕d4 ♖fc8 *(93)*

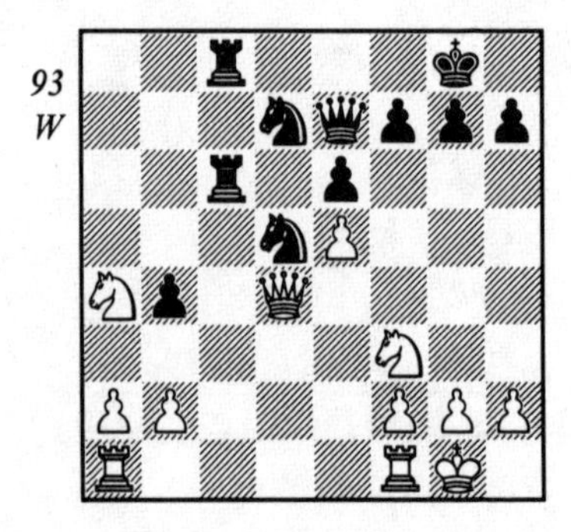

21 b3 ♘c3 was sufficient for Black in Piket-Kaidanov, Ca'n Picafort 1991. A simple idea, in which with his king safe, it appears that Black's positional trumps – the strong knight on d5; its poor counterpart on a4 and control of the c-file – give enough for a pawn.

c2) **13...♗xc5** 14 ♘g5 (14 ♘xc5 ♗xc5 15 ♗b5+ ♗c6! reveals another point of Black's 12th, but 14 ♗g5!? or the quiet 14 ♖e1 improve) 14...♗e7 15 ♕g4?? ♖xc1 0-1 Timoschenko-Kaidanov, Vienna 1989.

13 0-0 ♗xc5
14 ♘xc5

This exchange gives Black some activity (which White hopes to prove will be temporary) in exchange for the two bishops. The resulting position is more commonly reached from 12 ♘xc5, and with White's move order here he does have alternatives:

a) **14 ♖e1!?** ♘5b6 15 ♘xb6 ♕xb6 (15...axb6 Δ16 ♗e4 0-0-0 may be better according to Donaldson) 16 ♕e2 ♖c8 17 a3 ♗xf3 18 gxf3! (18 ♕xf3? would allow 18...bxa3 19 bxa3 ♗d4) 18...b3 19 ♖d1 ♖c7 20 ♗f4 0-0 with an edge for White in an unbalanced position; Rukavina-Korchnoi, Leningrad 1973.

b) **14 a3** ♗e7! (14...bxa3 15 ♘xc5 ♕xc5 16 ♖xa3 h6 17 ♕e2 ♕b6 18 ♗b5+ ♗c6 19 ♘d4 ♗xb5 20 ♘xb5 ♔f8 {20...0-0 21 ♗xh6!} 21 ♖f3 was awkward for Black in Timoshchenko-Smagin, Moscow GMA 1989) 15 ♗d2 0-0 16 ♖e1 (16 ♗e4 looks a little more testing, but 16...♖fd8 17 axb4 ♗xb4 18 ♗g5 ♖e8 19 ♘c3 ♕c7 20 ♘xd5 exd5= Schneider-Maximenko, Kherson 1989) 16...♖fd8 17 ♕b3 ♖ab8 18 ♗e4 ♗c6 19 axb4 ♗xb4 and Black had no problems in Uhlmann-Larsen, Monte Carlo 1969.

14 ... ♘xc5
15 ♗c2 ♖d8

Black never fully equalized with the previously played **15...♗a6**: 16 ♖e1 ♖d8 17 ♗g5! (17 ♕d4?! ♘e7! 18 ♕f4 ♗d3 allows Black to effect a positionally and defensively very desirable exchange) 17...♖d7 (17...♘e7 18 ♘d4!±) 18 ♕d4 ♘b6 (18...0-0 19 ♕g4!) 19 ♕g4 h5 20 ♕h4 ♗d3 21 ♗xd3 ♘xd3 22 ♖e2 ♕b5 23 b3± was Aseev-Dokhoian, Klaipeda 1989 when Black was lacking a safe haven for his king. Black could consider **15...0-0-0** however, which has often been suggested but not taken up in practice. One significant point is that **16 ♗g5** is no longer attractive in view of ...f6, and **16 ♗d2** (to parry the threat of ...♘e3 and to prepare a3) 16...♕b6 Δ17 a3 b3 looks OK for Black. Tests please!

16 ♘d4 ♘e7
17 ♗e3 0-0

17...♘d7?! 18 f4 ♘b6 19 ♘b3! ♕b5 20 ♕g4± was Pinter-Smagin, Paris 1990.

18 ♕h5 ♘g6
19 f4 ♘d7

20 ♕h3	**♖fe8**
21 ♘b3	**♕c7**
22 ♖ac1	**♕b8** *(94)*

94
W

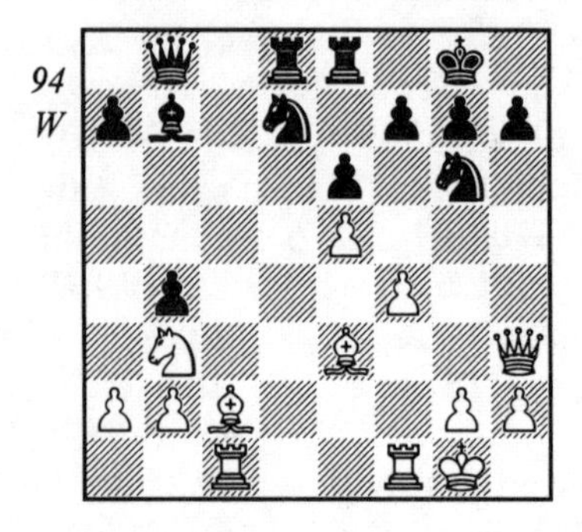

White has more space, but Black is solid and retains trumps such as the d5 square and the a8-h1 diagonal. White's next plan neutralizes the latter, but in the absence of a good break to further open the position, Black's two knights combat the two bishops remarkably effectively.

23 ♘a5	**♘b6**
24 ♕g3	**♕a8!**

It shows excellent understanding that Chernin realizes that far from undesirable, the exchange of White's knight is something that ought to be encouraged before White can make trouble with ♕f2.

The game continued: **25 ♘xb7 ♕xb7 26 ♕f2 ♘d5 27 ♗d2 ♖c8 28 ♗e4 a5 29 g3?!** (Either 29 h4 or g4 looks more challenging. The text allows Black to follow up shortly with ...h5, 'strong-pointing' the square f5 and seizing the initiative on the kingside) **29...♘ge7 30 ♖c5 ♖xc5 31 ♕xc5 ♕a6 32 ♖e1 ♖c8 33 ♕f2 h5! 34 h3 a4 35 a3 bxa3 36 bxa3 ♕c4 37 ♔h2 ♕b3 38 ♗c1 ♘f5** (The contrast from the diagram above is striking. Black has secured outposts or open files for all his pieces, and, although White is not yet lost, the defensive task is very difficult. This kind of 'slow infiltration chess' is a hallmark of Chernin's style. See also Game 27 where he does something similar to Malaniuk. White is able to evict the knight from f5, but only at the expense of creating weaknesses for Black to target) **39 g4 hxg4 40 hxg4 ♘h6 41 ♕g2 ♕c3 42 ♖f1 ♘e3 43 ♗xe3 ♕xe3 44 g5! ♘g4+ 45 ♕xg4 ♕xe4 46 ♕f3?** (Pinter misses his last chance to gain active play with 46 g6! ♖c2+ 47 ♔g1 ♕xg6+ 48 ♕xg6 fxg6 49 ♖b1 ♖c4 50 ♖b8+ ♔h7 51 ♖b6 ♖xf4 52 ♖xe6 ♖f3 53 ♖a6 ♖xa3 54 e6∓ {Chernin}. The poor placing of the black king means that despite the two pawn minus White can exchange e-pawn for Black's a-pawn and should draw. Having missed this chance, the rest needs little explanation. Black is able to use both the h-file and the eighth rank to access the white king's position and create a mating attack) **46...♕f5 47 ♖f2 g6 48 ♖d2 ♔g7 49 ♔g3 ♖h8 50 ♕g2 ♖b8 51 ♕h2 ♕b1 52 ♖f2 ♖h8 53 ♕g2 ♖h1 54 ♕f3 ♕g1+ 55 ♕g2 ♕c1 56 ♕f3 ♖e1 57 ♔h4 ♖e3 0-1**.

12 Wade Variation without 9 e4: Introduction and 9 a3

As we have seen, White still has some interesting possibilities to explore after 9 e4 despite the mass of theory which has accumulated. However, the move does commit White to making positional concessions as I have discussed above, and since the decline of the pawn sacrifice examined in Chapter 9 there has been a growth of interest again in White's ninth move options. Of these the most important is 9 0-0. This move is highly logical since White castles short in most lines of the Meran anyway and as we shall see, both of Black's most reliable options (9...a6 and 9...b4) result in play developing a very different character from that seen in the 9 e4 chapters. In fact, after 9...a6 10 e4 c5 11 d5 the position is closely related to that dealt with in Chapter 15 and 16 on Reynolds' variation against 8...a6, and presents some problems of transposition. I should explain here how I have decided to deal with these. Since 9...a6 10 e4 c5 11 d5 c4 12 ♗c2 is both invariably reached by this Wade Variation move order and currently very popular, it is dealt with in Chapter 13, as is 12 dxe6 fxe6 which is very closely connected to it. However, after 12 dxe6 cxd3 the insertion of 8...♗b7 9 0-0 gives no special flavour to the play and so is dealt with in Chapter 16. I hope this all makes sense! Naturally there is a strong case for studying the two chapters in conjunction since the strategic ideas are very similar.

The main alternative 9...b4, considered in Chapter 14, naturally bears comparison with Lundin's variation 8...b4 which has lost much of its topicality and will hence be briefly dealt with in the same chapter. This time however the insertion of the extra moves seems to be an unambiguous gain for Black, cutting out some of White's more threatening lines. Indeed, 9...b4 was for many years quoted as the reason why 9 0-0 was allegedly not very dangerous. However, things are by no means so simple, and White has recently been posing problems here.

In this chapter we shall start by examining 9 a3 which has recently received renewed attention, buoyed by the idea 10 ♘e4.

Game 16
Gelfand-Brenninkmeijer
Wijk aan Zee 1992

1 ♘f3 d5 2 c4 c6 3 e3 ♘f6 4 ♘c3 e6 5 d4 ♘bd7 6 ♗d3 dxc4 7 ♗xc4 b5 8 ♗d3 ♗b7

9 a3 *(95)*

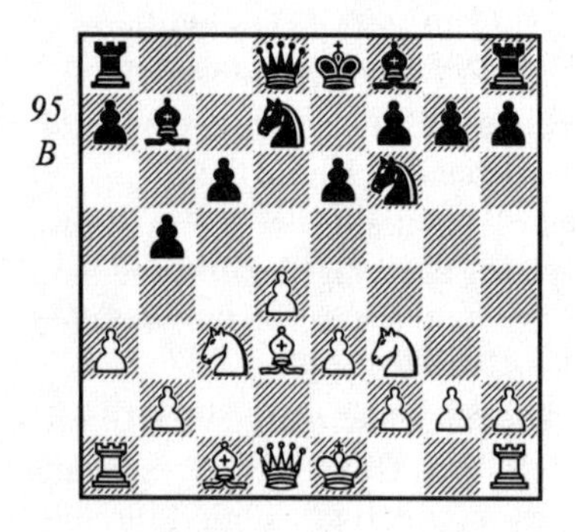

9 ... b4

With 9 a3 White intends in some circumstances to play b4 and try to prove the backward c-pawn weak, in others to play e4 without the danger of having the c3 knight kicked, and hence the text, currently by far Black's most frequent response, is also the most direct way to cross these plans. It is worth comparing the line with 8 ♗e2 ♗b7 9 a3, where 9...b4 from the 1984/5 World Championship match (see Chapter 18) looks the cleanest equalizer. Here however, Black has played other moves which are by no means bad:

a) **9...a6 10 b4**:

a1) **10...♗d6** 11 0-0 (11 ♘d2 is also interesting) 0-0 12 ♘e4 ♘xe4 13 ♗xe4 a5 14 ♖b1 ♕e7 15 ♗d2 gave White the edge in Gligorić-Sanguinetti, Buenos Aires 1959.

a2) **10...a5!?** (Black's ...a6-a5 implies that 10 b4 may be premature, and hence this loss of tempo is justified by the chance to target White's b-pawn. Again compare Chapter 18) 11 ♖b1 axb4 12 axb4 ♘d5 13 ♘xd5 exd5 14 0-0 ♗d6 and now 15 ♕c2!? Δ15...♘f6 16 ♘e5 is perhaps the most promising. In Gelfand-Tukmakov, Wijk aan Zee 1993, Black kept an eye on the e5 square with 15...h6, but with 16 ♘d2 0-0 17 e4 dxe4 18 ♘xe4 ♘f6 19 ♖b3! ♖e8 20 h3 ♘d5 21 ♗d2 the opening of the position seemed to favour White.

b) **9...♗d6!?** 10 0-0 0-0 11 ♕c2 interestingly enough, transposes to note 'b22' to White's tenth move in Game 33.

c) **9...a5** 10 0-0 ♗e7 11 e4 b4 12 ♘a4 ♖c8 13 axb4 axb4 14 ♗e3 (14 ♕e2!? Δ14...0-0 15 e5 or 14...c5 15 dxc5 ♘xc5?! 16 ♘xc5 ♗xc5 17 ♗b5+) 14...0-0 15 ♖c1 ♘g4 16 ♗f4 ♘gf6 ½-½ was Andersson-Pinter, Reggio Emilia 1987

10 ♘e4!?

The new move of former World Under-18 Champion Konstantin Sakaev's with which the latest spate of 9 a3 games, particularly from Boris Gelfand, is associated. White's idea is to put the question to Black's advanced b-pawn. Black must either open the b-file from which White is the more likely to profit (the b7 bishop may become vulnerable), or always have to reckon with axb4.

a) The absence of material on 9 a3 between 1988 and 1992 testifies that the older **10 axb4 ♗xb4 11 0-0 c5** (11...♗e7 Δ...c5= Baumbach) was thought harmless. A summary:

a1) **12 ♗a6?!** ♕b8 13 ♗d2 0-0 14 ♕e2 cxd4 15 exd4 ♗e7 16 ♗g5 ♘d5! 17 ♘xd5 ♗xg5 18 ♗xb7 ♕xb7 19 ♘c3 ♗f6 ½-½ Gelfand-Oll, Klaipeda 1988. If anything Black is fractionally better.

a2) **12 ♘a2** (more critical) is best met by 12...a5(!) 13 ♘xb4 axb4 14 ♖xa8 (14 ♗d2!? ♖xa1 15 ♕xa1 ♗xf3!? would give more winning chances for both sides) 14...♕xa8 15 ♗e2 0-0 16 dxc5 ♘xc5 17 ♕d4 ♗a6! 18 ♗xa6 ♘xa6 19 ♗d2 ♖d8 20 ♕c4 ♘e4= Gelfand-Shirov, Klaipeda 1988.

b) Also harmless is **10 ♘a4** bxa3 11 bxa3 c5 12 dxc5 ♘xc5 13 ♗b5+ ♘cd7 14 ♗b2?! (14 0-0=) 14...♕a5+ 15 ♘c3 a6 16 ♗a4 ♖b8! 17 ♕c2 ♗d6 18 ♖d1 ♔e7 19 ♗xd7 ♘xd7 20 ♕d2 ♕c7 21 ♘d4 ♘e5! and White had serious light-square weaknesses in Alexandrov-Kharlov, Kherson 1991.

10 ... bxa3

Since Black soon soon encounters some difficulties on the b-file this may be a good moment to consider alternatives. Two have been tried:

a) **10...a5** enables Black to keep his queenside pawns intact, and prepares to try to trade light-squared bishops with ...♗a6. Nevertheless, White can initiate promising play in the centre along the lines of game at the end of this chapter. Moreover, remaining uncastled gives White some extra attacking possibilities leading to very sharp play.

a1) Dokhoian-M.Gurevich, Bundesliga 1992 continued **11 ♘xf6+** ♘xf6 12 e4 ♗e7 13 ♕e2 bxa3 (perhaps 13...♘d7!? Δ...c5 should be considered since there are obvious attractions in seeking counterplay without the necessity of castling here) 14 bxa3 **0-0** 15 e5! (15 ♖b1 ♕c8 Δ...♗a6 eases Black's task) 15...♘d5 16 ♕e4?! (Gurevich's suggestion 16 h4! threatens ♗xh7+ and looks very dangerous for Black) 16...g6 17 ♗h6 ♖e8 18 h4 c5! (threatens ...♘b4. The position of the white queen aids Black's counterplay) 19 ♗b5 (19 ♕g4 ♘c3! threatens ...♗xf3 and highlights the weakness of d4) 19...♗a6! 20 ♗xa6 (20 ♗xe8 leaves White's king irrevocably stranded in the centre) 20...♖xa6 21 h5?! (It was time to bail out with 21 dxc5 and 22 0-0=) 21...c4! 22 ♕g4 ♕d7 23 ♗g5 ♖b8 24 ♗xe7 ♕xe7 25 hxg6 fxg6 26 ♘g5 h5 27 ♕g3 ♖b3 28 f3 ♖xa3 and Black's counterplay crashed through. Black's blockade of the central light squares was particularly instructive. (Most comments based on Mikhail Gurevich's notes for *Informator 43*).

a2) Of course, White is not obliged to play so sharply but after **11 0-0** ♗e7 12 ♘xf6+ ♘xf6 13 e4 0-0 14 ♕c2 (14 ♕e2!?) 14...h6 15 axb4 ♗xb4 16 e5 ♘d7 17 ♗h7+ ♔h8 18 ♗e4 ♕b8!? 19 ♖d1 c5 20 ♗f4 (20 d5 ♘xe5 21 dxe6 ♘xf3+ 22 gxf3 ♗xe4 23 ♕xe4 ♖e8 24 e7 ♕a7∓ Anand) 20...cxd4 21 ♖d4 ♖c8 22 ♕e2 ♘f8∓ Karpov-Anand, Moscow 1992. White has no realistic kingside attack, and Black enjoys the customary positional pluses.

b) **10...c5!?** was tried in Dreev-Illescas, Logroño 1991. Semi-Slav expert Dreev's patronage of this line for White is no mean endorsement, but he was unable to prove an advantage after 11 ♘xf6+ gxf6 12 0-0 ♕b6 13 axb4 cxd4 14 exd4 ♗xb4 15 ♕e2 (Δ♗e4) 15...a5 16 ♗e3 ♗d5 17 ♘d2 ♕b7 18 f3 f5 19 ♘c4 0-0! 20 ♗h6 ♖fc8 21 ♖ac1 ♗xc4 (an excellent judgement that reorganizing his remaining minor pieces necessitates exchanging the best one! The text enables Black to provide cover for his weakened kingside while White's weak d4 and b2 pawns still offer potential for counterplay) 22 ♗xc4 ♗f8 23 ♗xf8 ♘xf8=.

c) **10...♘xe4(?!)** 11 ♗xe4 ♕c7 12 axb4 ♗xb4+ 13 ♗d2 ♗xd2 14 ♘xd2 c5 15 ♕c2! ♕b6 16 dxc5 ♕xc5 17 ♕a4! ♖b8 18 **0-0**± 0-0! 19 ♕xd7 (Gelfand feels that after 19 ♗xh7+ ♔xh7 20 ♕xd7 ♗d5! White can do no better than reach a drawn four *vs* three rook ending) 19...♖fd8 20 ♗xh7+!? ♔xh7? (20...♔f8 21 ♕a4 ♖xd2 22 ♗e4 ♗xe4 23 ♕xe4 g6 leaves White with only a symbolic advantage – Gelfand) 21 ♕xf7 ♖xd2? (21...♗g2 is a better try – Anand) 22 ♖a4! ♕g5 23 g3! and the threat of ♖h4+ is unstoppable and decisive; Gelfand-Anand, Biel IZ 1993.

11 bxa3 **♗e7**

Gelfand's suggestion **11...♗a6!?** looks interesting.

12 ♘xf6+ **♘xf6**

13 0-0 **0-0**

14 ♖b1! **♕c7** *(96)*

If **14...♕c8** then Gelfand's recommendation **15 ♕b3** ♖b8 16 ♕a4! looks awkward to meet. Such probing on the queenside looks more thematic here than playing in the centre, which can merely give Black counterplay. If instead 14...♕c8 **15 e4** c5 16 e5 then not **16...♘d5?** 17 ♗g5 ♘c3 18 ♕c2 ♗xg5 19 ♘xg5 ♘xb1 20 ♗xh7+ ♔h8 21 ♗g8 g6 22 ♕d3! Δ♕h3± (Ftacnik) but **16...♘d7!** when it is less clear how White builds an attack.

Similarly, if **14...♖b8**, then 15 ♕a4! is more convincing than 15 e4 ♗a8!.

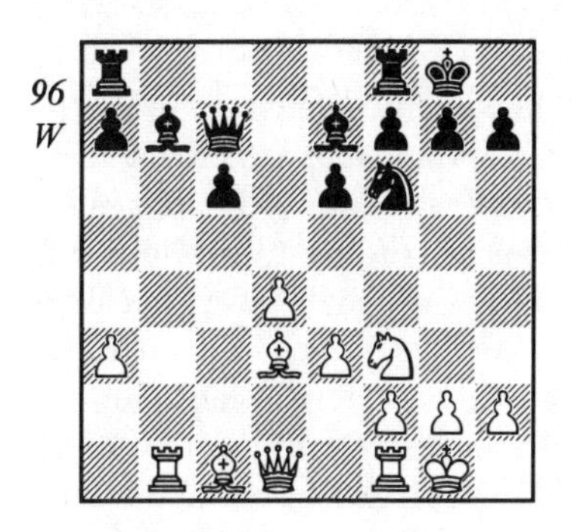
96
W

15 e4 **c5**
16 ♗f4! **♕c8**

16...♕xf4 17 ♖xb7 c4!? 18 ♗xc4 ♗xa3 19 ♕b3 ♖fc8 20 ♗xe6± (Ftačnik).

17 ♕e2 **c4**
18 ♗c2 **g6?!**

Black misses a chance to sacrifice the exchange to blunt White's attack and gain counterplay with **18...♗xa3!** 19 e5 ♗xf3! 20 ♕xf3 ♘d5 21 ♗h6!? c3! 22 ♕g4 g6 23 ♗xf8 ♔xf8. After the text White has the opportunity to launch a winning attack.

19 ♘e5 **♗xa3**
20 ♗g5?!

20 ♗h6! is more forceful, weakening f7, and indeed after 20...♖d8 21 ♕f3 ♗e7 22 g4! Black seems to have no defence.

20 ... **♘d7**
21 ♘xc4 **♗a6**
22 ♗d3 **♗xc4**
23 ♗xc4 *(97)*

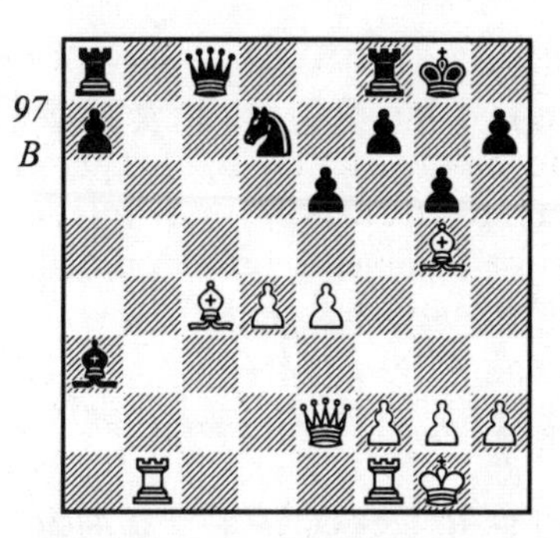
97
B

Black had no choice but to eliminate White's knight, but it will always be an uphill struggle against White's active bishops.

The continuation was: **23...♘b6 24 ♗a6 ♕d7 25 ♖fd1 f6** (If 25...♗e7 26 ♗b5 ♕b7 27 ♗c6!± Gelfand) **26 ♗h6 ♖f7 27 d5! exd5 28 exd5 ♗d6 29 ♗b5 ♕e7 30 ♕f3 f5 31 ♗f4! ♖d8 32 ♖e1 ♕f8 33 ♗e3 ♗c5 34 ♗g5 ♗e7 35 ♗f4 ♗d6 36 ♗c1!** (27 d5! helped to highlight Black's light-square weaknesses and opened lines against them. The text reminds Black that the long dark-square diagonal is none too healthy either) **36...♘d7 37 ♗b2 ♕h6 38 g3 ♕d2 39 ♗c3 ♕g5 40 ♖e6** (Perhaps 40 ♗xd7 ♖fxd7 41 ♖e6 was simpler) **40...♘c5 41 ♗a1 ♘e4 42 ♖d1** (Securing the passed d-pawn, and thus threatening ♖xe4 followed by ♕c3 winning material) **42...♕h5 43 ♕xh5 gxh5 44 ♔g2 ♗f8 45 ♗c4 ♘d6 46 ♗e2 h4 47 ♗f6 ♖c8 48 ♗xh4 ♖c2 49 ♗d3 ♖c5 50 ♗b1 ♖d7 51 ♗g5 ♘f7 52 ♗e3 ♖cxd5 53 ♖xd5 ♖xd5 54 ♖a6 ♖b5 55 ♗a2 ♖b7 56 ♗xa7 ♗g7 57 ♗e3 1-0**.

13 Wade Variation 9 0-0 a6

Game 17
Wells-Dreev
Cappelle la Grande 1992

1 d4 d5 2 c4 c6 3 ♘f3 ♘f6 4 ♘c3 e6 5 e3 ♘bd7 6 ♗d3 dxc4 7 ♗xc4 b5 8 ♗d3 ♗b7

9 0-0 a6

9...b4 is dealt with in Game 19.

Black has also tried **9...♖c8** which is based on a nice idea, but fails to equalize. If **10 e4?!** b4 11 ♘a4 c5 12 e5 c4! Black is even slightly better, since accepting the pawn with 13 exf6 cxd3 14 fxg7 ♗xg7 15 ♕xd3 gives Black vicious play on the light squares. Instead White has two good ideas:

a) **10 a3!?** when for most of the strategies available to Black in the analogous positions dealt with in the last game (9 a3) the rook is best left on a8. Two moves have been tested here:

a1) **10...a6** is best met by 11 b4! a5 when **12 ♕b3** is logical, to take advantage of the rooks absence from the a-file, while **12 bxa5** ♕xa5 13 ♗d2 ♕d8 14 a4!± Schroll-Shestiakov, Kecskemet 1991 is also quite promising.

a2) **10...a5** 11 ♕e2! b4 (11...♗e7!± is Marin-Spasov below) 12 axb4 axb4 13 ♘e4 ♘xe4 14 ♗xe4 ♕b6?! 15 ♘d2! gave White a large advantage in Wells-Collas, Capelle la Grande 1992.

b) **10 ♕e2** ♗e7 (10...a6 is interesting according to Maric, since it is known that the queen does not always stand well on e2 in positions where Black blocks with an early ...e5) 11 a3 a5 12 ♖d1 0-0 13 e4 b4 14 axb4 axb4 15 ♘a4 c5 16 e5 ♘d5 17 ♘xc5 ♘xc5 18 dxc5 ♖xc5 19 ♕e4 g6 20 ♗h6 ♖e8 21 ♕g4 with attacking chances, although Black is not without defensive resources; Marin-Spasov, L'Hospitalet de l'Infant 1992.

10 e4

10 a4 is dealt with in Game 20.

10 ... c5 *(98)*

10...b4 is weaker. White has only to find a version of the 9 e4 Wade Variation where ...a6 is a worse tempo than 0-0. One interesting example (by transposition) was Farago-Uržica, European teams 1977, which saw White obtain a powerful attack by 11 ♘a4 c5 12 e5 ♘d5 13 ♘g5! (13 ♖e1 cxd4 leads to the position from Game 14 which Lautier is trying to rehabilitate for Black) 13...cxd4?! 14 ♘xe6! fxe6 15 ♕h5+ ♔e7 16 ♗g5+ ♘5f6 17 ♖e1 ♕e8 18 ♕h4 ♗xd5 19 ♕xd4±.

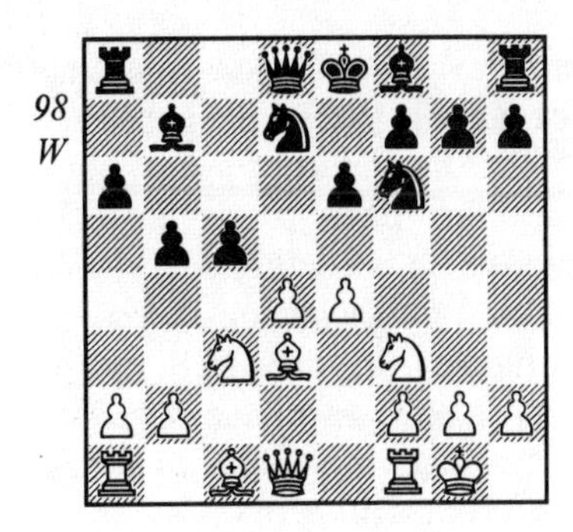
98 W

11 d5

It is this that gives the variation the characteristics of the Reynolds Attack which is often reached too from 8...a6 lines (see Chapters 15 and 16).

A recent idea with quite a different flavour is **11 e5!? ♘d5**:

a) **12 ♘g5!?** was played in the stem game, Sakaev-Dreev, USSR Ch 1991, which led to a difficult ending after fiery tactics: 12...♗e7 13 ♕h5 g6 14 ♕h6 ♘xe5!? (14...♗f8!?; 14...♘xc3!?) 15 ♘xd5 ♗xg5 16 ♕xg5 ♕xg5 17 ♗xg5 ♘xd3 18 ♘c7+ ♔d7 19 ♘xa8 ♖xa8 20 dxc5 (20 b3 c4!?) 20...♘xb2. Black has a pawn for the exchange and in addition, White's c-pawn may prove weak and Black's bishop has a perfect outpost on d5 to hinder the entry of the white rooks. The game is finely balanced.

b) An interesting attempt to refine White's play was seen in Nenashev-Oll, Moscow 1992: **12 a4!?** c4 (12...b4 13 ♘e4 cxd4 14 ♗g5 ♕a5∞ compare Game 26) 13 ♗b1 ♗e7 14 ♘d2 ♘7b6 15 ♕g4 ♔f8 16 axb5 ♘xc3 17 bxc3 axb5 18 ♖xa8 ♕xa8 19 ♘e4 h5 20 ♕f3 g6 21 ♖e1 when White has some initiative, but Black's position is sound, with solid positional gains. The line merits further tests.

11 ... c4

With Black's bishop on b7, **11...e5** (again compare chapter 15) is not very appealing after 12 b3!.

However, **11...exd5** is more playable here, although still not recommended. Kaidanov-Sveshnikov, Moscow 1987, continued 12 exd5 (12 e5 ♘e4 is OK for Black) 12...♗d6!? (12...♗e7 13 ♗xb5! axb5 14 d6 ♘e5 15 ♘xe5 ♕xd6 16 ♕xd6 ♗xd6 17 ♖e1 0-0 18 ♘xb5 was pleasant for White in Farago-Sveshnikov, Sochi 1980) 13 ♖e1+ ♔f8 and now **14 b3!** ♘b6 15 ♗b2 ♘bxd5 16 ♘e4 ♗e7 17 ♘e5 would have given White good compensation (Kaidanov). Also **14 ♘h4!?** ♕c7 (Høi-Rasmussen, Danish Ch {Århus} 1992) 15 g3 looks promising.

11...♕c7 may be OK too, but it is no more than transpositional.

12 dxe6

The alternative **12 ♗c2** is considered in Game 18. Partly influenced by the present game, I tend to the view that the exchange on e6 may be premature, needlessly helping Black's b7 bishop to play a significant role, but of course the play is very complicated. The rise and fall(?) of Marin's 15 ♘d4 (see below) is an example of how great caution should be exercised in making bald generalizations here. It is important to note that only a fear of 12...e5, which seems to be unjustified, requires White to rush the exchange on e6, since against all Black's other replies it remains an option.

12 ... fxe6

12...cxd3 is perfectly viable and transposes to Chapter 16.

13 ♗c2 ♕c7 *(99)*

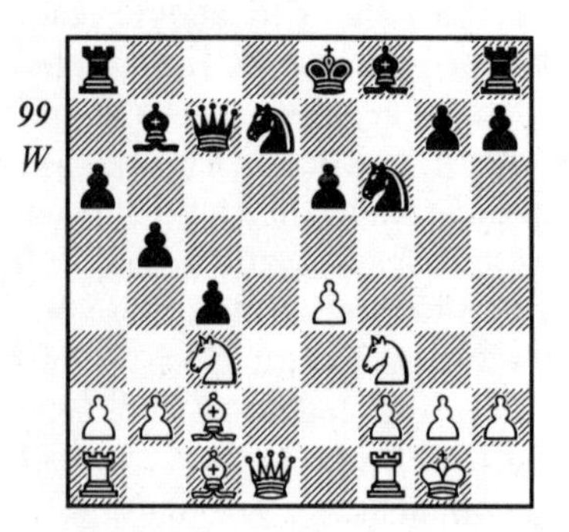

A good moment to pause and assess the situation. Black's e6-pawn is weak and may be attacked by ♘g5 or sometimes ♘d4. These moves may also liberate the f-pawn to support White's goal of playing e5 which, despite the fact that it clears the diagonal of the b7 bishop, also frees its c2 counterpart and is often dangerous for Black. Black has some difficulties with king placement, but also some choice. Crucial is the queenside pawn majority, which, while it can sometimes become weak after a timely a4 by White, can be a trump-card too. The status of these pawns is a key question in the variation. One unambiguous plus-point for Black is his potential outposts on the d-file, not only on d3, but, somewhat obscured and brought brilliantly to light by Dreev's play, on d4 too. 13...♕c7 seems clearly best since e5 should be prevented. Others:

a) **13...♕b6?!** 14 ♕e2 (14 e5!?) 14...0-0-0 15 a4! b4 16 a5 ♕c7 17 ♘a4 b3 18 ♗b1 ♗b4 19 ♗f4± Christiansen-Nikolac, Wijk aan Zee 1976.

b) **13...♗c5?!** gives White a very pleasant choice:

b1) **14 ♕e2 0-0** (14...♕c7 15 e5 ♘g4 16 ♗e4 {16 ♘g5 is dangerous too} 16...0-0 17 ♗xh7+ ♔xh7 18 ♘g5+ ♔g8 19 ♕xg4 ♕xe5 20 ♕xe6+ ± Partos-Inkiov, Lucerne OL 1982) 15 ♘g5 ♕b6 16 e5 ♕c6 17 ♘ce4 h6 18 exf6 hxg5 19 fxg7 ♔xg7 20 ♕g4 was very unpleasant for Black in Chekhov-Raičević, Kecskemet 1989.

b2) **14 e5(!)** may be even better since after 14...♗xf3 15 ♕xf3 ♘xe5 16 ♕e2 ♘d3 (Brenninkmeijer-Van der Sterren, Wijk aan Zee II 1990), 17 ♕xe6+! ♕e7 18 ♕c6+ would have been strong.

14 ♕e2

a) **14 ♘g5** Δ15 f4 is a very sharp but seemingly dubious alternative. After **14...♘c5**:

a1) **15 f4** h6(!) (If 15...♖d8?!, Anikaev's 16 ♕f3 h6 17 ♕h3 is interesting) 16 e5 (16 ♘h3 ♖d8

Δ...♘d3 is no problem for Black either) 16...♘d3 (16...hxg5 17 fxg5 is unclear and self-evidently dangerous; the strength of the text renders it unnecessary) 17 ♗xd3 (17 ♘xe6 ♕b6+ 18 ♔h1 ♕xe6 19 exf6 0-0-0 with excellent counterplay) 17...**0-0-0**! 18 ♘f3 **♖xd3** and Black assumed a serious initiative in Gligorić-Yusupov, Vrbas 1980, although according to Yusupov **18...♗c5**+ 19 ♔h1 ♘g4! was even stronger.

a2) However, the quieter **15 ♕f3!?** (Δ15...h6 16 ♕h3 Korchnoi) is quite playable, though not too terrifying:

a21) Seirawan-Ribli, Skellefteå 1989 unfortunately terminated peacefully after **15...♗d6** 16 ♕h3 **0-0-0 17 f4**. If instead **17 ♘xe6** presumably Ribli intended 17...♘xe6 18 ♕xe6+ ♔b8 (threatening ...♗c8) 19 ♕h3 b4 which looks very active for Black.

a22) Deserving attention too is Sergei Ivanov's analysis **15...0-0-0** 16 ♕h3 ♔b8 17 ♗e3 h6! 18 ♗xc5 hxg5 19 ♕xh8 ♗xc5 20 ♕h3 ♖d2 with a lot of compensation on the dark squares.

b) **14 ♘d4** ♘c5 15 ♕e2 0-0-0 16 ♘dxb5!? axb5 17 ♘xb5 ♕a5 18 a4 ♘d3 19 b4!? ♗xb4 20 ♗g5, Camara-Dorfman, São Paolo 1978, looks a bit hard to believe, and White has yet to repeat the experiment. Still, White has some threats, and for some enterprising soul...

c) **14 e5** looks aggressive but is really very innocuous. In Greenfeld-Pinter, Beersheba 1988 Black had the edge after 14...♘xe5 15 ♘xe5 ♕xe5 16 ♖e1 ♕d6 17 ♗g5 (17 ♕xd6?! ♗xd6 18 ♖xe6+ ♔d7 19 ♗f5 ♔c7 20 ♗h6 gxh6 21 ♖xf6 ♖af8 left Black very active in Herb-Speelman, French League 1992) 17...0-0-0 18 ♕e2 ♕c6 19 ♕xe6+ ♕xe6 20 ♖xe6 ♗c5 in view of his mobile queenside majority.

14 ... ♗d6

Westerinen's 14...0-0-0?! allows 15 e5 ♘d5 16 a4! b4 17 ♘xd5 ♗xd5 18 ♗g5 ♖e8 19 ♖fc1 ♘c5 20 ♘d2± (Bukić). Black's queenside looks extremely shaky.

15 ♘g5

By far the most popular, but currently the theoretical onus is very much on White. White has tried three alternatives, of which 'c' in particular requires an accurate knowledge of the theory:

a) **15 ♖e1** threatens e5 which Black has countered in two ways:

a1) **15...♘e5** 16 ♘g5!? ♕e7 17 f4 ♗c5+ 18 ♔h1 (18 ♗e3? ♘eg4) 18...♘d3! 19 ♗xd3 cxd3 20 ♕xd3 ♘g4 21 ♘h3 0-0 22 ♕g3 h5 23 ♘d1 ♖ad8 with good compensation; Torre-Mikhalchishin, Baku 1980.

a2) **15...♗c5?!** looked risky in Tunik-Sorokin, Sochi 1989: 16 e5 ♘g4 17 ♘e4 ♘gxe5 18 ♘fg5 ♗d5 19 ♗f4 although Black eventually won.

b) **15 ♔h1** deserves attention.

c) **15 ♘d4!?** *(100)* looked for a while the best territory for White to investigate in the entire variation.

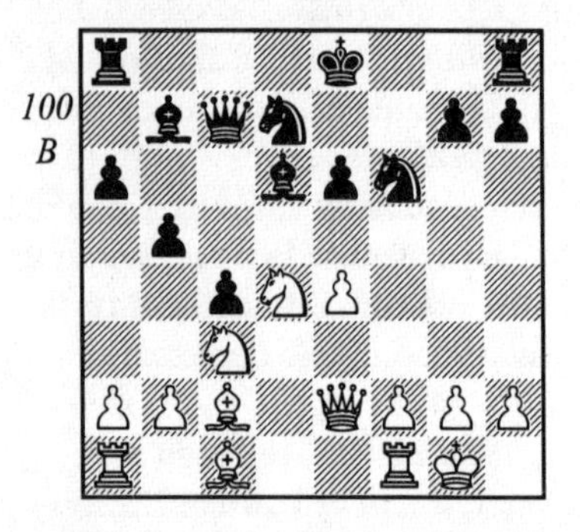

100
B

However, the antidote has now it seems been found, and even Mihai Marin, the originator of the idea, seems to believe that its time has passed:

c1) Shirov in *Informator 49* suggested **15...♗xh2+(!?)** 16 ♔h1 ♘c5 17 f4 0-0-0(!). However both **18 ♘dxb5** axb5 19 ♔xh2 b4 20 ♘b5 ♕b6 21 a4! and **18 ♗e3** Δ18...e5 19 ♘dxb5! seem to present some problems.

c2) **15...♘c5 16 f4 e5 17 ♘f5** and now Black should definitely castle short:

c21) Black was crushed in Marin-Delgado, Seville 1992 with **17...0-0-0?** 18 ♘xd6+ ♕xd6 19 fxe5 ♕xe5 20 ♖f5 ♕c7 21 a4 ♘fxe4?! (but what else?) 22 ♘xe4 ♗xe4 23 ♗xe4 ♖he8 24 ♗f4 ♕b6 25 ♕e3 1-0.

c22) Black fared better with **17...♘d3 18 ♗xd3** cxd3 19 ♕xd3 ♗c5+ 20 ♔h1 0-0 21 fxe5 ½-½ in Kharlov-Scherbakov, RSFSR Ch 1990 although it is not totally clear to me that Black's compensation suffices. Nonetheless, Marin preferred another route after 17...♘d3, namely **18 ♘xd6** ♕xd6 19 fxe5 ♘xc1 (19...♕xe5 20 ♖f5 ♕e7 21 e5 ♘d5 22 ♗d3 gives White pressure too) 20 ♖axc1 ♕xe5 21 ♖f5 ♕d4+ 22 ♔h1 0-0-0 23 a4± Marin-Guerra Bastida, Sitges 1992.

c23) **17...0-0!**:

c231) **18 ♖d1** ♘d3! (Pinter's recommendation, after his very unpleasant experience with 18...♖ad8? 19 ♖xd6! ♖xd6 20 fxe5 ♖e6 21 exf6 ♖fxf6 22 ♘d4 ♖e8 23 ♗g5± Marin-Pinter, French League 1992) 19 ♘xd6 ♕xd6 20 ♗xd3 cxd3 21 ♖xd3 ♕c7. The assessment of '=' generally attributed to this position is no doubt fair. Still, I must confess to a sneaking feeling that with the possible exception of **22 f5(!)** b4 23 ♘d5 ♘xd5 24 exd5 ♖xf5=, Black's practical chances are overall to be preferred here. Not, e.g. **22 ♗d2?** exf4 23 ♘d5 ♕c5+ ∓ Marin-San Segundo, Zaragoza 1992.

c232) **18 ♘xd6** ♕xd6 19 fxe5 ♕xe5 20 ♖f5. The right place for the rook, which in my view clearly does not belong on the d-file. Still after 20...♕c7! (20...♕e7 21 ♗g5±) 21 ♗f4 the players agreed a draw in Marin-Kuczynski, Debrecen 1992.

15 ...	**♘c5**
16 f4	**h6(!)**

The move that has been causing White problems. The older move **16...e5** weakens d5 and is less convincing. 17 a4! b4 (17...h6 Δ18 Nf3 Nd3 is still possible, but the pawn sac is better without ...e5; bad for Black was 17...Qb6? 18 axb5 axb5 19 Rxa8+ Bxa8 20 Be3 exf4 21 e5! Bxe5 22 Bd4 Nfe4 23 Bf2! f3 when 24 Qxf3! would have left Black in great difficulties; Marin-Shirov, Manila IZ 1990) 18 Nd5 Nxd5 19 exd5 0-0-0 20 Qxc4 looks good for White. If now **20...h6** 21 Nf7! Qxf7 22 fxe5 Qxd5 23 Qxd5 Bxd5 24 exd6 Rxd6 25 Be3± Gheorghiu-Schön, New York 1987, or **20...exf4** 21 Bxf4 Bxf4 22 Rxf4 Rxd5 23 Rf7± Tukmakov-Dolmatov, Frunze 1979. Oddly, Gligoric and several later sources suggest 23...Rd7(??) here, but 24 Bf5 looks like 1-0.

17 Nh3

a) After the main alternative **17 Nf3 Nd3!** (not 17...Bxf4 18 e5! Bxc1 19 exf6 Bf4 20 f7+! winning – Shirov) **18 Bxd3 cxd3 19 Qxd3** *(101)* Black seems to have excellent compensation:

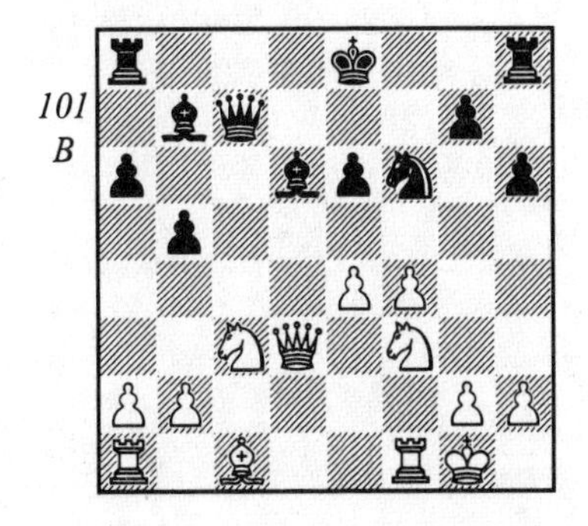
101
B

a1) **19...Rd8** 20 Qe2 b4!? (20...Bxf4 21 Bxf4 Qxf4 22 a4 was only equal in Brenninkmeijer-Zso.Polgar, Amsterdam 1990) 21 e5 Bc5+ 22 Kh1 Ng4 23 Nd1 Bc6 24 Nd4 Bxd4 25 Qxg4 Qf7 with compensation in Gschnitzer-Lukacs, Budapest 1990.

a2) **19...0-0!?** 20 Kh1 (20 e5 is the critical test but Black's play holds up well with 20...Bc5+ 21 Kh1! Nd5 22 Nxd5 Bxd5 23 b3 Rad8 24 Qe2∞ Shirov) 20...Rad8 21 Nd4 Bc5 22 Be3 Ng4 23 Nce2 Nxe3 24 Qxe3 Rxd4 Δ...Qb6, Rd8∓ Bareev-Shirov, Hastings 1991/2.

b) After **17 e5!?**, Se.Ivanov gives 17...hxg5 18 Bg6+ **Ke7** 19 exd6 Qxd6∞. However, 20 Qe5! would be irritating for Black. In Anić-Lukacs, Budapest 1992, Black found the right way with **18...Kf8!** 19 exd6 Qxd6 20 Qe5 Qc6 21 Qxg5? (Losing the possibility of opening the f-file also closes off the majority of White's play. Better according to Lukacs was the tricky 21 Ne4! Ncxe4 22 fxg5 Qb6+ 23 Kh1 Qd4!! 24 Qxd4 Ng3+ 25 Kg1 Ne2+ 26 Kh1=) 21...b4! 22 Be3 Rc8 23 Ne2 Nce4 24 Qa5 Ng4∓.

17 ... e5

Much more logical than with the knight on g5. Suddenly White's d4 square looks more of a factor. Shumiakina has played **17...Nd3** which gives fair compensation after 18 e5 Bc5+ 19 Be3 (!) Nd5 20

♘xd5 ♗xd5 21 ♗xd3 cxd3 22 ♕xd3 0-0 since the knight on h3 is not well placed to contest Black's light-square superiority.

18 a4 0-0!! *(102)*

102
W

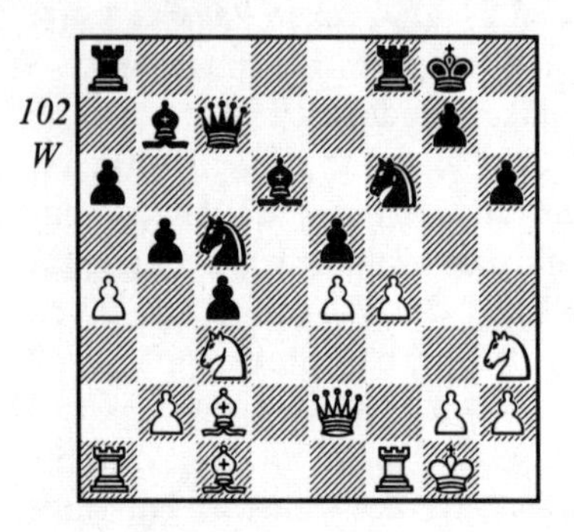

A brilliant and original concept, the product of a 45 minute think. Dreev correctly assesses that White is going nowhere serious on the queenside, and Black will be much better in the centre so long as his king finds safety. The game which had attracted me to the line was Butnoiris-Sveshnikov, Jurmala 1980 where after **18...♘d3** 19 axb5! ♘xc1 20 ♖axc1 axb5 21 ♔h1 ♕c5 22 ♘d5! (since if 22...♘xd5, 23 ♕h5+) 22...0-0 23 b4! ♕a7 24 fxe5 ♗xe5 25 ♘e7+ White stood very well.

19 axb5 ♘e6!∓

White can hardly capture on e5 since the black bishop will be in total command. Also there is no way to cover d4. White is virtually lost.

20 bxa6 exf4
21 e5 f3!
22 gxf3 ♘d4
23 ♕g2 ♗xe5

Black deftly refuted White's desperate 21 e5, and his pieces dominate the board. My next move is a time-trouble blunder which shortens the agony.

24 ♗xh6? ♘xc2
25 ♕xc2 ♗c8!
26 ♔h1 ♗xh3
27 ♖g1 ♘g4
0-1

The decision to include such an unpleasant defeat is not taken lightly! Although some of the sidelines may be worth investigating for White, the current trend is away from an early clarification of the centre, either delaying dxe6 until a more appropriate juncture, or inducing Black to play ...e5. It is to these developments that we now turn.

Game 18
Beliavsky-Khalifman
Manila OL 1992

1 ♘f3 ♘f6 2 c4 c6 3 ♘c3 d5 4 e3 e6 5 d4 ♘bd7 6 ♗d3 dxc4 7 ♗xc4 b5 8 ♗d3 ♗b7 9 0-0 a6 10 e4 c5 11 d5 c4

12 ♗c2 *(103)*

103
B

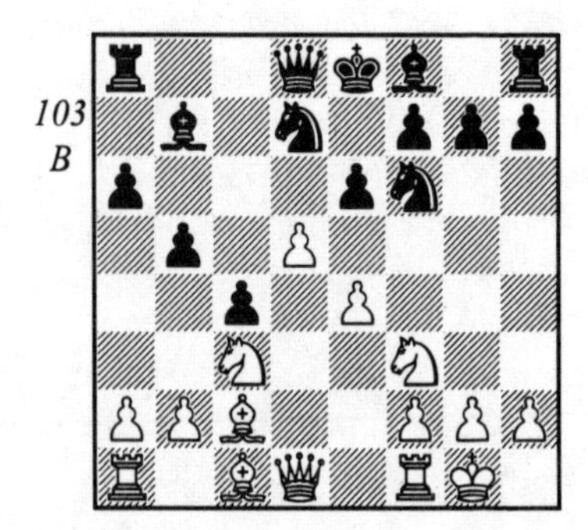

12 ... ♕c7

For many years the idea of playing 12 ♗c2 here (and especially the analogous 11 ♗c2 in Chapter 15) was regarded suspiciously in view of the reply 12...e5. Here there was admittedly more justification since the bishop on b7 is misplaced after 12...e5 but Black still gets mobile queenside pawns without the drawback of a weak e-pawn. Recently more players have been turning to the flexible text and whilst **12...e5** remains an important choice it certainly does not suit all styles, e.g. 13 ♕e2 ♕c7 14 ♗g5! h6 15 ♗d2 ♖c8 (15...♘b6? 16 a4 b4 17 a5± was Akopian-Shirov, USSR 1988) 16 ♖fc1 ♗d6 17 a4 b4 18 ♘d1 a5 19 ♗b3 ♗a6 20 ♘e3 ♘b6 21 ♘f5± Akopian.

By contrast **12...♗c5** is clearly inferior, since by 13 dxe6 White may transpose to Brenninkmeijer-Van der Sterren above. It is well worth remembering that until Black clarifies the centre he must always reckon with dxe6.

13 ♕e2

The regular choice, but **13 ♗g5** ♗d6 14 ♔h1 was tried in Tunik-Filipenko, Sochi 1989. This turned out well for White after 14...0-0 15 dxe6 fxe6 16 ♘d4 ♘c5 17 f4 **♘fxe4?**, but simply **17...b4** 18 e5 bxc3 19 exd6 ♕xd6 20 bxc3 ♘fe4 favours Black according to Sorokin.

Another original idea for White to consider is Yakovich's **13 ♘d4!?**, the logic being that prior to dxe6 the move is sounder in that White will not suffer any d-file embarrassment but recently the idea received a bit of a blow since it appears that with **13...e5(!)** 14 ♘f5 g6 15 ♘h6 ♘h5! 16 ♕f3 (16 g3 ♗d6=) 16...♘f4 17 ♘xf7 (17 ♘g4 ♗d6 Δ...h5∓) 17...♔xf7 18 g3 g5! 19 gxf4 gxf4, Gelfand-Dreev, Tilburg 1993, White is left with nothing better than a perpetual with 20 ♕h5+ ♔e7 21 ♕h4+ ♔f7 22 ♕h5 (in the game the exchange sacrifice 21 ♗d1 ♖g8+! 22 ♔h1 ♘f6 23 ♗h5+ ♖g6!! proved effective). This could put 13 ♘d4 out of commission.

13 ... ♗d6
14 ♗g5 *(104)*

104
B

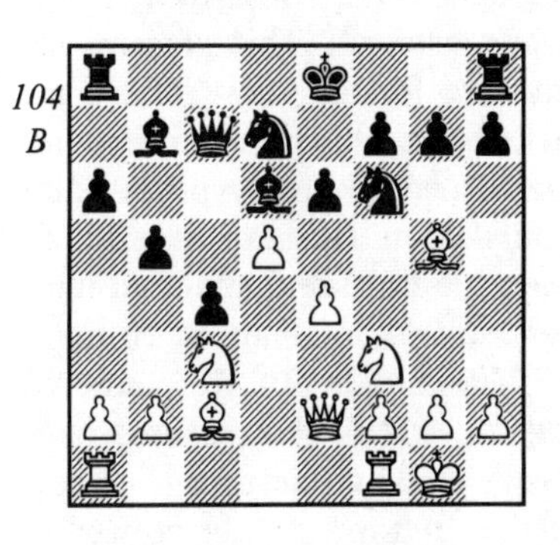

14 ... e5

Black becomes impatient with White's waiting game and decides to remove the option of dxe6 once and for all. At the same time he is hoping to show that ♗g5 and ♕e2 are not ideal developments for the new structure. Two other moves have been tried here. The first now seems condemned as inferior, since White can force weaknesses on both sides of the board, but the second remains interesting:

a) **14...h6?!** 15 ♗xf6 gxf6 16 a4! (This causes many more problems than 16 ♘d4 ♘c5 17 b4 cxb3 18 axb3 ♗xh2+ 19 ♔h1 ♗e5 20 ♕e3 ♗f4 21 ♕h3 ♗e5 22 ♕e3 ♗f4 23 ♕h3 ♗e5 24 ♕e3 ½-½ Khalifman-Dreev, Lvov Z 1990; Black must repeat with 24...♗f4, since otherwise White's threats of f4 and b4 are very unpleasant) 16...b4 17 ♘d1 ♘e5 18 ♘xe5 ♗xe5 19 ♘e3 ♖c8 (19...♗xb2 20 ♖ad1 c3 21 ♗b3!± Gelfand. As has been mentioned previously, the big issue in this variation is frequently whether Black's queenside pawns are strong or weak. This game is instructive for the way Gelfand attacks against the weakened centre, attacks the queenside pawns, and taunts them forward in order to blockade them and attain an utter light-square domination) 20 ♖ad1 h5 (20...♗xh2+ 21 ♔h1 ♗f4 22 ♘g4 ♗e5 23 d6! is no improvement) 21 ♔h1 (Gelfand is critical of this, retrospectively preferring the immediate 'blockade' strategy 21 b3 c3 22 ♘c4±) 21...b3 22 ♗b1 a5 23 ♕d2 c3 (tempting, but 23...♗a6 held out better chances of survival) 24 bxc3 ♕xc3 25 ♕e2! ♕b4 26 ♗d3 ♔e7 27 ♗b5 ♖cd8 28 ♘c4 ♗b8 29 ♕e3 ♗a8 30 ♖d3 ♖c8 31 d6+ ♗xd6 32 ♘xd6 ♖cd8 33 ♕a7+ 1-0 Gelfand-Illescas, Linares 1992.

b) **14...0-0-0**:

b1) **15 ♖fd1** h6!? 16 ♗xf6 gxf6 17 b3 (In the absence of a possible ♘d1, there is no realistic strategy based on a4) 17...♗b4 18 dxe6 fxe6 19 ♘b1 ♘e5 20 ♘bd2 c3 21 ♘f1 ♗c5 22 ♘xe5 fxe5 23 ♖xd8+ ♖xd8 and Black stood very well in Gelfand-Timman, Linares 1992.

b2) **15 dxe6** fxe6 16 ♘d4!? (The text looks much more promising than 16 b3 ♘e5 {16...b4!?} 17 bxc4 {More troublesome for Black would be 17 ♘d4 ♖he8 18 ♘dxb5 axb5 19 ♘xb5 ♕c5 20 bxc4 with compensation - Se.Ivanov} 17...♘xf3+ 18 ♕xf3 ♗xh2+ 19 ♔h1 ♗e5!-+ Sakaev-Se.Ivanov, Leningrad 1990) 16...♕b6! (16...♗xh2+ 17 ♔h1 ♘c5 18 ♘dxb5 axb5 19 ♘xb5 ♕b6 20 ♕c4 ♗a6 21 a4 gives White a very strong attack) 17 ♘xe6 ♗xh2+ 18 ♔xh2 ♕xe6 19 ♔g1 h6 20 ♗e3 ♘g4 21 b3 h5! with enough play to hold the balance; Hraček-Bagirov, Debrecen 1992.

15 a4

15 ♘h4 is an interesting alternative. 15...g6 (15...0-0 16 ♘f5 ♘e8 17 ♕g4 f6 18 ♗e3 ♗c8 19 ♕h4 b4 20 ♘e2 ♗c5 21 ♖ad1 ♘d6 22 ♘e7+ ♔f7 23 ♘c6± was Akopian-Sorokin, Minsk 1990) 16 ♕f3 ♕d8?! (Ribli gives 16...♗e7! 17 ♖ad1 ♕d6!∞ despite the queen's unorthodox role as blockader) 17 ♖ad1 ♖c8 18 a3 ♕e7 19 ♘e2 h6

20 ♗d2 ♘c5 21 ♗c3 ♘fxe4 (Black seeks to counteract has problems by initiating complications, but this should not have been successful) 22 ♘xg6 ♘xg5!? and now instead of the messy **23 ♕h5**, simply **23 ♘xe7** ♘xf3+ 24 gxf3 ♔xe7 25 ♘g3 favours White in view of the strong f5 square; Lobron-Ribli, Bielefeld 1992.

With 15 a4, Beliavsky seeks to prove that the black queenside will be vulnerable. However, Black's position is much sounder than in the analogous case with the doubled f-pawns that we saw in Gelfand-Illescas above. Although quickly drawn, the game is interesting as an example of the equilibrium between attack and defence in a genuinely finely balanced position.

15 ...	**b4**
16 ♘d1	**a5**
17 ♖c1	**♗a6**
18 ♘e3	**0-0**
19 ♗xf6	

White would not relish this decision, but the need to attack c4 further takes priority. The immediate 19 ♘d2?? fails to 19...c3 20 ♗d3 ♗xd3 21 ♕xd3 ♘c5-+, so White deflects the knight to the kingside.

19 ...	**♘xf6**
20 ♘d2	**♖fc8**
21 ♗b1	**c3**
22 ♗d3	**♗xd3**
23 ♕xd3 *(105)*	

105
B

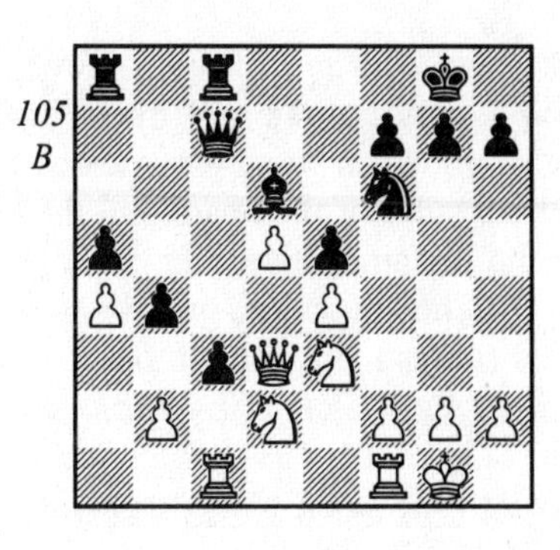

Here as in the aforementioned game Gelfand-Illescas, White has ceded the dark squares to pursue a single-minded attempt to control the light squares. However, after Black's strong 23rd it is impossible for White to maintain a blockade since **24 ♘dc4** fails trivially to 24...cxb2, and **24 ♘b3** ♕d7!? also gives the impression that White has lost control. Hence White has no choice but to exchange on c3, and then initiate a sequence which prevents Black from supporting his advanced passed pawn with ...♗b4.

23 ...	**♖ab8**
24 bxc3	**bxc3**
25 ♘f5	**♗f8**
26 d6	

26 ♘f3?! ♘e8!?∓.

26 ...	**♕c6**
27 ♘e7+	**♗xe7**
28 dxe7	**♕c5**
29 ♘f3	**h6**

½-½

14 8...♗b7 9 0-0 b4 and Lundin's 8...b4

Game 19
Serper-Shirov
USSR ch (Moscow) 1991

1 d4 d5 2 c4 c6 3 ♘c3 ♘f6 4 e3 e6 5 ♘f3 ♘bd7 6 ♗d3 dxc4 7 ♗xc4 b5 8 ♗d3

8 ... ♗b7

In modern practice Black usually prefers ...b4 only in the move order introduced in our main game. This of course allows White the possibility of 9 e4, but it also avoids some of the lines that have tended to push Lundin's immediate 8...b4 out of favour. In both cases, ...b4 has the plus point of saving time otherwise wasted on ...a6, but the drawback of making c4 available to the white pieces. At this point I shall give a summary of all important lines which give Lundin's variation an independent flavour. After **8...b4** *(106)*, White has two important choices:

106
W

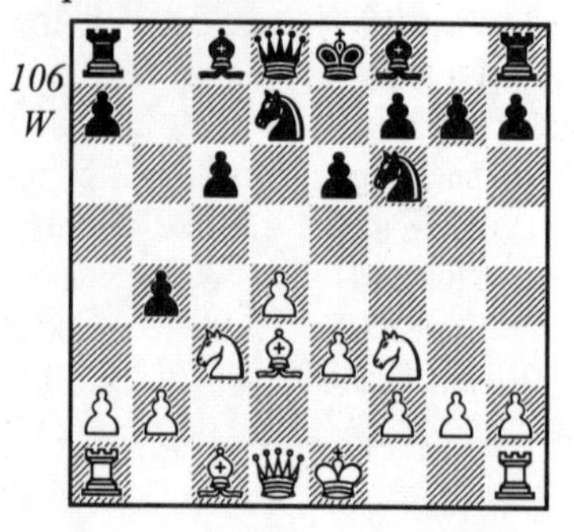

a) **9 ♘a4 c5!** and now:

a1) **10 0-0** cxd4 11 ♘xd4 ♗b7 12 ♗d2 ♗d6 13 ♕e2 a6! (otherwise 13...0-0 14 ♗a6±) Hort-Ciric, Athens 1968.

a2) **10 e4 cxd4**:

a21) **11 e5** ♘d5 12 0-0 ♗e7!? (12...♗b7 would transpose directly to Chapters 9 and 10) 13 ♖e1 0-0 14 ♘xd4 ♕c7 (14...♗b7 15 ♕h5! see line 'b2' in the note 13...g6 in Game 14) 15 ♕h5 g6 16 ♕e2 (Of course here the queen is tied to the defence of the e-pawn, so ♕h6 is not possible) 16...♗b7 17 ♗h6 ♖fc8 18 ♖ac1 (18 ♗a6?! ♗xa6 19 ♕xa6 ♕c4!∓) 18...♕a5∓ Taimanov.

a22) **11 ♗b5!?** ♕a5 (11...♗b7 12 ♕xd4!? Conquest; 11...♖b8!?) 12 ♗c6 ♖b8 13 0-0 (13 e5 ♘d5 14 0-0 may give some play too, but not 13 ♗f4? b3+ ∓) 13...e5! 14 ♗f4! *(107)*

107
B

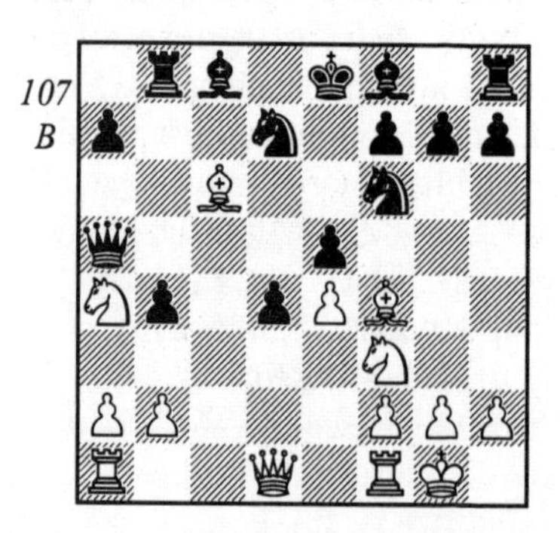

A remarkable move based on generating enough threats against the black king in the variation **14...exf4** 15 e5 ♘d5 16 ♘xd4, threatening 17 ♘b3, and intending to answer 16...♗b7 with the cool 17 ♖c1!?. Black did not like the look of it and declined with **14...♗d6**. This by no means killed the fun after 15 ♗g3! ♗c7?! (15...0-0 16 ♘xd4 ♕c7! 17 ♘f5∞) 16 ♖c1 0-0 17 b3! ♖d8?! 18 ♗xd7 ♘xd7 19 ♘xd4 ♘f6 20 ♘c6?! (20 ♖c5!±) 20...♖xd1 21 ♖fxd1 ♕b5 22 ♘xb8 ♗g4! (22...♕xb8 23 ♗xe5!+-) 23 ♖xc7 ♗xd1 24 ♖c8+ ♘e8 25 ♘c6 h5! and now White could have maintained some advantage with **26 ♖xe8+** ♔h7 29 ♖d8! ♕xc6 30 ♖xd1 ♕c2, though Black is not without play. After **26 h4?** White won only after extraordinary time-trouble induced randomness, in Wells-Conquest, London 1991.

a3) **10 dxc5** ♘xc5 11 ♘xc5 (11 ♗b5+ ♗d7 12 ♗xd7+ ♘fxd7 13 0-0 ♗e7 14 ♗d2 a5, Tylor-Alekhine, Hastings 1936/7, was very comfortable for Black. The possibility of ...♗d7 is one reason why 9 ♘a4 is rather innocuous. More difficult to explain is why it is nonetheless more popular than 10 ♘a4 after 8...♗b7 9 0-0 b4 which at least gives Black cause for thought before so lightly recapturing on c5) 11...♗xc5 12 ♕c2 (12 0-0 0-0 13 e4 ♗b7 14 ♕e2 {14 e5?! ♗e4! Kondratiev} 14...h6 15 ♗f4 ♕e7 16 ♖ac1 ♖ac8 17 e5 ♘d7 with equal play in Reshevsky-Mecking, Buenos Aires 1970. White's knight can aspire to reach d6, but Black's minor pieces notably the bishop on b7 are good, and his king secure) 12...♕b6 13 ♘d2 ♗b7 14 ♘c4 ♕c7 15 f3 **0-0** 16 b3 h6 17 ♗b2 ♘d5 18 e4 ♘f4 19 **0-0-0** ♖fd8 20 ♗e5 with complicated play in which Black's chances are somewhat preferable; Bareev-Sveshnikov, USSR 1992.

b) **9 ♘e4** is by far the most popular and challenging option. In principle the play can now take two directions. Either Black permits White to capture on f6 and to play a subsequent e4, after which Black's counterplay with ...c5 is similar to Wade's variation; or Black himself exchanges, and seeks to prove that White's play on the c-file, particularly against c6, is of a transitory nature. This basic dichotomy, however, comes with a number of interesting nuances, and here Black has four important continuations, as well as one which can be dismissed quite lightly:

b1) **9...♕b6?!** was tried in the game F.Olafsson-Pomar, Las Palmas 1974. Unfortunately, the idea of exchanging light squared bishops fails to address Black's structural problems and White stood much better after 10 ♘xf6+ ♘xf6 11 0-0 ♗a6 12 e4 ♗e7 13 ♗g5! h6 14 ♗xf6 ♗xf6 15 ♗xa6 ♕xa6 16 ♕b3!.

b2) **9...c5** is probably somewhat suspect, but interestingly not for the reason given in many opening manuals.

b21) The apparently logical **10 ♕a4?!** fails tactically to yield a plus, viz. 10...♗e7! 11 dxc5 (If 11 ♘xf6+ ♗xf6 12 dxc5 0-0 13 ♕xb4 ♘xc5! looks strong) 11...♘xe4! (Euwe's 11...0-0!? 12 ♕xb4 ♖b8 13 ♕xd4 ♘xc5 looks unclear) 12 ♗xe4 0-0! 13 ♗xa8 ♘c5 14 ♕xa7 ♗a6, although it is sad that all this excitement fizzles out to a draw after **15 ♗d2** ♕d3 16 0-0-0 ♘b3+ 17 axb3 ♖c8+ 18 ♗c3 ♖xc3+ with perpetual to follow; or **15 ♘e5** ♕d6 16 ♗f3 ♕xe5 17 ♗e2 ♗xe2 18 ♔xe2 ♕d5! (otherwise Black has insufficient for the exchange) 19 ♕xe7 ♕c4+ 20 ♔d1 b3!= (Euwe), since if **21 axb3?** simply 21...♘xb3 is strong, or **21 ♗d2** ♕c2+ 22 ♔e2 ♕c4+ 23 ♔d1 ♕c2+ etc.

b22) Until recently **10 ♘xf6+ ♘xf6** 11 ♘e5! seemed a fairly simple route to a plus (Taimanov) since Black can suffer problems on both the f3-a8, and a4-e8 diagonals. However, with **10...gxf6!?** Sveshnikov has given a new, although I suspect not quite sufficient, dimension to Black's play. 11 0-0 (11 ♗e4 ♖b8 12 0-0 and 11 e4!? deserve attention according to Sveshnikov) 11...cxd4 12 ♘xd4 ♕b6 (12...♗b7 13 e4 ♗c5) 13 a4!? a5 14 ♗b5 ♗b7 and instead of **15 ♕h5** ♖d8! 16 ♖d1 ♖g8 17 g3 ♖g5!∓ Dreev-Sveshnikov, Russia 1992, White should have tried **15 e4!** 0-0-0 16 ♗e3 ♗c5 17 ♕c2 with play for both sides.

b3) **9...♗b7** invites White to transpose to Serper-Shirov by either simply 10 0-0, or 10 ♘xf6+ ♘xf6 11 e4 ♗e7 12 0-0 etc. The interesting question is whether White has better, and it seems that he has, if only another transposition – to 'b4' below: 10 ♘xf6+ ♘xf6 (In general ...gxf6 is not so attractive when White can prepare to answer ...c5 with d5) 11 ♕a4!? (11 e4 ♗e7 12 ♕e2!? transposes to 'b4' in which White also enjoys some interesting possibilities by virtue of not committing his king too early. In view of the note to Black's 13th below, this may be the best option. I hope that the reader will agree that the detailed coverage of 11 ♕a4 is merited because sometimes wonderful chess must take precedence over current theoretical relevance!) 11...♗e7 12 ♗d2 a5 13 e4 0-0?! (A case of castling into it, although if it had been played against a lesser opponent, 'theory' could easily have overlooked the fact! Much better is 13...♘d7 which is generally marked ± without further ado, but to me Black looks fine {14 e5? ♘c5!}. It is hard for White to find a move which will make 14...0-0 Δ...c5 as dangerous for Black as one move earlier. Is 14 h4!? far-fetched?) 14 e5 ♘d7 15 ♕c2 h6 16 h4! c5 17 ♖h3! ♗xf3 18 ♗xh6!! *(108)*.

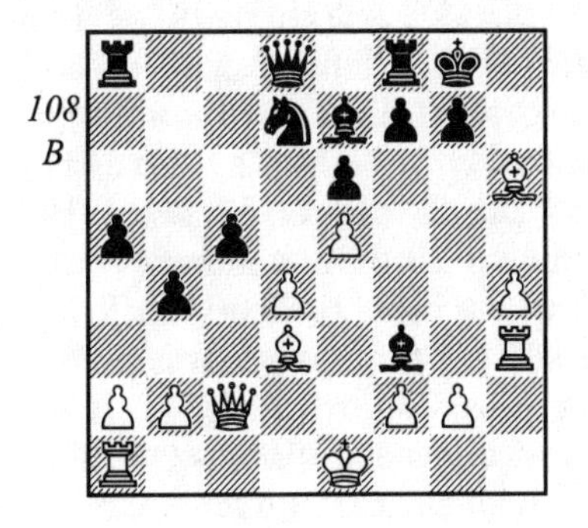

Truly beautiful and far from obvious. In the game Black now lost with **18...♗xh4** 19 gxf3 gxh6 20 ♔e2! ♘xe5!? 21 dxe5 ♕d4 22 ♖xh4! ♕xh4 23 ♖g1+ ♔h8 24 ♕c1! (Δ♖h1) 24...f6 25 ♖g6! 1-0 Portisch-Johannessen, Havana 1966. Also very fine is the variation **18...♗g4!?** 19 ♖g3 f5 20 ♖xg4! fxg4 21 ♗h7+ ♔h8 22 ♗xg7+! ♔xg7 23 ♕g6+ ♔h8 24 ♗g8!!± (strangely Varnusz mentions only 24 ♕h6 ♖f7 25 ♗g6+ ♔g8 26 ♗xf7+ which is just a draw) 24...♖f7 25 ♗xf7 ♕f8 26 ♕h5+ ♔g7 27 ♗xe6 with great advantage.

b4) **9...♗e7 10 ♘xf6+** (10 ♕a4?! c5! see 'b21') **10...♘xf6 11 e4** and now:

b41) **11...c5** looks suspect: 12 0-0 0-0 (12...cxd4 13 e5 ♘d7 {maybe 13...♘d5} 14 ♗e4 ♖b8 15 ♘xd4± Gheorghiu/Samarian) 13 ♕c2 ♘d7 14 ♖d1 ♕a5 15 d5!± Ragozin-Lundin, Saltsjöbaden 1948.

b42) **11...♗b7** 12 ♕e2(!) (12 0-0 transposes to the main game. Less testing is 12 ♗g5 ♘d7! 13 ♗xe7 ♕xe7 14 ♕a4 a5 15 ♖c1 0-0 Δ...c5=) 12...♕b6 (If 12...0-0?! 13 e5 ♘d7 14 ♕e4 g6 15 h4 is very dangerous - Korchnoi; or 12...♘d7 13 0-0 0-0 14 ♖d1 ♕a5 15 ♗f4 c5 16 d5! Szabo-Kottnauer, Szczawno Zdroj 1950) 13 0-0 ♖c8 (13...c5!? – Polugaevsky) 14 ♗g5 h6 15 ♗h4 c5 16 ♗xf6! (Also worth attention is 16 ♘e5 g5 17 ♘c4! {17 ♗g3 cxd4 18 ♘c4! ♖xc4 19 ♗xc4 ♘xe4 worked well for Black in Tal-Ljubojevic, Milan 1973} 17...♕d8 18 ♗g3 cxd4 19 ♗e5! Δf4 with strong pressure) 16...♗xf6 17 d5± Korchnoi.

b5) **9...♘xe4 10 ♗xe4 ♗b7** *(109)* and now:

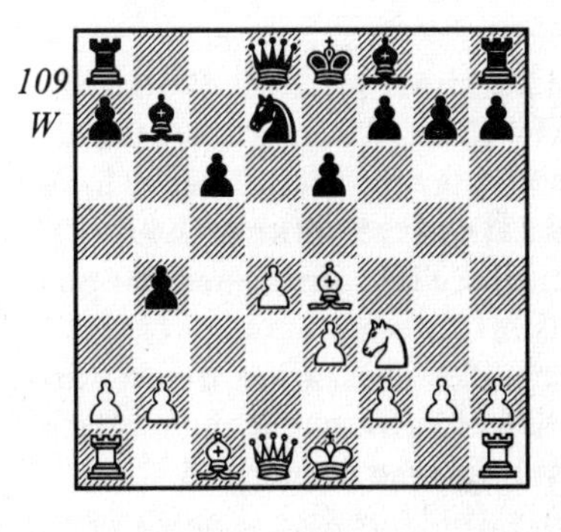

b51) **11 ♕c2** is not a very clever fork! 11...♖c8 12 ♗xh7 c5 13 ♗e4 cxd4 14 ♕d3 ♗xe4 15 ♕xe4 dxe3 was comfortable for Black in Malich-Kostro, Århus 1971.

b52) **11 ♕a4** is the most ambitious, initially extolled, certainly sound, but it is unclear whether White obtains a significant plus after **11...♕b6 12 ♘d2**:

b521) **12...♖b8!?** is suggested by Ornstein, who has been one of the most important advocates of this line. In a sense, the move is a mark of optimism. If things go badly the rook will be needed on c8, but if Black is successful in implementing ...c5, supporting the bishop is the chief task. However, White can play for a plus with either **13 ♘c4** ♕a6 (13...♕b5 14 ♕xb5 cxb5 15 ♗xb7 bxc4 16 ♗c6±) 14 ♕xa6 ♗xa6 15 ♘a5!? c5 16 ♘c6 ♖b7 17 a3!⩲; or **13 a3** Δ13...bxa3 14 bxa3!? since ...♗a6 is not now available to Black.

b522) **12...♖c8 13 a3! bxa3**:

b5221) The experimental **14 b4!?** was tried in Ogaard-Sveshnikov, Bucharest 1976. **14...♗xb4?!** 15 ♗xa3 c5 16 ♗xb4 cxb4 17 0-0 ♔e7 and now 18 ♕xa7 should favour White. Better looks **14...♕xb4** 15 ♕xb4 ♗xb4 16 ♗xa3 ♗c3!? with chances for both sides.

b5222) The earlier try **14 ♘c4** still looks OK, but has had some of its sting removed after 14...♕a6 15 ♕b3 ♖b8! (Ornstein again!) 16 **0-0** c5 17 ♗xb7 ♕xb7 18 ♕xa3 cxd4 19 ♘d6+ ♗xd6 20 ♕xd6 ♕b6 21 ♕a3 ♕c5 22 ♕xa7 ♕xa7 23 ♖xa7 ♘f6 24 exd4 **0-0**= Tukmakov-Ornstein, Vrnjacka Banja 1979.

b5223) **14 b3!?** ♗a6 15 ♘c4 ♕b4+ (15...♕b5? 16 ♖xa3!! is a terrific exchange sacrifice: 16...♗xa3 17 ♕xa3 ♔d8 18 **0-0** ♖c7 19 ♗d2 ♘b6 20 ♗d3+- Tarjan-Silva, Odessa 1976) 16 ♕xb4 ♗xb4+ 17 ♗d2 ♗xc4!? (17...♗xd2+ 18 ♔xd2 ♗xc4 19 bxc4 c5 20 d5!± Kondratiev) 18 ♗xb4 ♗xb3! 19 ♖xa3 ♗d5 20 ♗xd5 (At first I was intrigued by the possibility of 20 ♗d3!? Δe4, but it seems that Black is OK here too with 20...c5! 21 dxc5 ♘xc5 22 ♗b5+ ♗c6 23 ♗xc6+ ♖xc6 24 **0-0** {24 ♖c3 ♖b6!=} 24...♘a6! 25 ♗c3 0-0=) 20...cxd5 21 ♖xa7 ♘b8! (Ginsburg). The text is a very important idea, after which I must confess that like Donaldson I can find nothing special for White, e.g. **22 ♗c5** ♘c6 23 ♖b7 ♖b8! 24 ♖xb8+ ♘xb8 25 ♔d2 ♔d7 26 ♖b1 ♔c7= or **22 ♖b7** ♘c6 23 ♗d6 ♘a5!=.

b53) **11 0-0** is a more realistic route to a small plus:

b531) **11...♘f6** 12 ♗c2! ♗e7 13 e4 0-0 14 e5 ♘d7 15 ♕d3 g6 16 ♗h6 ♖e8 17 ♕e4 ♕b6 18 ♕f4 c5 19 ♗a4 gave White a powerful initiative in Chernin-Borkowski, Polanica Zdroj 1988.

b532) **11...♗e7** 12 ♘d2 (12 ♕c2 h6 13 ♗xc6 ♖c8 14 ♗xd7+ ♕xd7 gives good light-square compensation – Uhlmann) 12...♕c7 (12...**0-0** 13 b3 ♖c8(?!) 14 ♘c4 ♘f6 15 ♗f3 ♘d5 16 a3! a5 17 ♗d2 c5 18 dxc5 ♗xc5 19 ♘xa5! cost Black a full pawn in Portisch-Polugaevsky, Portoroz IZ 1973) 13 b3 0-0 14 ♗b2 f5 (Black seeks some central counterplay, but White's positional trumps on the queenside keep him on top) 15 ♗f3 e5 16 ♘c4 e4 17 ♗e2 c5 18 ♖c1 ♖ad8 19 ♕c2± Tukmakov-Mikhalchishin, Frunze 1979.

9 0-0 b4
10 ♘e4

As discussed above, **10 ♘a4** is here almost unseen, strangely, since with the bishop already on b7, Black's course of action after **10...c5 11 dxc5** is not so clear:

a) **11...♘xc5?!** 12 ♗b5+ ♘cd7 13 ♘e5 ♕c7 14 ♕d4 ♖c8 15 ♗d2± Cvetković-Bagirov, Vrnjacka Banja 1974.

b) **11...♗xc5** 12 ♘xc5 ♘xc5 13 ♗b5+ ♔e7 14 ♕e2 ♕b6 15 ♘d4 ♖hd8 16 b3 a6 17 ♗c4 ♗d5 18 a3 with advantage in a game Hort-Lombardy.

In general, White's structure here is much sounder with the pawn on e3 rather than on e5 as in the 9 e4 Wade Variation. Better possibilities are:

c) **11...♕a5** 12 ♘d4! (12 a3!?) 12...♘xc5 13 ♘xc5 ♗xc5 14 ♗b5+ which Donaldson gives as ±, but this seems a little harsh after 14...♔e7 15 ♘c6+ ♗xc6 16 ♗xc6 ♖ad8±.

d) Still, perhaps Black could also explore further with **11...a6!?** 12 a3!? (12 ♕c2 ♖c8 13 ♕e2 ♕a5!; or 12 c6 ♗xc6 13 ♘d4 ♗b7 are no big deal) 12...♗xc5! (12...bxa3 13 b4!±) 13 ♘xc5 ♘xc5 14 ♗e2±.

10 ... ♗e7

10...♘xe4 11 ♗xe4 transposes to 'b53' above.

11 ♘xf6+

11 a3 is also interesting, with obvious similarities to Game 16.

11 ... ♘xf6 *(110)*

Chekhov suggests **11...gxf6!?**.

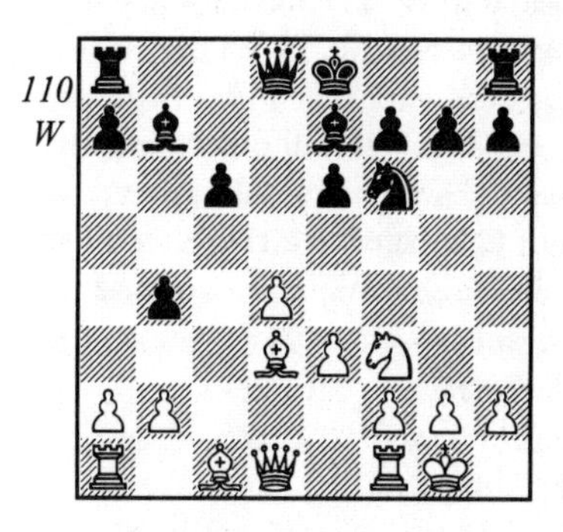

12 ♕e2

The text is currently highly regarded, although it has little independent significance as against 12 e4 0-0 13 ♕e2. Perhaps the best way to understand the thinking behind it is to first examine the alternatives after **12 e4 0-0** (12...♖c8 13 a3! bxa3 14 b4! ♗xb4 15 ♕b3± {Kondratiev} is by now a familiar motif) and now:

a) **13 e5**. White seeks to drive the knight from the defence of Black's kingside and to construct an attack there, but with the help of a novelty from Anand it now seems that Black can begin liquidating White's pieces before things get dangerous. The resulting positions moreover, although objectively equal, are just sufficiently unbalanced that Black can contest the full point. **13...♘d7** (13...♘d5?! 14 ♕c2 g6 15 ♗h6 ♖e8 16 ♘d2± Mednis; worse still would be 14...h6 15 ♕e2! Δ♕e4±. In principle Black's priority must be to support ...c5 not to occupy the 'outpost' at d5) **14 ♗e4** (14 ♕c2 transposes to 'b') with the following:

a1) **14...♕b6**, though tempting since Black would, given the choice, recapture on b7 with queen rather than rook, allows White just the sort of chances he seeks after **15 ♗g5!**:

a11) **15...♖fe8** 16 ♗xe7 ♖xe7 17 ♕c2 h6 18 a3! b3 (sad necessity in view of 18...a5 19 axb4 axb4 20 ♖xa8+ ♗xa8 21 ♖c1 ♖e8 22 h3 ♗b7 23 ♕c4 ♖c8 24 ♘d2 c5 25 ♗xb7 ♕xb7 26 ♘b3+- Averkin) 19 ♕c3 c5 20 ♗xb7 ♕xb7 21 dxc5 ♖c8 22 ♕b4 ♘xc5 23 ♖ac1 ♕c6 (Polugaevsky-Mednis, Riga IZ 1979) when 24 ♖c4! ♖ec7 25 ♖fc1 ♕d5 26 ♕b5! would have been unpleasant for Black.

a12) **15...♗xg5** 16 ♗xh7+! ♔xh7 17 ♘xg5+ ♔g6 18 ♕g4 f5 19 ♕g3 c5! (19...♖h8 20 ♘xe6+ ♔f7 21 ♕b3! ♔e7 22 ♘xg7 ♖ag8 23 ♘xf5+ ♔d8 24 ♘d6 ♔c7 25 ♖ac1 ♔b8? {25...♗a8⩲} 26 ♘xb7 ♕xb7 27 ♕f3± was Grigorian-Dobosz, Erevan 1980) 20 ♘xe6+ ♔f7 21 ♘xf8 ♖xf8 22 dxc5 ♘xc5 23 ♖ad1 ♔g8 24 ♖d6 ♕b5 25 ♖fd1 f4 26 ♕g4, unclear according to Dobosz, but the rook here seems for preference.

a2) **14...f5** is interesting: 15 exf6 ♘xf6 16 ♗c2 (16 ♕e2!? ♗d6⩲ Tal, who says that 16...♘xe4 is bad after 17 ♕xe4 and if 17...♕d5 18 ♕xd5 cxd5 19 ♗g5!±, but are 19...♗d6 or even 19...♖xf3 20 ♗xe7 ♖d3 so catastrophic?) 16...c5 17 ♗b3 ♗d5! 18 dxc5 ♗xc5 19 ♗g5 ♕b6 with approximate equality in Tal-Sveshnikov, Sochi 1986.

a3) **14...♖b8!?** *(111)*

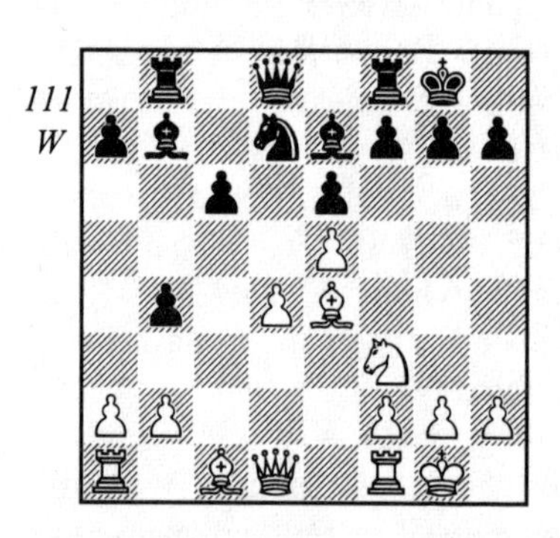

This seemingly very natural move had not been 'discovered' until very recently. On current evidence it should supersede other tries, although Black has to take care. **15 ♕c2 h6 16 ♗e3 c5 17 ♗xb7 ♖xb7**:

a31) White's initiative was rapidly neutralized in Beliavsky-Anand, Reggio Emilia 1991/2 after **18 dxc5?!** ♘xc5! 19 ♖fd1 (19 ♗xc5 ♕c8∓) 19...♕b8!

(19...♕b6 20 ♘d2!) 20 ♕c4 (White should already look to bail out with 20 ♗xc5 ♖c8 21 ♗xa7 ♖xc2 22 ♗xb8 ♖xb8 with an equal ending) 20...♘d7! (headed for d5) 21 ♕e4 ♖c8 22 ♖d2 ♖bc7 and White has insufficient kingside play to compensate for Black's control of the c-file and impending occupation of d5.

a32) Anand suggests **18 ♕e4** ♕a8 Δ...cxd4 assessing it as ±. White could try to make trouble with **19 ♕g4** but after 19...♔h7 Black looks quite safe and always has long term trumps. Also possible is **19 ♖fd1**± (Gelfand).

a33) In Gelfand-L.B.Hansen, Wijk aan Zee 1993, White preferred **18 ♖fd1** ♕c8!? 19 dxc5 ♘xc5 20 ♖ac1 when he believes that 20...♖d8 21 ♖xd8 ♕xd8 22 ♗xc5 ♖c7 23 ♕d2 ♕xd2 24 ♘xd2 ♖xc5 would have given full equality.

b) **13 ♗e3** c5 14 dxc5 ♗xe4 15 ♗xe4 ♘xe4 16 ♕c2 ♘xc5 (16...♘f6!? and 17...♘d5 also looks quite OK and perhaps safer than the text) 17 ♗xc5 ♕c7 Van der Sterren-Bagirov, Ter Apel 1990 and now 18 ♖ac1!? ♖fc8 19 ♕e4 ♗xc5 20 ♘g5 would have given interesting play for the pawn.

c) **13 ♕c2 h6** and now:

c1) **14 ♖d1** (14 ♕e2!? is untried) 14...♖c8 15 ♗c4 c5 16 d5 exd5 17 exd5 ♗d6 18 b3 ♖e8 19 ♗b2 ♖c7= Karasev-Klovan, USSR 1974.

c2) **14 e5 ♘d7**:

c21) **15 ♕e2!?** threatens ♕e4 with great force since Black's kingside is already weakened by ...h6. White did well after 15...c5 16 ♖d1 ♕c7 (16...♕b6; or 16...cxd4 17 ♘xd4 ♕b6 look better) 17 ♗f4 ♖fd8 18 ♖ac1 ♕c6 19 ♗b1 ♖ac8 20 ♘e1 ♕b6 21 ♕g4 with a strong attack in Holm-Sigurjonsson, Oslo 1983.

c22) **15 ♗h7+ ♔h8 16 ♗e4 ♕b6 17 ♗e3 c5! 18 dxc5**. The recapture with the knight now seems essential:

c221) Before its demise, **18...♗xc5** had an interesting history. After **19 ♗xc5?** ♗xe4! 20 ♗xb6 ♗xc2, Black with the d5 square and White's weak e-pawn stood better in Polugaevsky-Larsen, Palma de Mallorca IZ 1970. However, Polugaevsky seven years later playing Black was shown the right way: **19 ♖ad1!** ♗xe3 20 ♖xd7 ♖ac8 21 ♖xb7 ♖xc2 22 ♖xb6 ♖xf2 23 ♖xf2 ♗xb6 24 ♔f1 ♗xf2 25 ♔xf2 ♖c8 26 ♘d4 ♖c1 27 ♘b3, and since the pieces control the key entry squares of the rook, White enjoyed a large endgame plus in Korchnoi-Polugaevsky, Evian Ct 1977.

c222) **18...♘xc5!** is Byrne's move, which has rehabilitated the variation for Black. White seems to have nothing e.g. **19 ♗xb7** ♕xb7 20 ♗xc5 ♖fc8= or **19 ♗xc5** ♗xe4=.

c3) **14 ♗e3** ♖c8 15 ♖fd1 c5 16 dxc5 ♘g4 17 ♗d4 e5 18 h3 exd4

19 hxg4 ♖xc5 20 ♕d2 a5 21 ♖ac1 (all known also from the Korchnoi-Polugaevsky match, and thought to be better for White, an impression which Polugaevsky did much to enhance with the mistake 21...♕d7? 22 ♖xc5! ♗xc5 23 g5! and suddenly White has dangerous kingside chances. However, if Black keeps g5 covered and appreciates that the d4 weakness is more significant than the c- file he has no real problems) 21...♖xc1 22 ♖xc1 ♕d7 (22...♕d6!?) 23 ♕f4 ♖c8 24 ♖c4 ♗f6 Nenashev-Novikov, USSR Ch 1991.

12 ... 0-0
13 e4 c5

13...♘d7!? 14 ♖d1 c5 has been recommended but not yet tested. It seems well worth considering since in the most common line (see note to Black's 14th) the possibility of gaining time with c6 guarantees White at least a small plus.

14 dxc5 ♖c8?!

Shirov has brought to chess a great tactical flair, and in the openings a very individual approach of which aggression and ambition are the chief hallmarks. The text involves an ambitious plan which in fact Black is quite successful in implementing. Still, with **15 ♖d1!** ♖xc5 16 ♗e3 ♖a5 17 ♘d2! (Serper) White could now have severely embarrassed the black rook.

However, it appears that Black is having a tough time in the main line too. After **14...♘d7 15 c6! ♗xc6 16 ♗e3 ♗b7** (16...♘c5?? 17 ♗xc5 ♗xc5 18 ♖ac1+-) **17 ♖ac1 ♕b8** (17...♕a5 18 ♘d4! ♖ac8 {18...♘c5? 19 ♖xc5!±} 19 ♗b5!±):

a) **18 ♘d4** ♖c8 19 ♖xc8 ♕xc8 20 ♖c1 ♕d8 21 ♗b5 ♗xe4 22 ♗c6 ♗xc6 23 ♘xc6 ♕e8 was only slightly better for White (24 ♕a6!) in Chekhov-Novikov, USSR Ch 1991.

b) **18 g3** (an imaginative plan to weaken Black on the light squares, but it is hard to believe that it is so critical) 18...♖c8?! (Novikov's 18...a5!? would enable 19 ♗f4 ♗d6=) 19 ♗f4! e5 20 ♖xc8 ♗xc8 21 ♗g5 ♗f8? (21...♗xg5 was preferable) 22 ♖d1 ♘b6 23 ♗b5 ♗b7 24 ♗d8! *(112)*

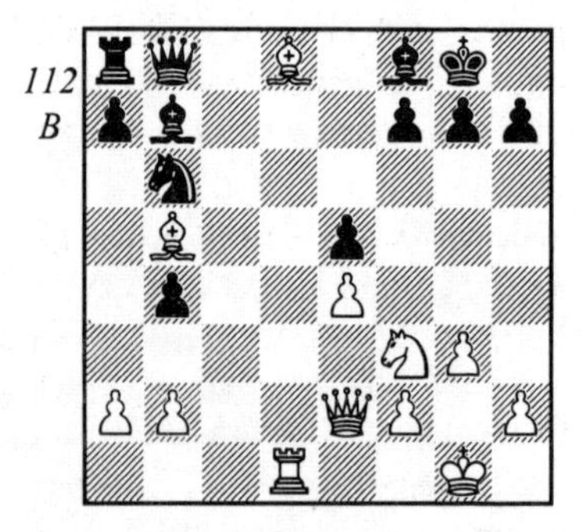

A very fine and instructive idea. Quite simply, White wants to consolidate his hold on the key light squares (d7, c4, d5) and to attack against f7. To further this end, he exchanges a piece which cannot contest these squares for a piece which had a key defensive role.

The following moves confirmed the correctness of this thinking: 24...h6 25 ♗xb6 axb6 26 ♕c4 ♕c8 27 ♘xe5 ♕xc4 28 ♗xc4 ♗xe4 29 ♗xf7+ ♔h8 30 ♗g6± Chekhov-Bagirov, USSR Ch 1991.

c) **18 ♗b5!** ♘f6 19 ♘d4± (Chekhov), looks very strong. Also if 18...♘e5 19 ♘d4 Δ19...a6 20 ♗a4 ♗xe4? 21 ♗f4+-. If Black can not find a serious improvement here, then the whole line looks quite suspect.

15 ♗f4?!	**♖xc5**
16 ♖ac1	**♖xc1**
17 ♖xc1	**♕a8!**
18 ♖c7	**♗d8!**
19 ♖c4	**♗e7**
20 ♖c7	

White's poor decision to exchange rather than harass Black's rook has given Black a very comfortable set-up where the pressure on e4 prevents White from strengthening the position of his forces. White has no good alternative to offering the repetition, since **20 ♘g5** h6 21 e5 ♘d5 22 ♕e4 g6 (22...♘f6 23 ♕e2=) 23 ♘xf7 ♘xf4 24 ♕xf4 ♖xf7 25 ♕h6 ♕f8 is speculative and risky.

20 ...	**♗d8**
21 ♖c4	**a5?**

A serious error, based upon a laudable but misguided attempt to play for more than the draw. Until now White has refrained from playing e5 since it would involve both opening the long light-square diagonal for Black, and leaving the f4 bishop looking less than happy. Shirov's move gives White the chance first to activate his bishop, and then to play e5 in circumstances where White's control of squares crucial to Black's defence will more than compensate for Black's control of a8-h1.

22 ♗d6	**♖e8**
23 e5!	**♘d5**

23...♗xf3 24 ♕xf3 ♕xf3 25 gxf3 ♘d5 26 ♖c8 wins for White.

24 ♖g4	**f5**
25 exf6	**♘xf6**
26 ♖f4	**♘h5??**

An absolutely incredible blunder from one of the world's most dangerous tacticians, albeit in a now very difficult position. To struggle on Black should try **26...♕c8**.

27 ♕xe6+ *(113)*

1-0

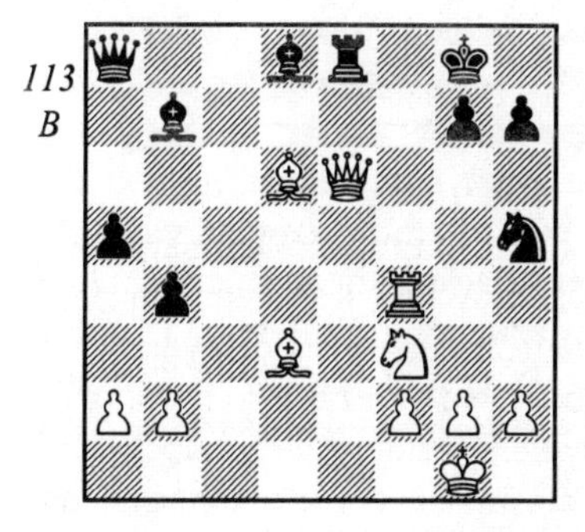

15 The Old Meran 8...a6: Introduction and Reynolds' Variation with ...fxe6

Game 20
Marin-Knaak
Stara Zagora Z 1990

1 ♘f3 d5 2 c4 e6 3 d4 c6 4 e3 ♘f6 5 ♘c3 ♘bd7 6 ♗d3 dxc4 7 ♗xc4 b5 8 ♗d3

8 ... a6 *(114)*

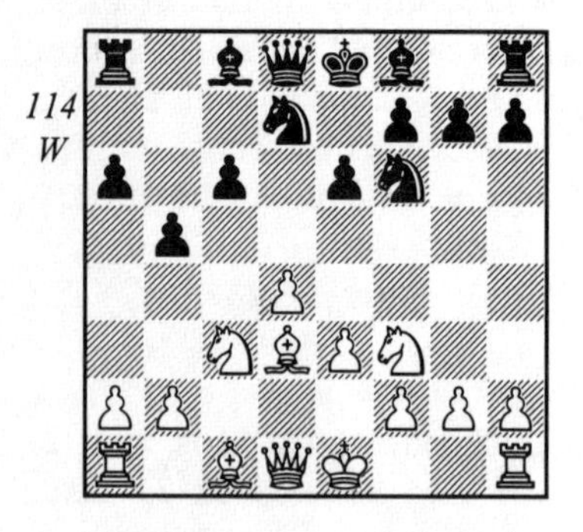

114
W

9 e4

In the overwhelming majority of games White takes up the challenge in this way. However, White does have the option of heading for much quieter waters, albeit with little prospect of an opening advantage, with **9 0-0 c5 10 a4** (even less troublesome are 10 ♕e2 ♗b7 11 ♖d1 ♕b6 12 ♗c2 ♗e7 13 e4 cxd4 14 ♘xd4 ♖c8 15 ♗e3 ♕c7= Rossolimo-Pachman, Hilversum 1946 and 10 b3 ♗b7 11 ♗b2 ♗e7 12 ♖ac1 0-0 13 ♕e2 ♖c8 14 ♖fd1 ♕b6= Prasad-Torre, Bangalore 1981) **10...b4 11 ♘e4 ♗b7** and now:

a) **12 ♘xf6+** ♘xf6 13 ♕e2 cxd4 14 ♘xd4 ♗e7 (More sensible than 14...♗c5?! 15 ♘b3 ♕d5 16 f3!+= with which I once lost to Michael Adams at a quickplay, the where and whenabouts of which I have successfully forgotten!) 15 ♖d1 0-0 16 ♗d2 ♕a5 17 f3 ♖fd8= Hort-Whiteley, Hastings 1967/8.

b) **12 ♘ed2** ♗e7 13 a5!? 0-0 14 ♘c4 ♕c7 15 h3 (If 15 ♕e2 cxd4 16 cxd4, then both 16...♘g4 and 16...♘d5 give Black very satisfactory play) 15...♗d5 16 ♕e2 ♕b7 17 ♖e1 ♗e4 (17...♗xf3!? 18 ♕xf3 ♕xf3 19 gxf3 cxd4 20 exd4 ♘d5 leads to an interesting position where White's bishops compensate for a variety of weaknesses. The text is safer) 18 ♗d2 ♗xd3 19 ♕xd3 ♖fd8 20 ♕e2 ♘e4 with balanced chances in Korchnoi-Nogueiras, Wijk aan Zee 1987.

It should be noted that White can also play this way against 8...♗b7 9 0-0 a6 with 10 a4 when 10...b4 11 ♘e4 c5 is a direct transposition.

9 ... c5
10 d5 c4

The text, which ensures that Black's queenside majority will not be immobilized by a later b3 by White, is generally regarded as the best move here. However, several others have been seen in practice, and 10...e5 in particular requires careful study:

a) **10...♗b7 11 0-0** leads to Chapter 13 in all cases except 11...c4 12 fxe6 cxd3 which is covered in the next game. Especially in the cases where White answers ...c4 with ♗c2, not capturing immediately on e6, it is far from clear that Black wants to be committed to ...♗b7 so early. In addition White may consider **11 dxe6** fxe6 12 b3!? - Müller/Haberditz.

b) **10...exd5?!** gives White a very dangerous lead in development after 11 e5! ♘g4 (11...d4 12 exf6 dxc3 13 ♕e2+ costs a piece) 12 ♗g5! f6 (also horrible was 12...♗e7 13 ♗xe7 ♔xe7?! 14 ♘xd5+ ♔f8 15 ♗e4 ♗b7 16 e6 fxe6 17 ♘f4 ♕a5+ 18 ♔f1 ♗xe4 19 ♕xd7 ♖e8 1-0 Yakovich-M.Lazić, Munich 1992, since 20 ♘g5 is instant catastrophe) 13 exf6 ♘dxf6 (13...♘gxf6 14 ♘xd5 ♗e7 15 ♘f4 ♘b6 16 0-0 0-0, Taimanov-Trifunović, Dortmund 1961, and now 17 ♕b1! with a powerful attack) 14 h3 ♘h6 15 0-0 ♗b7 (15...d4 16 ♖e1+ ♗e7 17 ♗xf6 gxf6 18 ♘d5!±) 16 ♖e1+ ♗e7 17 ♗xf6 gxf6 18 ♕d2 ♘f7 19 ♕f4± (Trifunović). Black's position is a mess!

c) **10...♘b6?!** is an attempt to avoid the weakening of the e6 pawn. However, the knight is not well placed, and the move fails to equalize:

c1) **11 d6?!** sets a nice trap since **11...e5?** 12 ♗xb5+! axb5 13 ♘xb5 (Uhlmann-J.Szabo, Dresden 1959) wins for White, but **11...c4** 12 ♗c2 e5! is unproblematic for Black.

c2) A good alternative for White though is **11 0-0** exd5 12 e5 ♘fd7 13 ♖e1 ♗e7 14 e6 fxe6 15 ♖xe6 0-0 (15...♘f6 16 ♘g5! keeps the attack) 16 ♕e2 c4 (16...♗f6 17 ♘xd5 ♘xd5 18 ♕e4±) 17 ♖xe7 (17 ♗xh7+ looks very strong too) 17...cxd3 18 ♕e6+ ♔h8 19 ♘g5 ♘f6 20 ♘f7+ ♔g8 21 ♘xd8+ ♗xe6 (Gligorić-Dahlberg, Lone Pine 1981) and now instead of **22 ♘xe6** ♖ae8∞ White could have maintained a clear plus with **22 ♖xe6** ♘c4 23 ♘c6 d2 24 ♗xd2 ♘xd2 25 ♖d1 – Gligorić.

c3) **11 dxe6** ♗xe6 12 ♕e2 ♗e7 13 0-0 b4 14 ♘d1 c4 15 ♗c2 ♗c5 16 ♘e3 ♕c7 17 ♗d2 h6 18 ♖fc1 0-0 19 e5 ♘d5 20 ♘f5 with a dangerous attack building for White in Suvalić-Trifunović, Yugoslav Ch 1961.

d) **10...e5** also prevents the damaging of Black's pawns by dxe6, but both clarifies the centre where

White has a protected passed pawn and affords White a tempo to restrain the Black queenside majority. Moreover, once White has controlled the Black pawns he can target them with a4, after more or less preparation. If Black is forced to advance ...b4 the pawns will lose their mobility and White's advantage will be clear. Hence much of the play revolves around attempts by Black to cross this plan, often by sacrificing a pawn. At the moment these all look dubious, and although the ever-fertile mind of Australian GM Ian Rogers recently unearthed a new approach I suspect that this too will prove insufficient, and 10...c4 will remain almost universal here. **11 b3** *(115)* is critical (if 11 0-0 c4 we reach a position considered under the note to 12 ♗c2, albeit also quite promising for White) and then Black has:

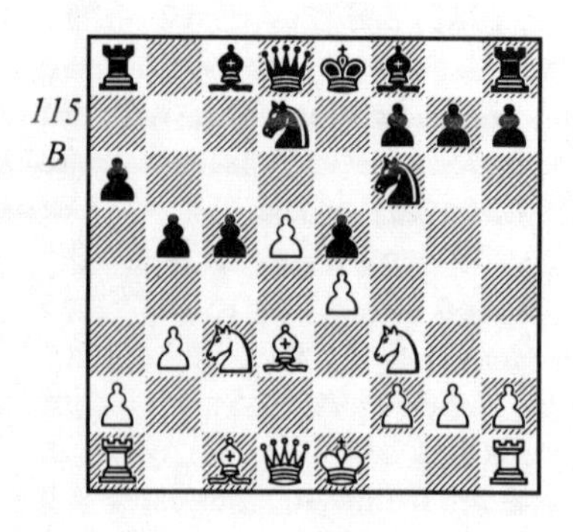

d1) **11...c4** is an old, but now somewhat discredited attempt to solve positional problems immediately by tactical means. 12 bxc4 ♗b4 (12...bxc4 13 ♗c2! ♗b4 transposes) 13 ♗d2 bxc4 (Boleslavsky's convincing analysis seems to put 13...♘c5 out of business too after 14 ♕e2! bxc4 15 ♗c2 ♘d3+ 16 ♗xd3 cxd3 17 ♕xd3 a5 18 0-0 ♗a6 19 ♘b5 ♗xd2 20 ♘xd2 a4 21 ♖fb1 Δ21...♕d7 22 ♘c4! or 21...♖b8 22 ♘c7+) 14 ♗c2! ♕a5 15 ♘e2 ♘xe4! (The best chance. Black must keep the momentum or White consolidates his positional plus and 15...c3 16 ♗e3 ♘xe4 fails to 17 a3!±) 16 ♗xe4 c3 17 ♘xc3 ♗xc3 18 0-0 ♗xd2 19 ♘xd2 0-0 20 ♘c4 ♕b4 and now 21 d6! seems much the simplest: 21...♖b8 (or 21...♗b7 22 ♖b1; 21...♖a7 22 ♗d5 ♖d8 23 ♖e1± Honfi-Kempe, corr. 1978-9) 22 ♗d5 ♖e8 23 ♖e1 with a difficult position for Black.

d2) **11...♗d6 12 0-0 0-0** and now if White proceeds with the immediate implementation of his plan with 13 a4 Black does not concede c4 lightly with 13...b4? when 14 ♘b1 followed by ♘d2-c4 is strong but initiates a pawn sacrifice with 13...c4! 14 bxc4 b4 for which he obtains an excellent outpost on c5 for his knight, and a passed b-pawn. It is not clear that this is enough, but it gives Black better counterchances than **13 ♖e1!**. It seems that thus White can avoid the pawn sac and implement his plan at a more leisurely pace, e.g. 13...♖b8 (the

13...c4 14 bxc4 b4 idea is clearly inferior here since 15 ♘a4 is available; for 13...♕c7!? see 'd3') 14 ♗f1! ♖fe8 (With 14...♘e8 15 a4 ♘c7 16 axb5 axb5 17 ♗g5 f6 18 ♗e3 Black can hold the queenside structure, but only at the cost of a very passive position) 15 a4 b4 (the main point is that when the bishop is not on d3, 15...c4 is answered by 16 axb5 axb5 17 bxc4 b4 18 ♘b5± since this excellent outpost squashes Black's counterplay) 16 ♘b1 ♘b6 17 ♘bd2 ♖e7?! (17...a5 was better, but the defensive task is still unenviable) 18 ♗b2 (18 a5!) 18...♘e8 19 ♖c1 f6 20 a5 ♘a8 21 ♘c4 ♖c7 22 ♘fd2 ♗d7 and now 23 f4! was the break that turned a large positional plus into a strong attack in Polugaevsky-Biyiasas, Petropolis IZ 1973. Black seriously needs an improvement to make this line playable again.

d3) **11...♕c7!?** 12 0-0 ♗d6 13 ♖e1 0-0 14 ♗f1 c4 (the point) 15 bxc4 bxc4 (Marin suggests 15...♘b6 but 16 a4! b4 17 a5 ♘xc4 18 ♘a4 ♘xa5 19 ♗e3 Δ♖c1-c6 is strong) 16 ♕c2 (16 ♗g5 h6!∞; 16 ♘d2 ♘b6 17 a4 ♗b4!; 16 ♕a4 ♘b6 17 ♕a5!?) 16...♘b6 17 ♗g5 (17 a4 ♗d7 18 a5 ♘c8 19 ♘d2 ♗b4∞) 17...♗d7! (17...♘fd7 18 a4 is strong since ...♗d7 is unavailable; also favourable for White is 17...♘e8 18 a4 ♗d7 19 a5 ♘c8 20 ♘d2!) 18 ♗xf6 gxf6 19 ♘h4 ♔h8 (19...♗c5!? Marin) 20 ♕d2 Δ♕h6 with a slight pull for White. This certainly looks like the most likely territory for Black after 10...e5.

11 dxe6

11 ♗c2 has become increasingly popular since the feeling has emerged that 11...e5 is no panacea. Among its virtues is that it avoids the 11...cxd3 of Game 21.

We shall consider the following in addition to **11...♗b7** 12 **0-0** which is considered in Chapter 13.

a) **11...e5**. It used to be thought that if Black both avoided the weakness of an isolated pawn on e6 and kept his queenside mobile he had a pleasant task. Recent practice has questioned this view.

12 **0-0** ♗d6 (12...♗b4!? 13 ♗d2 0-0 14 a4 ♖b8 15 axb5 axb5 16 ♘a2!? ♗d6 17 ♘b4 ♗b7 18 ♗c3 ♕e7 19 ♕d2 ♘c5 looked OK for Black in Tukmakov-Nogueiras, Biel 1988; Black had some problems however after 12...♗c5 13 ♘h4 0-0 14 ♘f5 g6 15 ♘h6+ ♔g7 16 ♗g5 ♕c7 17 ♕d2 ♘h5 18 ♘g4 ♔h8 19 ♗h6 ♖e8 20 ♘e2± Maksimenko-Rodin, Moscow 1991) 13 ♘e2!? ♘c5 14 ♘g3 0-0 15 b3 a5? (15...cxb3 16 axb3 a5 17 b4 ♘a4∞) 16 bxc4 b4 17 ♗g5± Chekhov-Haba, Halle 1987.

b) **11...♘c5!?** has a justified reputation as an interesting and exceedingly sharp continuation. There is unanimous support for **12 ♗g5 b4** *(116)* but here the clarity ends. White has three possibilities:

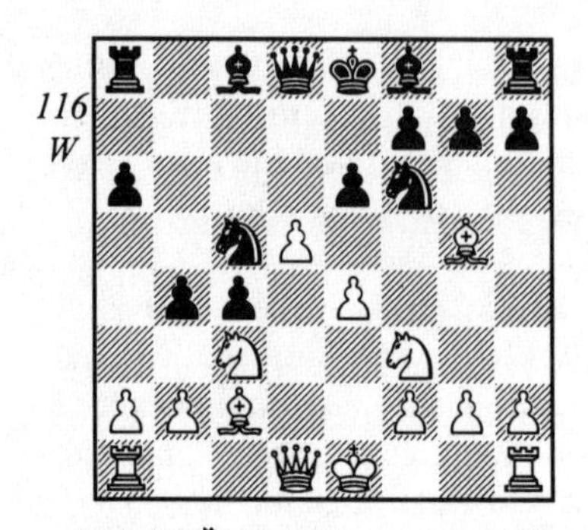

b1) **13 ♘e2** is known only from the game Van der Sterren-Donaldson, Reykjavik 1986. Although White was successful, Black has found improvements after 13...exd5 14 e5 h6 15 ♗h4 g5 16 ♘xg5 hxg5 (16...♕a5 17 0-0! hxg5 18 exf6 ♖xh4 19 ♕xd5 ♕c7 20 ♘g3 looks much too risky for Black - Donaldson) 17 ♗xg5 ♕a5 18 ♗xf6 b3+ 19 ♕d2 ♕xd2+ 20 ♔xd2 ♖g8 (The whole line is forcing and hence very easy to learn. 20...bxc2 21 ♗xh8 ♗h6+ 22 f4 ♗f5 is probably not sound but I must admit it looks like a lot of fun and may be worthy of the microscope) 21 axb3 cxb3 22 ♗h7 ♖xg2 23 ♖ag1 and now instead of **23...♗h3?** 24 ♖xg2 ♗xg2 25 ♖g1 ♗e4 26 ♗xe4 ♘xe4+ 27 ♔d3±, Donaldson and Seirawan suggest **23...♖xf2!** 24 ♔e3 ♗f5! with dangerous counterplay if White takes the exchange. No one seems to have been moved to put this assessment to the test, probably with good reason.

b2) **13 ♘a4** exd5! (Again seems best; 13...b3? 14 axb3 cxb3 15 ♘xc5 bxc5 16 ♗d3! ♕b6 17 0-0 exd5?! 18 ♗xf6! gxf6 19 exd5± Van der Sterren-Kuijf, Montpellier Z 1985, was the inauspicious debut for 11...♘c5. The move ...b4-b3 here, as so often in the Semi-Slav, packs more punch as a threat than when executed early) 14 e5 h6 15 exf6 (15 ♘xc5 has little independent significance) 15...hxg5 16 ♘xc5 (16 fxg7 seems inferior after 16...♗xg7 17 ♘xc5 ♕e7+ 18 ♕e2 ♗xb2 19 ♖b1 ♗c3+ 20 ♔d1 g4! with full compensation -- Korchnoi) 16...♗xc5 17 fxg7 ♖g8 18 ♗a4+ ♔e7! (18...♗d7 is weaker since simply 19 0-0! ♗b5 20 ♖e1+ ♗e7 21 ♘e5 is horrible; Brglez-Arkhangelsky, corr. 1987) 19 ♗c6 ♖a7 20 ♗xd5 (perhaps 20 ♕xd5!? is more promising: after 20...♕xd5 21 ♗xd5 ♔f6 Black's two bishops and activity give fair compensation for the pawn, but there is nothing concrete) 20...♔f6! 21 ♗xc4 (21 ♕d2 ♔g7! 22 ♕xg5+? ♕xg5 23 ♘xg5 ♖e8+ Δ...♖e5∓/-+ Berry) 21...g4! 22 ♕xd8 ♖xd8 23 ♘g1 ♔xg7 24 ♘e2 ♖e7 with lots of play for Black in Bang-Berry, corr. 1990.

b3) **13 ♗xf6!?** gxf6! 14 ♘a4 exd5 15 exd5 b3 (Donaldson and Seirawan give 15...♕e7+ 16 ♔f1 ♗b7 17 ♗f5(?) ♖d8 18 ♘b6 c3 19 bxc3 ♕d6 with counterplay. This seems to cause White more disruption) 16 axb3 cxb3 17 ♗xb3 ♘xb3 18 ♕xb3 ♕a5+ 19 ♔f1 ♗b4 20 ♕e3+ ♔f8 21 ♕h6+ ♔e7 22 ♘d4

Bd7 23 d6+ Bxd6 24 Re1+ Be5 25 Qe3 Qc5 and Black was fine in Gligorić-Todorović, Yugoslav Ch 1990. Still this would not be everybody's cup of tea.

c) **11...Qc7** (Inviting a return to the main lines of ...fxe6) 12 Qe2 Bd6 (12...Bc5 13 Qe2 {13 dxe6 is Marin-Knaak} 13...e5!? 14 Bg5!? {14 Nh4 0-0 15 Kh1 Bd4∓ Kharitonov-Ivanchuk, USSR 1988} 14...0-0 15 Nd1 h6 16 Bd2 Ne8 17 Ne3 Nd6 18 b4!? Bd4∞ Groszpeter-Kallai, Hungarian League 1991) 13 Nd4!? Nc5 14 dxe6 fxe6 15 a4?! b4 16 Ncb5 axb5 17 Nxb5 Qb8 18 Nxd6+ Qxd6 19 e5 Nd3+ 20 Bxd3 cxd3 21 Qe3 Qd5 22 exf6 Qxg2 23 Rf1 gxf6 24 Bd2 Ra5!∓ Anić-G.Flear, French League 1992.

11 ...	**fxe6**
12 Bc2	**Qc7** *(117)*

Throughout this section Black has various possibilities to play ...Bb7 which will transpose to Game 17. Here for example **12...Bb7** 13 0-0. However, after 12...Bb7 White can also consider **13 Ng5!?** at a moment when **13...Nc5** 14 Be3! is strong. Hence Black must defend e6 with **13...Qb6** when 14 Qf3 (Δ14...h6 15 Qh3) 14...Bc5 15 Qh3 Ke7± (Zarnicki), has clearly interrupted the flow of Black's development.

The text thus not only introduces the very important material examined here, it may also be the most accurate move order to reach Game 17 from 8...a6. The move is logical since controlling the key e5 square should be the priority for the black queen. Two weaker options merit a mention:

a) **12...Nc5?!** is illogical since several of the strengths of Black's position are of a 'middlegame' nature. The endgame after 13 Qxd8+ Kxd8 14 Be3 Ke8 15 Rd1 Bb7 16 Ng5 Nfd7 17 e5! Nxe5 18 Bxc5 Bxc5 19 Nxe6 Rc8 20 0-0 left White clearly better in Averbakh-Szabo, Hamburg 1965.

b) **12...Qb6?!** 13 e5(?!) (also good, and safer is 13 0-0(!) Bb7, covered in Chapter 13. In both cases the abdication of the black queen from e5 guarding duties dictates the course of the play) 13...Ng4 14 0-0 Ngxe5 15 Re1 Bd6 16 Nxe5 Bxe5 17 Qh5+ g6 18 Bxg6+ hxg6 19 Qxg6+ Kf8 20 Rxe5 Nxe5 21 Bh6+ Ke7 22 Qg5+ Ke8 23 Nd5 with a fair attack but no clear route to victory; T.Taylor-Pupols, Lone Pine 1974.

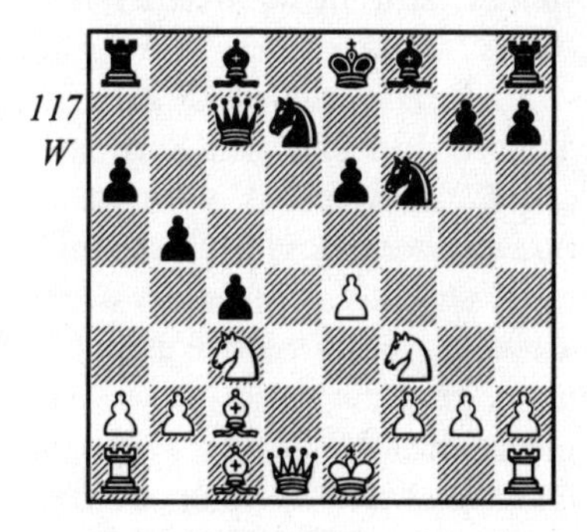

13 0-0

The sharpest option **13 ♘g5 ♘c5 14 f4** is complicated but manageable:

a) **14...♗b7** 15 e5 ♖d8 16 ♗d2 (16 ♕e2 ♘d5 and White loses the valuable 0-0-0 option) 16...♘d5 17 ♕h5+ g6 18 ♗xg6 hxg6 19 ♕xh8 ♘xf4 20 0-0-0 (Farago-Chandler, Belgrade 1982) 20...♕g7!⩲ 21 ♕xg7 ♘fd3+ 22 ♔b1 ♗xg7 with some, but maybe not full compensation.

b) **14...h6(!)** 15 e5 hxg5 16 exf6 gxf6 17 ♗g6+ ♔e7 18 ♕d4 (since fxg5 can always be answered by ...f5, the black king is much safer than would appear at first sight. 18 ♘d5+ is another try. However, after 18...exd5 19 ♕xd5 ♗e6! 20 ♕xa8 f5 Δ21 fxg5 ♕e5+ and ...♕g7, the bishop encounters some problems – Donaldson and Silman) 18...♖g8 19 ♗h7 ♖g7 20 ♗e4 ♕a7 21 ♗e3 Guseinov-Ziatdinov, Tashkent 1985, and now Ziatdinov seems to be right in claiming that 21...♘xe4 22 ♘xe4 ♕xd4 23 ♗xd4 ♖g6 24 fxg5 f5 would have favoured Black.

13 ... ♗c5

Again, **13...♗b7** will reach Game 17. Indeed, this is the most accurate move order to achieve this from 8...a6 and a good option here. The text move is attractive in that it comes with a clear plan - to use the two diagonals b8-h2 and a7-g1 in conjunction with the half open f-file to generate kingside counterplay.

Also possible is **13...♗d6** but it is not seen so often, although unrefuted. White can choose between:

a) **14 ♕e2** 0-0 (14...♗b7 is another route to Game 17, although if this is Black's intention it is illogical to permit so many deviations) 15 ♘g5 ♘c5 (15...♘b6 is also fairly safe) 16 f4 e5 17 ♘d5 (17 a4 ♗g4!?) 17...♘xd5 18 exd5 ♘d3! (18...♗f5 19 fxe5 ♗xc2 20 exd6 ♕b6 21 ♗e3 ♗d3 is also playable, but the text will surely supersede) 19 ♗xd3 (19 fxe5 ♗g4 20 ♕xg4 ♕c5+ 21 ♗e3 ♕xe3+ 22 ♔h1 ♖xf1+ 0-1 Mirallès-Neverov, Voskresensk 1990) 19...cxd3 20 ♕xd3 ♗f5∓.

b) **14 ♘d4!?** ♘b6 (In this moment, 14...♘c5 is weaker due to 15 f4 e5 16 ♘f3 and if 16...0-0 17 fxe5 ♗xe5 18 ♘xe5 ♕xe5 19 ♗f4±) 15 ♔h1 (A good useful half-waiting move, which also threatens ♘(either)xb5. The immediate 15 f4?! e5 16 ♘f3 ♗g4! – the point behind Black's 14th – is at least comfortable. Worth exploration is 15 a4 b4 16 a5! with complicated play) 15...♗d7 16 f4 e5 17 ♘f3 (If 17 ♘f5 ♗xf5 18 exf5 0-0∓; Black has a fair share of central control, a mobile queenside, and it is hard for White to open the position further to make the two bishops count) 17...♗g4! 18 a4 b4! (18...exf4?! 19 axb5 a5 20 ♕e1± Furman-Bronstein, USSR Ch 1975 cannot be right since it makes a fair mess of Black's queenside and light squares) 19 a5! ♗xf3! 20 ♖xf3 ♘bd7 21 ♘d5 ♘xd5 22 ♕xd5 0-0-0! 23 ♗e3 ♗c5 and Black is perhaps slightly for preference in this complex position.

c) **14 ♘g5** ♘b6 15 f4 e5 16 ♘d5 ♘bxd5 17 exd5 Ghitescu-Fuchs, Miskolc 1963, and now 17...0-0 seems quite safe for Black.

14 ♕e2

The main move here. White aims to play e5, and also in some lines ♗e3 to exchange the bishop on c5 and blunt Black's aggressive ambitions. Two reasonable alternatives have been tried of which the latter demands accurate defence:

a) **14 ♘g5** ♘e5! 15 ♗f4?! (15 ♔h1 h6 16 ♘f3 ♘xf3 17 ♕xf3 ♗b7= Yusupov) 15...0-0 16 ♗g3 h6 17 ♘h3 ♗b7 18 ♕e2 ♗d4∓ Georgadze-Yusupov, USSR Ch 1980. White's pieces have been pushed to rather passive positions, while Black's queenside has the customary expansive potential.

b) **14 e5** is an interesting pawn sacrifice. White can exchange off some of the more hostile Black forces and open the half open e-file against the black king. However, with careful defence, theory suggests that the chances are still about level. 14...♘xe5 15 ♗f4 ♗d6 (part of the justification for the gambit is this unavoidable loss of time by Black) 16 ♗xe5 (16 ♖e1?! ♘xf3+! 17 ♕xf3 ♗xf4 18 ♕xa8 ♗xh2+ 19 ♔h1 0-0 gives Black too much play for no real material deficit) 16...♗xe5 17 ♘xe5 ♕xe5 18 ♖e1 ♕c5! (18...♕c7?! {Gleizerov-Ulybin, Cheliabinsk 1991} 19 a4 b4 20 ♘d5 is strong since 19...♘xd5 20 ♕xd5 ♖a7 21 ♕h5+ ♕f7 22 ♕c5 is unpleasant for Black) 19 ♘e4 ♘xe4 20 ♗xe4 ♖a7 21 b4 (thus can White keep the black king in the centre, but this is not fatal for the defence) 21...♕g5 22 ♗c6+ ♔f7 23 a4 ♖d8 24 ♕f3+ ♔g8 25 axb5 ♖f7= Korchnoi-Torre, Brussels 1987.

14 ... ♘e5

Black has also tried to meet the threat of 15 e5 with the aggressive-looking **14...♘g4**. After 15 h3 ♘ge5 16 ♘xe5 ♘xe5 17 ♗e3 0-0 Engsner-Sigfüsson, Saltsjöbaden Rilton Cup 1988, White should probably play 18 f4 ♘g6! 19 g3 with a slight edge in an albeit sharp and demanding position.

15 ♘xe5

Absolutely not **15 ♗e3?** ♗xe3 16 ♕xe3?? ♘fg4 and wins. However, **15 ♗f4** is an interesting alternative since Black will be obliged to play ...e5 and hence lose use of this square for his pieces. After 15...♘xf3+ 16 ♕xf3 e5 17 ♗g5 0-0 18 ♗xf6 gxf6 19 a4! (seeking to ruffle black's queenside pawns a bit and improving on the immediate 19 ♘d5 ♕g7 20 b3 ♗g4 21 ♕g3 f5!? 22 bxc4?! {22 exf5∞} 22...f4! 23 ♕h4 ♗e2∓ Suba-Vera, Timișoara 1987) 19...b4 20 ♘d5 ♕g7 21 ♗d1! (planning ♖c1 and ♗e2 to target the freshly-made weakness on c4) 21...a5! 22 ♗e2 ♗a6 23 ♖ac1 ♖fc8! and Black's threat of counterplay with ...♗d4 kept White's plus to a bare minimum in Milovanović-Blagojević, Tuzla 1990.

15 ... ♕xe5 *(118)*

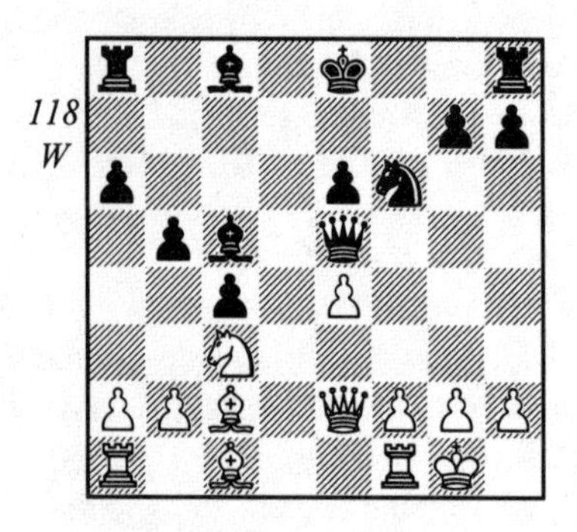

16 ♗e3

16 ♔h1!? preparing f4 is more ambitious but also involves some risk, since the black bishops remain unchallenged on their strong diagonals.

a) Still, after **16...0-0** 17 f4 ♕h5 18 ♕xh5 ♘xh5 19 e5! (19 ♗d1 ♘f6 20 e5 ♘d5 21 ♗f3 ♗b7 gave Black no problems in Marin-O'Donnell, Novi Sad 1990. The position of the knight on h5, for all that it may sometimes support counterplay against the f4 pawn, is on balance more likely to prove a liability than an asset) 19...g5 20 ♘e4! (20 f5 exf5 21 ♗xg5 ♗e6 is not so clear) 20...♗e7 21 f5 exf5 22 ♗xg5! ♖f7! 23 ♗e3!! (23 ♗xe7 ♖xe7 24 ♘f6+ ♘xf6 25 exf6 ♖e2∓) 23...♗b7! (23...fxe4 24 ♗xe4 ♖xf1+ 25 ♖xf1 ♖b8 26 ♗d5+ ♔h8 27 ♖f7 {27 ♗a7 ♗b7!∓} 27...♗b7 28 ♗xb7 ♖xb7 29 e6 ♔g8 30 ♗d4 ♖c7 31 g4±) 24 ♘c5 (24 ♘d6 ♗xd6 25 exd6 f4!?) 24...f4 White would have stood very well with 25 ♗d1!± in Chekhov-Blagojević, Pula 1990.

b) As an alternative, Black might consider **16...♗b7!?** 17 f4 ♕h5 18 ♕xh5 ♘xh5 19 e5 **0-0-0!?** 20 f5 ♖d4 with counterplay in Lukacs-Vera, Cienfuegos 1983. It is not clear to me why castling long in this line has not been more widely adopted.

16 ... ♗xe3
17 ♕xe3 0-0

17...♘g4!? 18 ♕h3 h5 19 ♗d1 (19 ♖ad1 0-0 20 ♖d2 ♕g5 21 f4 ♕c5+ 22 ♔h1 ♕e3 23 ♕xe3 ♘xe3 24 ♖ff2 ♘xc2 25 ♖xc2 ♗b7∓ Tarjan-Remlinger, Los Angeles 1981) 19...0-0 20 ♗xg4 hxg4 21 ♕xg4 b4 22 ♘a4 ♖a7! 23 ♘b6 ♖c7 where the possibility of pushing the c-pawn gives Black enough play. As we shall see, in these lines Black is frequently better off activating his queenside majority rather than merely keeping it solid.

18 ♖ad1

White has also tried his luck in the middle game: Vlastimil Hort, understandably after his experience against Sehner (see below), prevented Black's intended liquidation by **18 h3!?**. Hort-Torre, Biel 1988 continued 18...♘h5 19 g3 ♗b7 20 f4 ♕c7 21 e5 ♖ad8? (21...g6!) 22 ♖ad1?! (22 g4! ♘xf4

23 ♖xf4 ♖xf4 24 ♕xf4 ♕c5+ 25 ♔h2 ♖f8 26 ♘e4!±) 22...g6! 23 a3 ♖xd1! 24 ♗xd1 (24 ♖xd1 g5! and suddenly the long diagonal becomes an urgent problem!) 24...♖d8 25 ♗c2 ♕c6 Δ26 ♗e4 ♕c7 27 ♗c2 and Black had sufficient counterplay.

18 ... ♘g4
19 ♕g3 ♕xg3
20 hxg3 ♖a7!
21 ♖d2 g5

Understandable, to hold up a potential f4 and e5, which would give the white bishop on c2 new life. Still, the game Hort-Sehner, Bundesliga 1985/6 suggested that Black might fare better with the more active **21...b4**. After **22 ♘a4** ♖c7 23 ♖fd1 a5 24 ♖d8 ♖xd8 25 ♖xd8+ ♔f7 26 ♘b6 ♗b7 27 ♖d1 ♔e7 the mobile queenside pawn majority gave Black a plus which he subsequently converted. Although Marin-Knaak deserves close study as a masterly realization of White's assets, the possibility of 21...b4 might encourage White to deviate earlier, at moves 16 or 18. It would be interesting to know what Marin had in mind. Perhaps **22 ♘d1!?** intending to reroute the piece with f3 and ♘e3 is a better bet.

22 f3 ♘e5

If **22...♘e3** 23 ♖fc1 ♘xc2 24 ♖1xc2 White's control of the d-file leaves him with the better prospects. It is hard for Black to make play without his knight here.

23 ♔f2

Not **23 ♖c1?** ♖xf3!∓.

23 ... ♗d7
24 ♖c1 b4
25 ♘d1 ♗b5
26 ♘e3 ♖af7 *(119)*

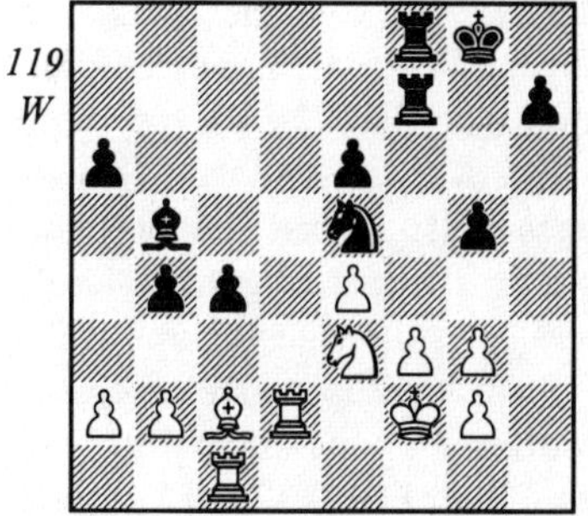

119
W

A very interesting moment. White has quite logically placed one rook on the open d-file, and the other ready to control Black's potentially threatening c-pawn. However, Black has concentrated on the f-file, not only containing White's majority but creating the dangerous threat of 27...♘xf3 28 gxf3 ♖xf3+ 29 ♔e2 c3+ -+. This looks quite hard to meet, but Marin has judged superbly that he can give material to avert Black's threats and expose his many weaknesses.

27 ♗d1!! ♘d3+

Black has little choice since the bishop threatens to come to e2, the perfect square for both attack and defence.

28 ♖xd3 cxd3
29 ♗b3 ♖e8
30 ♖c5 h6

It appears that Black has thus covered all immediate threats, but Marin's calm reply highlights the paucity of counterplay that Black can muster. White can henceforth probe Black's weak points at his leisure. Black would have greatly improved his practical chances by returning a little of the material to interrupt White's smooth co-ordination with **30...d2** 31 ♖xg5+ ♔f8 32 ♖e5 ♖d7 33 f4 when Black's d-pawn will not queen, but of course restricts the activity of White's forces and still makes a game of it.

After the actual move he chose, he suffered a long and painful demise: **31 ♔e1 ♔g7 32 ♔d2 ♔g6 33 ♖e5 ♖fe7 34 f4 ♗d7?!** (It was somewhat better to meet the threat of ♗xe6 with 34...♔g7. Now Black's queenside can be effortlessly attacked too) **35 ♗c4 a5 36 ♖xa5 gxf4 37 gxf4 e5 38 ♖a6+ ♔h5 39 f5 ♖g7** (Otherwise White would play 40 ♖g6 and the king could be added to Black's list of critical weaknesses!) **40 f6 ♖h7 41 f7 ♖f8 42 ♖a5** *(120)*

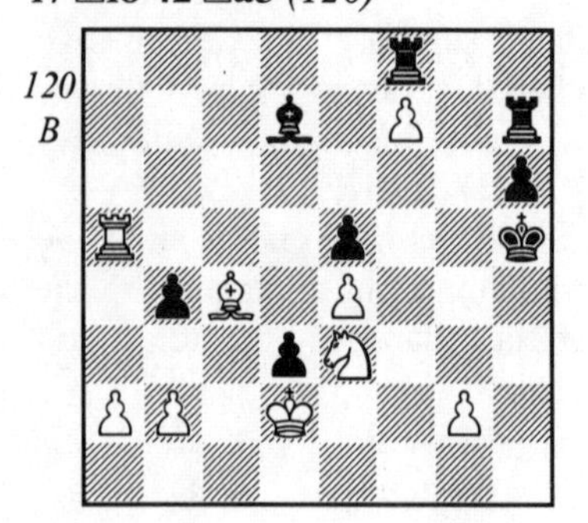
120
B

42...♖hxf7 (There is no longer any choice but to return the exchange, since otherwise the rook will languish permanently on h7. The resulting rook ending, however requires only a modicum of care from White, and his technique proves ample for the task) **43 ♖xe5+ ♔h4 44 ♗xf7 ♖xf7 45 ♘f5+ ♗xf5 46 exf5 ♔g3 47 ♔xd3 ♔xg2 48 ♔e4 h5 49 f6!** (Much more clinical than 49 ♖e8 h4 50 ♖g8+ ♔f2 51 ♖h8 ♔g3 52 ♔e5. Since the black king will be cut off at such a distance from the queenside it makes much more sense to liquidate the kingside pawns than to race them. Black has little choice since now since 49...h4 50 ♖g5+ ♔f2 51 ♔f5 is not much of a contest) **49...♖xf6 50 ♖xh5 ♖f2 51 ♖g5+ ♔h3** (Sadly for Black if he goes to the f-file the rooks are instantly traded) **52 b3 ♖xa2 53 ♔d3 ♔h4 54 ♖b5!** (Clearer than **54 ♖g8** ♖a7 when White must contest with frontal checks) **54...♔g4 55 ♔c4 ♔f4 56 ♔xb4 ♔e4 57 ♖h5 ♖a8 58 ♔c4 ♖c8+ 59 ♖c5 1-0.**

With his king cut off along the fifth rank and the white king shielded further resistance is futile. White revealed excellent judgement and technique in each of the game's phases.

16 Reynolds' Variation with ...cxd3

With 11...cxd3 Black avoids the weakness on e6 associated with Game 20, but in return for gaining the two bishops, his pawn on d3 is much more often a liability than a trump. In fact adoption of 11...cxd3 should indicate a willingness to sacrifice it in several lines. The principal compensation is to be found in control of the light squares. Not only has White lost his light-squared bishop, but winning Black's d-pawn usually entails executing the advance e5 which clearly does White's prospects of contesting the light squares no good at all. Black's initiative can often endure right into the endgame. Recent reinforcements of Black's play in two of the most critical lines leave the current theoretical status of 11...cxd3 looking rather rosy. However two slight reservations should be borne in mind:

1) The line is unsuitable for players needing to win at all costs against a peacefully-inclined opponent. Whereas it is true that many openings have 'drawing variations' they are at least often of some complexity. Here the variation 14 ♘e5, note 'a' to White's 14th, is trivially easy to learn, and affords Black no real chance to deviate.

2) More and more White players are experimenting with 11 ♗c2 (and 12 ♗c2 arising from the 'Wade' move order). Players who wish to avoid the ...fxe6 lines altogether would have to play 11...e5 or 12...e5, or in the former case 11...♘c5, two approaches whose theoretical pedigrees are not quite watertight.

So, on to the game, which at the time opened up a whole new theoretical debate. Black's important 16th move innovation is still looking healthy and critical. As a consequence, the recent trend has been towards the omission of ♗g5 and in favour of 14 ♖e1, often in conjunction with 15 e5, in which regard the perhaps prematurely terminated but extremely fascinating encounter between Curt Hansen and Alexander Chernin may prove to be crucial.

Game 21
Gavrikov-Chernin
USSR Ch (Minsk) 1987

1 d4 d5 2 c4 c6 3 ♘c3 ♘f6 4 e3 e6 5 ♘f3 ♘bd7 6 ♗d3 dxc4 7 ♗xc4 b5 8 ♗d3

8 ... a6

I have taken a few liberties with the move order of the main game here in order to be able to illustrate variations along the way. In fact, Chernin for the record played 8...♗b7 and only after 9 0-0 a6 10 e4 c5 11 d5 c4 12 dxe6 cxd3 13 exd7+ ♕xd7 do we return to strict historical truth!

9 e4 **c5**
10 d5 **c4**
11 dxe6 **cxd3**

Kondratiev and Karpov both mention the 'interesting pawn sacrifice' **11...♘c5** 12 exf7+ ♔xf7 *(perhaps they meant 12...♔e7 -editor's note)*. However, after 13 ♗xc4+ it looks suspiciously like a not very interesting double pawn sac!

12 exd7+

It is probably fair to say that recent practical trials with the astonishing sacrificial alternative **12 exf7+** have revealed two things: it is unsound, but quite dangerous in practice. After **12...♔xf7 13 e5 ♕e7** White has tried:

a) **14 ♘g5+** ♔e8 15 0-0 (Not 15 f4? ♘xe5! 16 0-0 ♕a7+ ∓ Korchnoi) 15...♘xe5 16 ♖e1 h6 17 f4? (Better was 17 ♘ge4 ♘xe4 18 ♘xe4 ♗g4! 19 f3 ♗e6 20 ♘f2 although Korchnoi's assessment of ∞ looks a bit optimistic to me) 17...hxg5! 18 ♖xe5 ♕xe5! 19 fxe5 ♗c5+ and ...♘g4 and Black had a very strong attack in Seirawan-Korchnoi, Barcelona 1989.

b) **14 ♗f4** ♘b6 (returning the material with 14...h6!? 15 ♕b3+ ♔e8 16 0-0 ♘h5 17 ♗e3 ♘c5! 18 ♕d5 ♗b7 19 ♗xc5 ♗xd5 20 ♗xe7 ♗xf3=+ Van der Wiel looks interesting too) 15 ♕b3+?! (The less direct 15 ♘g5+ ♔e8 16 ♕xd3 may have offered more enduring pressure) 15...♘c4! 16 0-0 ♘h5 17 ♗e3 ♗b7 18 ♘d2 ♖c8 19 a4 ♕xe5 20 axb5 ♗d6 21 g3 ♕e6!∓ Korchnoi-Van der Wiel, Amsterdam 1989.

12 ... **♕xd7** *(121)*

121
W

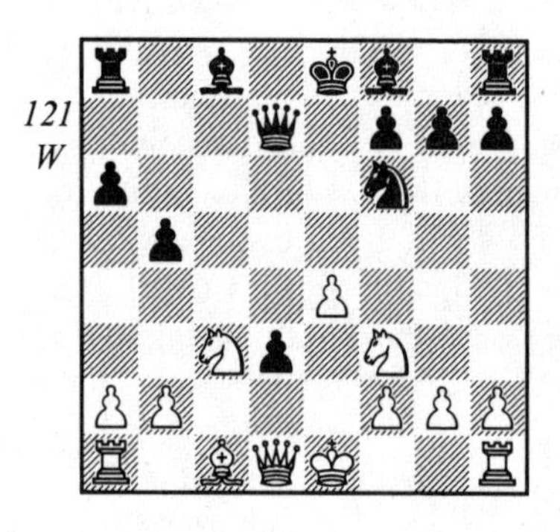

13 0-0

Three other moves have been tried here, but the text is by far the most popular and flexible. Note again that it often also arises through the 8...♗b7 9 0-0 a6 10 e4 move order which has in recent years been the most frequent route to Reynolds' variation. A brief look at the alternatives:

a) **13 ♘e5** is no problem for Black while the white king is still in the middle. Whereas in later critical lines Black often has to seek compensation for the loss of his vulnerable d-pawn, here

White's e-pawn falls easily in return. After 13...♕e7 14 ♗f4 (14 ♘xd3 b4 15 ♘e2 ♕xe4 16 0-0 ♗e7 17 ♘g3 ♕b7 18 ♗g5 0-0 19 ♘h5 (otherwise Black's two bishop's may make him slightly for preference) 19...♘xh5 20 ♗xe7 ♕xe7 21 ♕xh5 gave full equality in Gligorić-Torre, Bugojno 1984) 14...♘xe4! (looks simpler than 14...b4 15 ♘d5 ♘xd5 16 exd5 f6 17 ♕a4+ ♗d7 18 ♕xd7+ ♕xd7 19 ♘xd7 ♔xd7 20 0-0-0 although Black found activity to compensate for his e-pawn in Tal-Bagirov, Erevan 1982 by 20...♖c8+ 21 ♔b1 ♗c5 22 f3 ♖he8 23 ♖xd3 ♖e2 24 ♖d2 ♖xd2 25 ♗xd2 ♖e8=) 15 0-0 ♘xc3 16 bxc3 ♕b7 17 ♖e1 ♗e7 18 ♕xd3 0-0 19 ♘d7! ♕xd7 20 ♕xd7 ♗xd7 21 ♖xe7 ♗e6 with a rather sterile equality; Chekhov-Alexandria, Halle 1981.

b) **13 e5** virtually forces Black to sacrifice a pawn, but it seems to be a very favourable version, partly because the dark squared bishops stay on in contrast to some later lines, and ironically Black's uncastled king can be a plus point here since at critical points it defends the queen on d7. After 13...♘d5! 14 ♕xd3 ♘xc3 15 ♕xc3 (15 ♕xd7+ ♗xd7 16 bxc3 ♖c8 17 ♗d2 ♗a3 may be safer than the text, but the two bishops and vulnerable white pawns on c3 and e5 grant Black full compensation) 15...♗b7 16 0-0 ♖c8 17 ♕d4?! (17 ♕b3 ♗d5 {17...♗c5!? Polugaevsky} 18 ♕d3 ♕b7 or 18 ♖d1) 17...♗xf3 18 ♕xd7+ ♔xd7 19 gxf3 ♔e6 20 ♗f4?! ♖c4 and Black's activity more than outweighs White's weak extra pawn; Ivanov-Sakharov, Kislovodsk 1976.

c) **13 ♗g5** generally transposes to the main game. However, there are some independent possibilities: 13...♗e7 (whether 13...♗b7 14 ♗xf6 gxf6 weakens Black's kingside too much has yet to be tested. If White's play in Vaganian-Cirić can be strengthened then Black may have to try this) 14 ♗xf6 (14 0-0 ♗b7 is transpositional; 14 e5?! ♘g4 15 ♗xe7 ♕xe7 16 ♘d5?! ♕c5 is inferior) 14...♗xf6 15 ♘d5 ♗b7! 16 ♘xf6+ gxf6 17 0-0 0-0 (Black's play against White's e-pawn should be just sufficient to prevent White building a significant kingside attack) 18 ♖e1 ♖fe8 19 ♘d2 f5 20 ♕h5 (Vaganian-Cirić, San Felieu de Guixols 1975) when 20...fxe4! should encourage White to force a draw according to Cirić.

13 ... ♗b7
14 ♗g5

Again it is White who has the greater range of possibilities, and in fact, although the text is an important line, it is again arguably the most flexible option – 14 ♖e1 – which now has main line status. Two others also merit discussion:

a) **14 ♘e5** is unfortunately significant on spoiling grounds. After 14...♕d4 15 ♘f3 (15 ♘xd3? 0-0-0∓) 15...♕d7 Black has no satisfactory means of avoiding the draw; Suba-Chernin, Tunis IZ 1985, and countless others.

b) **14 e5?!** is still premature. Black should reply 14...♘d5! 15 ♕xd3 ♘xc3 which will transpose into 13 e5?! above.

c) **14 ♖e1!?** is best met by **14...♗e7** when White can transpose with 15 ♗g5 to the note 'b' to 15 ♖e1 in the main game. The other critical line is **15 e5 ♘d5 16 ♘e4!** (Since Portisch-Yusupov, Montpellier Ct 1985, White has understandably shied away from 16 ♕xd3 ♘xc3 17 ♕xc3 {as ever, 17 ♕xd7+ and 18 bxc3 gives Black full structural compensation} 17...0-0 {17...♖c8? 18 e6!} 18 ♗g5 {18 ♗f4 ♖ac8 19 ♕b3 ♕g4} 18...♖ac8 19 ♕g3 ♗xg5 20 ♕xg5 ♗xf3 21 gxf3 ♖c6! when Black had successfully converted his more active forces into a strong direct attack) **16...0-0 17 ♕xd3** *(122)*.

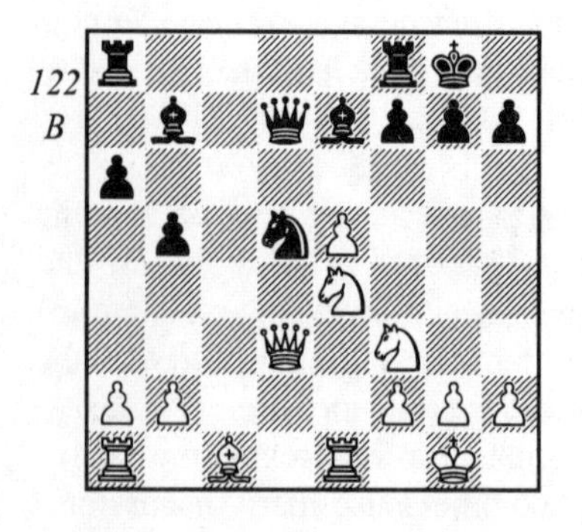

Perhaps one of the two most critical positions for the assessment of the validity of 11...cxd3. It seems clear that in comparison with Portisch-Yusupov above, the retention of the knights helps White. In the first place they simply serve to block the key long light-square diagonal. Secondly, White also has the option of playing ♘g3 seeking to occupy f5 with queen or knight. Thirdly White's queen has not been subjected to attack with gain of tempo as above. However, despite all this, practice suggests that Black's compensation may still be adequate after 17...♕g4!:

c21) **17...h6**:

c211) **18 ♗d2** ♖ad8 gives Black fair counterplay (Barbero).

c212) **18 ♘g3** ♖ad8 19 e6!? (Barbero gives 19 ♘f5 ♘b4! with compensation. White should indeed be careful, e.g. 20 ♕xd7 ♖xd7 21 e6? fxe6 22 ♘e5 ♖xf5 23 ♘xd7 ♘c2 24 ♖xe6 ♖d5∓ is too ambitious) 19...fxe6 20 ♗xh6 (Marin-Barbero, Thessaloniki OL 1988) and now Black can choose between **20...♖xf3(!)** 21 gxf3 gxh6 22 ♕g6+ ♔f8 23 ♕xh6+ ♔f7 24 ♕h7+ ♔f8 when perpetual looks more convincing than 25 ♘h5 ♗f6!; and **20...♗f6** 21 ♗g5! ♘c7 22 ♕xd7 ♖xd7 23 ♗xf6 gxf6 when Black has some play, but perhaps not quite enough.

c22) After **17...♕g4!**, White has:

c221) **18 h3?!** ♕g6 19 ♗d2 ♖ac8 20 ♘d4 ♘b4 with excellent play for a pawn; Vaganian-Yusupov, USSR 1981.

c222) **18 ♘g3!?** and now:

c2221) **18...♘b4** is the old move: 19 ♕f5 ♕g6 (19...♗xf3 20 gxf3 ♕d4 Groszpeter) 20 ♖d1 ♖fd8 (20...♖ad8!? {Δ21 ♗g5 ♗xf3!} 21 ♖xd8 ♖xd8 22 ♗g5 ♕xf5 23 ♘xf5 ♗xg5 24 ♘xg5 ♘xa2 25 ♘d6(?!) ♗d5= Donaldson, but stronger is 25 e6! to meet 25...fxe6 with 26 ♘e7+! ♔f8 27 ♘xe6+ ♔xe7 28 ♘xd8 ♗d5 28 ♘c6+ ±) 21 ♗g5! ♗xg5 22 ♘xg5 ♗d5 23 a3 ♘c6 24 ♕xg6 hxg6 25 f4± Groszpeter-Lukacs, Hungarian Ch 1986.

c2222) **18...f5!!** is an amazing discovery of the world-famous Russian trainer Mark Dvoretsky, tested in practice in C.Hansen-Chernin, Tåstrup 1992. The move, elevating White's e-pawn to 'passed' status with no ideal blockader ready, is quite counter-intuitive. The idea is simply to prevent White's planned occupation of f5, in some cases to use the f-pawn as part of a kingside attack, sometimes to take control of e4. The justification is that **19 exf6** ♗xf6 **20 h3** ♘b4! gives good play according to Chernin. Also **20 ♘e4** ♗xb2! Δ21 ♗xb2 ♘f4 22 ♕f1 ♗xe4 23 ♖xe4 ♘h3+ or 21 h3 ♖xf3 look good for Black. Overall it looks too frisky for White to open the f-file. Curt Hansen found a fine tactical solution to White's predicament, and the game continued blow for blow: **19 ♗d2** ♖ad8 20 ♕b3 ♔h8 21 h3 ♕g6 22 ♖ac1! (the start of a very imaginative solution. Already Black's threats are serious. The casual 22 ♖ad1? would meet a nasty shock after 22...f4 23 ♘f1 ♘e3!. Neither is 22 ♔h2 ♗c5 comfortable for White) 22...f4 23 ♘e4!⩲ (23 ♘e2 ♘e3! 24 ♘xf4 ♖xf4 25 ♖xe3 ♖xd2 26 ♖c7 ♗d5∓ Chernin) 23...♘e3 24 ♗xe3 ♗d5! (24...♗xe4 25 ♗c5 ♖d3 {25...♗xc5 26 ♖xc5 ♖d3 27 ♘h4! ♕g5 28 ♕b4 ♗xg2 29 ♘xg2 f3 30 ♕g4±} 26 ♕xd3 ♗xd3 27 ♗xe7 gives sufficient material for the queen and some chance for White to utilize his assets) 25 ♗c5!⩲ and now ½-½. Chernin gives 25...♗xb3 when White has a choice between **26 ♗xe7** which is similar to the note above, or the more speculative **26 axb3!?** ♗xc5 27 ♘xc5 Δe6 and again White seems to have enough since Black is rather devoid of counterplay. Much scope for further research!

14 ... ♗e7
15 e5

This advance seems thematic, but it is still White who has choices:

a) **15 ♘e5** ♕d4 16 ♘xd3 ♖d8! 17 ♗xf6 ♗xf6 18 ♘f4 **0-0** with excellent compensation.

b) **15 ♖e1!?**. White's intention is to prevent ...♘e4 and in the event of 15...**0-0** to hinder ...♘d5 too as an answer to e5, since 17 ♕xd3 would pin d5. Black has two reasonable responses:

b1) **15...0-0** 16 e5 ♘g4 17 ♗xe7 ♕xe7 18 ♕xd3 ♗xf3 19 ♕xf3 ♘xe5 20 ♕g3 ♖ae8 21 ♖ad1 f6 with at most a fractional edge for

White in Korchnoi-Flear, Wijk aan Zee 1987.

b2) **15...♖d8!?** and now:

b21) **16 e5?!** ♘g4 17 ♘e4 0-0 18 ♕d2 (18 h3 fails tactically to 18...♗xe4 19 ♖xe4 ♘xf2! 20 ♔xf2 ♗xg5 21 ♘xg5 ♕f5+ Gligorić-Ljubojević, Belgrade 1979) 18...♗xg5!? 19 ♕xg5 ♗xe4 20 ♖xe4 f6 21 exf6 ♘xf6∓ Nenashev-Kaidanov, Pinsk 1986.

b22) Quieter is **16 ♕b3** 0-0 17 ♖ad1 h6 18 ♘e5 ♕c7 19 ♗xf6 ♗xf6 20 ♘xd3 ♗xc3 21 bxc3 ♖c8 **22 f3** ♕xc3= Hort-Van der Wiel, Amsterdam 1988. White could try **22 ♖c1** Δ22...♕c4 23 ♘b2!?, but 22...♖fd8 looks like enough activity for a pawn.

b23) **16 ♗xf6** ♗xf6 17 ♘d5 (consistent; 17 e5?! ♗e7 18 e6 fxe6 19 ♘e5 ♕d4∓) 17...♗xd5 18 exd5+ ♔f8 19 ♕xd3 ♕xd5= P.Nikolić-Van der Wiel, Tilburg 1988; Black's excellent minor piece compensates for the temporary king misplacement.

15 ... ♘e4

This has largely replaced the older **15...♘d5** where Black must sacrifice a pawn for uncertain compensation:

a) **16 ♘xd5** ♕xd5 17 ♗xe7 ♔xe7 18 ♕d2 ♖hc8 19 ♕b4+ ♔e8 20 ♕g4! (if Black's king is allowed to rest in peace then with a strong passed d-pawn he will simply stand better) 20...♔f8 21 ♖ad1 ♔g8 (21...♖c4!?) 22 b3 ♖c2 23 ♘h4 ♕e4 24 ♕xe4 ♗xe4 25 f3 bg6 26 ♘xg6 hxg6= Groszpeter-Donaldson, Strasbourg 1985.

b) After **16 ♕xd3** ♘xc3 17 ♕xc3 ♗xg5 18 ♘xg5 ♕f5 **19 f4!?**. It looks risky to expose g2 further, but it seems that White can consolidate and the text thus improves on **19 ♕e3** h6 20 ♘h3 (20 ♘f3 ♗xf3 leads to an equal ending) 20...0-0 21 ♘f4 ♖fe8 22 ♖fe1 ♖ac8 23 f3 ♖c2 24 ♘d3 f6 25 ♖ac1 ♖xc1 26 ♖xc1 ♗d5 27 b3 (Chekhov-Bagirov, Yaroslavl 1982) when 27...♗f7 Δ...♗g6 would have maintained just enough play to hold the balance.

16 ♗xe7 ♔xe7! *(123)*

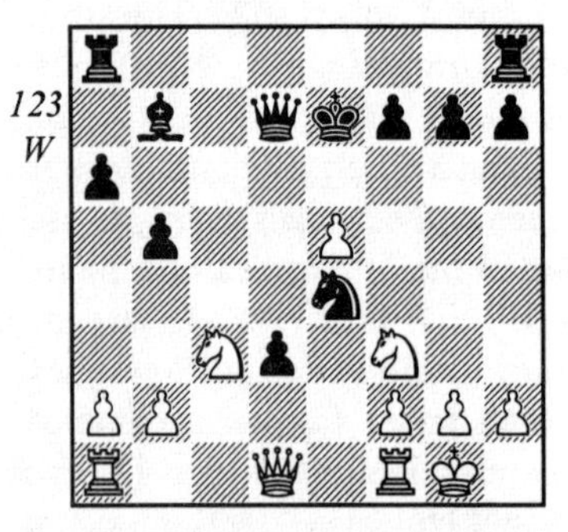

Chernin's fine novelty, which revived 15...♘e4. Unpalatable was 16...♘xc3 17 bxc3 ♕xe7 18 ♕xd3 0-0 19 ♖fe1 ♖ac8 20 ♘d4 ♕a3 21 ♖e3 when far from being a problem, the pawn on c3 provides useful support for the knight on d4, and clarifies White's advantage.

17 ♖e1

Since this stem game, various other solutions have been posited, but whilst perhaps preferable, none have seriously challenged the validity of Black's play:

a) **17 ♕b3** ♘xc3 18 ♕xc3 (18 ♕b4+ ♔e8 19 bxc3 ♗xf3∞) 18...♖hc8 19 ♕b4+ (19 e6?! ♖xc3 20 exd7 ♗xf3! 21 bxc3 ♗e2 was quite promising for Black in I.Farago-Tukmakov, Dortmund 1987) 19...♔e8∞ (Tukmakov).

b) **17 ♘xe4!?** ♗xe4 18 ♘g5!? (If 18 ♖e1, then 18...♕g4! 19 h3 ♗xf3= is better than 18...♕d5?! 19 ♘d2! Δ♕g4± Tukmakov-Nogueiras, Leningrad 1987) 18...♗b7 19 e6 ♕d5 20 ♕g4 f6 21 ♕b4+ ♔e8 with a complex struggle ahead; Hjartarson-Speelman, Belfort 1988.

17 ...	**♘xc3**
18 bxc3	**♕g4**
19 h3?!	

Capturing on d3 gives Black too much of a head start in claiming the open files: **19 ♕xd3** ♖hd8 20 ♕e3 ♗xf3 21 ♕xf3 ♕xf3 22 gxf3 ♖ac8∓. However, the endgame which arises from the text move favours Black too, and White should have tried **19 ♖e3!** to keep queens on the board. Here, too, Black has a pleasant game.

19 ...	**♗xf3**
20 hxg4	**♗xd1**
21 ♖axd1	**♖hd8**
22 ♖e3	**d2**
23 f3	

If **23 ♖e2** ♖ac8 24 ♖(either)xd2 ♖xd2 25 ♖xd2 ♖xc3 Black has a clear plus based on his more active rook and king, the vulnerability of the e5 pawn and the possibility of creating a passed pawn with his mobile two vs one queenside majority.

23 ...	**♖ac8**
24 ♔f2	**♖c4**
25 ♖e2	**♔e6**
26 ♖dxd2	**♖xd2**
27 ♖xd2	**♔xe5**

As in the previous note White has rounded up the advanced black d-pawn at the expense of one of his own. The weakness of White's a- and c-pawns is enough to give Black a great advantage, but **29 ♖b7!** would have at least complicated Black's task since White threatens to create counterplay with ♖b6+ and then back to b7.

After move 29 in the game White's rook is quite passive: **28 ♖d7 ♔e6 29 ♖a7? ♖a4 30 ♔e3 g5 31 g3 ♖xa2 32 ♔e4 ♖a4+ 33 ♔d3 ♖a2 34 ♔e4 ♔f6 35 ♖b7?! ♖e2+ 36 ♔d4 ♖e6** (Black's extra pawn is thus consolidated. The technical task from here is not too taxing, but a couple of errors from Gavrikov aid Black in his task of holding the kingside with the rook and switching his king to attack c3) **37 ♖a7 h6 38 ♖a8 ♔g7 39 ♔d3 ♖c6 40 ♔d2 ♔g6 41 ♖g8+?** (White was presumably worried about ...f5, but it was better to allow this but prevent the king's immediate journey by trying 42 ♖h8) **41...♔f6 42 ♖a8 ♔e5 43 ♖f8 0-1**.

Since 43...♖f6 44 ♔e3 ♔d5 45 ♖c8 ♖c6 46 ♖f8 ♔c4 47 ♔d2 ♔b3! 48 ♖xf7 ♖d6+ and Black's queenside pawns will have their day.

17 Old Meran with 10 e5

Game 22
Speelman-Ribli
Subotica IZ 1987

1 d4 d5 2 ♘f3 ♘f6 3 c4 c6 4 ♘c3 e6 5 e3 ♘bd7 6 ♗d3 dxc4 7 ♗xc4 b5 8 ♗d3 a6 9 e4 c5
10 e5 *(124)*

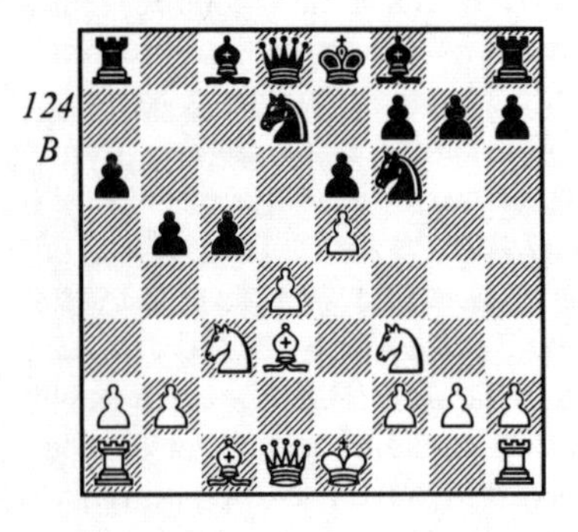

10 ... cxd4

In the early days of the Meran, the immediate 10...♘g4 was commonplace. Now it has fallen right out of favour. We shall consider two options for White – 'a' generally regarded as the main line, but 'b' perhaps more convincing:

a) **11 ♗e4** ♖a7 12 0-0 (12 ♘g5 is messy) 12...cxd4 13 ♕xd4 ♗c5 14 ♕d3 ♘gxe5 15 ♘xe5 ♘xe5 16 ♕c2 ♖c7! 17 ♗f4! ♕f6 18 ♗g3 with ideas of ♕e2, ♖ad1 or 17...♗d6 18 ♖ad1 ♕f6 19 ♗g3 when White's compensation looks dangerous, but there is certainly nothing like a clear win.

b) **11 ♗g5!?** ♕b6 12 ♗e4 ♗b7 13 ♗xb7 ♕xb7 14 0-0 h5 15 d5! ♘dxe5 16 ♘xe5 ♘xe5 17 dxe6 f6 18 ♕e2 ♗e7 19 ♖ad1 h4 20 f4 (20 h3!? keeps a simple plus too) 20...h3 21 fxe5 ♕xg2+ 22 ♕xg2 hxg2 23 ♔xg2 fxg5 (Botvinnik-Rabinovich, Leningrad 1926), when Botvinnik claims that the interesting knight manoeuvre 24 ♘d5! ♖a7 25 ♘e3 g6 26 ♘g4 was the best route to clarify White's advantage.

11 ♘xb5

The text, the so-called Blumenfeld Attack, dates back to 1925, and was for decades the main focus for research on the Meran. White's 'desperado' capture serves to weaken Black's queenside, and when Black declines to capture, for example with 11...♘g4, the knight can be *en route* for d6. In the 11...axb5 lines most graphically, Black plays with significant weaknesses on both flanks but with dynamic compensation in the form of an often mobile central majority. Needless to say, with such structural imbalance, the resulting positions are frequently very sharp. The immediate **11 exf6?!** is weak since only White's structure suffers after, e.g. 11...dxc3 12 ♗e4 ♖b8 13 fxg7 ♗xg7 14 bxc3 ♘c5∓ Euwe. Neither is **11 ♘e4** dangerous, provided Black knows what he is doing. The acknowledged antidote is **11...♘d5!** 12 0-0 (12 a4 ♘b4 13 axb5 ♗b7∓ Gligorić) and now:

a) **12...♗e7** is possible, although it is not clear that Black can dispense with ...h6 indefinitely. Gligorić gives 13 a4 b4 (although Black was successful in Nenashev-Yuneev, USSR 1989 with 13...bxa4 14 ♖xa4 0-0 15 ♖xd4 ♕c7 16 ♖e1 f5 17 exf6 ♘7xf6 18 ♘eg5 ♕b6 19 ♖xd5 ♘xd5 20 ♗xh7+ ♔h8 21 ♗e4 ♗xg5! eventually parrying White's attack, it looked very shaky along the way, and a simple move like 19 ♗b1 might have kept the exchange and a positional plus) 14 ♖e1 h6 15 ♗c4 ♗b7 16 ♕xd4 ♕b6 with a solid position for Black, structurally similar to the Wade Variation.

b) **12...h6** 13 a4 b4 14 a5 ♗b7 15 ♖e1 ♗e7 16 ♗c4 ♘c5 17 ♕xd4 ♘xe4 18 ♕xe4 ♕d7 19 ♗b3 ♔f8! 20 ♗d2 g6= Bronstein-Dorfman, Kishinev 1975.

11 ... ♘g4

11...axb5 and **11...♘xe5** are considered in Games 23 and 24 respectively.

12 ♕a4

Almost certainly still the critical move. White has two reasonable alternatives (12 ♗e4?! axb5 13 ♗xa8 ♕a5+ 14 ♘d2 ♘gxe5 15 ♗e4 f5 16 ♗b1 ♗b7 17 0-0 ♕a8 18 f3 ♗c5 gives Black good counterplay according to Polugaevsky). The first leads only to simplified equality, and the second, after a brief spell of relative popularity has perhaps had its sting removed:

a) **12 ♘bxd4**:

a1) **12...♘gxe5!?** is possibly simplest: 13 ♗e4 ♗b4+ 14 ♗d2 ♖b8 15 0-0 ♗xd2 16 ♕xd2 ♕b6!= Kaminsky-Kupreichik, USSR 1977.

a2) **12...♗b7** is also interesting: 13 0-0 ♘dxe5!? 14 ♕a4+ ♕d7 15 ♕xd7+ ♘xd7 16 h3 ♘gf6 17 ♗e2 ♗c5 18 ♘b3 ♗b6 19 ♗d2 a5 20 ♖fd1 0-0= Hartman-Bagirov, Sweden-USSR 1986.

a3) **12...♗b4+** 13 ♗d2 ♗xd2+ 14 ♕xd2 ♗b7 15 ♖d1 (15 ♗e2 is rather insipid, for example 15...♘dxe5 16 h3 ♘xf3+ 17 ♗xf3 ♗xf3 18 ♘xf3 ♕xd2+ 19 ♘xd2 ♘f6 20 ♔e2 ♔e7 with full equality; Seirawan-Chernin, Montpellier Ct 1985) 15...0-0 16 0-0 ♘gxe5 17 ♗e2 ♕b6 18 ♘xe5 (18 b3 ♘xf3+ 19 ♗xf3 ♘f6 20 ♗xb7 ♕xb7 21 ♘c2 a5 22 ♘e3 ♖fb8 23 ♕b2 ♕c7 ½-½ Miles-Kasparov, Basle (4) 1986) 18...♘xe5 19 ♕e3 ♘g6 20 ♖d2± Agzamov-Smagin, Tashkent 1984 and Cvitan-Rogić, Zagreb Z 1993. In the latter game Black sharpened the play with the slightly risky 20...e5 21 ♘f5 ♕e6 and lived to tell the tale. Still, it is possible that the 12th move alternatives are preferable.

b) **12 ♘d6+** ♗xd6 13 exd6 is very adequately met by **13...♕a5+!** 14 ♗d2 ♕d5 15 **0-0** (15 ♕a4!? e5∞ Ftacnik) 15...♘ge5 16 ♘xe5 ♘xe5 17 ♗f4 ♗b7∓ Cvitan-Chernin, Debrecen 1992.

12 ... ♘gxe5

Looks risky, but still unrefuted, and still the main line. However the pawn sacrifice commencing 12...♗b7!? retains some supporters, including Alexander Chernin who may be the world's strongest regular 8...a6 practitioner. Alternatives:

a) **12...♘c5?** 13 ♘d6+ ♔e7 14 ♕xd4 ♕a5+ 15 ♗d2 ♘xd3+ 16 ♕xd3 ♘xe5 17 ♕e3! ♘xf3+ 18 gxf3 Δ♗b4 gives White a fierce attack (Euwe).

b) **12...♖b8?! 13 ♘d6+! ♗xd6+ 14 exd6 ♕b6** (14...♗b7 15 ♕xd4 ♗xf3 16 gxf3 ♘ge5 17 ♗e2 ♕f6 18 ♕c3± Neikirkh) and now:

b1) Perhaps the best justification for trying 12...♖b8?! is that White may follow the analysis quoted by Harding and *ECO* {Korchnoi} - namely **15 ♕xd4??**, which in fact loses to 15...♘de5!.

b2) **15 0-0** doesn't give too much after 15...♕xd6 16 ♕xd4 ♕xd4 17 ♘xd4 ♗b7 18 ♗e2 ♘gf6 19 ♗d2 0-0 20 ♖fc1 ♘d5 Blagojević-Stanojovski, Kladovo 1990.

b3) **15 h3!** ♘gf6 16 ♕xd4 ♕xd4 17 ♘xd4 ♖b6 18 ♗e2 0-0 19 b3 ♖xd6 20 ♘f3 ♖b6 21 0-0 ♗b7 22 ♘d2 ♘d5 23 ♘c4 ♘c3 24 ♗d3 ♖b5 25 ♗a3 ♖g5 26 f3± Gelfand-C.Horvath, Halle 1987. Compared with line 'b2', Black had to spend much time recovering his pawn here, and this enabled White to activate his bishop pair.

c) **12...♗b7!?** *(125)*

125
W

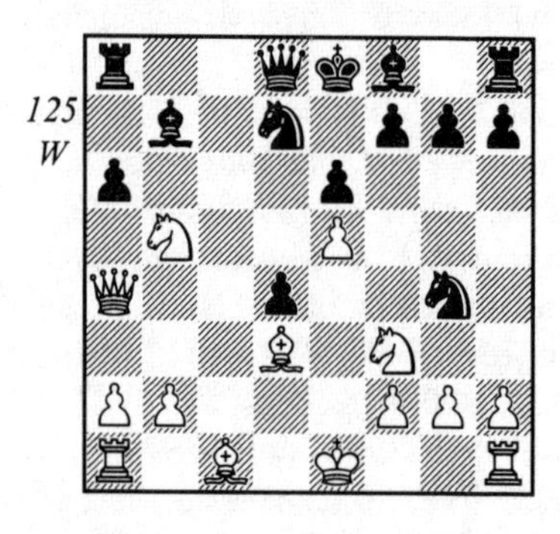

13 ♘bxd4 ♕b6 14 0-0 (14 h3?! ♘gxe5! 15 ♘xe5 ♕b4+ Taimanov) **14...♗c5** and now:

c1) **15 h3!?** is regarded highly in the theoretical works. I have long speculated upon what Messrs Van der Wiel and Chernin have in mind here. Perhaps a clue, and certainly food for thought, can be found in Alterman-Rogić below:

c11) **15...♘xf2** 16 ♖xf2 ♗xf3 17 ♖xf3 ♗xd4+ 18 ♔h1 ♖a7 19 ♗d2 0-0 20 ♗a5 ♕c5 21 ♗b4 ♕xe5 (Bozić-Rabar, Yugoslav Ch 1949) 22 ♖e1! ♕d5 23 ♗xf8 ♘xf8 24 ♖d1 e5 25 ♖df1+- (Euwe) looks pretty convincing.

c12) **15...♗xf3** 16 hxg4 ♗b7 (Others are inadequate) 17 ♘f3 h5 18 ♗d2 (18 g5 **0-0**! 19 ♕xd7 ♖ad8 is only equal) 18...♗xf3! (Rogić's important novelty, improving on 18...h4?! 19 ♘g5 ♔e7 20 ♕f4 f6 21 exf6+ gxf6 22 ♖ae1 with dangerous threats in Sorokin-Kirilov, corr. 1967) 19 gxf3 hxg4 20 fxg4 ♕xb2! 21 ♖ad1 (21 ♗f4 fails to 21...♗xf2+) 21...♔e7!! (intending ...♘xe5 and also ...♖h3 and ...♖ah8) 22 ♔g2 ♘xe5 23 ♗g5+?! f6 24 ♗f4 ♖h4 25 ♗xe5 ♕xe5 26 ♖h1 (Alterman-Rogić, Zagreb Z 1993) 26...♕d5+ 27 ♗e4 ♖xg4+ 28 ♔f3 ♕f5+ ∓. White now needs to find something new here.

c2) **15 ♗e3** (most recent attention has been focused here) **15...♘xe3 16 fxe3 h6! 17 ♔h1** (17 ♘d2? 0-0! 18 ♘c4 ♕c7 19 ♘f3 ♗xf3 20 ♖xf3 ♘xe5 21 ♕xe5 ♕xe5 22 ♕e4 ♕xe4 23 ♗xe4 ♖b8 24 b3 ♖fd8!∓ Bates-Wells, Hastings Challengers 1993/4) **17...♖d8 18 ♖ad1** (18 b4?! ♕xb4! 19 ♕c2 ♗xd4 20 ♖b1 {20 ♘xd4!? ♗d5 21 ♗xa6 0-0∓} 20...♕c3 21 ♖xb7 ♗xe5! 22 ♘xe5 ♕xc2 23 ♗xc2 ♘xe5 24 ♗a4+ ♔f8∓ Alterman-Chernin, Beersheba 1992) **18...0-0** and White seems to be hard pressed to prove a plus:

c21) **19 ♕c2?!** ♖c8 20 ♕f2 (Douven-Van der Wiel, Wijk aan Zee 1989) 20...♕c7 21 ♕g3 ♗a7 with an edge to Black. White should at least neutralize the bishop pair with 22 ♕f4 ♗b8 23 ♗e4∓.

c22) **19 ♗b1** ♕xb2 20 ♘xe6 fxe6! 21 ♖xd7 ♗xf3 22 gxf3 ♕xe5∓.

c23) **19 ♘b3** ♗xe3 20 ♗e4= Van der Wiel.

13 ♘xe5 ♘xe5
14 ♘d6++

Clearly **14 ♘c7++** needs to be well studied by Black too, but the consensus seems to be that there is no clear route to an advantage for White here. After **14...♔e7** White has:

a) **15 ♕b4+** ♕d6! (if 15...♔f6? 16 ♘e8+! ♕xe8 17 ♕xd4 ♔e7 18 ♕xe5 f6 19 ♕c3±) 16 ♕xd6+ ♔xd6 17 ♘xa8 ♘xd3+ 18 ♔e2 ♘c5! 19 ♘b6 ♗b7 20 ♘c4+ ♔d5 21 b3= (Rawie). Black has bishop and pawn for rook, with a strong passed pawn and active play.

b) **15 ♘xa8** ♘xd3+ 16 ♔e2 (16 ♔f1?! fails to attack the knight and thus gives Black time for 16...♕d6! 17 ♕c4 ♗d7! 18 a4 ♘xc1 19 ♖xc1 g6! when the possibility of rapid mobilization with ...♗h6 and ...♖c8 both with tempo gave Black excellent play in Toran-Trifunović, Oberhausen 1961) 16...♗d7!? (16...♘c5!? awaits trial, but 16...♘e5?! now seems to fall short after 17 ♕b4+ ♔f6 {17...♔e8 18 ♕b6±} 18 ♕d2! ♔e7 19 ♕g5+ f6 20 ♕xe5! – a familiar liquidating theme in this variation) 17 ♕xd4 ♘xc1+ 18 ♖axc1 ♕xa8 19 ♖c7 (The roles have been reversed. White has shed material for the initiative, but according to Christiansen, Black's resources are sufficient) 19...♕d8 20 ♖hc1 ♔e8 21 ♖a7 ♗e7 22 ♖cc7 ♗b5+ 23 ♔e3 ♗d6! 24

♖xf7 e5 with prospects of a successful defence.

14 ... ♔e7
15 ♘xc8+ ♖xc8

15...♕xc8 is much weaker after the simple 16 ♕xd4.

The outrageous-looking **15...♔f6?!** was very heavily analysed after Garry Kasparov sprung it on an unsuspecting Tony Miles in the sixth game of their match in Basle 1986. Refuting it over the board was not so easy and Black won following **16 ♗e4?** ♖xc8 17 h4?! (misplaced ambition; safer was 17 0-0) 17...h6 18 0-0 (since 18 ♗g5+? hxg5 19 hxg5+ ♔xg5 20 ♖xh8 ♖c4! {Δ...♗b4+} 21 ♖xf8 ♕xf8 gives Black a pawn and the initiative) 18...♖c4 19 ♕d1 d3 20 ♖e1? ♖xc1! 21 ♖xc1 d2 22 ♖f1 ♕d4∓ 23 ♖c2 ♕xe4 24 ♖xd2 ♗c5 25 ♖e1 ♕xh4 26 ♕c2 ♗b4 27 ♖xe5 ♗xd2 28 g3 ♕d4 29 ♖e4 ♕d5 0-1.

Subsequently it was found that the simple **16 ♗xa6! ♘d3+ 17 ♔f1** is very good for White. A sample of the lines:

a) **17...♘b4** 18 ♕b3 d3 19 ♕c4 ♕d5 20 ♘b6+-.

b) **17...♘c5** 18 ♕d1 ♕d5 19 ♘b6+-.

This analysis by Velicković has, it seems, finished off Kasparov's extraordinary idea once and for all.

16 ♗xa6 ♖a8
17 ♕b5 ♕d5!

Much better than **17...f6** 18 0-0 ♖b8 (18...♔f7 19 f4!) 19 ♕xe5 fxe5 20 ♗g5+ with a large endgame advantage in Spassky-Novotelnov, Leningrad 1961.

18 ♕xd5 exd5
19 ♗b5 ♔f6
20 0-0!? *(126)*

This ending is almost certainly critical for the assessment of 11...♘g4 as a whole. The text, played for the first time in this game clearly improved upon **20 ♔e2?!** ♗d6! 21 ♗f4 d3+ 22 ♗xd3 ♘xd3 23 ♗xd6 ♘xb2 24 ♖hc1 Ftačnik-Nogueiras, Szirak 1986, when 24...d4!? may even leave Black with a slight initiative. Speelman showed excellent judgement in seeing that the king in the centre can be more of a liability than an asset in this position. The third destination for the monarch was tested in Chekhov-Dzhandzhgava, Pavlodar 1987. Here White did seem to acquire a slight edge too with **20 ♗f4** d3 21 0-0-0!? ♖xa2 22 ♔b1 ♖a5 23 ♗xd3 ♗b4 24 h4!, but I feel that Speelman's approach will prove the most enduring.

126
B

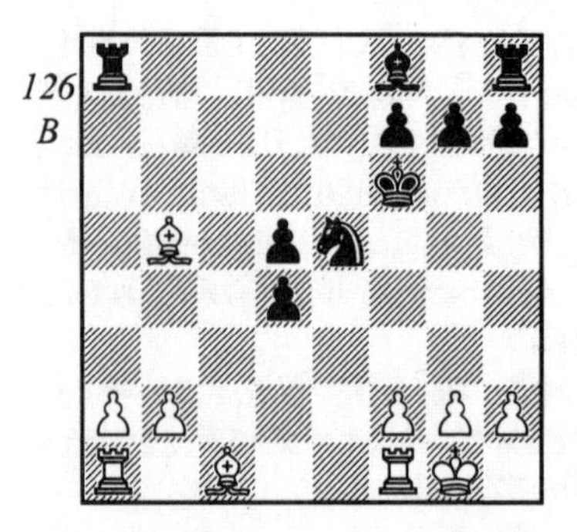

20 ... ♗b4

Less logical was **20...♖b8** 21 a4 ♗b4?! 22 ♖d1 ♗c5 23 b3 ♖hc8 24 ♗b2 d3 25 ♔f1 d4 26 f4± ♘c6? 27 ♖ac1 1-0 Wells-Lacrosse, Cappelle la Grande 1990.

However, **20...♗d6!?** (Ribli) merits attention since **21 ♗f4?** is ruled out by check on f3. Speelman then gives **21 a4** ♖hc8 22 ♗f4 (or 22 ♗g5+ based on the idea that after 22...♔xg5 23 f4+, f7 will be in trouble – pure Speelman!) 22...♘f3+ 24 gxf3 ♗xf4 25 ♖ad1 which retains a small plus. Presumably if 25...♗e5, then 26 f4 should be considered.

21 ♗f4 ♖hc8

22 a4

White can also strongly consider the very simple and direct 22 ♖fd1!? ♘g6 23 ♗d2 ♗d6 24 a4 ♖c2 25 ♖ab1 ♘e5 26 ♗e1! d3 27 b3 ♗c5 28 ♗xd3 ♘xd3 29 ♖xd3 ♖e8 30 ♔f1 and the queenside pawns met with few obstacles in Khalifman-Kuijf, European Club Cup 1988.

22 ... ♘c4?!

The alternative for Black is to penetrate on the c-file with 22...♖c2 planning to answer 23 ♖ad1 with 23...d3! (not 23...♗c5?! since 24 b4 merely helps White). After 23...d3!, White reacted badly in Tesić-M.Ivanović, Yugoslavia 1987 with 24 ♗e3 d2 25 ♗d4 ♔e6 26 b3 g5 27 f4 gxf4 28 ♖xf4 ♖c1 29 ♖ff1 ♖ac8. However, if White is really obliged to remove Black's greatest asset before it becomes too much with 24 ♗xe5+ ♔xe5 25 ♖xd3 ♖xb2 then the ending as a whole holds no terrors for Black.

23 ♖ad1! ♘xb2

If Black tries to hold d4 with **23...♗c5** then 24 b3! ♘a3 25 ♗d7! ♖d8 26 ♗g4 is strong according to Speelman. Ribli suggests rather that **23...g5!?** was the best defence. He gives 24 ♗c1 ♗c5 25 b3 ♘d6 26 ♗d3 ♖ab8 when White's advantage would be very hard to convert to the full point.

24 ♖xd4 ♗c3

25 ♖xd5± h6

If **25...♘xa4** 26 ♗g5+ ♔e6 27 ♖fd1 and the position of the black king suddenly becomes a key factor.

26 ♖d6+

Perhaps even stronger was **26 ♖c1!** since 26...♘xa4? would lose material to 27 ♖d3 ♖a5 28 ♗xa4 ♖xa4 29 ♗e3.

26 ... ♔e7

27 ♖d7+ ♔f8?!

The possibility of a check on d6 helps White's cause. It was better to return to f6, preparing to answer 27 ♖a1? with ...♘d3.

28 ♖a1 ♗f6?

Even now **28...♔g8** was preferable, again forcing White to consider the ...♘d3 idea. The text is a loss of tempo which enables White to take a time out to put an end to back rank problems.

29 g3! ♔g8

30 ♖a3 ♖c5

31 ♖b7 ♗d4
32 ♗e3 ♗xe3
33 ♖xe3 ♘xa4?

A final error, which has the virtue of circumventing the painful technical phase. Ribli had presumably reckoned only on 34 ♗xa4 ♖xa4 35 ♖e8+ ♔h7 36 ♖xf7 when Black can struggle on, but...

34 ♖a3!

1-0

Game 23
Cs.Horvath-Feher
Hungarian Ch (Budapest) 1989

1 d4 d5 2 ♘f3 ♘f6 3 c4 c6 4 ♘c3 e6 5 e3 ♘bd7 6 ♗d3 dxc4 7 ♗xc4 b5 8 ♗d3 a6 9 e4 c5 10 e5 cxd4 11 ♘xb5 axb5

12 exf6 *(127)*

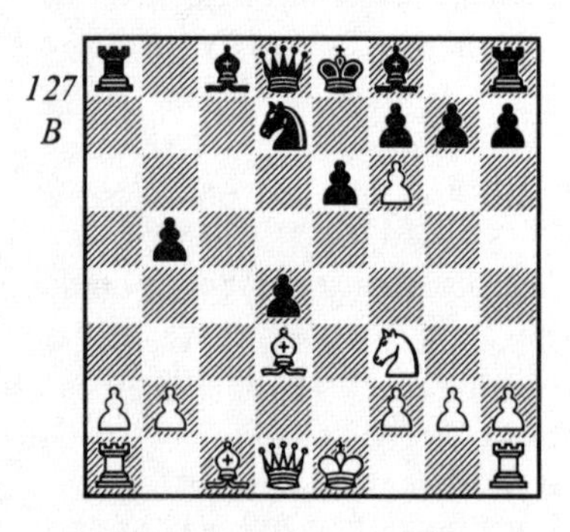
127
B

12 ... ♕b6

Black defends his d- and b-pawns and seeks to force White to clarify the situation on the kingside, i.e. whether to capture on g7. **12...♕xf6??** loses immediately to 13 ♗g5. **12...gxf6** 13 ♘xd4 may appear to give Black no real compensation for his weakened structure but 13...♕b6 14 ♗e3 ♗b4+ 15 ♔f1 ♗c5 16 ♗xb5 e5 17 ♗xd7+ ♗xd7 18 ♕f3 ♕a6+ 19 ♘e2 ♖g8! 20 ♗xc5 ♗c6 led to a quick win for Black in Alterman-Chernin, Groningen PCA 1993. Of the three other possibilities two are also inferior, but instructive:

a) **12...e5?!**. In general the central majority is Black's trump-card, but its utilization requires a bit of finesse. In particular Black should avoid a blockade on the light squares when especially f5 can be a very ugly weakness. This theme will recur. 13 fxg7 ♗xg7 14 ♕e2 ♕e7 (14...0-0 15 ♕e4) 15 0-0 ♗b7 16 ♖e1 ♕d6 17 ♘h4!± Bogoljubow-George Thomas, Baden-Baden 1925.

b) **12...♗b4+** 13 ♗d2 ♗xd2+ 14 ♕xd2 gxf6 15 ♗e4 ♖b8 16 ♘xd4 with an enduring structural plus – Polugaevsky.

c) **12...♗b7** is perfectly playable although often transpositional; thus the majority of 11...axb5 games reach the key position after move 16 in the main game. Still there are some interesting and perhaps unfairly neglected choices along the way:

c1) **13 0-0!?**:

c11) It is an important question whether **13...♕b6** would secure a main line. In Fernandez-Rivas, Cienfuegos 1983 White continued to avoid fxg7 and tried instead 14

♕e2. Black's reaction 14...♗c6 looks too passive, and he found himself in trouble after 15 ♗e4 ♗xe4 16 ♕xe4 ♖d8 17 fxg7 ♗xg7 18 ♗g5 f6 19 ♗d2 with positional plus for White.

c12) Also interesting and original was **13...♕xf6!?** which worked out OK in Hort-Vaganian, Moscow 1975 after 14 ♗xb5 ♗c5 15 ♗d2 ♗d6 16 ♖e1 h6 17 a4 ♔e7!? 18 ♘xd4 ♘e5 19 ♕e2 ♖hd8 20 ♗c3 ♕g6 21 g3 ♖ac8 with enough play for the pawn. The lack of subsequent tests reflects a certain suspicion but I think the idea merits further study.

c13) **13...gxf6!?** and now White has a choice:

c131) Worthy of note is **14 ♗xb5!?** ♖g8 15 ♗f4 ♖a5(!) (Seeking compensation with 'normal moves' here is inadequate since White's dark-squared bishop will shield the g-file, Black's king lacks a haven, and his centre can as so often become blockaded on the light squares, e.g. 15...♕b6?! 16 a4 e5 17 ♗g3 ♗d6 18 ♖e1 ♔d8 19 ♘d2! ♗b4 20 ♖e2 ♘c5 21 ♘c4 ♕e6 22 ♘xe5!± Cvitan-Thorhallsson, Oberwart 1991) 16 a4 ♖xb5 17 axb5 ♘e5 18 ♘xe5 fxe5 19 ♖a7 ♕d5 (Vainstein suggests the more ambitious 19...♗d5 although without the queen able to reinforce pressure on the diagonal it seems doubtful that Black has enough) 20 ♖xb7 ♕xb7 21 g3 when Black's structure looks a little loose, but the plan of ...f6 and ...♖g7-c7 may equalize; Botvinnik-Simagin, USSR Ch 1951.

c132) **14 ♘xd4** ♖g8 15 f3 ♗c5 16 ♗e3 ♖g5!? (This interesting rook manoeuvre which provides the b-pawn with a crucial indirect defence and prepares to strengthen the pins on the White knight via either d5 or e5, has given Black's 13th a new lease of life) 17 ♘c2 (17 ♗xb5 ♖d5 18 ♗c4 ♖d6 19 ♕b3 ♖xd4) 17...♕b6 (If 17...♗xe3 18 ♘xe3 ♕b6 turns out to be an improvement then White should prefer first 17 ♕e2 ♕b6 18 ♘c2) 18 ♕e2 0-0-0!? (Possible too is 18...♔e7, but the black king seems surprisingly secure on the queenside as well. The immediate 18...♖e5 is interesting. Sorokin and Scherbakov give 19 ♖fe1 {19 ♗xc5!? ♘xc5 20 ♕f2 looks reasonable to me too. Black looks quite active, but it is not so clear how to use this and positionally White has some trumps} 19...♗xe3 {19...f5!?; 19...♖a4!?} 20 ♘xe3 ♖a4 21 ♕f2!±. Overall I prefer the text) 19 ♔h1 ♖e5 20 ♖fe1 f5 (20...♗xe3+ 21 ♘xe3 ♔b8 looks OK too) 21 ♗xc5 ♖xe2 22 ♗xb6 ♖xe1+ 23 ♖xe1 ♘b6 24 ♗xb5 ♖d2 25 ♖e2 ♖d1+ 26 ♖e1 ♖d2 27 ♖e2 ♖d1+ and now White deviated with 28 ♘e1 but he never looked in any serious danger of winning since Black's forces are so active; Scherbakov-Sorokin, USSR 1991.

c2) **13 fxg7 ♗xg7 14 0-0 0-0**:

c21) **15 ♗xb5?!** ♘c5 16 ♗f4?! e5! 17 ♗g3 (17 ♘xe5 fails to 17...♘e6 18 ♗g3 ♕d5∓. This tactical justification is critical, since if White could hold up Black's centre the pawn sacrifice would be suspect) 17...♘e6 18 a4 e4 19 ♘e5 d3 20 ♘d7 ♘d4! with excellent play in Sakaev-Belikov, USSR 1990.

c22) **15 ♖e1** seems very sensible when Black probably has nothing better than **15...♕b6** transposing to the main game. In Wells-Murshed, British Ch (Eastbourne) 1990, Black blundered with **15...♘c5?** which allowed 16 ♗xh7+ ♔h8?? (relatively best was 16...♔xh7 although after 17 ♘g5+ ♔g6 18 ♕g4 f5 19 ♕g3 White has a very strong attack) 17 ♘g5 f5 18 ♕h5 ♖f6 19 ♖xe6! ♗h6 20 ♗g6 ♔g7 21 ♘f7! 1-0. Donaldson mentions *en passant* the possibility of **15...♕c7**. This is perhaps the most likely alternative, preventing ♗f4, but now perhaps White is more justified in testing Black's offer with 16 ♗xb5 since 15 ♖e1 is unambiguously useful.

13 fxg7

Trying to avoid the main line positions merits attention here too:

a) **13 ♗e4** ♗b7 14 ♗xb7 ♕xb7 15 0-0 ♘xf6 16 ♘xd4 ♖d8 17 ♗e3 ♗c5= A.Greenfeld-Van der Wiel, Groningen 1987 looks quite innocuous.

b) **13 0-0** gxf6 (13...♗b7 14 ♕e2!? is Fernandez-Rivas, note 'c11' to Black's 12th) 14 ♗e4 ♗b7 15 ♗xb7 ♕xb7 16 ♘xd4 ♖g8 17 ♕f3 ♕xf3 18 ♘xf3 Alekhine-Keres, Prague 1943.

13 ... ♗xg7
14 0-0

With **14 ♕e2** White hits the b5 pawn, prepares ♕e4 in some cases, and sometimes seeks to develop the king's rook to d1. In fact the 'threats' prove to be somewhat illusory, but, although out of fashion, the move is complex and by no means bad. **14...0-0! 15 0-0** (15 ♗xb5? ♘c5 threatens ...d3; 15 ♕e4 f5 16 ♕xa8 ♗a6 17 ♕xf8+ ♔xf8 and again the greed backfires since Black is so active and can easily support his strong d-pawn) and now **15...♗b7** (Konstantinopolsky) is soundest. White can try:

a) **16 ♗xb5** ♗xf3 17 gxf3 ♘c5 with enough play for the pawn.

b) **16 ♗f4?!** is met by Simagin's idea 16...f6! intending ...e5, ...♘c5 when Black is fine. It is harder for White to implement a light-square blockade with ♕e2 than with ♖e1, since ...f5 and a pin on the e-file to answer a capture on e5 can be embarrassing.

c) **16 ♖d1** (the most testing) 16...e5 (Vainstein suggested 16...b4, since 17 ♘xd4 ♗xd4 18 ♗xh7+ ♔h8! is good for Black. This could well be a more practical solution than the text) 17 ♗xb5 (17 ♘h4 e4! again highlights the down-side of 14 ♕e2) 17...♗xf3

18 gxf3 ♘c5 19 b4! (Eventov-Siroton, corr. 1950) and now 19...d3!? leads to immense complications.

14 ... ♗b7

a) **14...0-0** is fine when merely transpositional. Bad for Black was 15 ♖e1 e5? 16 ♗f5 ♕d6 17 ♕c2 h6 18 ♗d2 ♗b7 19 a3 Larsen-Mestel, Hastings 1972/3 with a classic light square control.

b) **14...♘c5** has also been overshadowed by the text. Although Black initially gains the bishop pair, he is virtually obliged to return this favour or lose further development tempi, and White retains a pull – **15 ♗f4 ♗b7 16 ♖e1** and now:

b1) The speed of Black's mobilization is again called into question after **16...♖d8** 17 ♖c1! ♖d5 18 ♗e5! (the exchange of the dark-squared bishops nicely highlights the lack of a safe haven for Black's king) 18...♗xe5 19 ♖xe5 ♖xe5 20 ♘xe5 ♘xd3 21 ♕xd3 f6 22 ♕g3! with a powerful attack in Botvinnik-Euwe, The Hague-Moscow Wch 1948.

b2) **16...♘xd3 17 ♕xd3** with a further division:

b21) **17...0-0??** 18 ♘g5±.

b22) **17...♕c6!?** is an ambitious move, and probably Black's best since at least he retains the one trump of his position, the bishop pair. However White is still for preference after 18 ♖ac1 ♕d5 19 b4! ♖c8 20 ♖xc8+ ♗xc8 21 ♗e5 f6! 22 ♗xd4 0-0 (Barczay-Tompa, Hungarian Ch 1976) 23 ♕e2! ♗d7 24 ♖d1! (Donaldson).

b23) **17...♗xf3** 18 ♕xf3 0-0 19 ♖ac1 ♖ac8 20 ♕g3 ♔h8 21 h4 with a strong initiative; Szabo-Foltys, Budapest 1948.

15 ♖e1 0-0

16 ♗f4 ♗d5 *(128)*

Not **16...f6** 17 ♘xd4! e5 18 ♘f5 exd4 19 ♕g4 ♖f7 20 ♘h6+ ♔f8 21 ♘xf7 ♘c5 22 ♗xh7 ♔xf7 23 b4 with a crunching attack for White in Chekhlov-Nekrasov, USSR 1981.

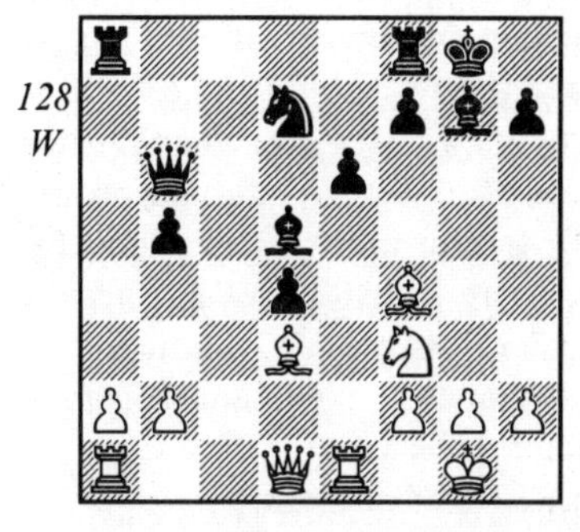

128
W

A very important position for the theory of 11...axb5. Black's 16th emphasizes both the offensive and defensive aspects of his position. His main problem is the weakness of the kingside, and 16...♗d5 is crucial to the ability to advance the f-pawn to shield h7 in particular. A secondary problem is that c7 offers White a dangerous entry-point on the only open file. On the plus side are the open a-file (White often jettisons the a2 pawn in the interests of getting on with his kingside play) and as usual in this variation the latent power of his central majority if it can be mobilized. Also we shall see instances where Black is able to trade the right pieces on the kingside and use the half-open g-file to his advantage. The position is unbalanced, practice slightly favouring White, but the only real drawback is that if White is peacefully-inclined it is difficult to play for a win against 17 ♘e5.

17 ♖c1

Directed towards penetration to c7, but Black seems to have two reasonable defences. In addition to the text, White has tried 17 ♘e5 when it is probably risky for Black to play for a win, but when it is far from clear that White can profitably try for more either. Recently the more brutal 17 h4 has been a focus of attention too, although it is still unclear how dangerous this attack really is:

a) **17 ♘e5** and now:

a1) **17...♘xe5 18 ♗xe5**:

a11) **18...♗xe5** 19 ♖xe5 (19 ♗xh7+ ♔xh7 20 ♕h5+ ♔g7! {20...♔g8?? 21 ♖xe5 f6 22 ♕g6+ ±} 21 ♕g5+ ♔h7 22 ♕h5+ etc ½-½ Golombek-Szily, Trencianske Teplice 1949 and others) 19...f5 20 ♕d2 (20 ♕h5!? Δ♖xd5) 20...♖a7∞.

a12) **18...f5?!** grants White the benefits of the exchange of dark-squared bishops and the consequent weakening of Black's king without the arguably awkward placing of the rook on e5. In Granda Zuñiga-Van der Wiel, Wijk aan Zee 1989 White quickly built a strong attack: 19 ♗xg7! (19 ♕d2?! ♖f7 20 ♕b4!? ♖xa2 Wells-Blauert, Lubeck 1990 was less convincing. Occupying g7 with Black's king rather than rook should be a priority) 19...♔xg7 20 ♕e2! ♖xa2 21 ♕e5+ ♔g8 22 ♖xa2 ♗xa2 23 ♖c1! ♗c4?! (It was necessary to try 23...♕d8 24 ♖c7 ♕f6) 24 b3!! ♗xd3 25 ♕g3+ ♔f7 26 ♖c7+ ♔e8 27 ♕g7 and Black had to give his queen with 27...♕xc7 when White had a decisive plus.

a2) **17...♖a7** the main intention behind which is to avoid the draw, is reputedly rather risky. White has tried:

a21) **18 ♕d2?!** ♘xe5 19 ♗xe5 ♗xe5 20 ♖xe5 f6! 21 ♖h5 ♖g7= reveals one point of ...♖a7.

a22) **18 ♖c1** ♘xe5 19 ♖xe5!? f5 (19...♗xe5 is too risky, e.g. 20 ♗xe5 f5 21 ♕d2 ♕d8 22 ♕f4 with a powerful attack) 20 ♖xd5! exd5 21 ♕b3. An interesting position – White has given the exchange to remove the bishop on d5 which affords Black's position so much of its dynamic energy. Black is left with a string of weaknesses, and the consensus is that although White did not convert in Dautov-Ruzhale, Riga 1988, this is not satisfactory for Black: 21...♔h8 22 ♕xd5 b4 **23 g3?!** ♕a5!=, but stronger was **23 ♗d6!** ♖d7 24 ♖c6! ♕b7 25 ♕c5 ♖e8 26 ♔f1! (± at least).

a23) **18 ♕g4!?** ♘c5 (18...f5!? – I have reservations about voluntarily taking pressure off the key e5 point) 19 ♗c2 f5 20 ♕d1 (20 ♕g3!?± Nogueiras) 20...♘e4 21 ♗b3 ♖d8 (21...♗xe5! 22 ♗xe5 ♗xb3∞ Nogueiras) 22 ♘d3!± Nogueiras-Beliavsky, Barcelona 1989.

b) **17 h4!?** is a very aggressive try. White threatens to march the pawn up to h6, which both creates threats against the black king and removes the g7 square from Black's rooks. If Black is obliged to play ...h6, then he will be weak on the light squares, in particular vulnerable to the manoeuvre ♘h4-g6. 17...♔h8 (17...♖a7 was suggested by Shabalov but after 18 h5 Black still needs to sort out his fundamental approach to the threat of 19 h6) 18 ♖ac1 (18 h5 f5!? 19 h6 ♗f6 20 ♘e5 ♘xe5 21 ♖xe5 ♖ad8!; 21 ♗xe5!?) 18...♖c7 19 ♗e4! ♗xe4 20 ♖xe4 ♖xa2 21 ♗c7 (Shabalov-Kishnev, Barnaul 1988) and now 21...♕a7 is best, but still leaves White for preference. 17 h4 deserves a lot of further investigation.

17 ... ♖a7!?

Defends c7, and as the course of the game brilliantly highlights, the rook has an interesting 'swinging' capability from here. Still, the alternative **17...♖ac8!?** seems satisfactory too, based on an extremely lengthy and complex analysis of White's most direct try in *New In Chess Yearbook 14*. After 18 ♘g5 h6 19 ♖xc8 (19 ♗h7+ ♔h8 20 ♘xf7+ ♖xf7 21 ♖xc8+ ♘f8!) 19...♖xc8 20 ♗h7+ ♔h8! 21 ♘xf7+ ♔h7 22 ♕d3+ ♔g8 23 ♘xh6+ ♔f8 24 ♕h7 e5! with the intention of meeting 25 ♘f5 with 25...♕f6 26 ♘xg7 (26 ♗d2 ♔f7 27 ♗h6 ♖g8!∓) 26...♕xf4 27 ♕h8+ ♔f7 28 ♕xc8 ♕g4!∓.

18 a3

18 ♘e5!? would transpose to Dautov-Ruzhale, note 'a22' to White's 17th above.

18 ... f5
19 ♕e2?! e5! *(129)*

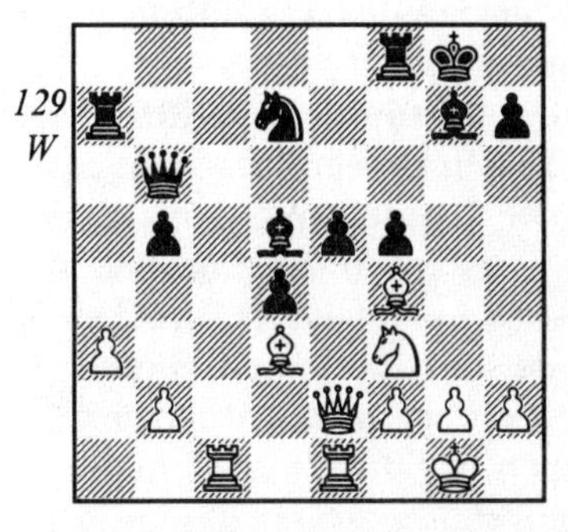

129
W

A very fine illustration of Black's possibilities for active play in the centre and on the g-file. On move 19, White should have bailed out with 19 ♘e5. Now Black takes advantage of the white queen's awkward position to force f4, which seriously weakens the g2 point.

20 ♘xe5 ♘xe5
21 ♗xe5 ♖e7!
22 f4

Forced as the attempt to solve tactically with **22 ♗xd4?** runs into 22...♕g6!-+.

22 ...	**♗xe5**
23 fxe5	**♖g7**
24 ♖c2!	

Stubborn defence! White gives the queen for rook and bishop in a bid to wrest the g-file and some initiative. By contrast **24 g3?!** would have led to a fierce attack for Black after 24...f4 opening another file against the white king.

24 ...	**♖xg2+**
25 ♕xg2	**♗xg2**
26 ♖xg2+	**♔f7!**

It is necessary to approach white's passed e-pawn. **26...♔h8** 27 e6 would give White good counterplay.

27 e6+	**♔f6?**

This however, is a serious error which throws away Black's advantage. Black must blockade the passed pawn with **27...♔e7!**. It is understandable that instinctively Black hesitated before allowing 28 ♖g7+, but after 28...♔f6 this danger is shown to be an illusion since the rook cannot leave the g-file (e.g. 29 ♖xh7?) because of 29...♖g8+ and suddenly White's king is again in mortal danger. After the text move, the rook on g2 does find a career.

28 e7	**♖e8**
29 ♖f2!	**♔g7**
30 ♖xf5	**♕d6?**

This time Black is jeopardizing the draw! It was necessary first to play **30...♕g6+!** 31 ♔f2 and only then 31...♕d6 also hitting h2. Then after 32 ♖ge5 Black has 32...♔f6 when 33 ♖f5+ ♔g7 34 ♖e5 ♔f6 35 ♖f5+ or 33 ♗xb5 ♖xe7 34 ♖xe7 ♕xh2+ both look like plausible ways to bring proceedings to a peaceful close. After Black's mistake he has to resort to attempting to permanently harry the white king, but this should not be successful...

31 ♖fe5 ♕f6 32 ♗xb5 ♕f4 33 ♗xe8 ♕g4+ 34 ♔f2 ♕f4+ 35 ♔g2 ♕g4+ 36 ♔f2 ♕f4+ 37 ♔e2 ♕xe5+ 38 ♔d1 ♕f5 39 ♗c6? (Just at the point where White has done everything right and is on the verge of victory he returns the compliment just before time control. Correct was 39 ♗a4 when the bishop is secure and the checks evaporate after 39...♕b1+ 40 ♔e2 ♕e4+ (or 40...♕xb2+ 41 ♔f1+-) 41 ♔d2 ♕f4+ 42 ♔d1 and the king can run to a1. Now Black can capture the bishop and thus force White to queen at a moment that allows the long-awaited perpetual) **39...♕b1+ 40 ♔e2 ♕c2+ 41 ♔f1 ♕xc6 42 e8♕ ♕f3+ 43 ♔g1 ♕g4+ 44 ♔f2 ♕f5+ 45 ♔e2 ♕c2+ 46 ♔f1 ♕f5+ 47 ♔g2 ♕g4+ 48 ♔f2 ♕f5+ 49 ♔g3 ½-½.**

Game 24
Ibragimov-Lukacs
Budapest 1992

1 d4 d5 2 c4 e6 3 ♘c3 c6 4 e3 ♘f6 5 ♘f3 ♘bd7 6 ♗d3 dxc4 7 ♗xc4 b5 8 ♗d3 a6 9 e4 c5 10 e5 cxd4 11 ♘xb5

11 ...	**♘xe5**

Although the 8...a6 Meran has not been so fashionable in recent years, the theory has still undergone quite a change. 11...♘xe5 used to be quite clearly Black's chief response to the Blumenfeld, developing a mass of theory. This is no longer so, and when Black does play 11...♘xe5, White has almost completely abandoned the moves 13 ♕f3 – which seems to fizzle to about equality and – 13 **0-0** which can give a strong attack, but at the same time allows Black a lot of positionally well-based counterplay. Consequently, I too, have reacted to space restrictions by concentrating on the unbalanced structure that arises after 13 ♗b5+, once awarded '?', now the most dangerous try. We have seen the contest between the black centre roll and either weaknesses on the flank or a queenside majority in several lines of the Meran. Here it is at its sharpest, in both middlegame and endgame settings.

12 ♘xe5 axb5 *(130)*

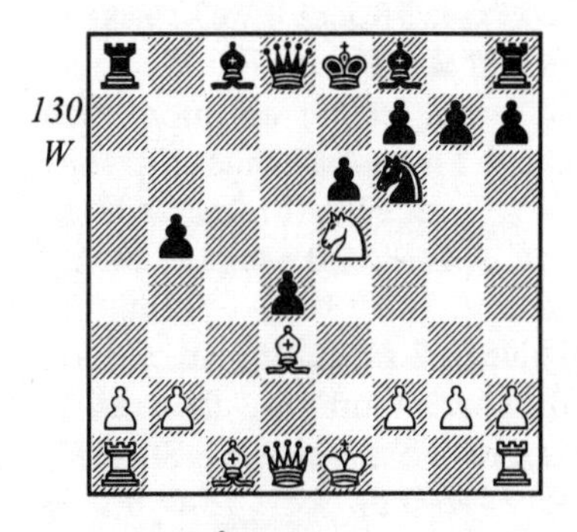

13 ♗xb5+

Three other moves, one dubious, two unfashionable but still requiring a certain basic knowledge:

a) **13 ♕b3** ♕a5+ 14 ♗d2 b4 15 f4 (15 ♘c6 ♕b6 16 ♘xb4 ♗b7 17 0-0 ♗d6 gives Black excellent activity) 15...♗b7 16 0-0 ♗e7 17 ♗c4 0-0! 18 ♗xe6 ♘d5 19 ♗h3 ♘e3 20 ♖fc1 ♕d5 21 ♕xd5 ♗xd5∓ Vaganian-Dolmatov, USSR Ch 1979.

b) **13 ♕f3** requires care from Black. 13...♖b8? for example fails to the simple 14 ♘c6 ♗b7 15 ♗xb5+-. Black can choose between two checks on a5 – a summary:

b1) **13...♕a5+!?** 14 ♔e2 (14 ♔d1!? {Vera} could be tested, but not 14 ♗d2? ♗b4∓) 14...♗d6 15 ♗d2 (White has the solid option 15 ♕c6+ ♔e7 16 ♗d2 b4 17 ♕xd6+ ♔xd6 18 ♘c4+ ♔d7 19 ♘xa5 ♖xa5 {Agzamov-Vera, Sochi 1985} 20 ♖hc1=) 15...♕a6 (not 15...♕a4 16 b3 ♕a6 17 a4 0-0 18 axb5! ♕xa1 19 ♖xa1 ♖xa1 20 ♘g4! with good play for White in Lalić-Mnatsakanian, Varna 1986) 16 a4 0-0 17 ♗xb5 ♕a7!? (Opinions differ on the queen sacrifice first analysed by Reshevsky, 17...♗xe5!? 18 ♗xa6 ♗xa6+ 19 ♔d1!. I am a bit sceptical, and it remains untested, but Black does have definite counterplay) 18 ♘c6 ♕b6 19 ♘e7+ ♗xe7 20 ♕xa8 ♗b7 21 ♕a5 ♕d6 and the unfortunate placing of both the white royals gives fair compensation for the exchange.

b2) **13...♗b4+** is perhaps more solid and reliable:

b21) **14 ♔f1** ♖b8 15 ♕g3 ♕c7! 16 ♘c6 {16 ♕xg7? ♕xe5! 17 ♕xh8+ ♔e7 18 ♗h6 ♗b7 19 ♕g7 ♖g8-+; 16 ♘f3!=} 16...♗d6! 17 ♕xg7 ♖g8 18 ♕xf6 ♕xc6 gave Black a tremendous initiative in Kramer-Bisguier, New York 1955.

b22) **14 ♔d1** ♗d7 15 ♘c6 ♗xc6 16 ♕xc6+ ♔e7 17 ♕xb5 ♖b8 18 ♕g5 h6 19 ♕xg7 ♕d5 20 ♕g3 ♖hg8 gave Black a strong initiative in Ree-Torre, Wijk aan Zee 1984.

b23) **14 ♔e2** ♖b8 15 ♕g3 (others seem weaker: 15 ♘c6 ♗b7 16 ♘xd8 ♗xf3+ 17 ♔xf3 ♔xd8 18 ♗f4 ♖b7 19 ♗e5 ♔e7= or 15 ♗g5?! ♗b7! 16 ♗xb5+ ♔e7 17 ♗c6 ♗a6+ 18 ♔d1 ♕a5! with strong counterplay) 15...♕d6 16 ♘f3 ♕xg3 17 hxg3 ♗d6 18 ♗f4 ♔e7 19 ♘xd4 ♗d7 20 ♗xd6+ ♔xd6 21 ♖hd1 ♔e7= De Boer-Kuijf, Dutch Ch 1990.

c) **13 0-0** *(131)* is still the most important alternative, but the sting has been substantially removed.

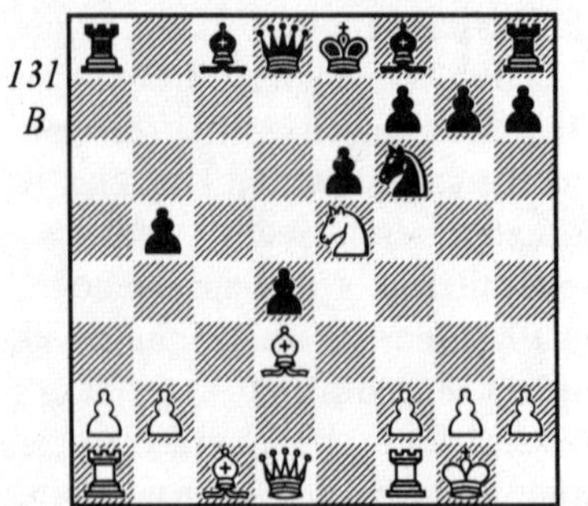

131
B

13...♕d5! 14 ♕e2 ♗a6! (14...♖b8 looks weaker since the rook on the a-file can be an important counterattacking asset for Black, e.g. 15 ♗g5 ♗d6 16 f4 h6 17 ♗h4 g5!? 18 ♗g3 gxf4 19 ♗xf4 ♖g8 Toshkov-Bagirov, Baku 1983, and now best is probably to dampen Black's play on the g-file with the all-purpose 20 ♘g6!. If now 20...♗xf4 21 ♘xf4 ♕g5 simply 22 ♖ac1 looks at least ±, or 20...♘d7!? 21 ♕f2!± Christiansen. No better was 15...♗e7 16 ♖ac1! 0-0 17 ♘c6 ♖b7 18 f4! ♖c7? 19 ♘e7+ ♖xe7 20 ♗xf6 gxf6 21 ♕g4+ ♔h8 22 ♕h4 1-0 Dreev-Sakaev, Moscow 1992) **15 ♗g5** (15 a4 is weak: 15...♗d6 16 axb5 ♗b7 17 ♖xa8+ ♗xa8 18 ♘c6 ♗xc6 19 bxc6 ♔e7 20 ♗c4 ♕xc6∓ Lilienthal-Botvinnik, Moscow 1941; 15 f4 should also be innocuous after 15...♗d6 16 ♗d2 0-0 17 ♖f3 ♗b7 18 ♖h3 Cifuentes Parada-Ribli, Dubai OL 1986, and now 18...g6 is very solid) and now Black can try:

c1) **15...h6!?** and now:

c11) **16 ♗xf6** gxf6 17 ♘g4 (If 17 ♗e4 ♕xe5 18 ♗c6+ ♔e7 19 ♕xe5 fxe5 20 ♗xa8 ♗g7 Black's pawn and strong centre are more than enough for the exchange) 17...♗g7 (also 17...♗e7!? 18 ♗e4 ♕d8 19 ♗c6+ ♔f8 20 ♗xa8 ♕xa8 {Δ...h5} 21 f3 b4∓ S.Ivanov, Polovez) 18 ♗e4 ♕d8 19 ♗c6+ ♔f8 20 f4 with mutual chances in M.Gurevich-S.Ivanov, USSR 1987.

c12) **16 ♗h4** ♗e7! 17 f4 0-0 18 ♖f3 (The position is similar to 'c2', and current praxis seems to suggest that the slight weakening of Black's kingside with ...h6 may count for less than the reduced options available to the white bishop on h4. If 18 ♗xf6 ♗xf6 19 ♗e4 b4! 20 ♘d3 ♕b5 21 ♗xa8 ♕xd3! 22 ♕xd3 ♗xd3 23 ♖fd1 ♗c2 24 ♖d2 d3∓ S.Ivanov, Polovez) 18...♗b7 19 ♖g3 ♖fc8 and now neither **20 a3** b4 21 a4 ♖c7 22 ♕d2? ♘h5!∓ Kamsky-S.Ivanov, USSR 1987, nor **20 b3** b4 21 ♖e1 ♖c7 22 f5 ♘e4! Seres-P.Kiss, Eger 1991 inspires confidence for White.

c2) **15...♗e7 16 f4 0-0 17 ♖f3** (Less committal is 17 ♔h1 g6 18 a4 ♔g7 19 ♖ae1 ♖ac8 20 axb5 ♗b7∞ Speelman-Nogueiras, Brussels 1988; the text threatens 17 ♗xf6 and ♗xh7+) **17...♗b7**:

c21) **18 ♖h3** g6 19 b3 (19 a3!?) 19...♖fc8 20 ♗xb5 d3 21 ♖xd3 ♕c5+ 22 ♔h1 ♕xb5!? (Weinstein) 23 ♖d8+ ♖xd8 24 ♕xb5 ♖xa2 25 ♖g1 ♘e4 26 h3 ♗xg5 27 hxg5 ♗d5∓.

c22) **18 ♖e1** g6 19 ♕f2 (19 a3 is better, but should not trouble Black) 19...♖xa2 20 ♗b1 ♖a1∓ Miles-Yusupov, Bugojno 1986.

c23) **18 ♖g3** ♖xa2! 19 ♖e1 (19 ♖xa2 ♕xa2 20 ♗h6 g6 is fine for Black since the white bishop is so off-side if it is not helping to deliver mate, but 20 ♗xf6 ♗xf6 21 ♘d7 ♗e7 22 ♗xh7+! ♔xh7 23 ♖xg7+ with perpetual to follow, may already be theoretically best) 19...g6 20 h4 ♖fa8! 21 h5 ♖xb2! 22 hxg6 hxg6 23 ♗xg6 (23 ♕xb2 ♖a2 24 ♗c4 ♖xb2 25 ♗xd5 ♘xd5 also gives Black a large plus) Salov-Nogueiras, Brussels 1988, and now 23...♖xe2! 24 ♗xf7+ ♔g7 25 ♗xf6+ ♔xf6 26 ♖g6+ ♔f5 27 ♖xe2 ♖a3! would have exhausted White's attack.

13 ...	**♗d7**
14 ♘xd7	**♕a5+**
15 ♗d2	**♕xb5**
16 ♘xf8 *(132)*	

132
B

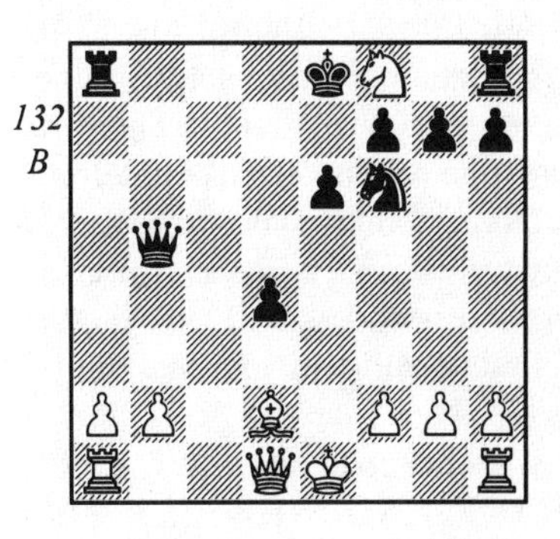

16 ...	**♖xf8!?**

For several years 16...♔xf8 was the automatic choice in this complex position.

At first White consistently sacrificed the b-pawn with 17 a4 and there was a constant see-saw of refutations followed by rehabilitations of Black's play. In addition to all this, the text move may well have been motivated by a fear of the simple 17 b3!? which at the time this game was played looked rather dangerous. Playing in 'endgame style' seemed to pose more dangers than seeking to exploit the black king's position, although ironically, the stem game with 17 b3 also saw the black king on the receiving end of a very violent onslaught. Now again Black's play in the endgame has been revived, and the theoretical situation is unclear.

It is worth mentioning that Black has also tried 16...♕xb2 here, which is possible because the knight is trapped on f8, and interesting since it cuts out the 17 b3 approach, but still clearly rather committal. The main problem is that if he refrains from counterproductive attempts to bring the knight out unscathed, White can use the tempo expended on 17 a4 in 'b1' below to build a dangerous initiative:

a) **16...♕xb2**:

a1) **17 ♘xe6?!** fxe6 18 0-0 0-0 19 a4 ♘e4 is good for Black; White should not grant the right to castle so lightly.

a2) **17 ♖b1?!** ♕xa2 18 ♗b4 (or 18 0-0 ♔xf8 19 ♗b4+ ♔g8 20 ♕d4 ♕d5 21 ♕f4 h5 and White is a bit short on compensation) 18...♕c4! 19 ♕e2 ♕xe2+ 20 ♔xe2 ♘d5.

a3) **17 0-0!** ♖xf8 18 ♗f4! ♔e7 19 ♖ab1 ♕xa2 20 ♖b7+ ♘d7 21 ♕xd4 ♕d5 22 ♕b4+ ♔f6? (22...♔e8 is a better try, but can be met by 23 ♖c1 Δh3 and ♖cc7 or ♖a7; in view of 23...e5 24 ♗xe5 the bind is hard to break) 23 ♗d6!± Utemov-Ioffe, USSR 1988.

b) Of much more moment is a detailed overview of **16...♔xf8** when as discussed White has two major options:

b1) **17 ♕e2** is interesting since 17...♕xb2 is risky for Black. Perhaps 17...d3!? 18 ♕f3 ♘d5 19 0-0 ♔e7 ...♖fc8 should be considered.

b2) **17 a4** ♕xb2 18 0-0 ♔g8!? (18...h5 19 ♗f4 h4?! 20 ♗e5 h3 21 ♕f3 ♖c8 22 a5 hxg2 23 ♖fb1 ♕c3 24 ♕b7!± Chekhov-Neverov, USSR 1988; 18...♘e4!? 19 ♕f3! f5 20 ♗f4 ♕c3 21 ♕e2 d3 22 ♕a2!? ♕xe6 and ♖fc1⩲) 19 ♗f4 h6 20 ♗e5 ♖d8 21 ♕d3 ♕c3! (Not 21...♘g4 22 ♗c7 ♖c8 23 ♖ac1 f5 24 ♕b5! ♕a2 25 h3 ♘f6 26 ♗e5± Ftačnik-Pinter, Warsaw 1987) 22 ♕xc3 (Black is also OK with accurate defence after 22 ♖fd1 ♕xd3 23 ♖xd3 ♖d5! 24 f4 ♘d7 25 ♖xd4 ♘xe5 26 ♖xd5 exd5 27 fxe5 ♔f8 28 ♖d1 ♔e7 29 ♖xd5 ♖c8∞ Ftačnik) 22...dxc3 23 ♗xc3 ♔h7 (23...♘d5!?) 24 ♗xf6 gxf6 25 ♖fd1 ♖a8! 26 ♖d7 ♖h8 27 ♖xf7 ♔g6 28 ♖e7 ♖xa4 ½-½ Ribli-Nogueiras, Barcelona 1987.

b3) **17 b3!?** and now:

b31) **17...♔e7** 18 a4 ♕d5 19 0-0 ♖hc8 20 b4 ♘e4 21 b5 ♖ab8 22 ♗b4+ ♔f6 23 ♕f3+ ♔g6 24 ♕g4+ ♔f6 25 ♖ae1 ♘d6 26 f4 1-0 in Timman-Nogueiras, Lucerne 1989.

b32) Black should hence try Timman's own suggestion **17...♘d5** to enable the queen to go to d3. After **18 a4 ♕d3** White can choose between an endgame or further complications with a pawn sacrifice:

b321) **19 ♕f3!?** ♕xf3 (19...♕c2 20 ♖c1 ♕b2 21 ♕d3 and White can castle without hinderance, with a clear plus) 20 gxf3 ♔e7 (20...♘c3 21 0-0 ♔e7 22 ♖fe1+) 21 ♔e2 ♖hb8 22 ♖hb1+ Schneider. This looks promising but 22...♘b4! (the key move I had underestimated) Yusupov believes that Black has enough counterplay. It is not easier for White to unleash his pawns than for Black.

b322) **19 ♕e2** ♕xb3 20 0-0 ♘c3 (Black sought to ease the defence with 20...♕c2 21 ♖fc1 d3 22 ♕e1 {22 ♖xc2=} 22...♕b2 23 ♖c4?! {23 a5} 23...♖b8! 24 a5 ♔e7 25 a6 in Bareev-Yusupov, Linares 1993 and now 25...♖b6! would have left Black better) 21 ♗xc3 dxc3 22 ♕e5 c2 23 ♕c5+ ♔g8 24 ♖a3 ♕b2 25 ♕c6! ♕xa3 26 ♕xa8+ ♕f8 27 ♕c6 g6 28 ♕xc2 ♕e7 29 ♕c3 h6 30 a5 with some advantage, but perhaps not enough to win against best defence; Schneider-Payen, Lyon 1990.

17 a4 ♕c4!?

Revealing one interesting possibility unique to the 16...♖xf8 line, namely keeping the queen on the a6-f1 diagonal since the square d3 is not taboo. The text is my favourite for Black here, but we consider also, in ascending order of merit:

a) **17...♕e5+?!** 18 ♕e2 ♕xe2+ 19 ♔xe2 e5 20 ♖hc1 ♔d7 21 b4 ♖fc8 22 ♖xc8 ♖xc8 23 ♔d3± Mikhalchishin-Panchenko, USSR Ch 1988. In several of the typical endings from this variation it is an improvement for Black to have played 16...♖xf8 since the black king is that much nearer the scene of the action, this alone is by no means enough to justify willingly accepting the endgame with no special concessions from White.

b) **17...♕d5** 18 **0-0** ♔d7 19 a5 ♖fc8 20 ♕a4+ ♔d8 21 a6! ♘e4 22 ♗b4 ♘c5 (Khalifman-Dokhoian, Vilna 1988) 23 ♕b5! ♘b3 (23...♕c6 24 ♕a5+ ♔d7 25 ♖c1!+-) 24 ♕xd5+ exd5 25 ♖a3+-. Again, Black's move can be faulted in that it neither snatches material, nor hinders the smooth course of White's development.

c) **17...♕xb2**:

c1) **18 ♖b1!?** ♕a2 19 **0-0** (19 ♗b4?! ♕xa4!) and now 19...♕d5! covers a lot of key squares and places many more difficulties in the way of White developing his initiative.

c2) **18 0-0** ♘e4! 19 ♗f4 ♘c3 20 ♕f3 ♔e7 (White blundered horribly in Titov-S.Ivanov, USSR 1988 after 20...♖a6!? 21 ♗e5?! {21 ♖fe1!?} 21...f6 22 ♕d3? ♕e2! 23 ♕xd4 ♕xe5-+) 21 ♖fe1! ♖fd8 (not 21...f6 22 ♗c1 ♕xa1 23 ♕b7+ ♔d6 24 ♗f4+) 22 ♗c1! and now **22...♕xa1!** is forced; Black fell victim to a terrible attack after **22...♕b6** 23 ♗a3+ ♔e8 24 ♕g4 d3!? 25 ♕xg7 ♘e2+ 26 ♔f1 ♖xa4 27 ♕f8+ ♔d7 28 ♕xf7+ ♔c8 29

♗c5 in Kishnev-S.Ivanov, USSR 1988.

18 b3 ♕d3
19 ♕e2

Clearly, White has to put the question to the black queen in order to make further progress with mobilization. The text involves a pawn sacrifice the danger from which Lukacs' excellent defence seems to neutralize. White can also consider:

a) **19 ♕f3** ♕e4+! (19...♕xf3 would lead to an endgame which would bare obvious comparison with the controversial position examined under note 'b3' to Black's 16th. White has gained a4, Black's king can go to d7 in one move. In fact the text is super-accurate since in the battle of passed pawns White wishes to keep bishop vs knight, but after the exchange of queens on e4 there is no convenient flight square from d2) 20 ♕xe4 ♘xe4 21 ♗b4 ♖g8 22 ♔e2 ♔d7 Δ...♖gb8= I.Sokolov-Todorović, Vrnjacka Banja 1990.

b) **19 ♗b4!?** ♕e4+ 20 ♕e2 **♕xg2!?** 21 0-0-0 ♕b7 (21...♖c8+ 22 ♔b2 ♖g8? 23 ♕b5+ ♕c6?? 24 ♖c1+-) 22 ♗xf8 ♔xf8 23 ♕b5 ♕f3 24 ♕c5+ ♔g8 25 ♕xd4 ♕xb3 ½-½ Morović-Korchnoi, Novi Sad OL 1990. Black seems to have sufficient counterchances at the end, but it should be noted that the more conservative **20...♖g8** leaves White nothing better than 21 ♕xe4 transposing to 'a'.

19 ... ♕xb3
20 0-0 ♖xa4
21 ♕e5!?

White makes a real gambit of it, but whilst dangerous, the attack does not seem to be worth more than at best a draw. **21 ♖xa4?!** would be worse since after 21...♕xa4 22 ♖b1 ♔d7 23 ♕f3 Black can utilize the weakness of White's back rank with the resource 23...♖b8∓. White's only real alternative is to head for winning the exchange for his two pawns with **21 ♖ab1** ♕c4 22 ♕xc4 ♖xc4 23 ♖b8+ ♔e7 24 ♗b4+ ♖xb4 25 ♖xb4 e5=.

21 ... ♘d7!

In all the best defensive traditions, Black returns part of the material, here to control key squares such as c5 and e5. By contrast the greedy **21...♔d7?** would allow White to penetrate by 22 ♖ac1! (the right rook, since it negates resources based on White's potentially vulnerable back rank) 22...♖c8 23 ♖xc8 ♔xc8 24 ♕c5+! ♔d7 25 ♖c1 ♕b7 26 ♕f8!±. An instructive reminder of White's attacking potential.

22 ♕xg7 ♖xa1
23 ♖xa1 ♕b2!

Defending, attacking and forcing White to declare his hand, Lukacs has calculated finely that far from in grave danger, the black king will be surprisingly safe in the middle of the board.

24 ♖a8+

Of course **24 ♖d1** ♕c2 25 ♕g4 ♘e5 26 ♕e2 d3 27 ♕h5 ♖g8∓ (Lukacs) is much too passive.

24 ... ♔e7

25 ♗g5+

25 ♕g5+ f6 would not worry Black.

25 ... ♔d6

26 ♖a6+ ♔d5!

Lukacs gives **26...♔c7** 27 h4 and White has good compensation for the pawn. The text move has dual purpose. If now **27 ♕xh**7 Black would reply 27...♖b8! forcing the exchange of queens in view of the threat of back rank mate, when the black king would be perfectly situated to escort the d-pawn to higher things. Moreover, since **27 g3?!** ♕b1+ 28 ♔g2 ♕e4∓ Δ...♖b8 is no good either, White is obliged to play **27 h4**, when Black can now use the b8-h2 diagonal.

27 h4 ♕b1+

28 ♔h2 ♕b8+

29 f4?!

This is too ambitious, since the need for the bishop on g5 to stay defending f4 will help Black to unravel. **29 g3?!** would also create a slight weakness which black can exploit in the interesting variation 29...♘c5 30 ♖a5 ♕c7! 31 ♕xf8 ♕xa5 32 ♕xf7 ♕e1! and despite level material it is Black who now enjoys the more active chances. Hence White should acquiescein **29 ♔g1** when according to Lukacs he would have had nothing preferable to repeating.

After the text the game continued: **29...♘c5 30 ♖a5 f6!?** (30...♕c7!?∓Lukacs) **31 ♗h6 ♖g8 32 ♕xf6?** (A blunder after which the position rapidly clarifies to both a material and positional advantage for Black. White had to force the black queen away from the b-file with 32 ♕d7+ ♕d6! {32...♔c4? looks risky and indeed with 33 ♕c6! ♕b4 34 ♖a1! ♕c3 35 ♖a4+ White suddenly turns the tables} 33 ♕xh7 ♖b8 with complicated play in which I slightly prefer Black) **32...♖xg2+! 33 ♔xg2 ♕b2+ 34 ♔f3 ♕c3+ 35 ♔g4 ♕xa5 36 ♕e5+ ♔c4 37 ♗f8** (In view of the power of the b-pawn, this attempt to tie down the black pieces is in vain. However, 37 f5 is clinically refuted by the precise 37...♕a8! 38 fxe6 ♕g2+ 39 ♕g3 ♕e4+ -+) **37...d3 38 ♗xc5 ♕xc5 39 ♕xe6+ ♔c3 40 ♕a2 d2** (The rest is simple since the white forces inhibit their own queen's checking power) **41 ♕a1+ ♔d3 42 ♕b1+ ♕c2 43 ♕b5+ ♕c4 44 ♕f5+ ♔e2 45 ♕e5+ ♔f2 0-1.**

At present the new trend towards 16...♖xf8 makes this line look quite attractive for Black. The onus seems to be on White to come up with something new in order to prove a plus.

18 Meran: 8 ♗e2 and 8 ♗b3

Once the regular choice of Capablanca, the apparently modest retreat 8 ♗e2, has enjoyed a steady following for some time. The reasons for this are not hard to discern. Firstly, in comparison with the main line 8 ♗d3, the demands placed upon White's theoretical knowledge are not too onerous. Moreover, this relative simplicity is not attained at the expense of all excitement. In several lines, most obviously the 'four queens' variation covered in Game 25 the play is extremely sharp. There has recently been something of an explosion of interest in 8 ♗e2, and this is in no small part due to a refinement in White's handling of the once feared 8...b4.

Before looking at the games, it is worth drawing attention to three features of the variation which give it a distinctive character.

1) In contrast to 8 ♗d3 lines the white queen defends d4. This is of great significance if Black seeks to play analogously with the old main lines of the Meran, i.e. after 8...a6 9 e4 c5? 10 e5 cxd4 11 ♕xd4! ♗c5 12 ♕f4 ♘g8 13 ♕g4 ♔f8 14 0-0 White stands very well (Najdorf-Lederman, Netanya 1975).

2) The bishop is defended and hence ideally placed on e2 for the Four Queens line. Again a comparison may be useful. The line analogous to that examined in our first game but with White's bishop on d3 is clearly advantageous for Black, viz: 8 ♗d3 ♗b7 9 e4 b4 10 e5?! bxc3 11 exf6 cxb2 12 fxg7 bxa1♕ 13 gxh8♕ ♕a5+ 14 ♘d2 ♕5c3! 15 ♗c2 (forced) 15...♗a6! and White cannot develop.

3) Approaches with ...b4, however, gain in force since ♘e4 is not available to White.

By contrast, 8 ♗b3 looks a pretty lame duck these days. A few games have been played with 8...b4 9 ♘a4, but this seems to cause Black even less problems than the traditional 9 ♘e2 and has done nothing to enhance the line's flagging reputation. In view of this, I have settled for just a brief coverage of the main lines in the notes to Malaniuk-Chernin.

Game 25
Sadler-Kaidanov
Andorra 1991

1 d4 d5 2 c4 e6 3 ♘c3 c6 4 e3 ♘f6 5 ♘f3 ♘bd7 6 ♗d3 dxc4 7 ♗xc4 b5

8 ♗e2 *(133)*

133
B

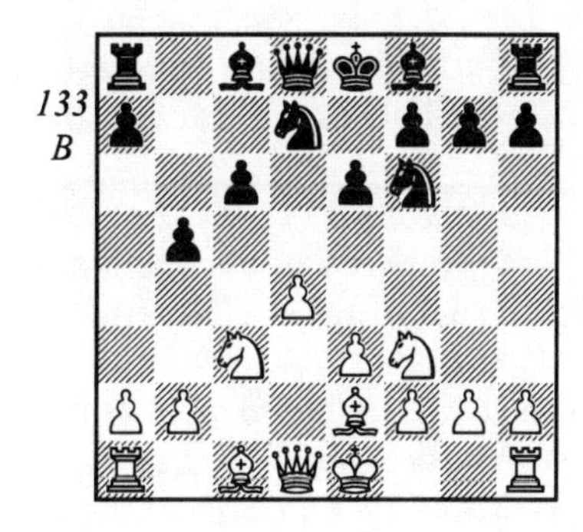

8 ... ♗b7

8...a6 has once again become an important alternative, and the 'modern' lines will be examined in game 26. Here we shall consider only the version of the four queens variation that it generates (which clearly favours White) and the last minute deviation 12...♗xg7!?.

After **8...a6 9 e4 b4 10 e5 bxc3 11 exf6 cxb2 12 fxg7** Black has:

a) **12...bxa1♕?!** 13 gxh8♕ ♕a5+ 14 ♗d2 (also strong is 14 ♘d2 ♕f5 15 0-0 ♗b7 16 ♕b3 ♘c5 17 ♗a3! ♘xb3 18 ♕xf8+ ♔d7 19 ♕e7+ ♔c8 20 ♘xb3 with a crushing attack; Krogius-Kamyshev, USSR 1949) 14...♕xd1+ 15 ♗xd1 ♕f5 (otherwise 16 ♕xh7 leaves Black short on compensation) 16 0-0 ♗b7 17 d5! (the point – in this line ...a6 was a wasted tempo and White can profitably open the position with Black's development lagging) 17...♕xd5 18 ♕xh7 c5 19 ♗a4 0-0-0 20 ♗a5 ♘e5 21 ♘e1!± Benko-Pytel, Hastings 1973/4.

b) **12...♗xg7(!) 13 ♗xb2 ♕a5+** (If White can develop smoothly Black's pawn weaknesses will begin to tell. Black's other attempt at disruption is 13...c5 14 0-0 ♗b7 15 ♖b1 ♖b8!? {15...♗e4 met with a swift *denouement* after 16 dxc5! ♗xb1 17 ♗xg7 ♖g8 18 c6 ♘c5 19 ♗d4 in Taimanov-Onat, Albena 1974} 16 dxc5! ♗xf3 17 ♗xg7 ♖xb1 18 ♕xb1 ♗xe2 19 ♖e1 ♖g8 20 ♕xh7 ♖xg7 21 ♕xg7 with advantage according to Seirawan's convincing analysis) **14 ♘d2**:

b1) The rather materialistic **14...♕b4** is far from stupid. Buchman-Karasev, USSR 1975 continued **15 ♕c2(!)** ♗xd4 16 ♗xd4 ♕xd4 17 0-0 ♖b8 18 ♘b3 ♕g7 19 ♖ad1 c5 20 ♖d3 ♗b7 21 ♖g3 and although matters are not clear, I tend towards Donaldson's view that White has good compensation. Korchnoi is less impressed and suggests instead **15 ♖b1**. However after 15...♗xd4 16 a3 ♕c5(!) his idea is not clear, since **17 ♘b3** can be answered by 17...♗c3+, or **17 ♘e4** by 17...♕a5+.

b2) **14...♖b8**:

b21) **15 ♕c2** gives Black a choice between **15...c5** 16 ♗c3 ♕c7 17 dxc5 ♕xc5 18 ♘c4 ♗xc3+ 19. ♕xc3 ♖g8! 20 0-0 ♗b7 21 g3 h5 22 ♖fd1 ♗d5 when Black was fine in Pytel-Izeta, Clermont-Ferrand 1986, and Seirawan's enterprising continuation of the disruption theme **15...♕f5**; if 16 ♕xf5 exf5 17 ♘b3 then both 17...c5 and 17...♘c5 offer interesting counterplay.

b22) **15 ♕c1** is Schneider's novelty after which no clear equalizing line has emerged, e.g. 15...♕g5 16 0-0 c5 17 ♘b3 ♕xc1 18 ♖axc1 ♗b7 19 ♗a3 cxd4 20 ♗d6 ♖d8 (20...♖c8 21 ♘a5) 21 ♖c7 with strong pressure in Schneider-Kishnev, USSR 1993.

9 e4

The important alternatives **9 0-0** and **9 a3** are considered in game 26.

9 ...	**b4**
10 e5	**bxc3**
11 exf6	**cxb2**

11...♘xf6 is quite a respectable option here, but strangely untested in practice. Taimanov gives simply 12 bxc3 ♗d6 followed by ...♕c7, and ...c5=. Compare with 8...♗b7 9 0-0 ♗e7 10 e4 examined in a note to Game 26, and with the 8...a6 and 11...♘xf6 also of Game 26.

12 fxg7 bxa1♕

The alternative **12...♗xg7** has a bad reputation. Compared with the 8...a6 variation above, the bishop on b7 blocks Black's potential counterplay on the b-file. After **13 ♗xb2**:

a) **13...♕a5+ 14 ♘d2 ♗h6** (14...c5 15 0-0 cxd4 16 ♘c4 ♕d5 17 ♗f3 ♕xc4 18 ♗xb7 ♖b8 19 ♗a3 is no improvement) Sveshnikov gives **15 ♕c2** ♘b6 16 ♗c3 ♕a4 17 ♕xa4 ♘xa4 18 ♗a5 ♖c8 19 ♖b1 and **15 d5** ♖g8 16 dxe6 0-0-0 17 0-0! ♗xd2 18 exd7+ ♖xd7 19 ♗f3 which both yield a significant plus.

b) However, in Garcia-Illescas, Spanish Ch 1991 Black equalized by surprisingly quiet means with **13...0-0!?** 14 0-0 c5 15 dxc5 ♗xb2 16 ♖b1 ♗f6 17 ♖xb7 ½-½.

13 gxh8♕ ♕a5+

Much weaker was the **13...♕b1** of Zsu.Polgar-V.Dimitrov, Ivailovgrad 1984. Black was crushed after 14 0-0 ♕f6 15 ♕xf6 ♘xf6 16 ♘e5 ♕xa2 17 ♗c4 ♕a5 18 ♕f3 ♗e7 19 ♗g5 ♕d8 20 ♗xe6 fxe6 21 ♗xf6 ♕xd4 22 ♕h5+ 1-0.

14 ♘d2 *(134)*

134
B

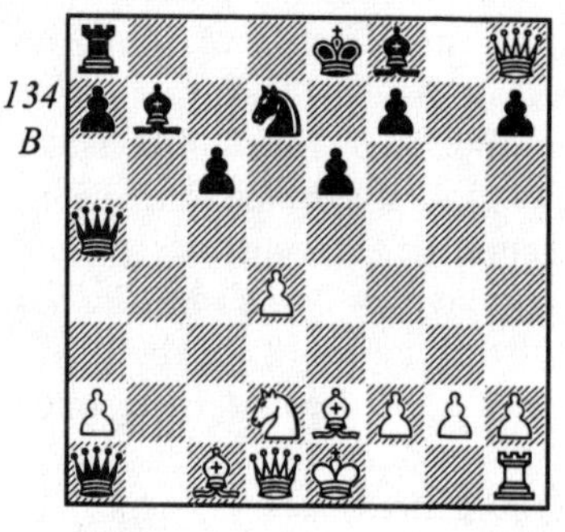

The reduction to a more manageable number of queens with **14 ♗d2** is no longer very dangerous since Black has the time both to guard h7, and complete development with ...0-0-0. After 14...♕xd1+ 15 ♗xd1 ♕f5 16 0-0 0-0-0 17 ♕g8 (17 d5? is now quite inappropriate: after 17...♗d6 18 ♕d4 c5 19 ♕a4 ♕xd5 20 ♗e2 ♖g8 21 ♖d1 ♕e4 22 ♕xe4 ♗xe4 23 ♘g5 ♗d5 24 f3 f5 25 ♘xh7? ♗e7 Black was already winning in Pliester-Dreev, New York 1989) 17...♗e7 18 ♕g7 ♕g6 19 ♕xg6 hxg6= Chekhover-Suetin 1951.

14 ... ♕f5.

In this highly complicated position Black has tried several alternatives.

a) **14...♕d5** 15 0-0 ♕1xd4 16 ♕xh7 ♘f6 17 ♕b1! ♕b6 18 ♗b2 ♗e7 19 ♘c4 ♕c7 20 ♗e5 ♕cd7 21 ♗xf6! ♗xf6 22 ♗f3 ♕d4 23 ♕a4± is an instructive demonstration of how easily Black's queens can become exposed in this line; Blackstock-Crouch, London 1980.

b) **14...c5** is a recent try. Chatalbashev-Sveshnikov, Anapa 1991 continued 15 **0-0** ♕xd4 **16 ♘b3** ♕xh8! (16...♕xd1 17 ♖xd1 ♕a4 18 ♕xh7 clearly favours White) 17 ♘xa5 ♗d5 and now Sveshnikov gives 18 ♗f3 ♕d4 19 ♕xd4 cxd4 20 ♗xd5 exd5 21 ♖e1+ ♔d8 22 ♘c6+ =. However, **16 ♕xh7**, previously played by Matthew Sadler, looks a stiffer test of Black's idea: 16...♕xa2 17 ♗c4 ♕aa1 18 ♗xe6! 0-0-0 (if 18...fxe6 simply 19 ♕h5+ and 20 ♘b3±) 19 ♕xf7 ♗d6 20 ♘c4 ♗c7 21 ♗d5! (nullifying any possible counterplay) 21...♗a6 22 ♕xd4 ♕xd4 23 ♗b2 ♕d3 24 ♕e6 ♗b5 25 ♖e1 ♔b8 26 ♘e3 ♕d2 27 ♖b1 ♘b6 28 ♗e5 ♕d3 29 ♗e4! ♕e2 30 ♗xc7+ ♔xc7 31 ♕e5+ ♔c8 1-0 Sadler-Payen, Hastings Challengers 1990.

15 0-0 0-0-0

Vidoniak suggests instead **15...♕xa2!?** 16 ♘c4 0-0-0 17 ♗d3 ♕f6 18 ♕xh7 ♘b6 19 ♕e2 ♕xe2 20 ♗xe2 ♘xc4 21 ♗xc4 ♕xd4 as ∓.

16 ♕b3 ♘c5

Awarded a '!' by Kaidanov.

In Koziak-Vidoniak, USSR 1991 White soon obtained a decisive advantage after the inferior **16...♗d6?** which exposes the bishop unnecessarily. After 17 ♘c4! ♗e7 18 ♕g7 ♘c5 19 ♕b4 (or 19 ♕a3) 19...♗h4 (19...♕xa2 20 ♗g4±) 20 ♗e3 White was winning. However, Vidoniak's recommendation **16...♗e7** 17 ♕xd8+ (17 ♕g7 ♘c5 18 ♕b4 transposing to the note to Kaidanov's 17th looks more promising for White) 17...♗xd8 18 ♗b2 ♕xf1+ = looks prudent.

17 ♕b4! ♕c2?

A serious error as Sadler's superb reply demonstrates. Kaidanov gives instead **17...♗e7** 18 ♕g7 ♗f6 19 ♕xf7 ♗xd4 20 ♕xf5 exf5 21 ♘f3 although White retains some positional pluses. Also possible is **17...♘d7**. In Sadler-Neverov, Hastings Challengers 1992 a draw was agreed after **18 ♕b3** ♘c5 etc. However this suited White's tournament aims, otherwise he might have investigated **18 ♕a4!?**.

18 ♕f6! *(135)*

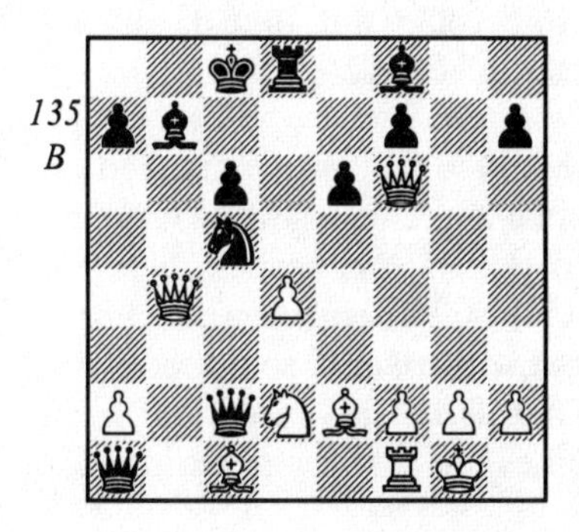
135
B

A very fine move based around a willingness to part with one queen to smash Black's king's defences. White wins after either **18...♘d7** 19 ♕xb7+! ♔xb7 20 ♕xd8 ♕xd4 21 ♘b3+- or **18...♖d7** 19 ♘b3 ♕ac3 20 ♕xc3 ♕xc3 21 ♕h8 ♖d8 22 ♕xh7 ♘xb3 23 axb3+- since Black's major pieces cannot defend f7. After the move played, though, the position simplifies and Black's kingside pawns are routed.

18 ...	**♕cc3**
19 ♕xc3	**♕xc3**
20 ♘f3±	

The game now concluded: **20...♘e4** (if 20...♖d7 21 ♕h8 ♖d8 22 ♕xh7) **21 ♕xf7 c5 22 ♗f4 ♗d6 23 ♕xe6+ ♔b8 24 ♗xd6+ ♘xd6 25 ♕e7 ♕a5 26 dxc5 ♘c8 27 ♕e5+ ♕c7 28 ♕xc7+ ♔xc7 29 ♖d1 ♖e8 30 ♗b5 ♖g8 31 ♖d7+ ♔b8 32 c6 ♗a8 33 ♘e5 a5 34 ♖xh7 1-0**.

Game 26
Vyzhmanavin-Sorokin
USSR Ch 1991

1 d4 d5 2 c4 e6 3 ♘c3 c6 4 e3 ♘f6 5 ♘f3 ♘bd7 6 ♗d3 dxc4 7 ♗xc4 b5 8 ♗e2

8 ...	**♗b7**

8...b4 will be considered in Game 27. As we saw in Game 25, the text is the best prelude for Black to enter into the 'four queens' variation, so much so that White frequently, as in our main game here, avoids this option.

8...a6 has recently enjoyed a revival of popularity, although I feel it probably still merits a lower profile. After **9 e4** (others allow Black to free himself simply with ...c5) **9...b4** (not 9...c5? – see introduction to the chapter) **10 e5 bxc3 11 exf6 ♘xf6!?** (for 11...cxb2(?!) see Game 25). Black's eighth move has the merit over 8...♗b7 of simply not leaving the bishop loose as a target on b7. After **12 bxc3 ♗d6**:

a) In Seirawan-Kramnik, Manila OL 1992 Black soon gained the upper hand after **13 0-0** 0-0 14 c4? (It is not easy to understand White's thinking here. Did he believe that the passed, but isolated c-pawn would be an asset?) 14...c5 15 ♗a3 ♕a5 16 ♗xc5 (16 ♗b2 was still equal according to Kramnik, but not 16 dxc5 ♗xh2+ ∓) 16...♗xc5 17 dxc5 ♖d8 18 ♕b3 ♕xc5 19 ♖ab1 ♗d7 with the better structure and active pieces.

b) Not surprisingly, White can do a lot better. Interesting is that this had already been demonstrated some years ago. The right way seems to be to delay castling in favour of **13 ♘d2!** (headed for c4) **13...0-0**:

b1) **14 ♗f3** ♗d7 {14...♘d5!? may be worth a look. The solid 14...♕c7 also performed well in its first outing after 15 ♘c4 ♗e7 16 ♗g5 ♘d5 17 ♗xe7 ♕xe7 18 ♕d2 ♖b8 19 0-0 c5 20 ♗xd5 exd5 21 ♖fe1 ♗e6 22 ♘e5 ♖fc8= Ehlvest-Lesiège, New York 1993} 15 ♘c4

♗e7 16 ♘e5 ♖c8 17 0-0± {at least} Pytel-Lederman, Bagneux 1979.

b2) **14 ♘c4** ♗e7 (14...♘d5!? 15 ♘xd6 ♕xd6 16 ♕d2! {with an eye to posting the c1 bishop actively on a3} 16...a5 {16...e5!?} 17 0-0 ♖d8 18 ♖b1 ♗a6 19 ♗xa6 ♖xa6 20 ♕d3 ♖a7 21 ♖d1 h6 22 c4 ♘e7 23 ♗a3 ♕f4 24 ♕e3!± L.B.Hansen-Mat.Müller, Groningen 1992. White has the better minor piece, and with 24 ♕e3 ensures that his d-pawn will be safer than Black's c-pawn) 15 ♗f3 ♗b7 (15...♗d7?! – see 'b1'; 15...♘d5 16 ♘e5 ♕b6 17 ♗d2 f6 18 ♘c4 ♕c7 19 0-0 c5 20 ♕e2 ♖e8 21 ♖fe1± since Black has a new weakness on e6; Polugaevsky-Arakhamia, Aruba 1992) 16 ♖b1 ♖a7 17 ♘e5 ♕c8 (17...♕c7 18 ♗f4!) 18 0-0 c5 19 ♗a3 ♗xf3 (19...cxd4? 20 ♕xd4!±) 20 ♕xf3 ♖c7 21 ♖fd1 cxd4 22 ♗xe7 ♖xe7 23 ♖xd4 ♖c7 24 c4 with an edge for White; L.B.Hansen-Bagirov, Debrecen 1992.

8...♗e7? is rightly criticized on the grounds of 9 a3! when **9...a6?** 10 e4 ♗b7 11 e5 ♘d5 12 ♘xd5 Pytel-T.Horvath gives a clear advantage. Also on **9...♗b7**, 10 e4 is strong, as is **9...a5** 10 e4! (10 0-0?! ♗b7 is Speelman-Bareev below).

9 0-0

If **9 a3** b4! (The exclamation mark is for 'clean' equalization. Also sufficient, and perhaps suitable for a game where the half point is not enough, is 9...a6 10 b4 a5! 11 ♖b1 axb4 12 axb4 ♘d5 13 ♘xd5 exd5 14 ♘e5 ♖a4!? 15 0-0 ♗d6! (15...♖xb4 16 ♖a1!) 16 f4 0-0 17 ♗d3 ♘f6! 18 ♕c2 ♕b6 19 ♗d2 ♖fa8 with about equal chances; Bönsch-Pinter, Budapest 1986) 10 ♘a4 bxa3 11 bxa3 ♗e7 12 0-0 0-0 13 ♗b2 c5 ½-½ Karpov-Kasparov, Moscow Wch (29) 1984/5.

9 ... a6

The text move is probably the most complicated and ambitious in the position, and its supporters have been quite loyal during some shaky times. **9...b4** is again dealt with in the next game, note to move 10. Another possibility, developing, again inviting e4, to be answered with ...b4 and enjoying modest popularity in the recent 8 ♗e2 boom is **9...♗e7!?** *(136)*.

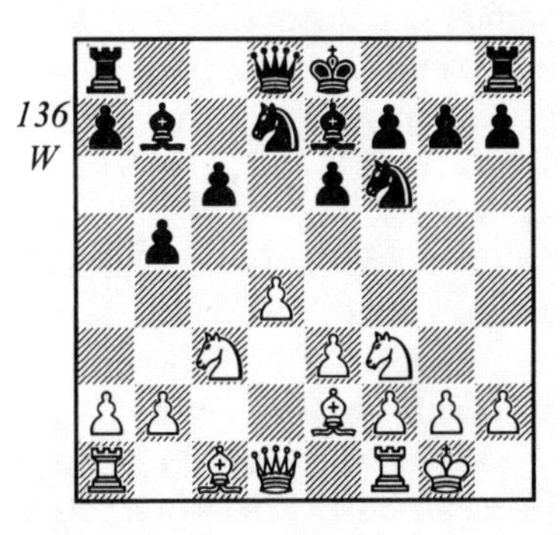

White has tried:

a) **10 a3?!** a5 11 ♕c2 0-0 12 ♗d2 (12 e4 b4 13 ♘a4 c5 14 e5 ♗e4! Bareev) 12...♕b8 13 ♘e4?! ♘xe4 14 ♕xe4 c5 and already Black has a slight initiative; Speelman-Bareev, Hastings 1992/3.

b) **10 e4** b4 11 e5 bxc3 12 exf6 ♘xf6 (12...♗xf6 13 bxc3 0-0 14

♖b1 ♕c8 15 ♕b3 ♗a6 16 ♗xa6 ♕xa6 17 ♕a3 ♕xa3 18 ♗xa3 ♖fb8 19 ♗d6 ♖b6 20 ♖b3± was Stohl-Akopian, Chalkidiki 1992) 13 bxc3 0-0 14 ♖b1 ♕c7 15 ♗f4!? ♕xf4 16 ♖xb7 ♘d5!? and now it looks more testing to keep the White structure intact with **17 ♕c2** or **17 ♕b3**, rather than the **17 g3** ♕d6 18 c4 ♘c3 19 ♕c2 ♘xe2+ 20 ♕xe2 ♗f6 of Lobron-Gelfand, Wijk aan Zee 1993, when Black was fine.

10 e4

The only critical move in the position. The alternative **10 a3?!** must be one of the limpest moves to have been played by two great World Champions. Black can carry out his freeing break ...c5 without difficulties, and for the impending symmetrical queenside structure the d7 knight is better posted than its counterpart on c3. After 10...c5 11 dxc5 ♗xc5!? (11...♘xc5 12 b4 ♕xd1 13 ♖xd1 ♘ce4 14 ♗b2 ♘xc3 15 ♗xc3 ♗e7= Capablanca-Alekhine, New York 1927) 12 b4 ♗e7 13 ♕b3 0-0 14 ♖d1 ♕c7 15 ♗b2 ♖ac8 16 ♖ac1 ♕b8 17 a4 (otherwise ...♘b6 is ∓) 17...bxa4 18 ♕xa4 ♘b6 19 ♕b3 ♘g4! 20 e4 ♗f6 21 ♗d3 ♘d7! and Black has some initiative; Karpov-Illescas, Wijk aan Zee 1993.

10 ... c5

The idea of **10...b4** is, as we have seen, playable after either ...♗b7 or ...a6. After both it is a bit of a liberty, since White has 0-0 for free. Nogueiras gives 11 e5 bxc3 12 exf6 cxb2 (12...♘xf6 13 bxc3 c5 14 ♘e5 ♘d7 15 ♗f3 ♗xf3 16 ♕xf3 ♘xe5 17 dxe5 ♕c8 18 ♖b1 ♖a7 19 ♖d1± Bogdanovski-Alexeev, Warsaw 1990) 13 fxg7 ♗xg7 14 ♗xb2 0-0 15 ♖b1! Δd5±.

11 e5

11 d5 is quite dangerous, and possibly a little unfairly neglected. After 11...exd5 12 e5! ♘e4 13 ♘xe4 dxe4 14 e6 fxe6! (14...exf3 15 ♗xf3 ♗xf3 16 exd7+ ♕xd7 17 ♕xf3± leaves Black's king horribly stranded in the centre; Lysenkov-Sharov, corr. 1976) 15 ♘g5 ♗d5. White has fair compensation, and after 16 ♗g4 some attacking chances, although I suspect Black is OK.

11 ... ♘d5
12 a4! b4

This is now clearly taken over as the main line. After the alternative **12...♘xc3 13 bxc3 c4** White has two possibilities: to attempt to undermine Black's queenside pawn chain; or to attack directly on the other wing. It is his attacking chances in 'b' that have pushed the line out of favour, but the older variation 'a2' is not so pleasant either:

a) **14 ♗g5 ♗e7 15 ♗xe7 ♕xe7** and now:

a1) **16 ♕b1** ♖b8! 17 axb5 axb5 18 ♘e1 0-0 19 ♗f3 ♗xf3 20 ♘xf3 b4 with counterplay in Portisch-G.Flear, Szirak IZ 1987.

a2) **16 axb5** axb5 17 ♖xa8+ ♗xa8 18 ♕a1 0-0 19 ♕a6 may be

more promising – it is logical to remove the most natural defender of Black's queenside. 19...♖b8 20 ♖b1 ♗b7! 21 ♕xb5! ♗c8 22 ♕xb8 ♘xb8 23 ♖xb8 ♕c7 24 ♖b4 (Tatai-Nogueiras, Thessaloniki OL 1984) and now Nogueiras gives 24...♕a5(!), but Donaldson continues with 25 ♘d2! g6 (25...♕a1+? 26 ♗f1±) 26 ♖xc4 ♗a6 27 ♖c5 ♕a1+ 28 ♗f1±.

b) **14 ♘g5!?** ♗d5!? (14...♗e7!? 15 ♗f3! ♗xf3 16 ♕xf3 0-0 17 ♕g4 ♘b6 18 axb5 axb5 19 ♖xa8 ♕xa8 20 ♘e4 ♔h8 21 ♖e1 Christiansen-G.Flear, Szirak IZ 1987 gives quite a strong attack, but at least with 21...♕a5!± Black could discourage the transfer of White's rook to the kingside too. 14...h6?? is of course disastrous after 15 ♘xe6!+-) 15 ♗h5! g6 16 ♗f3 ♘b6 17 ♘e4∞ (Christiansen) but I am at a loss for how he intends Black to proceed; if **17...♗e7** both 18 ♗a3 and 18 ♗h6 look good value, or **17...♗xe4?!** 18 ♗xe4 ♘d5 19 ♕f3±.

13 ♘e4 *(137)*

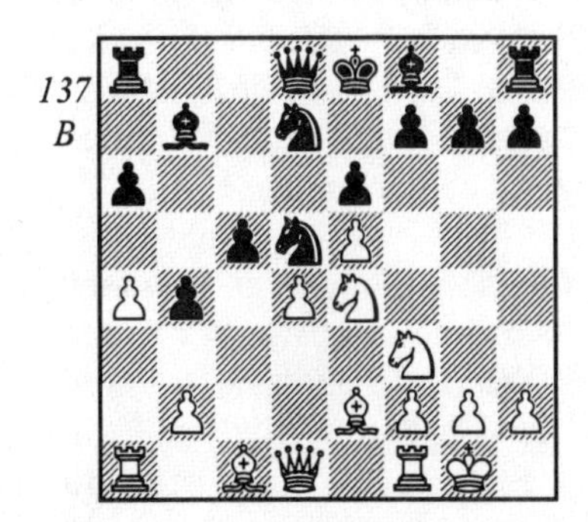

13 ... cxd4

A major parting of the ways. The key question revolves around whether Black should feel obliged to give a tempo to prevent his queen being driven away by ♗g5.

a) **13...♖c8** has both intrinsic and historical interest, since the little-known Finnish player Böök used it to attain excellent play against the mighty Keres, viz. 14 ♗g5 ♕b6 15 ♘fd2! cxd4 16 ♘c4 ♖xc4 (The point! This exchange sacrifice is a known idea from similar lines) 17 ♗xc4 ♘xe5 18 a5 ♕a7 (18...♕c6?! 19 ♕xd4! ♘xc4 20 ♖ac1±) 19 ♖c1 f5 (19...f6?! 20 ♗xd5 ♗xd5 21 ♗xf6 gxf6 22 ♘xf6+ ♔d8 23 ♘xd5 exd5 24 ♕h5 ♗d6 25 ♕f5!+- Speelman) **20 ♘g3?** ♔f7 21 ♗b3?! h6 22 ♗d2 ♗d6∓. Clearly in purely positional terms the message is clear. Black's two pawns and central control is well worth the exchange. So, White has to make trouble, and Jon Speelman, renowned expert in messy positions took us much nearer the truth with instead **20 ♗xd5!** ♗xd5 21 ♖c8+! (21 ♘d6+ ♗xd6 22 ♖c8+ wins further material, but Black has fair compensation. The text keeps firm hold of the initiative) 21...♔f7 (21...♔d7 22 ♖d8+ ♔c7 23 ♕c2+ ♗c6 24 ♖c1 h6 25 ♖xf8! ♖xf8 26 ♗f4+- Speelman) 22 ♕h5+ g6 23 ♖xf8+! ♔xf8 24 ♕h6+ ♕g7 (the best chance; if the black king stays on the back rank, White's rook enters on the c-file with decisive effect) 25 ♕xg7 ♔xg7 26 ♗f6+ ♔g8 27 ♗xe5 fxe4 28 ♗xd4! with few conversion problems; Speelman-Van der Oudeweetering, Netherlands 1992.

b) **13...h6 14 ♘fd2! ♗e7 15 ♘c4 0-0 16 ♘cd6 ♗c6** (best; 16...♗xd6?! 17 ♘xd6 ♗c6 18 a5! cxd4 19 ♕xd4 f6 20 f4± gave White a problem-free positional advantage in Piket-Brenninkmeijer, Groningen 1991) **17 ♘xc5 ♗xd6 18 exd6** *(138)*.

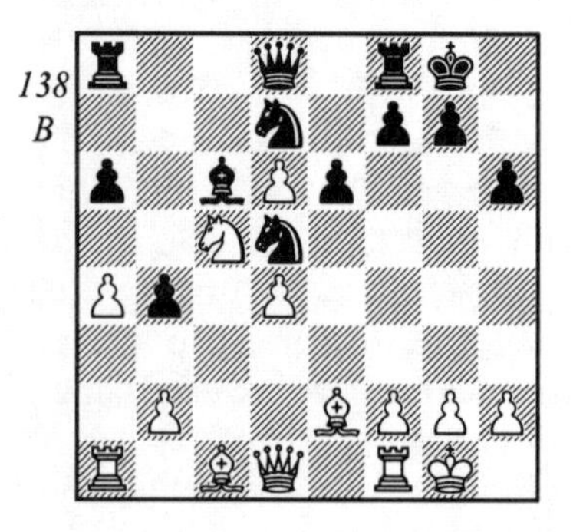

138
B

So far (virtually) forced, at least for Black. Now he has a choice of ways to try to recover the pawn, but neither looks quite enough for equality:

b1) **18...♘b8** 19 ♘e4 (If Black can simply recapture on d6 without concessions, then with his excellent knight on d5 he will always stand quite well) 19...a5 (19...f5?! 20 ♘c5! ♕xd6 21 ♖e1± would constitute just such a concession) 20 ♖e1 ♘d7 21 ♗d3 ♕b6! (The plausible 21...♘7f6 22 ♕f3! would leave Black rather embarrassed) 22 ♗c2 ♖ac8? (critical is 22...♖ae8 with the direct intention of winning back the pawn with ...f5 and ...♕b8, which at the same time is the most efficient way to safeguard Black's king along the b1-h7 diagonal. Perhaps 23 ♗xh6 is worthy of analysis, but it is hard to find more than a draw) 23 ♕d3 ♘5f6 24 ♘xf6+ ♘xf6 25 ♗f4 Δ♗e5± Khenkin-Shabalov, Minsk 1990.

b2) **18...♕b8** 19 ♘xa6 ♕xd6 20 ♕b3 ♗b7 21 ♘c5 ♘xc5 22 dxc5 ♕xc5 23 ♕g3!? (23 ♗f3 and 24 ♗d2 targeting b4 may be more realistic) 23...♔h8 24 ♗e3!± Alonso-Guerra, Ciego de Avila 1991. If Black liquidates bishop and queen, White's passed a-pawn will become the key player.

14 ♗g5

14 ♕xd4 immediately is not threatening if only because after 14...♕b6 15 ♕d3 **♕c7** White is obliged to repeat with 16 ♕d4. If Black is more ambitious, though, matters are not so clear. In Peshina-Ruzele, Lithuanian Ch 1993 Black tried **15...h6**, but after 16 ♗d2 ♗e7 17 a5 ♕a7 18 ♖fc1 0-0 19 ♖c4 ♖fc8 20 ♖ac1 ♖xc4 21 ♖xc4 ♖d8! 22 ♘g3 ♘f8 23 ♕c2! White enjoyed a certain initiative.

14 ... ♕a5

Probably the best, and certainly the most common choice. **14...♕b6?!** 15 a5 ♕a7 16 ♘xd4! ♘xe5 17 ♕a4+ ♘d7 18 ♘c6± (Dreev) looks horrible, but

14...♕b8!? is playable, if a little difficult for Black. 15 ♕xd4 h6 16 ♗h4 ♕a7 17 ♕xa7 ♖xa7 18 ♗g3!? (Or 18 ♖fc1 – Dreev; the text supports e5, freeing the f3 knight for a more ambitious role, and the passed pawn which will ensue in the event of ♘d6+) 18...♘c5 19 ♘fd2 ♘xe4 20 ♘xe4 ♗e7 (20...♘e3? 21 fxe3 ♗xd5 22 ♖ac1 and ♖fd1 with a later e4 to open the d-file) 21 ♖fc1 0-0 22 ♘d6± Seirawan-Cabrilo, New York Open 1990.

15 ♕xd4 h6 *(139)*

139
W

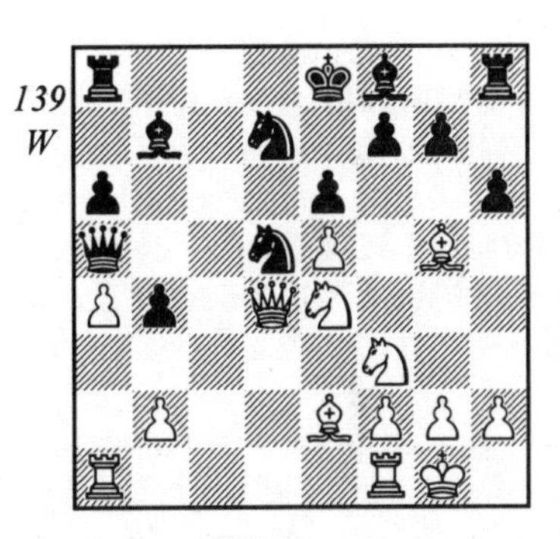

16 ♗h4

As we shall see, there is sufficient ambiguity in this game prior to White's success that White too has felt moved to search for improvements. **16 ♗d2!?** is among the most critical:

a) **16...♖c8?!** 17 ♖ac1 ♘c5 18 ♘d6+ ♗xd6 19 exd6 **0-0** 20 ♕g4 (20 ♗c4!?; 20 ♗xh6!? gxh6 21 ♕g4+ ♔h8! {21...♔h7 22 ♘g5+!} 22 ♕h4 ♔g7 23 ♖c4!? {22 ♕g4=} looks dangerous too) 20...f5 21 ♕h5 ♕d8 22 ♗xh6 ♕xd6 23 ♗e3 ♘e4 and the worst was over for Black in Soffer-G.Flear, Biel 1991.

b) **16...♕b6(!)** 17 ♕xb6 ♘5xb6 18 ♘d6+ ♗xd6 19 exd6 ♘d5 (Speelman-Scherbakov, London Lloyds Bank 1992) when 20 ♖fc1 ♘7f6 21 ♘d4 ♘e4 22 ♘b3 was the simplest route to a small plus – Speelman. If 22...♘xd6?! then 23 ♘a5 **0-0** 24 ♗f3 looks pleasant for White.

16 ... ♕b6
17 ♕d2 ♘c5

Interesting too was **17...b3** (to give the black queen extra space) 18 a5 (18 ♖fc1 looks logical too; Belov gives 18...♗b4 19 ♘d6+ ♗xd6 {19...♕xd6!?} 20 exd6 ♕xd6 21 ♖a3!±) 18...♕b4 19 ♘c3! g5 (Belov-Zviagintsev, Russia 1992) when 20 ♖a4! ♘xc3 21 ♖xb4 ♘xe2+ 22 ♕xe2 ♗xb4 23 ♗g3 would have somewhat favoured White. Black has good play on the light squares, but his king lacks a safe haven in view of which the queen's value is enhanced.

18 ♘xc5 ♗xc5
19 a5 ♕a7
20 ♖fc1! 0-0

Bravely deciding to face White's aggressive idea of ♖-c4-g4 head-on. If **20...♗e7** White has a choice between a safe but small positional edge with **21 ♗xe7** ♔xe7 22 ♕d4 ♕xd4 23 ♘xd4, hoping to make use of Black's dark square weaknesses on the queenside, and the more ambitious **21 ♖c4** ♗xh4 22 ♖xh4.

21 ♗d3 ♖fc8
22 ♖c4 ♗c6
23 ♖g4 ♔f8?!

Too risky. Black needs the extra defensive possibilities offered by the transfer with tempo of his knight towards the kingside via **23...♘e3!** 24 ♖g3 ♔f8 with reasonable chances to defend; Khenkin-Scherbakov, USSR 1989.

24 ♖e1 ♕c7

Rather nonchalant in view of the coming blitz! There was still a strong case for heading the knight towards f5 with **24...♘e7,** e.g. 25 ♗f6!? gxf6 26 exf6 ♗xf2+ (If Black does not return the material and liquidate, White's attack will be too strong) 27 ♕xf2 ♕xf2+ 28 ♔xf2 ♘d5 29 ♘e5! ♘xf6 30 ♖xb4 when White is restricted to a positional advantage.

25 ♗h7! g5 *(140)*

Forced, in view of the elegant threat of 26 ♕xh6!.

140
W

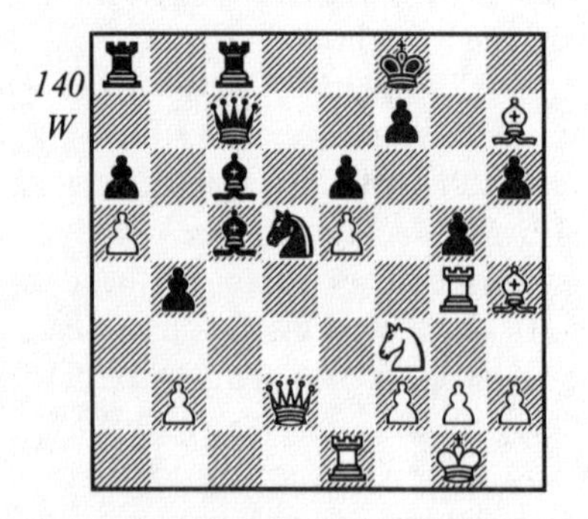

26 ♘xg5! hxg5
27 ♕xg5 ♔e8
28 ♕g8+ ♔d7
29 ♕xf7+ ♘e7

29...♗e7 30 ♖g6! ♖e8 31 ♕xe6+ ♔d8 32 ♖d1 is also crushing.

30 ♗xe7 ♗xe7
31 ♖d4+ ♗d5
32 ♖xd5+ 1-0

In view of 32...exd5 33 ♕xd5+ ♗d6 34 ♗f5+. A fine attacking finish by White, but from the theoretical standpoint it seems that with care Black's resources ought to be adequate, and the quiet 16 ♗d2!? harassing b4 may promise more.

Game 27
Malaniuk-Chernin
USSR Ch (Minsk) 1987

1 d4 d5 2 c4 c6 3 ♘c3 ♘f6 4 ♘f3 e6 5 e3 ♘bd7 6 ♗d3 dxc4 7 ♗xc4 b5

8 ♗e2

In contrast to the text which has benefitted from the continued viability of Black's game in the main line Meran, 8 ♗b3 has almost completely disappeared. Although the bishop looks somewhat blunted on the a2-g8 diagonal, the original idea of the move was highly aggressive, looking to intensify the pressure on e6 with ♘c3-e2-f4, and often ♘g5 too. Often White sacrifices a pawn with e4 to give the extra impetus to justify a sacrifice on e6 or f7. The problem is that if Black plays carefully and in particular is willing to liquidate one of the attacking white pieces with ...♗xf4 at a moment when White is heavily committed, he has a sound position and often some counter-punch with ...c5. After **8 ♗b3 b4!** *(141)* we consider:

141
W

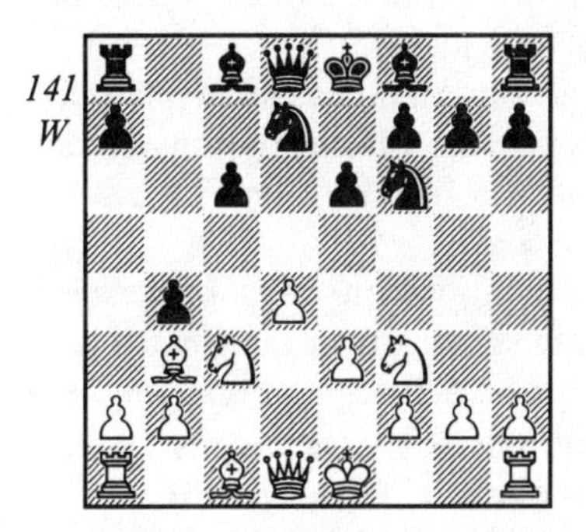

a) **9 ♘a4?! ♗a6** (the difficulty White has in organizing castling is a serious strategic flaw in this line) **10 ♗d2 c5!** (If Black delays White can use the c-file. In Speelman-Yusupov, Lucerne 1985 Black settled for 10...♗e7?! 11 ♖c1 0-0 12 ♗c4! ♗xc4?! 13 ♖xc4 ♘b6 14 ♖xc6 ♕d5 when with 15 ♖xb6! White could have clarified his advantage) **11 dxc5 ♘xc5!** (the previously-played 11...♗xc5 is not bad either; Vulfson-Lepeshkin, USSR 1988 proceeded sharply with 12 ♘xc5 ♘xc5 13 ♗a4+ ♘fd7 14 ♗xb4 **0-0** {14...♘d3+ 15 ♕xd3 ♗xd3 16 ♘e5 is surprisingly awkward} 15 ♗c2 ♕b6 16 ♕d4 ♖fc8 17 ♗c3 f6 18 0-0-0∞) **12 ♘xc5 ♗xc5**:

a1) **13 ♖c1** ♕b6 14 ♗c4 ♗b7 15 ♕a4+ ♗c6 16 ♕c2 ♗d6 17 ♗d3 ♗b7 18 ♕a4+ ♔e7! 19 ♘d4 ♖hc8 20 ♔e2?! ♘e4 21 ♗xe4 ♗xe4 22 f3 ♗d5 and White had a horrible position in Costa-Kramnik, Debrecen 1992.

a2) Maybe **13 ♗a4+** ♔e7 14 ♘e5 ♕b6 15 ♕b3 is relatively best, although it should not threaten Black.

a3) **13 ♗xe6** 0-0! (13...fxe6 of course fails to 14 ♕a4+) 14 ♕b3 ♗b7 15 ♗c4 a5 16 ♖d1 ♕c7 17 0-0 ♖ad8 18 h3 ♗a7! 19 ♗c1 ♖c8 with excellent compensation for the pawn in Costa-Bagirov, Debrecen 1992.

b) **9 ♘e2 ♗b7 10 0-0 ♗d6!** (The safest. The immediate 10...c5 gives White the interesting option of 11 ♗a4!? ♗e7 12 dxc5 ♗xf3 13 gxf3 ♗xc5 14 ♔h1!± Vilela-Vera, Cuban Ch 1985) and now White has:

b1) **11 ♘f4** 0-0 12 ♘g5 and now the cleanest equalizer seems to be 12...♗xf4! 13 exf4 c5 14 ♗e3 h6 15 ♘f3 ♖c8 16 ♖ac1 ♘g4 with a full share of the play; Butnoiris-Panchenko, USSR 1975.

b2) **11 e4!?** *(142)*:

142
B

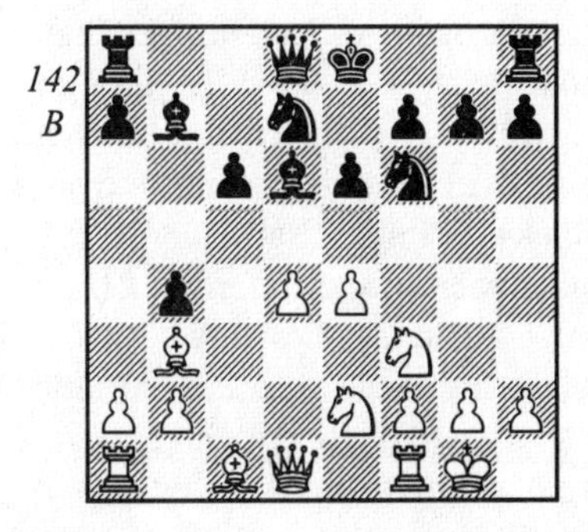

This leads to forcing and unclear complications which might be worth investigating further viz: 11...♘xe4 12 ♘f4 0-0 13 ♖e1 ♘df6 14 ♘e5 c5 15 f3 cxd4 16 ♘xf7 ♖xf7 17 ♘xe6 ♗xh2+! 18 ♔h1 ♘f2+ 19 ♔xh2 ♕a5! 20 ♕xd4 ♕h5+ 21 ♔g1! (21 ♔g3 ♘ge4+!! favours Black) 21...♘h3+ 22 gxh3 ♕xf3 23 ♘f4 and Black should take perpetual with 23...♕h1+ 24 ♔f2 ♕f3+.

8 ... b4

Before discussing the positional themes, a word on move order. Chernin has been one of the chief enthusiasts for the approach with ...b4, and heads for it immediately. Another route to similar positions is 8...♗b7 9 0-0 b4. The differences are only in the deviations that they allow. After 8...♗b7, as we have seen, Black must also be prepared for 9 e4 or 9 a3. After 8...b4, Black must also be ready to meet 10 ♗d2 (see note to 10 0-0 below). Theoretically none of these three are terribly terrifying, and either choice can be justified more in terms of the alternatives it encourages than those that it avoids! (Although 8...♗b7 9 e4 clearly requires a fair level of preparedness from Black). I think that the relative prevalence of the order 8...♗b7 9 0-0 b4 can be explained by the belief that ideas with ...b4 are the best after 9 0-0, but there is no great enthusiasm for the move since the resultant positions have drawish tendencies.

After 8...b4 9 ♘a4, the play revolves around two sequential issues:

1) Whether Black can liquidate his backward c-pawn and free his game with ...c5.

2) Assuming he can, will his active pieces sufficiently compensate for his potentially vulnerable queenside.

The position begs interesting comparisons with the Open Catalan where Black must play for ...c5, but it does not necessarily end his problems. Although here Black has played ...b4, which generally is not undertaken lightly in the Catalan, the relatively passive placement of White's king's bishop here should I believe be the most important difference, considerably easing Black's task.

9 ♘a4 ♗b7 *(143)*

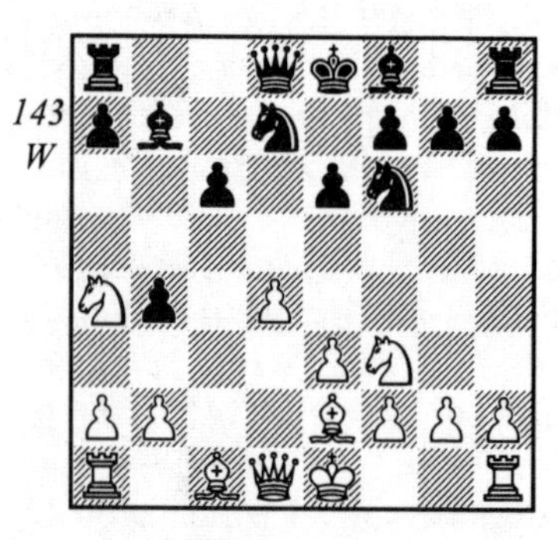

10 ♗d2

White tries to create problems for Black on the queenside (sometimes attacking the b4 point, sometimes trying to hold up ...c5 with a quick ♖c1) and considers castling a low priority. Still, **10 0-0** is an important alternative and not surprisingly there is also a wealth of transpositions between the two (generally badly dealt with by the literature). **10...♗e7** (10...c5?! 11 dxc5 ♗xc5 12 ♘xc5 ♘xc5 13 ♕d4±) and now:

a) **11 b3?!** causes no problems after 11...0-0 12 ♗b2 c5 13 ♖c1 ♖c8 14 dxc5 ♘xc5 15 ♘xc5 ♗xc5 16 ♕xd8= Zsu.Polgar-Knaak, Hamburg 1991.

b) **11 a3!?**:

b1) **11...bxa3?!** 12 b3! (12 bxa3 is rarely dangerous and here 12...0-0 13 ♗d2 c5 14 ♘xc5 ♘xc5 15 dxc5 ♗xc5= Marszalek-Kirov, Pernik 1981 was no exception) 12...c5 (Black was probably worried about ...c5 being prevented if it was not effected immediately, e.g. 12...0-0 13 ♗xa3 ♗xa3 14 ♖xa3 ♕e7 15 ♕c1!± {Oll} but it was the lesser evil) 13 dxc5 ♘xc5 14 ♗b5+ ♘cd7 15 ♘e5 ♕c7 16 ♕d4± Oll-Wolff, Wijk aan Zee 1993.

b2) Clearly better seems to be **11...a5!**.

b21) Then **12 ♕c2 0-0**:

b211) **13 ♖d1** c5!? could transpose, after 14 ♘xc5 ♘xc5 15 dxc5 ♕c7 to the critical line 'd22' below – as was the case in Timman-Lautier.

b212) *editor's note:* **13 axb4!** axb4 (13...♗xb4 might be worth trying since Black is now stuck with a weak b-pawn which makes the ...c5 advance difficult) 14 ♗d2 ♕a5 (what else? White threatened ♘c5) 15 b3! ♖fc8 16 ♕b2 ♕d8 17 ♖fd1 ♕f8 18 ♖ac1± S.Pedersen-Lukacs, Budapest 1993.

b213) **13 ♗d2 c5!? 14 dxc5 ♗e4**= Akhmylovskaya-Alexandria, Kislovodsk (m) 1980 gave Black no trouble, but **14 ♘xc5** ♘xc5 15 dxc5 ♗e4 16 ♕c1 may make life more difficult. However, Black has generally preferred after 13 ♗d2 to preface ...c5 with **13...bxa3** now that b-pawn moves other than recapturing are ruled out for White: 14 bxa3 c5 15 dxc5 ♗e4 16 ♗d3!? (16 ♕c4 ♖c8= is still simpler for Black; Bönsch-Smagin, Berlin 1988) 16...♗xf3 17 gxf3 ♘xc5 18 ♘xc5 ♗xc5 19 ♗c3 ♖c8 20 ♗a6!? ♖a8 21 ♗e2 Müller-Knaak, Hamburg 1991 with equal chances and a little unbalance in the position too.

b22) So why does Oll give **12 ♗d2** as ± ? After 12...0-0 White can try the slightly more challenging 13 ♕b3!? which Trostjaneski gives as ± after **13...♖b8** 14 axb4 axb4 15 ♖fc1. If Black must so lightly relinquish the a-file then I agree with this, but **13...♘e4!?** looks a better try, e.g. 14 axb4 (14 ♗e1 c5 should not be a problem) 14...♘xd2 15 ♘xd2 axb4(!) (It is not so easy to organize ...c5 in the event of 15...♗xb4 16 ♘e4± as given by Chernin, who considers this by transposition) 16 ♘e4 (16 ♖fc1 c5 17 dxc5 ♘xc5!=) 16...c5! (16...♖a5?! 17 ♖ac1! {17 ♖fc1? ♕a8!} 17...c5 18 ♘exc5 ♘xc5 19 ♘xc5 ♗xc5 20 dxc5 ♕g5 21 g3 ♖xc5 22 ♕xb4 ♖xc1 23 ♖xc1 ♕d5 24 f3±) 17 ♘exc5 ♗xc5 18 dxc5 ♕g5 19 g3 (19 f3 ♘xc5=) ♘xc5 20 ♕xb4 ♕d5 21 f3 ♖xa4 22 ♖xa4 ♘xa4 23 ♕xa4 ♕d2 24 ♔f2! ♕xb2=. This variation is very important, and if this analysis holds up Black seems to have few problems in attaining equality (albeit drawish).

c) **11 ♗d2 0-0** 12 ♕c2 (12 ♕b3 a5 13 ♖fd1 {13 a3 see 'b22'} 13...c5= was Pinez-Bronstein, Mar del Plata 1955) 12...a5 and now 13 a3 transposes to note 'b213' and was indeed the move order of Müller-Knaak for example.

d) **11 ♕c2!?** is the latest try to attract attention since Polugaevsky last year gave an excellent lesson in how to exploit the small pluses in a 'classic' 8 ♗e2 b4 ending. It now seems that Black can reach approximate equality but care is required, viz. **11...0-0** (Black achieved equality with 11...♖c8 in Alexandrov-Kherson, USSR Ch 1991, but after 12 a3! bxa3, 13 ♘c5!± would have been much stronger than 13 bxa3?! c5 14 ♘xc5 ♘xc5 15 dxc5 **0-0**=) **12 ♖d1**:

d1) **12...♖c8** is not so good in view of 13 a3! (The point is that although the immediate 13 ♘c5? is bad since the c-pawn cannot be supported after 13...♘xc5 14 dxc5 ♕a5, this key move is easily prepared) 13...a5 (worse is 13...bxa3 14 ♘c5!±) 14 axb4 ♗xb4 15 ♘c5! ♘xc5 16 dxc5 ♕e7 17 ♗d2 ♗xc5 18 ♗xa5 ♗d6 19 e4 ♘g4! 20 ♗c3⩲ L.B.Hansen-B.Kristensen, Espergærde 1992, although 20...♗c5! would have minimized Black's coming troubles.

d2) **12...c5! 13 ♘xc5 ♘xc5 14 dxc5 ♕c7 15 a3!**:

d21) **15...♕xc5?!** 16 ♕xc5 ♗xc5 17 axb4 ♗xb4 18 ♗d2 a5 (18...♗xd2 19 ♖xd2 ♗d5 20 ♘d4!⩲, since White will 'blunt' Black's bishop with f3) 19 ♘e5 h5?! 20 ♗xb4 axb4 21 ♖xa8 ♖xa8 22 f3! ♖c8 23 ♖d4 ♘d5 24 e4 ♘f4 25 ♗c4± Polugaevsky-Speelman, Monaco 30 min 1992.

d22) The crucial improvement comes here courtesy of Swedish Grandmaster Jonny Hector whose usually maverick approach to the opening seems to calm down a little when he is put behind a Semi-Slav. The right way is **15...a5!** 16 axb4 axb4 **17 ♖xa8** ♖xa8 18 ♗d2 ♕xc5, and White, unwilling to bring out his microscope to check the advantage, acquiesced in a draw in L.B.Hansen-Hector, Espergærde 1992. This idea held up at top level, in Timman-Lautier, Wijk aan Zee Ct (7) 1994, though this was a game in which a draw was sufficient for Timman to qualify: **17 ♗d2** ♕xc5 18 ♕xc5 ♗xc5

19 ♘e5 ♗e7 20 ♗f3 ♘e4 21 ♗e1 f6 22 ♘d3 b3 23 ♖xa8 ♖xa8 24 ♘c1 ♗d5 25 ♗xe4 ♗xe4 26 ♘xb3 ♖b8 27 ♖d7 ♖xb3 28 ♖xe7 ♖xb2 29 f3 ♗d5 30 e4 ♗c4 31 ♖c7 ♗d3 32 ♖c3 ♗b5 33 ♖c8+ ♔f7 34 ♖b8 ♖b1 ½-½.

d23) **15...bxa3** 16 b4 a5 17 ♗a3 (± Ftačnik) 17...axb4 18 ♗xb4 ♘d5 19 ♗a3 ♖a5 Δ...♖fa8 is also possibly enough.

10 ... ♗e7

11 ♖c1

White has one other independent idea delaying 0-0, namely **11 a3!?** after which Chernin gives **11...a5** 12 ♕b3 ♘e4 13 axb4 ♘xd2 14 ♘xd2 ♗xb4 (14...axb4 15 ♘e4 0-0 16 ♖c1!±) 15 0-0 c5!? with interesting complications. However, with the bishop already committed to d2, why not simply **11...bxa3** ?

11 ... 0-0

12 0-0 a5

13 ♘e1?!

Perhaps the most important message to come from contemporary praxis in this variation as a whole is that White should try from the start to make problems for Black's b-pawn. Merely concentrating on preventing ...c5 is the wrong approach. Barring a mistake on Black's part this goal is unattainable. Already, White should probably be thinking in terms of an equal game – the ambitious text hands Black a clear initiative. Chernin's analysis of **13 ♕b3** is highly instructive: 13...c5! 14 dxc5 ♗d5! 15 ♗c4 (15 ♕c2 ♖c8∓) 15...♗xf3! 16 gxf3 ♘e5 17 ♔g2! and now not **17...♕xd2?** 18 ♖fd1, but **17...♘g6!** with excellent kingside play for the pawn.

13 ... ♘e4! *(144)*

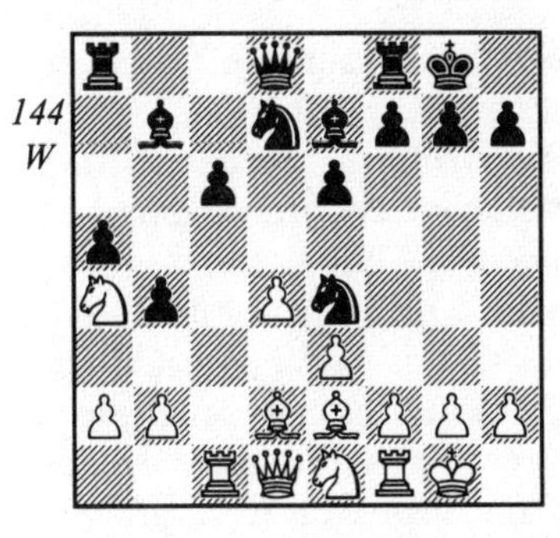

144
W

An important moment. Of course Black can here obtain level chances with **13...c5** 14 dxc5 ♖c8 15 ♗f3! ♗xf3 16 ♘xf3 ♘xc5. Chernin's move shows that he is alive to the right moment to retain pieces, tension and imbalance in the bid for the full point.

14 ♘d3 c5

15 dxc5

15 ♘axc5 ♘dxc5 16 dxc5 ♖c8 also leaves Black with the initiative, but there must be a strong case for not leaving the knight stranded on a4.

15 ... ♖c8

16 ♖c2

The bishop on d2 needed more support as Chernin demonstrates with the variations **16 ♗f3** ♗c6! 17 b3 (17 ♗e1 is relatively best, but White would be very passive. Not 17 ♗xe4 ♗xe4 18 ♕e2 ♗c6!∓)

17...♘xd2 18 ♕xd2 ♗xf3 19 gxf3 ♘e5∓.

16 ...	**♘dxc5**
17 ♘axc5	**♘xc5**
18 ♘xc5	**♖xc5!**
19 ♖xc5	**♗xc5**
20 ♕c2	**♕g5**

A typical example of successful Black strategy in this line. Far from being weak, the advanced Black pawns have a useful cramping effect on the White pieces. Meanwhile, although the pawn formation is symmetrical, Black begins to use his more active pieces to probe and create more tangible weaknesses. Clearly **21 g3** ♕d5 would be most unappetizing, but from this point, the e4 pawn is a target to the defence of which White's pieces will be further tied.

21 e4	**♕e5**
22 ♗f3	**♖c8**
23 ♕b1	**♗d4!**
24 b3	**♗a6**
25 ♖c1	**♖c5!?**

An interesting decision. In general with such a space advantage, Black would aim to avoid exchanges. However, the rook is White's best piece, and Chernin wants the c-file too.

26 g3	**♕c7**
27 ♖xc5	**♕xc5**
28 ♗e1	**♕b5**
29 ♗d2	**♕d3!** *(145)*

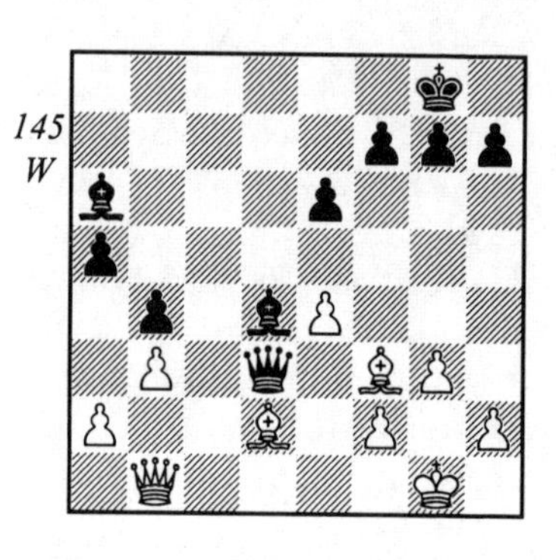

Another virtue of the variation (and perhaps yet another argument for the lines where White essays an early a3) – if Black's advanced pawns do not prove to be weak, then White must watch out for the safety of his own queenside. The gradual squeezing of White's pieces is most elegantly effected: **30 ♕d1 e5 31 ♔g2 ♗b7 32 ♕c1 h6 33 ♗e3 ♗xe4 34 ♗xe4 ♕xe4+ 35 f3!** (A bit transparent to be an effective trap, but White can dream of 35...♕xe3?? 36 ♕c8+ with a perpetual) **35...♕d5 36 ♕c8+ ♔h7 37 ♕c2+ g6 38 ♗d2 ♗c5 39 ♕c1? e4 40 ♗e3 exf3+ 41 ♔f2 ♕d3! 0-1**.

Since if 42 ♗xc5 ♕e2+ mates. This game should serve as a model for exploiting passive play in this line.

Section 3 6 ♕c2 Introduction

Of itself the move 6 ♕c2 does not yet betray any particular disposition by White. In this section can be found the full range from the most critical 'violent' approaches such as 7 g4!? recently brought to prominence by the talented and supremely uncompromising young Latvian Alexei Shirov, to the unashamedly quiet 7 ♗e2.

The meteoric rise of the latter to astonishing popularity is *the* fashion development in the Semi-Slav in the past five years. For a time it was more popular than either 5 ♗g5 or the Meran (although perhaps already a slight waning can already be detected as Black has unearthed a diverse selection of fairly acceptable approaches). A clue to its status around 1987 can be found in the fact that the lines where Black captures on c4 (here comprising three chapters) are classified apart under D46 on the *ECO* key by virtue of a single note to 8 ♕c2 dxc4 in the 6 ♗d3 ♗d6 lines!

It has been hinted elsewhere that the rise of 7 ♗e2 is in part a tribute to the success of the Meran for Black. However, as we shall see, the system does contain a little poison in its own right, and positional players (notably Karpov and Epishin) have been clocking up a good score with it. The initial appeal of 7 ♗e2 may have included the motive of theory avoidance, but whilst only now beginning to be sorted out into book form there is already a mass of material which inevitably renders it theoretical. More on this key section later.

In view of the very varied nature of the lines introduced by 6 ♕c2, this introduction will be curtailed in favour of more detailed chapter discussions. First to take the chapters in order we return to the more aggressive approaches.

19 Aggressive ideas for White

Here we shall look at the various lines, 7 h3, 7 ♗d2 and the recent addition 7 g4. The latter two generally imply queenside castling followed by an attempt to blast Black from the board. The most interesting and topical of these is 7 g4, and here the chess world at first reacted strangely. Usually it is difficult to dissuade a mass-following of any opening idea which the World Champion has so much as touched, be it good or bad. With his reaction to 7 g4, namely the simple capture on c4 with which he so efficiently despatched Michael Adams, it was a very different story. Despite appearing at the very least among Black's best choices, it experienced initially very limited take-up. At the same time, paradoxically, it seems that the possibility of 7...dxc4 lessened enthusiasm for 7 g4. Recently, the move has again enjoyed a resurgence, and although 7...dxc4 has now taken up its rightful place as a principal defensive try, White's approach has been sufficiently refined that the theoretical position is fascinatingly unclear.

Although at present Black's resources against 7 ♗d2 are looking more than sufficient and 7 g4, whilst more dangerous, does not refute the Semi-Slav either, Black would be well advised to prepare the material in this chapter with a special thoroughness.

Game 28
Krasenkov-Sveshnikov
Moscow 1992

1	**♘f3**	**d5**
2	**d4**	**♘f6**
3	**c4**	**e6**
4	**♘c3**	**c6**
5	**e3**	**♘bd7**
6	**♕c2**	**♗d6**
7	**g4!?** *(146)*	

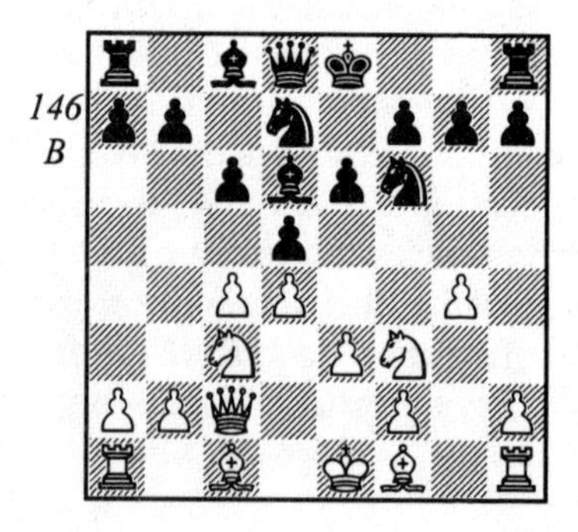

146
B

The text is the most direct way of initiating a speedy assault on Black's kingside. Originally an idea of Shabalov's, it has since Shirov-Thorhallsson, Reykjavik 1991 (see below) been a hot topic amongst those aggressive players who want the guarantee of a sharp game without stepping into the theoretical minefield of 5 ♗g5. Shirov is on record as saying that it seems that he always plays other people's ideas rather than his own. Since he has suggested 7 ♖g1?! here, it is probably a good moment to uphold this practice. 7...♘xg4 is not so strong that this loss of tempo can be justified.

However 7 ♗d2, aiming to complete queenside mobilization before striking at Black's king, remains an interesting option, and for those seeking to maintain the option of play on either wing, 7 h3 is possible, although in conjunction with a quick g4 I believe it is inferior.

We shall consider:

a) **7 h3**. The main appeal of this move is its flexibility. It does not yet commit White to an all-out kingside strategy. After **7...0-0**, White has two possibilities of which I prefer 'a2':

a1) **8 g4** seems to lack the flexibility of 8 ♗d2, and also the punch of 7 g4. Black has fared well after **8...e5** (8...♕e7 is also good, so that, albeit promising, Black is not obliged to give a pawn, e.g. 9 g5 ♘h5 10 ♗d3?! {Shabalov suggests 10 ♗d2!, claiming that the 10...b5 11 cxb5 c5 gambit is promising} 10...g6 11 ♗d2 dxc4 12 ♗xc4 b5 13 ♗e2 ♗b7 14 ♘e4 c5∓ Djurhuus-Shabalov, Oslo 1991) 9 g5 ♘e4 10 ♘xe4 (10 cxd5 ♘xc3 11 dxc6 ♘d5 12 cxd7 ♗xd7 13 dxe5 ♘b4! gave good compensation for Black in Shabalov-Sveshnikov, Torcy 1991) 10...dxe4 11 ♕xe4 f5 12 ♕h4 exd4! 13 ♕xd4 ♕e7∞ (Shabalov) but I believe in Black's counterplay.

a2) **8 ♗d2!?**:

a21) **8...b6!?** 9 e4 e5! 10 cxd5 cxd5 11 exd5 ♗b7 Tisdall-G.Flear, London 1990, was an original approach which worked out well. Normally, Black plays a more conventional preface to ...e5.

a22) The immediate **8...e5** is perhaps a little premature: 9 cxd5 cxd5 10 ♘b5 ♗b8 11 ♗b4 ♖e8 12 ♖c1 e4 13 ♘d2 ♘f8 14 ♘c7 ♗xc7 15 ♕xc7 ♗d7 16 ♕xd8 ♖exd8 17 ♗e2 with a queenside initiative in Lechtynsky-Thesing, Nettetal 1992.

a23) However, **8...a6** is likely to be enough to persuade White to switch plans, e.g. 9 g4!? (9 0-0-0 b5!? 10 c5 ♗c7 11 g4 leads to unclear and very sharp play) 9...b5 10 c5 ♗c7 11 ♗d3 ♔h8 12 ♘e2 ♕e7 13 0-0-0 e5 14 dxe5 ♘xe5 15 ♘xe5 ♗xe5 16 ♘d4 ♗d7 17 f3 a5 18 h4 Malaniuk-Shestiakov, Kecskemet 1991. White's attack looks promising enough to encourage Black to seek alternatives.

a24) **8...♖e8!?** 9 a3!? (9 0-0-0 e5 10 cxd5 cxd5 11 ♘b5 ♗b8 12 dxe5 ♘xe5 13 ♔b1 ♗d7 is nothing special for White; Agdestein-Smyslov, Aker Brugge 1989) 9...e5?!

(The chief virtue of White's ninth move seems to be that he is not yet determining where will be his focus of attack. Given this, it seems much more logical to avoid the game problems of ♘b5 with 9...a6!, with equal chances) 10 cxd5 cxd5 11 ♘b5 ♗b8 12 ♖c1 e4 13 ♘g1!? ♘f8 14 ♘c7 (Speelman-Bagirov, London Lloyds Bank 1991) with a similar queenside pull to Lechtynsky-Thesing. Black's defence will require great care.

b) **7 ♗d2 0-0** and now apart from 8 h3 transposing to 'a' above, White has in ascending order of merit:

b1) **8 e4?!** (There is no check on b4, but otherwise the move is quite illogical. When the position opens up, 7 ♗d2 looks like a loss of tempo) 8...c5! 9 cxd5 exd5 10 exd5 cxd4 11 ♘xd4 ♗e5! 12 ♘f3 ♗xc3 13 ♗xc3 ♖e8+ and Black stands well; Banas-Dreev, Cappelle la Grande 1992.

b2) **8 cxd5** looks strange since the open e-file often gives Black a useful outpost on e4. The structure is like an Exchange Variation of the Queen's Gambit, but Black has done nothing unnatural enough to compensate for White blocking his own dark-squared bishop. It was nevertheless tested at the highest level and the result was highly entertaining. Agdestein-Shirov, Gausdal 1992 saw the young Latvian at his tactical best after 8...exd5 9 0-0-0 ♖e8 10 ♗d3 (Shirov prefers 10 ♔b1 ♘e4 11 ♗c1 ♘df6 12 ♘e1!? to break out again with f3, but the plan looks rather artificial) 10...c5! 11 dxc5 ♘xc5 12 ♘d4 (12 ♗b5 ♗d7 13 ♗xd7 ♕xd7 14 ♗e1 ♖ac8 leaves Black very comfortable in both static and dynamic terms) 12...a6 13 f3 b5 14 ♔b1 b4 15 ♘ce2 (Shirov gives 15 ♘a4 ♘xd3 16 ♕xd3 ♗d7 17 b3 as unclear, but Black seems to retain the initiative) 15...♘xd3 16 ♕xd3 a5 17 ♗e1 ♗a6 18 ♕d2 ♘d7 19 ♗g3 ♘b6 20 b3 a4 21 ♘c6 ♕d7 22 ♘ed4 ♗f8 23 ♘xb4?! axb3 24 axb3 *(147)*

147
B

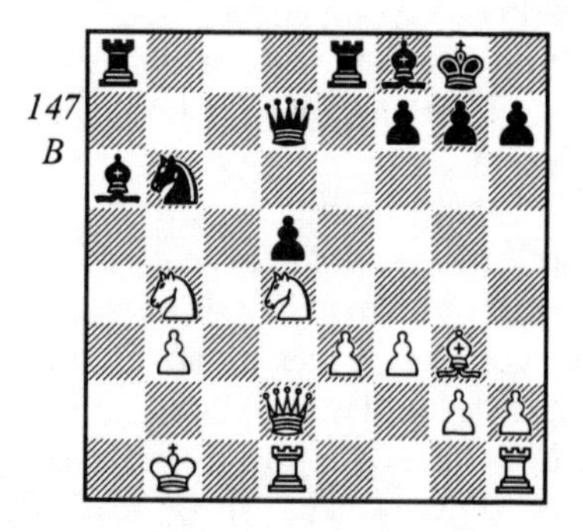

24...♗c4!! 25 ♘bc2 (acceptance of the offer also gives Black a crushing attack, e.g. 25 bxc4 ♘xc4 26 ♕c3 ♖a3 27 ♘b3 ♕a4) 25...♖ec8 26 ♘a1 ♗d3+ 27 ♕xd3 ♕a7 28 ♘dc2 ♕a2+ 29 ♔c1 ♕xa1+ 30 ♔d2 ♕b2 31 ♖c1 ♗b4+ 32 ♔d1 ♖c3 33 ♕d4 ♖xc2! 0-1.

b3) **8 0-0-0** *(148)* is very much the main line, after which Black has many interesting options:

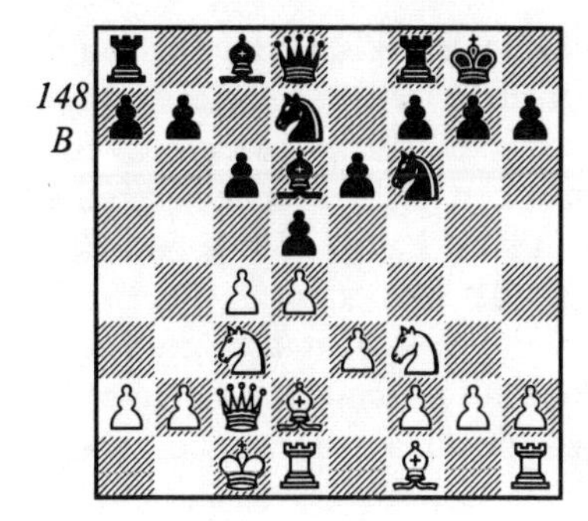
148
B

b31) **8...♕e7?!** 9 e4! (With White's king in safety, and the black queen on a potentially vulnerable square this opening of the position makes much more sense than in 'b1' above) 9...dxe4 10 ♘xe4 ♘xe4 11 ♕xe4 e5?! 12 ♗g5! f6 (Neither is 12...♕e6 any great panacea since after 13 dxe5 ♘xe5 White has 14 ♖xd6 ♕xd6 15 ♘xe5 f6 16 ♗d3±) 13 ♗d3! (a well-known sequence which we shall again see in Game 35 with 8...♕e7) 13...g6 14 ♗h6 ♖e8 15 c5 ♗c7 16 ♗c4+ ♔h8 17 ♖he1± Taimanov-Gromek, Moscow OL 1956.

b32) **8...♘g4?!** is quite an original idea, exploiting White's temporary neglect of f2 to attempt to set up a Stonewall formation while White's queen's bishop is rather passive. Unfortunately, White can drive the errant black knight to an unfavourable square, and indeed far from holding back White's kingside ambitions, the f5 pawn even provides a target for them, e.g. 9 ♗e1 f5 10 h3 ♘h6 (10...♘gf6 11 g4! is strong, threatening not only to open the g-file but also to undermine Black's d5 pawn) 11 ♗e2 (11 ♗d3!? Watson) 11...♘f6 12 ♘e5 ♘f7 13 f4 ♘e4 14 ♘xe4 dxe4 15 g4 ♗d7 16 c5 ♗xe5 17 dxe5 ♕e7 18 ♖g1 with a large plus; Taimanov-Karaklajić, USSR 1957.

b33) **8...dxc4** is interestingly, and somewhat curiously, praised by both Shirov and Ftačnik. The former, perhaps a little glibly, offers **9 ♗xc4** b5 10 ♗d3 ♗b7∓. Most textbooks prefer **9 e4** which would indeed appear to be more testing, e.g. 9...e5 10 ♗xc4 b5 11 ♗b3! ♕e7 (±/∞ Sokolov) 12 ♖he1 a5 13 a4 b4 14 ♘e2 c5 15 ♘g3!± J.Watson. In any case, the move is almost untested in practice.

b34) **8...e5** by contrast has a quite solid reputation. **9 cxd5** and now:

b341) Bilek-Neikirkh, Leipzig 1960 revealed a nice tactic after **9...exd4?** 10 dxc6! dxc3 11 ♗xc3 ♘b6 12 ♘g5 g6 13 ♗xf6 ♕xf6 14 ♘e4 and ♘xd6±.

b342) However, **9...♘xd5** may be worth considering since freeing White's development also involves loosening his king. In Radev-Lukov, Bulgaria 1983 Black sacrificed a pawn for dynamic counterplay and the play rapidly became very sharp after 10 ♘xd5 cxd5 11 dxe5 ♘xe5 12 ♗c3 ♕e7! 13 ♖xd5 f6 14 ♘xe5 ♗xe5 15 ♕e4 ♗e6 16 ♗d3!? ♖fc8 17 ♕xh7+ ♔f8 18 ♖xe5 fxe5∞.

b343) **9...exd5** 10 ♘b5 ♗b8 11 dxe5! ♘xe5 12 ♗c3 ♕e7 13 ♗d4 (Δ♗c5, ♘c3) 13...♖d8 (13...b6 is regarded as adequate in several opening works, but I agree with Donaldson that after 14 ♘c3 ♗b7 White should avoid the complications arising from the 15 ♕f5 ♘eg4 of Tal-Trifunović, Munich OL 1958, since he can retain a plus with 15 ♔b1! keeping ♕f5 in reserve) 14 ♘c3 g6!? (Again the American analysis seems the most perceptive. The text which encourages White to commence exchanging to forestall ...♗f5 seems more logical than 14...♘xf3 15 gxf3 ♗e5 {= Taimanov} when 16 ♔b1! {Watson} keeps some pull. The opening of the g-file seems to help only White, e.g. 16...g6 17 ♖hg1±) 15 ♘xe5 ♗xe5 16 ♗xe5 ♕xe5 17 ♖d4 ♗e6 18 ♗d3 a6 19 ♕d2 b5 and Black was solid with some prospects of counterplay too, in Åkesson-Dlugy, Gausdal 1982.

b35) **8...c5** *(149)*

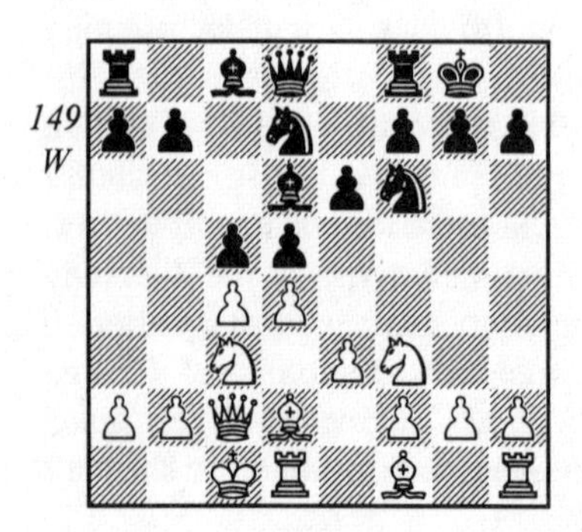
149
W

Again, Black's willingness to accept an 'isolani' is enhanced by the somewhat passive placing of the bishop on d2. Now apart from the main line, 9 cxd5, White has tried two other moves:

b351) **9 ♔b1** was Smyslov's move but its tendency still to crop up in practice does not seem merited:

b3511) **9...cxd4** 10 exd4 dxc4 11 ♗xc4 a6 12 ♗d3 b5 13 ♘e4 ♗e7 14 ♘e5 ♗b7 15 ♘g5 (15 ♘xd7!?) 15...g6 was also nothing special for White in Smyslov-Whiteley, Hastings 1976/77.

b3512) **9...a6!?** 10 cxd5 exd5 11 ♗c1 b5!? (11...c4 12 g4 ♘b6 13 h3 ♖e8 14 ♗g2 ♗b4 led to an interesting position in Taimanov-Botvinnik, match 1953, when with 15 ♘d2! – Botvinnik – White's threat to break in the centre with e4 would have been at least sufficient to stem Black's queenside initiative) 12 dxc5 ♘xc5 13 ♘xd5 ♘xd5 14 ♖xd5 ♗b7 15 ♖d4 ♕e7 16 ♗d3 g6 17 ♖d1 ♖ac8 Cifuentes Parada-Barbero, Buenos Aires 1991. Black's chances on the c-file and the light squares seem very attractive compensation for a pawn.

b352) Interesting, but not only for White, is **9 e4!?** which leads to great complications, e.g. 9...cxd4 10 ♘xd4 dxc4 (10...♗e5!? looks better since if 11 ♗g5?! h6 12 ♗h4 ♕b6! Black is fine; Åkesson-Andrianov, Groningen 1981. Perhaps

11 ♗e1 improves) 11 ♗xc4 a6 (Euwe's 11...♘b6 12 ♗e2 ♗d7 is a bit passive, and I agree with Kondratiev that after 13 ♔b1 ♖c8 14 ♕b3 White is for preference) 12 ♗e3 ♕e7 13 ♗e2 ♘e5 14 h3 ♘g6 15 ♔b1 ♗f4 16 ♕d2± Taimanov-Fichtl, Vienna 1957.

b353) **9 cxd5 exd5**. Now immediately 'saddling' Black with the IQP only serves to free his game. After 10 ♔b1 the structure is very similar to Agdestein-Shirov, seen under 'b2' above. However, perhaps more obstacles are put in the way of Black's successful implementation of his light-square strategy too after 10 ♗e1!?:

b3531) **10 ♗e1!?** c4 (10...♘b6!?) 11 g4 ♘b6 12 h3 (12 g5 is false aggression; its most important consequence is to give Black the f5 square) 12...♖e8 13 ♗g2 ♗d7 14 ♘d2 ♗b4! 15 ♘db1! (control of e4 is all!) 15...h6 (Pinter gives 15...♗c6 16 g5 ♗xc3 17 ♘xc3 ♘e4 as ∓, but as Donaldson points out 18 ♗xe4 dxe4 19 d5! breaks the light-square bind) 16 a3 ♗a5 17 ♗f3 ♖c8 18 ♖g1± Bischoff-Pinter, Plovdiv 1983.

b3532) **10 ♔b1** c4 (as above, not forced but here rather tempting!) 11 ♗c1 a6 12 g4 ♘b6 13 h3 ♖e8 14 ♗g2 ♗b4 15 ♘e5?! ♗xc3 16 ♕xc3 ♘e4 17 ♕c2 (17 ♗xe4) 17...♘d6!∓ Taimanov-Botvinnik, match 1953.

b36) **8...b5!?** *(150)*

150
W

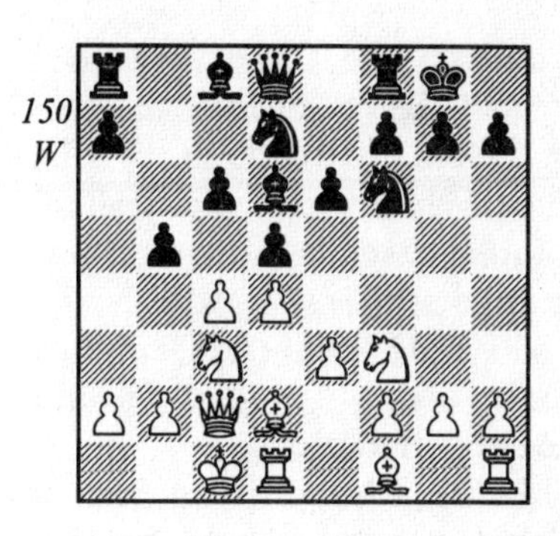

A fascinating gambit designed both to open lines against the white king, and to reduce pressure on d5 in preparation for ...c5. Theory was initially sceptical but the current state of play looks promising for Black:

b361) **9 cxd5** exd5 10 e4 dxe4 11 ♘xe4 ♘xe4 12 ♕xe4 ♘f6 is fine for Black.

b362) Polugaevsky suggests **9 c5** which is interesting but Black is fairly well placed to prepare ...e5, backed by the possibility that e4 often can be met with ...b4. Keipo-Lugo, Camaguey 1988 continued 9...♗c7 10 ♗d3 b4 11 ♘a4 a5 12 ♖dg1 ♗a6 13 ♗xa6 ♖xa6 14 g4 ♘e4 15 ♗e1 f5 with satisfactory play.

b363) **9 cxb5 c5! 10 e4!** (White should immediately strike in the centre before Black can open lines with ...a6) **10...♗b7 11 exd5** (weaker is 11 e5 cxd4 12 exd6 ♘e4 with good counterchances - Euwe) **11...♘xd5!** (This was the improvement which did much to enhance the theoretical status of 8...b5.

Weaker was 11...exd5? 12 ♕f5! ♕c7 13 ♗d3 cxd4 14 ♘xd4 ♘c5 15 ♗c2 ♗c8 16 ♕g5 h6 17 ♕h4 when White was a pawn ahead with the attack in Åkesson-Iskov, Stockholm 1978/79) and now:

b3631) **12 ♘xd5** ♗xd5 13 ♗c4 ♗xf3! and 14...cxd4 is fine for Black – Kupreichik.

b3632) **12 ♘g5!?** is logical with Black's knight dragged towards the centre, e.g. 12...g6 13 ♘ge4 ♗e7 14 dxc5 ♘xc5 15 ♘xc5 ♗xc5 16 ♗h6 ♖e8. De Firmian and Donaldson give this as OK for Black. However, Black should be ready to meet 17 ♘xd5 since 17...♗xd5 18 ♕c3! e5? 19 ♗c4 ♗d4 20 ♖xd4 is a disaster. Probably 17...exd5 is OK, with ideas of ...♖c8, ...♕h4, or ...d4. In general I am sympathetic to the case for Black's compensation in all these lines, but this may well be White's best version.

b3633) **12 ♘e4** ♗e7 13 dxc5 ♘xc5 14 ♘xc5 ♗xc5 15 ♘g5 g6 16 ♘e4 ♗d4! 17 ♔b1 ♖c8 with excellent play in Marović-Kupreichik, Medina del Campo 1980.

7 ... ♘xg4

Obviously the text is a critical test, but four other moves have been tried, of which I believe that only 'a' can be lightly regarded as inferior:

a) **7...0-0?!** was Black's reaction in the stem game Shirov-Thorhallsson, Reykjavik 1992. However, it is likely that Black cannot so lightly allow his king's knight to be so misplaced. The result was a virtuoso Shirov performance which should be given in full, if only on entertainment grounds: 8 g5 ♘h5 9 ♗d2 (White intends 0-0-0 and e4 with the initiative both on the kingside and in the centre) 9...f5 (White also obtains a very dangerous attack after 9...a6: 10 e4 dxc4 11 e5 ♗e7 12 ♗xc4 c5 13 ♘e4! cxd4 14 ♘g3! g6 15 ♘xh5 gxh5 16 ♗d3 ♘c5 17 ♗xh7+ ♔g7 18 b4 d3 19 ♕c4 ♕d5 20 ♕f4 ♗d7 21 ♔f1 ♖g8 22 g6! fxg6 23 ♗xg6 1-0 Lima-Lesiège, Biel IZ 1993) 10 gxf6 ♘hxf6 11 ♘g5 ♕e8 *(151)*

151
W

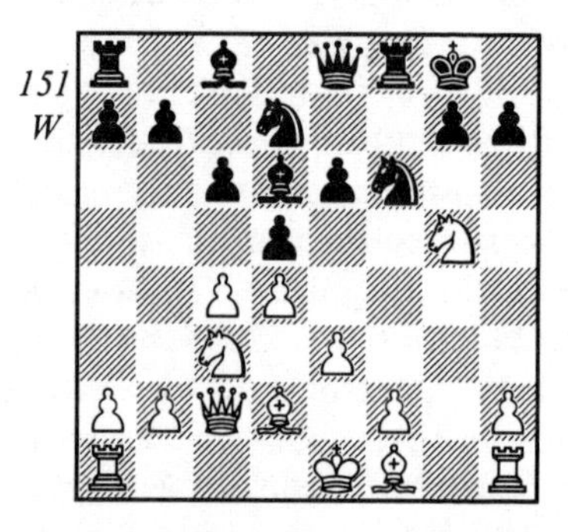

12 0-0-0 (Shirov's tactical alertness is quite even-handed; he points out that 12 f4 may allow Black to sacrifice a piece for counterplay with 12...e5 13 dxe5 ♘xe5!∞) 12...h6 13 h4 ♗b4! (13...hxg5? 14 hxg5 ♘e4 15 ♘xe4 dxe4 16 ♕xe4 ♖f5 17 c5! Δ♗c4 with a decisive attack – Shirov. Black's resourcefulness contributes much to the quality of this game throughout. Threatening to

control e4 renders White's 13th a genuine sacrifice) 14 ♗d3! ♗xc3 15 ♗xc3 hxg5 16 hxg5 ♘e4 17 ♗xe4 dxe4 18 ♕xe4 ♖f5 19 ♕h4 ♕g6 20 ♕h8+! (A very important check. White no longer has immediate prospects of a mating attack, but a clear strategy of creating mayhem by the advance of his centre pawns. To this end the weakness of Black's king's rook is crucial, and the text prevents its retreat) 20...♔f7 21 f4 ♘f8 (such is Black's coordination that 22 ♕d8 Δ♖h8 would have been instantly decisive) 22 ♕h4! ♔e8 23 e4 ♖f7 24 ♖he1 ♔d8 25 d5! cxd5 26 cxd5 ♗d7 (26...exd5? 27 ♖xd5 ♗d7 28 f5 is murder, but now White sacrifices one pawn to liberate his two centre pawns while keeping Black's pieces passive) 27 f5! exf5 28 e5 f4!? 29 e6 ♗a4 30 ♖d2 ♖f5 31 ♕f2! (it is much more important to keep Black's king hemmed in and the d6 square vulnerable to a decisive invasion, than to win back material with e7+ when Black would enjoy some freedom) 31...f3!? 32 ♖e4?! (as Shirov points out 32 ♕c5! ♔e8 33 ♕b4! b5 33 ♕c5! Δ♕c6+ was much more clinical) 32...♖g5 33 ♖xa4 ♖g1+ 34 ♖d1 ♖g2? (In time trouble Black eases White's task. More stubborn was 34...♕h6+ 35 ♕d2 f2 although White has a slightly intricate win with 36 ♖f4 ♖xd1+ 37 ♔xd1 ♕h1+ 38 ♔e2 ♘g6 39 ♖xf2 ♕e4+ 40 ♔d1! ♕b1+ 41 ♕c1 ♕d3+ 42 ♖d2 ♕f3+ 43 ♔c2 ♕e4+ 44 ♔b3 and finally the checks are exhausted) 35 ♕h4+ ♔e8 36 ♖e4 ♖c8 37 d6 ♖d8? 38 ♕e7# (1-0). An excellent initial piece of publicity work for 7 g4 !

b) **7...h6** appears to be a rather modest reaction, but White seems to be forced to seek an advantage along positional paths, which was clearly not his intention. White can switch to play along the lines of 7 h3 and ♗d2 considered above, when Black's counterplay will be a bit delayed. On the other hand White must never lose sight of the fact that 7 g4 is very committal. At the moment I prefer White, but not by much. Two moves have received attention in theory and practice:

b1) Pein gives **8 ♗d2!?** ♕e7! (8...♘xg4 9 ♖g1 ♘xh2 10 ♖xg7 still gives White good compensation. Compared with the main game, White has the useful ♗d2 preparing 0-0-0, and although ...h6 removes the inclination to defend h7, it is far from clear that this is Black's most urgent priority. Of course 8...0-0 looks premature since it invites g5) 9 h3 (9 ♗e2?! dxc4!; and 9 0-0-0? ♘xg4∓ are clearly inferior. 9 ♖g1 looks more aggressive than the text, but so long as Black avoids ...0-0, it is perhaps a good idea for White to retain the option of castling short. White tried another tack in the game Djurhuus-Grønn, Norwegian Ch

1993 with the simple exchange 9 cxd5!? which forces at least some unbalance since 9...cxd5? would be refuted by 10 ♘b5!. The game led to a slight plus for White after 9...exd5 10 ♗d3 c5 {10...♘xg4 11 ♖g1 ♘xh2 12 ♘xh2 ♗xh2 13 ♖xg7 gives play for the pawn closely resembling the main lines} 11 **0-0-0** c4 12 ♗e2±) 9...e5 10 cxd5 ♘xd5 (There seems to be no clear road to equality either with 10...cxd5 11 ♘b5 e4 12 ♖c1! ♘b6 13 ♘h4 ♘b6 14 ♕b3 {∞ Pein} when I think White's queenside pull counts for something) 11 ♘xd5 cxd5 12 dxe5 ♘xe5 13 ♘xe5 ♗xe5 14 ♗g2. Again White has a small plus, since **14...d4** 15 0-0 gives Black a slightly weak b7 and a lag in development, and **14...♗e6** 15 ♕a4+ the prospect of a pleasant ending for White.

b2) **8 ♖g1** dxc4?! (8...e5 9 cxd5 ♘xd5 {∞ Shirov} looks worth investigating, or simply 8...♕e7!? – Bareev) 9 ♗xc4 b5 (9...♘d5 should not be sufficient for equality. In Bagirov-Guliev, Berlin 1993 Black compounded his problems with passive play: 10 ♗d2 {a common theme in all the ...dxc4 positions, covering b4 and hence preparing ♘e4} 10...a6?! 11 ♘e4 ♗f8 {11...♗c7 12 g5! hxg5 13 ♘exg5 ♕f6 14 e4 ♘f4 15 e5!±} 12 a3 b6 13 h4?! {the immediate 13 g5 is more logical since if Black captures on g5 White would reply 14 ♘exg5 with serious threats against f7 in particular. If Black does not intend to capture, then h4 is a waste of tempo} 13...♗b7 14 g5 ♖c8 15 b4 hxg5 and even now 16 ♘exg5! would have given Black's king a serious headache) 10 ♗e2 ♗b7 11 e4 e5 12 ♗e3!? (Initiating an interesting pawn sacrifice which should be more than adequate. Bareev also regards 12 h4 as promising. Although there is a good deal of tension in the centre, White does not have to worry too much about starting a flank assault since if Black seeks clarification in the centre the white knight will come to f5 with great effect. To this end he also mentions the very direct 12 dxe5!? ♘xe5 13 ♘d4. The overall conclusion must be that Black's position is not satisfactory) 12...exd4 13 ♘xd4 ♗xh2 14 ♖h1 ♕c7 15 g5! hxg5 16 ♘cxb5 ♕b8 17 ♘c3 c5 18 ♘f3 g4 19 ♘xh2 ♖xh2 Dreev-Bareev, Biel IZ 1993, and now 20 ♖xh2 ♕xh2 21 0-0-0 would have given White a clear plus according to Bareev.

c) **7...dxc4!?**. As mentioned above, this was the World Champion's choice, found incidentally over the board. In the game Adams-Kasparov, Dortmund 1992, it led to rapid success after **8 e4?** (Of course Michael knows better than the rest of us that the text gives a very anti-positional impression. However he apparently simply overlooked Black's 10th, without which he would have been fine. The natural and best move 8 ♗xc4 will be considered below) 8...e5 9 g5 exd4 10 ♘xd4 *(152)*

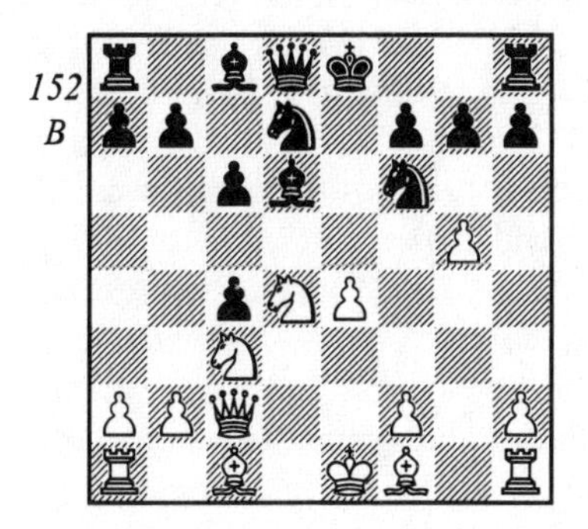

10...♘g4! (Clearly stronger than 10...♘h5 11 ♗xc4 when the thematic positional move 11...♗f4 fails tactically to 12 ♗xf7+ ♔xf7 13 ♕b3+ and 14 ♘e6. 11...♘b6 avoids this but White is very much in the battle) 11 h3 ♘ge5 12 ♗e3 ♘c5 (Black's control of d3 is already decisive, although it takes Kasparov's technique to make it look easy) 13 0-0-0 ♘ed3+ 14 ♔b1 ♕e7! (14...0-0?! 15 ♘f5! still gave counterchances. If now 15 ♘f5, then 15...♗xf5 16 exf5 0-0-0!) 15 ♖g1 g6 16 ♗g2 0-0 17 ♔a1?! ♗f4! 18 ♗xf4 ♘xf4 19 h4 ♖d8 20 ♕d2 ♘cd3 21 ♕e3 ♗g4 22 ♖d2 ♕e5 0-1. This game has historical interest, being Michael's first tournament encounter with the World Champion. More crucial to the understanding of 7...dxc4 are:

c1) **8 g5?!**. Motivated by the desire to exchange knights rather than have his own knight driven to the side of the board by ...b4, this move seems to be misguided. I am baffled by its appearance twice at the Interzonal in Biel, since there was nothing in that experience to revive its reputation. After the exchange of knights Black can apparently break in the centre and leave White's kingside looking distinctly loose. **8...♘d5 9 ♗xc4** and now:

c11) **9...e5** transposes to note 'c2' to Black's 8th.

c12) **9...b5** 10 ♗e2 (Shirov gives 10 ♗xd5 cxd5 11 ♘xb5 ♕a5+ 12 ♘c3 ♗a6∓ which looks horrible for White. 10 ♗f1 is similar to the text; maybe 10 ♗d3!? with similarities to Shirov-Akopian covered under 'c2') 10...♘xc3 11 bxc3 ♗b7 12 e4 e5 13 ♗e3 ♕e7 14 a4 a6 15 0-0 0-0 was Gomez-Baigorri, Zaragoza 1992. White has held up ...c5, but his kingside pawn thrust still seems very out of place.

c13) **9...♘xc3!? 10 bxc3** with two examples:

c131) **10...♕e7** 11 a4 e5 (11...b6!? M.Gurevich) 12 a5 (White is trying to tie the black pieces down and prevent obvious methods of development. The pawn storm on both wings is quite unusual but it is hard to believe it can be correct. Black also obtained good play against the immediate 12 h4 with 12...exd4 13 cxd4 ♘b6 14 ♗e2 ♘d5 15 ♘e5 ♗xe5 16 dxe5 ♗g4! in Goldin-B.Ivanović,

Yugoslavia 1993) 12...♖b8 13 h4 c5 (13...b5!?) 14 h5!? *(153)*

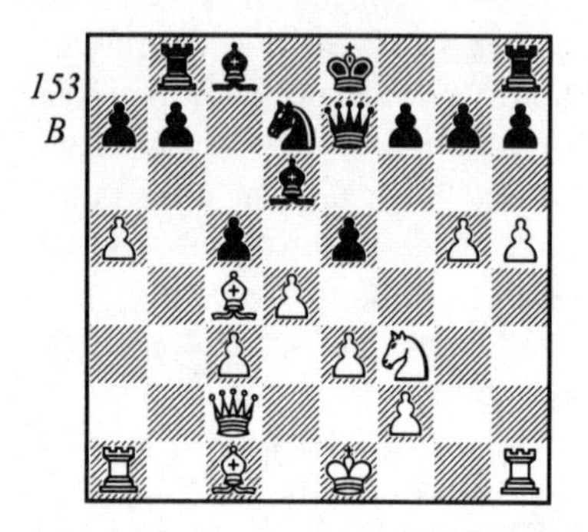

14...b5 15 axb6 axb6 16 ♗d5 ♗b7 17 ♗xb7 ♖xb7 18 ♖a8+ ♖b8 19 ♖a7 ♕e6 20 ♖h4!? ♖d8 21 dxe5 ♗b8! and White's position looks rather loose and later 0-1 (39); Dreev-M.Gurevich, Biel IZ 1993.

c132) **10...e5** 11 ♖g1!? (Δg6) 11...g6 (Illescas criticizes this and recommends instead 11...♕e7!∞) 12 ♗b2 ♕e7 13 h4 b5 14 ♗d3 ♗b7 15 ♗e4 ♖b8 16 ♖d1 (16 a4!?) 16...0-0 17 h5 c5! (the classic defensive/counterpunching break in the centre. It is clear that whilst in both these games White tried an interesting blend of attacking and consolidating moves, there is a diverse range of approaches for White here. Still, I stand by my gut feeling that after 8 g5?! White is a bit too overextended. Interestingly, Illescas is still quite positive about White's chances here) 18 hxg6 fxg6 19 ♗xb7 ♖xb7 20 ♕e4 ♖b6 21 dxe5 (21 ♕d5!± Illescas) 21...♘xe5 22 ♕d5+ ♘f7 23 ♖g4 c4 24 ♖e4 ♕b7 25 ♕xb7 ♖xb7∓ D.Gurevich-Illescas, Biel IZ 1993.

c2) **8 ♗xc4(!)**. It is unresolved as to how Black should best continue:

c21) Uhlmann mentions **8...♘xg4** 9 ♖g1 h5!? 10 h3 ♘h6 11 e4 ♔f8∞ but it would take a quite special breed of player to want to defend this.

c22) **8...e5!?** looked interesting on the strength of its first trial, but matters are no longer so clear. Black's break in the centre will leave White's kingside looking rather vulnerable. Krasenkov-Dokhoian, Bundesliga 1993 posed more questions than it answered: 9 g5 ♘d5 10 ♗d2(!) (10 ♘e4 ♗b4+ 11 ♗d2 ♕e7∞ or 10 ♗xd5?! cxd5 11 ♘xd5 0-0 which looks excellent value for Black) 10...exd4 **11 ♘xd5(?!)** cxd5 12 ♗xd5 dxe3 when according to Dokhoian the very double-edged **13 ♗c3!?** exf2+ 14 ♔xf2 0-0 15 ♖ad1 ♕c7! 16 ♖he1 ♘b6 17 ♗e4 g6; or **13 ♕e4+** ♕e7 14 ♕xe7+ ♔xe7 15 ♗e3 ♘b6 16 ♗e4 ♖e8 17 0-0-0 ♘c4 18 ♗d4 ♔f8∞ were both more promising than **13 fxe3?!** ♘b6 which was very comfortable for Black. In all cases, however, White's king looks every bit as vulnerable as Black's. Bagirov's **11 ♘xd4(!?)** looks like an improvement which yielded a strong attack after 11...♘7b6 (11...♘e5 is too extravagant, and 11...♕xg5? is much too greedy, being punished by an immediate piling in of the knights: 12 ♘e4 ♕g6 13 ♘f5!±) 12 ♗e2 ♘xc3 13 ♗xc3 ♘d5 (13...♕xg5 14 0-0-0 is still risky) 14 0-0-0 ♘xc3 15 ♕xc3 0-0 16 h4 ♕e7 17 ♖hg1⩲ (at least) Bagirov-Rai.Kleeschaetsky, Giesen 1993.

c23) **8...b5** leaves White with an important decision to make:

c231) **9 ♗d3!?** is Shirov's latest interesting contribution. 9...♗b7 10 g5 ♘d5 11 ♘e4 ♗e7 12 ♗d2! ♕b6 13 ♖c1 ♘b4 14 ♗xb4 ♗xb4+ 15 ♔e2 c5 16 a3 c4 17 axb4 ♗d5 18 ♘fd2 0-0 19 ♖hg1 e5 20 dxe5 ♖ad8 *(154)*

154
W

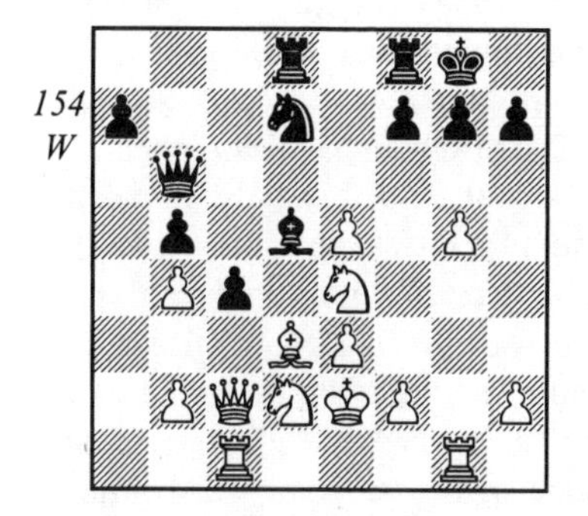

21 ♘f6+! ♘xf6 22 ♗f5± Shirov-Akopian, Biel IZ 1993. If Knaak's assessment of the important position in the next diagram is correct, White should try this, but I am not so sure.

c232) **9 ♗e2** ♗b7 (with 9...b4?! Black shows his hand much too soon, which eases White's task, e.g. 10 ♘a4 ♗b7 11 g5 ♘d5 12 ♗d2 c5 {12...♖c8? 13 ♘c5± Kasparov} 13 ♘xc5 ♗xc5 14 dxc5 ♖c8 {∞ Kasparov !} 15 e4! ♘e7 16 ♗xb4 ♘c6 17 ♗a3 and Black was very short on compensation in Krasenkov-Heyken, Bundesliga 1992) 10 g5 (10 ♗d2 is possible too, but Black can play 10...♖c8 when I can see nothing better than 11 g5, transposing to the line below. Also 10...h6 might be possible) 10...♘d5 11 ♘e4 (11 ♘xd5?! is almost certainly a bad exchange. After 11...cxd5, White's self-inflicted kingside weaknesses count for more than the passive bishop on b7) 11...♗e7 12 ♗d2! ♖c8! 13 ♘c5!? (Black's plan was executed without inconvenience in Michaelson-Knaak, Bundesliga 1992 after 13 ♖c1?! c5 14 dxc5 ♘xc5 15 ♘xc5 {15 ♗xb5+ ♘d7 16 ♕a4 ♖xc1+ 17 ♗xc1 0-0! Δ18 ♗xd7 ♘b6∓} 15...♖xc5 16 ♕b3 ♖xc1+ 17 ♗xc1 0-0∓. 13 ♖g1!? is a further possibility for those who do not like White's compensation in the main line) 13...♘xc5 14 dxc5 ♗xg5 15 ♘xg5 ♕xg5 16 0-0-0 e5 *(155)*.

155
W

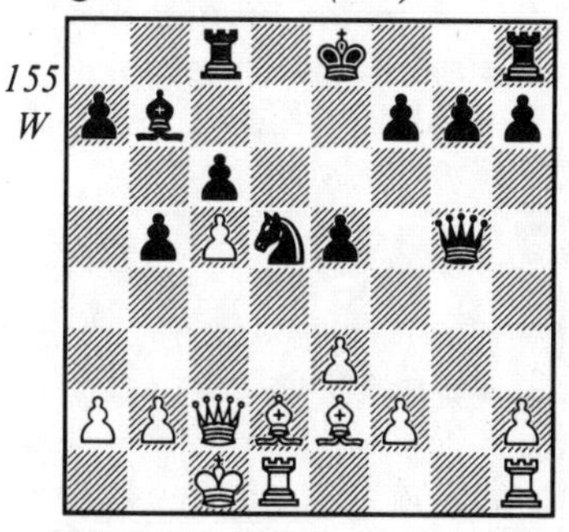

Knaak gives this position as ∓, but I had earlier analysed this and come to the conclusion that it is worth a try for White since the black bishop on b7 really is bad, and White has immediate attacking chances which may prevent the black king from fleeing the centre. For example White can try 17 ♖g1 ♕f6 18 ♗g4! ♖a8! 19 e4 ♘f4 20 ♗d7+! when either **20...♔xd7** 21 ♗xf4+ ♔c7 22 ♗g5 or **20...♔e7** 21 ♗a5! give Black real problems.

d) **7...♗b4!?** looks strange, but Black's plan of creating a square for the knight on e4 was by no means refuted in Krasenkov-Pekarek, Germany 1993. After 8 ♗d2 a5 (8...♕e7!? Krasenkov) 9 g5 ♗xc3 10 ♗xc3 ♘e4 11 ♖g1 ♕e7 12 ♗d3 ♘xc3 13 ♕xc3 ♕b4 14 ♔e2 ♕xc3 15 bxc3 Black could according to Krasenkov obtain equal play with 15...b6 Δ...♗a6, although I still slightly prefer White with 16 cxd5 exd5 17 ♖ab1 when 17...♗a6 18 ♗xa6 ♖xa6 19 ♖fc1 (Δc4) 19...b5?! 20 a4 bxa4 21 ♘e5 is rather awkward to meet.

8 ♖g1 ♘h6?!

Again a major parting of the ways. Black has also tried:

a) **8...♘xh2!? 9 ♘xh2 ♗xh2 10 ♖xg7** *(156)* and now:

156
B

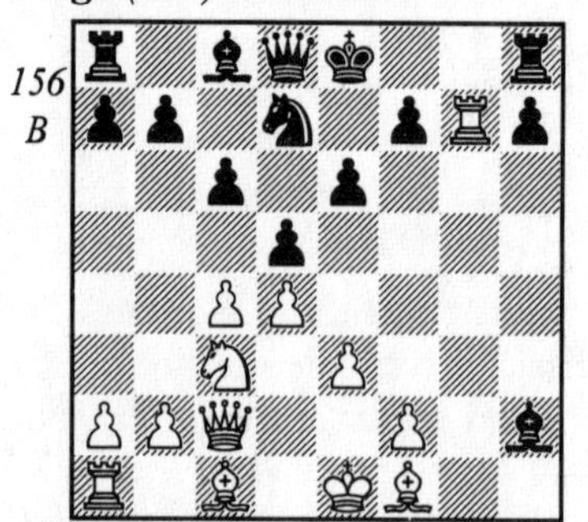

a1) **10...h6??** overlooks White's principal threat; it is interesting that a very strong computer should have made such an 'oversight'. Shabalov-*Mephisto Risc*, Neu Isenburg 1992 continued 11 f4 ♕h4+ 12 ♕f2 ♕xf2+ 13 ♔xf2 ♘f6 14 ♖g2! h5 15 ♖xh2 ♘g4+ 16 ♔g3 ♘xh2 17 ♔xh2+-.

a2) **10...♗d6** and **10...♕f6!?** have been variously suggested and the latter received a test in Rogozenko-Golubev, European Junior 1992 when after a few natural moves White initiated a very sharp sequence, viz. 11 ♖xh7 ♖xh7 12 ♕xh7 ♗d6 13 ♗d2 ♘f8 14 ♕c2 ♗d7 15 e4!? ♕xd4 16 ♗e3 ♕f6 and now instead of 17 0-0-0? d4!∓ White should play 17 exd5 exd5 18 0-0-0± (although still complicated).

a3) **10...♘f8(!)** neatly intends to meet White's threat to trap the bishop on h2 with a counter-trap of the rook by ...♘g6, whilst at the same time holding on to the extra pawn. If Black is willing to experience some temporary discomfort, then the text seems to be one of the most interesting counters to 7 g4. Interestingly Lukacs and Hazai have challenged the underlying premise of the move by recommending 11 f4 ♕h4+ 12 ♕f2 ♕xf2+ 13 ♔xf2 ♘g6 14 ♔g2 ♔f8 15 ♖xg6 hxg6 16 ♗d2 'and the bishop is trapped'. However Black should examine 16...e5!? 17 dxe5 g5∞; 17 fxe5 ♗h3+ 18 ♔f2 ♔g7∞ and if simply 17 ♗e2, 17...♗xf4!? 18 exf4 exd4 comes into consideration.

Practice has seen 11 ♖g2 and then:

a31) **11...♗c7?!** 12 e4! ♘g6 (12...dxe4 13 ♕xe4 is full compensation, whilst 12...dxc4!? – Djurhuus – is interesting but risky, e.g. 13 ♗g5 ♕xd4 14 ♖d1 ♕e5 {If 14...♕g7?! not 15 ♗f4? ♕xg2 16 ♗xg2 ♗xf4∓ but 15 ♕d2! with a very strong attack} 15 f4 ♕c5 16 ♗f6 and Black's compensation will be inadequate) 13 ♗g5! f6 14 ♗h6! ♘h4 15 0-0-0 ♘xg2 16 ♗xg2 dxc4 (the only try to keep the centre closed, but White's play down the g-file is fierce too) 17 ♗f3! ♕e7 18 ♗h5+ ♔d8 19 e5! ♖g8 (19...f5 20 ♖g1 is crushing) 20 ♘e4 f5 21 ♘f6 ♖g2 22 ♕xc4 ♗d7 23 ♕f1 (the last outpost on the g-file is undermined) 23...♖g7 24 ♗xg7 ♕xg7 25 ♕g1! ♕h6+ 26 f4 ♔c8 27 ♕g8+ ♗e8 28 ♗e8 ♗xf6 29 ♗xd7+ (29 exf6! was even clearer) 29...♔xd7 30 ♕xa8 ♕xf4+ 31 ♔b1 ♗d8 32 ♕xb7+ ♗c7 33 ♖g1 ♕h6 34 ♖c1 1-0 Djurhuus-Grønn, Oslo 1992.

a32) **11...♗d6** *(157)* is more natural, and probably stronger too.

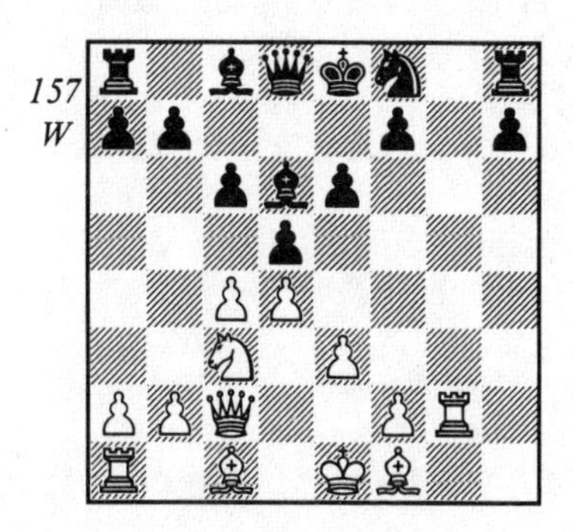
157
W

12 ♗d2 (12 e4 is less critical than above since Black's bishop can go to e7 in the event of ♗g5) 12...♗d7 13 0-0-0 a6 14 e4 ♖c8 15 ♖e1 ♗e7 16 f4 b5 17 c5 dxe4 18 ♘xe4 f5 was Garcia Ilundain-Illescas, Leon 1992, when instead of 19 ♘d6+, which just served to free Black, White could have posed interesting problems with 19 ♗e2. Overall, Black's plan of ...a6 and ...b5 looks over-ambitious and I think he should be alright in general here.

b) **8...f5** 9 h3 ♘gf6 10 ♖xg7 ♘e4 was given as unclear by Kasparov but it seems Black's task is unenviable after 11 ♗d2! ♕f6?! (11...♔f8± Krasenkov) 12 ♖g2 b6 13 ♕a4 ♗b7 14 cxd5 b5 (14...exd5 15 ♗a6! b5?! 16 ♕a5±; it is interesting how often White can switch to a positional approach in this line) 15 ♘xb5 cxb5 16 ♗xb5 ♖d8. This occurred in Krasenkov-Filipenko, Moscow 1992, when White could have best clarified his advantage and nullified Black's key resource ...f4 by the materialistic 17 ♗a5! ♔e7 18 ♗xd8+ ♖xd8 19 ♗c6 f4 20 ♕c2! (Krasenkov).

c) **8...h5!?** is a better version of the ...♘h6 idea, but I still prefer White's attacking chances, e.g. 9 h3 ♘h6 10 e4 (10 ♖xg7?? ♕f6 11 ♖h7 ♖xh7 12 ♕xh7 ♘f8∓/-+; 10 ♗d2!?) 10...dxe4 11 ♘xe4 ♗b4+ 12 ♗d2 ♗xd2+ 13 ♕xd2 ♘f6 14 ♘c3 ♘f5?! (Shirov gives 14...♖g8 15 0-0-0 ♗d7 16 ♘e5 ♕e7 as an improvement, but White could also investigate 16 d5!? or even 15 ♘e5 ♗d7 16 ♗d3 Δ16...♕e7 17 ♗h7!?) 15 0-0-0 ♔f8 16 ♗d3! ♗d7 when 17 ♕f4! would have given White a very strong initiative for the pawn in Shirov-Akopian, Oakham 1992.

d) **8...♕f6!?** is Black's most recent try, which also deserves further tests. **9 ♖xg4 ♕xf3 10 ♖xg7** and now:

d1) **10...♘f8** 11 ♖g1 ♗xh2 (12...♕h5!?) 12 ♗e2 ♕f6 (12...♕h3!? 13 ♖f1 Δ♗d2, 0-0-0, ♖h1∞) 13 e4! ♕xd4 14 cxd5 exd5 15 ♗e3 gives White a good attack for the pawn.

d2) **10...♘f6 11 ♖g5!?** (or 11 ♖g1 ♘e4 12 ♘xe4 ♕xe4 13 ♕xe4 dxe4 14 ♗g2 f5 15 f3 h5 16 ♗h1 exf3 17 ♗xf3 h4 18 h3 ♗d7 19 ♗d2± Fedorowicz-Vučić, New York 1993; maybe 11...♕h5) with these possibilities:

d21) **11...♕h1** 12 f4!±.

d22) **11...♘e4** 12 ♘xe4 ♕xe4 (12...dxe4(!) 13 ♗d2! ♗d7 14 ♗c3! 0-0-0! is unclear, but not 13 ♗g2? ♕f6! Δ14 ♖g4 e5!; or 14 ♖h5 ♕g6+-) 13 ♕xe4 dxe4 14 ♗g2 f5 15 h4!±.

d23) **11...♘g4?!** 12 h3! ♘h2 (12...♘h4 13 ♗g2 ♕f6 14 e4±) 13 ♗g2 ♕f6 14 f4 h6 15 ♖g3 ♕h4 16 ♕f2 ♗e7 (16...♗d7 17 ♗h1! {17 ♖g8+? ♖xg8 18 ♕xh4 ♖xg2∞/∓} 17...0-0-0 18 ♕xh2 ♖g8 19 ♘e2+-) 17 ♗h1 ♕h5 18 ♕xh2 (18 ♕e2!? ♕f5 19 ♖g2+-) 18...♗h4 19 ♔f1+- Wells-Dankers, Antwerp 1993.

9 e4

Again not **9 ♖xg7??** ♕f6 10 ♖xh7 ♖xh7 11 ♕xh7 ♘f8∓/-+, but **9 ♗d2!?** avoiding simplification is probably even stronger. Shirov-Bangiev, Hamburg 1993 looked very convincing for White after 9...♕e7 10 e4 dxe4 11 ♘xe4 ♘f5 12 0-0-0 ♘f6?! (Shirov offers nothing better than 12...b5± for Black here) 13 ♘xf6+ ♕xf6 14 ♗g5 ♕g6 15 c5 ♗c7 16 ♘e5 *(158)*

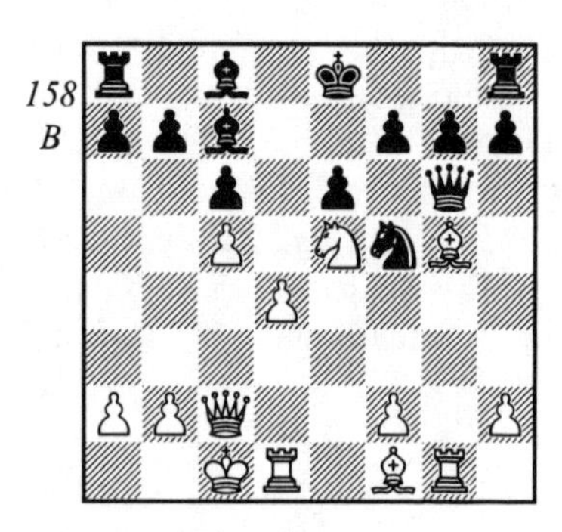

16...♕h5 (16...♗xe5 17 dxe5 f6 {17...0-0 18 ♗e2! Δh4-h5} 18 exf6 gxf6 19 ♕c3! e5 20 ♗c4! Δ21 ♕xe5+!+- is a nice illustration of White's possibilities here) 17 h4! ♗d8 18 ♕e4 0-0 19 ♗e2 ♗xg5+ 20 hxg5 ♕h4 21 f4 ♖d8 (21...f6!±) 22 ♖h1 ♘g3 23 ♖xh4 ♘xe4 24 ♗d3 ♘g3 25 ♖xh7 ♘e2+ 26 ♔b1 ♘xd4 27 g6! fxg6 28 ♗xg6 ♖d5 29 ♖dh1 ♔f8 30 ♖h8+ ♔e7 31 ♖e8+ ♔f6 32 ♖f8+ 1-0.

9 ...	**dxe4**
10 ♘xe4	**♗b4+**
11 ♗d2	**♗xd2+**
12 ♕xd2	**♘f5**

Krasenkov mentions the possibility of **12...♘f6** here, but either 13 ♘c3 or 13 ♗d3 with play similar to the game look good.

13 0-0-0 ♘f6

14 ♗d3

If Black's defensive resources around about move 17 are deemed adequate, then White may here investigate **14 ♘c3**, not so much to keep pieces on the board for the sake of it, but more to deny access to f6 for the black queen to join the defence. If Black elects to castle short, then the plan of ♘e5, ♗xf5 and ♕h6, in conjunction with doubling on the g-file is sufficiently dangerous for me to be unwilling to defend Black's position.

14 ... 0-0

15 ♖g2

Again perhaps **15 ♘e5!?** is more direct.

15 ... ♘xe4

16 ♗xe4 ♕f6

17 ♘e5 ♖d8?!

A clear error which gives White attractive combinational possibilities. Better chances were offered by either **17...♕h6** 18 f4 ♖d8, or even **17...g6!?** (Krasenkov).

18 ♘g4! ♕e7?

A second mistake is more than the critical Black position can stand. For better or worse, Black had to try his luck in the unpleasant exchanges arising from **18...♕xd4** 19 ♘h6+! ♔h8 (19...♔f8? 20 ♕b4+ +-) 20 ♘xf7+ ♔g8 21 ♘xd8 ♕xe4 22 f3! when material will be fairly balanced but Black's development problems and White's enduring pressure down the g-file add up to a large plus. The text allows a swift and pretty *denouement*.

19 ♗xf5 exf5

20 ♘h6+ ♔h8

21 ♖xg7!! *(159)*

159
B

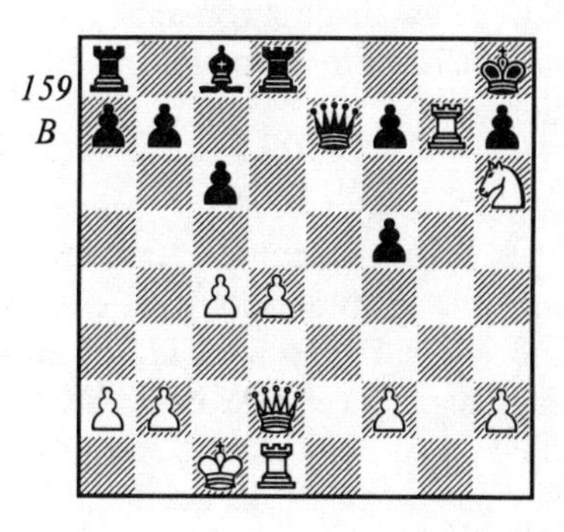

21 ... ♔xg7

Neither can Black politely decline with **21...♗e6** since White can initiate an onslaught on the diagonal too with 22 d5! ♕f6 23 ♖dg1 cxd5 24 ♖xf7! ♕e5 25 ♖xf5! and wins.

22 ♖g1+ ♔h8

23 ♕e2!

Neatly overworking the black queen. If 23...♗e6 24 ♘xf7+! and 25 ♕e5+ will decide.

1-0

20 7 e4

In this chapter we shall concentrate on 7 e4, which was the original intention behind 6 ♕c2, and for some time the main line. It received an outing and an apparent blow in the 1984 World Championship match when Kasparov countered with the surprising 7...e5 and equalized in a straightforward manner.

The recent evidence suggests that White can probably create rather more difficulties here, and hence the simple capture on e4 is once again recommended. After this Black has a choice of two lines which seem both viable, and less deadening than 7...e5 even in its successful form.

We shall also deal here with some rarely seen possibilities for both sides. For White, the move 6 ♗e2 had a brief vogue after Portisch used it to defeat Timman in their candidates match. If 6...dxc4 White plans the positional idea 7 a4 and ♘-d2xc4 which I feel thematically belongs better here than in the Meran section. It is quite playable, but not, I feel, too threatening.

Deviations for Black are considered here at two points. On move five, 5...a6 appears from time to time. Black prepares ...b5, with the additional point that 6 ♗d3 dxc4 7 ♗xc4 b5 and ...c5 leads to a QGA where White's knight is perhaps a bit prematurely committed to c3. Still, the move is a bit committal, and White can use this fact to secure some plus. Black's options at move six include Ljubojević's favourite 6...♗e7, but it is too passive to catch on widely.

Game 29
Gorelov-Kishnev
USSR 1984

1 c4 ♘f6 2 ♘f3 e6 3 ♘c3 d5 4 d4 c6 5 e3

5 ... ♘bd7

Rare alternatives for which White should be prepared:

a) **5...♘e4!?** (Speciality of the highly original Swedish GM Jonny Hector) 6 ♘e5!? (6 ♗d3 f5 7 ♘e5 ♕h4 8 0-0 ♗d6 9 ♗xe4!? dxe4 10 f4 0-0 11 ♕b3 b6 12 ♗d2± Farago-Hector, Geneva 1989) 6...♗b4 7 ♗d2 ♘xd2 8 ♕xd2 0-0 9 c5! ♘d7 10 ♘d3 ♗a5 11 ♗e2 ♗c7 12 f4!± Kupreichik-Hector, Torcy 1989.

b) **5...a6** and now:

b1) **6 b3** (6 cxd5?! still gives White a bad QGD exchange, which ...a6 in no way justifies) 6...♗b4 7 ♗d2 ♘bd7 (7...0-0 8 ♗d3 b5!? 9 0-0 bxc4 10 bxc4 dxc4 11 ♗xc4 c5 12 a3 cxd4 13 axb4 dxc3 14 ♗xc3±

but quite playable for Black; Salov-P.Nikolić, Wijk aan Zee 1992) 8 ♗d3 0-0 9 0-0 ♗d6 10 e4 dxc4 11 bxc4 (11 ♗xc4!?) 11...e5 12 c5!? ♗c7 13 ♘a4 exd4 14 h3 ♖e8! 15 ♖e1 with chances for both sides in a very complex position; Kasparov-Gelfand, Linares 1991 (by transposition).

b2) **6 c5!?** ♘bd7 (6...b6 7 cxb6! ♘bd7 8 ♘a4 ♘xb6 9 ♗d2±) 7 b4 g6 8 ♗b2 ♗g7 9 ♗e2 0-0 10 0-0 ♕e7 11 ♘a4 ♘e4 12 ♗d3 f5 13 ♘e5± *ECO*.

b3) **6 ♕c2** ♘bd7 (6...b5!?) 7 b3 (7 e4 dxe4 8 ♘xe4 ♘xe4 9 ♕xe4 ♗b4+ is similar to note 'c' to Black's 9th in our main game, except that Black has the extra move ...a6. This should by no means harm his prospects) 7...b5 (7...♗d6 8 ♗b2 0-0 9 ♗e2 dxc4 10 bxc4 c5!? 11 d5?! exd5 12 ♘xd5 ♘xd5 13 cxd5 ♕e7 14 0-0 ♖e8 with counterplay; Schlosser-Chernin, Altensteig 1991) 8 ♗d3 ♗e7 9 0-0 0-0 10 ♗b2 ♗b7?! (10...bxc4!?) 11 c5 ♕c7 12 ♘e2 ♔h8 13 ♘g3± Kharitonov-Barczay, Sochi 1979.

6 ♕c2

Two other moves merit a mention. 'b' in particular has again fallen from favour after a brief flurry of interest, but it is not yet clear which is Black's best approach:

a) **6 a3** ♗d6 (6...g6!? Smyslov) 7 b4 0-0 8 ♗b2 ♕e7 9 ♕c2 e5 (9...♖e8!? 10 h3 a6 11 c5 ♗c7 12 ♗d3 e5 13 dxe5 ♘xe5 14 ♘xe5 ♗xe5 15 0-0 ♗c7 16 ♖ae1 ♘e4∞ Tisdall-Skembris, Gausdal 1993) 10 cxd5 e4?! (10...cxd5∞) 11 dxc6 exf3 12 cxd7 fxg2 13 ♗xg2 ♗xd7± Kir. Georgiev-Lukacs, Bulgaria 1990.

b) **6 ♗e2!?** and now Black has:

b1) **6...dxc4** 7 a4!? (7 ♗xc4 is of course Section 2) 7...♗d6 (7...♗b4!? 8 0-0 0-0 9 ♗xc4 ♕e7 10 ♕c2 e5 11 h3 a5 12 ♖d1 e4 13 ♘g5 ♘b6 14 ♗b3 ♗f5 15 f3 ♘bd5 16 fxe4 ♗g6 17 ♕f2 ♘xc3 18 bxc3 ♗xc3 19 ♗a3 ♗b4∞ Finegold-Kuijf, Wijk aan Zee 1991) 8 ♘d2 0-0 9 ♘xc4 ♗c7 10 b3 ♘d5 (10...e5 11 ♗a3!±) 11 ♗b2 b6 12 0-0 ♗b7 13 ♗f3 ♖b8 Portisch-Timman, Ct 1989, 14 g3! (Timman) Δe4±.

b2) **6...♗d6** 7 0-0 0-0 8 b3 ♘e4!? (The other main point of 6 ♗e2, this time an advantage over 6 ♕c2, is seen after 8...♕e7 9 ♗b2 dxc4 10 bxc4 e5 11 ♕b3! ♖e8 12 ♖fe1 e4 13 ♘d2 ♘f8 14 a4± Dzhandzhgava-Testa, Rome 1990 since White's queen has a more active posting than in the analogous positions from Chapter 21) 9 ♗b2 (9 ♘xe4 dxe4 10 ♘d2 f5 11 c5 ♗c7 12 ♘c4 ♘f6 13 f4 exf3 14 ♗xf3 ♗d7= Miles-Smagin, Philadelphia 1989) 9...f5 10 ♖c1 (10 ♘e1!? b6 11 f4 ♗b7 12 ♘f3 ♘df6 13 ♘xe4 ♘xe4 14 ♗d3 c5 15 ♕e2 ♖c8 16 ♖fd1 ♕e7 17 a4± Larsen-Smagin, Valby 1991) 10...♕f6 11 ♖c2?! ♕h6 12 ♘a4 g5 13 ♘e5 g4 14 ♕e1 ♕g7 15 ♘d3?! ♖f6 16 ♘f4 ♖h6 with strong kingside counterplay in Rohde-Machulsky, New York 1990.

6 ... ♗d6

Almost universally played, since it is appropriate to the full range of plans outlined in the introduction. Others:

a) **6...♗e7** 7 b3 (7 ♗e2 0-0 8 0-0 b6 9 cxd5?! {9 b3} 9...exd5 10 b3 ♗b7 11 ♗b2 ♖e8 12 ♘e5 c5∞ Epishin-Ljubojević, Reggio Emilia 1991; not 7 e4? dxe4 8 ♘xe4 e5! 9 dxe5 ♘xe5∓) 7...0-0 8 ♗e2 b6 9 0-0 ♗b7 and White plays for e4, with a slight edge, but Black is very solid.

b) **6...♗b4** 7 ♗d3 (7 ♗e2, 7 a3 and 7 ♗d2 are all reasonable too) 7...0-0 8 0-0 ♕e7 9 ♗d2 dxc4 10 ♗xc4 ♗d6 11 h3 a6 12 ♗b3 (12 a3!?; basically White is a tempo up on positions similar to Game 34) 12...c5 13 ♘e4 ♘xe4 14 ♕xe4 e5 15 ♖fe1 ♘f6 16 ♕h4 e4 17 dxc5 ♗xc5 18 ♘d4± Krasenkov-Serper, USSR Ch 1991.

7 e4 *(160)* **dxe4**

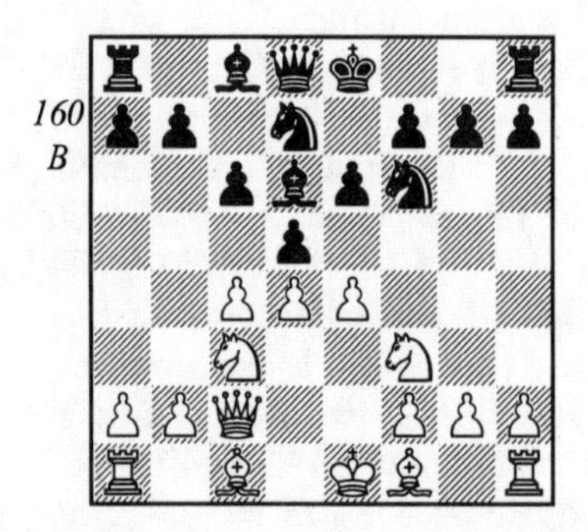

160
B

7...♘xe4 of course has no independent significance. However, since the 33rd game of the Karpov-Kasparov, Moscow 1984/85 World Championship marathon, where Black equalized with some ease, **7...e5** has been regarded as a legitimate alternative. Latest evidence confirms that the ensuing central clearance does indeed solve the majority of Black's problems, but perhaps because Black aspires to little more than sterile equality it has never really caught on, e.g. **8 cxd5 cxd5 9 exd5 exd4 10 ♘xd4 0-0**:

a) **11 ♗e2 ♘b6** and now:

a1) **12 0-0** ♘bxd5 13 ♘xd5 ♘xd5 14 ♖d1 ♕e7 15 ♗f3 ♖e8! 16 g3 ♗h3 17 ♗d2 ♗e5 18 ♗xd5 ♗xd4 19 ♗c3 ♗xc3 20 ♕xc3 ½-½ Karpov-Kasparov, Moscow Wch (33) 1984/85.

a2) **12 ♗g5** and now:

a21) Gufeld's suggestion **12...♘bxd5!?** 13 ♘xd5 ♕a5+ 14 ♕c3 (14 ♕d2 avoids a subsequent pin on the h8-a1 diagonal, but invites one on the d-file and is hence no improvement) 14...♕xd5 15 ♗xf6 gxf6 looks quite interesting for Black. In general the dark squares should be enough to balance the split pawns, and here 16 0-0? ♗e5 17 ♖ad1 ♖d8 is embarrassing.

a22) **12...h6** (this looks adequate) 13 ♗h4 ♗e7! 14 ♕b3 ♘bxd5 15 ♖d1 ♕a5 16 0-0 ♘xc3 17 bxc3 ♗d7! 18 ♕xb7 ♖ab8 19

♕a6 ♕xc3= Mascariñas-Flear, Aosta 1989.

b) **11 ♘f5** ♘b6 12 ♘e3 (after 12 ♘xd6 ♕xd6 Black's extra mobilization is worth the bishop pair) 12...♗e5=.

c) **11 ♗g5!?** is met logically by 11...♘b6.

8 ♘xe4 **♘xe4**
9 ♕xe4 **c5** *(162)*

An important moment since Black's various possibilities can lead to quite different styles of game. In recent years Black's defences have been considerably strengthened after the text (this game playing no mean role in that!) and it has emerged as the most popular, but others are still important. To summarize the main lines:

a) **9...♘f6** is a reasonable try since White's queen reaches a less active posting. It is still a bit passive though. **10 ♕c2** ♗b4+!? 11 ♗d2 ♗xd2 12 ♕xd2 and now 12...♘e4! is the justification of Black's idea. Neither the ending after **13 ♕e3** ♕a5+ (Donchev-Stefanov, Bulgaria 1984) nor **13 ♕b4** c5! 14 dxc5 ♕c7 (Donaldson/Silman) looks to give anything clear.

b) **9...♗b4+** seeks both to simplify and, albeit temporarily, to misplace White's knight. Black has chances to break subsequently with either ...c5 or ...e5. **10 ♗d2 ♗xd2+ 11 ♘xd2** and now:

b1) **11...♕a5** 12 0-0-0! ♕xa2 13 ♗d3 looks good value for a pawn.

b2) **11...c5!?** is an interesting option. In Kindermann-Tatai, Dortmund 1981, Black had few problems after 12 dxc5 ♕a5 **13 ♗e2** ♕xc5 14 0-0 ♘f6 15 ♕c2 ♗d7 16 a3 0-0 17 b4 ♕c7. If **13 c6** ♘c5 14 ♕e3 bxc6 15 a3 ♖b8. The onus is on White here.

b3) **11...0-0** (preparing to strike in the centre with ...e5) 12 0-0-0 e5!? 13 dxe5 ♕a5 14 ♗d3 g6 15 ♗b1 ♕xe5! 16 ♖he1 ♕g7 17 ♕f4 ♘b6 18 ♖e7 ♘a4! 19 ♕e5 ♕xe5 20 ♖xe5 ♖d8 21 ♗c2 and White was for preference in Chandler-Torre, Hastings 1980/81, but Black need not lose this position.

c) **9...e5!?** is by far the most combative of Black's alternatives. Its credentials have for some time been rightly judged by the validity (after 10 dxe5) of 10...0-0, which for a while looked wholly adequate. Then White's impressive performance in Mikhalchishin-Flear led to the belief that White's queen sacrifice was just too strong. Since then new ideas have been found for the Black and the situation now is unclear.

Thus after **10 dxe5** (10 ♗d3?! f5! Δ11 ♕xf5 ♘f6 12 ♕g5 e4 13 bxe4 ♘xe4 14 ♕xg7 ♕f6∓ is a nice trap; and 10 c5?! ♗e7! 11 ♘xe5 ♘xe5 12 ♕xe5 0-0 is too greedy by half) **10...0-0!** is without doubt Black's best, leaving White no good alternative to 'sacrificing' his queen for rook, piece and pawn, with **11 exd6! ♖e8 12**

♕xe8+ ♕xe8+ 13 ♗e3 *(161)* and now:

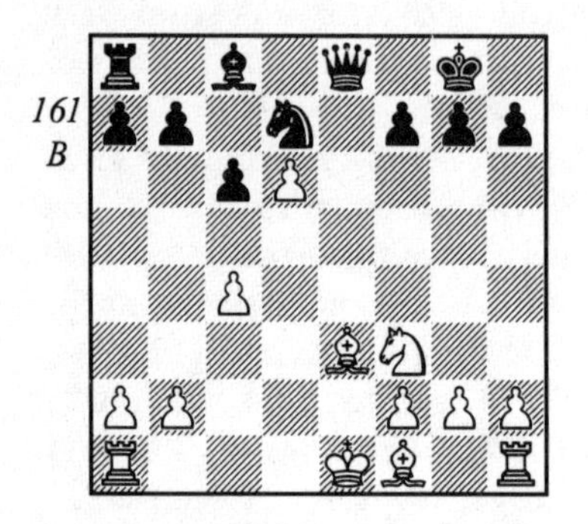

161
B

c1) The stem game for the entire line was Black's decidedly unpleasant experience in Mikhalchishin-G.Flear, Mexico 1980: **13...♘e5?** 14 0-0-0 ♘xf3 (14...♘g4 15 ♗d3 ♘xe3 16 ♖he1± Mikhalchishin) 15 gxf3 ♗d7 16 ♗d3 ♕e5 17 ♖hg1 g6 18 f4 ♕f6 19 f5! b6 20 ♗c2 ♕h4 21 ♔b1 c5 22 ♗g5 ♕xf2 23 fxg6 hxg6 24 ♖df1 ♕d4 25 ♗e7 a5 26 h4 and Black was under serious pressure.

c2) **13...♕e6** seeks to create counterplay on the queenside.

c3) **13...♘b6!?** 14 ♗d3 ♗e6 15 0-0-0! ♖d8 16 ♖he1 h6 17 ♘e5 ♖xd6!? 18 c5 ♖xd3 19 ♖xd3 ♘d5 and Black's domination of the light squares and queenside counterplay produce a situation where the queen outweighs the two rooks.

c4) **13...♘f6 14 0-0-0** and now:

c41) **14...♗e6** 15 ♗d3 b5 (after 15...♖d8 16 b3 ♗g4 17 ♗f4! ♗xf3 18 gxf3 ♘h5 19 ♖he1± Dorfman-Sveshnikov, USSR 1980) 16 c5! ♗xa2 17 ♖he1 (John Watson) and the weakness of c6 is a key factor in several variations, e.g. **17...♕e6** 18 ♗g5 ♕g4 19 ♗xf6 ♕f4+ 20 ♖d2 ♕xf6 21 ♘e5 Δ21...♗d5 22 ♗xb5!±; or **17...♗b3** 18 ♗g5 ♕d8 19 ♘d4!, in both cases with a clear plus.

c42) **14...♗f5** 15 ♗d3 ♗xd3 16 ♖xd3 ♕e6 17 b3 a5 (17...♘d7 18 ♖hd1 ♕g6 19 g3 ♖e8 20 ♗d4! {threatening ♘e5} 20...♕xd6 Andruet-Bryson, Lucerne OL 1982, could have been strongly met with 21 ♗xg7! ♕g6 22 ♗c3 when White has a new front of attack) 18 ♖hd1 a4!? 19 d7 ♖d8 20 ♗g5 ♖xd7 21 ♖xd7 ♘xd7 22 ♖e1 ♕g4 23 ♖e8+ ♘f8 24 ♗e7 h6 25 ♖xf8+ ♔h7 26 ♗c5 f6 and strangely Black's queen gives sufficient play on the light squares which White's pieces are ill-suited to counter; Shneider-Chekhov, USSR 1982.

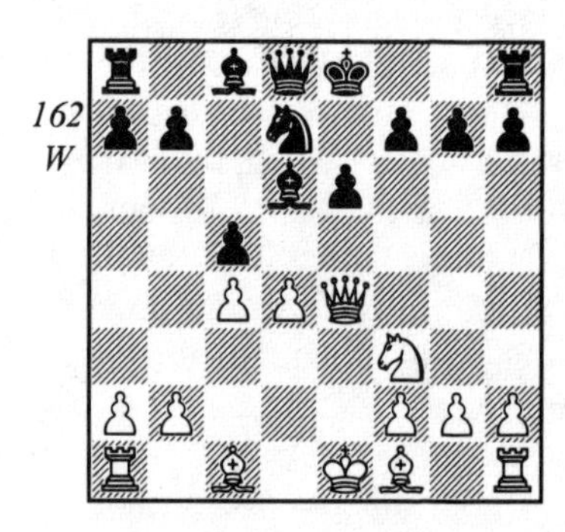

162
W

10 ♗g5

Also important, indeed probably to be preferred, is **10 ♗d2 ♘f6** and now:

a) **11 ♕h4?!** cxd4 12 ♕xd4 (12 ♘xd4 ♗e5! 13 ♗c3? g5!) 12...e5!

13 ♕e3 (13 ♘xe5 ♕e7 14 f4 ♗c5 with excellent play -Chernin/Dvoretsky) 13...0-0 14 h3 ♕c7 15 ♗e2 b6 16 0-0 ♗b7 17 ♕b3 ♘e4 18 ♗e3 ♘4c5 19 ♕c2 a5 20 ♖ad1 f5 with active play for Black in Grønn-Shabalov, Gausdal 1991.

b) **11 ♕d3** cxd4!? 12 ♘xd4 0-0 13 ♗e2 e5 14 ♘b5 ♗c5 15 b4 ♗e7 16 ♕xd8 ♖xd8 17 ♘c7 ♖b8 and White was looking a bit over-stretched in Burnett-Kaidanov, USA 1992.

c) **11 ♕c2** cxd4 12 ♘xd4 ♗c5 (I prefer Chernin's later suggestion of 12...♗d7 and ...♕c7, hindering short castling) 13 ♘b3 ♗e7 14 ♗e2 ♕c7 15 0-0 ♗d7 16 ♖ac1 ♖ac8 17 ♘d4 0-0 18 ♖fd1 a6 and White's queenside majority gives at best a nominal plus; Smyslov-Chernin, Subotica IZ 1987.

10 ... ♗e7

Again the text is not compulsory, but the main alternatives perhaps represent an unnecessary risk:

a) **10...♕a5+?!** 11 ♗d2 ♕c7 12 0-0-0! ♘f6 13 ♕h4 cxd4 14 ♘xd4 ♗d7 15 ♔b1 a6 16 ♗d3 0-0-0? 17 c5! ♗e5 18 c6 ♗xd4 19 cxd7+ ♕xd7 20 ♗a5 with a crushing attack in Silman-Pollard, San Francisco.

b) **10...♘f6** 11 ♕h4 cxd4 12 0-0-0 e5 (otherwise after 12...♗e7 White is again able to reach the 'ideal' attacking formation with 13 ♗d3 and ♖he1) 13 ♗d3 h6 (Polugaevsky suggests 13...♗e6!?) 14 ♖he1 (14 ♘xe5!? is interesting too, since 14...♗xe5 15 ♖he1 0-0 16 ♖xe5 hxg5 17 ♖xg5 gives an overwhelming attack, and 14...0-0 15 ♗xh6! is dangerous) 14...0-0 15 ♗xh6 gxh6 16 ♕xh6 ♖e8 17 ♘g5 ♗e6 18 ♗h7+ ♘xh7! 19 ♕xh7+ ♔f8 20 ♕h6+ ♔e7 (after 20...♔g8, 21 ♖e4!? is an interesting alternative to repeating) 21 ♘xe6 ♖h8! 22 ♘xd8 ♖xh6 23 ♘xb7 ♔d7 24 ♘xd6 ♔xd6 25 f4 f6 and despite the two pawn deficit Black's mobile centre pawns gave him sufficient counterplay to hold the balance in Dorfman-Dolmatov, Rostov 1980.

11 ♗xe7 ♕a5+! *(163)*

163
W

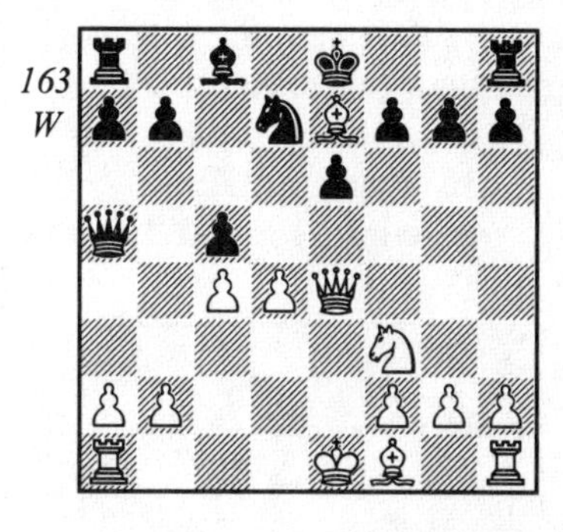

The novelty which did much to put 9...c5 back on the map. The obvious but inferior **11...♕xe7** had led, after 12 0-0-0 cxd4 13 ♕xd4 to a comfortable plus for White in Dorfman-Sveshnikov, USSR 1980. Kishnev's excellent discovery is that the misplacement of White's knight on d2 is much more disruptive than the slight inconvenience to the black king, especially since the black rook develops in one go to its best square, d8.

12 ♘d2 ♔xe7
13 0-0-0 ♖d8!

Black correctly assesses that the priority for both attack and defence is to bring the rook with all haste to harry White's centre. By contrast the greedy **13...♕xa2?!** 14 ♗d3 would turn out to be no more than a gesture of counterplay after which the situation of Black's king would become a serious question.

14 ♕xh7

For White too, development with **14 ♗d3** should have been given priority. White's kingside pawn-snatching only serves to enable Black to dominate the d-file and harass the white queen.

14 ... ♘f6
15 ♕xg7 ♖xd4
16 ♕g5 ♗d7! *(164)*

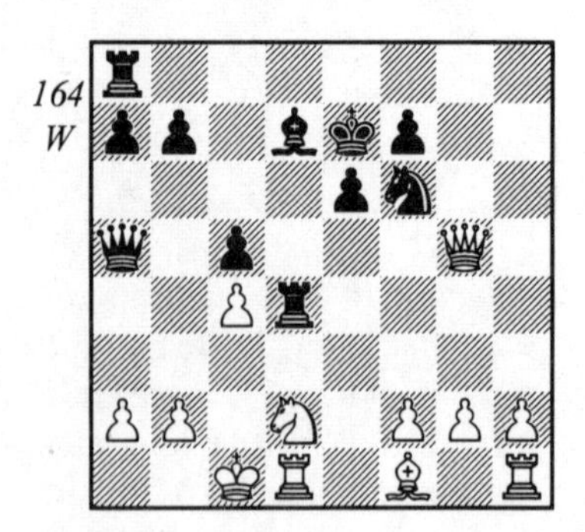

Directed against White's intended **17 ♘b3** which could now be well met with 17...♖xd1+ 18 ♔xd1 ♗a4!.

17 ♗d3 ♖g8

Of course not **17...♖xd3??** 18 ♘e4! and the direction of the play shifts 180 degrees. After the powerful text White must seek refuge in the exchange of queens, but Black's pressure persists.

18 ♘b3 ♖xg5
19 ♘xa5 ♖xg2
20 ♘xb7 ♘g4!
21 ♘xc5 ♘xf2
22 ♖d2 ♗c6

Also very strong was **22...♘xd3+** 23 ♘xd3 ♖xc4+ 24 ♔d1 ♖xd2+ 25 ♔xd2 ♖h4! 26 h3 ♔d6 and Black's e- and f-pawns should decide.

After the text, the battle proceeded: **23 ♖f1 ♘xd3+ 24 ♘xd3 ♖xc4+ 25 ♔d1 ♖d4 26 ♖ff2** (26 ♖f4 promised no joy either after 26...♖xd2+ 27 ♔xd2 ♗e4! 28 ♔e3 ♖xd3+ 29 ♔xe4 ♖d2 and White's pawns will be 'Hoovered') **26...♖xf2 27 ♘xf2 ♖h4 28 h3 e5 29 ♖d3 ♖a4!** (By forcing a3, Black prevents counterplay against the a7 pawn and thus frees the rook for exclusively offensive duties).

Henceforth with the superior minor piece and two mobile pawns Black encountered no real resistance: **30 a3 ♖f4 31 ♔e1 f5 32 ♖c3 ♔d6 33 ♘d1 ♖e4+ 34 ♖e3 ♖d4 35 ♖e2 ♖h4 36 ♖e3 e4 37 ♖c3 f4 38 ♔f2 ♖h6 39 b4 ♗b5 40 ♖c5 ♗d3 41 ♘b2 ♖xh3 42 ♘xd3 ♖xd3 43 ♖a5 0-1.**

21 7 b3

This chapter considers in detail the quite varied structures arising from 7 b3. This seems to me to be an interesting alternative to 7 ♗e2, although there are considerable transpositional possibilities between the two. These I shall try to point out, but the most obvious is that Game 35 should certainly be studied in conjunction with 7 b3. Indeed the whole approach with ...♖e8, and ...b6, which Kramnik's enormous talent has revealed to be more than just a passive waiting strategy, is highly pertinent to the assessment of both 7 b3 and 7 ♗e2. The main game considers the popular structures which arise after Black captures at some stage on c4 and White replies bxc4. These lead to situations of enormous tension in the centre, but White has more space if Black subsequently exchanges on d4, and queenside chances after ...e4.

Game 30
Karpov-M.Gurevich
Reggio Emilia 1991/2

1 d4 d5 2 c4 c6 3 ♘f3 ♘f6 4 ♘c3 e6 5 e3 ♘bd7 6 ♕c2 ♗d6
7 b3 *(165)*

165
B

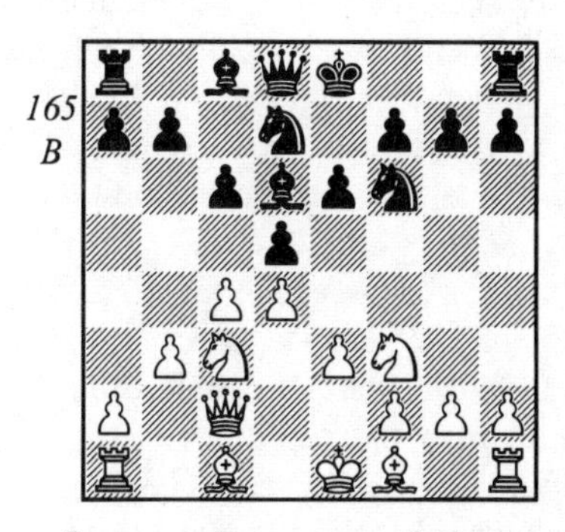

In my view, one of the most promising set-ups for White after 6 ♕c2. White delays playing for e4 until he has completed his development and places his queen's bishop on a diagonal which, whilst temporarily blocked, will become opened in the event of Black effecting either of his 'freeing breaks' ...e5 or ...c5. In addition White gains the important option of answering ...dxc4 with bxc4, giving him a central majority, and sometimes play on the b-file too. The line has many similarities with those variations of 7 ♗e2 where Black eschews the early capture on c4. Indeed, whilst here we shall touch upon lines with ...b6 which are independent to 7 b3, the main treatment of this recently very fashionable approach will be found in Game 35.

7 ... 0-0

8 ♗e2

Clearly the right square for this bishop, since ♗d3 would run into ...e5, the text is also regarded as more accurate than the immediate **8 ♗b2**. This is principally because Black can then reply **8...e5** 9 cxd5 cxd5 10 dxe5 ♘xe5 when **11 ♘b5?!** is dubious on account of 11...♗b4+ 12 ♗c3 ♗xc3+ 13 ♕xc3 ♘e4 14 ♕c7 ♘xf3+ 15 gxf3 ♕f6 16 ♘d4 ♘g5∓ Antoshin-Nei, Zinnowitz 1966. Of course, White could play the more circumspect **11 ♗e2**, but comparing Game 35, the general feeling is that White's b3 and ♗b2 is a bit committal here.

When White has chosen 8 ♗b2, the motivation has usually been an early long castling which has led to a couple of examples which deserve a mention. For example **8...dxc4** 9 ♗xc4 e5 10 0-0-0 ♕e7 11 ♘b1!? a5 with sharp play; Bronstein-Dvoretsky, Tbilisi 1980. Otherwise 8 ♗b2 loses flexibility. Our main game shows this well – White adopts a very modern approach where ♗b2 is delayed in the interests of direct pressure on the b-file.

8 ... dxc4

The relative leisureliness of White's build-up has the corollary of widening Black's choice of defensive set-ups. In addition to the text Black can consider 8...♖e8, often as a preparation for similar play; the immediate break in the centre with 8...e5 (which however seems less favourable than in Chapter 22), the same idea with the preparatory ...a6; or simple completion of mobilization with ...b6.

a) **8...e5 9 cxd5** and now:

a1) **9...cxd5!?** is generally regarded as dubious on account of the immediate **10 ♘b5 ♗b4+** (the point is that 10...♗b8?! 11 ♗a3 and ♘d6 favours White) 11 ♗d2 ♗xd2 12 ♘xd2, but Black's task does not seem unacceptably onerous after 12...a6! (12...e4?! 13 0-0 a6 14 ♘c3 ♘b6 15 a4 ♗e6 16 a5 ♘c8 17 b4 with a queenside initiative in Lputian-Anastasian, Protvino Z 1993) 13 dxe5 ♘xe5 14 ♘d4 ♗g4!? (14...♗d7 is not so bad either. The exchange of dark-squared bishops in such IQP positions does reduce Black's kingside counterchances a little, but White's queenside is a little weakened, and Black is quite solid) 15 ♗xg4 ♘eg4 16 h3 ♘e5 17 0-0 ♖c8 without serious problems for Black in Lev-Dreev, Arnhem 1988. Of course White can also choose the quieter **10 dxe5** ♘xe5 11 **0-0** but this would not threaten the validity of 9...cxd5.

a2) **9...♘xd5 10 ♘xd5 cxd5 11 dxe5 ♘xe5**. Now praxis has shown that while the check on b4 (which it seems White should allow) is slightly inconvenient, the weakness of d5 more than compensates:

a21) The exchange of knights on d5 is revealed very graphically to favour Black if White incautiously castles. **12 0-0?** is quite rightly one of chess's famous opening traps (observe the quality of the victims!) since after 12...♘xf3+ 13 ♗xf3 ♕h4! White has no good reply, e.g. **14 g3** ♕f6 15 ♗xd5? (but even 15 ♗g2 ♗f5! 16 e4 ♖ac8 17 ♕b1 ♗xe4 costs a pretty clear pawn) 15...♗f5! 16 e4 ♗h3 17 ♖d1 ♗e5! (17...♕f3?? 18 e5) **0-1** L.Lengyel-Hamann, Barcelona 1973; or **14 h3** ♗xh3! 15 ♖d1 ♗h2+ 16 ♔f1 ♕f6 17 ♗xd5 ♗f5 18 e4 ♗g4 19 ♗a3 ♕a6+ 0-1 Portisch-Ribli, Montpellier Ct 1985.

a22) **12 ♗b2! ♗b4+** *(166)*:

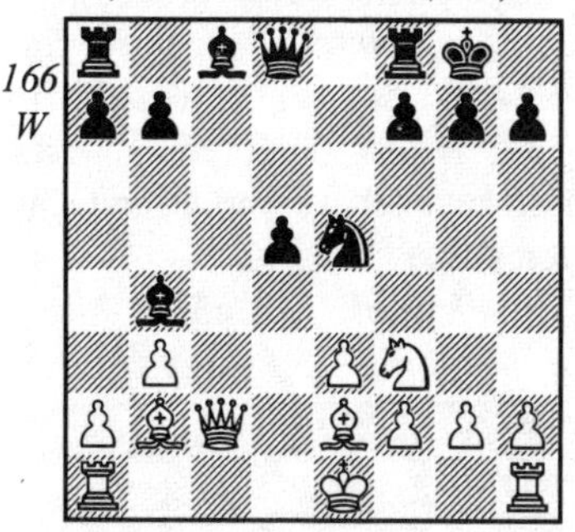
166
W

a221) **13 ♗c3** causes no problems after 13...♘xf3+ 14 ♗xf3 ♗f5!? (14...♕c7!? 15 ♖c1 ♗a3 16 ♗b2 ♕a5+ 17 ♗c3 ♕c7= Foisor) 15 ♕d2 ♗xc3 16 ♕xc3 ♖c8!? (Hübner also gives 16...♗e4 as dead equal) with balanced play.

a222) **13 ♔f1!** ♘xf3 (In principle Black would prefer not to simplify, but 13...♘c6?! allowed White to weaken Black's structure further in Portisch-Lukacs, Budapest 1986 with 14 h4! ♗e7 {14...h6? fails to discourage 15 ♘g5!} 15 ♘g5 g6 16 ♖d1 ♗f6 17 ♘e4±; maybe 13...♘g4 is worth consideration) 14 ♗xf3 ♗e6 15 ♕d3 (Rogozenko suggests 15 ♔e2 ♗e7 16 ♖hd1 ♗f6 17 ♖ac1± where again Black has little clear counterplay) 15...♗e7 16 ♔e2 (16 h4!? is also reasonable, intending to secure the white king on g2, without allowing ...♗h3+, e.g. 16...♗f6 17 ♗d4 ♖c8 18 g3 ♗xd4 19 ♕xd4 ♕a5 20 ♔g2± although Black has some c-file chances; Borges Mateos-Diaz, Cuban Ch 1991) 16...♕a5 (16...♗f6!?) 17 ♖hc1 ♖ac8 18 a3 h6 19 ♔f1 ♕b6 20 ♔g1 ♕d6 21 ♗d1! ♖c6 22 ♖xc6 bxc6 23 ♗c2 f5 24 b4± Portisch-Hübner, Brussels OHRA 1986, although Black held on.

b) **8...a6** is generally played as a preparation for ...e5. The move of course is played in many IQP positions, but here is directed against the immediate ♘b5 (see 'a' above) as well as White's longer-term blockading aspirations. The move has Garry Kasparov's stamp of approval. We shall consider:

b1) **9 0-0 e5 10 cxd5 cxd5 11 dxe5** (In Panno-Morović, Buenos Aires 1992, White tried the strange-looking 11 a4 to exchange dark-squared bishops, but after 11...e4 12 ♘d2 ♘b8 13 ♗a3 ♘c6 14 ♗xd6 ♕xd6 15 ♖fc1 ♗g4 Black was already for preference) **11...♘xe5 12 ♗b2**:

b11) **12...♗e6** 13 ♖ac1 ♖c8 14 ♕b1 ♘fg4!? 15 ♘xe5! ♗xe5 16 ♗xg4! (16 h3 ♗h2+ 17 ♔h1 ♗b8

– Kasparov – gives Black good attacking chances) 16...♗xg4 17 ♘a4 ♗b8 18 ♖xc8 ♗xc8 19 ♗d4 ♖e8 20 ♕b2 ♕d6 21 f4 f6 with only a slight edge for White in Portisch-Kasparov, Dubai OL 1986.

b12) **12...♗g4!?** 13 ♘xe5 (13 ♘d4 ♗xe2 14 ♕xe2 ♖c8 Δ...♗b8 also causes Black no difficulties) 13...♗xe5 14 ♗xg4 ♘xg4 15 h3 ♘f6= Rogozenko-Vidoniak, Romania 1991.

b2) **9 ♗b2**:

b21) **9...b5** turned out badly for Black after 10 0-0 (10 c5!?) **10...♗b7?!** 11 c5! ♗c7 12 b4 a5 13 a3 e5 14 e4! in Lerner-Cuijpers, Nîmes 1991 since White was better placed to benefit from the opening of the centre. However, Lerner suggests the reasonable freeing break **10...bxc4** 11 bxc4 dxc4 12 ♗xc4 c5=.

b22) **9...dxc4 10 bxc4 c5!?** is interesting:

b221) **11 d5** exd5 12 ♘xd5 ♘xd5 13 cxd5 ♕e7 14 0-0 ♖e8 15 ♗d3 ♘f6 and Black can create enough counterplay before White can roll his centre pawns; Schlosser-Chernin, Altensteig 1991.

b222) **11 0-0** cxd4 12 exd4 b6. Now in Ree-Kupreichik, Hastings 1981/2, White tried **13 a4** ♗b7 14 ♗a3 (14 ♖fd1 or even 14 ♘g5!? - Polugaevsky) 14...♗xa3 15 ♖xa3 ♖c8 and Black had quite sufficient play against the hanging pawns. Instead Donaldson gives **13 ♘e4 ♘xe4** 14 ♕xe4 Δ♗d3, but it seems to me that Black is safer with **13...♗e7(!)** when it is not so easy to find a testing follow-up for White.

b3) **9...e5** 10 0-0-0 (Alternatives are similar to 'a') 10...exd4 (10...♕e7!? – Dreev – is also worth attention since if White plays to win the d5 pawn he will face fierce pressure on the c-file in conjunction with a possible ...♗a3) 11 ♘xd4 ♘b6 12 h3 ♕e7 13 g4 ♗a3 14 ♗xa3! ♕xa3+ 15 ♕b2 ♕e7 16 cxd5 and now instead of **16...cxd5?!** when ♔b1 and a4 should together have put a stop to Black's counterplay on the c-file and with ...a5-a4 in Bischoff-Dreev, Brno 1992, **16...♘bxd5** would have left a complex and balanced game.

9 bxc4	**e5**
10 0-0	**♖e8** *(167)*

167
W

11 ♖d1

The play here is interesting and complex in that Black can still largely determine the nature of the game according to how he chooses to resolve the central tension. White's aim is to play moves which are useful in the event of either ...e4 or ...exd4. In the event of ...e4, with which Black establishes a pawn wedge in the centre and then seeks to generate play on the kingside, White has in turn two possible plans:

1) Challenge Black's central pawn directly with f3, exchange it off and then mobilize two centre pawns to smother Black.

2) Attack on the queenside, using the b-file, the possibility of a4-a5 (sometimes even a6 too) as a lever, maybe in conjunction with c5 and ♘c4 to highlight Black's weak d6 point.

Clearly it is wise to select during this period of 'shadow boxing' which plan is to be preferred, and Karpov's move reflects the increasing trend towards plan no. 2, since to effect the f3 break a rook is required at e1 to defend the e-pawn. In general, the preference for play on the queenside has also, logically enough, been related to a tendency to delay or even avoid ♗b2 altogether (again epitomized by Karpov's model here). As we shall see, after the old move 11 ♗b2, there seems little doubt that 11...e4 poses more questions for White than 11...exd4. The danger for White to bear in mind is that in preparing too dedicatedly for ...e4, he may find his pieces ill-placed for the hanging pawn structure after ...exd4.

First we must examine **11 ♗b2**, both as an important line in its own right, and as an important starting point for understanding the modern trends. Black has:

a) **11...exd4 12 exd4 ♘f8 13 ♖ad1** (13 h3!? is an old move which has also held up well, e.g. 13...♘g6 14 ♖fe1 ♕a5?! {14...♕c7!?} 15 c5! ♗f8 16 ♗c4!± Müller-Kopecky, Vienna 1953) and now:

a1) **13...♘g6?!** 14 ♘e5! ♘xe5 15 dxe5 ♖xe5 *(168)*

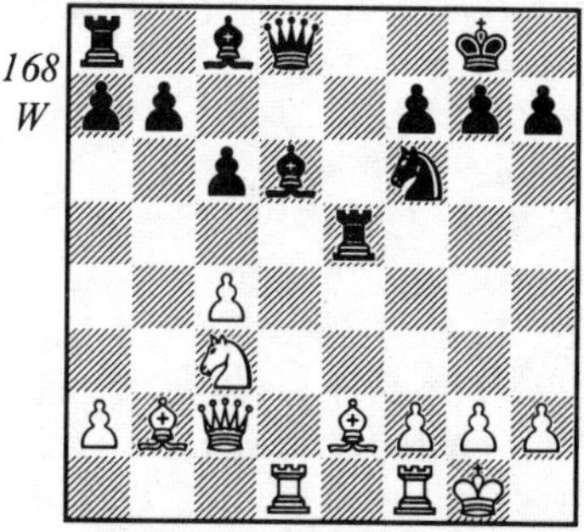

168
W

16 ♕d2!± (at least) Donaldson, but, as he points out, not the oft-recommended **16 ♘b5?** since 16...♖xe2! 17 ♕xe2 cxb5 18 c5 ♕e7! wins for Black.

a2) **13...♗g4** 14 ♘e5 ♗xe2 15 ♘xe2 ♕c7 gives White a pleasant choice between **16 c5** ♗xe5 17 dxe5 ♘g4 (otherwise a knight will simply land on d6 with great effect) 18 ♘g3 ♘xe5 19 ♘f5 f6 20 ♘d6 ♖e7 21 ♗xe5! fxe5 (21...♖xe5 22 ♕b3+) 22 f4! with a strong attack in Ligterink-Ree, Wijk aan Zee 1985, or simply **16 ♘f3** ♘e4 17 ♘g3 ♘xg3 18 hxg3 with a slight plus according to Hübner.

a3) **13...♕c7** 14 c5!? (14 h3!?) 14...♗e7 15 ♘e5 (15 ♖fe1 ♗e6 16 ♘e5 ♖ad8 17 ♗f3 Plachetka-

Sveshnikov, Torcy 1991, should not be too dangerous for Black after 17...♗d5! instead of 17...♘d5?! 18 ♘e4! which gave fair attacking chances) 15...♗e6 16 f4 ♘d5! (by contrast, this is now clearly superior to 16...♗d5 after which Black was forced into a passive position by 17 f5 ♘8d7 18 ♘xd5 ♘xd5 19 ♗h5! ♖f8 20 ♖fe1± in Groszpeter-Pinter, Budapest 1984) 17 f5 ♘xc3 18 ♗xc3 (18 fxe6!? ♘xe2+ 19 ♕xe2 f6 {19...fxe6 20 ♕g4 with good play} 20 ♕g4 ♗d8 21 d5 cxd5 22 ♖xd5 ♕e7! 23 ♘f7 ♕xe6 24 ♘h6+ ♔h8 25 ♕xe6! ♘xe6 26 ♘f7+ ♔g8 27 ♘d6 ♖e7 28 ♗a3 followed by ♖b1 gives good play for the pawn - Taimanov) 18...♗d5 with a balanced game; Tisdall-Sigurjonsson, Brighton 1982.

b) **11...e4 12 ♘d2** (If 12 ♘g5 Black should avoid 12...♕e7? 13 c5! ♗c7 14 ♗c4!± in favour of Chernin's 12...♘xg4 13 ♗xg4 ♕xg5=. If the latter does not appeal, there is nothing wrong with the move order 11...♕e7 12 ♖fe1 e4 – see also 'c') **12...♕e7** *(169)* and now:

169
W

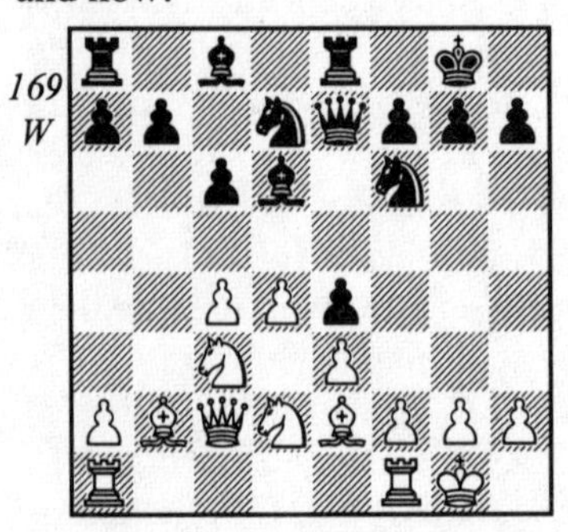

b1) **13 c5** is consistent with the fashionable view that the queenside should be White's chosen battleground here, but as the plan of ♘c4, ♗a3 and ♘d6 involves here a loss of tempo it probably should not be too dangerous. White did stand well in Plachetka-Zso.Polgar, Rimavska Sobota 1991 after 13...♗c7 14 ♘c4 b5 15 cxb6 axb6 16 a4 **♘f8?!** 17 ♘e5!, but Csom's suggestion of **16...♗a6!** seems fine for Black.

b2) **13 ♖ae1**. White would like to keep a rook on f1 for his coming break, but if anything the text seems to help Black to organize kingside counterplay around White's centre operations, not least because f1 is denied to the white knight. 13...♘f8 14 ♗d1 (played to prepare f3 with the intention to meet ...exf3 by recapturing with the knight. However, the immediate 14 f3!? may be more testing, e.g. 14...exf3! 15 ♗xf3 ♘g4 16 ♗xg4 ♗xg4 17 c5! ♗c7 18 ♘de4 ♗h5!? {18...♖ad8 19 ♗a3 ♕e6 20 ♘d6⩲ was Skembris-Vouldis, Komotini 1992} 19 d5 and now not 19...exd5?? 20 ♘f6+ +-, but 19...♗g6!∞ Skembris) 14...♗c7! 15 f3 exf3 16 ♘xf3 ♗e6 (highlighting a drawback of ♗d1) 17 ♗e2 ♗g4 18 ♗d3 ♖ad8 19 ♔h1 ♘g6 20 ♘d1 ♘h5 21 ♕f2 f5 22 e4 ♘hf4 23 ♗c2 fxe4 24 ♖xe4 ♕d7∓ Co.Ionescu-Chernin, Sochi 1986.

b3) **13 ♖ad1** ♘f8 14 c5 ♗c7 15 ♘c4 (a similar idea to 'b1' above, but 15...b5? is not here available in view of 16 ♘e5± but on the other hand with the knight already on f8 Black can prevent ♘e5) 15...♘g6 16 d5 cxd5 (16...♘xd5!? looks better) 17 ♘d6 ♗xd6 18 cxd6 ♕d8 19 ♘xd5 with some advantage in Kuzmin-Tatai, Dortmund 1981.

b4) **13 ♖fe1 ♘f8 14 f3 exf3** (14...♕c7!? 15 f4± Barbero) **15 ♗xf3 ♘g4** (again here the case made by Donaldson for a rarer approach is interesting: 15...♘e6 is dismissed by, for example, Tal, on account of '16 ♘de4±', but after 16...♘xe4, 17 ♗xe4 ♕h4 is counterplay, and on 17 ♘xe4 Black has the plan of ...f5 and ...♘g5 which at least merits examination) **16 ♘f1** and now:

b41) **16...♕g5**:

b411) **17 ♕d2** ♗f5 18 ♖ad1 ♖ad8 19 g3 ♕g6 20 ♕g2 ♗b4 21 e4 ♗c8 22 h3 ♘h6 23 g4 ♘e6 24 ♕f2 ♘g5 25 ♕g3 f5!! 26 e5 (26 exf5 ♘xf5 27 ♖xe8+ ♖xe8 28 gxf5 ♘xf3+ 29 ♔xf2 ♕xg3+ 30 ♔xg3 ♘g1! 31 ♔g2 ♘e2! Ligterink) 26...fxg4 27 ♗xg4 ♘xg4 28 hxg4 ♗xg4 0-1 Gelpke-Van der Wiel, Hilversum 1986.

b412) **17 e4** ♘e6 18 e5! (since if 18 ♖ad1 c5! 19 ♘b5! ♗b8 20 d5 ♘f4∓; this is incidentally the rationale for 17 c5 above) 18...♘xd4 19 exd6 ♗d7 20 ♕d2! ♕c5 21 ♔h1 ♘e2! 22 ♖xe2 ♖xe2 23 ♘xe2 ♘f2+ 24 ♔g1 ♘h3+ 25 ♔h1= Van der Wiel.

b413) **17 c5!? ♗c7 18 e4 ♘e6**:

b4131) In Agdestein-Tal, Taxco IZ 1985, the great champion's tactical alertness was in good shape after **19 ♘e2?** ♗xh2+! 20 ♘xh2 ♕e3+ 21 ♔h1 ♘f2+ 22 ♔g1 ♘e4+ 23 ♔h1 ♘f2+ 24 ♔g1 ♘d3+ 25 ♔h1, but here he could have continued the struggle with the interesting 25...♘xe1! 26 ♖xe1 ♘f4 with lots of play.

b4132) After **19 ♖ad1!** White is probably theoretically a little better, although Black retains fair chances against the white king.

b42) **16...♕h4!? 17 g3** (17 h3? ♘f6 18 e4 ♘e6! and ...♘g5 gives excellent chances of landing something on the kingside) **17...♕g5** *(170)*

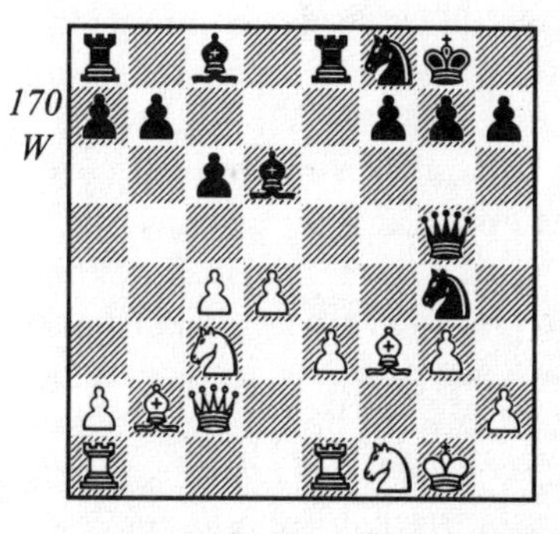

170
W

b421) **18 ♘e4?!** ♕g6 19 ♕g2 ♗b4 20 ♖e2 ♗f5 21 ♘f2 ♘xf2 22 ♖xf2 ♗e4 was very comfortable for Black who had successfully blockaded White's centre in Taimanov-Barbero, Montpellier 1986. In comparison with 'b41', the diagram position differs only in the insertion of g3, which sometimes gives White valuable control of f4 and the possibility of ♕g2, but sometimes merely weakens f3.

b422) **18 e4** may be better than above, since after **18...♘e6** (18...c5!?) 19 ♖ad1 c5 20 ♘b5! ♗b8 21 d5, Black's knight is denied f4. Also, **18...♕f6** 19 ♗xg4! (19 ♕d3? ♗c5!) 19...♕xd4+ 20 ♘e3 ♗xg4 21 ♘b5! wins material.

b423) However, again the best move may be **18 c5!?** ♗c7 (18...♘xe3 19 ♕d2 ♗f4 20 ♘e4! ♘xf1 21 ♕xf4! ♕xf4 22 gxf4 and the knight will not emerge) 19 e4 and if 19...♕f6 simply 20 ♕d3 is fine.

c) **11...♕e7!?**. We have already seen that the text is a quite legitimate move order for reaching 'b' above, and indeed occurs quite frequently due to transpositions from Game 35 when White delays b3. However, it can also initiate a very different, and seemingly quite promising plan for Black. White must of course bear in mind that Black can push ...e4 leading to 'b':

c1) **12 ♖ae1** b6!? 13 ♘e4 ♘xe4 14 ♕xe4 ♘f6 was very comfortable for Black in Tal-Van der Wiel, Wijk aan Zee 1988.

c2) **12 c5** ♗c7 13 ♗c4 h6 14 ♖ae1?! (14 ♘h4!?) 14...e4 15 ♘d2 ♗xh2+ 16 ♔h2 ♘g4+ 17 ♔g3 ♘df6! 18 ♘cxe4 ♘xe4 19 ♕xe4 ♕xe4 20 ♘xe4 ♖xe4 and Black is not worse; Boissonet-Dreev, 1989.

c3) **12 ♖fe1** b6 13 a4 (13 ♖ad1 ♗b7 14 ♘e4 ♘xe4 15 ♕xe4 ♘f6 16 ♕h4 exd4 17 ♘xd4 ♘e4!∓ Tai-Lukacs, Rome 1988) 13...a5 14 ♖ab1 ♗a6 15 ♗a1 e4! 16 ♘d2 ♗b4 17 ♗f1 ♘f8 18 g3 ♗c8 19 ♗g2 ♗f5= Hübner. This method of keeping the central tension clearly merits further outings.

11 ... ♕e7

As I am regularly suggesting, **11...exd4** looks logical at several points here as an alternative to the regular kingside *vs* queenside tussle presaged by ...e4. It received a recent outing, and Black was soon better after 12 exd4 ♘f8 13 ♘e5?! (13 h3) 13...♕e7 14 ♗f4 ♘e6 15 ♕d2 ♘xf4 16 ♕xf4 c5∓ Zsu.Polgar-Ioseliani, Monaco wom Ct 1993, although it would not be too hard to improve White's play.

12 ♖b1

Another recent try both to further White's queenside ambitions, and to afford the possibility of ♗a3 is **12 a4!?** *(171)*.

171
B

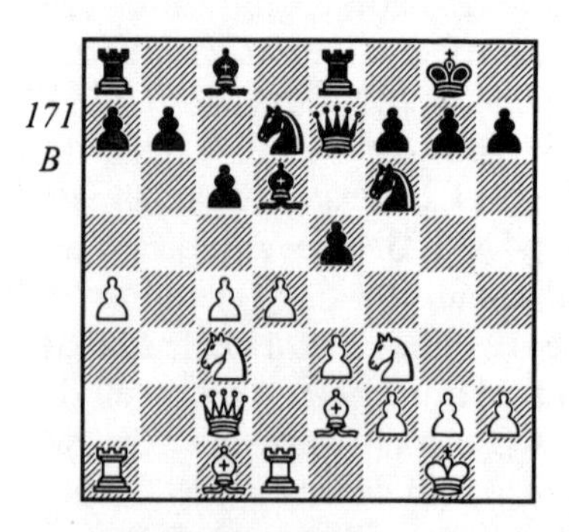

a) This has fared well after **12...e4 13 ♘d2 ♘f8**:

a1) **14 a5?!**:

a11) **14...a6?!** 15 ♘f1 ♘g6 16 ♕b3 h5 17 ♗a3! h4 18 ♗xd6

♕xd6 19 ♕a3 ♕d8 20 h3 ♘h7 21 ♕c5 ♕f6 22 ♘h2 ♘g5 23 ♘g4 ♗xg4 24 ♗xg4 ♘e7 25 ♖ab1 with a large positional plus in Speelman-Anand, Monaco (30 min) 1992. After the initial hiccup, a model execution of White's plan.

a12) **14...♘g4!** is strong according to Mikhail Tseitlin, who backs his case with some convincing variations: **15 h3** ♘xf2! 16 ♔xf2 ♕h4+ 17 ♔g1 ♗xh3∓; or **15 ♘f1** ♕h4 16 g3 ♕f6!∓. All in all, when White's knight is still on d2, and the bishop on e2, White should show a little more caution regarding defence along the second rank. White could of course try **15 ♗xg4**, but this is certainly not going to trouble Black unduly. Perhaps the best is **15 g3** ♘xh2! 16 ♕xe4 ♕d7, '∓' says Tseitlin but after 17 ♕h4 it seems messy and unclear to me.

The analysis of 14...♘g4 gives a flavour of how careful White must be on the kingside, and a clue to the appeal of the approach with ...e4 for Black.

a2) **14 ♘f1** ♗f5 (14...h5 15 ♕b3 ♗g4 16 ♗a3! also gives White an edge according to Tseitlin) 15 a5 a6 16 ♕b3 ♖ad8 17 ♗a3! taking the sting out of Black's counterattack, and leaving White better; Lputian-Mi.Tseitlin, Moscow 1992.

b) However, particularly after 12 a4, there seems to be a strong case for switching back to **12...exd4!?** 13 exd4 ♘f8 (or perhaps 13...c5) since neither ♖fd1 or a4 seem ideally suited to the new circumstances, and Black can seek play with ...♘g6, ...♗g4 etc.

12 ... e4

The same argument for **12...exd4** largely applies here too. Indeed Portisch-Godena, Reggio Emilia 1991/2 gave White at best a slight pull after 13 exd4 c5 (13...♘f8 also seems logical) 14 ♗e3 cxd4 15 ♘xd4 ♘c5 16 ♘cb5 ♗b8 17 ♖e1 ♘g4 18 ♗xg4 ♗xg4 19 ♘f5?! ♕e4 with no problems.

It is not so easy to fathom the logic behind Black's play in Kir.Georgiev-Granda Zuñiga, Manila OL 1992. After **12...h6?!** 13 a4 e4?! (13...exd4⩲) 14 ♘d2 ♘f8 15 c5! (Black's planless play fully justifies a more aggressive set-up from White) 15...♗c7 16 ♗a3 ♗g4 17 ♗xg4 ♘xg4 18 g3 ♗a5, the simple 19 ♗b4 ♗xb4 20 ♖xb4 ♘f6 21 ♖db1 would have given White a huge advantage.

Another familiar mode of development can also be tried here, namely **12...b6!?** although the natural plan of a4-a5 does at least justify White's ♖b1. Bischoff-Schlemermeyer, Bundesliga 1993 continued 13 a4 e4 14 ♘d2 ♘f8 15 a5 ♘g6 16 ♘f1 ♘h4 17 ♘g3 bxa5 18 c5 ♗c7 19 ♕a4 ♗d7∞.

13 ♘d2 ♘f8

In Portisch-Zsu.Polgar, Hungarian Ch 1991, Black tried to first slow White down on the queenside before furthering her attack, but according to Portisch, **13...c5(?!)**

only served as a target for White. After 14 ♘f1 b6 15 a4 ♗b7 16 ♘g3 g6 17 ♘b5 ♗b8 18 ♗a3 h5 19 ♘f1 ♕e6 20 a5! ♗a6 21 d5 (this central breakthrough is often important in White's whole plan, behind which, it should be mentioned, Portisch himself was the brains) 21...♕e5 22 ♗b2 ♕g5 White could have obtained a decisive advantage with 23 d6! ♗xb5 24 axb5 ♖e6 25 f4! ♕h6 26 ♗c4 ♖xd6 **27 ♘g3**, or even **27 ♖e1** further emphasizing the terrible lack of coordination of Black's forces.

14 ♘f1

Here White has an interesting choice between the solid text, and the more ambitious routing of the knight via c4 to d6. This plan has since been preferred by Karpov himself. We shall examine:

a) **14 a4** h5 (14...♘g4!? seems very closely analogous to Tseitlin's analysis above {see note to 12 a4}. It is arguable that ♖b1 is fractionally more useful than a5 but not enough to change the assessment that the idea is a good one) 15 c5 ♗c7 16 ♗a3 h4 (16...♗g4!? Skembris; 16...♘g4!?) 17 ♘c4 (17 h3 ♘8h7 ...♘g5 with attacking chances) 17...h3 18 g3 ♕e6 19 ♘d6 ♗xd6 20 cxd6 ♘8h7 21 d5! (it must be right to open the position for the bishop pair and the better developed rooks before Black has time to organize his kingside strike) 21...♕f5! (21...♘xd5 22 ♘xd5 cxd5 23 ♖b5 ♘f6 is too passive, and 21...cxd5 22 ♘b5 is simply bad) 22 a5 ♘g5 (Skembris gives the interesting line 22...♘xd5 23 ♘xd5 cxd5 24 f4! with some advantage. Perhaps better were 22...a6 or 22...♘g4. Black must either block White's threat or create a more concrete counterthreat) 23 a6! *(172)*

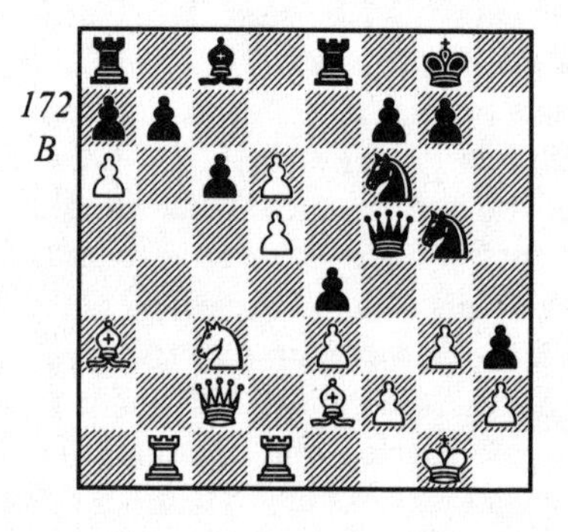
172
B

A very visual queenside breakthrough. However, the next few moves still require very careful defence. The dedication of both players to their respective attacks makes this game an instructive example. **23...♘f3+** 24 ♔h1 ♘g4?! (24...♘e1!? 25 ♖xe1 ♕xf2 26 ♗d3! ♕f3+ 27 ♔g1 exd3 28 ♕f2±; or 24...♘xh2!? 25 f4! ♘hg4 26 ♗xg4 ♕xg4 27 ♕e2±. White's far-advanced onslaught enables quite ugly and extreme measures to be employed to keep the king intact) 25 ♖f1 ♗d7 26 axb7 ♖ab8 27 ♗c5 ♘fxh2 28 ♗xg4 ♘xg4 29 f3 with great advantage; Skembris-Delchev, Mangalia 1992. As soon as Black's attack peters out, the writing is on the wall.

b) **14 c5(!)** ♗c7 15 ♘c4 ♘g4!? 16 h3 (With the white knight already on c4, defending e3, the sacrifice 16...♘xf2 is inadequate after 17 ♔xf2 ♕h4+ 18 ♔g1 ♗xh3 19 gxh3 ♕g3+ 20 ♔f1 ♖e6 21 ♘xe4 and Black cannot mobilize further forces. Another interesting variation from Karpov is 16...♗h2+ 17 ♔h1 ♘xf2+ 18 ♔xh2 ♕h4 19 ♗f1 ♖e6 20 g3 ♘g4+ 21 ♔g2, when 21...♕xh3+ and 24...♖h6+ will merely exchange queens leaving Black a piece to the bad) 16...♘f6 17 ♗a3 ♘d5 18 ♘d6 (If 18 ♘xd5 cxd5 19 ♘d6 ♗xd6 20 cxd6 ♕g5 21 ♔h2 ♖e6 Black can build sufficient counterchances around the d6 pawn according to Karpov) 18...♗xd6 19 cxd6 ♕g5 20 ♘xe4 ♘xe3!? *(173)*

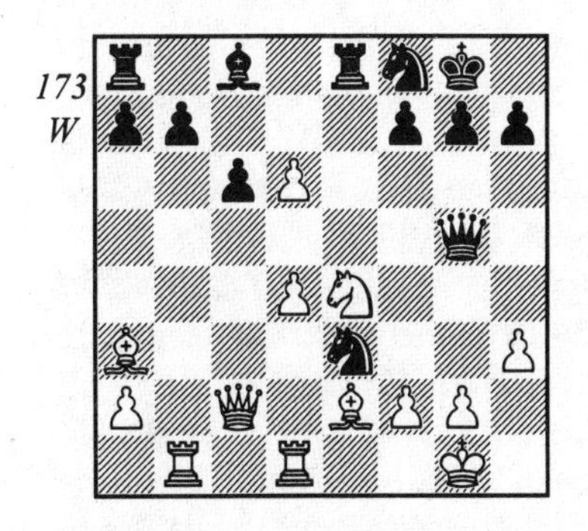

21 ♘xg5 ♘xc2 22 ♗c4 ♘e6 23 ♗xe6 ♗xe6 24 ♘xe6 ♖xe6 25 ♗c5! b6 26 ♖b2 bxc5 27 dxc5! ♖e1+ (since 27...♘a3 fails to the pretty 28 d7 ♖d8 29 ♖b8!) 28 ♖xe1 ♘xe1 29 ♖d2 ♔f8 30 ♔f1 ♖e8 31 d7 ♖d8 32 ♔xe1 ♔e7 33 ♖d6 with an excellent ending for White; Karpov-Knaak, Baden-Baden 1992. Such long sequences, combining exact calculation with fine judgement are a mark of Karpov at his very best.

14 ... ♘g6

14...h5 is Karpov's recommendation, and it seems very logical. Whilst 14 ♘f1 gives extra cover to h2, it does not especially help White against the plan ...h4 and ...h3, and neither does it help much to enable h3 to meet this, since the manoeuvre ...♘f8-h7-g5 still gives good prospects. White would have to be careful to avoid a position similar to Skembris-Delchev only with a slower queenside build-up. I think Karpov's later preference for 14 c5 is not without significance.

15 a4 ♘h4

16 ♘g3

16 a5 is unnecessarily risky. 16...♘xg2! 17 ♔xg2 ♕e6 18 ♘g3 ♕h3+ 19 ♔g1 ♘g4 20 ♗xg4 ♗xg4 21 f4 exf3 gives good value for the investment.

16 ... ♘f5

17 ♖b3 ♘xg3

18 hxg3 h5

Unfortunately for Gurevich, it is harder to create threats against the new kingside formation. The text moreover justifies a White breakthrough in the centre without further ado.

19 c5 ♗c7

20 d5! ♗e5

20...♘xf6 is clearly bad after just 21 ♘xd5 cxd5 22 ♗xh5. **20...cxd5** also gives White a choice between **21 ♘xd5** ♘xd5 22 ♖xd5 ♗e6 23 ♕xe4 when Black's exposed kingside and White's two bishops and control of the b-file give excellent compensation and **21 ♘b5!?** with many positional trumps for the pawn.

21 ♘xe4 ♘xd5
22 ♘d6! *(174)*

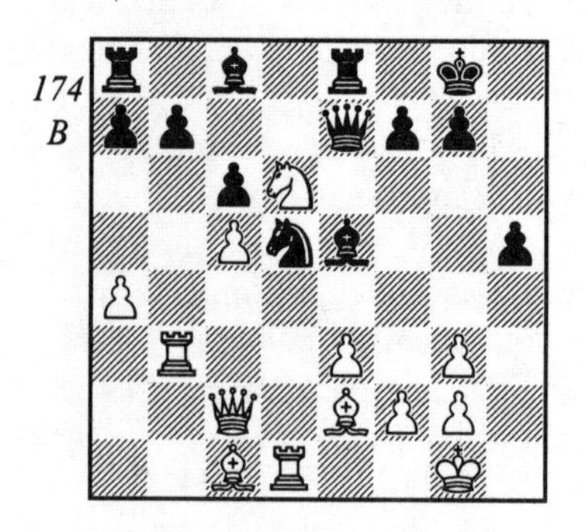

174
B

22 ... ♗xd6
23 cxd6 ♕xd6
24 ♗xh5

Not however **24 e4?** ♕g6!. White's combination has netted the bishop pair, and since he also ties the bishop to c8, and has the possibility of e4, Black cannot even maintain the knight on d5.

Play proceeded: **24...♕h6 25 ♗f3 ♘f6 26 ♖d6 ♕g5 27 ♗b2 a5 28 ♕d2 ♘d5** (Black tries to give a pawn to break the bind. Still, the resulting position has more of the middlegame characteristics where the opposite-coloured bishops benefit the attacker than those where they increase the prospects of peace) **29 ♗xd5 cxd5 30 ♖xd5 ♕g6 31 ♖bb5!** *(175)*

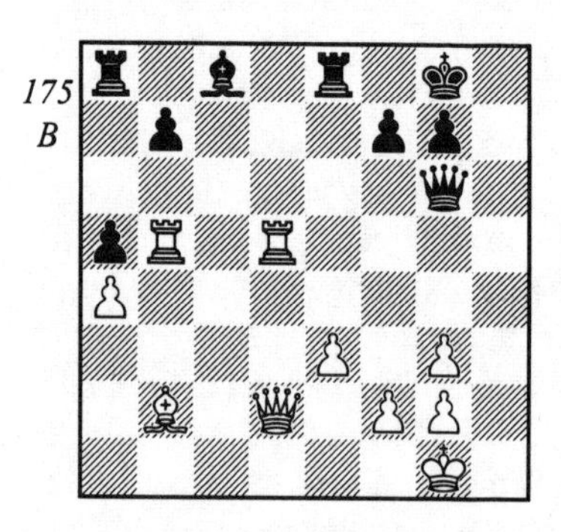

175
B

White is not content with just dominating files and diagonals! The text forces a further weakness. Note how by contrast White's kingside formation permits Black's queen and bishop to make no threats: **31...f6 32 ♗c3 ♗e6 33 ♖d4 ♖ac8 34 e4 ♕f7 35 ♗xa5 ♖c6 36 f3 ♔h7 37 g4 ♖ec8 38 ♖h5+ ♔g6 39 e5 ♖c5 40 ♖d6 ♕e7** (White switches to direct attack. Clearly 40...♖xe5 41 ♕d3+ f5 42 ♖xf5 ♖xf5 43 gxf5+ ♕xf5 44 ♖xe6+ wins for White. The rest is simple for Karpov) **41 ♗d8 ♖xd8 42 ♖xd8 ♕c7 43 ♕d6 ♕a5 44 exf6 ♕e1+ 45 ♔h2 ♖d5 46 ♕e7 1-0**.

22 7 ♗e2: Introduction and 8...e5

In this and the next three chapters we consider the topical 7 ♗e2. This complex of lines in fact contains a good deal of variety. Hence I shall restrict my remarks here to a few general points which strike me. The good news is that although the whole system does have something of the safety first about it, it is not dull and Black has a good deal of choice too over the direction of the play in the next few moves. One consequence of the less critical nature of the early play is that some of the lines are less distinctive than those in for example the Meran. 8...e5 for example leads to isolated queen's pawn (IQP) positions similar to those arising from some lines of the Caro-Kann, or the Tarrasch. Black's compensation for the allegedly gloom-spreading weakness is just as viable here as elsewhere, but of course this kind of thing is very much a matter of taste. Lines where Black keeps the central tension, plays ...b6 and White counters with e4 have a distinctly Caro-Kannish feel about them, and after 8...dxc4 Black often follows up with ...c5 and ...cxd4 when White is the IQP bearer and the Nimzo-Indian comes to mind. For those who have found my advocacy of the Semi-Slav convincing, this loss of distinctiveness may seem a shame. However, most openings have some close relationship to others; not to do so is usually a fair indication of unsoundness! I mention this at some length because these comparisons may be useful in considering the style of variation to play, and indeed as an aid to studying the types of positions arising. White's less critical play has the flipside of vastly increasing Black's options.

The lines where Black captures on c4 are particularly full of nuance.

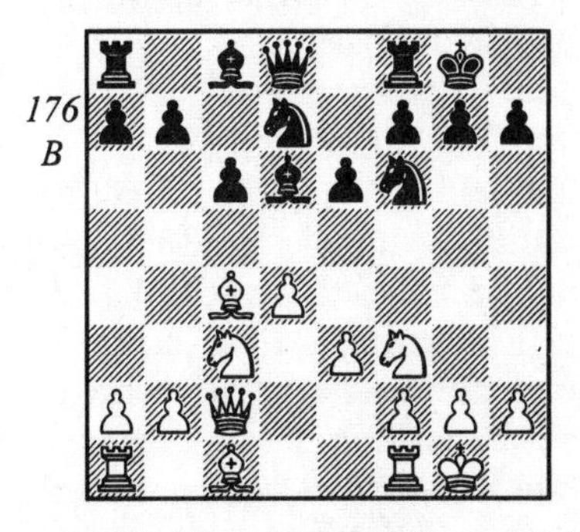
176
B

From a Semi-Slavists point of view I feel very drawn to 9...b5. White's whole system is based on the premise that if Black plays in Meran style the bishop on d6 will be worse placed than the queen on c2. Certainly Black's approach has to adapt (any subsequent e4 will threaten to win a piece!) and if

White avoids e4, then a freeing ...e5 can leave Black's queenside structure looking a little clumsy, but the line remains unrefuted. Recent examples leave White short of any clear route to a plus, and the line is thus growing in popularity. 9...e5 is Black's other immediate break, but it has declined in popularity. Perhaps the clearest strategic advice I can give on the entire variation is **avoid capturing on d4 too early**. White's compensation for the IQP is too great since Black's f7 weakness means that White will enjoy unchallenged e-file dominance. In general after ...e5, Black has the nagging difficulty that f7 is vulnerable, and the attempt to mitigate this weakness with an early ...h6 often invites the manoeuvre ♘h4-g6.

More popular are Black's less committal 9th move options. Van der Wiel has stated the belief that 9...♕e7 (Anand's leading and hence much-discussed Candidates match choice) is wrong in principle, preferring it a move earlier to keep the position closed. However, while Karpov's clever semi-waiting move 10 a3 preparing to meet both ...c5 and ...e5 remains a critical test, several players of repute have been willing to follow in Anand's footsteps. Also worthy of note is that several commentators have underestimated 10 h3, since Anand's 10...c5 probably has tactical flaws.

Black's last choice, 9...a6, keeps options of both ...c5 and ...b5 and creates no weakness in the event of 10 e4 e5. As with 9...♕e7, both sides often indulge in some subtle semi-waiting moves, and the evidence seems to suggest that in many circumstances an early e4 is premature. Epishin's beautiful win in Game 32 should not be seen as a condemnation of 9...a6 although according to the current state of theory I would not recommend it. In general the positions arising from each of Black's 9th moves have considerable similarities. I have tried wherever possible both to point out transpositions and to deal with them under their most probable move order.

Game 31
Cu.Hansen-L.B.Hansen
Wijk aan Zee 1993

1 d4 d5 2 c4 c6 3 ♘c3 ♘f6 4 e3 e6 5 ♘f3 ♘bd7 6 ♕c2 ♗d6

7 ♗e2	**0-0**
8 0-0	**e5** *(177)*

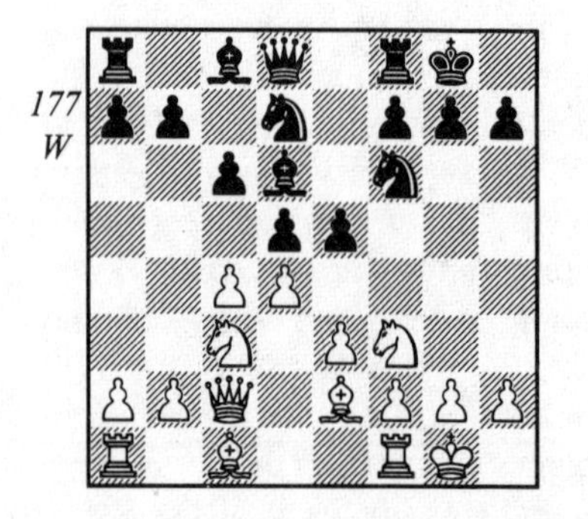

With 8...e5 Black uses the possibility opened up by White's rather slow build-up to obtain active piece play in return for an isolated d-pawn – a classic trade-off. In fact Black's pieces are well situated to generate counterplay against the white king. Equally, with the possible exception that the queen is committed a little early to c2, White's pieces also stand well for the new structure. White has an interesting choice of two approaches now. The textbooks always, and with some justification, stress the importance of blockading the 'isolani'. I think it was Larsen who said that sometimes a little more emphasis could be put on simply trying to take it off, or at least tying down pieces to its defence. White's 10th move choices reflect well this dichotomy. In our main game White effects the blockading manoeuvre ♘b5-d4 with tempo. However, in several games the efficacy of Black's counterchances have been demonstrated. Whichever approach wins the theoretical vote, I believe that the frontal assault on the d5 pawn forces Black into greater passivity, and even if he can equalize, it is less enjoyable to meet.

9 cxd5 cxd5
10 ♘b5

This is the aforementioned point of departure, and **10 dxe5** is the very important alternative. Practice after **10...♘xe5 11 ♖d1** has seen three moves tried, although the transpositional possibilities are numerous:

a) **11...♗e6** 12 ♗d2 (12 e4!? completely changes the character of the position. White liquidates Black's weakness, but on the evidence of Panno-Milos, Santiago 1989 White's pieces come rapidly to life. Black held, but had to be careful after 12...♖c8 13 exd5 ♗xd5 14 ♘xe5 ♗xe5 15 ♗g5 ♕a5 16 ♗xf6 gxf6 {16...♗xf6? 17 ♕f5} 17 ♗d3 ♗xc3 18 bxc3 ♕xc3 19 ♕e2 ♕e5 20 ♕xe5 fxe5 21 ♗xh7+ ±) 12...♘xf3+ (12...♖c8!?) 13 ♗xf3 ♕c7 14 g3 ♗e5 15 ♗e1 ♖fd8 16 ♕e2 a6 17 ♖ac1 ♖ac8 18 a3 ♕b8 19 ♘a4 ♖xc1 20 ♖xc1 ♘e4 21 ♕d3 ½-½ Panno-Barbero, Buenos Aires 1991.

b) **11...♘xf3+ 12 ♗xf3 ♕c7!?** and now:

b1) **13 h3** is by far the most popular. **13...♗h2+! 14 ♔h1 ♗e5 15 ♗d2 ♗e6** *(178)* and now:

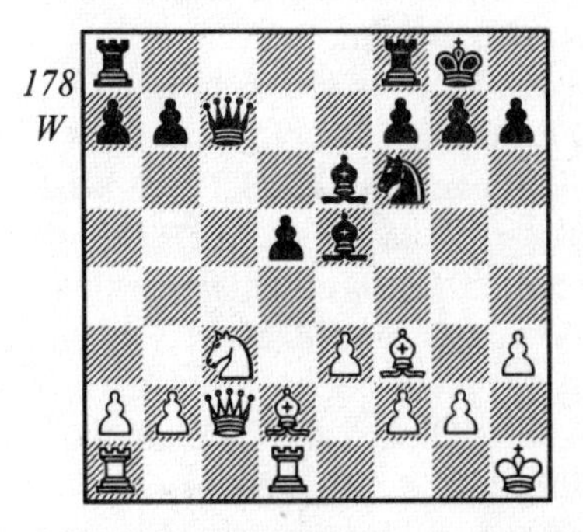

b11) **16 ♕d3** ♕d7 17 ♗e1 ♖fd8 (Very misguided would be

17...♗xh3 18 ♘xd5 ♘xd5 19 ♕xd5 ♕f5 20 ♔g1! with great advantage) 18 ♔g1 ♖ac8 19 ♖ac1 d4 20 exd4 ♗xd4 21 ♕e2 h6 22 b3 a6 (22...♕e7 would be significantly weaker after 23 ♘d5 ♘xd5 24 ♖xc8 ♖xc8 25 ♖xd4) 23 ♖c2 b5 24 ♖cd2 ♕a7! 25 ♘e4 ♘xe4 26 ♕xe4 ♗b6 was dead equal and shortly drawn in Karpov-Kasparov, Linares 1991.

b12) **16 ♗e1!?** seems to pose more questions:

b121) **16...♖ac8?!** is not particularly accurate, since by 17 ♕e2! White threatens both ♘xd5, and the positional ♘b5 Δ♗c3. Black's attempted solution 17...♕c4 18 ♔g1 ♕xe2 19 ♗xe2 a6 20 f4 ♗b8 (20...♗xc3 21 ♗xc3 ♘e4 22 ♗d4± Lputian) 21 ♗f3 ♖fe8 22 ♗f2 left d5 much weaker than e3 in Lputian-Dreev, Manila OL 1992.

b122) **16...♖fd8!** and now:

b1221) **17 ♕d3** (Akopian-Illescas, Chalkidiki 1992) is best met by 17...♕d7! transposing to Karpov-Kasparov in 'b11'.

b1222) **17 ♕e2** looks more risky: 17...a6 18 ♖ac1?! (18 ♘a4= Khalifman) 18...♖ac8 19 a3 ♕d7 20 ♔g1 ♗b8 21 g3 ♗a7 22 g4? (Unjustifiably weakening the kingside further, but Black already enjoyed a sneaking initiative) 22...h6! 23 ♗g2 d4! 24 exd4 ♗b3 25 ♖d2 ♗b8! left White's kingside full of little perforations in M.Gurevich-Khalifman, Biel IZ 1993.

b2) **13 g3** may not be so good since the majority of Black's efforts to take advantage of 13 h3 too directly – such as landing a queen on h2 – have tended to backfire. However Farago-Blauert, Vienna 1991 saw Black underestimate the importance of his dark-squared bishop: 13...♗e5 14 ♕d3!? ♗xc3? (14...♗e6! Ribli, when if White captures on d5, Black can simply trade everything and win control of the d-file and White has no real chances of conversion) 15 ♕xc3 ♕xc3 16 bxc3 ♗e6 (The position resembles a Nimzo-Indian – two bishops against weak c-pawn. The problem for Black is that he is powerless to stop the following manoeuvre after which White's 'extra' bishop dominates the board) 17 ♖ab1 ♖ab8 18 ♗a3 ♖fe8 19 ♗d6! ♖bd8 20 ♗e5 ♘g4 21 ♗d4±.

c) **11...♕c7** is similar to 'b' but both sides may try to deviate:

c1) **12 h3** leaves Black a choice between 12...♘xf3+ (see 'b'), and 12...♗e6 13 ♗d2 ♖ac8 14 ♖ac1 ♕e7 15 ♕b1 ♘xf3+ 16 ♗xf3 ♗b8 17 ♘e2 ♖xc1 18 ♖xc1 ♕d6 19 ♘g3 ♘e4! with enough counterplay; Kohlweyer-Barbero, Buenos Aires 1991.

c2) **12 ♘e1!?**. White avoids the exchange of knights and, by defending the queen threatens both ♘xd5 and ♘b5. On the minus side Black is developing and may generate enough play to compensate for positional concessions. 12...♘eg4 13 b3 ♗e6 14 ♘b5 ♕e7 15 ♘xd6 ♕xd6 16 ♕a4 ♕e5 17 ♕f4 ♕h5 18 h4 ♕g6 and Black has made enough trouble on the light squares around White's king to compensate for the loss of his dark-squared bishop; Atalik-Lukacs, Miskolc 1991.

10 ... **♗b8**
11 dxe5 **♘xe5** *(179)*

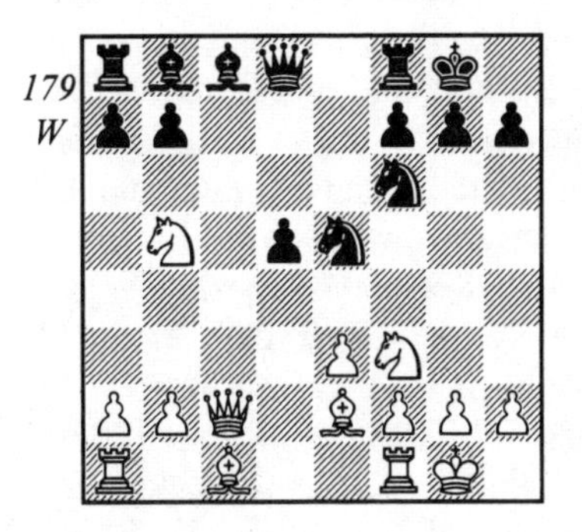

12 ♗d2

This has served White best in practice. Two other moves merit a mention:

a) **12 ♖d1?!** is not so logical now that White has rescinded the direct attack on d5. In Granda Zuñiga-Illescas, Pamplona 1991/2, Black rapidly seized the initiative with 12...a6 13 ♘c3 (or 13 ♘bd4 ♕d6 14 g3 ♗g4 Ribli) 13...♕c7 (also good is 13...♕d6 14 ♘xe5 ♕xe5 15 f4?! ♕c7 16 ♗f3 ♗e6 17 ♕e2 ♗a7∓ Krasenkov-S.B.Hansen, Copenhagen 1992, when Black no longer possessed the weakest pawn on the board!) 14 g3 ♘eg4 15 ♗d2 ♗e6 16 ♖ac1 ♕e7 17 ♘d4 h5! 18 ♘a4 ♗d6 19 ♘f5?! (19 ♘b6!?) 19...♗xf5 20 ♕xf5 g6 21 ♕f3 ♕e6∓.

b) **12 b3** looks very natural, but Black has a choice of routes to create play:

b1) **12...♗g4** 13 ♘bd4 ♕d6 14 g3 (14 ♘xe5 ♕xe5 15 g3 ♖c8 16 ♕d3 ♗h3 17 ♖d1 ♘e4 18 ♗b2 ♕f6 19 ♗f3 ♗g4! 20 ♕e2 h5 21 ♖f1 ♕g6 ½-½ Smejkal-Franke, Bundesliga 1987 also looks at least very comfortable for Black) 14...♖c8 15 ♕b2 ♗h3 16 ♖d1 ♘e4 17 ♘xe5?! ♕xe5 18 ♗d2 ♕f6 19 ♗e1 ♗e5∓ 20 ♖ac1 ♖e8 21 ♖c2 ♖ad8 22 ♕a3?! ♘g5! 23 f4 ♗xd4 24 exd4 ♕f5! 25 ♕c1 ♕e4 26 ♗d3 ♕xd4+ 27 ♔h1 ♕f6 28 fxg5 ♕f3+ 29 ♔g1 ♖e2!! (not a difficult motif, but very attractive nonetheless) 30 ♗xh7+ ♔xh7 0-1 Martin-Borik, Bundesliga 1992.

b2) **12...♘fg4!?** is another attractive possibility, specific to 12 b3, since 13 ♘xe5 ♗xe5 is embarrassing. Thus White has tried 13 ♘bd4 ♕d6 (again Black has satisfactory alternatives: 13...♘xf3+ 14 ♘xf3 ♕d6 15 g3 ♗d7 16 ♗b2 ♕h6 also gave fair counterplay in Arlandi-Zso.Polgar, Portoroz 1991) 14 g3 a6 15 ♘xe5 (15 ♗b2 ♕h6!?) 15...♕xe5 16 ♗a3 ♖e8 17 ♖ad1 (17 ♖ac1 ♕h5; 17...♗a7∓) 17...♕h5 18 ♗xg4 ♗xg4 19 f3 ♗h3 with the initiative in Popchev-Bönsch, Polanica Zdroj 1987.

12 ... **♗g4**

Again in the absence of direct threats from the first player, Black has several ways to try to make something of his active pieces. In approximate reverse order of importance:

a) **12...♕b6** looks a bit strange since usually Black aims much more single-mindedly at the kingside, and indeed after 13 ♘xe5 ♗xe5 14 ♗c3 ♗xc3 15 ♕xc3 ♗g4 16 ♗d3! ♖fc8 17 ♕d4 ♖c5 18 ♘c3 ♖c6 19 ♕xb6 ♖xb6 20 f3 ♗e6 21 ♖f2 I think most players would opt for the white pieces in this endgame. Still, Black, a great IQP specialist, drew without apparently great difficulty in Dokhoian-Bareev, Bundesliga 1992.

b) **12...a6** 13 ♘bd4 ♖e8 14 ♗c3 (14 ♖ac1!?) 14...♘e4 15 ♖ad1 ♕d6 16 ♘xe5 ½-½ Miles-Adianto, San Francisco 1987.

c) **12...♘e4!?** *(180)* and now:

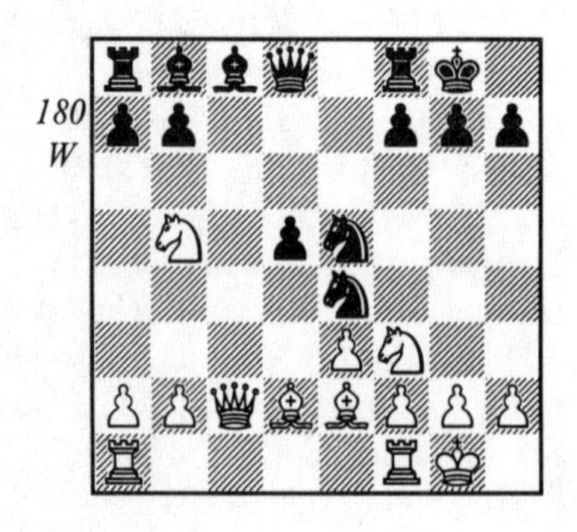

c1) Not **13 ♗b4?** ♘xf3+ 14 ♗xf3 ♕h4! 15 g3 ♘xg3∓.

c2) **13 ♗e1** ♕b6 (13...a6, and ...♕d6 is again valid too) 14 ♘bd4 ♕h6 15 ♗b4 ♖e8 16 ♘xe5 ♗xe5 17 ♘f3 ♗b8 18 ♕a4 ♖d8 19 ♗e7 ♗d7 with interesting well-balanced play in Adorjan-Ka.Müller, Balassagyarmat 1990.

c3) **13 ♖ad1** ♗g4 14 ♘bd4! ♕f6 (Zsuzsa Polgar gives 14...♕d6?! 15 ♘xe5 ♕xe5 16 f4 as ±) 15 ♕b3 ♕h6 16 ♘xe5 (16 g3 is interesting because Black is very heavily committed to the kingside, and consequently d5 and b7 are very weak. However, if less ambitious tries fail, Black can at any rate hold the balance with 16...♕h5 17 ♘xe5 ♗xe2 18 ♘xe2 ♗xe5 when White must avoid 19 ♕xd5? ♕xe2 20 ♕xe4 ♗xg3±) 16...♗xe5 17 f4 ♗xd4! 18 ♗xg4 ♗b6 19 ♗c1 ♖fe8! 20 ♗f3 (20 ♖xd5 ♘f6 21 ♖g5 ♘xg4 22 ♖xg4 ♖ac8! 23 ♗d2 ♕e6 24 ♕xe6 ♖xe6 25 f5 ♗xe3+ 26 ♗xe3 ♖xe3 27 f6 g6 28 ♖d4 ♖e2 29 ♖fd1 h5= Ribli) 20...♖ac8 21 ♖xd5 ♕c6! (21...♘f6 22 ♖d3 ♕xf4 23 ♕xb6! ♕xf3 24 gxf3 axb6 25 e4±) 22 ♖d3 ♕c2! 23 ♗xe4 ♖xe4 and Black's active pieces, plus the weakness of e3 gave full compensation for the pawn in Browne-Zsu.Polgar, San Francisco 1991.

13 ♘bd4 ♕d6

Black also fared OK with **13...♘e4** 14 ♗b4 ♖e8 15 ♖ad1 ♕b6 16 ♘xe5 ♗xe2 17 ♘xe2 ♗xe5 18 ♗c3 ♕c7 19 h3 ♕c4= Karpov-Korchnoi, Amsterdam

1991. The text is more ambitious, although the consequent exchanges give White chances for a small edge.

14 ♘xe5 ♗xe2
15 ♘xe2 ♕xe5
16 g3 ♘e4

Lars Bo Hansen comments interestingly that if **16...♕h5** 17 f3! and far from being actively placed, the queen may simply find herself cut out of the play.

17 ♖ad1 a6 *(181)*

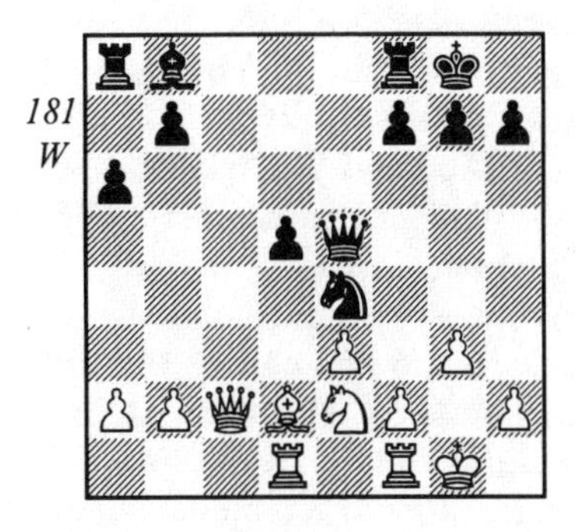
181
W

18 ♕b3?!

White identifies what is undoubtedly a weakness on b7, but L.B.Hansen's convincing notes suggest that Black has a harder time when d5 is targeted, e.g. **18 ♗b4!?** ♖d8 19 ♗a5 ♖e8 20 ♗b6!± (20 ♘f4 d4∞); or **18 ♗c3!?** ♕h5 19 ♕d3! ♖e8 20 ♕xd5 ♕xe2 21 ♕xe4 ♗xg3 22 ♕xb7 ♖ab8! 23 ♕g2 ♗e5 with some compensation for the pawn, but clearly Black interested in holding the balance.

18 ... ♕h5
19 ♘c3 ♘f6!

White has missed his chance to activate his bishop and create threats which Black could not ignore. The cost of this failure is that Black has concrete counterplay in the form of ...♕h3 and ...♘g4 which is not so easy to meet. White's next permits f3 by bolstering the g3 pawn. It seems that White could also try **20 ♕xb7** when **20...♗a7!** 21 ♗e1 ♖d8 is the game, but not **20...♕h3?** 21 ♘xd5! ♘g4 22 ♘e7+ and 23 ♕g2+-.

20 ♗e1 ♖d8
21 ♕xb7 ♗a7
22 ♔g2 ♗xe3! *(182)*

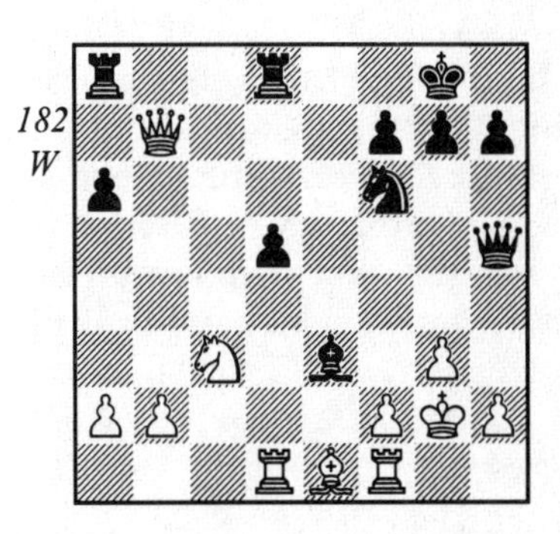
182
W

23 ♗d2

Since if **23 fxe3?** ♘g4 24 ♘xd5 ♕xh2+ 25 ♔f3 ♘e5+ White's king is in grave danger.

23 ... ♖ab8
24 ♕xa6 ♗c5!
25 h4?!

White still seems to underestimate Black's counterplay. Of

course it would be nice to activate the bishop with ♗g5, but thoughts of consolidation, perhaps with **25 h3** would be more appropriate.

25 ...	**d4**
26 ♘a4	**♕d5+**
27 ♔g1	**♗d6**
28 ♕d3	

Virtually forced in view of the threat of ...♕f3. White's kingside extravagance comes home to roost, and after Black re-establishes material parity he stands better since his d-pawn can become dangerous and his knight's placing is more convincing.

28 ...	**♕xa2**
29 ♖a1	**♕d5**
30 ♗g5	**♖b3**
31 ♘c3!?	

Impatient with the sad state of his knight, White takes advantage (probably correctly) of a tactic to return it to the play. If Black were now to shy away from investing a little material in his passed pawns future White would stand fine, e.g. **31...♕c5?!** 32 ♗xf6 gxf6 33 ♕d1! Δ♘e4 etc.

31 ...	**dxc3!**
32 ♕xd5	**♘xd5**
33 ♗xd8	**cxb2**
34 ♖ad1	

34 ♖a8 loses very prettily to 34...b1♕ 35 ♗c7+ ♗f8 36 ♗d6 ♖xg3+!! (the only move to net the full point).

34 ...	**♖b5!**
35 ♗g5	**♗b4!** *(183)*

183
W

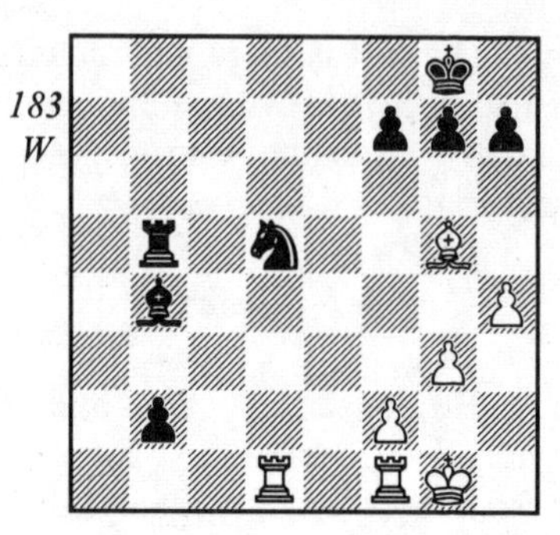

Otherwise 36 ♗d2, and it is not so easy to make progress.

36 ♔g2?

The decisive error! White should remove Black's b2 monster even at heavy cost with **36 ♖b1** ♗a5 37 ♗c1! bxc1♕ 38 ♖fxc1 ♖xb1 39 ♖xb1 ♗b4 and White should not lose although Black can still have a little fun.

White's punishment was as follows: **36...h6 37 ♗e3 ♘c3 38 ♖de1 ♗a3 39 ♖b1 ♘xb1 40 ♖xb1 ♖b3 41 ♗d4 ♖d3** (It would be more accurate first to fix White's kingside pawns with 41...h5! since Black has all the time in the world to win the exchange) **42 ♗xb2 ♖b3 43 ♗xa3 ♖xb1 44 h5 ♖b5 45 g4 f5 46 f3 ♔f7 47 ♗d6 ♔e6 48 ♗f8 ♖b7!** (Black's rook takes over the defensive task to free the king to invade White's position. White lacks any useful check when the king reaches e5; thus penetration to f4 cannot be stopped, and the rest is easy) **49 ♔g3 ♔e5 50 ♗c5 fxg4 51 fxg4 ♖b3+ 52 ♔h4 ♔f4 53 ♗d4 ♖b1 54 ♔h3 ♖h1+ 0-1**.

23 8...dxc4: 9...a6 and 9...b5

With the flexible move 9...a6 Black avoids commiting his queen and retains a choice of his three reasonable breaks in the position: ...b5, ...c5 and ...e5. The move has retained a certain popularity, but I feel that against accurate play from White it should be regarded with a little suspicion. After 10 ♖d1(!) ♕c7 11 ♘e4 our main game sees White achieve very pleasant prospects, but instead 10...♕e7 looks to be the right method.

Game 32
Epishin-Brenninkmeijer
Wijk aan Zee 1992

1 d4 ♘f6 2 c4 c6 3 ♘c3 d5 4 ♘f3 e6 5 e3 ♘bd7 6 ♕c2 ♗d6 7 ♗e2 0-0 8 0-0

8 ... dxc4
9 ♗xc4 a6 *(184)*

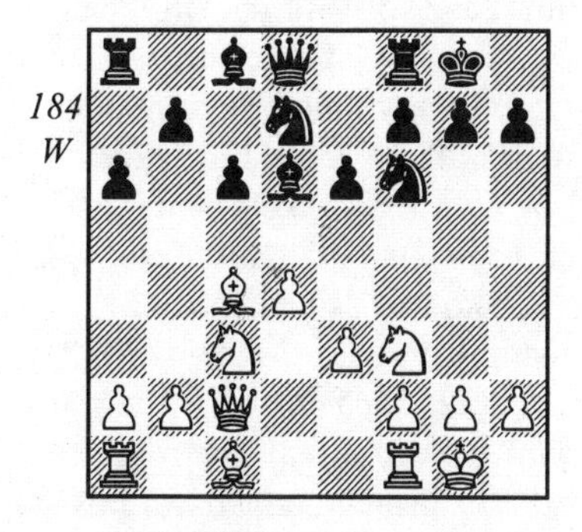

10 ♖d1

This logical developing move is slowly emerging as the main line, but White has tried almost every half-sensible move here. Starting with the more insipid:

a) **10 ♗e2?!** anticipates ...b5, but the whole virtue of Black's 9th is its flexibility. In Groszpeter-Lukacs, Kecskemet 1988 Black was able to switch to a set-up where the voluntary ♗e2 cannot be critical, viz: 10...e5 11 ♖d1 ♕c7 12 h3 h6 13 b3 ♖e8 14 ♗b2 exd4 15 ♘xd4 ♘e5 with equal play.

b) **10 ♘e4?!** is as usual not dangerous with the black queen still at home. 10...♘xe4 11 ♕xe4 ♕e7 12 b3 e5 13 ♗b2 ♘f6 14 ♕h4 e4 15 ♘e5 ♗e6 16 f3 exf3 17 ♖xf3 ♘d5 18 ♕xe7 ½-½ Krasenkov-Lukacs, Lillafüred 1989. In the final position Black's prospects are very pleasant.

c) **10 a4** also looks like a move which tackles only one of Black's ideas. However, it has been quite popular. Presumably approaches with ...e5 come into consideration, but practice has mainly seen **10...c5**:

c1) **11 h3** does not look dangerous. 11...♕c7 12 b3 cxd4 13 ♘xd4 b6 14 ♗b2 ♗b7 15 ♖fd1 ♘e5= Fyllingen-Kharlov, Gausdal 1992.

c2) **11 dxc5** ♗xc5 12 ♗d2 b6!? 13 ♘e4 ♗b7!= Stangl-Lukacs,

Budapest 1990. If 14 ♘xc5 ♘xc5 it is typical that Black's activity on the light squares fully compensates for the bishop pair.

d) **10 ♗d2** c5 (10...b5 is an inaccuracy which would receive an instructive punishment with 11 ♗d3 ♗b7 12 ♘g5! gaining a tempo for the restraining ♘e4; at least ⩲) 11 a4 (11 ♗d3 ♕c7 12 ♖ac1 cxd4 13 exd4 h6 14 ♖fe1 b6 15 ♕d1!? ♗b7 16 ♘e4 was perhaps a fractional edge for White in Polugaevsky-Pinter, Haninge 1988) 11...♕c7 12 ♕d3 (12 dxc5 ♘xc5!? 13 ♖fc1 b6 14 b4 ♘cd7 15 ♘e4 ♘xe4 16 ♕xe4 ♗b7 17 ♕h4 ♕d8!= Portisch-Pinter, Reggio Emilia 1987/8) 12...cxd4 13 exd4 b6 14 ♖ac1 ♗b7 15 ♗b3 (Van der Wiel suggests either 15 ♘a2 15...♕d8?! 16 ♘b4±; or 15 ♘e2 Δ♘g3. My feeling is that Black should overall be absolutely OK here) 15...♖ac8 16 ♖fe1 ♕b8 17 h3 (Vyzhmanavin-Novikov, USSR Ch 1990) and now the pragmatic and sensible 17...♗f4 would have given White nothing.

e) **10 e4?!** seems to fall in with the idea behind the flexible ...a6. After 10...e5 11 ♗e3 (11 ♖d1 is Kamsky-Anand in the note to White's 11th) 11...♕c7 (the best queen development for this central tension) 12 h3 b5 13 ♗b3 exd4 14 ♗xd4 c5 15 ♗xf6 (already White is forced to find equality in exchanges) 15...♘xf6 16 ♘d5 ♘xd5 ½-½ Schlosser-Chernin, Altensteig 1990.

10 ... ♕c7?!

This removal of the queen from the d-file looks perfectly natural, especially since Black was obliged to attend to the threat of 11 e4±. It is a tribute to Epishin's excellent understanding of this opening that he identifies a possibility for a really dangerous kingside attack arising from the absence of Black's queen from the h4-d8 diagonal. In view of White's aforementioned threat, Black has only three viable alternatives, all of which have been tried, but the last of which, rightly in my view, has generally been preferred:

a) **10...c5!?** 11 dxc5 ♗xc5 12 ♗d3!? h6 (12...b5 13 ♘e4! ♗e7 14 ♘xf6+ ♗xf6 14 ♗h7+ ♔h8 15 ♗e4 ♖b8 16 ♗d2±) 13 b3 ♗e7?! 14 ♗b2 b6 15 ♗e4! (the coming initiative more than outweighs the bishop pair) 15...♘xe4 16 ♕xe4 ♖a7 17 ♘e5 ♕e8 18 ♘c6 ♘f6 19 ♘xe7+ ♕xe7 20 ♕d4 ♕b7 21 ♘a4!± since ...b5 gives White tremendous play on the dark squares; Adorjan-Zsu.Polgar, Budapest 1991. A model in the construction of a plan with a symmetrical formation.

b) **10...b5** 11 ♗f1 (11 ♗e2 ♕c7 12 e4 e5 13 g3!? ♖e8 14 a3 ♗b7 15 ♗g5 h6 16 dxe5!⩲ also resolved the tension to White's benefit in Epishin-J.Polgar, Madrid 1992) 11...c5 12 dxc5 ♗xc5 13 ♘g5! (again it seems that when Black heads for these symmetrical positions in the absence of slow play by

White, the first player's initiative causes persistent problems) 13...♗b7 14 ♘ce4 ♘xe4 15 ♘xe4 ♗e7 16 ♘d6! ♗d5 17 e4! ♗xd6 18 exd5 ♖c8 19 ♕e2 Karpov-J.Polgar, Madrid 1992, and in the absence of the light-squared bishop, Black's queenside is potentially very weak.

c) **10...♕e7** and now:

c1) **11 a3** is considered under the note to Black's 10th in Game 34, but looks fairly harmless.

c2) **11 h3** b5 12 ♗d3 c5 13 ♘e4 c4! 14 ♘xd6 ♕xd6 15 ♗e2 ♗b7 (Black's initiative on the light squares more than compensates for the bishop pair) 16 ♗d2 ♖fc8 (Anand also suggests that the very direct 16...♘e4 17 ♗a5 f5 Δ...♖f6-g6 gives a promising attack) 17 ♖dc1 ♘e4 18 ♗a5 f5∓ Karpov-Anand, Brussels Ct (2) 1991.

c3) **11 e4(!)** is the most likely to cause problems, and the reason for my caution about 9...a6. After 11...e5 12 h3! we have transposed to Karpov-Anand, 4th match game, examined under note 'a2' to White's 10th below. Improvements suggested for Black there are not enough to make it an enticing prospect.

11 ♘e4!

A very important novelty after which Black seems unable to equalize and must tread very carefully. Much less convincing was **11 e4?!** (not particularly logical since in the resultant positions of central tension the black queen sits more comfortably on c7 than e7 where it is not vulnerable to a later ♘f5) 11...e5 (11...c5 12 d5 ♘b6 13 ♗e2!? Browne) 12 h3 exd4! (improving on 12...b5 13 ♗e2 ♗b7 14 dxe5 ♘xe5 15 ♗g5 ♘xf3+ 16 ♗xf3 ♗e5 17 ♗xf6 gxf6! 18 ♗g4± Browne-Renet, St. Martin 1991) 13 ♘xd4 ♖e8 14 a3 ♗e5 15 ♗e3 ♘f8 16 ♖d2 b5 17 ♗a2 c5 18 ♘de2 c4 19 ♘d5 ♘xd5 20 exd5 ♘g6 when Black had assumed some initiative in Kamsky-Anand, Tilburg 1991.

11 ... ♘xe4
12 ♕xe4 e5

12...c5 13 ♗d3 ♘f6 14 ♕h4± (Epishin) also gives White the makings of an attack.

Also unsatisfactory for Black is **12...♗e7** 13 ♗d2 b5 14 ♗d3 g6 15 ♖ac1 ♗b7 16 ♕g4 ♕b6 17 b4± Danielsen-L.B.Hansen, Danish Ch (Århus) 1992.

13 ♕h4 ♘f6

'Saddling' White with an isolated pawn only aids White's development: **13...exd4?!** 14 exd4 ♘f6 15 ♗d3 Δ♗g5±. Indeed, Epishin is about to sacrifice two pawns for just such a prize.

14 e4!

There is nothing to be gained by **14 dxe5** ♗xe5 15 ♘xe5 ♕xe5 16 ♕d4 (it is hard to develop otherwise) 16...♕xd4 17 ♖xd4 c5 Δ...♗e6 neutralizing White's bishop pair. Development and threatening the knight on f6 –

Black's only piece on kingside duty – is the priority, and the immediate refutation of the superficially attractive **14...♗g4?** by 15 ♗g5! ♗xf3 16 ♗xf6±.

14 ... exd4
15 e5!! *(185)*

185
B

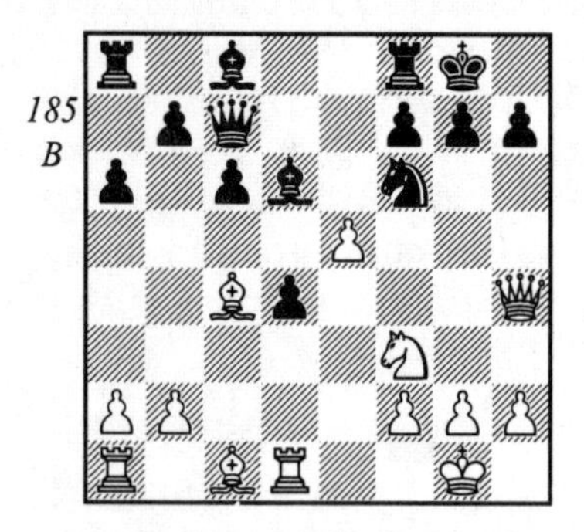

A beautiful clearance sacrifice opening diagonals for both the white bishops to participate in the onslaught. Epishin's appreciation of the dangers for Black in a fairly innocuous looking situation makes this game very striking and instructive.

15 ... ♗xe5
16 ♖e1?!

An inaccuracy which gives Black a little extra time to organize a defence and restrict White to just a positional advantage. As Epishin points out the immediate **16 ♗d3!** was better and gives a very dangerous attack after 16...♖e8 17 ♖e1! (17 ♗g5 h6 gives defensive chances) 17...♗g4 18 ♗g5 ♗xf3 19 ♗xf6 gxf6 20 ♕xh7+ ♔f8 21 gxf3 f5 22 ♔h1 ♗f6 23 ♖g1!±.

16 ... ♗d6
17 ♗d3 ♕a5!
18 ♗g5 ♗f5
19 ♗xf6 ♗xd3
20 ♗xg7! ♔xg7
21 ♕xd4+ ♔g8
22 ♕xd6 ♖ad8
23 ♕g3+

23 ♕e7 would have restricted Black's mobilization better. Epishin gives 23...♕b5 24 b3 ♖d5 25 h4±.

23 ... ♗g6
24 h4 ♖fe8
25 ♔h2 ♔g7
26 ♖ad1 ♖xe1
27 ♖xe1 ♖d5
28 a3 ♕d8
29 ♖e5

White has retained a positional advantage due to Black's split pawns on the kingside and inferior minor piece. He now sensibly seeks to realize this in a pure queen and minor piece ending in which the generic superiority of the knight is well documented. Black is not yet lost and a move later could have substantially stiffened his resistance by 30...f6 31 ♘c4 ♔f8 instead of further weakening his vulnerable structure. Still, the practical task of defending this ending is not to be relished.

Events unfolded in the following manner: **29...♖xe5 30 ♘xe5 h5?! 31 b4 ♕d4 32 ♘f3 ♕d7 33 ♕f4 f6 34 ♘d4 b6 35 ♕e3** (The knight is headed for the f4 square now that the bishop on g6 has been weakened) **35...♔f7 36 ♘e2 ♕d6+?!**

(36...♕g4 would have at least caused White some inconvenience) **37 ♘f4 c5 38 bxc5 bxc5 39 ♕g3! ♗f5 40 ♘xh5 ♕xg3+ 41 ♔xg3! c4 42 ♔f3** (White has brought his king into the 'square' of the passed pawn, and the rest is simple) **42...c3 43 ♔e3 ♔e7 44 ♘g3 ♗h7 45 ♘e2 c2 46 ♔d2 1-0**.

Game 33
Khalifman-Tukmakov
Sverdlovsk Teams 1987

1 d4 ♘f6 2 c4 c6 3 ♘c3 d5 4 e3 e6 5 ♘f3 ♘bd7 6 ♕c2 ♗d6 7 ♗e2 0-0 8 0-0 dxc4 9 ♗xc4

9 ... b5
10 ♗e2

Increasingly this modest retreat is looking like the best. The alternatives:

a) **10 ♗b3?!** looks a little odd since Black has alternatives to playing for ...e5, and can leave the bishop 'biting on granite' as they say. **10...♗b7** and now:

a1) **11 ♖d1** ♕c7 12 ♕e2?! a6 13 h3 c5∓ 14 ♗d2 c4 15 ♗c2 b4 16 ♘a4 ♕c6 17 ♖ac1 ♖ac8 18 ♖fe1 ♕b5! (Δ19 e4 ♗xe4∓) 19 a3 c3 20 bxc3 b3 and Black won material in Umanskaya-Dreev, Calcutta 1992. A typical punishment of passive planless play in these lines.

a2) **11 e4** c5! 12 ♘xb5?! (12 e5 ♗xf3 13 gxf3 cxd4! 14 exd6 ♕b6∓; or 12 dxc5 when 12...♗xc5 is safe, or 12...♘xc5 13 e5 ♗xf3 14 exf6 is messy and unclear) 12...♗xe4 13 ♕e2 ♗xf3 14 gxf3 (14 ♕xf3 ♗xh2+ ∓) 14...♗b8 15 f4 (otherwise ...♘h5 is strong) 15...a6!? 16 ♕f3 ♗xf4 17 ♗xf4 axb5 18 ♗d6 cxd4! 19 ♗xf8 ♕xf8 20 ♖ac1 ♖d8! 21 ♖c7 ♘c5 and Black had two pawns and weaknesses to target, which were good value for the exchange in Korchnoi-Tukmakov, Reggio Emilia 1987/8.

b) **10 ♗d3** can be met by:

b1) **10...♕c7** 11 e4 e5 12 ♘e2!? exd4 (12...♗b7!?; 12...a6 13 a4!?) 13 ♘exd4 ♗b7 (13...♘e5 14 ♘xe5 ♗xe5 15 ♘f3!?±) 14 ♘f5 c5 15 ♕d2! ♗e5 16 ♕g5 ♘xe4 17 ♕g4 g6 18 ♗xe4 ♘f6 19 ♕g5 ♘xe4 20 ♘e7+ ♔g7 21 ♕xe5 ♕xe5 22 ♘xe5 ♖fe8 23 ♘5c6 and White's extra piece was safe in Jo.Horvath-Smagin, Stary Smokovec 1990.

b2) **10...♗b7** and now:

b21) **11 e4** e5 12 dxe5 ♘xe5 13 ♘xe5 ♗xe5 14 h3 (14 ♕e2?! ♖e8 15 ♗e3 ♗xc3 16 bxc3 ♘xe4 17 ♕c2 ♘f6 18 ♖fd1 ♕c7 19 h3 h6 and White's compensation does not look sufficient; Fokin-Dreev, Gorky 1989) 14...♖e8 15 ♗e3 (15 f4!? is a bit loose: 15...♗d4+ 16 ♔h1 ♗xc3 17 bxc3 ♘h5!?) 15...♕e7 16 ♖ae1 a6 17 ♘e2 c5! 18 ♗xc5 ♕c7 (Δ19...♘xe4, 19...♗xb2) 19 ♗d4 ½-½ Portisch-Tukmakov, Reggio Emilia 1987/8.

b22) **11 a3**:

b221) **11...♕e7** is playable. Vyzhmanavin-Shirov, Tilburg 1992 took an interesting and surprising course: 12 ♘g5 ♗xh2+ 13 ♔xh2 ♘g4+ 14 ♔g1 ♕xg5 15 f3 ♘gf6 16 e4 ♕h4 17 ♕f2 ♕xf2 18 ♔xf2 e5 19 ♗e3 and White's bishop pair along with Black's inactive minor pieces gave enough for a pawn.

b222) **11...♖c8!?** 12 ♖d1 (12 b4 a5 13 ♖b1 axb4 14 axb4 ♕e7 15 e4 e5 16 h3! exd4 17 ♘xd4 ♗xb4 18 ♗e3 g6 19 ♖fe1∞ Epishin. White has undisputable compensation, but maybe 19...♗c5!? Δ...b4, ...♗xd4 and ...c5 is an interesting way to generate counterplay) 12...c5! (12...♕e7 13 e4 e5 14 h3± Epishin) 13 ♘xb5 (13 ♘e5 a6!=) 13...♗xf3 14 gxf3 ♗b8 15 ♕e2 ♘d5 16 f4 **cxd4?** 17 ♘xd4 e5? 18 ♘f3± since after 18...exf4 19 ♗xh7+ Black would pay dearly for undermining his once strong knight on d5. That was Epishin-Shabalov, USSR Ch 1990. **16...a6** is better, but after 17 ♘c3 cxd4 18 ♘xd5 exd5, instead of 19 exd4 a5= (Epishin), Lukacs/Hazai suggest 19 ♗f5 dxe3 20 ♗xe3±.

b223) **11...a6!** is a very logical suggestion also from Lukacs and Hazai. The inserted moves by no means help White after **12 e4** e5, and **12 b4** a5 13 ♖b1 axb4 14 axb4 ♕e7 15 ♕b3 e5 16 dxe5 ♘xe5 17 ♘xe5 18 f4 ♕e7 19 e4 c5! seems to give Black good counterplay.

10 ... ♗b7

Natural and best in my opinion. Other moves have been tried, but they are less flexible and their compensating merit is unclear:

a) The immediate **10...♖e8** has sometimes been favoured by Shirov, but from the evidence I expect he will tire of it soon, e.g. **11 ♖d1 ♕c7**:

a1) **12 ♘e4!?** (a similar idea to Game 32) 12...♘xe4 13 ♕xe4 e5 14 dxe5 ♘xe5 15 ♘g5 f5 16 ♕d4 ♗e7 17 ♘f3 ♘f7 18 ♕c3 a6 19 a4 b4 20 ♕c2 and White had many positional trumps in Brenninkmeijer-Shirov, Ter Apel 1991.

a2) Still more instructive was the beautiful lesson in strategic judgement and the transformation of advantages to which Karpov treated us in his game against Shirov at Biel 1992. The game proceeded **12 b3** e5 13 h3 ♗b7 14 ♗b2 a6 15 dxe5! ♘xe5 16 a4! ♖ad8 (16...b4 17 ♘b1 Δ♘d2-c4 is unsatisfactory for Black) 17 ♘g5! ♕e7 18 ♘ce4 ♘xe4 19 ♘xe4 ♗b4 20 ♘g3 f6 (White was actually threatening 21 ♖xd8 ♖xd8 22 ♕e4+-) 21 ♗xe5!! *(186)*.

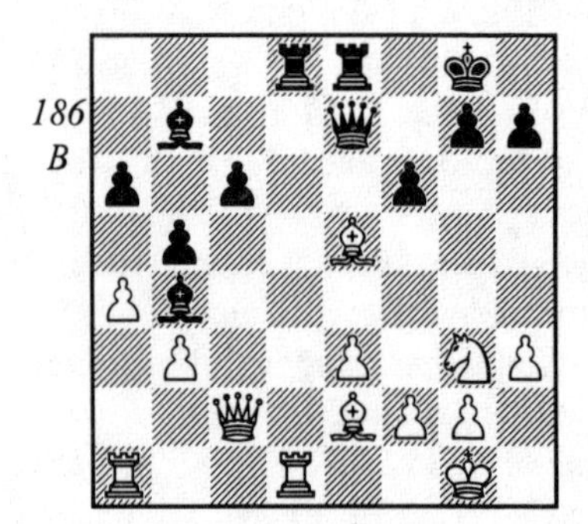

186
B

It takes a special level of judgement to take such decisions, and in this case, a little calculation too. Of course White is better, but Karpov sees a way to magnify greatly the light-square weaknesses which ...f6 has helped to create, and the poor scope of the bishop on b7 does nothing to combat. Such a structure, where White is preventing ...c5, is the nightmare of 9...b5 players. 21...♕xe5 22 ♗d3 h6 (It is this necessity which justifies White's 21st. The point is that 22...g6, desirable on positional grounds, loses tactically to 23 ♗xg6 hxg6 24 ♕xg6+ ♔h8 25 ♕h6+ ♔g8 26 ♘h5+-) 23 ♗g6 ♖f8 24 ♘f5 c5 (Sadly for Shirov the text adds more scope to the white rook on a1 than to his own hapless bishop) 25 axb5 axb5 26 ♖a7 ♕c7 27 ♘h4 ♖xd1+ 28 ♕xd1 ♖a8 29 ♕g4! ♕c6 30 ♖xb7! (there is a nice irony that White ends up sacrificing the exchange to rid Black of the bishop which up until now has been his Achilles' Heel) 30...♕xb7 31 ♕e6+ ♔h8 32 ♗e4 1-0 Karpov-Shirov, Biel 1992. Karpov offers the following pretty line 32...♕a6 33 ♘g6+ ♔h7 34 ♘e5+ ♔h8 35 ♘f7+ ♔g8 36 ♘xh6+ ♔h8 37 ♕g8+ ♖xg8 38 ♘f7#. A nice variation on Philidor's famous theme.

b) **10...♕c7** 11 ♗d2 ♖e8 (11...a6!?) 12 ♖ac1 ♕b8 13 ♘e4 ♘xe4 14 ♕xe4 ♗b7 15 ♕h4! (A standard idea when ...♕d8 cannot be effected in reply without a price. Here if 15...♕d8 White has 16 ♕xd8 ♖axd8 17 ♗a5! ♖c8 18 ♘d2± Karpov/Zaitsev) 15...h6 16 ♖fd1 a5 17 ♗e1± Karpov-Van der Wiel, Tilburg 1988.

11 a3?!

Here again White has tried a variety of moves, and the rather passive text seems far from the most critical. The pecking order among the others is still a matter for debate, so:

a) **11 b3** e5 12 ♗b2 ♖e8 13 dxe5 (13 ♖fd1 e4 14 ♘e5 ♕e7! 15 ♘xd7 ♕xd7∓ Lobron) 13...♘xe5 14 ♖ad1 ♕c7 15 ♘g5 (15 h3=) 15...♘g6 16 g3 (Δ♘ge4 hindering ...c5) 16...♗e5! 17 ♗f3? (17 ♘f3 ♗d6=) 17...♕e7 and White's pieces were coordinating badly in Bischoff-Lobron, Hamburg 1991.

b) **11 e4** e5 12 dxe5 ♘xe5 13 ♘xe5 ♗xe5 14 ♗g5 h6 15 ♗h4 ♕b6!? 16 ♖ad1 ♖fe8 17 ♗f3 ♖e6 18 ♗g3 ♗xg3 19 hxg3 a5 20 ♖d2 ♖ae8 21 ♖fd1 c5 and Black was certainly no worse in P.H.Nielsen-Knaak, Bad Lauterberg 1991.

c) **11 ♗d2** has been quite popular, but Black seems to have little to fear: **11...a6** (11...♖e8 12 ♖fd1 ♕c7 13 ♖ac1 ♖ac8 14 ♘e4 ♘xe4 15 ♕xe4 c5 16 ♕h4 ♗e7! {16...c4?! 17 e4} 17 ♕h3 c4 18 b3 ♗a3 19 ♗d3 ♘f6 20 ♖c2 ♗e4! 21 ♗xe4 ♘xe4 22 ♕h5 ♕b7∓ was Stangl-Kuporosov, Brno 1991) and now White has tried two distinct approaches:

c1) **12 e4** e5 13 dxe5 ♘xe5 14 ♘xe5 ♗xe5 15 f4 ♗d4+ 16 ♔h1 b4 17 ♘d1?! (17 ♘a4 c5 18 ♗f3 ♖c8 19 ♖ae1 ♖e8 20 b3 ♗c6 21 e5

♗xf3 22 ♖xf3 ♘g4 23 h3 ♕h4 24 ♖ef1 ♘f2+ 25 ♔h2 ♘g4+ 26 ♔h1 etc ½-½ Schlosser-Kuporosov, Brno 1991) 17...♕b6! (Black successfully interferes with White's intended ♘e3 and ♖ae1) 18 ♗d3 g6 19 ♖e1 ♖ad8 20 ♘e3 c5 21 ♘c4 ♕e6 (White's king is surprisingly weak. If now 22 e5 ♘h5 23 f5 ♕e7 24 f6 ♕e6 25 ♗e4 ♕g4! threatening ...♘g3+ mating) 22 ♖e2 ♕g4 23 ♖f1 ♖fe8 24 ♗e1 ♘h5 25 h3 ♕d7!? (25...♘g3+ would have yielded a thematic edge; Black tries for more) 26 ♖f3 ♕c7! 27 ♗h4 ♖d7 28 f5 g5! 29 ♗e1 ♖de7 and White was under pressure in Douven-J.Piket, Dutch Ch 1990.

c2) **12 ♘e4** ♘xe4 13 ♕xe4 ♖b8 (looks the simplest recipe) 14 ♕h4 ♕xh4 15 ♘xh4 c5 ½-½ Portisch-Ivanchuk, Linares 1989. In general, as we have observed, ideas with ♘e4 are only dangerous when the black queen is committed to c7 and hence h4 is available to her white counterpart.

d) **11 ♖d1** (probably the most testing) and now:

d1) **11...♕e7?!** is unpalatable: 12 e4! e5 13 dxe5 ♘xe5 14 ♘d4 ♗c5 15 ♘f5 ♕c7 16 ♗e3 ♗xe3 17 ♘xe3 ♕b6 18 ♖d6 ♕c5 19 ♕d2 b4 20 ♘a4± Cvitan-Panchenko, Moscow 1989.

d2) **11...♕c7** and now:

d21) The apparently unassuming **12 ♗d2** is important:

d211) **12...♖ae8** 13 ♖ac1 ♕b8 14 ♗d3 a6 15 ♘e4 ♘xe4 16 ♗xe4 f5 17 ♗xc6 ♖c8 18 d5 ♘f6 19 ♕d3 ♘xd5 20 ♗d7 was much better for White in Adorjan-G.Flear, Polanica Zdroj 1992.

d212) **12...a6!** 13 b4 a5 14 ♖ac1 ♖fc8 15 ♕b3 ♗xb4 16 ♘xb5 ♕b8 17 ♘c3 c5 18 a3 cxd4 19 axb4 dxc3 20 ♖xc3= Ftačnik-Piket, Groningen 1988; Black's activity is worth as much as the bishop pair.

d22) Another possibility is **12 ♘e4!?**, but Black fared OK in M.Gurevich-Thorhallsson, Reykjavik 1988 with 12...♘xe4 13 ♕xe4 ♖ae8 14 a4 e5 15 h3 c5 16 ♕c2 exd4 17 exd4 ♗e4 18 ♕d2 ♘f6. See also 11...♕b8!? for discussion of the analogous position from J.Horvath-Wells.

d23) **12 e4!? e5 13 dxe5 ♘xe5 14 ♘d4**. With White's king's rook on d1, 14 ♘xe5 Δa later f4 is not so appropriate. The position after 14 ♘d4 has occurred quite frequently in practice, and we have another parting of the ways, and some doubt concerning Black's best approach:

d231) **14...b4** looks dubious. In Kir.Georgiev-Dreev, Manila IZ 1990, Black eventually won but White missed several chances for advantage: 15 ♘f5! ♗c5 16 ♘a4 ♗xf2+ (positionally virtually forced, but definitely unsound) 17 ♔xf2 ♘eg4+ 18 ♗xg4 ♘xg4+ 19 ♔f3 (19 ♔e1 ♕h2 20 ♕e2± Dreev, was simpler) 19...♘xh2+ 20 ♔f2 (20 ♔e2 ♗a6+ 21 ♔e1 ♖fe8 22 g3! Δ♗f4 is another Dreev self-refutation. Still, the text is fine so long as White intends to transpose to proceed as in the note to his 19th) 20...♘g4+ 21 ♔e1 ♕h2 22 ♗g5?? (22 ♕e2! as indicated would have consolidated) 22...♗a6! (Suddenly Black's attack has enough reserves!) 23 ♘c5 ♕g1+ 24 ♔d2 ♖fd8+! 25 ♗xd8 ♖xd8+ 26 ♔c1 ♖xd1+ 27 ♕xd1 ♕xc5+ 28 ♔b1 h5 29 ♕d4 ♕xd4 30 ♘xd4 ♗d3+ 31 ♔c1 ♗xe4 and Black's kingside pawns gave him a decisive endgame advantage.

d232) **14...♘ed7** 15 g3 b4 16 ♘a4 (16 ♘f5 ♗e5 17 ♘a4 c5 probably gives Black sufficient counterplay too) 16...♖fe8 17 ♘f5 ♗f8 18 ♗f4 ♕a5 19 f3 ♘b6 20 ♘xb6 axb6 21 ♘d6 ♗xd6 22 ♖xd6 c5 23 a4 ♗a6 looked OK for Black in Adorjan-J.Piket, Novi Sad OL 1990 although White later won.

d233) **14...♗c5** 15 h3 (15 ♘f5? fails simply to 15...♘eg4) 15...♕b6 (15...♖fe8 16 ♗e3 a6 17 ♖ac1 ♗b6 18 b4 ♖ac8 19 ♗g5 ♗xd4! 20 ♖xd4 c5 21 bxc5 ♕xc5 22 ♕d1 ♘f3+ 23 ♗xf3 ♕xg5 left Black more actively placed in Cs.Horvath-O'Donnell, Siofok 1990) 16 ♗e3 ♖ad8 17 ♘f5 ♗xe3 18 ♘xe3 g6 19 ♖ac1 ½-½ Adorjan-Jo.Horvath, Hungarian Ch 1991. White is yet to prove an advantage here either.

d234) **14...♘g6** was originally suggested as an improvement by Dreev himself. Brenninkmeijer-Kuijf, Dutch Ch 1991 tested this out and Black was virtually equal after 15 g3 ♖fe8 16 ♗f3 ♖ad8 17 ♘f5 ♗c5 18 ♗e3 ♗xe3 19 ♘xe3 a6 20 ♗g2 ♕b6.

d3) **11...♕b8!?** *(187)*.

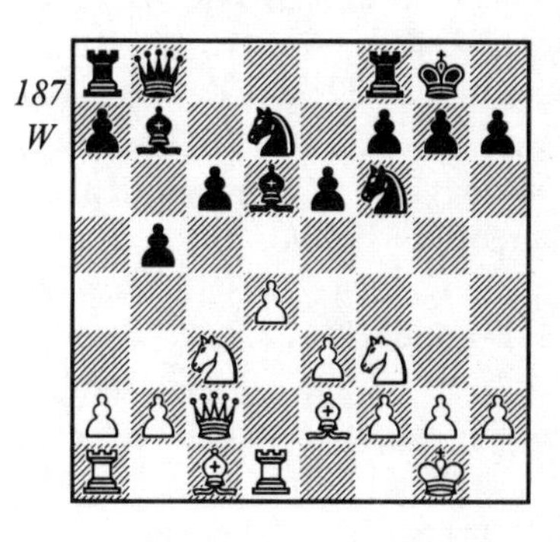
187
W

A recent idea which I believe Black should consider seriously. The point is simply that on b8 Black's queen is not vulnerable to tricks on the c-file. The claim is that this outweighs the temporary embarrassment of the rook on a8. I think the idea is very interesting. A few possibilities:

d31) **12 ♗d2** a6! and b4 is not possible. Black will play ...c5 with a comfortable game.

d32) **12 e4** e5 13 dxe5 ♘xe5 14 ♘d4 ♘g6(!) 15 g3 ♖e8 16 ♘f5 ♗f8 (In the analogous position with ...♕c7, this would of course not be possible) 17 ♗g5 ♕e5 18 ♗f3 h6 19 ♗xf6 ♕xf6 20 ♗g2 ♘e5 21 f4 ♘g4 22 e5 ♕g6 23 ♘e4 (A mistake which allows a very 'visual' winning combination. Better was 23 ♘e2 ♗c8 24 ♘ed4 when taking twice on f5 followed by 26...♗c5+ is a draw, but Black may also consider 24...c5!? 25 ♗xa8 cxd4 with interesting compensation) 23...♕xf5 24 ♘f6+ gxf6 25 ♕xf5 ♗c5+ 26 ♔h1 ♘f2+ 27 ♔g1 ♘xd1+ 28 ♔h1 ♘f2+ 29 ♔g1 ♖ad8! 30 exf6 ♖d5!! 31 ♗xd5 ♘d1+ 32 ♔h1 ♖e1+ 33 ♔g2 ♘e3+ 34 ♔f3 ♘xf5 35 ♖xe1 cxd5 36 ♖e8+ ♔h7 0-1 Lingnau-Knaak, Bundesliga 1992/3.

d33) **12 ♘e4** ♘xe4 13 ♕xe4 c5 14 ♕h4 c4!? (14...a6 15 dxc5 ♘xc5 16 b3 leaves White with a nagging edge) 15 e4 e5 (I rejected 15...♕d8 ♗g5 f6 16 ♗e3 f5 17 ♗g5 ♕b6 as too risky, but the positional prizes are quite high, and Joszef Horvath felt it was well worth consideration) 16 d5 (16 ♗e3!?) and now instead of **16...a6?!** J.Horvath-Wells, Budapest First Saturday 1993, Black could obtain good play on the queenside by **16...♘c5** 17 ♗e3 ♘a4!? 18 ♖d2 c3∓.

11 ...	**a6**

White's rather uncritical 11th move choice affords Black the luxury to prepare ...c5 at relative leisure. At the same time, 12 b4 a5! would not be in White's favour.

12 ♖d1	**c5**
13 dxc5	**♘xc5**
14 b4	**♘ce4**
15 ♘xe4	**♘xe4**
16 ♗b2	**♖c8**

Of course the game is equal, and with correct play should result in a draw. Still, the next few moves confirm my feeling that Black's pieces (especially ♗b7 *vs* ♗e2) are slightly more active, and the speed with which Tukmakov whips up an attack is notable. There are many such positions that arise in chess theory when White plays in the opening phase not weakly but uncritically, and it is important that in such a quiet position that the draw should not be inevitable.

17 ♕d3	**♕e7**
18 ♖ac1	**♖xc1**
19 ♖xc1	**♖d8**
20 ♕c2	**h6**
21 ♗d3	**f5!**

An excellent decision. **21...♘g5** looks tempting, but White has a good choice between the solid and simplifying **22 ♘xg5** ♕xg5 23 ♗f1=; and **22 ♘d4** asking Black's knight to justify itself.

22 ♘e5	

The tactical justification of ...f5 is that the natural positional/defensive **22 ♗e5?** fails to 22...♘xf2 23 ♔xf2 ♗xf3∓ utilizing the 'loose' situation of the bishop on d3.

22 ...	**♘xf2!** *(188)*

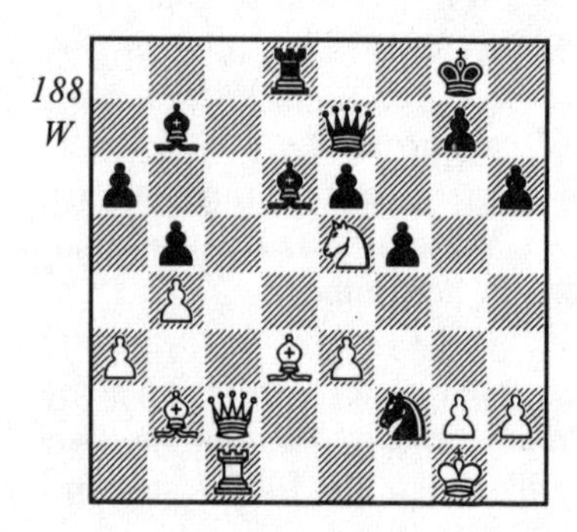
188
W

The same motif as in the last note, except in a far less obvious and more complex circumstance. It does not lead to a clear theoretical advantage, but it does at a stroke succeed in utterly unbalancing the play.

23 ♔xf2 **♕h4+**
24 ♔f1

Since if **24 ♔g1** ♕g5 which neatly 'forks' the e3 pawn and an overworking of the white queen.

24 ... **♕xh2**
25 ♘f3 **♗xf3**
26 gxf3 **♕h1+**
27 ♔f2 **♕h4+!?**
28 ♔e2?

Black's enterprising play is rewarded by a time-trouble induced error; White had to try **28 ♔g1** when he can insist on a draw by perpeetual. Tukmakov mentions the possibility 28...♕g5+ 29 ♔f1 ♕xe3 30 ♕e2 ♗f4 31 ♕xe3 ♗xe3 32 ♖d1 g5 33 ♔e2 ♗f4∞, but 34 ♗xf5 seems to win on the spot, so maybe 32...♔f7.

28 ... **♗g3!**
29 ♖g1

29 ♕c3? fails to 29...♕h2+ 30 ♔d1 ♗e5!; **29 ♖f1** ♕h2+ 30 ♔d1 ♖xd3+ 31 ♕xd3 ♕xb2 gives Black a clear plus too – Tukmakov.

After the text Black should win the ending, and White's 33rd is a mistake which eases the technical task: **29...♕h2+ 30 ♔f1 ♖xd3!∓ 31 ♕xh2 ♗xh2 32 ♖xg7+ ♔f8 33 ♔e2 ♖xa3 34 ♖g2 ♖b3 35 ♗g7+ ♔f7 36 ♗xh6 ♖b2+ 37 ♔f1 ♖xg2 0-1.**

24 8...dxc4: 9...♕e7 and 9...e5

Matches at all stages of the World Championship cycle attract great attention from opening theorists. 9...♕e7 was an important topic of the Karpov-Anand candidates match and also a game from the Korchnoi-Timman match, the theoretical importance of which may well have been underestimated. To some critics the whole idea of 9...♕e7 was wrong, and it is true that the commitment of the queen to this square can prove problematic, for example when White plays e4 with correct timing as in Karpov-Anand, 4th game, which was a fine strategic display from the former champion. The main focus of criticism arose from the opening of the 8th game, where Karpov introduced 10 a3(!), supposedly an improvement on 10 h3 which permitted 10...c5(!). Despite White's alleged advantage in the 8th game several players have been willing to defend the Black side of 10 a3 e5. One of these later encounters forms the main game, chosen as lesser known than the candidates matches and a really entertaining tactical *mêlée*. Recently, Alexander Chernin has gone still further towards strengthening Black's case.

Game 34
Stohl-Rogers
Brno 1991

1 d4 ♘f6 2 c4 c6 3 ♘c3 d5 4 e3 e6 5 ♘f3 ♘bd7 6 ♕c2 ♗d6 7 ♗e2 0-0 8 0-0

8 ...	**dxc4**
9 ♗xc4	**♕e7**

As with 9...a6, flexibility is a major motive behind the text. Black can consider ...e5, ...c5 and even ...b5 according to circumstances.

The immediate **9...e5** *(189)* makes less frequent appearances now, but is still important. Since 10 h3 ♕e7 is considered below, we look here at:

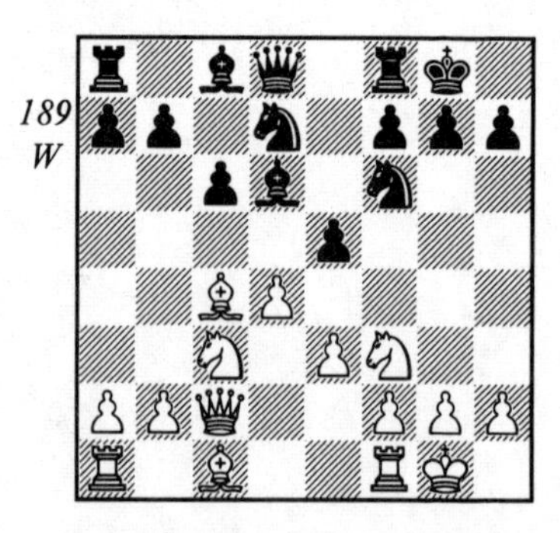
189
W

a) **10 ♗b3(!)** and now Black has no clear route to equality. Practice has seen:

a1) **10...exd4?!** as usual frees White's game a little too much for comfort. One warning: 11 exd4

♘b6 12 ♗g5 ♗g4?! 13 ♘e5 ♗h5 14 ♘e4± ♗e7 15 ♘g3 ♕xd4 16 ♖ce1 ♗b4 17 ♗xf6 ♗xe1 18 ♘xh5 gxf6 19 ♘xf6+ ♔g7 20 ♕f5 ♗d2 21 ♘h5+ ♔h6 22 ♕f6+ 1-0 Zviagintsev-Whiteley, Cappelle la Grande 1993.

a2) **10...♕e7** and now White has two good lines:

a21) **11 ♗d2** e4 12 ♘g5! ♗xh2+ 13 ♔xh2 ♘g4+ 14 ♔g1 ♕xg5 15 ♕xe4 ♘df6 16 ♕f4! ♕xf4 17 exf4± Polugaevsky-Pinter, Zagreb 1987.

a22) **11 ♖e1(!)** ♖e8(?!) (11...e4 12 ♘d2 ♖e8 13 f3!± Miles) 12 ♘g5 ♖f8 13 ♗d2 h6 14 ♘ge4 ♘xe4 15 ♘xe4 ♗b8 16 f4! exd4 17 exd4± ♘f6?! 18 ♗b4 ♕xb4 19 ♘xf6+ gxf6 20 ♕g6+ Δ♖e3+- Miles-Summerscale, Dublin Z 1993.

a3) **10...h6 11 h3** ♖e8 12 a3 ♗c7 13 ♗a2 exd4 14 exd4 ♘f8!? 15 d5 cxd5 16 ♘xd5 ♘xd5 17 ♗xd5 ♕xd5 18 ♕xc7= Panno-Granda Zuñiga, Buenos Aires 1992. What however of **11 ♖d1!?** since if 11...♕e7 12 ♘h4! or 11...♕c7 12 ♕g6! ?

a4) **10...♕c7** does not seem to solve all of Black's problems either: 11 h3 (11 ♗d2!?) 11...b5 12 ♘g5 ♗b7 13 ♖d1 ♖ad8 (Black already had to be very careful, e.g. 13...exd4 14 ♖xd4 a6 15 ♖h4! h6 16 ♖xh6!; and 13...a6 14 ♘ce4 ♘xe4 15 ♘xe4 ♗e7 16 d5! were two unpleasant ways to go down) 14 a4 a6 15 ♘ce4 ♘xe4 16 ♘xe4 ♗e7 17 axb5 axb5 Rohde-Shabalov, Philadelphia 1990, when instead of **18 d5** ♘b6!∓ White could have kept a bind with **18 ♗d2!** Δ18...♖c8 19 ♗a5 ♕b8 20 ♘c5!.

b) **10 h3** exd4?! (10...♕e7 see note 'a' to White's 10th below) 11 exd4 ♘b6 12 ♗b3 ♘bd5 (not 12...h6 13 ♗xh6! gxh6 14 ♕g6+ ♔h8 15 ♕xh6+ ♘h7 16 ♘e4 ♗e7 17 ♘f6! ♗f5 18 ♘h5 ♗f6 19 ♘g5! ♗xd4 20 ♘xh7 ♗xh7 21 ♖ad1 f5 22 ♖fe1!+- Smagin-Monin, Pinsk 1986) 13 ♗g5 ♘c7 (13...♗e6!?) 14 ♖ad1 ♗e6 15 ♖fe1 ♗xb3 16 ♕xb3 ♖b8 17 ♘e5 ♗e7± Stangl-Renet, Dortmund 1991.

10 a3

As mentioned above the text received much acclaim after Karpov's success with it in the last of the Semi-Slav clashes with Anand. It has since eclipsed alternatives, but this is perhaps not fully justified:

a) **10 h3!?** *(190)* was previously Karpov's choice, when Black can choose from:

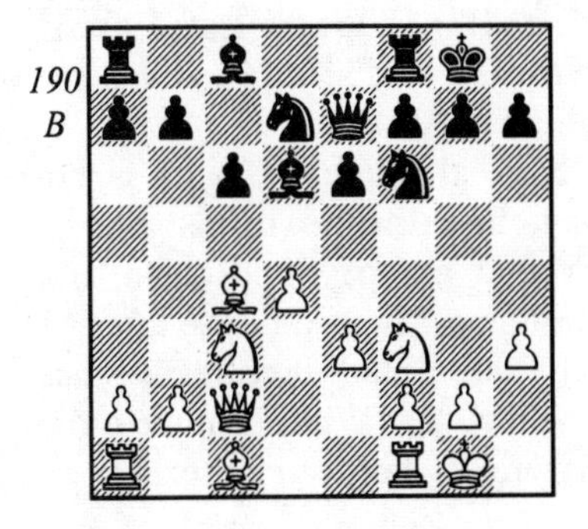

a1) **10...e5** transposes to the current main line if White continues 11 a3, but White has some independent tries too:

a11) **11 ♗d2(?!)** and now:

a111) **11...exd4?!** is a classic case of the premature capture on d4 giving White an easy attacking game: 12 exd4 ♘b6 13 ♖fe1 ♕c7 14 ♗b3 ♗f4 15 ♖e5! ♗xd2 (15...♗xe5 16 dxe5 ♘e8 17 ♘g5±) 16 ♕xd2 ♕d6 17 ♖ae1 ♗d7 18 ♘g5 ♖ae8 19 ♖xe8 ♗xe8 20 ♘e6+- Smagin-Govedarica, Trnava 1987.

a112) **11...♗c7?!** 12 ♗b3 h6 13 ♘h4 ♖e8 (13...exd4 just falls short of equalizing. Dreev-Wessman, Reykjavik 1990 continued 14 exd4 ♕d6 15 ♘f3 ♘b6 16 ♖fe1 ♘bd5 17 ♖ac1 ♗e6 18 ♘a4 ♖ac8 19 ♘c5 ♗c8± but playable for Black) 14 ♘b5?! (As usual, 14 ♘g6 serves only to transfer the initiative after 14...♕d6 15 ♘xe5 ♘xe5 16 dxe5 ♕xe5. However, 14 ♘f5 ♕f8 15 ♘b5 merited attention) 14...♗b8 15 ♘g6 ♕d8 16 dxe5 ♘xe5 17 ♘d4 ♘xg6 (Black could also consider 17...♕d6!? 18 ♘xe5 ♕xe5 19 f4 ♕e4!?) 18 ♕xg6 ♘d5 19 ♕d3 ♕d6 20 ♘f3 ♘f6= Farago-Chernin, Austria 1993.

Still, although 11...♗c7 is not bad, and the positions arising from it are of importance, not least since they can arise after 11 ♗b3 too, I mark it critically since I believe that White's move order is careless and can be exploited. Black has two more enticing options:

a113) **11...b5!?** worked out well in Timoshchenko-Ivanov, Vienna 1991: 12 ♗d3 ♗b7 13 ♘e4 ♘xe4 14 ♗xe4 g6 15 ♖ac1 ♖ac8 16 ♖fe1 f5∓.

a114) **11...e4!?** 12 ♘g5 ♘b6 13 ♗b3 ♗f5 14 f3 ♖ae8 15 fxe4 ♗g6 16 ♕d1! h6 17 e5 hxg5 18 exf6 gxf6 19 ♕f3 ♔g7 20 e4 ♕d6 with counterplay in Wojtkiewicz-Arakhamia, Bern 1991.

a12) **11 ♗b3!?** b6 (for 11...♗c7 12 ♗d2 see line 'a112' above. In view of Black's alternatives studied above, 11 ♗b3 seems to be a more accurate move order if White wants to reach this position) 12 e4 (12 ♖d1!? is more logical since developing naturally with ...♗b7 can weaken f5 when the centre becomes open) 12...exd4 13 ♘xd4 ♕e5! (13...♘c5?! 14 ♗g5 ♘xb3 15 axb3 ♗d7 16 f4 ♗c5 17 ♖ad1 ♕d6 18 ♕f2 with a strong initiative; Khalifman-Khuzman, USSR 1987) 14 ♘f3 ♕h5= Khalifman.

a2) **10...a6** is not well timed here since h3 was a good reparation for 11 e4! e5 12 ♖d1! b5 (12...exd4 13 ♘xd4 ♘e5 14 ♗f1±, but could Black try 12...♘b6 here along the lines of Salov-Ivanchuk {see Game 35} although ...a6 weakens this piece somewhat?) 13 ♗f1 c5 14 d5 c4 15 a4 ♖b8 16 axb5 axb5 17 ♖a5! and Black's queenside pawns were being undermined in Karpov-Anand, Brussels Ct (4)

1991. Compare again 10 a3 against which the approach with 10...a6 has more validity since White has not yet taken the g4 square away from Black's knights.

a3) **10...c5** was the reason why 10 a3 was deemed to be more accurate, but this is unclear. **11 dxc5 ♗xc5 12 e4(!) ♗d6** and now:

a31) **13 ♘d4?!** (preparing to advance the f-pawn after due preparation, but Anand's knight manoeuvre prevents this and renders it less than harmless) 13...♘e5! 14 ♗b3 ♗d7 15 ♗e3 ♘g6! (Anand gives the variation 15...♖fd8 16 f4 ♘c6 17 e5 ♘xd4 18 ♗xd4 ♗c5 19 ♖ad1 ♗xd4+ 20 ♖xd4 ♘e8 21 ♖fd1± which well illustrates the dangers if Black does not respond with enough energy) 16 ♖ad1 ♖fd8 17 ♘f3 ♗c6 18 ♖fe1 ♖dc8! (An excellent move which prepares ...♗b4 and the focusing of pressure on White's e4 pawn) 19 ♕b1 ♗b4! 20 ♗d2 ♖d8! 21 a3 ♗c5 22 ♘a4 ♗d6! 23 ♘c3 (The tempting 23 e5 is too risky after 23...♗xf3 24 exd6 ♕xd6 25 gxf3 ♘h4 26 ♖e3 ♕f4; or 24 exf6 ♕xf6 25 gxf3 ♗f4!) 23...♕c7 24 ♗a2 a6 25 ♗e3 b5 with good counterplay in Karpov-Anand, Brussels Ct (6) 1991.

a32) **13 ♘b5!** is most testing. After **13...♘e5! 14 ♘xe5 ♗xe5 15 f4 ♕c5+ 16 ♔h2 ♗d7** *(191)* the critical position is reached.

191
W

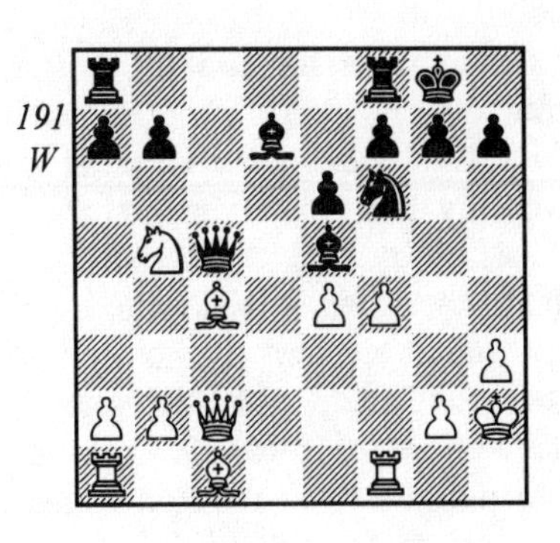

a321) In the game Korchnoi-Timman, Brussels Ct (6) 1991, Black's play was not seriously tested, and after **17 a4** ♗xb5 18 axb5 ♗d4 19 ♕e2 e5! the crisis had passed with Black enjoying a slight positional plus.

a322) **17 fxe5** is not dangerous either since 17...♗xb5 18 exf6 ♕xc4 is a fully adequate reply.

a323) However, **17 b4** is interesting, and after 17...♕c8, instead of **18 ♘xa7** ♖xa7 19 fxe5 ♘g4+! 20 hxg4 ♗xb5∞ Timman, when Black indeed seems to have sufficient compensation, I would suggest **18 fxe5!?** ♗xb5 19 exf6 when 19...♕xc4 20 ♕d2 ♕xf1? 21 ♗b2! leads to big trouble for Black.

b) **10 ♗d2** a6 11 a4 c5 (11...e5!?) 12 dxc5 (12 ♖ae1 b6 13 d5 ♘e5 14 ♘xe5 ♗xe5 15 e4 exd5 16 ♘xd5 ♘xd5 17 ♗xd5 ♗b7= Vyzhmanavin-Akopian, Moscow 1992) 12...♗xc5 13 e4 ♘g4 (13...♗d6!? 14 ♖ae1 ♘e5!?∞) 14 ♗f4 (14 ♖ae1?! ♘xf2!) 14...♗d6 15 ♕d2 ♘de5 16 ♘xe5 ♗xe5 17 ♖ad1±

Vyzhmanavin-Savchenko, Moscow 1992.

c) **10 e4** looks too committal to be really dangerous even though e7 is not always the ideal square for the black queen in these situations of central tension. Karpov gives 10...e5 11 ♗e3 (11 ♖d1 would transpose to Salov-Ivanchuk, Dortmund 1992, covered under note 'a' to 8...♕e7 in Game 35) 11...exd4 12 ♗xd4 ♘g4! 13 h3 ♘ge5 14 ♘xe5 ♘xe5 15 ♗e2 ♘g6=.

10 ... e5

Part of the motivation behind 10 a3 is to discourage **10...c5** which can indeed be answered here by 11 dxc5 ♗xc5 12 e4!? (12 b4 is also possible, but Karpov's more sophisticated idea has other designs for the b4 square) 12...♗d6 (12...♘g4 13 ♗f4! ♗d6 14 ♕d2!± Karpov) 13 ♘b5! ♘e5 14 ♘xe5 ♗xe5 15 ♗d2!± with the unpleasant threat of 16 ♗b4.

However, whilst **10...b5** 11 ♗a2 ♗b7 remains an untested suggestion of Jozsef Horvath, 10...a6!? has established itself as a quite respectable waiting move. Compare 9...a6 10 ♖d1 ♕e7 – which of White's moves is the more relevant? After **10...a6**:

a) As hinted at above, **11 e4** is nothing special with the h-pawn still at home.

b) **11 b4!?** is possible.

c) **11 ♖d1** should not be too problematic. After 11...e5 (11...c5!? or even 11...b5!? look reasonable too) 12 h3 b5 (Tukmakov suggests 12...e4!? since Black is in a position to support e4 rapidly, viz. 13 ♘g5 ♘b6 14 ♗a2 ♗f5 15 f3 ♖ae8 which looks quite a viable approach) 13 ♗d3?! c5 14 ♘e4 exd4 15 exd4 c4 16 ♘xd6 ♕xd6 17 ♗e4 ♖b8 18 ♗g5 ♖e8 19 ♗f5 ♗b7 20 d5 ♘c5 21 ♗h4 ♖bd8 the play was very complicated in Maiwald-Sakaev, Manila 1992 but I would prefer Black, since any attempt to push the white d-pawn unleashes the full force of Black's minor pieces.

d) **11 ♗d2** b5 12 ♗d3 c5 13 ♘e4 ♗b7 14 dxc5 ♘xc5! 15 ♘xf6+ ♕xf6 (seems fully adequate, but 15...gxf6!? is also very interesting when 16 ♗xh7+ ♔h8 would manifestly court danger for White down the g-file) 16 ♗xh7+ ♔h8 17 e4 ♔xh7 and now instead of the misguided **18 ♘g5+** of Sokolin-Ionov, St. Petersburg Ch 1992, **18 e5+** ♗e4 should liquidate to something resembling equality.

11 h3 ♗c7

Black fared OK with **11...a5** 12 ♗d2 ♗b8 **13 ♖fd1?!** h6 14 ♗a2 ♖e8 15 ♘h4 ♘f8 16 ♘f5 ♕c7= in Gurevich-Nogueiras, Leningrad 1987. However, White should try **13 ♗a2** and if 13...h6 14 ♘h4 it is not clear what the change of move order has added to Black's cause.

Van der Wiel mentioned **11...♔h8** in his notes, but after 12 ♗a2 h6 13 ♘h4 Black must play

13...g6 too which looks unappealing, since if **13...♘b6**, 14 ♗xf7! is strong.

11...♗b8!? however, is an interesting attempt by Chernin to prevent the ♘b5 problems of Karpov-Anand and the main game. So far the evidence is very encouraging for Black: **12 ♗a2 h6 13 ♘h4 ♖d8!? 14 ♘f5 ♕e8** (keeping f8 open for the knight) and now:

a) **15 ♘e4** ♘xe4 16 ♕xe4. White is looking for tricks based on the unusual placement of the black queen, e.g. **16...♘f6?** 17 ♘xh6 or **16...exd4?** 17 ♕g4!, but **16...♘f8!** 17 ♗d2 exd4 18 ♕e8 ♖xe8 19 ♘xd4 ♘e6 20 ♘xe6 ♗xe6 ½-½ Akopian-M.Gurevich, Wijk aan Zee 1993 seems to establish the case for the defence.

b) **15 ♘e2** is a similar idea of playing the knight to g3 to support its colleague on f5 that we shall see in Epishin-Akopian note 'b' to White's 15th below. Here again, though, the defence benefits from the possibility of 15...♘f8 16 dxe5 ♗xf5! (16...♕e5 allows White to execute his plan of ♘eg3 followed by f4 and e4) 17 ♕xf5 ♕xe5 18 ♘g3 ♕xf5 19 ♘xf5 ♘e6 20 b4 ♗e5 21 ♖b1 ♘e4 22 ♗b2 ♗xb2 with at the most a very slight edge for White in Karpov-Chernin, Tilburg 1992.

c) **15 ♗d2** ♘f8 16 ♖ad1 ♕d7!? (cleaner than 16...exd4 17 ♘xd4 ♗c7 18 ♗c1 ♗b6 19 ♖fe1 ♗xd4! {19...♘e6 20 ♘f5} 20 exd4 ♗e6 21 d5!?∞ Stangl-Chernin, Munich 1992) 17 ♘g3 exd4 18 exd4 ♕c7! 19 ♘ce2 ♗e6 20 ♗f4 ♕b6 21 ♗xe6 ½-½ Portisch-Chernin, Budapest Z 1993. Black is very comfortable here. According to Chernin, it is White who should be looking to equalize here by liquidating his d-pawn with 22 ♗e5 ♘d7 23 ♗xb8 ♖axb8 24 d5=.

12 ♗a2	**h6**
13 ♘h4	**♖e8**
14 ♘f5	**♕f8**
15 d5?!	

The above-mentioned Karpov-Anand match triggered a flurry of activity in this variation, despite some scepticism at the entire black approach. The text was an interesting attempt to improve on Karpov's 15 ♘b5 which despite his success is not totally clear in the face of possible improvements.

a) After **15 ♘b5 ♗b8 16 ♗d2! a5 17 dxe5** *(192)*.

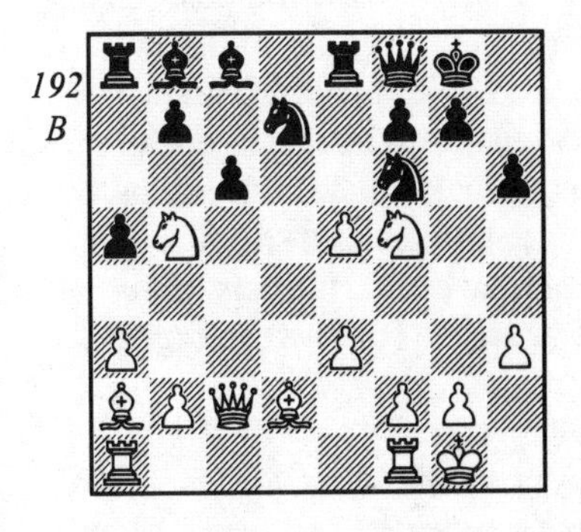

a1) The stem game went **17...♗xe5** (17...♘xe5 18 ♘c3) 18 f4! ♗b8 19 ♘c3 ♖d8 (19...♗a7!?±)

20 ♗e1! ♘h7 21 ♗h4 ♘df6 22 ♖ad1± Karpov-Anand, Brussels Ct (8) 1991.

a2) So far so good for White, but **17...♖xe5!** which Rogers intended here, and which I believe he said Anand had suggested to him by telephone (a handy service!), is much more testing since after 18 ♘c3 ♘c5! Black is claiming his fair share of the centre.

b) By contrast the recent idea **15 ♘e2** does not look very much to the point. After 15...♘b6 16 dxe5 ♖xe5! 17 ♘eg3 ♗e6 18 b4 ♗xa2 19 ♖xa2 g6 20 ♘d4 ♖ee8! 21 ♘de2 (If 21 ♗b2 Black can exchange with 21...♗xg3!, and follow up with 22...♘e4, ...♘d5 before neutralizing the a1-h8 diagonal with ...f6, with good play) 21...h5 22 ♖d1 ♖ad8 23 ♖xd8 ♖xd8 24 e4 ♖e8 White had at best a fractional initiative in Epishin-Akopian, Novosibirsk 1993.

The text is in fact a positionally motivated idea, but in the event it initiates an extremely complex tactical battle. White succeeds in ruffling Black's queenside pawns, but Rogers' excellent reply emphasizes that ceding the very important e5 square to Black was a high price to pay.

15 ... e4!

Variations such as **15...♘b6?!** 16 dxc6 bxc6 17 e4 ♗xf5 18 exf5 e4 19 ♘b5± would fully justify White's idea. It is possible that Stohl had dismissed Black's brave reply as too costly in material, and underestimated the new life which this sacrifice of the exchange would breathe into Black's entire position.

16 dxc6 bxc6
17 ♘b5

The only critical test. Not **17 ♘d5?** ♘xd5 18 ♗xd5 ♘f6! 19 ♗xc6 ♗xf5 20 ♗xa8 ♕d6-+.

17 ... ♗b8
18 ♕xc6 ♘e5
19 ♕xa8

Prefacing this capture with the desperado **19 ♘xh6+** is bad after 19...gxh6 **20 ♕xa8** ♕g7! 21 ♔h1 ♗d7 22 ♕b7 ♔h8 Δ...♖g8 with a very strong attack. In this line the more modest **20 ♕xf6** is possible too, but all roads still lead to the g-file and good counterplay with 20...a5! Δ...♖a6

19 ... ♗xf5
20 ♕b7?!

It is natural to want to extricate the queen at once, but after this Black is able to send Her Majesty far enough from the action to commence a very dangerous attack. The critical lines (albeit not sufficient to make 15 d5 dangerous) arise after 20 ♘d4! which provides f3 with much needed cover and whilst permitting ...♕d6, in general this is not immediately dangerous in view of 21 f4!. After **20 ♘d4** Black can choose between:

a) **20...♗d7** 21 ♕b7 ♕d6 22 ♕b4! ♕c7 23 ♕c3 ♕d6 and White

must force a draw by pursuing the black queen thus.

b) **20...♗xh3!?** may well lead to the same result, but is fraught with interesting possibilities for both sides to go wrong. Since Stohl is a pupil of the Lubomir Ftačnik school of voluminous analysis, I offer a critical assessment of the highlights – 21 gxh3 ♕d6 22 ♔g2 ♘g6! 23 ♖h1 (Stohl mentions 23 ♖g1'!', but 23...♘h4+ 24 ♔f1 {24 ♔h1 ♕c8!} 24...♕a6+ 25 ♔e1 ♗c7 looks good since if 26 ♕c6? ♘f3+) 23...♘h4+ 24 ♔g1 ♘f3+ 25 ♘xf3 (25 ♔g2!=) 25...♕d1+ 26 ♘e1 ♗h2+ 27 ♔xh2 ♖xa8 28 ♘g2 ♕e2 when although White has rook and two bishops for the queen and pawn, his problems completing development are so great that I think I would choose Black.

20 ...	**♖e7**
21 ♕a6	**♗c8**
22 ♕a5	**♗xh3!** *(193)*

193
W

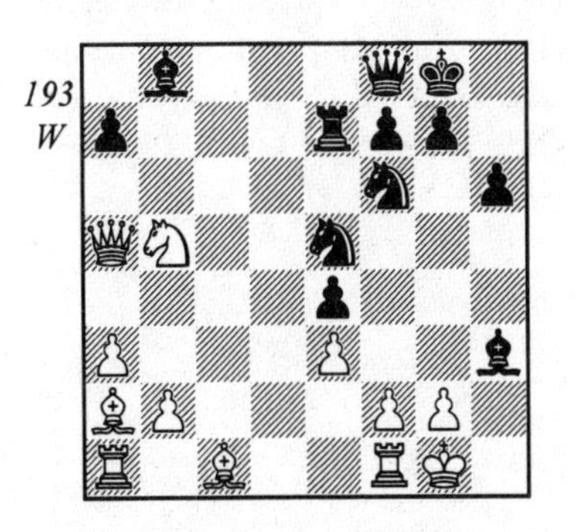

Having driven the white queen from the defence of c8, the bishop is immune as **23 gxh3** ♘f3+ 24 ♔g2 ♘h4+ 25 ♔h1 ♕c8 would decide immediately.

23 ♖d1	**♘d3**
24 ♕c3	

Still not **24 gxh3** ♕c8 25 ♔g2 ♕f5 with a decisive attack.

24 ...	**♕d8**

24...♗g4 to answer 25 f3 by 25...♘xc1 26 ♖axc1 exf3 was a simpler way to keep strong pressure for a minimal material deficit.

25 ♗c4	**♖d7**

And here Rogers definitely gets carried away. After sufficient preparation White can finally capture the provocative bishop on h3. Black still had the interesting possibility **25...♗g4!** 26 f3 ♘d5 27 ♕d4 ♖d7! which in view of 28 ♕e4 ♘f6! 29 ♕c6 ♘e5 leaves the white queen rather embarrassed.

26 gxh3	**♘d5**
27 ♗xd5	

Returning the compliment. White had to prioritize the removal of the knight on d3. The no-nonsense **27 ♕c2!** ♕g5+ 28 ♔f1 ♕h4 29 ♗xc3 ♕xh3+ 30 ♔e1 would remove enough of Black's firepower to win.

27 ...	**♖xd5**
28 ♘d4	**♕d7?**

Errors are the inevitable consequence of such complicated play. Still **28...♕h4** looks natural once Black has established that 29 ♕c8+ ♖d8 30 ♕f5 is no defence of f2 after 30...g6!. Also 29 ♖xd3 ♕xh3 30 f4 ♖h5 looks pretty nasty.

29 ♔f1	**♕xh3+**

30 ♔e2 ♘xf2! *(194)*

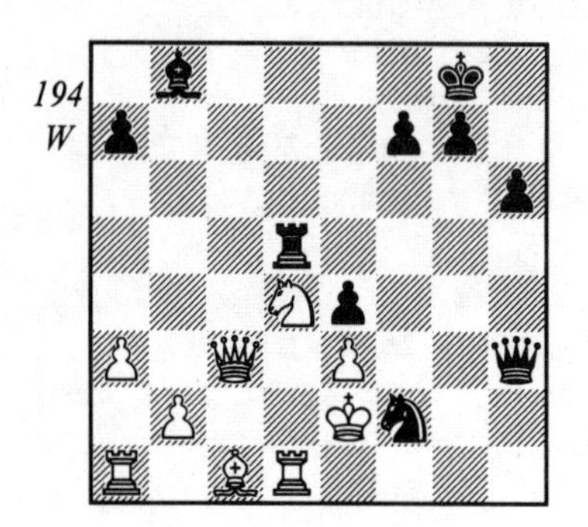

31 ♖g1!

31 ♔xf2 ♗g3+ is clearly bad. Running with **31 ♔d2** is also insufficient since 31...♘xd1 32 ♔xd1 ♕h5+ 33 ♔d2 ♖c5 is ∓.

The game continued its uneven course thus: **31...♕h2 32 ♖xg7+ ♔h8 33 ♖xf7 ♘d3+ 34 ♔d1 ♕h1+ 35 ♔c2** (A regrettable necessity since 35 ♔e2 fails neatly to 35...♖c5 36 ♖f8+ ♔h7 37 ♖f7+ ♔g6 38 ♖g7+ ♔h5 39 ♕d2 ♖c2!!-+) **35...♖c5 36 ♖f8+ ♔h7 37 ♖xb8** (Presumably the product of time pressure. Better was 37 ♕xc5 ♘xc5 38 b4 when Black is still for preference, but the game continues) **37...♖xc3+??** (37...♕h2+! 38 ♔b1 ♖xc3 Δ39 ♖b7+ ♖c7-+) **38 ♔xc3 ♘xc1 39 ♖b7+ ♔g6 40 ♘b3** (40 ♘c2 might have done a better job of covering White's various weaknesses) **40...♘e2+** (40...♕h3! {threatening ...♕c8+} 41 ♔d2! ♘xb3+ 42 ♖xb3 ♕h2+ 43 ♔c3 h5 should still be enough to win) **41 ♔c4 ♕h3 42 ♖d1! ♕xe3 43 ♖d6+** (Against active rooks Black's winning chances are already much reduced) **43...♔g5 44 ♖g7+ ♔h4 45 ♘d4 ♕c1+ 46 ♔b3 ♕d1+ 47 ♔c4 ♕c1+ 48 ♔b3 ♕e3+ 49 ♔c4 ♔h3!? 50 ♖h7! ♘xd4 51 ♖xd4 ♔g4 52 ♖xa7 ♔f3** (Not the careless 52...h5? 53 ♖e7 ♔f3 54 ♖exe4 when suddenly White is winning) **53 ♖f7+ ♔e2 54 ♖e7 ♕c1+ 55 ♔b3 e3 56 ♖de4 h5 57 a4! ♕d1+ 58 ♔a2 ♕d5+ 59 ♔a3 ♕c5+ 60 ♔a2 ♕d5+ 61 ♔a3 ♕d3+ ½-½.**

A game of several halves in which the many imperfections merely served to enhance a great fight.

25 Maintaining the Central Tension

Game 35
Grivas-Kramnik
Dortmund 1992

1 d4 d5 2 c4 e6 3 ♘f3 c6 4 ♘c3 ♘f6 5 e3 ♘bd7 6 ♕c2 ♗d6 7 ♗e2 0-0 8 0-0

8 ... ♖e8

Whilst 8...dxc4 and 8...e5 remain very important options, there has been in the last couple of years increasing interest in lines where Black at least initially maintains the central tension. One reason for this has been the realization that the 'modest' development of Black's queenside with ...b6 and ...♗b7 need not be a merely passive strategy. The text carries the added virtue that 9 e4 is easily countered by 9...dxe4 10 ♘xe4 ♘xe4 11 ♕xe4 e5 12 ♗g5 exd4!∓. Black has tried two other moves which fit in with the strategy under discussion here:

a) **8...♕e7** *(195)* had for some time been considered simply inaccurate, and increasingly Black was preferring 8...♖e8 first. This was perhaps at the theoretical level a bit harsh as Black was holding his own in 'a512' below. Now, the apparent validity of Ivanchuk's 12...♘f6 makes the move a good deal more attractive again. It is no longer so self-evident that White should strike with the immediate 9 e4, although it is fair to comment, as Ribli for example does, that all of White's alternatives, with the possible exception of 9 b3, play to the strength of 8...♕e7 - its flexibility:

195
W

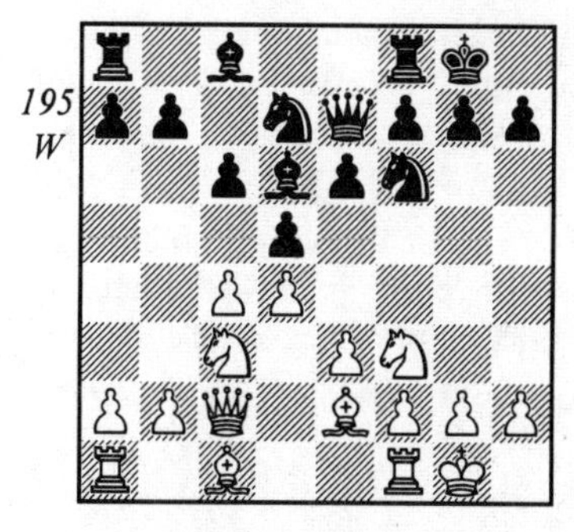

a1) **9 ♗d2?!** will prove to be a loss of tempo in positions where White wishes ultimately to open the centre. Hence 9...b6! is a convincing answer.

a2) **9 h3** is possible but compared with the positions examined later under 8...♖e8, 9 ♖d1 ♕e7 10 h3!? Black may be able to dispense with ...♖e8 saving a tempo to execute the ...c5 break more quickly. Therefore 9...b6! again seems appropriate.

a3) By contrast ♖d1 is not so critical in the variation where Black captures on c4 and plays ...e5, and hence **9 ♖d1** here encourages **9...dxc4!? 10 ♗xc4 e5**:

a31) **11 h3** e4! 12 ♘g5 ♘b6 13 ♗b3 ♗f5 14 f3 ♖ae8 with good counterplay – Ribli. This received a test in M.Gurevich-Bareev, Biel IZ 1993, which continued 15 ♘gxe4 ♘xe4 16 fxe4 ♗xe4 17 ♘xe4 ♕xe4 18 ♕xe4 ♖xe4 19 ♗c2 ♖ee8 20 e4 ♖d8 21 ♗g5 ♖d7 22 ♖ab1 ♖e8 23 ♔f2 ½-½. Black's pressure against the hanging pawns compensates for White's bishop pair.

a32) **11 e4** was tried in Salov-Ivanchuk, Dortmund 1992, but Black still obtained good play after 11...exd4 (11...b5!?) 12 ♘xd4 ♘b6! (12...♘e5 13 ♗e2 ♘g6 14 g3 ♖e8 15 ♘f5! – Mikhalchishin – reveals another drawback to having the queen on e7) 13 ♗e2 ♖e8 14 ♗e3 ♗d7 15 f3 ♖ad8 16 ♗f1 ♘bd5! 17 ♗f2 ♘xc3 18 bxc3 ♗c8 19 ♖ab1 ♕c7 20 g3 h5!.

After 9 ♖d1 Black may in any case continue with **9...♖e8** which is considered in note 'b' to White's 9th, or **9...b6** after which Epishin-Dreev, Russia 1992 continued 10 e4 ♘xe4 11 ♘xe4 dxe4 12 ♕xe4 ♗b7 13 ♗f4 (13 ♗g5 ♘f6! Δ...c5) 13...♖ad8 14 ♗xd6 ♕xd6 15 ♖d3?! (15 ♘e5! along the lines of Karpov-Lautier must be right) 15...♕c7 16 ♖ad1 c5 17 ♕e3 h6 with a comfortable game.

a4) After **9 b3**, Black also has a variety of approaches. **9...♖e8** Δ...dxc4 would lead to play similar to Game 30 whereas **9...b6** is naturally also playable and can lead to play similar to several of the notes below. One example with an independent twist was M.Gurevich-Lesiège, Biel IZ 1993: 10 e4 ♘xe4 11 ♘xe4 dxe4 12 ♕xe4 ♗b7 13 ♗f4!? ♗xf4 14 ♕xf4 ♖ac8 (the position seems more comfortable for Black than that where White has played ♖d1 instead of b3; one consequence is that here the immediate 14...c5! is possible, planning to answer 15 ♕c7 with 15...♗xf3 16 ♗xf3 ♖ac8 17 ♕f4 cxd4=) 15 ♖ad1 c5 16 ♘e5 cxd4 17 ♘xd7 ♕xd7 18 ♖xd4 ♕e7 19 ♖fd1±.

a5) After **9 e4 dxe4 10 ♘xe4 ♘xe4 11 ♕xe4** we shall consider:

a51) **11...e5 12 ♗g5!** *(196)* (not 12 c5? exd4!∓). Now Black has tried a number of different replies, only the last of which looks a really plausible route to equality:

196
B

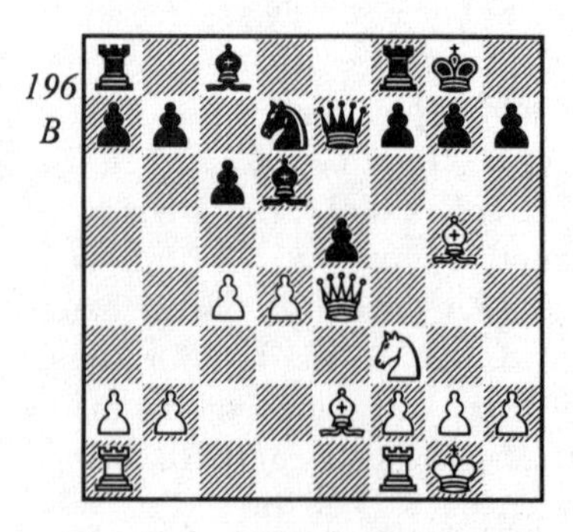

a511) **12...♕e6!?** 13 c5 ♗c7 14 ♗d3 ♕g6 15 ♕xg6 hxg6 16 ♖fe1! exd4 17 ♗e7 ♖e8 18 ♗c4 ♘f8! 19 ♘d4 ♗e6 20 ♘xe6 ♘xe6 21 ♗d6 ♗xd6 22 cxd6 ♖ad8 23 ♖ad1 b5!= Ribli. I would not be surprised if

White can find something here, but for the moment Black seems to be just OK.

a512) **12...♘f6(!)** is Ivanchuk's suggestion, which held up well to a practical test in M.Gurevich-Bareev, Munich 1993 after **13 ♗xf6** gxf6 14 dxe5 fxe5 15 c5 ♗xc5 (15...♗c7 is also fine) 16 ♗c4 ♔g7 (16...♗e6! Bareev) 17 ♘e5 f6 18 ♗d3 ♖h8 19 ♘c4! ♕xe4 20 ♗xe4 ♖d8 21 ♖ac1 f5 22 ♗f3 ♔f6 23 a3 a5 24 ♘xa5 ♖xa5 25 b4=. Clearly, it was White who needed to show accuracy to maintain the balance. Unconvincing too is Bareev's **13 ♕h4** h6 14 ♗xh6 gxh6 15 dxe5 ♗xe5 16 ♖ae1. This appears dangerous, and indeed, several moves seem to hand White the chances he is looking for: **16...♕c7?!** 17 ♗d3 ♗xb2 18 ♖e2! ♗c3 19 ♖ac1 ♕a5 20 ♕xh6±. Strangely, apparent greed with **16...♗xb2!** is Black's best course, although the real motive for the move is not further material gain but to enable the black queen to go immediately upon being attacked to its best square d8. Since ♕xh6 is always then answered by ...♘g4, I can find no good line for White here.

a52) **11...c5!?** is a speciality of Dreev's, but he is experiencing increasing problems:

a521) **12 ♗g5** (12 ♗d3!? Ribli) **12...♘f6** and now:

a5211) **13 ♕h4!?** h6 (13...b6? 14 ♗d3! h6 15 ♗xf6 ♕xf6 16 ♕e4+-) 14 ♗xf6 ♕xf6 15 ♕xf6 gxf6 16 ♖ad1 b6 17 dxc5 ♗xc5 18 ♘d4 ♗d7?! (18...♗b7 19 ♘b3 ♖fd8!) 19 b4!± (since if 19...♗xb4?? 20 ♘c2) Eingorn-Dreev, USSR Ch 1989.

a5212) **13 ♕c2** b6 (13...cxd4 14 ♘xd4 ♗xh2+ 15 ♔xh2 ♘g4+! 16 ♗xg4 ♕xg5 17 ♕g4! f5 18 ♗xf5 {18 ♘xf5 exf5 19 ♕d5+ ♖f7 20 ♗f3 ♕h6+ 21 ♔g1 ♗e6 22 ♕e5! Dydyshko-Panchenko, Bratislava 1992 also gives White excellent activity for the pawn} 18...exf5 19 ♕d5+ ♔h8 20 ♖fe1 with much better centralized pieces and development for White) 14 dxc5 bxc5 15 ♖ad1 ♗b7 16 ♗xf6 gxf6 17 ♘d2 f5 18 ♗f3 (it must be right to exchange off half of Black's bishop pair, but Black still has the better minor piece to compensate for his weakened structure) 18...♖fd8 19 ♕c3 ♖ab8 20 ♗xb7 ♕xb7 21 b3 ♗f8 ♘f3 ♗g7 with balanced chances; Akopian-Dreev, Tilburg 1992.

a522) **12 ♗f4!?** (Dreev punctuated this still more positively!) 12...♗xf4 (12...cxd4 13 ♗xd6 ♕xd6 14 ♕xd4; or 12...♘f6 13 ♗xd6 ♕xd6 14 ♕e5! both lead to more pleasant endgames for White) 13 ♕xf4 cxd4 (since the simple 13...b6 14 ♖fd1 ♗b7?! 15 ♕c7! is unpleasant) 14 ♘xd4! ♕b4 (14...e5 15 ♕e3!±) 15 ♕e3! e5 16 ♘f5 g6 17 a3 ♕c5 (unpleasant necessity; if 17...♕xb2 18 ♖fb1 ♕c2 19 ♗d3 ♕c3 20

♖c1 ♕b2 21 ♖ab1 ♕xa3 22 ♕h6! gxf5 23 ♗xf5 ♘f6 24 ♕g5+ wins) 18 b4 ♕xe3 19 ♘xe3 and White's mobile queenside pawn majority and better development should give Black an unenviable defensive task; G.Georgadze-Dreev, Podolsk 1992. It will be interesting to see Dreev's next move, since his annotations seem quite pessimistic.

b) **8...b6!?** is the latest try, leaving the queen on d8 being perhaps motivated by the desire to avoid the simplification which results from White's ♗f4 and subsequent ♗xd6 (with tempo) seen below - Karpov-Lautier and so on. So far Black has fared OK, but it would be surprising if White's spatial plus counts for nought.

b1) Kramnik mentions **9 b3** ♗b7 10 ♗b2 **c5** 11 ♖fd1 ♖c8=. Perhaps a slight over-simplification, but the current feeling is that in all such positions White can only make trouble with e4. Instead **10...♕e7** 11 e4 dxe4 12 ♘xe4 ♘xe4 13 ♕xe4 ♘f6?! 14 ♕c2 ♖fd8 (14...c5 15 ♘g5 e5∞) 15 ♗d3 c5?? 16 dxc5 ♗xc5 17 ♗xf6 Δ♗xh7+, ♗e4, with a winning advantage was Akopian-Jirovsky, Mamaia Wch jr 1991. Since Grivas-Kramnik, the tendency is for Black to have few reservations about playing ...f5 rather than the modest ...♘f6.

b2) **9 e4 ♘xe4 10 ♘xe4 dxe4 11 ♕xe4 ♗b7** and now:

b21) **12 ♗f4?!** ♘f6 13 ♕e3 ♘g4!? 14 ♕d2 c5 15 h3 ♘f6= Kramnik.

b22) **12 ♖e1** ♘f6 13 ♕h4 c5= Vyzhmanavin-Sveshnikov, St. Petersburg Z 1993.

b23) **12 ♖d1** ♖b8!? (12...♕c7!? – the possibility of this queen development is another motivation for 8...b6 – 13 c5 bxc5 14 ♕h4 ♖fe8 15 dxc5 ♗e7 16 ♗g5 ♘xc5 17 ♖ac1 ♗a6 18 ♗xe7 ♕xe7 19 ♕xe7 ♖xe7 20 ♘d4 ♗xe2 21 ♘xe2 ♘a6 22 ♖xc6 ♘b4 23 ♖c4 ♘d5 24 ♘c3 ♘xc3 25 ♖xc3 g6 26 ♔f1 a5 27 ♖d4 ♖b7 28 b3 ♖b4 29 ♖cc4 ♖xc4 30 ♖xc4 ♖d8 31 ♖c5 a4 32 bxa4 ♖d2 33 a3 ♖d3 34 ♔e2 ♖xa3 35 a5 ♔f8 36 h4 ♔e7 37 ♖c7+ ½-½ Karpov-Ivanchuk, Tilburg 1993) 13 ♗d3 g6 14 ♘g5!? ♖e8?! (14...c5 15 ♕h4 ♘f6 seems surprisingly hard to break down, since if 16 dxc5 bxc5 17 b3 ♗e5!∓) 15 ♕h4 ♘f8 16 c5! ♗c7 17 ♗f4 ♖c8 18 ♕g3 ♗xf4 19 ♕xf4± Vyzhmanavin-Yakovich, St. Petersburg Z 1992.

b24) **12 ♗d3** g6 (12...♘f6 is riskier but 13 ♕h4 c5 14 d5(!) exd5 15 ♗g5 h6 16 ♗xh6 – Sorokin, is not so obviously clear after 16...dxc4!) 13 b3 (13 ♗f4 c5!=; or 13 ♗h6 ♖e8 14 ♖ad1 ♖b8!? {Black leaves his queen on d8 to prevent the aggressive White transfer to h4; 14...f5 15 ♕e3 c5 16 ♗e2 ♕e7 17 ♗g5 ♕g7 18 ♕c3 ♗e7 19 ♗xe7 ♖xe7 20 ♖fe1 ♖ae8 21 h3 e5 22 dxc5 ♘xc5 23 b4 ♗xf3

24 ♗xf3 e4 25 ♕xg7+ ♔xg7 led to a draw in Karpov-Kaidanov, Tilburg 1993} De Boer-Sorokin, Groningen 1992, 15 ♕e2 c5 16 ♗e4= Sorokin) 13...♖b8 14 ♕e3?! (14 ♕e2!) 14...c5 15 ♗e4 cxd4 16 ♕xd4 ♗c5! 17 ♕d3 ♘f6 18 ♕xd8 ♖fxd8 19 ♗xb7 ♖xb7 20 ♗g5 ♔g7 and Black was more comfortable in Schneider-Kramnik, Moscow 1992.

9 b3

As mentioned above, Black's eighth move renders the immediate 9 e4 harmless. Grivas' choice invites a transposition into lines considered in Chapter 21. However, Kramnik remains true to the ...b6 idea, and indeed whilst there is certainly nothing objectionable in 9 b3, this game suggests that against an early commitment of the bishop to b2 this may well gain in force. This, of course also has implications for move order in Game 30. Overall though, here it can be argued the most flexible and certainly the most popular choice is **9 ♖d1** *(197)*:

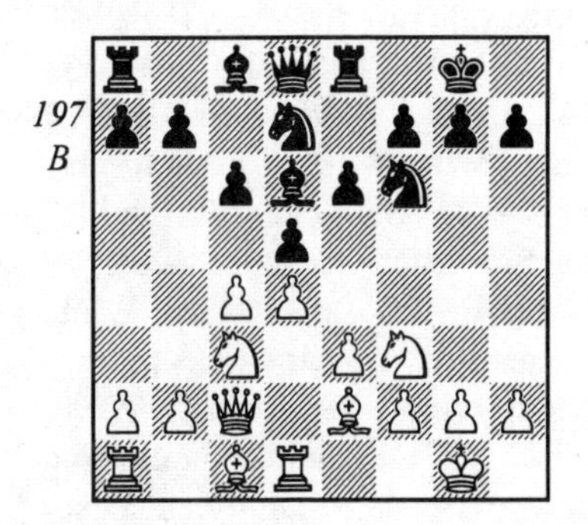

a) **9...♕c7!?** 10 c5!? (10 e4 dxe4 11 ♘xe4 ♘xe4 12 ♕xe4 c5 justifies the black queen's unusual placement) 10...♗e7 (10...♗f8!?) 11 e4 dxe4 12 ♘xe4 b6 (12...e5?! 13 dxe5 ♘xe4 14 ♕xe4 ♘xc5 15 ♕f4±) 13 ♗g5 ♘xe4 14 ♗xe7 (14 ♕xe4 is also good, e.g. 14...♗xg5 15 ♘xg5 ♘f6 16 ♕xe5!) 14...♖xe7 15 ♕xe4 bxc5 16 ♖ac1 ♘f6 17 ♕c2 cxd4 18 ♘xd4 ♗b7 19 ♘xc6 ♗xc6 20 ♕xc6 ♕xc6 21 ♕xc6 with an ending in which Black can really suffer; Kuzmin-Yasseen, Doha 1992.

b) After **9...♕e7** White has tried as many as four moves, although with the exception of 10 e4, which simply looks like bad timing, the play after each has many similarities:

b1) **10 e4** dxe4 11 ♘xe4 ♘xe4 12 ♕xe4 e5 13 ♗g5 ♕f8! (Even in apparently innocuous positions there is no safety from the World Champion's preparation. 13...f6 14 ♗h4 exd4 15 ♕xd4 ♗c5 16 ♕c3 ♘f8= was Maiwald-Kramnik, Guarapuava 1991) 14 ♗d3? (Not the ideal blunder for a televized match!) 14...f5! 15 ♕xf5? ♘f6 0-1 Hübner-Kasparov, Cologne TV 1992.

b2) **10 h3** and now:

b21) **10...b6 11 e4 dxe4 12 ♘xe4 ♘xe4 13 ♕xe4** *(198)*:

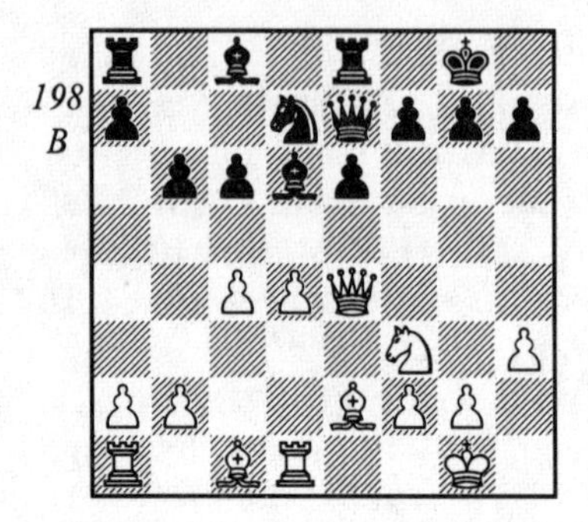
198
B

b211) **13...♗b7 14 ♗f4!?**. The key moment from a theoretical angle, since after his next move in Karpov-Lautier, Black's task was never enviable.

b2111) **14...♖ad8?!** 15 ♗xd6 ♕xd6 16 ♘e5! ♘xe5 (Karpov gives also 16...♘f6 17 ♕e3 c5 18 dxc5 ♕xc5 19 ♕xc5 bxc5 20 f3±. Note the consistent desire, epitomized by 20 f3, to limit the scope of Black's queen's bishop. After 16...♘xe5, White's whole strategy revolves around killing it off completely!) 17 dxe5 ♕c7 18 ♗f3 ♗a8 19 ♖xd8 ♖xd8 20 ♖d1! (Karpov already has his eye on a bishop ending, and is hence absolutely not afraid of simplification. The most impressive feature of the game for me is Karpov's willingness to cede Black some temporary activity, even to sacrifice a pawn, for the greater gain of restricting the bishop to a8) 20...♖xd1+ 21 ♗xd1 ♕d8 22 ♗f3 ♕d2 23 b3 ♕xa2 24 b4! ♕a1+ 25 ♔h2 ♕a6 26 ♕d4! (avoiding 26 b5 ♕c8 27 bxc6 h6 28 g3 a5 when Black has a plan too!) 26...♕c8 27 c5 bxc5 28 ♕xc5 a6 (28...♕b8! was more stubborn) 29 ♕e7 g6 30 h4 h5? (seriously weakening the dark squares which it will be hard to contest if White's king seeks to invade) 31 ♔g3! ♕b7? (Nervous about the combined attacking potential of White's king and queen, but the pure bishop ending holds few technical problems) 32 ♕xb7 ♗xb7 33 ♔f4 ♔f8 34 ♔g5 ♔e7 35 ♗e4 ♗a8 36 f3! (Black is utterly helpless against the simple plan of creating a passed h-pawn) 36...♗b7 37 g4 ba8 38 gxh5 gxh5 39 f4 ♗b7 40 ♗f3 ♗a8 41 ♔xh5 1-0 Karpov-Lautier, Biel 1992.

b2112) **14...c5?!** 15 ♗xd6 ♗xe4 16 ♗xe7 ♖xe7 17 dxc5 ♘xc5 18 b4 ♘a4 19 ♖ac1±; Black's knight is badly off-side and White's pawn majority mobile.

b2113) **14...♘f6** 15 ♕e3 ♗xf4 16 ♕xf4 ♖ad8 17 ♖d2 c5 18 ♖ad1 ♗xf3! 19 ♕xf3 cxd4 20 ♖xd4 ♖xd4 21 ♖xd4 ♕c5 (Ribli) is a better possibility, but here too Black must exercise great care that White's minor piece does not prove superior.

b2114) Probably best is **14...♗xf4!** 15 ♕xf4 c5 16 ♕c7 ♖ab8! when **17 ♘e5** leads to play similar to 'b3' and 'b4', and **17 dxc5?!** ♘xc5 18 ♕xe7 ♖xe7 19 ♖ac1 ♖c7 20 ♘d4 a6 gave White absolutely nothing in Cosma-Kir.Georgiev, Budapest Z 1993.

b212) Black found an interesting new twist in M.Gurevich-Yusupov, Bundesliga 1993, eschewing the natural move above in favour of **13...♘f6!?** 14 ♕h4 (14 ♕xc6 ♗d7 15 ♕b7 ♖eb8 16 ♕a6 ♘e8! causes the white queen some embarrassment; 17 c5 bxc5 18 dxc5 ♗xc5∞ – Gurevich, although perhaps White can claim a tiny initiative after 19 ♘e5) 14...♗b7 15 ♗f4 ♖ad8 16 ♗xd6 ♖xd6?! (16...♕xd6 is approximately equal) 17 ♕g5! h6 18 ♕e3 c5 19 dxc5 ♖xd1+ 20 ♖xd1 ♗xf3 21 ♗xf3 bxc5 22 ♕e5 and White had something to work for.

b22) **10...h6!?** was tried in Karpov-Illescas, Wijk aan Zee 1993 which saw a structure familiar from Game 30. After 11 a3 a6!? (11...b6!? 12 e4 ♘xe4 13 ♘xe4 dxe4 14 ♕xe4 ♗b7 15 ♗f4 ♗xf4 16 ♕xf4 c5 17 ♕c7 ♖ab8 18 dxc5 {18 ♘e5!? would bear comparison with Dokhoian-Bangiev examined under 'b4' below. The text is harmless} 18...♘xc5 19 ♕xe7 ♖xe7 20 b4 ♘e4 21 ♖ac1 e5= Ljubojevic-Illescas, Linares (1) 1993) 12 b3 (In the absence of the temporary weakness of the c6 pawn which ...b6 permits, 12 e4?! would allow Black very easy play with 12...dxe4 13 ♘xe4 ♘xe4 14 ♕xe4 e5 15 dxe5 ♘xe5 16 ♘xe5 ♕xe5∓ Karpov) 12...dxc4 13 bxc4 (13 ♗xc4 b5 14 ♗f1 e5= Karpov) 13...e5 14 ♘h4! (Karpov is very alert to the impact of the various waiting moves. Most important is that if White plays all-out on the queenside, he will find that 10 h3 created an unfortunate target for Black's counterplay with, e.g. ...♘d7-f8-g6. On the other hand, Black's ...h6, weakening g6 and hence f5, affords White a useful alternative plan) 14...♘f8 15 ♘f5 ♗xf5 16 ♕xf5 exd4 (16...e4 threatens the queen with some embarrassment, but after 17 h4! g6 18 ♕h3± {Karpov} White's positional gains are the more relevant) 17 exd4 c5 18 ♗e3! cxd4?! (18...♘e6! 19 dxc5 {19 d5 ♘d4 20 ♕d3 ♕e5 21 g3⩲ Karpov, but maybe 19...g6!? preserving the option of ...♘f4 as well depending on where the queen chooses to go} 19...♗xc5 20 ♘d5 ♘xd5 21 cxd5 ♗xe3 keeps White's plus to a bare minimum) 19 ♗xd4 ♗e5 20 ♗xe5 ♕xe5 21 ♕xe5 ♖xe5 22 ♖ab1± with enduring pressure on Black's queenside.

b3) **10 b3 b6** (If here 10...dxc4, 11 bxc4 and 11 ♗xc4 lead to lines considered elsewhere) **11 e4** (The message on this move seems to be now or never. If first 11 ♗b2 ♗b7 12 e4 we reach play similar to Ftačnik-Blatny {see note to 14 ♗d3 in the main game} except that White possibly has the wrong rook on d1. Black should have no problems there. White can also eschew e4, but Black proceeds calmly with ...♗b7, ...♖ac8 and at leisure ...c5, and is well placed to defend and use the resulting hanging pawns) **11...dxe4 12 ♘xe4 ♘xe4 13 ♕xe4 ♗b7**:

b31) **14 ♘e5!?** ♘f6 (14...f5!? 15 ♕e3 ♘xe5 16 dxe5 ♗c5 17 ♕g3 ♖ad8! 18 ♗g5 ♖xd1+ 19 ♖xd1 ♕c7 is at worst fractionally ±) 15 ♕e3 c5 16 ♗b2 ♖ad8(?!) 17 ♗f3 cxd4 18 ♗xd4 ♗xf3 19 ♕xf3 and although the threat of ♘c6 looks strong, it was revealed as somewhat illusory in Karpov-Morović, León 1993 since 19...♕c7 20 ♘c6 ♖d7 21 ♗xf6 gxf6 22 ♘xa7 ♖ed8! 23 ♘b5 ♗xh2+ 24 ♔h1 ♕f4 25 ♖xd7 ♖xd7 was OK for Black. This idea, unlike 14 ♗f4 is, of course, specific to 10 b3.

b32) **14 ♗f4** ♗xf4! (see also notes to Karpov-Lautier in the analogous position) 15 ♕xf4 c5 (15...e5 16 ♘xe5! ♘xe5 17 dxe5 c5!?±) 16 ♕c7 ♖ab8! 17 ♘e5 ♘xe5 18 ♕xe7 ♘f3+ 19 ♗xf3 ♖xe7 20 ♗xb7 ♖exb7 21 dxc5 bxc5 22 ♖d6 ♖c7 23 ♖ad1 ♔f8 24 ♖a6 ♔e7= Stohl-Skembris, Burgas 1992. If Black is content with a peaceful outcome then this line seems sufficient.

b4) **10 a3!?** On the evidence of Dokhoian-Bangiev, Bundesliga 1992, White's new idea does not too seriously disturb the equilibrium: 10...b6 11 e4 ♘xe4 12 ♘xe4 dxe4 13 ♕xe4 ♗b7 14 ♗f4 ♗xf4 15 ♕xf4 c5 16 ♕c7 ♖ab8! 17 ♘e5 ♘xe5 18 ♕xe7 ♘f3+ 19 gxf3!? (White is willing to make a structural concession since he believes that Black's bishop impedes his efforts to combat White's mobile queenside) 19...♖xe7 20 dxc5 (Bangiev's 20 b4!? may be more flexible) 20...bxc5 21 b4 ♔f8! (21...cxb4? 22 axb4±) 22 ♖d2 ♖c7=.

9 ... ♕e7

10 ♗b2

10 ♖d1 is of course note 'b3' above.

10 ... b6 *(199)*

Here, **10...dxc4** 11 ♗xc4!? or 11 bxc4 leads to Chapter 21.

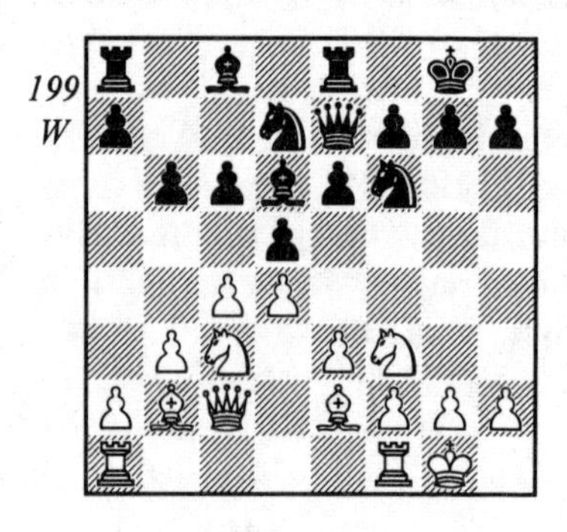
199
W

11 e4

This is of course not compulsory, and with the bishop already committed to b2, it may not be recommended for reasons we have already touched upon. The main alternative is playing ♖ac1, ♖ad1 and waiting in many cases for ...c5. It seems that this does not promise too much either. Portisch recently tried to play for e4 with the intention of landing a knight there. However, Black easily foiled the plan with his own central strike, viz: **11 ♖fe1** ♗b7 12 ♘d2!? ♖ac8 13 e4 e5! (White's knight is poorly placed to contest this) 14 dxe5 ♗xe5 15 exd5 cxd5 16 ♗f3 ♕d6

17 h3 ♕b8 18 cxd5 ½-½ Portisch-Topalov, Budapest Z 1993. Black is at least no worse.

10 ... dxe4
12 ♘xe4 ♘xe4
13 ♕xe4 ♗b7
14 ♗d3?!

Against **14 ♖ad1** too, Black's basic plan seems quite relevant:

a) **14...f5** 15 ♕e3 c5 16 ♘e5 (16 ♕g5 ♘f6! 17 dxc5 ♗xc5 18 ♗xf6 ♕xf6 19 ♕xf6 gxf6 20 ♖d7 ♗c6 21 ♖c7 ♖ec8 and the two bishops give Black good play) 16...cxd4 17 ♗xd4 ♖ad8 18 a4?! (18 f4 or 18 ♘xd7 both give rough equality, but certainly no more) 18...♗e4! 19 ♘xd7 ♖xd7 20 ♗d3 ♗xd3 21 ♖xd3 e5 and Black's centre is mobilized with advantage; Ftačnik-Blatny, Brno 1992.

b) Similar, equally valid and merely enhancing my curiosity as to why White still ventures here, was **14...♖ad8** 15 ♗d3 f5! 16 ♕e2 c5 17 dxc5 ♘xc5 18 ♗c2 ♘e4 19 ♗xe4 ♗xe4 20 ♗e5 ½-½ Wojtkiewicz-Kolev, Budapest Z 1993. Again, I feel that it is White who is fighting for level play.

Kramnik gives as best **14 ♕e3** c5 15 ♖fd1 ♖ad8 16 dxc5=.

14 ... f5!

14...♘f6?! is less ambitious.

15 ♕e2 c5
16 ♖ad1?

White fails to appreciate the dynamic potential in Black's position. It was already time to consider **16 h3!?** to prevent the coming onslaught.

16 ... cxd4
17 ♘xd4 ♕h4
18 g3

Positionally, White would prefer to play **18 h3**, but in this case simply 18...♕f4! 19 g3 ♕h6 20 h4 ♘e5 would force still greater weaknesses.

18 ... ♕h3
19 f3 ♗c5+
20 ♔h1 ♘f6
21 ♘c2?

This is weak, since only the knight can hope to stem the in-coming tide. White had to try **21 ♕g2**.

21 ... e5
22 ♕g2 ♕xg2+
23 ♔xg2 e4
24 fxe4 ♘xe4
25 ♔h3 ♖ad8!!

Of course Black is winning too with the simple **25...♘f2+**, but White could certainly struggle on. The text is a wonderful piece of virtuoso calculation based on the following: 26 ♗xe4 (otherwise 26...♘f2+ is much nastier than before) 26...♗xe4 27 ♘a1 (27 ♘d4? ♖d6!; or 27 ♘a3 ♖xd1 28 ♖xd1 ♖e6 29 ♖d8+ ♔f7 30 ♗c1 ♗xa3 deflecting the defender) 27...♖xd1 28 ♖xd1 ♗f3! 29 ♖d2 (otherwise White loses a piece along the second rank) 29...♗g4+ 30 ♔g2 ♖e1 31 h3 ♖g1+ 32 ♔h2 ♗f3 33 g4 with mate to follow. White had had enough.

0-1

26 5 ♕b3 and other Fifth move alternatives

Most of this book has been devoted to White's principal and sharpest 5th move choices 5 ♗g5 and 5 e3. However, whilst White's choices are limited a little by the threat of 5...dxc4, there are a few respectable alternatives. Of these 5 g3 and 5 ♕c2 may be of interest to those who wish to play in gambit mode, while avoiding highly theoretical routes. The main focus of attention here, 5 ♕b3, again has the virtue of not being too heavily analysed (although it is by no means rare) and also is a fairly solid, risk-free system for White. It is worth noting that the main line often arises too from the Queen's Gambit Accepted: 1 d4 d5 2 c4 dxc4 3 ♘f3 ♘f6 4 ♘c3 e6 5 ♕a4+ c6 6 ♕xc4 etc and other similar move orders. The main game here is of theoretical interest, and in a line that is often quite peaceful, has been selected as an example of the fun that can ensue when Black seeks to sharpen the play.

Game 36
Shipov-S.Ivanov
Cheliabinsk 1991

1 d4 ♘f6
2 c4 e6
3 ♘c3 d5
4 ♘f3 c6
5 ♕b3 *(200)*

Others in brief:

a) **5 cxd5** exd5 leads to a Queens Gambit Exchange variation in a rather comfortable version for Black. The early commitment of the knight to f3 removes much of the flexibility from White's structure. It is beyond our scope here, but suffice to say that 6 e3 ♗f5! is immediately = and after 6 ♕c2 Black can choose between 6...♘a6!? or 6...g6 both of which give fair chances.

b) **5 ♕c2** dxc4 6 e4 b5 7 ♗e2 (7 a4 looks the most likely to worry Black) 7...♗b7 8 a4 ♕b6 9 0-0 a6 10 ♖d1 ♘bd7 11 ♗g5 h6 12 ♗h4 ♗b4 with inadequate compensation; Spassky-Smyslov, USSR Ch 1960. The age of the reference reflects the prevailing view of 5 ♕c2.

c) **5 ♕d3** can transpose to our main game here after **5...dxc4**, but in my view **5...b6!** is a clear equalizer. Speelman-Wells, London Lloyds Bank 1990 went 6 cxd5 (6 e4 ♗a6! looks to me dubious for White) 6...cxd5 7 ♗g5 ♗e7 8 ♖c1 0-0 9 ♕b1 ♗a6 10 e3 ♗xf1 11

♔xf1 ♘c6= which should be enough to put White off the idea.

d) **5 g3!?** is by far the most serious challenge here. It is very closely related to the Catalan, but since it is important territory for prospective Semi-Slav players we shall examine it in sufficient detail to enable Black to meet it with confidence:

d1) **5...♘e4!?** 6 ♗g2 ♘xc3 (6...♗b4!? 7 ♕c2 ♕a5 8 ♗d2 ♘xd2 9 ♘xd2 ♘d7 10 0-0 0-0 11 e4 dxe4 12 ♘dxe4 e5 13 a3 ♗e7 14 d5 ♕a6 15 d6 ♗d8 16 ♘d2 ♗g5 17 ♘ce4 ♗h6∞ with an interesting battle between Black's bishop pair and White's spatial plus; Khalifman-Dreev, Simferopol 1988) 7 bxc3 ♘d7 8 ♘d2 ♗e7 9 0-0 0-0 10 a4 ♘f6!? 11 e4 dxe4 12 ♘xe4 ♘xe4 13 ♗xe4 ♕a5= Østenstad-Shabalov, Oslo Cup 1991.

d2) **5...dxc4** 6 ♗g2 ♘bd7 7 a4 (7 0-0 ♗e7 {7...b5!?} 8 e4!? 0-0 9 ♗f4 ♕a5 10 a4 ♗b4 11 ♕c2 h6 12 ♘d2 ♘b6 13 ♗c7!± Sosonko-Van der Wiel, Dutch Ch 1992) 7...♗e7 (7...♗b4 8 0-0 0-0 9 ♕c2 ♕e7 10 ♘a2 {10 ♗f4 ♘d5!? 11 ♗g5 f6 12 ♗c1 ♗a5 13 ♘a2 e5 14 ♕xc4 e4 15 ♘d2 f5∞ Urban-Kuczynski, Polish Ch 1993} 10...♗d6 11 ♕xc4 a5 12 ♘c3 e5 13 e4 exd4 14 ♘xd4 ♘e5 15 ♕e2 ♗c5= Poluliakhov-Sorokin, Alekhine mem 1992) 8 0-0 0-0 9 e4 e5! 10 dxe5 ♘g4 11 ♗f4 ♕a5 12 ♕d2 (12 e6!?) 12...♗b4! 13 e6 fxe6 14 ♗d6 ♗xd6 15 ♕xd6 ♘de5 16 ♘xe5 ♘xe5 17 ♕d4 Rd8 and White's compensation is looking ropey; Hausner-Kramnik, Bundesliga 1992.

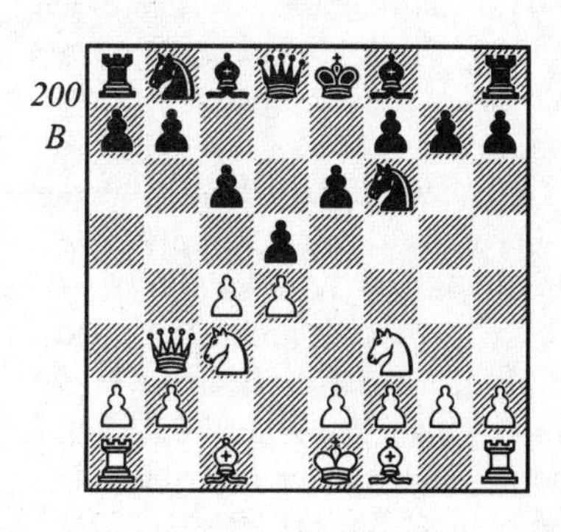

5 ... dxc4

With this capture Black hopes to exploit White's early queen sortie to gain time for queenside development. It is the most popular reply, but against a relatively uncritical move such as 5 ♕b3 it is no surprise that simple development is OK too, although more closely resembling the Orthodox Queen's Gambit Declined than most of the material in this book. In addition, Black can also delay ...dxc4, but keep this option against certain White set-ups. Also possible is to try to encourage c5 to take pressure off d5 and fix the central structure. For reasons of space, I shall discuss these lines only briefly, and restrict myself to those which retain at least some Semi-Slav flavour:

a) **5...♘bd7** 6 g3 (6 cxd5 is dull, and not especially promising) 6...♘b6!? 7 c5 ♘bd7 (7...♘c4!? –

Wojtkiewicz, might be a bit of fun) 8 ♕a4 (otherwise ...b6 is fine for Black) 8...e5 9 b4 exd4 (9...e4!?) 10 ♘xd4 g6 11 ♗g2 ♗g7 12 0-0 0-0 13 ♗f4 ♘h5 14 ♗e3±, although 14...♘e5 is not too bad; Wojtkiewicz-Smagin, Palma de Mallorca 1989.

b) **5...♕b6!?** 6 c5! ♕xb3 (maybe 6...♕c7, although simply 7 g3 should be ±) 7 axb3 ♘a6 8 ♘e5 (8 e3 ♘c7 9 b4 a6 is nothing) 8...♘d7 (8...♘c7!? 9 ♗f4 ♘h5±; 9 h3!?) 9 ♖xa6!? bxa6 (9...♘xe5 10 ♖a1 and there is no longer an impediment to the plan of b4-b5) 10 ♘xc6 ♘b8 11 ♘a5 ♗e7 12 b4 ♗d8 13 e4! with good activity and a pawn for the exchange in Rogers-Dragoljub Pavlović, Niš 1985.

c) **5...a5** 6 e3 ♘bd7 7 ♗d3 g6 8 0-0 ♗g7 9 e4 dxe4 10 ♘xe4 ♘xe4 11 ♗xe4 0-0 Uhlmann-Schön, German Ch 1991, when 12 ♖d1 looks ±. The plan of ...a5-a4-a3 carries much less sting than against the Moscow Variation (see Chapter 8) since White's dark squares on the queenside give much less cause for concern.

6 ♕xc4 b5
7 ♕b3

White has an interesting alternative here in **7 ♕d3** which has recently proved quite popular. The move is appealing since it helps to control the e4 square but sometimes the queen is vulnerable on d3. My personal view is that 7 ♕d3 causes rather more problems and it is debatable how Black should best respond. It now seems that the crude attempt to exploit the queen's position with 7...♗a6 is misguided, but it would be a pity to lose the possibility of placing the bishop on the a6-f1 diagonal altogether – an admirable aspiration, but finding a move to keep the option open is not such a trivial task. Practice has seen:

a) **7...♗a6?! 8 ♘e4!** *(201)* (much weaker is 8 ♕c2?! b4! 9 ♘a4 ♗b5!∓ Rivas-Dorfman, Barcelona 1992).

201
B

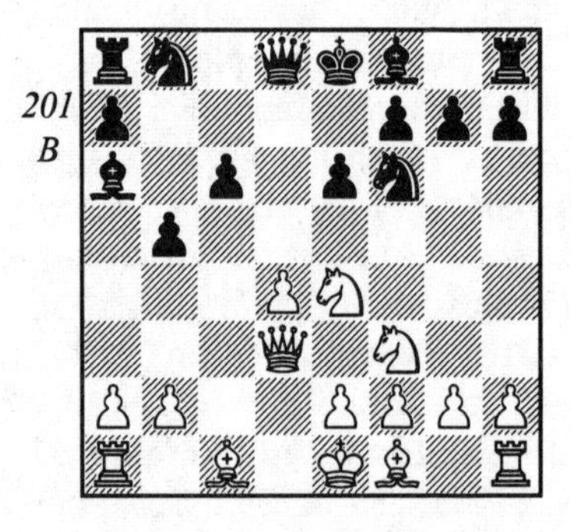

The value of controlling e4 with the queen is starkly revealed. 8...♕a5+ (8...b4 9 ♘xf6+ gxf6 10 ♕c2 Δg3, ♗g2, ♗e3± and 8...♘bd7 9 e3 simply with the idea of ♗d2 and ♖c1 both clearly favour White too according to Karpov. White's simple 8th move seems to leave the bishop on a6 dangling) 9 ♗d2 b4 10 ♘xf6+ gxf6 11 ♕c2 ♗e7 12 a3! ♕b6 (12...♗b5 13 a4 ♗a6 14 g3± Karpov) 13

♗xb4 ♗xb4+ 14 axb4 ♕xb4+ 15 ♕c3! ♕xc3 16 bxc3 ♔e7 17 ♔d2 c5 18 e3 bxf1 19 ♖hxf1 cxd4 20 cxd4 ♘d7 21 ♖hb1 ♖b8 22 ♖xb8 ♘xb8 23 ♖a5! ♘c6 24 ♖c5! with a large endgame plus, although Karpov's excellent conversion should not disguise the fact that it is still far from automatic to win; Karpov-Yudasin, Madrid 1992.

b) **7...♗e7** was awarded a '?' by Shirov, but this seems to me to be ungenerous. The move is motivated by the considerations mentioned above, namely to retain ...b4 and ...♗a6 ideas if and only if White commits himself to e4. Thus Black plays a developing move while studiously avoiding touching his queenside pieces. White does best to play **8 a3!** when Black has tried:

b1) **8...0-0** 9 e4 c5?! (9...a6± Shirov) 10 dxc5 ♗xc5 (Bareev-Shirov, Linares 1993) when Black's compensation is found wanting after 11 ♕xd8! ♖xd8 12 ♗xb5 ♗b7 13 ♗g5 ♘c6 14 ♔e2! ♘d4 15 ♘xd4 ♗xd4 16 f3± Shirov.

b2) **8...a6!?** 9 e4 ♗b7!? (9...c5 10 dxc5 ♕xd3 11 ♗xd3 ♗xc5 12 e5 Δ♗e4 is horrible for Black) 10 e5 (Otherwise ...c5 should be OK) 10...♘d5 11 ♘e4 ♘d7 12 ♗g5 f6 13 exf6 gxf6 14 ♗h6 c5 15 ♗e2± according to *Informator 57*, which concurs with Dharshan Kumaran's view at the time. Black's play involves an element of risk, but I do not believe that assessment now any more than I did then, since the undermining of White's centre should, I feel, be fast enough to compensate for Black's difficulties in finding a watertight haven for his king. The game proceeded (crazily) 15...c4 16 ♘fd2 ♕b6 17 ♗h5+ ♔d8 18 ♕g3 ♕xd4 19 ♗f7? (19 **0-0!**∞ although Black's task would not suit all tastes) 19...♘e5 20 ♗xe6 ♘d3+ 21 ♔e2 ♕xb2?? (21...♘xb2! was good and should have been obvious even in time-trouble) 22 ♘d6± ♘3f4+? 23 ♗xf4 ♗xd6 24 ♗xd6 ♖e8 25 ♖he1? c3 26 ♗c7+! **1-0** since White mates in two; Kumaran-Wells, Dublin Z 1993.

c) **7...a6?!** 8 e4 (also interesting was 8 ♗g5 c5?! {8...♘bd7} 9 a4!? bxa4 10 ♗xf6 gxf6 11 d5!⩲ Gofshtein-Zviagintsev, Cappelle la Grande 1993) 8...c5 9 dxc5 ♕xd3 10 ♗xd3 ♗xc5 11 e5 ♘fd7 12 ♗e4⩲ Browne-Saeed, Taxco 1985.

d) **7...♘bd7** with the following possibilities:

d1) **8 ♗g5** ♗b7 9 a3 h6 10 ♗f4 (10 ♗h4 ♕a5!=) 10...b4! 11 axb4 ♗xb4 12 e3 ♘d5 13 ♗g3 c5 14 ♗e2 cxd4 15 exd4 a5 with comfortable equality in Portisch-Nogueiras, Brussels 1988.

d2) **8 g3** b4 (8...♗b7!?) 9 ♘e4 ♕a5 10 ♗g2 ♗a6 11 ♘xf6+ ♘xf6 12 ♕d1 ♖c8 13 0-0 ♗e7 14 ♘e5 ♕b5 15 a4 bxa3 16 bxa3 ♘d5 17 e4 ♘c3 18 ♕d2 ♘e2+ 19 ♔h1 0-0∞ I.Sokolov-Piket, Wijk aan Zee 1991.

d3) **8 e4!?** b4 9 ♘a4 ♗b7 (9...♕a5 10 b3 ♗b7 11 e5!? ♘d5 12 ♘g5!? ♗e7 13 ♕f3 ♗xg5! 14 ♗xg5 ♘5b6= Bareev-Sveshnikov, Biel IZ 1993) 10 e5 (Possibly better was 10 ♗e2 ♕a5 11 b3 c5 12 e5 ♘d5 13 0-0 ♖c8 14 ♗d2 ♗e7 15 ♖ac1 0-0 16 ♕b5! – a common theme in this variation – 16...♕xb5 17 ♗xb5 ♗c6 18 ♗a6 ♖cd8± Umansky-Dreev, Gorky 1989. Also very interesting is 10 ♗g5!? ♕a5 11 b3 c5 12 ♗xf6 gxf6 {12...♘xf6?! 13 ♕b5+ ±} 13 ♗e2 0-0-0 14 0-0 ♔b8 {14...cxd4±} 15 d5 ♘b6 16 ♘xb6 ♕xb6 17 ♖ad1 ♗h6 18 ♕c4 ♖d6 19 dxe6 ♖xe6 20 ♖d5!± Karpov-Gelfand, Linares 1993) 10...♘d5 11 ♗d2 ♕a5 12 b3 c5 13 dxc5 ♗xc5 14 ♕b5 ♕xb5 15 ♗xb5 ♗e7 16 ♖c1 a6= Portisch-Kuczynski, Budapest Z 1993.

7 ... ♘bd7

By far the most usual here. However, perhaps Black's very direct play in Korchnoi-Morovic, match 1991 merits a look. After **7...b4** 8 ♘a4 ♘bd7 9 ♗g5 ♕a5 10 ♗xf6 gxf6 11 e3 ♘b6! 12 ♘xb6 axb6 13 ♗d3 ♗b7 14 0-0 c5 Black had definite counterplay.

8 ♗g5

Alternatively White can opt for the Catalan style again with **8 g3** when Black can choose between a solid preparation of ...c5, or play on the a6-f1 diagonal:

a) **8...b4** 9 ♘a4 ♗a6 10 ♗g2 ♕a5 11 ♕d1 ♖d8 12 0-0 ♗e7 13 ♗d2 ♗xe2 (what else?) 14 ♕xe2 ♕xa4 15 ♘e5! ♘xe5 16 dxe5 ♘d5 17 ♕g4 with a dangerous initiative for the pawn in Speelman-Shvidler, Beersheva 1987.

b) **8...♗b7** 9 ♗g2 a6 10 0-0 c5 11 ♖d1 ♕b6 12 ♗g5 ♗e7 13 ♗xf6 ♗xf6 14 d5 c4 15 ♕c2 ♘c5 Titov-Ivanov, Azov 1991, looks more certain for Black.

8 ... c5!?

A very interesting sacrificial attempt to make Black's thematic break without what had previously been regarded as 'due preparation'. For the two pawns Black obtains a lead in development often aided by a rather embarrassed white queen, and good play down the b- and c-files. However, I am just a little suspicious that future trials might unearth a defence for White and it is handy that more sober approaches are also available to Black. In particular 'b' with 9...♗e7 seems quite promising:

a) **8...a6** 9 e4 (9 a4!?) 9...c5?! (9...h6! 10 ♗xf6 ♘xf6 11 e5 ♘d7! 12 ♗e2 ♗b7 13 0-0 ♗e7 14 ♘e4 ♖c8 15 ♖ac1∞ and not 15 ♖fc1? ♕b6! 16 a4 c5 17 ♘d6+ ♗xd6 18 exd6 c4 19 ♕b4 ♗xf3! 20 ♗xf3 0-0 21 axb5 axb5 22 ♖a5 ♖b8 23 ♖e1 ♖fd8 24 h3 ♘f6∓ Korchnoi-Ribli, Reggio Emilia 1987/8) 10 d5 c4 11 ♕c2 ♕c7 12 ♗e2 ♗d6 13 a4 exd5 14 axb5 dxe4 15 ♘xe4 ♗b4+ 16 ♗d2± Korchnoi-Novikov, Pamplona 1991.

b) **8...♕a5!?** 9 e3 ♗a6 (9...♗e7!? 10 ♗d3 and now

10...a6!? {Shipov} looks like a good idea. White should perhaps try 11 ♘e5!?∞ directed against the impending ...c5) 10 ♗xf6 gxf6 (10...♘xf6 11 ♘e5!) 11 ♗d3 (or 11 ♗e2± Karpov) 11...b4 12 ♘e4 ♖d8! 13 ♖c1! ♗xd3 14 ♕xd3 b3+ 15 ♘fd2 bxa2 16 0-0 f5 17 ♘c3 (17 ♘g3!?) 17...♗g7 18 ♖a1 0-0 19 ♖xa2 ♕c7 with at best a slight edge for White in Karpov-Timman, Tilburg 1991.

c) **8...♗e7** 9 e4?! (9 e3 a6 10 ♗e2 c5 11 0-0 c4 12 ♕c2 ♗b7= Gross-Polgar, Rimavska Sobota 1991) 9...b4 10 ♘a4 ♘xe4 11 ♗xe7 ♕xe7 12 ♗d3 ♘gf6 13 0-0 0-0∓ Korchnoi-Anand, Tilburg 1991. White's compensation is not sufficient.

9 d5

Best. Immediate captures on b5 are weak. **9 ♕xb5** ♖b8 Δ...♖xb2 allows too much counterplay, and **9 ♘xb5** ♖b8 is a bit embarrassing. Also innocuous is **9 dxc5** ♗xc5 10 ♘e4 ♗e7 when all three recaptures in reply to 11 ♗xf6 seem sufficient – even 11...♗xf6 12 ♘d6+ ♔f8 13 ♘xb5?! ♕a5+ Δ...♖b8 is fine for Black.

9 ... c4

Black is committed to this highly aggressive course, since **9 exd5** 10 ♘xd5 a6 11 ♕e3+ favours White.

10 ♕xb5 ♖b8

11 ♕xc4

11 ♕c6!? is worth a look, foregoing one pawn to encourage Black to block the b-file. After 11...♗b7 12 ♕xc4 exd5 13 ♕d3, Black can mobilize rapidly and put the question to the b2 pawn, but I slightly prefer White's defensive chances.

11 ... exd5

12 ♘xd5 ♕a5+

13 ♘c3 ♘c5! *(202)*

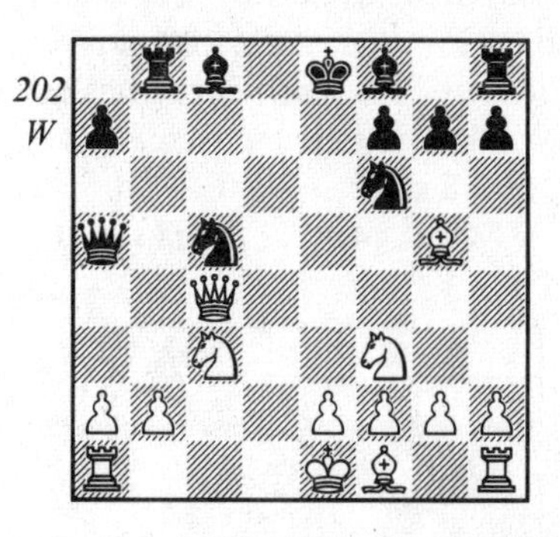

202
W

A good moment to take stock. Black has sacrificed two pawns, for which he has a lead in development and concrete threats to White's queenside. White's queen is vulnerable to attack, and the only convenient way to defend b2, namely **0-0-0** carries obvious risks.

14 ♗xf6

14 ♗d2, not relinquishing his hold on the important dark squares was also critical, but with **14...♗e6!** Black can generate good play:

a) **15 ♕f4** ♖xb2! 16 ♘d1 ♖xd2 17 ♘xd2 ♘fe4! with excellent attacking chances.

b) **15 ♘d5(!)** ♗xd5 16 ♕xd5 ♘xd5 17 ♗xa5 ♖xb2 with some play for the pawn.

14 ... gxf6
15 0-0-0 ♗e6

15...♖b4!? 16 ♕d5 ♗b7 looks interesting too.

16 ♕f4

16 ♘d5!?.

16 ... ♕b6
17 ♖d2 ♗e7

But not **17...♗xa2?** 18 ♘xa2 ♘b3+ 19 ♔d1 ♘xd2 20 ♕a4+! ♔d8 21 ♘xd2 when Black has no means to continue the attack.

18 e3 0-0
19 ♗c4 ♖fc8 *(203)*

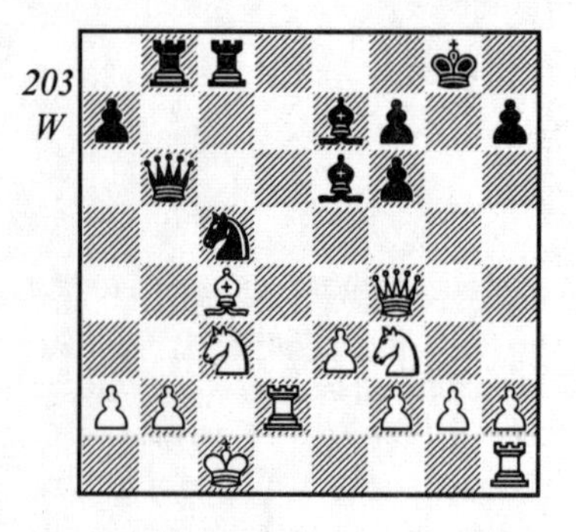
203 W

20 ♔b1?

The wrong direction! White had to try **20 ♔d1** ♘e4! 21 ♗xe6 ♘xc3+ 22 bxc3 ♕xe6 although Black has enough compensation since his queen is superbly placed for both attacking and defending, and 23 ♘d4 fails to 23...♖b1+ 24 ♔e2 ♕c4+ etc.

20 ... ♘d3!
21 ♗xd3 ♖xc3
22 ♕d4 ♕a5!
23 a4

There is no choice, since **23 b3** invites 23...♗xb3 24 axb3 ♖cxb3+ 25 ♖b2 ♖xb2+ 26 ♔xb2 ♕a3+ 27 ♔b1 ♖xd3-+.

23 ... ♖cb3
24 ♖c1 ♖3b4
25 ♖c4! ♕xa4?

Black's investment in his attack has reaped its reward, and now was the moment to cash in with **25...♗xc4** 26 ♗xc4 ♖xa4∓. The text allows White's bishop to remain momentarily pointed at h7, which allows White a counterattack.

26 ♕h4! ♔f8
27 ♕xh7 ♔e8
28 ♕g8+?

After **28 ♖xb4!** ♖xb4 29 ♘xd4 the position would be quite unclear. Once the queen has neglected the important defensive diagonal b1-h7, this resource is no longer available.

Black now wrapped up the game as follows: **28...♗f8 29 ♕g3 ♕a3! 30 ♖xb4 ♖xb4 31 ♔c1 ♕a1+ 32 ♗b1 ♗f5 33 ♔d1 ♕xb1+ 34 ♔e2 ♖xb2 35 ♖xb2** (Black was threatening 35...♗d3 mate, but a pretty sequence now leads to the same fate for White) **35...♗d3+! 36 ♔d2 ♗b4+ 37 ♖xb4 ♕c2+ 0-1**.

27 4 e4 Marshall's Gambit

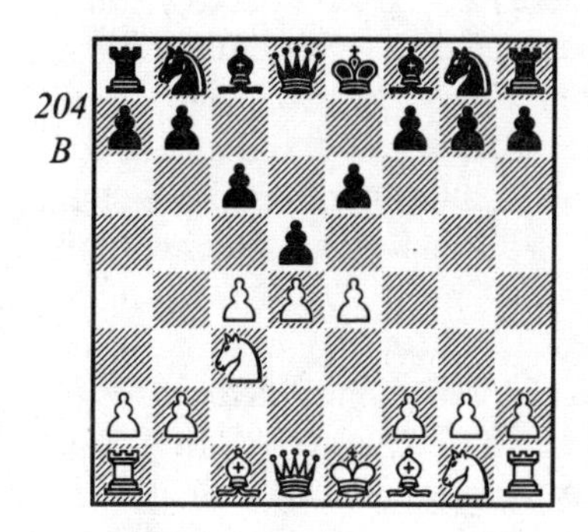

Frank Marshall has an interesting and impressive distinction. The strong American master was not only a daring and exciting player in his era, he also left an impressive array of gambits named, usually uncontroversially, after him. A few such as 5 e4 in the QG Tarrasch have lost their topicality, but what is remarkable about Marshall is that in an era when not so many old gambits are regarded as truly respectable, several of his are still theoretically crucial. This is certainly true of 4 e4 in the diagram position, and as discussed in the introduction, it is the main drawback for Black in an otherwise attractive move order for reaching the bulk of the book.

For his pawn White obtains the bishop pair and chances against the dark squares where the theoretical weakening implied by the moves ...e6 and ...c6 takes on a very real form in the absence of the dark-squared bishop and the opening of the position. White's gambit has the appeal of flexibility. The defects of the black position sometimes succumb to a violent onslaught, sometimes persist surprisingly awkwardly into the endgame. The main game here has been rightly hailed as a superb model for White.

Lautier's judgement that after the exchange of queens Black would still face a strong attack, with little counterplay to offer, was very fine, and has clearly put the burden of proof back on Black in the 8 ♗e2(!) ♘a6 9 ♗c3! main line. Lautier's comment on the position after 8 ♗e2 is interesting: 'For only a pawn, White has taken definitive control of the dark squares and enjoys a serious lead in development. Imagine a King's Gambit where Black is deprived of his king's bishop!'. Much of this is hard to dispute, but the reality is that Black is also finding new resources in a very fast-changing and topical theoretical debate. At the risk of preempting the coming material a little, I would suggest that the recent revival of 8 ♘e2 will prove short-lived, and that after 8

♗e2(!) Black will, failing an effective antidote to Lautier's play at a later stage, turn increasingly to a newer approach such as 8...♘d7 9 ♘f3 b6!?.

Game 37
Lautier-M.Gurevich
Biel IZ 1993

To appreciate the boldness of White's approach fully, it is worth mentioning here that both players were in the high-tension situation of needing the full point to qualify for the 1994 FIDE Candidates matches. Lautier was duly thus rewarded for his fine effort.

1 c4 **e6**
2 ♘c3 **d5**
3 d4 **c6**
4 e4 *(204)* **dxe4**

Alternatives are almost unheard of here, but **4...♗b4** has been suggested. Interestingly **5 exd5** cxd5 6 ♘f3 ♘f6 (6...♘e7!?) would transpose to the Caro-Kann Panov Attack. **5 e5** is independent and may be promising.

5 ♘xe4 **♗b4+**

The only response to challenge White's bold fourth move. Still, **5...♘d7**, though unambitious, has been tried. In comparison with either the 4...♘d7 Caro-Kann, or the Rubinstein French, Black has played both ...e6 and ...c6 which is unnecessarily passive. Still, a purist might try to claim that White's c4 may be a bit premature, weakening d4, albeit very marginally. One example: 6 ♘f3 ♘gf6 7 ♗d3 ♘xe4 8 ♗xe4 ♘f6 9 ♗c2 ♗b4+ (if 9...♗e7 10 0-0 0-0 11 ♗g5 White's space advantage assumes serious proportions) 10 ♗d2 ♕a5 11 a3 ♗xd2 12 ♕xd2 ♕xd2+ 13 ♔xd2 with a more comfortable ending for White in Karpov-Korchnoi, Vienna 1986.

Other fifth moves are weak. **5...e5?** fails since after 6 dxe5 ♕a5+ 7 ♗d2 ♕xe5 8 ♗d3! Karpov-Ivanović, Skopje 1976, Black loses in the event of 8...f5 9 ♕h5+ g6 10 ♕e2 fxe4 11 ♗c3 ♕e7 12 ♕xe4!. Also bad is **5...♘f6?!** 6 ♘xf6 ♕xf6 7 ♘f3 ♘d7 8 ♗d3 ♗b4+ 9 ♔f1! (Black's bishop shortly becomes stranded) 9...h6 10 ♕e2 ♕e7 11 c5! e5 12 a3± Ungureanu-Suba, Bucharest 1976.

6 ♗d2

The gambit continuation, after which White gains indisputable compensation in the form of greater development, the two bishops, and play on Black's weakened dark squares. However, the solid if unambitious **6 ♘c3**, in fact Marshall's own initial choice, still appears with perhaps surprising regularity. My impression is that Black has a choice of routes to equality after **6...c5! 7 a3** and now:

a) **7...♗xc3**+ 8 bxc3 ♘f6 9 ♘f3 ♕a5 (9...♘c6!? 10 ♗e2 0-0 11 0-0 h6 is also solid) 10 ♗d2 ♘e4!? 11 ♗d3 ♘xd2 12 ♕xd2 ♘d7 13 **0-0**

0-0 14 ♕c2 h6= Baburin-Malevinsky, USSR 1987.

b) **7...♗a5!?** 8 ♗e3 ♘f6 9 ♖c1 (9 ♘f3 cxd4 10 ♘xd4 ♘e4 11 b4 ♘xc3 12 ♕c2 ♗c7 13 ♕xc3 ♗e5 14 f4 ♗f6 15 ♖d1 **0-0** 16 ♕c2 ♕e7 17 ♘f3 b6= Gulko-Zsu.Polgar, Aruba 1992) 9...cxd4 10 ♕xd4 ♕xd4 11 ♗xd4 ♘c6 12 ♗xf6 gxf6 13 b4 ♗c7 (the bishop pair is quite sufficient compensation for a very modest structural minus) 14 ♘f3 ♔e7 15 g3 ♘e5= Groszpeter-Lukacs, Hungarian Ch 1991.

Recently, Black came up with a completely different idea, **6...e5!?**, which at least fared well in the stem game. After **7 dxe5(?!)** ♕xd1+ 8 ♔xd1 ♗f5 9 ♘ge2 ♘d7 10 ♘g3 ♗g6 11 f4 ♘h6 12 ♗d2 0-0-0 Black clearly had good compensation in Brklaca-Todorović, Yugoslavia 1993. **7 a3** looks more logical since **7...♗xc3+** 8 bxc3 looks ±, and if **7...♗d6** 8 dxe5 ♗xe5 9 ♕xd8+ Black will have to lose a little time, or in the event of exchanging on c3 risk embarrassment to his king. **7...♗a5** looks best, when White should perhaps grab the pawn and rely on the extra possibility of b4 to improve his defensive prospects. Black's idea certainly merits attention.

6 ...	**♕xd4**
7 ♗xb4	**♕xe4+**
8 ♗e2	

Until recently the alternative **8 ♘e2** was often awarded a ?!. Now some more positive aspects of the move have come to light. Although White's kingside development is temporarily blocked, he does retain the g2 pawn which is useful not so much on the material level but so as to prevent manoeuvres such as ...♕xg2-g5-e7 which can prove the most economical route to a greater role for the black queen (albeit after due preparation). Additionally, another natural route for Black's First Lady via g6, here runs into ♘f4 which can be awkward. Still, the jamming of White's mobilization looks to me the most important factor, and although Black is experimenting with a variety of replies, he seems to me to have at least one route to a very pleasant equality:

a) **8...♕xc4?!** does not appear to lose by force, but its untested status presents no great mystery: 9 ♕d6 c5 10 ♗xc5 ♘d7 11 ♗a3! is very dangerous for Black.

b) **8...♘e7?!** (by way of warning) 9 ♕d2! c5 (9...♘a6 10 ♗xe7 ♔xe7 11 **0-0-0** would give all the advantages graphically demonstrated in Vaiser-Namyslo – see 'e21' in the note to Black's 8th) 10 0-0-0 0-0 11 ♗xc5 ♘bc6 12 ♘d4 ♘xd4 13 ♗xe7± G.Georgadze-Cruz Lopez, San Sebastian 1991. The Georgian Grandmaster can take most of the credit for putting 8 ♘e2 back on the map.

c) **8...♘d7 9 ♕d6** and now:

c1) **9...c5?!** 10 ♗c3! (Georgadze's other novelty. 10 ♗xc5

♘xc5 11 ♕xc5 ♗d7= {Euwe} is of course harmless) 10...♘e7 11 0-0-0 ♘f5 12 ♕d2 0-0 13 ♘g3! ♕c6 (13...♘xg3 14 hxg3 f5 15 ♗d3 holds obvious dangers for Black too) 14 ♘xf5 exf5 15 ♗e2! ♘f6 16 ♕g5! with a fierce attack in G.Flear-Bryson, Hastings Challengers 1992/3.

c2) **9...a5!?** is the latest wrinkle, and on current evidence the most realistic alternative to 'd' below: 10 ♗c3 (10 ♗a3 ♕e5 {Stoica's suggestion 10...c5!? Δ...♖a6 is interesting too} 11 ♕d2 ♘gf6 12 0-0-0 ♘e4 13 ♕e3 b5!? 14 f4 ♕c7 15 ♕xe4 b4 16 ♗xb4 axb4 17 ♔b1 0-0 was complicated, but Black's chances looked fine in Hauchard-Dorfman, Brussels Z 1993) 10...♘gf6 11 b3 c5 12 ♖d1 ♖a6 13 ♕d2 0-0 14 f3 ♕h4+ 15 g3 ♕h5 16 ♗g2 e5 17 0-0 ♖e8∓ Grigore-Cozianu, Romanian Ch 1993. It is too early to pronounce definitively on this, but the idea looks well conceived.

d) **8...♘a6(!)** and now:

d1) **9 ♗c3?!** e5! (9...f6 should transpose) 10 ♕d6 f6 11 0-0-0!? (I must confess I had overlooked the feasibility of this and was happy at the prospect of 11 ♖d1 ♔f7! when I felt that White had about as many problems developing as Black does. In fact Malaniuk-Kharlov, Simferopol 1992 had already established that Black has fair prospects here: 12 f4 exf4 13 ♖d4 ♕e7 14 ♕xf4 ♘h6 15 ♖e4 ♕d8 16 ♕f3 ♗f5 17 ♖d4 ♕c8 18 h3 ♖e8∓. White has some compensation still for the pawn but it is not very convincing) 11...♗f5 12 ♘d4! *(205)*

205
B

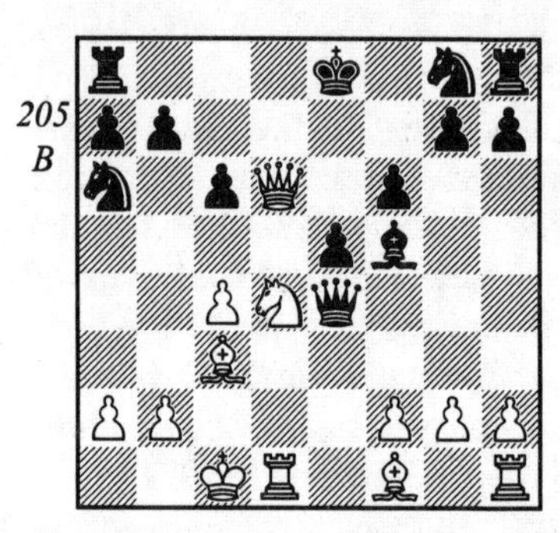

The only (but very embarrassing) time I can remember where my opponent had just one move to keep him on the board in the opening but I still contrived to overlook it! In fact it was mentioned as dangerous by Illescas in *Informator 57* but although Black has only one defence, it seems to be at least adequate: 12...♕b1+! 13 ♔d2 ♖d8 14 ♕xd8+ ♔xd8 15 ♘e6+ ♔e7 16 ♖xb1 ♗xb1 17 ♘xg7 ♗g6! T.Wall-Wells, Hastings Challengers 1993/4, with perhaps some positional plus for Black since White has to make concessions to extricate his adventurous knight. Still, if he gets on with this by 18 g4! there is still a lot of play.

d2) **9 ♗f8!** (WARNING – this bishop is immune!) **9...♘e7 10 ♗xg7** and now again an important parting of the ways:

d21) **10...♘b4** 11 ♗xh8 (11 ♕d6 leads to a forced sequence and a virtually equal ending after 11...♘d3+ {11...♘c2+?! 12 ♔d2 ♘xa1 13 ♗xh8 ♕c2+ 14 ♔e1 ♕b1+ 15 ♕d1 ♕xa2 16 ♘c1 ♕a6 17 ♗d3 gives White too much play for the pawn – Flear} 12 ♔d2 ♘f5 13 ♕xd3 ♕xd3+ 14 ♔xd3 ♘xg7= Vaiser-G.Flear, San Sebastian 1992) 11...e5 12 ♕d6 (12 ♔d2? ♗g4! 13 ♔c3 ♖d8 14 ♘g3 ♘ed5+! 15 cxd5 ♘xd5+ 16 ♕xd5 ♕xd5 17 ♗c4 ♕d4+ 18 ♗b3 b5∓ Flear) 12...♘c2+ 13 ♔d2 ♗f5 *(206)* (13...♘xa1? 14 ♕xe5±)

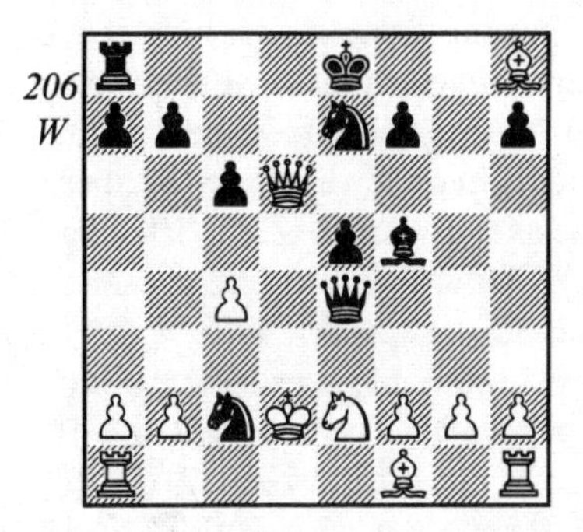
206
W

14 ♖d1!? (14 ♘g3 ♕f4+ 15 ♔c3 ♘d5+! 16 cxd5 ♕d4+ 17 ♔b3 ♘xa1+ 18 ♔a3 ♘c2+ 19 ♔b3 ♘a1+ ½-½ Gomez Esteban-Illescas, Lisbon Z 1993) 14...♖d8 15 ♕xd8+ ♔xd8. Here Illescas claims a small plus for White after 16 ♔c1+ ♔e8 17 ♘c3 ♕f4+ 18 ♖d2. This is interesting, and may well be White's best bet in the whole line. Not however 16 ♘g3(?) (!? Illescas) since 16...♕f4+ 17 ♔c3 ♘d5+! 18 ♔b3 (18 ♖xd5 cxd5 19 ♘xf5 ♕xf5 20 ♗d3 d4+ 21 ♔xc2 e4∓) 18...♗g6!? 19 a3 b5!∓ is much too dangerous for the white king.

d22) **10...♖g8!?** was tried in G.Flear-Zso.Polgar, Hastings Challengers 1992/3, where play continued **11 ♕d4** ♕xd4 12 ♗xd4 c5 13 ♗c3 **♘b4?!** ½-½. Glenn gives 14 ♗xb4 cxb4 **15 ♘g3** f5! and Black is fine, but **15 ♘d4!** is more accurate according to Stoica, who gives **15...♗d7** 16 0-0-0 0-0-0 17 f4!±, but Black equalized easily in G.Georgadze-Sveshnikov, Podolsk 1992 with the no-nonsense **15...♘c6** 16 ♘xc6 bxc6 17 g3 ♗b7 18 ♗g2 0-0-0. Black has I think a still more attractive alternative in **13...♘c6!?** aiming for the ambitious set-up of ...e5, ...♔e7 and ...♘d4. So, what should White do? **11 ♗c3?** is not the answer in view of 11...♘c5∓, but what of **11 ♗f6!?** ? As far as I can see, no one has considered this familiar idea here, but the threat of 12 ♕d6 appears to give White the tempo he needs to play ♕d2 and 0-0-0 liberating his kingside forces. If he can proceed so, then there is nothing wrong with exchanging ♗xe7 if provoked. Tests are required here, although White needs to reinforce 10...♘b4 too.

8 ... ♘a6

The text, gaining a much-needed tempo to bring the black forces into play, has long been the main line. The main game here is one of the greatest dents to its fortunes in the history of the variation, although I would be careful before writing it off. Still, in the meantime, the recently revived 8...♘d7, and the new idea 8...♘e7 will enjoy enhanced status. Also 8...c5 should be studied carefully. We shall examine no less than five choices here, although the first two are almost definitely inferior:

a) **8...♘f6?!** is an inflexible development which leaves e7 seriously weak. 9 ♘f3 (9 ♕d6 looks good too) 9...♘bd7 10 ♕d6 c5 11 ♗c3 ♕c6 12 ♕xc6 bxc6 13 ♘d2! with an excellent endgame in which Black's c-pawns are chronically weak; Flohr-Shamkovich, USSR 1942.

b) **8...♕xg2?!** has long been rightly regarded as too risky. White has two promising approaches, although the older is perhaps the more reliable: 9 ♕d6 (9 ♗f3!? ♕g6 10 ♘e2 ♘a6 11 ♗a3 ♘e7 12 ♖g1 ♕f6 13 ♘c3 ♘f5 14 ♘e4 ♕d8 15 ♖xg7! gave a clear plus in Wood-Alexander, London 1948; 9 ♕d4!? Polugaevsky, but perhaps 9...c5!? when 10 ♗xc5 transposes to a position considered under 'c' and if 10 ♕xc5 ♘d7 it is not clear how White should proceed) 9...♘d7 (if 9...c5 10 ♖d1! ♘d7 11 ♗f3 Δ♗xb7 seems to win) 10 0-0-0 ♕xf2 (White had a lot of pressure too after 10...♕g5+ 11 f4 ♕e7 12 ♕d2 c5 13 ♗c3 in Furman-Kopaev, USSR 1949) 11 ♗h5 ♕e3+ 12 ♔b1 ♕e5 13 ♗xf7+! ♔xf7 14 ♖f1+ ♘gf6 15 ♕e7+ ♔g8 **16 ♕d8+?** ½-½ Ree-Pliester, Amsterdam 1982. Sosonko and Pliester demonstrate convincingly that instead by **16 ♘f3!** intending ♖g1 and ♘g5, White's threats would be too strong: **16...♕e4+** 17 ♔a1 h6 18 ♖hg1 ♖h7 19 ♘d2! Δ♖xf6±; or **16...♕h5** 17 ♖hg1 ♕f7 18 ♕d8+ ♕e8 19 ♖xg7+! ♔xg7 20 ♖g1+ ♕g6 21 ♖xg6+ hxg6 22 ♕e7 and wins.

c) **8...c5!?** is an interesting attempt to improve on the immediate g2 capture. After White captures, Black hopes subsequently to gain a tempo against the 'loose' bishop on c5. The current assessment is that Black cannot equalize: 9 ♗xc5 (weaker is 9 ♗c3 ♘e7! 10 ♗xg7 ♖g8 11 ♗f6 ♘d7 12 ♗xe7 ♔xe7 and Black stands well) 9...♕xg2 10 ♗f3! (probably weaker is 10 ♕d6 ♘d7 which is considered in 'c1' 10...♕g5 11 ♗d6! ♘c6 12 ♘e2 (or 12 ♗xc6+!? bxc6 13 ♘f3 ♕a5+ 14 b4 ♕f5 15 ♕e2 ♘f6 16 ♖g1 ♗a6 17 ♖xg7 ♗xc4 18 ♕xc4 ♕xf3 19 ♗e5 ♘d7 20 ♗b2± Vaiser-Ermenkov, Odessa 1977) 12...♘ge7 13 ♖g1 ♕f6 14 ♘c3 and now instead of **14...♘f5** 15 ♗xc6! bxc6 16 ♘e4± Spraggett-Maiorov, Cannes 1992, Black should prefer **14...♘d4!** 15 ♗e4 ♘df5 16 ♗a3∞ (Spraggett).

d) **8...♘e7!?** recently made an appearance in the game Borisenko-Kalikstein, Uzbekhistan Ch 1992. After the natural 9 ♘f3, the novelty

9...♘d5!? was revealed. Play continued messily 10 ♗a3 ♘f4 11 0-0! ♘xe2+ (11...♕xe2?! 12 ♕d6 c5 13 ♗xc5 {13 ♕xf4 is good too but less incisive} 13...♘g6 14 ♖ad1 ♘d7 15 ♖d4 gives White a huge attack) 12 ♔h1 ♘d7 (12...♘f4!? 13 ♕d6 c5 14 ♗xc5 ♘g6 15 ♖ad1 ♘g6 16 ♘d4 ♕e5 17 ♘b5 ♕xd6+ probably leads to just a draw) 13 ♖e1 ♕xc4 14 ♖xe2 c5∞.

e) **8...♘d7!?** *(207)* may now be left looking the most promising. Black's resources seem sufficient after both:

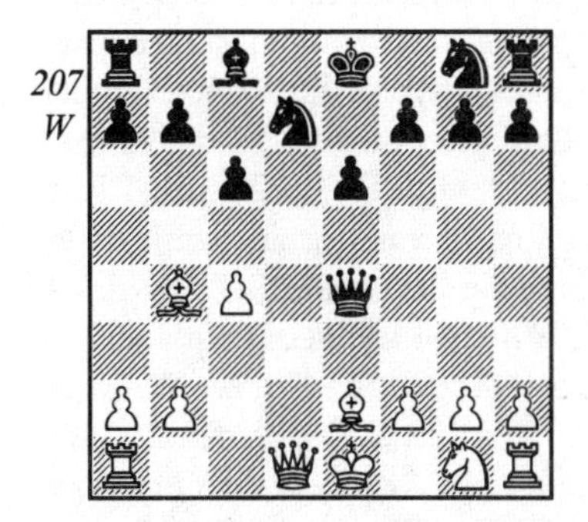

e1) **9 ♕d6** c5 10 ♗xc5 ♕xg2 leads to a position also reached when White tries 10 ♕d6 in line 'c' above. It is rightly reckoned to give Black a comfortable game: 11 ♗f3 (11 **0-0-0** should be met by the immediate 11...♕c6 since after 12 ♕xc6 bxc6 13 ♗f3 ♗b7 14 ♗d6 0-0-0 15 b4 ♘h6 {Donaldson} Black stands well) 11...♕g5 12 ♗e3 (12 ♗a3 ♘e7∓ Donaldson) 12...♕a5+ 13 b4 ♕e5 and the ending holds no terrors.

e2) **9 ♘f3!** is far more testing, and Black has tried several moves, two of which are serious candidates:

e21) **9...♘e7?** is weak. Black was crushed by 10 ♗xe7 ♔xe7 11 ♕d2 ♖e8 12 0-0-0 ♔f8 13 ♗d3 ♕g4 14 h3 ♕h5 15 g4 ♕c5 16 ♗xh7 ♕xc4+ 17 ♔b1 ♘f6 18 ♕d6+ ♖e7 19 ♘e5 ♕b5 20 ♕d8+ ♖e8 21 ♕c7 ♖e7 22 ♖d8+ ♘e8 23 ♘g6+!! in Vaiser-Namyslo, Bern 1992.

e22) **9...♘gf6?!** 10 ♗d6! is very awkward, since Black has problems contesting the diagonal and hence finding a home for his king.

e23) **9...b6!?** deserves further study. The stem game continued 10 ♘d2!? (10 ♕d2 ♘gf6 11 0-0-0 {11 ♗d6!?} 11...c5 12 ♗c3 ♗b7 looks OK for Black, and against 10 ♕d6 c5 11 ♗c3 ♘e7!? Δ...♘f5 looks worth a try) 10...♕f4 11 ♗f3 (11 g3 ♕c7 12 ♘e4 c5 13 ♘d6+ ♔e7 14 ♘b5 ♕b8 15 ♗c3 ♘gf6 16 ♗f3 a6! 17 ♗xa8 ♕xa8 18 ♕d6+ ♔d8 19 ♕c7+ and White should force the draw) 11...♘e5 12 ♗e4 (12 ♘e4!? may be the critical try in the whole line. Ionov gives 12...♘xf3+ 13 gxf3 c5 14 ♗d2! ♕c7 15 ♗c3 f6 16 ♕d2. White's structure is horrible, but the open g-file certainly gives his attack more bite) 12...♗b7 13 g3 ♕g4 14 f3 ♕h5 15 f4?! (15 0-0 ♘f6 16 ♕e2 gives better practical chances, but Black can feel satisfied with the theoretical outcome already)

15...♕xd1+ 16 ♖xd1 ♘d7 17 ♗f3 Ionov-Sorokin, Cheliabinsk 1991, and now 17...♘gf6! Δ18 g4 0-0-0 19 g5 c5!∓.

e24) **9...c5 10 ♗c3** and now there is a further choice, but I am not convinced that either leads to an easy game:

e241) **10...♘e7** 11 0-0!? (More dangerous in my view than 11 ♕d2 0-0 12 0-0-0 ♘g6 13 g3 h6 14 ♖he1 e5 15 h4 ♘f6! and Black was organizing a plausible defence in Danielian-Sakaev, Duisburg Wch U-18 1992) 11...0-0 12 ♗d3 ♕f4 13 ♖e1 ♘g6 14 g3 ♕h6 15 h4! e5 16 ♗e2! ♘e7 17 ♘xe5 ♘xe5 18 ♗xe5 ♘c6 19 ♕d6! ♘xe5 20 ♕xe5 gave Black a surprisingly unpleasant defence despite the simplification in Crouch-Wells, Dublin Z 1993.

e242) **10...♘gf6** 11 ♕d2 (Again the quiet approach has a claim: 11 0-0 0-0 12 ♖e1 b6 13 ♘d2 ♕f5 14 ♗f3 ♖b8 15 ♕a4 with enough pressure in Vera-Antunes, Cuba 1992) 11...♕g6 12 ♘e5! ♘xe5 13 ♗xe5 0-0 14 0-0-0 ♘e4?! (Black should try 14...♘d7 15 ♗d3 f5 16 ♗c3 b6 17 g4! ♘f6 with complicated play, but perhaps not the ultra-sharp 14...b5?! 15 ♗f3 ♘e4 16 ♕e3 f5 17 g4 ♗b7 {S.Ivanov} when Black looks loose, and I am not sure how to meet 18 gxf5 ♕xf5 19 ♖d7 ♕xe5 20 ♖xb7) 15 ♕e3 f6 16 ♗d3 fxe4 17 ♗xe4 ♕h6 18 ♕xh6 gxh6 19 ♖he1± (at least) S.Ivanov-Bashkov, Cheliabinsk 1991.

9 ♗c3(!)

This is now clearly established again as the main line. By contrast with the analogous position with 8 ♘e2, weak is 9 ♗f8 in view of 9...♕xg2 10 ♕d6 ♗d7 11 0-0-0 0-0-0 followed by ...♘h6 and Black will consolidate his material plus. That leaves two reasonable alternatives to the text:

a) **9 ♗a5** seeks to control d8, utilizing the fact that **9...b6?** would weaken c6 unacceptably, after 10 ♗c3 ♘f6 11 ♕d6±. Hence Black's reply is forced, but it also seems to be adequate and the line has largely fallen into disuse: **9...♗d7** 10 ♘f3 ♘f6 11 ♕d6 ♕f5! 12 ♘e5 (Black also has an important tactical resource in the event of 12 ♗c3 ♘e4 13 ♕d4 f6 14 ♘h4 e5! with advantage) 12...♕xf2+ 13 ♔xf2 ♘e4+ 14 ♔f3 ♘xd6 15 ♖ad1 ♔e7 16 ♖xd6! (16 ♖d2 uses the control of d8 to force Black to return the exchange, but the two pawns count for more after 16...♗e8 17 ♖hd1 ♘f5 18 ♗d8+ ♖xd8 19 ♖xd8 f6 20 ♘g4 c5 according to Shamkovich's analysis. Similar is 16 ♘xd7 ♔xd7 17 ♖d2 ♔e7 18 ♖hd1 ♖ad8!∓) 16...♔xd6 17 ♘xf7+ ♔e7 18 ♘xh8 ♖xh8 19 ♗c3= Taimanov. White has at best just enough for the pawn minus.

b) **9 ♗d6!?** and Black has several possibilities of which the first three are weak, but two merit special attention:

b1) **9...♕xg2?!** 10 ♕d2! (Δ10...♕xg2 11 ♕g5±) 10...♗d7 11 0-0-0 0-0-0 12 c5 ♗e8 13 ♗xa6 ♕xh1 14 ♕a5 ♖d7 15 ♗e2±.

b2) **9...♗d7** 10 ♘f3 c5 11 ♘e5 ♗c6 12 ♘xc6 bxc6 (12...♕xc6!±) 13 0-0 ♘e7 14 ♕a4 with clear advantage in Taimanov-H.Steiner, Stockholm IZ 1952.

b3) **9...♕f5** 10 ♘f3! ♕a5+ 11 ♘d2 ♘e7 12 0-0 ♘f5 13 ♘e4 ♘xd6 (13...c5!?) 14 ♘xd6+ ♔e7 15 ♕d3 ♖d8 16 ♖ad1 ♕c7 17 ♕xh7! ♖xd6 18 ♕xg7 (Δ♗h5) 18...e5 and now White could have obtained a decisive advantage with 19 ♖xd6 ♕xd6 20 ♖d1 ♕g6 21 ♕h8 ♗h3 22 ♕xh3 in Ivanchuk-Dreev, Leningrad 1985.

b4) **9...b6** 10 ♘f3 ♗b7 11 0-0 (Against the very sharp 11 ♘e5 Black's defences seem to hold up well. Maximenko-Sorokin, USSR 1989 continued 11...f6 12 0-0!? fxe5 13 ♗h5+ g6 14 ♖e1 ♕xc4! 15 ♖xe5 0-0-0 16 ♗e2 ♕h4 17 g3 ♕f6 18 ♖xe6 ♕xe6 19 ♗g4 ♖xd6 20 ♕xd6 ♕xg4 21 ♕f8+ ♔d7 22 ♖e1 ♕d4 23 ♕e8+ ♔c7 24 ♕f7+ ♕d7 25 ♕f4+ ♕d6 26 ♕f7+ ♘e7! 0-1) 11...♖d8! 12 ♘e5 ♘e7 13 ♖e1 ♕h4 14 g3 ♕f6 15 ♘g4 ♕g6! 16 ♘e5 ♕f6 17 ♘g4 ♕g6= since both sides have nothing better than a repetition (I.Sokolov).

b5) **9...e5(!)** 10 ♘f3 ♗g4 11 0-0 (11 ♘xe5 ♗xe2 12 ♕xe2 ♕xe2+ 13 ♔xe2 ♘h6 was nothing for White in Vaiser-Novikov, Volgodonsk 1983) 11...0-0-0 12 ♗d3 ♕f4 13 ♗xe5 ♕xe5 14 ♘xe5 ♗xd1 15 ♗f5+ ♔c7 16 ♘xf7 and now instead of **16...♘e7?** 17 ♗xh7± Tal-Dorfman, USSR Ch 1978, **16...♘h6!** 17 ♘xh6 ♗h5! 18 ♗g4 ♗xg4 19 ♘xg4 ♖d2 gives Black full compensation for the pawn in the ending.

9 ... ♘e7

In general Black's best development for the knight, reserving the possibility of a later ...f6 and ...e5 to give a stake in the fight for the centre.

None of Black's alternatives here look good enough for equality. We consider:

a) **9...♘f6?!** 10 ♘f3 ♗d7 11 0-0 (11 ♘e5 immediately also looks good, e.g. 11...♖d8 12 ♕d2 ♗c8 13 ♕g5 ♖g8 14 f3 h6 15 ♕c1 ♕h4+ 16 g3 ♕h3 17 ♗f1 ♕f5 18 ♕e3 c5 19 h4 and Black is in great difficulties; Flohr-Turn, USSR 1945) 11...0-0-0 12 ♗d3 ♕g4 (12...♕f4 may be a little better) 13 ♕c2 ♕f4 14 b4! (The position of the black king gives this advance a bit of added spice, but b4 aiming to exploit the poor situation of the knight on a6 is a theme common to the whole variation) 14...c5 15 b5 (15 a3 ♗c6! lets Black off the hook) 15...♘b4 16 ♗xb4 cxb4 17 ♖fe1 ♕c7 18 a3 b3 19 ♕xb3± ♔b8 20 ♖ac1 ♗c8 21 c5 ♖d5 22 b6 axb6 23 axb6 ♕d6 24 ♘e5! ♗d7 (24...♖xe5 25 ♖xe5 ♕xe5 26 ♕a4 and mate follows) 25 ♘xf7 ♖xd3

26 ♕c4 ♕b6 27 ♕xd3 ♖f8 28 ♕g3+ ♔a7 29 ♕xg7 1-0 I.Sokolov-Akopian, Groningen 1991.

b) **9...e5?!** is unambitious, since White's two bishops will always count for something: 10 ♕d6 ♘e7 11 ♖d1 ♗e6 12 ♘f3 ♘f5 13 ♕xe5 ♕xe5 14 ♘xe5 f6 15 ♘f3± Knaak-Dokhoian, Erevan 1988.

c) **9...f6?!** 10 ♕d6 ♗d7 (10...♘h6 11 ♗xf6 gxf6 12 0-0-0 with strong threats) 11 0-0-0 0-0-0 12 ♕g3 e5 (12...♕g6 13 ♕e3 b6 14 ♘h3! is dangerous too, Bronstein-Szily, Moscow 1946) 13 ♗d3 ♕f4+ 14 ♕xf4 exf4 15 ♘e2 g5 16 h4±.

10 ♗xg7!

Until recently this move tended to be dismissed based largely on the basis of the analysis of 11 ♗c3 given below. It is remarkable how quickly 11 ♗f6!, once dismissed so lightly, should have become the hot main line.

9...♘e7 can also be met more sedately, seeking compensation for the pawn by focusing on the position of the a6 knight with **10 ♘f3**. I believe this is maybe sufficient but not more: 10...0-0 11 0-0 (11 ♕d2 ♘g6 12 0-0-0 ♕f4 13 ♕xf4 ♘xf4 14 ♗f1 Δg3, ♗g2 and h4-h5 Pfleger-Czerniak, Bucharest 1967 merits attention; also interesting was here 12...f6 13 ♖he1 e5 14 ♗f1 ♕f4 15 ♖e3 ♗g4 16 h3 ♗xf3 17 ♖xf3 ♕xd2+ 18 ♗xd2 ♘h4 19 ♖a3 ♘f5 from Lobron-Knaak, Baden-Baden 1992. The exchange of queens again offers Black relief, but on the other hand the two bishops *vs* two knights inevitably gives play for the pawn. It's probably a matter of taste) 11...♘g6 12 ♖e1 (12 ♗d3 'with initiative' – Ragozin, is true after 12...♕f4 13 g3 ♕c7 14 h4, but 12...♕g4 Δ...♘f4, 13 h3 ♕h5 looks fine for Black) 12...f6! (looks better motivated than 12...♘h4?! 13 ♕d6 ♘xf3+ 14 ♗xf3 ♕xc4 15 ♗e4!± f6? {15...♕c5!} 16 ♗xh7+ ♔f7 17 ♗g6+ ♔g8 18 ♕g3 e5 19 ♖e4 ♕d5 20 ♕h4± Bönsch-Hamori, Hungary 1987; or 12...♕f4 – too soon to commit the queen to this route home - 13 b4! ♕c7 14 ♗d3 f6 15 ♕c2 ♕f7 16 h4± Rudnev-Mikenas, corr. 1982) 13 b4! e5 (or 13...♘f4!? 14 ♗f1 ♕g6 15 g3 e5 16 ♘h4 ♕g5 17 b5 Estévez-Diaz, Bayamo 1984, when perhaps Black's kingside aspirations have rendered key defensive pieces a bit offside) 14 b5 cxb5 15 cxb5 ♘c5 16 ♗f1 with fair compensation for White in Bronstein-Matlak, Polanica Zdroj 1988.

10 ... ♖g8 *(208)*

208
W

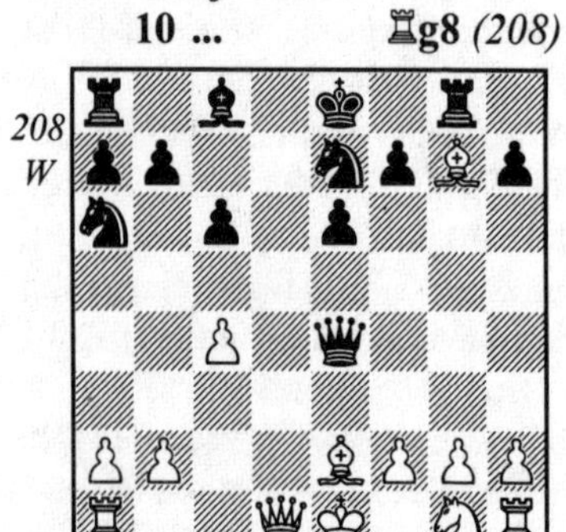

11 ♗f6!

The move that has turned theory's verdict upside down. Once dismissed with the laconic '11...♕f4! (Euwe) 12 ♗c3 ♖xg2∓', White first found 12 ♗xe7 to be a viable alternative, and then Euwe's assessment to be well wide of the mark.

The tactical justification of Black's play against 11 ♗c3? was discovered in two stages too, first a route to equality, and then a clear plus for the 'defender'.

For the record, Black answers **11 ♗c3** with 11...♘d5!! (This brilliant but thematic blocking of the d-file must not be delayed. If immediately 11...♕xg2? 12 ♕d2 ♕xh1 13 0-0-0 ♘d5 14 ♘f3 ♕xd1+ {14...♕g2 15 cxd5 cxd5 16 ♕f4 ♗d7 17 ♗xa6 bxa6 18 ♖g1±} 15 ♗xd1 ♘xc3 16 ♕xc3± Bronstein-Kotov, Budapest 1950) 12 cxd5 ♕xg2 13 dxe6 (13 ♗f3? ♕xh1 wins) 13...♗xe6! 14 ♗f6. This position is still given in several sources (notably and surprisingly *ChessBase Magazine*) as only equal, based on the old game Dukić-Seslija, Yugoslavia 1967 which continued **14...♕xh1** 15 ♕d6 ♖xg1+ 16 ♔d2 ♕d5+ 17 ♕xd5 ♗xd5 18 ♖xg1 ♔d7 19 ♖g7 ♖h8 20 ♗xa6=. However, thanks to a fantastic 16th move resource discovered by the Russian Razmoglin, it seems that White is unable to justify his material loss after **14...♖g6!** 15 ♗h4 ♕xh1 16 ♕d6 ♖g5!! (Δ17 ♗xg5? ♕xg1+), e.g. **17 0-0-0** ♖c5+ 18 ♔b1 ♕e4+ 19 ♗d3 ♕xh4 20 ♗xa6 ♖d8∓; or **17 ♗xa6** ♕xg1+ 18 ♔d2 (18 ♗f1 ♖d8∓) 18...♕xa1 19 ♗xg5 ♕b2+ 20 ♔e1 ♕c3+ and suddenly there is a mating attack, but it's not White's!

11 ... ♕f4

11...♖g6 has long been dismissed on the grounds **12 ♗c3!** ♘d5 (12...♕xg2 13 ♕d2 ♕xh1 14 0-0-0) 13 cxd5 ♕xg2 14 ♕d4! since in addition to the d-file threats, Black's rook has abandoned h8. It is not clear why in Vaiser-Savchenko, Moscow 1992 Black allowed this or White avoided it. After **12 ♗xe7** ♔xe7 13 ♕d2 e5 14 ♖d1 ♗e6 15 f3 ♕d4 16 ♕xd4 cxd4 White had at best a slight edge.

12 ♗c3(!) *(209)*

Lautier's contribution, which will probably prove to be more dangerous than **12 ♗xe7!?**, which however also has more sting than would appear at first sight. I discovered this first hand after 12...♔xe7 13 g3 ♕e5 (I would prefer 13...♕f6!? with hindsight. Black loses the possibility of ...♕a5+ but is not subject to loss of tempo upon ♘f3 and in addition 14 ♕b1?! e5! looks promising. So probably 14 ♕c1 but then just 14...b6 15 ♘f3 ♗b7 Δ...c5=) 14 ♕b1! (A very strong move which I had overlooked. If 14 ♕c1 ♘b4! is awkward, and 14 ♘f3 ♕xb2 15 **0-0**

♖d8 gives no real compensation. After the text White threatens to develop with tempo, and as soon as he has castled the pawn on h7 is genuinely hanging in many lines. I suspect this is ± already) 14...♗d7 (after a very extended think. I think the ending which follows 14...♘c5 15 ♘f3 ♕e4 16 ♕xe4 ♘xe4 is playable but a little uncomfortable. Still more uncomfortable was 14...♔f8 15 ♘f3 ♕a5+ 16 ♔f1 ♔g7 17 ♕e4± Danielian-Relange, Cannes (m) 1993) 15 ♘f3 ♕a5+ 16 ♔f1 ♕h5 17 ♕d3 ♖d8 18 ♖d1± ♗c8 19 ♕e3 ♕h3+ 20 ♔e1 ♖xd1+ 21 ♔xd1 ♕f5 22 ♗d3 ♖d8 23 ♔e2 ♕g4 24 ♖c1 ♕g7! with some counterplay, although later 1-0; G.Flear-Wells, London Lloyds Bank 1993.

209
B

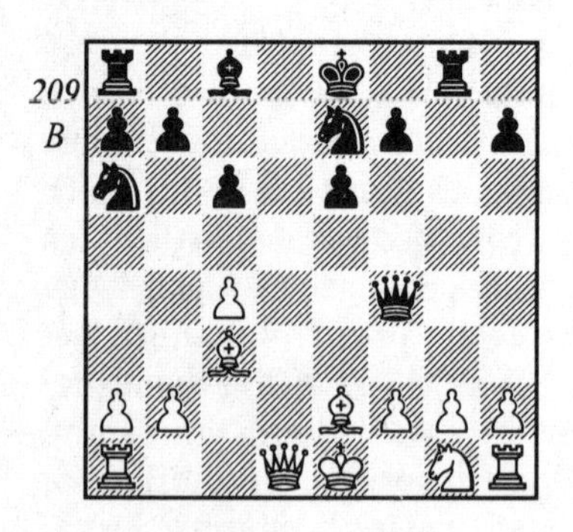

12 ...	**♖xg2**
13 ♘f3	**f6**

The text looks natural. Since White's compensation lies chiefly on the dark squares Black seeks to compete for them. The course of the game shows that White's supremacy there is sufficient that the pawns on f6 and e5 merely serve as targets. However, it is not easy to suggest good alternatives. Black also has a pressing problem that his rook can be in trouble in many variations. A sample, mainly based on Lautier's comments:

a) **13...♘g6** is positionally desirable, but enables White to painlessly hassle the errant black rook with 14 ♔f1! when neither **14...e5** (enterprising but unsound!) 15 ♔xg2 ♗h3+ 16 ♔xh3 ♕f5+ 17 ♔g2 ♘f4+ 18 ♔f1 ♕h3+ 19 ♔e1 ♘g2+ 20 ♔d2 ♖d8+ 21 ♔c2 ♖xd1 22 ♖axd1±; nor **14...♘h4** 15 ♗e5 ♕f5 16 ♗g3 ♕h3 17 ♔f1 ♖xg3 18 fxg3 ♕g2 19 ♖f1± is good enough for Black.

b) **13...♘c5** is directed against White's threat of ♗e5-g3, which could be answered with ...♘e4. However, White can gain time for a strong attack with 14 ♗e5 ♕h6 15 ♕d4! b6 16 ♖d1 ♗b7 17 ♗f6, followed by 18 b4+-.

c) **13...♘f5** was tried in G.Flear-Novikov, Antwerp 1993. White only obtained a slight plus after 14 ♗e5 ♕h6 **15 ♗d3** f6 16 ♗xf5 fxe5 17 ♗c2 ♗d7 18 ♕c1!±, but again Lautier's solution **15 ♕d2!** ♖g8 (15...♕xd2+ 16 ♘xd2 puts the white knight dangerously *en route* for e4 and beyond) 16 ♗f4 ♕f8 17 **0-0-0** ♕e7 18 ♖hg1 with a tremendous initiative.

d) Perhaps Black should look at **13...♖g8** Δ...♘g6, but White will retain a strong initiative with or without queens.

It is not easy to imagine where a really effective antidote to 12 ♗c3! will come from.

14 ♕d2!! *(210)*

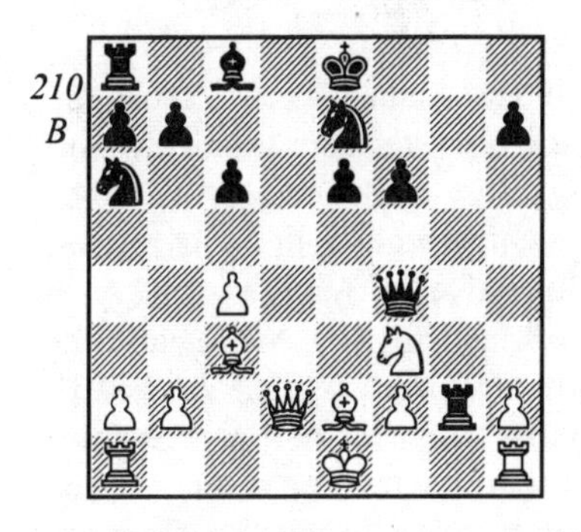

Excellent understanding of the position. The queen is Black's best piece for defending some dark squares and the exchange will leave White's knight perfectly placed for the attack. The 'middlegame solution' **14 ♕d3** allows Black to consolidate with 14...e5 15 ♕h7 ♗g4 16 ♗d2 ♕f5 17 ♕xf5 ♘xf5 with no serious problems.

14 ... ♕xd2+

Sad necessity. **14...e5** 15 ♕xf4 exf4 16 ♘h4! ♖g8 17 ♗h5+ ♘g6 18 0-0-0±, or **14...♘g6** 15 ♕xf4 ♘xf4 16 ♗xf6 ♘xe2 17 ♔xe2± (with the option of ♖hg1) both give White a powerful attack.

15 ♘xd2 e5

16 ♘e4 ♔f7

17 ♖d1!

The young Frenchman continues to concentrate on the initiative, eschewing material gains that would enable Black to consolidate, e.g. **17 ♘g3?!** ♘g6 18 ♗f3 ♘h4 19 ♗xg2 ♘xg2+ 20 ♔e2 ♘f4+ with good defensive chances.

17 ... ♖g8?!

Too passive. Black should, according to Lautier, force White to seek material by **17...♘c7!** although after 18 ♗h5+ ♘g6 19 ♗f3 ♘h4 20 ♗xg2 ♘xg2+ 21 ♔e2 ♘f4+ 22 ♔f3 ♗h3 23 ♖hg1 White still has a large plus.

18 f4! *(211)*

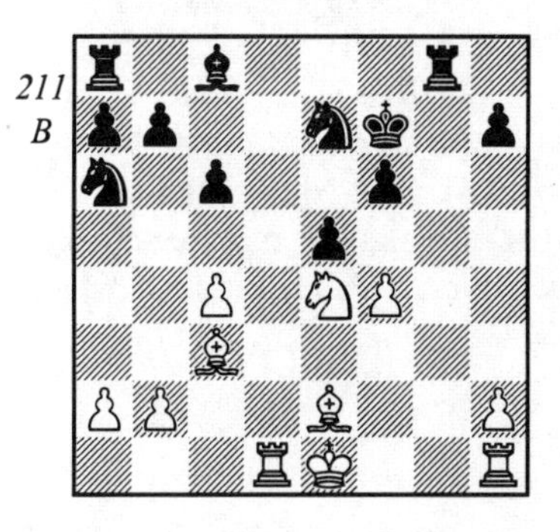

18 ... ♘g6

If **18...exf4** simply 19 ♗h5+ ♘g6 20 ♘xf6 would be crushing.

19 ♖d6 ♔e7

20 ♖xf6 ♘xf4

21 ♗xe5 ♘xe2

22 ♗d6+! ♔e8

23 ♔xe2 ♗h3

23...♗g4+ 24 ♔e3 ♖d8 25 ♖g1! would be no better. The smoke has cleared somewhat, White has regained his pawn and has a large advantage based on the embarrassment of the black king, the lack of coordination of the black pieces which this reinforces, and the absence of a safe posting for his bishop. Note how here the opposite-coloured bishops greatly aid the white attack. White's precise 24th forces Black to shed material.

24 ♖h6!	**♗g4+**
25 ♔e3	**♗f5**

If **25...♔f7**, 26 ♖f6+ ♔e8 (or 27...♔g7 28 ♖g1 ♔h8 29 ♗e5+-) 27 ♖g1 decides. Now the rest is not too problematic.

26 ♘f6+	**♔f7**
27 ♘xg8	**♖xg8**
28 ♔f4!	**♗g6**
29 ♖e1	**♖d8**
30 ♖e7+	**♔f6**
31 c5	**♘b4**

Black seeks last minute activity, but can create no real threats while White obtains a passed h-pawn that will decide the game.

32 ♖exh7!	**♘d5+**
33 ♔f3	**♖e8**
34 h4	**♖e3+**
35 ♔f2	**♔f5**
36 ♖g7	**♖e6**
37 h5	**1-0**

If 37...♗e8 38 ♖xe6 ♔xe6 39 h6 there is no stopping White promoting.

A superb game in all its phases, illustrative of White's strategy in the Marshall as a whole, and the latest word on 8...♘a6. Still, whilst the Marshall is clearly a dangerous try for which Black should be well prepared, there are enough avenues to explore in Black's 8th move possibilities, especially 8...♘d7!?.

Index of Variations